THE KENNEDY HALF-CENTURY

THE
KENNEDY
HALF-CENTURY

· · ·

THE PRESIDENCY,
ASSASSINATION, AND LASTING
LEGACY OF JOHN F. KENNEDY

LARRY J. SABATO

BLOOMSBURY

NEW YORK · LONDON · NEW DELHI · SYDNEY

Photo credits (numbers run sequentially from the first insert, top to bottom): 23 © AP/ AP/CORBIS; 30, 31 © Associated Press; 8 courtesy of Barry Webb Battle; s 1, 10, 11, 13, 15, 17, 18, 21, 22, 28, 35, 42 © Bettmann/CORBIS; 63 by Dennis Brack/Bloomberg News © Getty Images; 59 courtesy of the George Bush Presidential Library and Museum; 37 is from the archives of the *Chicago Sun-Times*, and the author's private collection; 61, 62 courtesy of the William J. Clinton Presidential Library; 2, 3, 16, 34 © CORBIS; 26 courtesy of the Tom Dillard Collection, *The Dallas Morning News*/The Sixth Floor Museum at Dealey Plaza; 7 © Randy Faris/CORBIS; 54 courtesy of the Gerald R. Ford Library; 44 © Bob Jackson; 55 courtesy of the Jimmy Carter Library; 12 courtesy of the John F. Kennedy Presidential Library and Museum, Boston; 47, 48 courtesy of the LBJ Presidential Library; 5 by Dan McElleney and © CORBIS; 4 courtesy of Reni News s, Inc. and © CORBIS; 50 by Yoichi Okamoto. Courtesy of the LBJ Presidential Library; 19 by Jerry Olsen, U.S. Navy and courtesy of the John F. Kennedy Presidential Library and Museum, Boston; 56, 57, 58 courtesy of the Ronald Reagan Library; 60 © Arnie Sachs/CNP/Corbis; 53 courtesy of Nate D. Sanders; 20 by Len Simon and courtesy of the John F. Kennedy Presidential Library and Museum, Boston; 32 courtesy of The Sixth Floor Museum at Dealey Plaza; 45 by Stan Stearns and © Bettmann/CORBIS; 29, 38, 40 by Cecil Stoughton, courtesy of the John F. Kennedy Presidential Library and Museum, Boston; 41 by Cecil Stoughton, courtesy of the LBJ Presidential Library; 14 by Stanley Tretick and © Bettmann/CORBIS; 6 ©Underwood & Underwood/CORBIS; 64 © Evan Vucci/AP/Corbis; 26, 27 are from the Warren Commission, exhibits #133A and #237, courtesy of the National Archives and Records Administration, College Park, Maryland; 46 by Harold Waters and © Associated Press; 33 by Jack A. Weaver; 51 by Frank Wolfe. Courtesy of the LBJ Presidential Library.

Published by Bloomsbury USA, New York

All papers used by Bloomsbury USA are natural, recyclable products made from wood grown in well-managed forests. The manufacturing processes conform to the environmental regulations of the country of origin.

LIBRARY OF CONGRESS CATALOGING-IN-PUBLICATION DATA

Sabato, Larry
The Kennedy half-century : the presidency, assassination, and lasting legacy of John F. Kennedy / Larry J. Sabato.
pages cm
Includes bibliographical references and index.
ISBN 978-1-62040-280-1 (hardback)
1. Kennedy, John F. (John Fitzgerald), 1917–1963—Influence. 2. Kennedy, John F. (John Fitzgerald), 1917–1963—Assassination. 3. Kennedy, John F. (John Fitzgerald), 1917–1963—Public opinion. 4. Public opinion—United States. 5. United States—Politics and government–1945–1989. 6. United States—Politics and government—1989- I. Title.
E842.1.S23 2013
973.922092—dc23
2013023969

First U.S. Edition 2013

1 3 5 7 9 10 8 6 4 2

Typeset by Westchester Book Group
Printed and bound in the U.S.A. by Thomson-Shore Inc., Dexter, Michigan

For all those who ask what they can do for their country

There is no present or future, only the past, happening over and over again, now.

—EUGENE O'NEILL, IRISH AMERICAN PLAYWRIGHT

CONTENTS

ACKNOWLEDGMENTS

THE KENNEDY HALF-CENTURY is the result of a research project stretching over five years, and many people have contributed much along the way. Without generous funding, this book would still be in my hard drive. The essential financial support came from the Reynolds Foundation, with special thanks to J. Sargeant Reynolds, Jr., Richard S. Reynolds III, Randolph N. Reynolds, David P. Reynolds, Glenn R. Martin, Dorothy R. Brotherton, and Victoria Pitrelli; our loyal Center for Politics backers, Paul and Victoria Saunders; McGuireWoods Consulting and McGuireWoods law firm, with special thanks to Frank B. Atkinson, Mark T. Bowles, and Richard Cullen; the Honorable William P. Hobby and Paul W. Hobby of the Hobby Family Foundation; James Falk and Martha Powell of the World Affairs Council of Dallas/Fort Worth; Dan Alcorn, a Center board member; and several sources at the University of Virginia, including the offices of President Teresa Sullivan and Provost John Simon.

It was my great pleasure to work with Hart Research Associates on the public opinion research that undergirds many of the book's findings. The pollsters at this firm are Picassos in their field, and their artistry drew out our participants about long-ago events. We extend our gratitude to Peter Hart, chairman; Geoff Garin, president; Molly O'Rourke, partner; Becca Mark, analyst; Kevin Schmidt, assistant analyst; and Leah Stecher, also an assistant analyst.

I am deeply indebted to the interviewees, reviewers, and professionals who have so willingly shared their time, memories, research, and impressions. Special thanks to former President Jimmy Carter for granting us an interview, as well as Dr. Stephen Hochman and Lauren Gay of the Carter Center. A special mention is also needed for JFK speechwriter Ted Sorensen, who was generous with his thoughts and counsel on several occasions before his passing in October 2010. Former Dallas mayor Tom Leppert and his wife, Laura, also deserve special acknowledgment for their hospitality and graciousness in showing me the critical locales of November 22, 1963, and giving me considerable access to people who understood the city of that time and our time. In addition, I am grateful to Bill Alexander, Pierce Allman, Hugh Aynesworth, James Barger, Eddie Barker, Barry Webb Battle, Gerald Blaine, Robert Blakey, Aniko Bodroghkozy, Julian Bond, Dan Bongino, David Bowers, Jim Bowles, Stephen Bryce, Joseph Califano, Tommy Caplan, Mortimer Caplin, Jim Carroll, James Carville, Phil Costello, Mal Couch, Senator John Culver, Jim Cunningham, Craig Daigle, Jerry Dealey, John Dean, Ralph Dungan, Frank Fahrenkopf, Dan Fenn, Ari Fleischer, Winfried Fluck, Frank Gannon, Bill Greener, Jeff Greenfield, Ken Holmes, Henry Hurt, Heinz Ickstadt, James Jones, Matthew Maxwell Taylor Kennedy, Ronald Kessler, Sergei Khrushchev, Chris Kincheloe, Mary Moorman Krahmer, Jim Leavelle, Jim Lehrer, Peter Leventis, Fred Malek, Chris Matthews, John McAdams, Paul McCaghren, Dr. Robert McClelland, Senator Mitch McConnell, H. B. McLain, Harry McPherson, Herbert Meza, Jefferson Morley, Bill Moyers, Bill Newman, Michael O'Dell, Robert Orben, Harold Pachios, Jerry Paul, House Speaker Nancy Pelosi, Barbara Perry, Gary Powers, Jr., Sandy Quinn, First Lady Nancy Reagan, Ron Reagan, Richard Reeves, Lynda Bird Johnson Robb, Jason Roberts, James I. Robertson, Jr., Ed Rollins, Jay Root, Sarah Collins Rudolph, Bob Schieffer, Bill Simpich, Gillian Martin Sorensen, Cliff Spiegelman, Oliver Stone, Kathleen Kennedy Townsend, Judge John R. Tunheim, Sander Vanocur, and David R. Wrone for their time and assistance.

The following people at the John F. Kennedy Presidential Library and Museum were helpful to us: Director Thomas Putnam and staff members Stephen Plotkin, Sharon Ann Kelly, Lara Hall, Stacey Bredhoff, Laurie Austin, and Sara Ludovissy.

Staff in other presidential libraries also lent a hand, and we thank Kevin Bailey at the Dwight D. Eisenhower Presidential Library; Tina Houston, Regina Greenwell, Claudia Anderson, Allen Fisher, Liza Talbot, Barbara Cline, Eric Cuellar, Lara Hall, Brian McNerney, Christopher Banks, and Margaret Harman at the Lyndon Baines Johnson Library and Museum; Greg Cumming, Jonathan Roscoe, and Jon Fletcher at the Richard Nixon Library; Nancy Mirshah and William H. McNitt at the Gerald R. Ford Library; James A. Yancey, Jr., Keith J. Shuler, and Polly Nodine at the Jimmy Carter Library; Ray Wilson, Jennifer Mandel, Shelly Williams, Shelley Nayak, and Michael Pinckney at the Ronald Reagan Library; Robert Holzweiss at the George Bush Library; Herbert Ragan and Lisa Sutton at the William J. Clinton Library; and Christine A. Lutz at the Seeley G. Mudd Manuscript Library, Princeton University.

We also thank several people at the National Archives and Records Administration, including David S. Ferriero, Archivist of the United States; Gary

M. Stern, general counsel; Mary Kay Schmidt and Amy DeLong, archivists working in the President John F. Kennedy Assassination Records Collection; Daniel Rooney, supervisory archivist of the Motion Picture, Sound, and Video unit, and Mark Meader, an archives specialist in the same department; Joseph A. Scanlon, FOIA / Privacy Act Officer, Office of General Counsel; the Honorable Frank Keating, a member of NARA's board of directors; and Kenneth Lore, president of the Foundation for the National Archives. Marc Oliver, production manager at Silver Spring Studios, deserves a special acknowledgment for copying essential audio files from NARA's College Park, Maryland, repository.

We relied extensively on the personnel and resources of the Sixth Floor Museum at Dealey Plaza for our chapters on President Kennedy's assassination, and we thank Nicola Longford, executive director; Gary Mack, curator; Stephen Fagin, associate curator; Megan Bryant, director of collections and intellectual property; and Pauline Martin and Krishna Shenoy, the Sixth Floor Museum's chief librarians. Their cooperation was crucial, although they have no responsibility for anything I have written.

Charles Olsen, a senior analyst at Sonalysts, Inc., assembled an extraordinary team of audio experts to reexamine the Dallas Police Dictabelt recording and the original report put together by Bolt, Beranek, and Newman for the House Select Committee on Assassinations. Mark Bamforth, Malinda Finkle, Jonathan Grant, Richard Hodges, Dr. John Jakacky, Lauren Logan, Scott Martin, Lisa Peringer, and Curt Ramm of Sonalysts teamed up with Brian Sargent of Aberrant Sound in Concord, Massachusetts, to produce a ground-breaking scientific study. These gifted men and women deserve the gratitude of everyone who has ever researched the Kennedy assassination.

A companion documentary based on the findings of this volume will air on PBS stations throughout the nation. We wish to acknowledge Curtis Monk, president and CEO of Commonwealth Public Broadcasting; John Felton, vice president and general manager of WCVE in Richmond and WHTJ in Charlottesville; Gene Rhodes; Mark Helfer; Leslie Custalow; and Paul Roberts, independent filmmaker.

Most of all, I am deeply appreciative for the fine team we assembled at the University of Virginia to work on this book. The team leader was Dr. Andrew Bell, a historian with a keen grasp of the subject, who worked directly with me on almost every aspect of the research. Andrew was the first to read each of my draft chapters and to fill in critical details that had escaped my attention or memory. Further, Andrew worked with Sean Lyons, who skillfully helped us conduct interviews, and he supervised a crack team of graduate and undergraduate interns and researchers. Several interns spent far more hours than they should have, but we are ever so grateful that they became a bit obsessed with the project. They include Josh Bland, Sophie Arts, Jonathan Elsasser, Nicholas Blessing, Valerie Clemens, Jack Jessee, Emma Paine, Blake Wheelock, James Yu, Cameron Cawthorne, Ann Laurence Baumer, Joseph Wilkinson, Brian Wilson, and Michael Bugas. Other students who made significant contributions were Andrew McGee, Aaron Flynn, Whitney Armstrong, Joe Wiley, Jeff Young, Tyler Matuella, Ethan Thrasher, Justin Lee, Scott Tilton, Michael Pugliese, Randy Pearson, Kasey Sease, and Reed Arnold.

The home base for this book project was the University of Virginia's Center for Politics, whose staff assisted us in countless ways. First mention must go to Kenneth Stroupe, the Center's associate director, whose hard work and creativity stitched together the pieces of the project in brilliant fashion. His patient, thorough work with the National Archives and on the evidence we have obtained of the assassination has been exceptionally diligent and creative. Also supporting the book in various vital ways were Mary Daniel Brown, Nyshaé Carter, Glenn Crossman, Joseph Figueroa, Geoffrey Skelley, Bruce Vlk, and Isaac Wood. Deb Maren and Donna Packard carefully transcribed interviews for us. Kyle Kondik, a daily generator of good ideas, proposed some gems we quickly adopted, and he served as a keen in-house critic of my arguments. A special shout-out to my executive assistant Tim Robinson, who performed many roles, not least keeping me on schedule and running interference as deadlines loomed.

No one has ever had a more caring, enthusiastic publisher than I have in George Gibson of Bloomsbury. George was as determined as my team to make this project all that it could be. Years ago, I was told that George was "one of the real gentlemen of New York publishing," and the description has proved completely accurate. He was so termed by my able agents, Susan Rabiner and Sydelle Kramer of the Susan Rabiner Literary Agency. In that spirit, I declare them to be two of the real ladies of their field. The Bloomsbury team is unmatched, and I thank Cristina Gilbert, director of marketing and publicity, Laura Gianino, publicist, Laura Keefe, director of adult marketing, Marie Coolman, director of adult publicity, Megan Ernst, marketing associate, Nathaniel Knaebel, managing editor, and Emily DeHuff, copy editor. I also wish to thank Gene Taft, owner of GTPR, for his tireless promotional efforts.

Over the course of this lengthy undertaking, we have endeavored to be fair at every juncture, taking care not to be "captured" by any interest group or camp (pro-Kennedy, anti-Kennedy, Kennedy family, the factions supporting various assassination theories, and so on). No doubt many of the people upon whom we relied for information will disagree with some of my observations, and inevitably, despite our best efforts, some errors of fact and interpretation remain in this volume. For all of these, I take the customary responsibility. For now, I can only hope that the book is worthy of the wholehearted efforts given by all the people acknowledged here.

Larry J. Sabato
Director, Center for Politics
University Professor of Politics
University of Virginia
Charlottesville, Virginia
June 2013

INTRODUCTION:
THE BIRTH OF A LEGACY

WHEN JOHN F. KENNEDY ENTERED THE presidential limousine at Love Field, he began his ride into history. The journey continues, and we call it the Kennedy legacy.

At its core, a legacy is a bequest.[1] Every president wants to hand down a dazzling record to posterity, and each occupant of the Oval Office dreams he will be elevated to the pantheon of "the greats." But what presidents imagine their legacy to be usually differs from what cruel fate dictates.

Every president's legacy is a strange, evolving thing. It transforms itself from year to year and generation to generation. Some memories fade while others come into sharper focus because of new circumstances, perhaps more revelations from the past or a transformation in the present that makes once-insignificant events loom large. A president's legacy is a struggle in public relations, too. The former chief executive and his family and staff seek to enhance it, to airbrush away the blemishes while emphasizing the achievements, as they conceive of them. Opponents of the president rarely go into hibernation with his retirement or death; old grudges and fresh agendas can make a former president a continuing target. Democrats ran against Herbert Hoover for forty years. Republicans have targeted Jimmy Carter for over thirty. This sad destiny is usually spared public figures who exit through the brutality of assassination. Martyrdom's blood and tears can wash away grievous sins—the martyr's and our own.[2]

Long after a president has left Washington, journalists ferret out hidden secrets that affect his image for good or ill.[3] Tidbits about their terms still dominate headlines with regularity. Far peskier and unrelenting than reporters are the historians and political scientists. For us, time stands still and there is never a final deadline. George Washington, Thomas Jefferson, and Abraham Lincoln are still being reevaluated virtually on an annual basis. There is value in such constant churning, in part because our society's unceasing search for the right path can be guided by roads already taken, and our developing values can find new expression in past precedent. The scholar

Merrill Peterson's view of Jefferson, one of Kennedy's favorite predecessors, applies just as well to JFK:

> The guiding concept, *the Jefferson image*, may be defined as the composite representation of the historic personage and of the ideas and ideals, policies and sentiments, habitually identified with him. The image is highly complex and never stationary. It is a mixed product of memory and hope, fact and myth, love and hate, of the politician's strategy, the patriot's veneration, and the scholar's quest . . . It is posterity's configuration of Jefferson. Even more, however, it is a sensitive reflector, through several generations, of America's troubled search for the image of itself.[4]

Not only is there a need for this presidential revisionism, there is—to judge by book sales—a popular appetite for statesmen's modified biographies centuries after they departed the scene. Such a prospect is both comforting and frightening to modern presidents. They know they will not be completely forgotten, and the less successful among them hope for redemption. Yet they also recognize history's unpredictability. Unforeseen circumstances may cause their administration's high points to appear irrelevant and their decisions unwise. While breath remains in their body, they work directly or through associates to spin pundits and commentators for generous evaluations.[5] Beyond the grave, former presidents will be unknowing, but their survivors often continue the effort.

Eventually, however, the public relations fog lifts. There are few or no people left with a personal stake in promoting or condemning long-past ex-presidents; this may be the first point of historical clarity. In the case of John Kennedy, we are almost at that moment. While JFK's family continues to be prominent and ever-vigilant about the Kennedy image, the clan's political power has waned enormously. With the death of Senator Edward Kennedy in 2009, the family's last political powerhouse left the scene. Few JFK aides remain alive. In another quarter century only a relative handful of Americans will personally recall the Kennedy years.

A half century from John Kennedy's death, we can finally see more plainly. We can separate fact from fiction and reality from myth. We can assess the true impact of a short presidency that has had a sharp silhouette. Has it really been fifty years? For those who lived during the Kennedy administration, the images of that brief epoch are still so vivid that time often seems to stand still. The vibrancy of those memories underscores this book's focus: the legacy left by John Fitzgerald Kennedy, the thirty-fifth president of the United States, in this, the fiftieth year since his life ended in a hail of gunfire.

Kennedy served less than three years as chief executive before he was brutally slain in Dallas on November 22, 1963. Many presidents who stayed four or even eight years in the White House have been largely forgotten. Yet JFK regularly ranks as one of the best in surveys of the public, and his words are employed more often than those of all but a handful of other statesmen by officeholders and candidates today.

What has set Kennedy apart? Was it singular style, exceptional substance, or a special mix of the two that has made his short presidency such a touchstone for other politicians, academics, everyday Americans, and people around the world?

In an age of punishing political polarization, when the right and the left are constantly at each other's throats, President Kennedy—a forceful partisan in his time—has become a standard exemplar of bipartisanship. For Democrats, he is in the permanent pantheon of party saints, the man who restored unto them the White House after an eight-year period of GOP control and whose popularity continued them in power even after his death. Of course, many modern Democrats have forgotten just how conservative many of JFK's policies were; they have blurred the Kennedy picture, confusing John with his brothers Robert and Edward, whose politics became much more liberal after JFK's assassination.

For Republicans, John Kennedy's muscular foreign policy (after a shaky start), his strong anticommunism, and his enthusiastic backing of free-market capitalism and broad-based income tax cuts have made him a favored, or at least an acceptable, Democratic president—one frequently cited in speeches and television advertisements by GOP politicians. The goal of this partisan cross-dressing is obvious: to portray Republicans as closer to the Kennedy tradition than some current Democrats.

A political party borrows only the brightest stars from the other party's firmament, so this establishes the standard: The legacy of John F. Kennedy has proven durable and popular, even in the face of many distasteful personal revelations about JFK. This book will explain how and why.

The initial focus here is Kennedy's prepresidential career, followed by an examination of his precedent-setting 1960 effort to win the White House—in many ways, the first truly modern campaign for the presidency. A look at the highlights of his abbreviated term in office follows. And then the moment no one will ever forget, the tragedy in Dallas, which has become an ongoing murder mystery and a fascinating Rorschach test about one's view of life, politics, and the nation's path since 1963. I will offer some new perspectives on a fifty-year-old puzzle and take a balanced look at the charges and countercharges in the crime of the century. I have also been able to make significant progress in analyzing a key piece of evidence that sheds light on the events of November 22.

John Kennedy's life and death were just the beginning of the legacy mak-ing. The notion of Camelot, invented shortly after the assassination by JFK's widow, Jacqueline, took hold immediately. Practically the entire JFK agenda, which had been stalled in Congress, was passed as a tribute to the late presi-dent. The new president, Lyndon Johnson, effectively used public remorse over Kennedy's killing to do far more than JFK had planned or even proba-bly hoped for in a second term. This book traces not just LBJ's use of JFK but the ways all nine of Kennedy's White House successors have drawn from his record and image to support their own initiatives and to deflect criticism from their own performance.

The source of this long-lasting Kennedy influence is not hard to deter-mine: It is public opinion. Americans had a positive view of JFK throughout his White House years, and the assassination solidified, elevated, and made inviolable the power of his name. For the first time ever, extensive polling and focus groups have been employed in the course of the research for this vol-ume to study how adult Americans of all ages remember a U.S. president. I believe the methods used for this book will become the standard for judging presidents' long-term influence. Conducted by the renowned polling firm of Hart Research Associates, and supervised by the firm's chairman, Peter D. Hart, and president, Geoff Garin, the study is the most extensive ever done to assess a long-ago White House. A large sample (2,009) of American adults was surveyed about every major facet of President Kennedy's record. The on-line poll included film clips of some critical moments in the Kennedy presi-dency. The sample was representative of the overall U.S. population and also big enough to allow for conclusions about change across generations. Hart and Garin separated out the people who had lived through (and presumably had some conscious memory of) the Kennedy years—those who were aged fifty-five and older at the time of the poll. The respondents younger than fifty-five perceive JFK in secondhand ways, from school textbooks, the media, older friends, and family members.

The quantitative survey was supplemented with six more qualitative, video-taped "focus groups" of fifteen to twenty people in each of three cities: Chicago, Los Angeles, and Richmond, Virginia. Focus group discussions can add depth to the bare-bones data yielded by a poll.[6] The entire survey and the focus group findings can be viewed at this book's website, TheKennedyHalfCentury.com. Only highlights are presented in the book, and I invite you to explore the rich trove of online information we have compiled about Kennedy. Supplement-ing the surveys are personal interviews with many individuals directly con-nected to the Kennedy administration, the assassination, and subsequent White House administrations.

This study of John F. Kennedy's life and legacy is far from dusty history; it is less about Kennedy in his time than about Kennedy in our time. I believe it reveals a great deal about our country, and about what matters to us as a nation as we cope with the enormous problems confronting us. Leaders want to create a positive legacy, and citizens should encourage them to travel that path. At the end of the book, I identify some useful lessons that can be learned by presidents, and the rest of us, from the Kennedy example.

Political power is created in many ways, such as winning an election, facing down an enemy, or skillfully riding the waves of popular opinion. But lasting power is accorded to only a handful of presidents, especially after their death. There is no doubt that John Kennedy is one of the few. How did it happen? Why does his influence persist, and will it continue? What are the effects? These questions and more are answered in the pages of this book.

1

"PRESIDENT KENNEDY DIED AT 1 P.M. CENTRAL STANDARD TIME"

"WE'RE HEADING INTO NUT COUNTRY today. But Jackie, if somebody wants to shoot me from a window with a rifle, nobody can stop it, so why worry about it?"[1]

Her husband's words brought little comfort to Mrs. Kennedy—she was still nervous about the trip to Dallas. The full-page ad she had just seen in the *Dallas Morning News* accused the president of supporting Communists and using the Justice Department to silence his critics. Were such extreme political views common in the city? If so, then perhaps they should cancel the final leg of the trip. She had even asked her primary Secret Service agent about it, but he replied that Dallas was probably no more dangerous than anyplace else. Plus, she knew that Jack would never agree to a last-minute change of plans. He had come to Texas to heal a rift between the liberal and conservative wings of the state's Democratic Party, and both sides wanted him to motorcade through Dallas.[2]

Moreover, the president himself knew that he needed to cut his losses in Dallas, which had voted Republican in 1960 and 1962. When John Connally was elected governor of Texas in November 1962, Kennedy called him to chew over the election results. The president asked how Connally had fared in Dallas, and in light of events to occur a year later, Connally gave an eerie reply: "They went crazy up there . . . They're in open rebellion . . . They just murdered all of us [in Dallas on election day]."[3] "They're . . . talking to me . . . about having that federal building down there and all the rest of that stuff," Kennedy grumbled in response. "I don't know why we do anything for Dallas." Still, he did not want to cede the city to the GOP without a fight.[4]

Air Force One landed at Love Field at 11:40 A.M. The rain clouds that had hung in the sky earlier were gone, replaced by a warm southern sun that raised the temperature to a comfortable 63 degrees. With the change in the weather, the president and First Lady would be able to ride through downtown Dallas without the Plexiglas bubbletop attachment on their 1961 Lincoln Continental convertible. JFK was delighted. He wanted the locals to get a good look at Jackie. This was her first trip with her husband since the death of their premature son, Patrick, in August. Her public appearances energized voters and gave newspaper reporters something positive to write about— important considerations for a president facing a reelection campaign.[5]

The president made sure that the cameras caught Mrs. Kennedy stepping off the plane first. She wore a pink Chanel suit with navy trim and a matching pillbox hat. Ward Warren, a fifteen-year-old high school student, recorded the event with his 8-millimeter camera. Fifty years later, we can look at Warren's film and see the Kennedys at the height of their power. Jackie looks stunning in her iconic outfit, and JFK appears tan, rested, and supremely confident.[6] Even after so many years, a viewer's first reaction is to wish someone on the scene had had an inkling of what was to come. We want a time tunnel to 1963 so we can shout, "Get back on Air Force One! Don't climb into the limousine!"[7] But the celluloid figures cannot hear a warning. The grief and tears will just have to flow.

As the Kennedys came down the plane's stairway, a cheer went up from a crowd of spectators gathered behind a five-foot-high chain-link fence. They had been waiting all morning to catch a glimpse of the world's most famous couple. Some of them waved placards that read HOORAY FOR JFK, WELCOME, MR. PRESIDENT, KENNEDY-JOHNSON, and NIXON GO HOME, a slap at the former vice president, who had left Dallas after his own visit earlier that morning. A few held signs that expressed contempt for Kennedy and his politics: YANKEE GO HOME, IN 1964, GOLDWATER AND FREEDOM, and YOU'RE A TRAITOR.[8]

The Kennedys shook hands with the official welcoming party waiting at the bottom of the stairs. It included Vice President Lyndon Johnson, Texas governor John Connally, and Earle Cabell, mayor of Dallas. Cabell's wife, "Dearie," handed Jackie a dozen red roses, which the First Lady happily accepted. JFK knew that his bodyguards wanted him to proceed directly to his car, but the soon-to-be candidate could not resist the adoring crowd on the other side of the fence. People were shouting, "Welcome to Dallas, Mr. President!" and "Jackie! Over here! Look over here!" He moved toward the fence. The spectators surged forward, desperate to clasp his outstretched hands. Jackie soon joined her husband, generating additional excitement. It was a dangerous moment, and a live TV announcer noted that the unscheduled, wide-open contact seemed to cause unease among the Secret Service agents.[9] Anyone with a pistol could have fired through or over the fence at point-blank range. The Secret Service crew did all they could to keep the Kennedys safe. They watched "every hand as it was held out, ready to jump if they saw so much as a flicker of metal or a grasp that held on a second too long."[10] Nothing untoward happened. Nothing had happened in a hundred similar situations over the past three years.

The agents were relieved when the Kennedys finally climbed into the backseat of their convertible, even though the bubbletop was down and they were still exposed from the shoulders up. Jim Lehrer, afterward for many years the host of PBS's *NewsHour*, remembers seeing the limousine with the bubbletop in place earlier that morning. At the time, Lehrer was a reporter for the *Dallas Times Herald* and had been assigned to cover the story at Love Field. When someone from his newsroom called to ask if the bubbletop would be on JFK's car during the parade, Lehrer passed the question on to an acquaintance in the Secret Service waiting on the tarmac. "And so the agent looks up at the sky," Lehrer recalls, "and he says, 'Well, it's clear here,' and he yells at another agent, he's got a two-way radio, and he says 'What's it like downtown?' The guy goes 'Clear downtown!' So the agent turns to another agent and says words to this effect: 'Take the bubbletop down.'"[11]

Texas governor John Connally and his wife, Nellie, sat in the jump seat right in front of the Kennedys, while two Secret Service agents, Bill Greer (the driver) and Roy Kellerman, rode up front. Most of the other agents piled into the follow car. Some rode on the car's running boards while others relaxed a bit in its leather seats. One agent put an AR-15 assault rifle on the floor of the automobile. Dallas County sheriff Bill Decker rode in the lead car, ahead of the presidential limo, along with Jesse Curry, the city's police chief, and two more Secret Service agents, Win Lawson and Forrest Sorrels.[12]

The president was scheduled to deliver a luncheon speech at the Dallas Trade Mart, a sprawling business complex that had opened its doors only five years earlier. The city's most prestigious civic groups, business leaders, and government officials had purchased tickets for the event and would all be there. But the upcoming political campaign mandated that the average citizens of Dallas—those who toiled on construction sites and in office buildings, flower shops, newsstands, restaurants, and dozens of other small businesses—see Kennedy first, on the theory that one is a little less likely to vote against a president one has seen up close and personal. Despite having a Texan on the ticket, Kennedy had won the state by only 46,257 votes in 1960; this was not a battleground that could be taken for granted in 1964.

Ralph Dungan, one of JFK's aides, remembers the president calling his staff together right before he departed for Dallas. "We had a little meeting in the cabinet room," Dungan told us. "It was the first meeting of the next campaign. He talked about being able to do some of the things in the second term that he wasn't able to do in the first, without specifying the kinds of things he had in mind. But he just felt that in the second term, he was going to be much freer to move." But first Kennedy would have to win the second term, and one big step in that direction was for the president to heal the split in the Texas Democratic Party.

KENNEDY'S MOTORCADE LEFT Love Field at 11:55 A.M for the 9.5-mile trip to the Trade Mart. Everyone in Dallas knew the precise details of the president's route; it had been printed in the newspapers and discussed on local television during the week.[13] The limo crawled along Mockingbird Lane for a few seconds before turning onto Lemmon Avenue. At the corner of Lemmon and Lomo Alto Drive (near Craddock Park), JFK spotted a group of schoolchildren frantically waving a sign that read MR. PRESIDENT, PLEASE STOP AND SHAKE OUR HANDS. He ordered the driver to pull over. The children, as well as giddy adults, squealed with delight and swarmed the convertible. "He shook my hand! The president shook my hand!" exclaimed one little boy. Dave Powers, JFK's political adviser, knew a campaign commercial when he saw one and filmed the encounter from the follow car. After a few moments, the president said, "All right. Let's travel on." But he ordered his limo to halt a second time when he saw a nun with a group of Catholic schoolchildren. It was "an irresistible temptation for America's first Catholic president."[14]

Meanwhile, on the sixth floor of the Texas School Book Depository building, a twenty-year-old African American man named Bonnie Ray Williams was eating lunch and wondering where his friends could be; hadn't they all agreed to meet on that floor to watch the presidential motorcade? The Kennedys would soon be passing underneath the large double windows facing Elm Street, but Williams was there by himself. He could hear pigeons cooing on the roof and someone moving around downstairs. He ignored the stacks of boxes in the southeast corner, knowing that they had been moved there by workers installing a new floor. He waited a few more minutes and then went to a lower floor to look for his colleagues, leaving behind a paper sack and an empty Dr Pepper bottle.[15]

As the president's limo drew closer to the downtown area, the crowds lining the road grew larger. On Turtle Creek Boulevard, people began spilling out into the street, forcing the police motorcycle escort to drop back. "[Secret Service agent] Clint Hill jumped off the left running board of the follow-up car, ran to the back of the limousine, and hopped onto the back foot stand," where he crouched down "in an uncomfortable squat" and "scanned the crowd."[16]

Hill and his fellow agents were part of the thinnest of thin blue lines, tasked with protecting the leader of the free world—an unenviable job that carried huge risks and a tiny paycheck. They knew that presidents had long

been the preferred target of America's madmen, and that one person armed
with a gun could change the course of history. Three presidents (Abraham
Lincoln in 1865, James A. Garfield in 1881, and William McKinley in 1901) had
been assassinated, and half a dozen others had been physically attacked.
President Kennedy had had more than his share of assassination threats since
the 1960 election. Sooner or later, someone else was bound to make an attempt on the president's life. Congress knew it and the Treasury Department
(which supervised the Secret Service) knew it, and yet a mere handful of Secret Service agents formed the nucleus of the government's response to the
looming threat.[17]

On Main Street in Dallas, people were hanging out of open windows and
throwing confetti at the motorcade. Buildings were festooned with red,
white, and blue bunting. Men with crew cuts and women in cat-eye glasses
stood on the streets and sidewalks, grinning and gawking at the sleek presidential auto. They shouted and clapped and whistled over the roar of the
motorcycles.[18]

At one point, a teenaged boy emerged from the crowd and sprinted toward
JFK's car. "Slow down! Slow down!" he shouted. Agent Jack Ready jumped off
the follow car and shoved the boy back into the crowd, causing several people
to crash into each other.[19] "The crowd appeared good natured and friendly and
no other agents reported seeing pickets or unfriendly signs other than one . . .
sign having something to do with Cuba."[20]

When the motorcade, nearly at the end of its route, reached the intersection of Main and Houston Streets, it turned right onto Houston; looming directly ahead was the nondescript Texas School Book Depository. Proud of her
fellow Texans for behaving themselves, Nellie Connally turned around in her
seat and uttered one of history's great ironic lines: "Well, Mr. President, you
can't say Dallas doesn't love you." A few seconds later, the motorcade slowed
for an unusual hairpin left turn onto Elm Street. The crowds were noticeably
thinner as downtown's landmarks receded in the rearview mirror. A handful
of people smiled and waved from the grassy strips inside Dealey Plaza. The
giant Hertz Rent-a-Car clock on top of the Depository changed from 12:29
to 12:30. The Trade Mart was but five minutes away.

And then . . .

Shots.

Bone, blood, and brain matter flying through the air.

The First Lady crawling on the trunk of the convertible.

Mothers and fathers lying on top of their children.

Screams.

People running in all directions.

Drained faces.

Shock.
Horror.
Bewilderment and disbelief.
Fear.
Crying and grieving.

BONNIE RAY WILLIAMS, James Jarman, and Harold Norman saw it happen from the fifth floor of the School Book Depository. Williams had found his co-workers there at 12:20 P.M. He hadn't paid much attention to the first shot because he "did not know what was happening." But other shots sent a chill down his spine. The reverberations from a gun rattled the building, causing a fine layer of plaster dust to fall on Williams's head. Harold Norman heard the *cha-chuck! cha-chuck*! of a fast-moving bolt action rifle and the *ping! ping! ping!* of brass cartridges falling on the floorboards above his head. After pausing a few minutes to assimilate what had happened, they went outside and found a policeman talking to a construction worker who had seen a man pointing a gun out of a window in their building. Williams and his co-workers told the officer their story.[21]

Another officer, Marrion L. Baker, also thought that the shots had come from the Depository. Was the assassin on the roof? Having recently returned from a hunting trip, Baker immediately recognized the sound of a high-powered rifle. He dashed into the lobby of the building and began searching for a way upstairs. Roy Truly, the building's superintendent, showed him the way to the freight elevators, both of which were up on five. "Let's take the stairs," said Baker, knowing that he didn't have a second to lose. He drew his revolver and followed Truly into the stairwell. On the second floor, through a small window in the stairwell door, he saw a man walking away from him into an employee lunchroom. Baker followed the man. "Come here," he commanded. The man stopped dead in his tracks and turned around; he was not out of breath and didn't appear ruffled to see an armed police officer. Truly, who up until this point had been a few steps ahead of Baker, bounded back down the stairs and stood behind the patrolman. "Do you know this man, does he work here?" Baker asked. "Yes," said Truly, immediately recognizing Lee Harvey Oswald. Satisfied, Baker turned around and raced back up the stairs toward the roof.[22]

A minute later, Geraldine Reid passed Oswald in an office on the second floor. He was walking toward the front stairwell, carrying a full bottle of soda. Reid had been watching the parade from the sidewalk in front of the building and had dashed inside when she heard gunfire. "Oh, the president has been shot, but maybe they didn't hit him," she offered optimistically.

Oswald mumbled an indecipherable response and continued toward the stairs and eventually the Depository's front exit. The building had not yet been sealed off by police.[23]

At 12:39 P.M., Oswald banged on the side of a bus stopped in traffic seven blocks east of the Depository. The driver let him in. This particular bus happened to be traveling west on Elm in the direction of the crime scene at Dealey Plaza. Once it became clear that the commotion up ahead was blocking traffic and that the bus would not be moving anytime soon, Oswald asked for a transfer and stepped out into the street. He then proceeded to a bus station on the corner of Lamar and Jackson to catch a cab. "I wonder what the hell is the uproar," said his driver. Police sirens were wailing in the background. Oswald kept his mouth shut.[24]

The cabbie dropped off his passenger in the Oak Cliff section of Dallas. Earlene Roberts, the housekeeper of a boarding house in Oak Cliff, was fiddling with the television in the living room when Oswald, one of her tenants, rushed in. "Oh, you are in a hurry," she teased. Oswald did not respond and went straight to his small adjacent bedroom. Shortly afterward, he emerged from his room wearing a windbreaker. Roberts watched him go out the front door and walk a few feet to a bus stop for buses headed into downtown Dallas. She later recalled hearing a car horn honk, and said she saw a police cruiser near her house.[25]

In the meantime, the news from Dallas had begun to rocket around the nation and the world. "Here is a bulletin from CBS News," said a tense announcer. Viewers who had been watching the soap opera As the World Turns suddenly saw letters flash across their screens at 12:40 P.M.:

CBS NEWS BULLETIN

"In Dallas, Texas, three shots were fired at President Kennedy's motorcade in downtown Dallas," the announcer continued. "The first reports say that President Kennedy has been seriously wounded by this shooting." The voice belonged to the veteran correspondent and anchorman Walter Cronkite. Viewers could hear Cronkite in the studio fumbling with a piece of paper. "More details just arrived," he continued. "These details about the same as previously. President Kennedy shot today just as his motorcade left downtown Dallas. Mrs. Kennedy jumped up and grabbed Mr. Kennedy. She called, 'Oh no!' The motorcade sped on. United Press International reports that the wounds perhaps could be fatal."[26] Remarkably—in part because the primitive TV cameras of the day needed time to warm up—CBS returned to As the World Turns after the shocking announcement. A short time later, however, all three networks canceled their regular programming to focus on the story in Dallas, which obliterated all other news—including the deaths later that day of the famous novelists Aldous Huxley and C. S. Lewis.[27]

The early reports were confusing, making it difficult to separate fact from rumor. At one point, viewers were told that the president was still alive, in critical condition and receiving blood transfusions at a local hospital. Live footage from the Trade Mart showed stunned guests, an empty presidential podium, and an African American waiter dabbing at his eyes with a handkerchief.[28]

The scene at Parkland Hospital was chaotic and frightening. At the emergency room entrance, the First Lady sat motionless in the limo, surrounded by a puddle of blood and brain matter, clinging to her husband's limp body. A large piece of hair-covered skull lay on the seat beside her. "Mrs. Kennedy, let us get the president," said Agent Emory Roberts in a soothing tone. Still in shock, unable to absorb the enormity of events, Jackie refused to let go. Roberts gently lifted her arm and looked at the president's wounds; he knew no one could survive such massive head trauma. Turning toward Agent Roy Kellerman, he said, "You stay with Kennedy. I'm taking some of my men for Johnson." Agent Clint Hill realized that Jackie didn't want the press and public to see her husband in his awful state, so he covered the president's head with his suit coat. Mrs. Kennedy yielded. Kellerman helped a grieving Dave Powers and two other agents hoist the president's body onto a stretcher. "When Agent Paul Landis helped Mrs. Kennedy out of the car he saw a bullet fragment in the back where the top would [normally] be secured. He picked it up and put it on the seat, thinking that if the car were moved, it might be blown off." Dallas officer H. B. McLain, whose motorcycle had accompanied the motorcade, also helped Jackie get out of the Lincoln and into Trauma Room One.[29]

Shortly after he escorted Jackie into the hospital, "an unnamed Secret Service agent asked Parkland personnel to clean the limo interior." Photos from the period show a slop bucket lying next to the presidential car. Gary Mack, curator of the Sixth Floor Museum at Dealey Plaza, which is located in the former Book Depository building and is dedicated to preserving the history of November 22, 1963, calls it "one of the really strange stories about Parkland Hospital . . . The car, of course, was a crime scene, and here's someone altering the crime scene! Is he sweeping up evidence? What's he doing? We don't know."[30] The cleanup removed vital, precise proof of the spray pattern of blood that could have helped determine the direction of the bullets. Afterward, Secret Service agents attached the bubbletop, drove the car back to Love Field, and loaded it onto an Air Force cargo plane for a flight to Washington.[31]

The president was received in Trauma Room One by a twenty-eight-year-old resident physician, Charles Carrico. After checking Kennedy's vital signs, Carrico ordered his assistants to make a small incision in the patient's ankle as an entry point for fluids, blood, and medicine. Carrico then checked for additional wounds by sliding his hands along the president's back; he did not find any more injuries using this method, but neither he nor anyone else at Parkland made a visual inspection of JFK's back. He also inserted a tube down Kennedy's throat to help him breathe. Other physicians soon arrived to lend a hand. Drs. Charles Baxter, Malcolm Perry, and Robert McClelland performed a tracheotomy and inserted a tube into the president's chest cavity "since there was obvious tracheal and chest damage." The tracheotomy widened the bullet hole in JFK's neck. Had the doctors cut through an entrance wound or an exit wound? It wasn't immediately obvious. Dr. Kemp Clark pumped the president's chest with the heel of his hand, but he knew that he was fighting a losing battle. John Kennedy's spirit was leaving—or had left—his body.[32]

Mrs. Kennedy had only reluctantly agreed to leave Trauma Room One to make space for the doctors trying to save her husband. She sat in the hallway with a blank expression, flanked by two Secret Service agents. She refused a nurse's offer to help her tidy up. "Absolutely not," said the First Lady. "I want the world to see what Dallas has done to my husband."[33]

AT THE SAME time, in another part of the hospital, Lyndon Johnson was wondering what his next move should be. Agents Emory Roberts and Rufus Youngblood, the latter LBJ's chief bodyguard, urged him to return quickly to Air Force One. "We should evacuate this hospital right away, get on that plane and get back to Washington," said Youngblood. "We don't know whether this is one man, two men, a gang or an army. The White House is the safest place to conduct the nation's business." Johnson knew that Youngblood was right. What was happening in Washington? Who was running the government? Was a nuclear attack imminent? Still, he did not know the full extent of JFK's injuries, and there were a number of important political factors to consider. What would the American people say if he fled Parkland while JFK was fighting for his life? What would they think if he abandoned Jackie during her hour of need? How would Kennedy loyalists interpret a decision to fly back to the White House before anything certain was known about the president? Some might see it as evidence of Johnson's overweening ambition. He had long coveted the presidency, had run against JFK in 1960 and planned to try for the White House again in 1968. Now he had the prize but couldn't look pleased or eager.

More important, the process of succession was unclear. Although Article

II, Section 1 of the U.S. Constitution states that "In case of the removal of the President from office, or of his death, resignation, or inability to discharge the powers and duties of the said office, the same shall devolve on the Vice President," the clause had always been viewed as a loose set of guidelines rather than an ironclad contract. What was the vice president supposed to do if the president was temporarily or permanently disabled? First Lady Edith Wilson had run the White House for several months in 1919 after her husband suffered a debilitating stroke. During the early days of the Kennedy administration, Johnson and JFK had agreed that if the president was alive but had become incapacitated, the vice president would consult with the cabinet, and especially the attorney general, before assuming the powers of the presidency.[34] And that would mean negotiating a truce with Attorney General Robert F. Kennedy, LBJ's archnemesis.[35]

What no one at the time realized was that Johnson was already president of the United States. The transfer had occurred on Elm Street at precisely 12:30 P.M., when JFK had an estimated one third of his brain blasted away. JFK was brain-dead before he left Dealey Plaza. Dr. Robert McClelland, one of the last surviving physicians who treated Kennedy in Trauma Room One, agrees Kennedy effectively died instantly, at least as we conceive of life and death today.[36]

At any rate, McClelland and his colleagues at Parkland soon resolved any lingering succession questions. Dr. Baxter broke the news as gently as he could: "Mrs. Kennedy . . . your husband is dead." Her brown eyes were filled with grief, terror, and bewilderment. Trying his best to comfort her, Baxter added, "We will not pronounce him dead until he has had the last rites." Catholic clergy were soon on hand to administer the sacrament of extreme unction.[37]

In a hallway near the hospital's main elevators, Darrell Tomlinson, Parkland's senior engineer, heard a metallic clink when he pushed a stretcher out of the way. He was surprised to see a bullet lying on the gurney and reported his discovery to O. P. Wright, the hospital's personnel officer. Wright in turn gave the projectile to a Secret Service agent named Richard Johnsen. Did the bullet drop from Kennedy's stretcher, or Connally's—or, as some would later insist, was it deliberately planted to be found there?[38]

A little over an hour after the shooting, CBS viewers watched as Walter Cronkite, hunched over a microphone and wearing a pair of thick-rimmed glasses, solemnly announced, "From Dallas, Texas, the flash, apparently official, President Kennedy died at one P.M. Central Standard Time, two o'clock Eastern Standard Time, some thirty-eight minutes ago."[39] Cronkite removed his glasses and choked back tears. "Vice President Johnson has left the hospital in Dallas," he continued, "but we do not know to where he has proceeded.

Presumably, he will be taking the oath of office shortly and become the thirty-sixth president of the United States."[40] America—indeed, most of the world—was frozen in place, unbelieving, uncomprehending, and unsure of the moment, much less the future.

IN THE BLINK of an eye, America had changed forever. The youngest elected chief executive in U.S. history became the youngest to die. A vigorous administration of 1,036 eventful days turned to dust in six seconds.[41] A beautiful wife was widowed in a savage way in front of her eyes. Two young children were made fatherless in an instant. The tragedy overwhelmed the public's senses and raised a host of painful questions. How could it happen? Why did it happen? Who did it? Was it a conspiracy? Were America's enemies plotting a takeover? Could war be imminent? Was Lyndon Johnson a fit successor?

People could not absorb the news, too shocked to make sense of the nonsensical and find a way forward. There is film of unknowing passersby on the streets, drawn to the crowds around car radios and TVs in storefronts; as they listened, some jumped in adrenaline-spiked horror, their mouths agape. Americans hurried to surround themselves with friends and family for comfort and reassurance. Spouses were called in a panic and phone lines were jammed. Parents rushed to schools that closed early, eager to embrace their children. Pastors were flooded with requests for spiritual guidance, and churches were as crowded as for a Christmas mass, with parishioners weeping openly in the pews. The lives of people, the business of a nation, simply—stopped. For the first time ever, all-day television became the nation's communal town hall. In ways that we have become accustomed to in times of great tragedy, viewers hesitated to break away from their TV sets. For four long days, they soaked up every word, every image, in the vain hope of solace.

Lyndon Johnson did not have time to watch television that afternoon. He needed to speak with Bobby Kennedy from the parked Air Force One at Love Field. Years later, the former attorney general remembered their conversation:

> First [Johnson] expressed his condolences. Then he said . . . this might be part of a worldwide plot, which I didn't understand, and he said a lot of people down here [in Dallas] think I should be sworn in right away. Do you have any objection to it? And—well, I was sort of taken aback at the moment because it was just an hour after . . . the president had been shot and I didn't . . . see what the rush was. And . . . at the time, at least, I thought it would be nice if [President Kennedy] came back to Washington [as president] . . . But I suppose that was

all personal . . . He said, who could swear me in? I said, I'd be glad to find out and I'll call you back.[42]

After checking with his staff, RFK told Johnson that anyone who administered oaths, including a district court judge, could perform the ceremony. In a sad comedy that could be excused under the circumstances, neither the new president nor the incumbent attorney general could recall the presidential oath or knew where to find it. Johnson had one of his aides phone Nicholas Katzenbach, the deputy attorney general.[43] "Katzenbach walked over to his bookcase and pulled out a copy of the Constitution and read the relevant sections of Article II."[44]

Johnson then contacted federal district court judge Sarah Hughes of Dallas and asked her to administer the presidential oath aboard Air Force One. She declined his offer to send a government car for her—it would be quicker if she drove herself, Hughes explained. Her car sped onto Love Field at around 2:30 P.M. LBJ met her at the door to the president's stateroom. "Thank you for coming, judge. We'll be ready in a minute," he remarked to the first woman who would swear in a president. He then told Larry O'Brien, JFK's chief political strategist, to find a Bible and ask Mrs. Kennedy, who was already on board with her husband's casket, if she would be willing to join them for the brief ceremony. Even though she was deep in grief, Jackie agreed, saying she owed it to her husband. Her bloody clothes, which she was determined to wear all the way back to Washington, caused some people to avert their eyes.[45]

The human tragedy was gripping, but the assassination's political implications were far graver. In this dangerous moment, America was in the throes of a major constitutional crisis. The bullet that had shattered Kennedy's skull had also scrambled the U.S. chain of command. "Officials at the Pentagon were calling the White House switchboard at the Dallas-Sheraton Hotel asking who now in charge. An officer grabbed the phone and assured the Pentagon that Secretary of Defense Robert McNamara and the Joint Chiefs of Staff 'are now the President.'"[46] Moreover, in the confusion of the moment, LBJ had gotten separated from Warrant Officer Ira Gearhart, the man who carried the "football" containing the ciphers needed to launch a nuclear strike. In 1963 the football was "a locked metal suitcase jammed with thirty pounds of codes and equipment" that allowed the president to initiate atomic war instantly. If November 22 had been a Soviet plot, or if the Communists had decided to capitalize on the disarray following the assassination, the United States would have been at a deadly disadvantage.[47]

Cecil Stoughton, JFK's official photographer, snapped the historic photograph of LBJ taking the oath in the crowded airplane stateroom. "He was the only photographer onboard Air Force One, swiftly reloading to black-and-white film, then struck with horror as the shutter jammed. After much jiggling, he obtained 20 shots of the swearing-in ceremony, [most of them] carefully cropped to cut out the bloodstains still showing on Jackie Kennedy's skirt and stockings." Johnson raised his right hand and placed his left hand on a Catholic missal that O'Brien had mistaken for a Bible. "I do solemnly swear," he said, repeating after Judge Hughes, "that I will faithfully execute the office of President of the United States and will, to the best of my ability, preserve, protect, and defend the Constitution of the United States, so help me God." Air Force One climbed into the sky a few moments later.[48]

WHILE AIR FORCE One had been grounded in Dallas, Officer J. D. Tippit was on patrol in the Oak Cliff neighborhood. At 12:45, 12:48, and 12:55 P.M., an announcement came over police channel 1 for all units to be on the lookout for a "white male, approximately thirty, slender build, height five foot ten inches, weight one hundred sixty-five pounds."[49] As he cruised past the intersection of Tenth Street and Patton Avenue, Tippit spotted a man who generally fitted the description. The patrolman pulled his car to the curb and exchanged a few words with the man through the passenger's side window. Tippit then climbed out of his car and started toward the sidewalk. A split second later, gunshots sounded and Officer Tippit fell dead, his body riddled with bullets. While the conclusion is not universally accepted—nothing much would ever be about the events of this day—eyewitnesses identified the shooter as Lee Harvey Oswald.[50]

Johnny Brewer, the acting manager of a Hardy's shoe store, saw Oswald nervously loitering outside of his business on Jefferson Boulevard. The former Marine kept his back to the street and peered anxiously over his shoulder as police sirens screamed in the background. Brewer remembered, "His hair was sort of messed up and [it] looked like he had been running, and he looked scared." Brewer watched as Oswald made the short walk to the Texas Theatre, which was showing a double feature about the ultimate form of violence, war. *Cry of Battle*, starring Van Heflin and James MacArthur, told the story of two Americans "caught in the wilds of the Philippines at the outbreak of World War II"; *War Is Hell* focused on the Korean conflict and a glory-seeking sergeant who refused to tell his men that there had been a cease-fire. The commotion of the police sirens prodded Julia Postal, the theater's ticket taker, to walk out to the curb. While she was distracted, Oswald ducked behind her into the theater. Brewer asked Postal if the man he had just seen going inside had purchased a ticket. "No, by golly, he didn't," she replied. At Postal's behest, Brewer and the concessionaire, Butch Burroughs, secured the exits while she telephoned police.[51]

At 1:45 P.M., a voice crackled over the Dallas police radio: "Have informa-tion a suspect just went in the Texas Theatre on West Jefferson." Every cop in the area immediately converged on the movie house. This was more than just a routine homicide case—one of their own had been gunned down. Officers M. N. "Nick" McDonald, Ray Hawkins, Thomas Hutson, and C. T. Walker entered the theater through the rear exits. "Put your hands up and don't make a move," Hutson demanded. "I'm not the one," Brewer replied tensely. "I just came back to open the door for you. I work up the street. There's a guy inside that I was suspicious of." "Is he still there?" asked Hutson. "Yes, I just seen him." Brewer led the officers into the theater and pointed at a man sit-ting near the doors to the lobby. Nick McDonald cautiously advanced up the left center aisle. In order to keep the suspect calm, he questioned a few of the other people in the theater. "Get on your feet," he snapped as he reached Oswald's row. The suspect stood up and raised his hands; the officer moved in to frisk him for weapons. "Well, it's all over now," Oswald announced before unexpectedly punching McDonald in the face. A mad scramble ensued. "He's got a gun!" someone shouted. As several officers piled on top of Oswald, McDonald heard the chilling sound of a clicking gun hammer. Detective Bob Carroll managed to wrest the weapon from Oswald's hand. "Don't hit me anymore. I am not resisting arrest!" Oswald screamed. "I want to complain of police brutality!"[52]

By this time, word had spread that a suspect in the president's slaying had been cornered; an angry, jeering crowd had gathered outside the theater. As the doors burst open, a freelance photographer, Jim MacCammon, snapped a picture that has become one of the memorable images of the assassination weekend. It shows a visibly agitated Oswald being dragged from the theater in handcuffs, flanked by Officer McDonald and Detective Paul Bentley. Dur-ing the scuffle inside the theater, Bentley punched Oswald in the forehead with his Masonic ring. The blow left a nasty wound, which is visible in subse-quent photographs of Oswald.[53] When asked about it by reporters later at police headquarters, Oswald huffed, "A policeman hit me."

Captain Will Fritz, chief of Dallas police's homicide bureau, returned to headquarters at 2:15 P.M. after investigating the whereabouts of a missing Book Depository employee. Fritz told Sergeant Gerald Hill to "get a search warrant, go to an address on Fifth Street in Irving, and pick up a man named Lee Oswald." When Hill asked why, Fritz said, "Well, he was employed down at the . . . Depository and he [was not] present for a roll call of employees." "Captain, we will save you a trip," replied Hill. "There he sits."[54]

When word leaked that the police had nabbed a possible suspect in the Kennedy murder, hundreds of journalists crammed into the narrow hallways and small offices of Dallas police headquarters. Security was loose. People without press credentials roamed freely through a main hallway. Captain Fritz actually invited Lonnie Hudkins, a reporter for the *Houston Post*, to attend one of Oswald's interrogation sessions. Hudkins asked Oswald, "'Why did you kill Officer Tippit?' And he threw the question right back at me and said, 'Someone get killed? Policeman get killed?' And at that time he had this little smirk on him and I wanted to hit him, but I didn't. And all of a sudden it dawned on me that he wasn't sweating; not a drop of sweat on him. He was cooler than all of the people around him—Secret Service, police, FBI, district attorney . . . *everybody* was in that office."[55]

Surprisingly, authorities acquiesced to reporters' requests to make Oswald available for what was then called a "showing." Although told they were not allowed to ask questions of the suspect, reporters did so after Oswald started talking to them. When one reporter asked if he had been in the Depository at the time of the shooting, Oswald said, "Naturally, if I work in that building, yes, sir." "Did you shoot the president?" asked another reporter. Oswald answered, "No. They've taken me in because of the fact that I lived in the Soviet Union. I'm just a patsy."*

Jim Lehrer was one of the reporters crammed into police headquarters, standing outside a door waiting for news. When the door opened, the Secret Service agent with whom he had had the conversation about the bubbletop at Love Field that Friday morning emerged. "He comes over to me and says, 'Oh, Jim, if I just hadn't taken the bubbletop down.' Of course I'm thinking to myself, 'Shoot, if I just hadn't asked the question.'"[56]

Oswald was allowed to talk to a large press contingent in a crowded room late on Friday. When asked if he had assassinated the president, the suspect said, "No, I have not been charged with that. In fact, nobody has said that to me yet. The first thing I heard about it was when the newspaper reporters in the hall asked me that question." "You *have* been charged," insisted a reporter, incorrectly. Oswald looked confused. "Sir?" he asked. "You *have* been charged," the reporter said a second time.[57] The police broke up the session before Oswald could respond.[58]

It is doubtful that Oswald noticed a man in the back of the room wearing sunglasses. But some Dallas police probably knew who he was and would not have been surprised to see him there. Jack Ruby usually showed up when something big was going on. Some officers had even been to Ruby's strip club

---

* Oswald's "patsy" remark is perhaps the most-quoted aspect of his short time in custody. Over the years, some have insisted that "patsy," meaning an easily blamed pawn, was a signal that Oswald was a low-level flunky in a larger conspiracy. Of course, it is just as possible that Oswald was simply providing himself cover for his actions, implying that he was an available scapegoat because of his Communist ties.

on Commerce Street, which featured attractive performers with names like Tammi True (the "Teacher Turned Stripper"), Kathy Kay, and Joy Dale. Ruby treated cops well, wanting to ensure that he never crossed the legal "decency line," and he was constantly "promoting some inane product, chasing fire trucks, pushing himself into public displays or passing out his Carousel Club calling cards at the fights, in the bars, or on downtown streets." On this particular historic night in Dallas, Ruby would later insist, all he could think about was Oswald's smirk.[59]

LYNDON JOHNSON HELD a much different kind of press conference when he landed at Andrews Air Force Base outside Washington, D.C., at approximately 5:58 P.M. EST. With his presidency barely five hours old, Johnson stood with his wife, Lady Bird, in front of a clutch of microphones and offered brief remarks that had been drafted for him during the flight: "This is a sad time for all people. We have suffered a loss that cannot be weighed. For me, it is a deep personal tragedy. I know that the world shares the sorrow that Mrs. Kennedy and her family bear. I will do my best. That is all I can do. I ask for your help—and God's."[60] Johnson was sincere, but his Southern drawl and unimpressive rhetoric probably caused many at home to say or think, "He's no John F. Kennedy."[61]

Professor James Robertson, a nationally renowned Civil War historian, was at home in northern Virginia glued to his TV screen when he heard the phone ring. "My wife came in, her eyes as big as two cue balls, and she said, 'It's the White House.'" The First Lady needed Robertson's help, said the caller. She had already begun planning her husband's funeral and wanted the White House to look the same way it had during Lincoln's funeral. Could he come to the executive mansion right away? Robertson said he could. In the meantime, he instructed, someone should gather as much black bunting as possible. Robertson then drove straight to the Library of Congress where he and a colleague, armed with flashlights, explored the bowels of the library until they found two newspapers—*Harper's Weekly* and *Frank Leslie's Illustrated*—that featured "woodcuts of the Lincoln coffin in the East Room." Next, Robertson made the quick trip to the White House and was waved in through the northwest gate. "It was driving rain, which seemed appropriate," Robertson recalls, "And there was a massive crowd just standing in the rain in Lafayette Square, staring at the White House seemingly helpless of what to do and where to go."[62] Security escorted him to the president's office. "Quite frankly that's when it all got to me. It was very touching to see the two white sofas and the rocking chair. All of the decorations, the murals and bric-a-brac were still up as if the president would be back."[63] He spread the newspapers out on the floor and began to discuss the details of the funeral with the president's staff. Robertson was then taken to the East Room and was stunned to see that a group of carpenters had already been assembled. They were awaiting his instructions amid a sea of black bunting, more than Robertson had ever seen in his life. In addition, Lincoln's catafalque—the wooden platform that had held the sixteenth president's coffin—had been retrieved from a subterranean storage room in the U.S. Capitol.[64] Robertson and his team worked through the night to prepare for the arrival of the thirty-fifth president's body. Unstated in this hurricane's eye of activity was the cool, shrewd decision by an anguished First Lady to link her husband to America's most beloved chief executive.[65] She wanted JFK's death to mean something, and civil rights, not just assassination, would connect the Lincoln and Kennedy legacies.

THE ASSASSINATION OF a president in the nuclear age came with an especially dark underbelly. Without public notice, those in military authority had to consider the possibility of attack by a hostile power, as well as the need for a massive, instant response that would have killed tens of millions. "At the Pentagon the military machinery stood at global readiness. On the news of the assassination and suspecting a coup, the director of the Joint Chiefs of Staff had immediately warned all of the nine great combat commands of the United States, which girdle the world, to hold themselves in readiness for action. One of them, on its own initiative, [elevated] its men to Defense Condition One, or combat alert. Within half an hour the command was called to order and restored to normal readiness. In Pennsylvania, state troopers sped over the roads to throw a guard around the farm of Dwight D. Eisenhower, lest assassination be planned for him, too."[66]

Once taken from Air Force One, JFK's body—accompanied by Jackie, Bobby, and other relatives and family friends—was transported to Bethesda Naval Hospital. Mrs. Kennedy had chosen this autopsy location because of her husband's service in the Navy.[67] John Stover, the commanding officer of Bethesda's medical school, ordered thirty-nine-year-old James J. Humes to perform the procedure. Humes supervised the school's research labs and had a background in pathology. Lieutenant Commander J. Thornton Boswell, another Navy pathologist, and Colonel Pierre Finck, an army ballistics expert, were selected to assist with the autopsy.[68] The autopsy was limited in scope and competence—another aspect of a terrible day that would haunt the nation for decades to come.

Having spent Friday night in a jail cell on the fifth floor of the Dallas police station, Lee Oswald was moved downstairs to the homicide bureau offices at ten thirty Saturday morning. Reporters he passed in the hallway kept quiet;

they were under strict orders from police not to ask questions. Behind closed doors, Captain Fritz resumed the interrogation. "Lee, did you bring curtain rods to work with you yesterday morning?" he twice asked. Oswald said he had not. "Well . . . ," began the captain, "the fella that drove you to work yesterday morning tells us that you had a package in the backseat. He says that package was about twenty-eight inches long, and you told him it was curtain rods." "I didn't have any kind of package," Oswald replied. "I don't know what he's talking about. I had my lunch and that's all I had."[69] The more Fritz pressed, the more Oswald denied. Toward the end of the session, Fritz sharpened his questions: "Mr. Oswald, did you view the parade yesterday?"

"No, I didn't."

"Did you shoot the president?"

"No, I did not."

"Did you shoot the governor?"

"No, I didn't know that the governor had been shot."[70]

Fritz then ended the session and sent Oswald back to his cell. By the end of the day, the Dallas police were even more convinced that they had JFK's killer. Early Saturday morning the FBI had tracked down an order for an Italian rifle that had been filled out by Oswald and sent to a mail order house in Chicago; the Dallas police found several photos of Oswald holding what appeared to be the assassination weapon along with two left-wing magazines; Oswald's Russian-born wife, Marina, had confirmed that her husband kept a rifle in a friend's garage; police discovered the rifle on the sixth floor of the Book Depository and found Oswald's palm print on a box inside the "sniper's nest." District Attorney Henry Wade, later remembered for his role in the controversial *Roe v. Wade* abortion case, told the press Friday night that he planned to seek the death penalty. It seemed like a classic open-and-shut case. Few observers in November 1963 could have imagined the tangled web that would be revealed in time.[71]

ON SATURDAY A steady rain fell on the streets of Washington. Inside the White House, Lyndon Johnson opened his first cabinet meeting with a moment of silent prayer for JFK. The president's broken body lay in a flag-draped closed coffin in the East Room, surrounded by soldiers, sailors, and airmen. The black bunting that had been hung by Robertson's crew gave the room an additional air of solemnity. Earlier in the day, former presidents Harry Truman and Dwight Eisenhower had stopped by to pay their respects. Now Johnson was asking the assembled members of the Kennedy cabinet to remain at their posts. The country needed continuity, and he said he needed them more than John Kennedy ever had.

What Johnson didn't know was that a few of JFK's most loyal staffers were actively plotting to replace him with Bobby Kennedy. Earlier that day, Arthur Schlesinger had convened a private lunch with John Kenneth Galbraith, Walter Heller, and other officials to discuss the 1964 Democratic Convention—*would it be possible to dump LBJ in favor of an RFK-Humphrey ticket?* they wondered.[72] Bobby Kennedy would have likely supported such a move. He despised Johnson, whom he viewed as a modern-day Cassius. Yet Bobby wanted to stick around long enough to see his brother's legislative proposals enacted to ensure a Kennedy legacy. Johnson, who nursed an enmity for RFK greater than for any other person, would have preferred a cabinet without him. But the Kennedys were now, more than ever, America's royal family, and the "usurper" could not cut loose the dead king's brother without jeopardizing his own reign.

Instead, Johnson moved to honor John Kennedy, ordering the closure of all federal offices on Monday, November 25, for President Kennedy's funeral. "I earnestly recommend the people to assemble on that day in their respective places of divine worship," said Johnson, "there to bow down in submission to the will of Almighty God, and to pay their homage of love and reverence to the memory of a great and good man. I invite the people of the world who share our grief to join in this day of mourning and rededication."[73] A national day of mourning was born, and it was observed in many countries around the world.

Men and women across the globe were already deeply grieving. James Michener, the Pulitzer Prize–winning author, was visiting Israel when news came over the radio of the assassination. "It was the Israelis who started to weep," he wrote, "for they had come to think of Kennedy as a trusted friend, and to lose him in this way was both intolerable and dangerous. 'What will happen now?' they asked me, and for the first time, I heard the comment that would be uttered frequently that night: 'I hope to God the assassin wasn't a Jew.'" Kusum Singh was riding a train across India when he heard that Kennedy had been shot. A hush fell over Singh's compartment, and when the train stopped, people got off to make sure that the news was accurate. One passenger compared JFK to Mahatma Gandhi—both leaders, he said, had been taken before their time. In Ireland, the scene of a triumphant visit by the Irish American president just a few months prior, people canceled weekend activities and crowded into churches to offer prayers for their transnational hero. In Mexico City, small business owners placed busts and pictures of the president in their windows. Mexico's head of state, Lopez Mateos, declared a three-day period of national mourning. Even America's enemies were moved by the events of November 22. Americans in Moscow "were stopped in the street by Soviet citizens wishing to express sympathy, and American students at the university reported that a number of their Soviet colleagues were in tears." Marina Tempkina was a high school student in Leningrad when she learned of the assassination. "I was deeply saddened by Kennedy's death because I liked him personally, and even more because he seemed to offer hope for a better world," she said. "When he died, I thought we had lost much of such hope."[74]

Americans everywhere were stunned, from the mightiest to the most humble. House Speaker John McCormack exclaimed, "My God! My God! What are we coming to?" Senator Ted Kennedy was presiding over the Senate, a task often assigned to junior senators, when he got word and quickly slipped out of the chamber. Every town, city, and school had its own story. At Temple University, students stared with "blank, expressionless faces" at a sign posted in the window of the school's communications building that read PRESIDENT KENNEDY IS DEAD. Some students cried while others prayed. Temple's faculty tried to cope with the crisis by offering instant analyses of the Kennedy presidency. "Not since Roosevelt has there been a president who had such a firm hold on his followers as well as his opponents," opined William McKenna, an associate professor of economics. "Even after his term of office, whether it might have been four or eight years, he still would have been able to perform valuable service for the United States," offered Professor Harry Tinckom, chairman of the history department.[75]

Bob Schieffer, now the host of CBS's *Face the Nation*, was a police beat journalist for the *Fort Worth Star Telegram* in 1963. Because of Kennedy's arrival in Fort Worth the night before and some wee-hours schmoozing with national reporters and Secret Service agents, Schieffer was still in bed when he learned from his brother that the president had been shot. "I didn't know what else to do so I just got dressed and rushed down to the office," Schieffer remembers. "By the time I got downtown it came over the radio that the president was dead and I really just lost it. It was total mass confusion. They closed the borders to Mexico. We didn't know if this was the beginning of World War III. We didn't know if there was some sort of attempted coup. And people were terrified. I never felt again the way I felt during those days until 9/11." Schieffer says that the traumatic event changed his personality for a time. "I had been a police reporter for a while and had seen about everything you could see. And about a week or so after this happened I covered this horrible automobile accident where an entire family . . . had run under a load of pipe [and] it literally sawed them in half along with the car. And I'm standing there looking at it and I realized I had no emotion whatsoever. None! I was like a dog watching television."[76]

Like most people of his generation, Senate Minority Leader Mitch McConnell—then a twenty-one-year-old college student at the University of Louisville—remembers precisely where he was when he first learned of the president's death. "I was watching a flag football game between my fraternity and another one and it had just ended," McConnell recalls. "As I was walking away from the [playing field], someone came up to me and said, 'the president's been shot.' I was obviously not a Kennedy supporter but it made no difference. It was such a stunning and traumatic event for the country." McConnell spent the whole weekend at his parents' house "glued to the television set" and saw "Jack Ruby shoot Lee Harvey Oswald in real time" while he was "sitting there eating a sandwich."[77]

LBJ's daughter, Lynda Bird Johnson, was a college student at the University of Texas-Austin, and was looking forward to attending the dinner with President and Mrs. Kennedy in Austin that evening. She had just arrived at her dorm room for lunch after class when a "former roommate called me and said, 'stay where you are, I'm coming to get you.' She had just heard from somebody that the president had been shot in Dallas. She took me to a room where they had a radio. Nobody had a television and I didn't even have a radio in my room. And so we went there and I listened and I just fell on my knees and started praying that it wasn't so. I loved President Kennedy, and I also loved John and Nellie Connally. They had been like parents to me. We called him 'Uncle Johnny.' I had spent many summers with them and their oldest daughter had spent summers with me. So I was scared for them. There were even some things on the news that maybe my father had had a heart attack. Just like a lot of people I didn't know what had happened."[78]

Joe and Rose Kennedy, JFK's aging parents, received an avalanche of sympathy letters and telegrams. "He asked not what his country could do for him," wrote astronaut John Glenn. "He gave his all. We draw an increased devotion from his example. May God grant you faith, understanding and courage." Actress Marlene Dietrich cabled a single, poignant sentence: "Cannot express the depth of my sadness."

Even J. Edgar Hoover, the strong-willed FBI director who had frequently crossed swords with the Kennedys, sent a sympathy letter to JFK's father. "It is impossible to express the depth of my sorrow," Hoover wrote. "I regret I have only condolences to offer since I know they can do but little to ease your grief."[79] Of course, it was Hoover's bureau that failed to keep close tabs on Lee Harvey Oswald. The director learned four days after the assassination that Oswald's name had never even been on the FBI's Security Index, a watch list of potential subversives with a history of violent tendencies.[80] In truth, despite his defection to Russia and various run-ins with military and civilian authorities over the years, there was nothing in Oswald's known background to suggest he was a violent threat to anyone. But in the hothouse of finger pointing following the assassination, the FBI would try to put as much distance as possible between itself and Oswald.

Average citizens poured their pain onto paper. Carolyn Williamson wrote about the reaction of the men who were serving on board her son's naval vessel. "The Captain of the ship ordered them to assemble on deck where he announced that he had 'grievous news' for them—their Commander-in-Chief had been taken. Their faces, my son wrote, were as wet as the waters of the Pacific." Williamson closed with a heartfelt good-bye to JFK: "We needed our president. I wish he could have been spared to us longer."[81]

Catholics were especially devastated by the president's death and sought solace in their faith. Gerald J. Murray, commander of a World War I veterans group in Scranton, Pennsylvania, assured Rose Kennedy that the "people of the world" would miss her son and expressed his desire to see JFK canonized as a saint. "May the good Lord take him to Paradise . . . where his great reward will be waiting him," Murray wrote tenderly. "And may God bless you and your family and his to carry on and bear your burdens with grace." It was not uncommon in Catholic homes, for years after 1963, to see photos of JFK next to images of the pope and Jesus Christ. "Dear Mrs. Kennedy," wrote Elaine McCluggage, "I am writing this letter as another mother who has a son named John, whose middle name is my maiden name, and who is also American, Irish and Catholic." McCluggage wanted Rose to know that she attended mass "most mornings" and would remember JFK "each morning for as long as I am able." Theresa Twaddle was just seventeen years old when she mailed a letter to the "finest parents of the finest president." "As a Catholic I have offered all my masses, communions and prayers for your son and you," Twaddle assured them.[82]

Pope Paul VI issued a special statement that included a reminder that JFK had been "the first Catholic president of the United States." "We remember that we had the honor of . . . knowing his great wisdom (*sagezza*) and his good intentions for all humanity," His Holiness observed. "We offer the Holy Mass tomorrow for the peace of his soul, and for those who mourn his death."[83]

After receiving a generous donation in JFK's name, the Seraphic Mass Association for the support of the Capuchin Foreign Missions promised that "the soul of the deceased John Fitzgerald Kennedy" would "share forever in:

1. 6,000 Holy Masses which will be said each year by the Capuchins exclusively for the members.
2. 500 Conventional Masses said daily.
3. All the prayers and good works of the religious of the Capuchin Order (who number 15, 624)."[84]

Not to be outdone, Protestants penned missives designed to ease the Kennedys' grief. R. Bresnahan complimented Rose for producing "wonderful sons" and behaving gallantly "throughout this unspeakable tragedy." Mindful of Rose's strict Catholicism, Bresnahan added, "Always in our hearts, you remain the mother second only to the Virgin Mary." Martin Maehr, a faculty member at a conservative Lutheran college in the Midwest, expressed his appreciation for the "testimony of religious conviction" that the Kennedys had displayed "under such trying circumstances. Maehr also singled out Rose for demonstrating "in a most exemplary way" that the "home is the cradle of Christianity and true citizenship."[85]

On Sunday, November 24, Americans flocked to their churches and synagogues seeking spiritual comfort and hoping that religious leaders could find meaning in a senseless act. Preaching at St. George's Episcopal Church in New York, the influential theologian Reinhold Niebuhr attributed the "dimension and universality" of the grief for JFK to three things: first, the assassination had "cut short the life of a promising career" and robbed the nation of an extraordinary leader; second, unlike some other presidents, Kennedy had perished before his "essential work was done"; and third, JFK took over the presidency at a time when the United States was the undisputed leader of the free world. "This concentration of power and prestige is so great," Niebuhr explained, "that we must view President Kennedy's death with mingled gratitude for the providential selection of so gifted a leader to exercise that power, and with an anxious and prayerful attitude about our American world responsibilities in the future."[86]

Some religious leaders perceived universal messages and warnings. Monsignor John S. Kennedy (no relation) told his flock, "The head of our nation was carried away in death a few days ago because of what has been in the hearts of too many of us. His death should sober those drunk on hatred of whatever sort and from whatever source." Rabbi Julius Mark delivered a similar message to a packed house at Temple Emanu-El. "[JFK's] tragic death was the direct result of the dark hatreds and insane hostilities which poison the hearts of otherwise decent and respectable citizens of our country," Mark insisted. Norman Vincent Peale—a famous Protestant preacher who had been one of Kennedy's persistent critics—blamed the crisis on America's moral decline: "I rode down a street in [New York] this morning looking at the signs on the marquees of the theaters," Peale said. "Every single one of them implied that the picture they advertised was either one of sex or violence. And if a nation becomes conditioned to violence they need not be surprised when some one man or a group of men take the law into their hands and destroy the man who has been elected by the sovereign people to enforce the laws of this land." Peale hoped that the shock of the assassination would lead Americans toward "a new appreciation of the fact that we must insist that this become a nation of reason and law."[87]

DALLAS CERTAINLY SEEMED like a lawless place on that Sunday. As Americans sat in their pews and prayed for peace, yet another loathsome act of violence occurred in the basement of the city's police headquarters. Just before 11:30 A.M., Lee Harvey Oswald emerged from an elevator handcuffed to Jim Leavelle, a detective in a beige cowboy hat. The suspect was being transferred to the Dallas County jail in a carefully choreographed attempt to make Oswald visible to the media to prove he wasn't being mistreated.[88] As Leavelle and his partner, Detective L. C. Graves, threaded their way through a mass of detectives and officers, a man in a gray fedora emerged from the crowd holding a snub-nosed revolver. Bob Jackson, a photographer for the *Dallas Times Herald*, captured the famous photograph of Jack Ruby shooting Oswald in the belly. It shows Oswald groaning in agony with his mouth open and his eyes shut. Jim Leavelle, who tried at the last second to pull Oswald out of the path of the bullet, grimaced. Astonishment best describes the reaction of millions at home, who witnessed television's first live murder. Tom Pettit, correspondent on scene for NBC News, uttered the simple lines that have echoed ever since: "He's been shot! He's been shot! Lee Oswald's been shot!" In the ensuing pandemonium, a scrum of officers wrestled Ruby to the ground and grabbed his revolver.

Oswald was rushed to Parkland Hospital, where some of the same doctors that had worked on President Kennedy attempted to revive him in the room across from where JFK had lain. The result was also the same. Oswald was pronounced dead almost exactly 48 hours after JFK (1:07 P.M. CST). The .38-caliber bullet had punctured his spleen, stomach, intestinal arteries, and right kidney. Behind closed doors, Ruby offered a motive: "When I saw that Mrs. Kennedy was going to have to appear for a trial, I thought to myself, 'why should she have to go through this ordeal for this no good son of a bitch?'" Was Ruby telling the truth? Or had he been hired to silence Oswald before he could disclose a conspiracy?[89]

Millions of people subscribed to the latter theory. But the answer to "Who killed JFK?" depended partly on one's political views and degree of trust in government. Conspiracy theorists across the political spectrum saw evidence of their enemies' handiwork in Dallas. The KGB quickly concluded that Kennedy had been killed "by a circle of reactionary monopolists in league with pro-fascist groups" who were upset with the president for supporting civil rights, peace with Russia, and higher taxes on oil profits. Khrushchev himself refused to believe "that the U.S. security services were so inept as to have allowed a madman to kill the president" and thought that the Dallas police must have been involved in the murder. Fidel Castro held similar views. He implicated American "ultrareactionaries," whom the Cuban media described as power brokers upset over Kennedy's "weak" handling of Cuba. Similar themes rippled across the Communist world. "Communist propaganda organs in East Europe suggested that the rightists, in their impotence to reverse President Kennedy's liberal policies," had "resorted to 'political terror' to gain their ends." A Communist newspaper in Hanoi blamed U.S. "financiers" for the shooting.

People living in other parts of the world put their own spin on the events of 11/22. Many sub-Saharan Africans thought that white racists had murdered Kennedy for his support of civil rights. Middle Eastern commentators viewed the JFK assassination as part of a Zionist plot. "One Cairo newspaper noted that Oswald's killer was 'one Jack Ruberstein [sic], a Jew of course.'" Right-wingers in Nationalist China and Latin America smelled a Red conspiracy, as did Herbert Philbrick, a rabid anticommunist and FBI counterspy who later expounded his theories in a manuscript entitled "The Strange Death of President Kennedy." In a matter of hours, JFK's assassination had become a reflection of each individual's ideology—people saw what they wanted to see in the events of 11/22 and created narratives that reflected their personal prejudices and predilections.[90]

Jackie Kennedy appeared less interested in theories of the assassination than in strategies to make sure that John F. Kennedy would be forever remembered as a great president.[91]* She was disappointed when she learned that a left-wing loner had been charged with murdering her husband. "He didn't even have the satisfaction of being killed for civil rights," she lamented. "It had to be some silly little Communist. It even robs his death of any meaning." Her first effort to assign significance to JFK's life and death was to orchestrate an unforgettable funeral, and she somehow found the physical and emotional strength to do so. On Sunday, three hundred thousand people lined the streets of Washington to watch a team of horses transport JFK's

---

* One of those strategies involved the location of her husband's grave. Most visitors to Arlington Cemetery do not consciously notice that the eternal flame above JFK's resting place aligns perfectly with the Lincoln Memorial, the Washington Monument, and the U.S. Capitol, which "confers upon the late President's grave a civic consequence comparable to that possessed by the Washington and Jefferson as well as the Lincoln memorials. This is doubtless what the Kennedys intended when they chose the site, and architect John Warnecke did not fail them. He . . . made inspired use of every dramatic, expressive and evocative potential the land provides." See "John Fitzgerald Kennedy Grave Research Report," LBJ Papers—EX FG 1 3/26/68, Box 18, FG 1 3/26/68 – 4/18/68, Lyndon Baines Johnson Library, Austin, Texas. The John F. Kennedy Center for the Performing Arts is also close by.

body from the White House to the U.S. Capitol. Hundreds of millions more around the globe watched the event on live television. A riderless black horse followed the cortege, twisting and turning but firmly under the control of its handler. The streets of Washington were silent except for the solemn sounds of drums, muffled sobs, and the clip-clop of horses' hooves.

The president's coffin was placed in the Dome Room of the Capitol, where Mike Mansfield, the Senate majority leader, delivered the most moving speech of his career. "There was a sound of laughter; in a moment, it was no more," Mansfield began. "And so she took a ring from her finger and placed it in his hands," a reference to Mrs. Kennedy's action in Parkland's Trauma Room One as she said good-bye to her husband. The senator offered a series of tributes, all ending with the same refrain about the transferred wedding ring. His address was a source of great comfort to Jackie. In her ears, it sounded "as eloquent as a Pericles oration, or Lincoln's letter to the mother who had lost five sons in battle." "A piece of each of us died at that moment," Mansfield continued. "Yet, in death he gave of himself. He gave us of a good heart from which the laughter came. He gave us of a profound wit, from which a great leadership emerged. He gave us of a kindness and a strength fused into a human courage to seek peace without fear. He gave us of his love that we, too, in turn, might give." When Mansfield finished, he approached Jackie and handed her the manuscript. "How did you know I wanted it?" she asked. "I didn't," said Mansfield. "I just wanted you to have it." Jackie then led daughter Caroline over to the president's catafalque—together they kneeled and kissed the flag that lay draped across his coffin. It was a fitting farewell that brought a shattered nation together.[92]

Hundreds of thousands of people waited in line for a chance to file past the president's casket. "The overflow spilled down the streets between the congressional office buildings, the Supreme Court, the Library of Congress, and the Folger Library, and to the west it ran from the Botanic Gardens to the Taft tower." Every citizen, it seemed, wanted to say good-bye in some personal, significant way. Filmmaker Robert Drew, father of the cinema verité movement, captured the sad expressions on the faces of those who shuffled through the Dome Room on that bleak autumn day. The resulting film, *Faces of November*, later won two first-place awards at the Venice Film Festival. We see black and white, old and young, men and women joined together in an outpouring of anguish, perhaps sad also for the loss of national innocence. Despite a long history of political violence, people were genuinely aghast that such a thing could have happened in the United States.[93]

Kings, queens, emperors, princes, ministers, chancellors, presidents, and ambassadors from a vast array of countries arrived for the Monday funeral. Jackie insisted on walking to St. Matthew's Cathedral, which meant that

President Johnson and visiting heads of state would walk in the open, too. The Secret Service objected strenuously, deathly afraid that something else might happen on their watch, but to no avail. Escorted by Bobby and Ted, the remaining brothers also frightfully exposed, Jackie stayed close to the caisson as it rolled toward the church. The Royal Highland Black Watch Regiment paid their respects with a somber bagpipe tune. The sound seemed to bring Mrs. Kennedy to the verge of tears, but she remained supremely disciplined. Hauntingly beautiful, she simultaneously projected strength and fragility beneath her black veil, which stirred gently in the breeze.

At Jackie's behest, the Most Reverend Philip Hannan, a young auxiliary bishop stationed in the nation's capital, delivered the president's eulogy. Hannan mentioned a few of JFK's favorite Bible verses (such as "Your old men shall dream dreams, your young men shall see visions"), and then he recited the 1961 inaugural address. It was an exquisite choice and temporarily lifted the spirits of those in attendance. Ted Sorensen, Kennedy's inaugural co-writer, later told Hannan that his eulogy would "be remembered . . . for a long time."[94]

Then it happened, the moment that no one alive at the time will ever forget. It was a child's simple gesture, and yet it brought home the true personal tragedy of November 22. As the president's flag-draped coffin was being removed from St. Matthew's Cathedral, Jackie leaned over and whispered in her son's ear. Just weeks before the assassination, the son had been taught by his father and several Secret Service agents how to salute the flag. John F. Kennedy, Jr., fatherless on his third birthday, dutifully stepped forward and pressed his tiny right hand against his forehead to say good-bye. America wept as one.[95]

President Kennedy's body was then taken across the river to Arlington National Cemetery, once the estate of Robert E. Lee, the Confederacy's greatest general. "Fifty jet planes of the Air Force and Navy, one for each state, roared low overhead as the caisson halted beside the grave. The apex of the last V formation was empty, symbolizing a fallen leader. The president's jet, Air Force One, trailed the formation and dipped its wings . . ." An honor guard of Irish military cadets, rifles reversed, executed a manual of arms in Gaelic. Next, Cardinal Richard Cushing, the Kennedys' chief spiritual adviser, led the assembled dignitaries in the Lord's Prayer and the Hail Mary. Cannon boomed a twenty-one-gun salute; a lone bugler blew Taps; a group of servicemen handed Mrs. Kennedy a folded American flag.

There was only one piece of unfinished business, one final gesture for the man who had carried the torch for a new generation. Bending down beside her husband's grave, Jackie (with help from Bobby and Ted) ignited a gas and electric jet that had been installed by the Washington Gas Company. This was no ordinary burner; it had come specially equipped so that the blaze could survive every kind of weather. The "eternal flame"—the symbol of her husband's life and legacy—would glow for as long as the American Republic endured.[96]

The fire was everlasting, yet America's and the world's premier leader had been snuffed out in a vicious, premature way. No one could have imagined it would end like this. No one could have guessed the misery that awaited John F. Kennedy and his family when his astounding political journey had begun a few short years earlier.

2

"ALL THE MARBLES"

AT HALF PAST EIGHT ON THE OPENING night of the 1956 Democratic National Convention, the Honorable Paul M. Butler stood on the main stage of Chicago's International Amphitheatre and made the following announcement: "Will the delegates please clear the aisles? The lights are going to be turned out, so you had better get into your seats, if you want to see." What they were about to see, explained the DNC chairman, was a documentary film on the history of the Democratic Party. The delegates should hold their applause until the movie ended.[1]

A few minutes later, a star was born. "Ladies and gentlemen, I am Senator John F. Kennedy of Massachusetts," said the boyishly handsome face on the screen. "To some, the Democratic Party represents a philosophy, a way of life, a point of view. Others think in terms of personalities—the great Democratic leaders of past and present . . . Whatever the unique quality of our party represents to each of you, I believe you will find it in the course of this film, which singles out the principal events which have given the Democratic Party special character and dignity—which make it now, as always, our nation's best and greatest hope."[2]

At the conclusion of the twenty-eight-minute film called *The Pursuit of Happiness* (which was shown on ABC and NBC, but not CBS), Butler thanked the narrator, referring to him as "one of our new young Democratic giants."[3] Kennedy "was introduced from the floor" and received "prolonged applause." A small group of New England delegates rushed the platform and waved Kennedy placards, but they instantly vanished when Butler "asked them to clear the aisles so [that] the keynoter, Gov. Frank G. Clement of Tennessee, could be introduced."[4]

Kennedy outclassed the parochial Clement, who delivered a partisan (and much parodied) speech.[5] The *New York Times* called the Massachusetts senator a "movie star" and described his delivery as "excellent." Eleven thousand delegates and millions of TV viewers witnessed Kennedy's exemplary performance. Historian Herbert Parmet says that it made the senator "an overnight hero in Chicago" and that people mobbed him "wherever he went, on the streets, on the convention floor." Dore Schary, the film's producer and one of California's delegates, later said that "the personality of the senator just came right out. It jumped at you on the screen. The narration was good, and the film was emotional. He was immediately a candidate. There was simply no doubt about that because he racked up the whole convention." Schary had cast Kennedy at the behest of Paul Butler, who recognized the young senator's potential. Kennedy threw himself into the film project, contributing his own lines and patiently enduring multiple takes and rehearsals.[6]

Jack Kennedy was one of the few politicians who understood the emerging power of televised images. His father had made millions in the 1920s off a Hollywood studio called Film Booking Offices (FBO). The elder Kennedy turned FBO into a profitable company by focusing on low-cost productions rather than big-budget blockbusters. Kennedy's target audience was theater owners in small towns and rural areas who usually featured new films every couple of days. Before long, Kennedy had established a lucrative niche for FBO. During the first year of his stewardship, the studio generated nearly $9 million worth of revenue. It remained a profitable company in the years that followed before merging with Keith-Albee-Orpheum (KAO) to form RKO Pictures, one of the studio giants of Hollywood's golden era. The money that came from FBO, the stock market, and other investments allowed Joe— FDR's ambassador to the United Kingdom between 1938 and 1940—to pamper his nine children. Although descended from poor Irish Catholic immigrants who had come to America in the nineteenth century, the twentieth-century Kennedys lived like Boston Brahmins. John Kennedy wore the nicest clothes, ate the best-prepared foods, and attended the finest schools, including Choate—a posh prep school in Connecticut—and Harvard. His father had taught him to play hard and to win at any cost. This lesson gave him the strength to rescue three sailors from a sinking PT boat during World War II, the ambition to run for Congress before he turned thirty, and the temerity to challenge and defeat an old-moneyed WASP named Henry Cabot Lodge, Jr., for a U.S. Senate seat in 1952. And in 1956, this same feisty, competitive spirit convinced JFK to try for the Democratic Party's vice presidential nomination.[7]

According to Ted Sorensen, Kennedy knew "early in 1956" that he was under consideration for the number two slot on the party's ticket. Adlai Stevenson's handlers told Theodore White (who in turn told Sorensen and Kennedy) that two southerners—Senator Al Gore, Sr., of Tennessee and Frank Clement—as well as two Catholics—JFK and New York Mayor Robert F. Wagner, Jr.—were under consideration for the running mate job. Connecticut governor Abraham Ribicoff was the first politician to publicly endorse Kennedy; Governor Dennis Roberts of Rhode Island quickly followed suit. So did Governor Luther Hodges of North Carolina, who thought that JFK would be acceptable to the southern wing of the party. Newspapers and magazines also played up the possibility of a Kennedy vice presidency during this period.[8]

During the convention, the delegates and media speculated on who Stevenson, the presumed nominee, would choose as a running mate. The influential former First Lady Eleanor Roosevelt made it clear that she did not want Kennedy on the ticket. Several weeks before the convention, she received a letter from a friend who wanted her to endorse the ambassador's son. "Across the bottom of her reply, Mrs. Roosevelt added that, before she would support Senator Kennedy for the second spot, he would have to declare his views on Senator [Joseph] McCarthy (R-Wis.) so that she could know 'how he really stands.'" McCarthy, a Kennedy family friend and enemy of the left, had made a name for himself in the early 1950s by accusing prominent people of supporting Communism without real evidence. Careers had been ruined and reputations besmirched as a result of the senator's witch hunts. Kennedy had never publicly denounced fellow Irish American McCarthy, aware that many of the voters in his district supported the Wisconsin senator. During the convention, Kennedy made a backhanded attempt to appease Mrs. Roosevelt by telling her that he would make his views on McCarthy known "when the occasion presented itself." Mrs. Roosevelt was not satisfied and continued giving JFK the cold shoulder.[9]

On August 14, the *New York Times* reported that Al Gore, Sr., was Stevenson's "personal choice" for vice president. But Gore was reluctant to pick a fight with Estes Kefauver, a fellow Tennessean, who he purportedly said would "attract more widespread voting support to Mr. Stevenson than any other Democrat." Gore was honest enough, however, to admit that Kefauver—perceived as too liberal by many southerners—might be a drag on the ticket in the former Confederate states. John Kennedy was Gore's second choice. On August 15, the *Times* reported that the Stevenson camp was leaning toward Kefauver or Minnesota's Hubert Humphrey but preferred a man who would be acceptable to the various factions represented at the convention. Thus, John Kennedy's name made Adlai's short list.[10]

The same day, Kennedy received word "by a circuitous route" that he was no longer under consideration as the party's vice presidential nominee. In response, Kennedy sought, and received, an audience with Stevenson, who insisted to JFK that he was noncommittal. The presidential nominee-to-be did, however, ask JFK to deliver his (Stevenson's) official nomination speech. Kennedy accepted but interpreted the offer as effective proof that he was no longer in the running for the vice presidential slot. One of Stevenson's aides delivered a prewritten speech to Kennedy that had been slap-dashed together, partly by Arthur Schlesinger. Kennedy and Sorensen worked late into the night redrafting it.[11]

The senator scored big political points the next day (August 16) when he read the new and improved speech before the convention. He received "a great cheer" when he appeared on the platform. "Sometimes in the heat of a political convention, we forget the grave responsibilities which we as delegates possess," said Kennedy.

> For we here today are selecting a man who must be something more than a good candidate, something more than a good speaker, more than a good politician, a good liberal, or a good conservative. We are selecting the head of the most powerful nation on earth, the man who literally will hold in his hands the powers of survival or destruction, of freedom or slavery, of success or failure for us all. We are selecting here today the man who for the next four years will be guiding, for good or evil, for better or worse, the destinies of our nation and, to a large extent, the destiny of the free world. I ask you, therefore, to think beyond the balloting of tonight and tomorrow—to think beyond even the election in November and to think instead of those four years that lie ahead, and of the crises that will come with them.[12]

Kennedy also took the required pot shots at the GOP, which entertained his partisan audience. He wisely chose to attack the often-reviled Nixon instead of the popular Eisenhower: "Our party will be up against two of the toughest, most skillful campaigners in its history—one who takes the high road, and one who takes the low." According to Sorensen, this line "was picked up by subsequent speakers and became part of that year's campaign vocabulary."[13]

Looking ahead to the 1960 presidential race (or perhaps worried about the current vice presidential one), the senator made passing reference to "the nation's distressed farmers." Kennedy had earned the ire of this group in April 1956 by voting against "90-percent-of-parity price supports for one year," which basically amounted to a new government welfare program for farmers.[14]

Kennedy closed his speech with a tribute to Stevenson, whom he described as a man of "compassion" and "courage" who also happened to be "the top vote-getter in the Democratic Party." "Fellow delegates," he proclaimed, "I give you the man from Libertyville—the next Democratic nominee and our next president of the United States—Adlai E. Stevenson." The crowd cheered. Jacqueline Kennedy, six weeks pregnant at the time, stood on her chair and waved a Stevenson placard from the convention floor.[15]

Shortly after eleven P.M., Stevenson threw the convention into an uproar when, in a move unprecedented in modern times and apparently with no advance word to any of the possible contenders, he asked the delegates to choose his running mate for him. "The choice will be yours," said the Illinois politician. "The profit will be the nation's." Stevenson wanted to highlight the differences between the two parties by showing that Democrats were the only true supporters of majoritarian rule. The decision also relieved him of the politically risky burden of choosing a running mate.[16] Kennedy and his energetic supporters instantly swung into action. Bobby and John Bailey held an impromptu meeting at the Stockyards Inn and began handing out assignments and lining up key backers. Eunice lobbied state delegations for support. Jack buttonholed Robert Wagner in the men's room of the Blackstone Hotel sometime after midnight and proposed a deal: the candidate who came up short after the first ballot would throw his support to the other. The New York City mayor agreed. "By sunrise that morning, overnight button factories had produced Kennedy-for-Vice-President stickpins, which went on sale outside the International Amphitheater."[17]

Inside the arena, the real work got under way. After the first ballot, Estes Kefauver led with 483½ votes; Kennedy came in second with 304 votes; Al Gore earned 178 votes, while Robert Wagner and Hubert Humphrey finished with 162½ and 134½ respectively. On the second ballot, the race broke open. Southerners who were anxious to stop Kefauver—an advocate of civil rights—began throwing their support to Kennedy. "Kennedy's supporters raised a yell as Arkansas switched its 26 votes from Gore to the young New England senator." Delaware soon followed suit. True to his word, Wagner delivered 96½ of New York's 98 votes to JFK, which sparked a spontaneous outburst of chanting on the convention floor: "We want Kennedy! We want Kennedy!"[18]

Kennedy watched the drama unfold from the comfort of his hotel room. Sorensen later recalled the scene: "Our television set showed wild confusion on the convention floor and a climbing Kennedy total. But the Senator was as calm as ever. He bathed, then again reclined on the bed. Finally we moved, through a back exit, to a larger and more isolated room."[19]

Though it wasn't recognized as such at the time, perhaps the most historically evocative moment came when Senator Lyndon Johnson hollered on the convention floor, "Texas proudly casts its vote for the fighting senator who wears the scars of battle, that fearless senator, the next vice president of the United States, John Kennedy of Massachusetts." Johnson had come to Chicago with his eyes on the top prize. But when Stevenson secured the nomination instead, LBJ decided to play vice presidential kingmaker. He threw Texas's 56 votes to Clement and then Gore and finally to Kennedy when it looked as if the Massachusetts senator had a decent shot at beating Kefauver, who was not one of Johnson's Senate favorites.[20] Johnson's announcement triggered a burst of applause and activity; California gave Kennedy 14½ more votes;

North Carolina contributed 17½; Kentucky switched its 30 votes from Gore to JFK. He was now leading Kefauver 618 to 551½. He needed 686½ votes to win the nomination. Back at the Stockyards Inn, Sorensen offered his boss a congratulatory handshake. "Not yet," said Kennedy. Even so, Kennedy was upbeat; he dressed, kept one eye on the TV, and discussed what sort of speech he would deliver if nominated. A cordon of cops arrived, ready to escort the thirty-nine-year-old senator to the convention center.[21]

And then the momentum suddenly, almost mysteriously, shifted. The young Kennedy had soared too close to the sun.

Al Gore withdrew from the contest and asked his supporters to back Kefauver. Oklahomans, unhappy at the prospect of having to vote for a Catholic from an industrial state, happily complied. Missouri and Michigan also jumped on the Kefauver bandwagon. South Carolina tried to stanch the bleeding, but without success. Pennsylvania added 74 votes to the Tennessee senator's column, which encouraged the delegations from Iowa, Montana, California, Delaware, West Virginia, and Maine to adjust their votes. At the end of the second ballot, Kefauver secured the nomination with 755½ votes. Kennedy finished with a respectable 589. Knowing that he'd been beaten, he headed to the amphitheater to congratulate Kefauver.[22]

Kennedy received a warm welcome as he took the stage. "Recognizing that this convention has selected a man who has campaigned in all parts of the country," he said just after four o'clock, "I hope this convention will now make Estes Kefauver's nomination unanimous." As the young senator started to leave the stage, Sam Rayburn called him back and handed him the chairman's gavel. Kennedy raised it and said, "I move we suspend the rules and nominate Estes Kefauver by acclamation." The crowd roared its approval. Kennedy's magnanimous concession endeared him to millions. His "near victory and sudden loss, the impression he gave of a clean-cut boy who had done his best and who was accepting defeat with a smile—all this struck at people's hearts in living rooms across the nation. In this moment of triumphant defeat, his campaign for the presidency was born." In private, JFK was hugely disappointed that he had lost. He flew to France for a vacation, leaving behind his pregnant wife, who had already had one miscarriage and would soon suffer another. But as events would show, losing the vice presidential nomination was the best thing that could have happened. If Kennedy had won the contest, he would have been blamed in part for Stevenson's subsequent defeat. Inevitably, the press would have cited the Catholic issue. Instead, he received extensive, positive media coverage yet was held harmless for Stevenson's November rout.[23]

Kennedy spent the next few months crisscrossing the country on Stevenson's behalf. These trips raised the senator's public profile and gave him the opportunity to chat up party leaders and build a loyal following. Stevenson and Kefauver were happy to ride Kennedy's coattails. J. Howard McGrath, Kefauver's special assistant, told the press that the Massachusetts senator would "play a leading role in the Democratic presidential campaign, second only to that of the presidential and vice presidential candidates."[24]

Kennedy's help, though, turned out to be the kind politicians often offer—me first, you second. While ostensibly stumping for the party ticket, he frequently promoted his own record. In California, he told a roomful of union workers about his time on the Labor Committee and how hard he had worked to boost the minimum wage. At the World Affairs Council luncheon in Los Angeles he bolstered his foreign policy credentials by lecturing on the security threats posed by "four Middle Eastern-Mediterranean areas—Suez, Cyprus, Israel, and French North Africa." In Springfield, Massachusetts, the topic turned to energy: "I was gratified when the Congress accepted my amendment to the Atomic Energy Act and gave preference to areas with high power costs in the location of reactors . . ." Thousands of people turned out to hear Kennedy, whose popularity began to transcend sectional boundaries.[25]

But endorsements from political celebrities were not enough to save Stevenson's campaign. Eisenhower trounced the Illinois senator at the polls by an even greater margin than in 1952. Without a discernible pause, JFK geared up for his own 1960 race. Shortly after the Democratic loss, he bluntly offered to a *Chattanooga Times* reporter, "Now, this is the time for me."[26]

Kennedy was still savoring the attention he'd received in Chicago. He knew that it meant he had a decent shot at the 1960 nomination. Over the Thanksgiving holiday, he told Dave Powers that he wanted to run for president. "With only about four hours of work and a handful of supporters, I came within thirty-three and a half votes of winning the vice presidential nomination," he said. "If I work hard for four years, I ought to be able to pick up all the marbles."[27]

In January of 1957, the *Los Angeles Times* reported on the "blossoming" of "a bumper crop of [Democratic] presidential hopefuls"—Senator Lyndon Johnson of Texas, Senator Stuart Symington of Missouri, Senator Frank Lausche of Ohio, Senator Paul Douglas of Illinois, Senator Hubert Humphrey of Minnesota, and of course Kennedy were among the names mentioned. The following month, the paper published a survey that showed JFK trailing Kefauver among the party faithful, 49 to 38 percent.[28]

In April, the influential journalist Stewart Alsop opined that one could not swing a cat "on the Democratic side of the Senate aisle" without hitting a presidential candidate. Still, Alsop thought that Kennedy and Johnson had the best chance of securing the nomination. "Kennedy . . . has great ability, as well as great appeal for the voters (the ladies especially) and unlimited financial backing. His Catholicism is no bar to the nomination, any more than

Johnson's heart attack—indeed, a good case could be made that his religion is a political asset."[29]

During the first half of 1957, Kennedy's stock climbed as a result of two major triumphs. First, he snagged a spot on the powerful Senate Foreign Relations Committee, which he knew would help him overcome concerns about his youth and inexperience. Second, he received a Pulitzer Prize for his best-selling book, *Profiles in Courage*. JFK's fellow senators were impressed that one of their own had won such a prestigious award. Congratulations—as well as invitations to speak—poured in from all over the country. The Massachusetts senator "braved bad weather and visited out-of-the-way places in small planes" in order to fulfill his many speaking engagements. Critics accused Kennedy of taking credit for someone else's work. On December 7, 1957, the journalist Drew Pearson went on ABC's *Mike Wallace Show* and charged that *Profiles in Courage* had been written by someone other than the senator. Incensed, JFK hired Clark Clifford, a Truman administration alumnus, as his attorney. Clifford sent ABC a sworn affidavit from Ted Sorensen (Pearson's prime suspect), who denied that he'd ghostwritten the book. On December 14, ABC issued a formal apology: "We deeply regret this error and feel it does a grave injustice to a distinguished public servant and author, to the excellent book he wrote, and to the prize he was awarded." Kennedy rewarded his lawyer with a Patek Philippe watch—arguably the finest timepiece in the world.

From the vantage point of the twenty-first century, the *Profiles in Courage* controversy appears quaint. After all, few politicians today write their own speeches or books and instead rely on ghostwriters and staff members to come up with memorable lines.[30] At the time, though, this was considered a serious charge that might have derailed Kennedy's presidential ambitions.

On Capitol Hill, Kennedy worked hard to maintain his reputation as a political moderate. He investigated cases of labor racketeering (an issue popular with voters) and tiptoed around the civil rights issue. Many younger Americans today associate the Kennedy name with liberalism, but it was the post-1963 Bobby and Ted who transformed the family name's ideology. JFK was first and foremost a pragmatic politician: tough on crime and Communism, fiscally conservative, and certainly not at the forefront of the civil rights movement. "I think [JFK's] legacy in the larger public mind is . . . one that's kind to him, probably kinder than he deserves," says Julian Bond, former chairman of the NAACP. "He had a chance to be a bigger fighter for civil rights than he was and didn't take that chance."[31]

Kennedy also formed lasting friendships with members of the opposition party at a time when bipartisan camaraderie was still possible in Washington. Senator John Sherman Cooper of Kentucky, who would later serve on the Warren Commission, was one of Kennedy's closest Republican pals. "When

Cooper was reelected in 1952, JFK was coming in as a freshman senator," recalls Senate Minority Leader Mitch McConnell, one of Cooper's former interns. "They socially played the same game and lived a block apart in Georgetown. John Sherman Cooper was every Democratic president's favorite Republican. One of the few private dinners that JFK had during the very busy time between his election and inauguration was with the Coopers in Georgetown. Loraine Cooper and Jackie Kennedy became buddies and since Senator Cooper voted with the Democrats a lot, it was a natural combination of political and social connections that intertwined."[32]

Cooper, the Republican, was actually more liberal than Kennedy on the issue of civil rights. When the Civil Rights Bill of 1957 came up for a vote, Kennedy cast his lot with Southern Democrats by sending the bill to the Judiciary Committee, then chaired by James Eastland, a Democrat from Mississippi and an unapologetic segregationist. But at the same time he voted for Title III of the bill, a provision supported by liberals who wanted the government to get serious about integration. This back-and-forth on civil rights became the template for Kennedy as president, at least until the summer of 1963. JFK always had his eye on Southern electoral votes.[33]

Other issues with less political risk engaged Kennedy more. For example, JFK stood up in the Senate on July 2, 1957, and called for an end to the French war in Algeria. He advocated a negotiated settlement, but also American recognition of Algerian independence in the event that negotiations failed. Eager that attention be given to his stand on a top-ranked international concern, the senator made sure that the French embassy and State Department received advance copies of his speech. The *New York Times* called it "perhaps the most comprehensive and outspoken arraignment of Western policy toward Algeria yet presented by an American in public office." Secretary of State John Foster Dulles remained skeptical. He thought that it would be a better idea to simply offer U.S. assistance rather than "openly intervene" in the situation. Dulles added that he would be "very sorry" to see the Algerian war become an American problem. The conservative *Wall Street Journal* worried that Kennedy's plan might lead to U.S. military intervention and rejected a comparison between the American and Algerian revolutions: "Any resemblance between the politically literate men who wrote the Declaration of Independence and the politically primitive Algerian nationalists is coincidental. It is important that we be able to make distinctions between different kinds of independence movements."[34]

The French response was understandably harsher. The French minister for Algeria, Robert Lacoste, accused Kennedy of being brainwashed by Arab propaganda and "badly informed" on the situation in North Africa. Lacoste drew cheers from a group of French veterans when he denounced JFK and "the old maids and Quakers of the United States." In Europe, French patriotic groups boycotted Fourth of July celebrations. France's minister of defense, André Morice, accused Kennedy of prolonging the bloodshed.[35]

In October 1957, JFK published an article in *Foreign Affairs* in which he accused the Eisenhower administration of diplomatic obtuseness. "To an observer in the opposition party there appear two central weaknesses in our current foreign policy," the senator argued. "First, a failure to appreciate how the forces of nationalism are rewriting the geopolitical map of the world—especially in North Africa, southeastern Europe and the Middle East; and second, a lack of decision and conviction in our leadership, which has recoiled from clearly informing both our people and Congress, which seeks too often to substitute slogans for solutions, which at times has even taken pride in the timidity of its ideas." Kennedy wanted the United States to provide more economic support for struggling countries (even Communist ones) and embrace a more flexible foreign policy. He accused Secretary of State Dulles of falling prey to a dangerous teleological rigidity, not unlike the kind that had convinced the Soviets of capitalism's imminent demise. Instead, the United States should show greater diplomatic flexibility by accepting "partial gains in order to undercut slowly the foundations of the Soviet order." Another part of the solution, argued Kennedy, lay in championing the nationalistic aspirations of people living in the world's newest nations. He again referenced the Algerian crisis, which he claimed had spilled "over into the rest of free Africa," and undermined the strength of NATO and the United Nations.[36]

Kennedy's opinions endeared him to "Third Word nationalists" and Frenchmen who were opposed to the war in Algeria. They also convinced some American political elites that he had a keen understanding of international affairs. Meanwhile, "a major publicity blitz accompanied Kennedy's heightened Senate activity. Joe Kennedy generated much of it, quietly using . . . friends such as [*Time* publisher Henry] Luce and [*New York Times* reporter Arthur] Krock." Kennedy staffers cranked out a steady stream of articles under their boss's byline for *Look*, *Life*, *McCall's*, and other popular periodicals. In October 1957, ABC television broadcast *Navy Log*, the story of JFK's PT-109 adventures, with the lead role played by actor John Baer.[37] Kennedy, who had served as a consultant during production, admitted that he was impressed by the show's special effects, but also "slightly embarrassed" by its campy dialogue. In December 1957, JFK made the cover of *Time*. The accompanying article described him as the Democratic Party's "Man Out Front" who was leaving "panting politicians and swooning women across a large spread of the U.S." in his "unabashed run" for the nomination.[38]

Kennedy was careful to cultivate ties with the various factions inside the Democratic Party—not easy given the uneasy marriage between Northern liberals and Southern conservatives that all gathered under the same party label. The civil rights issue in particular proved to be a bed of nails. On September 23, 1957, an angry mob harassed nine black students as they tried to enter Central High School in Little Rock, Arkansas. President Eisenhower responded by federalizing the Arkansas National Guard and deploying 1,000 paratroopers to quell the unrest. Prior to the incident, Kennedy had promised Congressman Frank Smith that he would address a group of Young Democrats in Jackson, Mississippi, but now it seemed a risky move. Yet Kennedy was determined to keep his promise to Smith even though he couldn't predict the outcome. White Mississippians were angry over the civil rights issue and outside interference in what they perceived as a strictly local matter, and Kennedy represented to them the Northern politicians pushing "too much change." Sensing an opportunity, Mississippi's Republican state chairman asked Kennedy to clarify his position on segregation. "I have no hesitancy in telling him . . . the same thing I have said in my own city of Boston," Kennedy replied, "that I have accepted the Supreme Court's decision on desegregation as the law of the land. I know we do not all agree on that issue—but I think most of us do agree on the necessity to uphold law and order in every part of the land. I now invite [the] Republican chairman . . . to tell us his views on President Eisenhower and Mr. Nixon." The crowd of fifteen hundred clapped and whistled. Carroll Kilpatrick, a reporter for the *Washington Post*, interpreted the applause as a sign of respect rather than full agreement. What is more likely is that the crowd was responding to Kennedy's dig at the administration. After all, Republicans were the ones sending troops into Arkansas, not Democrats, and most white Southerners at the time were still loyal members of the party of Andrew Jackson. Still, as this episode demonstrates, Kennedy's reputation as a leading civil rights supporter has been exaggerated. At least until his final months, JFK viewed civil rights as a distraction—a powder keg that could blow a hole in his political career. Although reckless in his private life, Kennedy usually took a cautious, pragmatic approach to politics and governing.[39]

The senator's public statements on organized crime were much more direct. During a speech in Gainesville, Florida, on October 20, 1957, he lambasted lawyers who accepted jobs from corrupt union bosses. JFK talked about his work on the McClellan committee and the ugly cases of professional misconduct that it had uncovered. Both he and Bobby were becoming known as honest reformers. In an earlier era, Theodore Roosevelt and Robert La Follette had battled corruption and corporate malfeasance; now two great-grandsons of Irish immigrants were following in the footsteps of Protestant patricians. The torch of American progressivism had been passed to a new generation. Of course, Kennedy's critics accused him of playing politics with the McClellan hearings. Why was a Republican such as Teamsters boss Jimmy Hoffa under investigation, they wondered, while allegedly corrupt liberals such as Walter Reuther, president of the United Auto Workers union, were exempt? JFK denied that he had a partisan agenda.[40]

John Kennedy also chose to identify with the battle against Communism. This was an easy decision, since any hint of being "soft on Communism" would have been a career breaker. If anything, Kennedy was more hawkish than many Republicans, at least while he was in campaign mode. His was a tough Democratic posture that left no room on the right for Republicans to claim to be the party of military might, as became the case in the 1970s and 1980s. The same month that JFK spoke in Florida, Americans learned that the Soviet Union had launched the world's first manmade satellite, a 22-inch orb known as *Sputnik*. The ensuing public panic led to "a crash program of upgrading mathematics and science teaching" and acceleration in the U.S. space program. Kennedy capitalized on the event by claiming that America was losing the "satellite-missile race" due to Republican parsimony and ineptitude. At the same time, he joined labor leaders in denouncing the Soviet occupation of Eastern Europe. Labor, one of the Democratic Party's most vital constituency groups, was traditionally anticommunist—reinforcement for Democratic candidates such as JFK in positioning himself as rough on the "Reds."[41]

Aware that his Catholic background offended many Democratic Protestants, Kennedy worked hard to neutralize the religious issue. On November 24, 1957, he told a television audience that there was no logical reason why Catholics should be prevented from seeking the presidency. "Now, what church I go to on Sunday or what dogma of the Catholic Church I believe in is a personal matter," he explained. "It does not involve public questions of policy or as the Constitution defines responsibilities of the president, senator, or member of the armed forces." Several months earlier, Kennedy had told the press that he thought the American public was running ahead of the political establishment on the faith issue: "People are more interested in a man's talent than his religious convictions." As the campaign progressed, Kennedy could be seen pretesting the themes that would enable him to sidestep, though never fully overcome, the Catholic issue in the general election of 1960.[42]

By June 1957, JFK was leading the pack of Democratic presidential contenders. A Gallup poll showed that a majority of Democrats favored his candidacy over Kefauver, a stark reversal from four months earlier.[43]

The Kennedy campaign continued to gather steam the following year. In March 1958, the senator introduced the Kennedy-Ives Bill, which targeted corruption among union leaders. Although the bill failed, Kennedy reinforced his image as a reformer. This was also another example of his political pragmatism. He supported anticommunist unions that advocated for fair wages but also distanced himself from the dishonesty that existed in parts of organized labor—a major reason for public distrust of unions. Further, Kennedy issued warnings about the alleged "missile gap" with the Soviet Union, which he said would place the United States in "a position of grave peril"—a charge he would often make during the 1960 presidential race. *Look, Life*, the *Saturday Evening Post, Redbook, Parade*, and other popular magazines ran favorable stories about the senator and his attractive family. In November, Massachusetts voters sent their favorite son back to the Senate with 1,362,926 votes. Kennedy's relatively unknown Republican opponent, Vincent Celeste, garnered 488,318 votes. It was "the largest [popular-vote] margin ever" achieved by a Bay State candidate.[44]

Not everyone backed Jack, though. Eleanor Roosevelt continued to criticize Kennedy for ducking the McCarthy issue, and in May she told a reporter that she doubted whether a President Kennedy would be able to make decisions without the Vatican's approval. In today's pluralistic society, it is hard to fathom Roosevelt's comments or understand why Kennedy's faith mattered so much to many Americans. But at the time, both conservative and liberal Protestants believed that Catholics took their marching orders from Rome, a situation they saw as antithetical to republican self-government.[45] Mrs. Roosevelt's comments reflected a deep strain of anti-Catholicism in American life that had been present since the nineteenth century, when large numbers of Catholic immigrants first began arriving in largely Protestant eastern cities. In addition, many Democrats were still haunted by the ghost of 1928, when the Catholic New Yorker Al Smith lost the White House in a landslide to Herbert Hoover, a conservative Quaker from the Midwest.

Of course the Catholic issue wasn't Kennedy's only hurdle. James Reston, the influential *New York Times* columnist, raised reasonable questions about his youth and inexperience, while *Washington Star* columnist William White attributed Kennedy's political successes to his father's deep pockets. Kennedy fought back against these attacks with humor. At the 1958 Gridiron Dinner, which annually brings together top journalists and politicians for good-natured roasting, he addressed the rumor that his father was trying to buy the election: "I have just received the following wire from my generous daddy: 'Dear Jack: Don't buy a single vote more than is necessary—I'll be damned if I'm going to pay for a landslide.'"* He went on to poke fun at his Democratic rivals: "I dreamed about 1960 the other night, and I told Stuart Symington and Lyndon Johnson about it in the cloakroom yesterday. I told them how the Lord came into my bedroom, anointed my head, and said: 'John Kennedy, I hereby anoint you President of the United States.' Stu Symington said: 'That's

---

* This invented anecdote received renewed attention after Kennedy's 1960 squeaker victory.

strange, Jack, because I, too, had a similar dream last night, in which the Lord anointed me and declared me, Stuart Symington, President of the United States *and* outer space.' And Lyndon Johnson said: 'That's very interesting, gentlemen: because I, too, had a similar dream last night—and I don't remember anointing either one of you!'"[46]

The speech was a hit, the result of careful preparation. According to Ted Sorensen, none of Kennedy's Senate speeches "worried him longer or more deeply." The senator enlisted the help of a number of "experts," including Clark Clifford, whom Kennedy referred to as "Washington's best wisecrack artist."[47]

In January 1959, Stephen Smith, Kennedy's brother-in-law, quietly opened the "first presidential headquarters of the Kennedy campaign" in Washington. Three months later, JFK met with his team in Palm Beach to discuss critical details. Which primaries should they enter? Who were the key decision makers in the various state delegations? Where and when should the candidate speak? Knowing that he had his work cut out for him, Kennedy stayed on the road and out of the Senate for much of the year giving "speeches, speeches, and more speeches." "In October and November, he spent four days in Indiana, one day each in West Virginia, New York, and Nebraska, two days in Louisiana, made a stopover in Milwaukee on the way to Oregon, flew back to New York, followed by three- and four-day stays in Illinois, California, and Oregon, and briefer visits to Oklahoma, Delaware, Kansas, and Colorado. He addressed audiences of every size on street corners, at airports, on fairgrounds, and in theaters, armories, high schools, state capitols, restaurants, gambling casinos, hotels, and pool, union, lodge, and convention halls. The groups he addressed were as varied as the venues—farmers, labor unions, chambers of commerce, bar associations, ethnic societies, state legislatures, college and university students and faculties, and civic organizations."

As candidates always do, Kennedy made sure that he ingratiated himself with each Democratic voting bloc. He told the National Rural Electric Cooperative Association, popular with farmers, that "REA rates must remain low—more generating capacity must be developed" and "the vast resources of nuclear energy must be tapped." In Indianapolis, he told a racially diverse audience that there were "few educational drives more important or of more vital significance than that of the United Negro College Fund." At the National Civil Liberties Clearing House Annual Conference, he recited the preamble to the Declaration of Independence. In August he told a roomful of AFL-CIO members to watch out for the "Republican-Southern Democratic coalition in the House of Representatives." "I come to you today as a friend of labor," he gushed. "I have never concealed or apologized for my friendship with labor, and I do not intend to start now."[48]

Kennedy also tried to stay out in front of the Catholic issue. In an interview with *Look* magazine, he expressed his opposition to U.S. diplomatic relations with the Vatican, thereby distancing himself from his father, who was a quiet supporter of such an official attachment. JFK also spoke out against federal aid for religious schools, which was a high priority for the Catholic community.[49]

At the end of the year, Kennedy overcame a short-lived controversy when a special presidential report showed the strength of U.S. foreign aid programs being undermined by a global population explosion. The report recommended help for those countries that wanted assistance in dealing with "the serious challenge posed by rapidly expanding populations." Catholic bishops immediately condemned the report's recommendations, since the bishops viewed birth control as immoral. When asked to weigh in on the issue, Kennedy said that he personally opposed U.S. support for overseas birth control programs, but also that "this was a question for other countries to decide for themselves." He added that if he won the White House, "he would decide any issue that came before him on this question on the ground of what was best for the interests of the United States." It was an effective tap dance that bought him time until the controversy died down.[50]

ON JANUARY 2, 1960, Kennedy made his candidacy official. Speaking from the Senate Caucus Room, he told the press that he was seeking "the most powerful office in the Free World." "Through its leadership can come a more vital life for our people," he said.

> In it are centered the hopes of the globe around us for freedom and a more secure life. For it is in the executive branch that the most crucial decisions of this century must be made in the next four years—how to end or alter the burdensome arms race, where Soviet gains already threaten our very existence; how to maintain freedom and order in the newly emerging nations; how to rebuild the stature of American science and education; how to prevent the collapse of our farm economy and the decay of our cities; how to achieve, without further inflation or unemployment, expanded economic growth benefitting all Americans; and how to give direction to our traditional moral purpose, awakening every American to the dangers and opportunities that confront us.

Kennedy would revisit these themes again and again during his campaign. He closed with details on how he would secure his party's endorsement: "I believe that any Democratic aspirant to this important nomination should be willing to submit to the voters his views, record, and competence in a series of primary contests. I am therefore now announcing my intention of filing in the New Hampshire primary and I shall announce my plans with respect to the other primaries as their filing dates approach." In truth, JFK didn't have a choice; he needed to enter the primaries to prove to his party that he could win in Protestant states. None of the other candidates had this problem.[51]

With his campaign officially under way, Kennedy began ratcheting up the partisan rhetoric.[52] During a speech at the National Press Club in mid-January, he listed the problems that he said had been mishandled by the Eisenhower administration—China, the missile gap, the needs of underdeveloped countries, Berlin, Formosa (today's Taiwan), NATO, the arms race, and various domestic issues such as education and agriculture.[53]

This was an era when only sixteen states held presidential primaries (in our century, more than forty do so), and candidates could pick and choose states in which to compete. In February, Kennedy accepted Humphrey's challenge to compete in the West Virginia primary. As events would show, it was a smart, perhaps essential, political decision. During the same month, he strengthened his prospects in Wisconsin by barnstorming five cities in the north central part of the state and telling farmers there that his vote against the 90-percent-of-parity bill had been a mistake. Humphrey fought back by calling Kennedy a Johnny-come-lately who flip-flopped on farm issues.[54]

Although Kennedy coasted to victory in the New Hampshire primary in early March, the triumph was seen as little more than a publicity coup—a pat on the back for New England's favorite son. Kennedy's next stop, Wisconsin, represented middle America, an area teeming with Protestants, independent shopkeepers, dairy farmers, factory workers, and a hodgepodge of ethnic and religious factions. More important, the state was smack dab in the middle of Humphrey territory. By the spring of 1960, Humphrey, who was Kennedy's only serious challenger in the Badger State, had represented Minnesota in the Senate for twelve years. As Sorensen later noted, "Minnesota and Wisconsin were distinguishable only by the invisible boundary between them. Both states had a surplus of farm products, a predominance of Protestant German and Scandinavian descendants, and aggressively liberal Democratic parties with farmer-labor backing." Kennedy's advisers had been divided over whether he should even run against Humphrey in Wisconsin, where the Minnesota pol "reigned unofficially as a sort of third Wisconsin Senator." But JFK saw it as a chance to prove to the eastern party bosses that he could garner votes outside New England and ease concerns about his youthfulness and religious affiliation. Of course, the age issue didn't matter as much as it once might have. The hundreds of thousands of young, victorious World War II vets were brimming with confidence and unwilling to defer to their elders in the same way that prior generations had. All across the country, Young

Turks were running against entrenched politicians. Ironically, Richard Nixon made it easier for JFK to run for high office by winning the vice presidency at the age of thirty-nine. In 1960 Nixon was forty-eight, only five years senior to JFK.[55]

In the months leading up to the primary, Kennedy campaign workers poured into Wisconsin's ten congressional districts. Pollster Lou Harris conducted the largest survey ever taken in the state while JFK's other aides recruited volunteers and lined up key endorsements. Thanks mainly to his father, Kennedy enjoyed the advantages of a large staff and nearly limitless supply of campaign funds here and elsewhere. In addition, appearances with his large, vivacious family attracted swarms of journalists and were people pleasers. Humphrey told the press that he felt like a "corner grocer running against a chain store."[56]

Actually, Humphrey had less of a chance in Wisconsin than is commonly supposed. He lacked two critical elements that JFK had in abundance— money and charisma. Robert Drew's landmark documentary film *Primary* reveals the differences between the two campaigns. In one segment, we see Hubert Humphrey standing on a Wisconsin city sidewalk, handing out business cards to passersby and delivering old-fashioned stump speeches to farmers; in the next, Kennedy is mobbed by autograph seekers and wildly enthusiastic supporters. Drew's camera documented the changes that were taking place in American life after World War II. Humphrey represented the past, a time when seasoned if dull politicians could run by-the-book, just-the-facts-ma'am campaigns that appealed mostly to voters' intellect and interests. Kennedy, on the other hand, enabled youth, energy, image, and a sense of possibility to overwhelm other considerations in a new mass marketing era. JFK was also the first presidential candidate to fully grasp the significance of a strategically chosen primary election. Prior to 1960, many politicians thought of primaries as unimportant or even dangerous popularity contests. Harry Truman had once referred to them dismissively as "eyewash." But thanks to the choices made by Kennedy in 1960, especially Wisconsin and West Virginia, party primaries became critical stepping-stones on the path to the White House, a nearly essential part of the campaign process. Kennedy rewrote the rules of the game.[57]

According to one of these new rules, presidential candidates had to work like sled dogs when they were on the campaign trail. JFK certainly did so in the seven days leading up to the Wisconsin election. On March 30, he began the day with an eight A.M. press conference at the Northland Hotel in Green Bay. An hour later, he was speaking at a high school in Kaukauna; an hour after that, it was the city hall in Chilton; then on to more speeches and more handshaking in Kiel, Manitowoc, Two Rivers, and Plymouth before ending the day with a reception in Sheboygan and a late-night trip back to Milwaukee. On April 1, he stumped Mount Horab, Dodgeville, Mineral Point, Darlington, Shullsburg, Argyle, Blanchardville, New Glarus, Monroe, Broadhead, and Beloit. Always energetic, Humphrey hustled as well, but he could not match Kennedy's personal magnetism.[58]

On election day, Kennedy captured 56 percent of the popular vote in Wisconsin. However, his margin of victory was derived from a quartet of overwhelmingly Catholic congressional districts; he had fared poorly with Protestants. Though triumphant, Kennedy was actually crestfallen and interpreted the result as proof that he would "have to do it all over again." "We have to go through every [primary] and win every one of them," he told his sister, "West Virginia and Maryland and Indiana and Oregon, all the way to the convention."[59]

West Virginia's primary became the most important, mainly because the leading candidates decided they could best make their case in the Mountain State. JFK's first priority there was to neutralize the Catholic issue. While Kennedy had once led in West Virginia, he had slipped behind Humphrey as the media focused on JFK's Catholicism in the heavily Protestant state. "I am a Catholic, but the fact that I was born a Catholic, does that mean that I can't be the president of the United States?" he asked a crowd in Charleston. "I'm able to serve in Congress, and my brother was able to give his life, but we can't be president?" Many West Virginians felt stereotyped and downtrodden themselves, and they could identify with Kennedy in this respect. Despite the religious question JFK generally received a warm welcome wherever he went in the Mountain State.[60] Bill Battle, Kennedy's campaign manager in West Virginia, reminded voters that JFK was an "Irish Catholic," not a "Roman Catholic." "There was always a big round of applause when he mentioned that and everybody would say, 'Oh! That's different!'" recalled Battle's widow, Barry.[61] Between April 5 and May 10, JFK crisscrossed the state, shaking hands, kissing babies, and promising to get West Virginia moving again. He wooed New Deal Democrats by asking Franklin Roosevelt, Jr., to help with the campaign. One West Virginia reporter noted that Roosevelt's visit to West Virginia was like "God's son coming down and saying it was all right to vote for this Catholic, it was permissible, it wasn't something terrible to do."[62]

"Dear fellow Democrat," began one letter from Roosevelt. "The people of West Virginia once again need the kind of understanding in Washington they had during the New Deal. There are many parallels." FDR Jr. went on to blame the Republicans for West Virginia's economic decline and drew comparisons between his father and JFK. "As in 1932, the people of West Virginia need strong, dynamic leadership in the White House. My father knew that all you want is a fair break and a decent chance to help yourselves; and you have justified his faith with miracles of labor and production. I believe that John F.

Kennedy is the only candidate for President who can furnish the needed leadership and understanding." Roosevelt showed a darker side when he falsely accused Humphrey of avoiding the draft during World War II. In reality, the Minnesota senator had been rejected by the military due to a disability. JFK and Bobby knew as much, but never made Roosevelt repudiate the charge. The spurious accusation embittered Humphrey, who gradually realized that he was fighting a hopeless battle against a well-oiled, richly financed machine.

Roosevelt told other whoppers as well. When introducing JFK to a crowd in Bluefield, the former car salesman mashed his fingers together and said, "My daddy and Jack Kennedy's daddy were just like that!" The senator was astonished by the audacity of FDR Jr.'s statement. In reality, President Roosevelt disliked JFK's father, once referring to him as "a temperamental Irish boy" who was "thoroughly selfish and thoroughly obsessed with the idea that he must leave each of his nine children with a million dollars apiece when he dies." However, throughout their careers, the Kennedys were never above using dirty tricks and delivering low blows if circumstances required. That is precisely what prompted them to flood West Virginia's impoverished counties with cold cash. An old political tradition in the state held that county bosses (usually sheriffs) were responsible for picking "slates" in order to simplify the voting process for their constituents. Any candidate who wanted his name on the approved slate had to grease the palm of the local boss. The Kennedys, accustomed to such shenanigans in Boston's boroughs, paid out thousands of dollars in "contributions" to Mountaineer kleptocrats.[63]

On May 10, West Virginians delivered JFK a 61 to 39 percent triumph over Hubert Humphrey, a margin so large that Kennedy won 48 of 55 counties. It was the campaign's turning point, the moment the Kennedys had been planning and hoping for since January. A despondent Humphrey withdrew from the race, and a confident Kennedy predicted that he would win the nomination at the Democratic National Convention. Moreover, Kennedy claimed, the West Virginia vote had proven that the religious issue would not be a major factor in the upcoming presidential contest.[64]*

THE SAME MONTH, the Soviets downed an American U-2 spy plane, which led to the cancellation of a summit meeting between Eisenhower and Khrushchev. The Cold War was getting chillier, and the public thought that the next president might need to save the world from annihilation. Kennedy

---

* It was wishful thinking, of course. Right through to election day, Americans weren't sure if they were ready for a Catholic president.

blasted the Eisenhower administration for lying about the U-2 program and authorizing reconnaissance flights in the weeks leading up to the summit. Lyndon Johnson and Harry Truman, united in their desire to stop JFK, told voters that the crisis revealed the need for a mature commander in chief who had plenty of experience in international diplomacy.[65]

But it was too late to stop the Kennedy machine, which was feared and revered in and out of the Democratic Party. By the summer of 1960, most party insiders believed the Kennedy nomination was a fait accompli. JFK arrived in Los Angeles for the Democratic Convention brimming with confidence. He had already chosen his Washington headquarters for the general election and determined his strategy for the fall. His challengers were desperate to stop his nomination. Johnson supporters told the press that Kennedy had Addison's disease and depended on cortisone treatments to stay alive. Robert Kennedy denied the charge, saying that Jack "does not now nor has he ever had an ailment described classically as Addison's disease." Bobby was lying, as were Drs. Eugene Cohen and Janet Travell when they published a report in June describing JFK's health as "excellent" and his "vitality, endurance and resistance to infection" as "above average." In reality, Kennedy had nagging health problems, including ulcers, colitis, and severe back pain as well as Addison's disease. Travell would later discover that Kennedy's left leg was three quarters of an inch shorter than his right leg, a defect that had worsened his back pain for years and would force him to wear special shoes during his presidency.[66] John Connally, one of LBJ's strongest supporters and a fellow Texan, said that he would be delighted "to submit Senator Johnson's medical record, since his recovery from a 1955 heart attack, and have it compared with that of Senator Kennedy and any other contenders." The Kennedy campaign refused to take the bait and the controversy was soon lost in the excitement of the convention.[67]

Joseph Kennedy was also trying to shield his son's reputation in another way. He wanted to ensure that one of the Kennedy family's darkest secrets remained hidden. He told the press that he had ordered a lobotomy for JFK's sister Rosemary in the 1940s because she was mentally retarded and would never lead a fulfilling life. Yet Rosemary suffered from mental illness rather than mental retardation and functioned at a decent intellectual level before the lobotomy went "horribly wrong" and turned her into a "zombie." Regrettably, mentally ill individuals were often severely stigmatized in the mid-twentieth century, and Joe Kennedy wanted no gossip about genetic "insanity" running in Jack's family.[68]

JFK arrived in Los Angeles with 600 delegate votes, 161 short of what he needed to secure the nomination. Although confident of victory, Kennedy refused to take anything for granted. He knew that Senator Stuart Symington controlled between 100 and 150 delegates, Adlai Stevenson had somewhere around 50, and the Kansas and Iowa delegations had pledged their 52 votes to their favorite-son candidates, Governor George Docking and Governor Hershel Loveless. Kennedy also understood that Lyndon Johnson posed the greatest threat to his nomination; even though the Texas senator had waited until the last minute to declare his candidacy—less than a week before the convention—LBJ had already lined up close to 500 votes. Five states were still up for grabs: Pennsylvania, California, New Jersey, Illinois, and Minnesota.[69]

On Monday, July 11, the opening day of the convention, JFK zipped between meetings in a white Cadillac that had a rare car telephone. At each stop, he glad-handed delegates and fielded questions from journalists. Meanwhile, at the Los Angeles Sports Arena, delegates had just settled in for a round of humdrum party speeches when a huge commotion erupted outside—hundreds of men, women, and children were marching back and forth in front of the arena, waving signs and shouting "We want Stevenson! We want Stevenson!" The demonstration encouraged the California delegation—which previously had been leaning toward JFK—to split its vote the next day between Kennedy and Stevenson. At the same time, Johnson kept up the pressure on the Kennedy camp, secretly encouraging his supporters to make hay out of the family's religion and accusing Joseph P. Kennedy, Sr., of harboring Nazi sympathies. Johnson also challenged the young senator to a debate in the week ahead of the convention before their home Texas and Massachusetts delegations. Kennedy accepted, and confident of his forthcoming convention majority, all but ignored the brickbats Johnson hurled at him. Kennedy even said he was "strongly in support" of Johnson . . . for Senate majority leader.[70]

Unknown to Johnson or almost anyone else, Kennedy was seriously considering the Texan for the vice presidential nomination. On the opening day of the convention, in a highly unusual intervention by journalists, the newspaper columnist Joseph Alsop and Philip Graham, publisher of the *Washington Post*, stopped by Kennedy's suite to urge him to select Johnson as his running mate. Having talked to friends of Johnson, they assured JFK that Johnson would accept the nomination if it were offered to him. Kennedy tipped his hand a bit when he readily agreed with their arguments.[71]

On Wednesday, the excitement of the convention reached a fever pitch when Senator Eugene McCarthy of Minnesota put Adlai Stevenson's name into nomination. "Do not reject this man who has made us all proud to be called Democrats," proclaimed McCarthy, his right fist clenched. "Do not, I say to you, do not leave this prophet without honor in his own party." Stevenson's supporters roared their approval and marched through the hall singing, clapping, and chanting. The sudden outburst irked Governor LeRoy Collins of Florida, chairman of the convention, who made a futile attempt to restore order. "Ladies and gentlemen, do you want this convention to be associated with hoodlumism? That is exactly what you are turning this demonstration into. Now will you please take your seats? Stop the music.... Now nobody can be nominated president of the United States if we are going to conduct ourselves like a bunch of hoodlums." Adlai's boosters booed. Watching the scene from the comfort of a posh Beverly Hills estate, JFK told his father not to worry because "Stevenson has everything but delegates." The Kennedy high command had made a science of delegate counting and was supremely confident. A bit later, Kennedy won the nomination on the first ballot with the support of 763 delegates—two more votes than he needed.[72]

The decision on the running mate was next. Kennedy's short list included Symington, Johnson, Humphrey, Minnesota governor Orville Freeman, and Senator Henry "Scoop" Jackson of Washington State. Ted Sorensen and many party stalwarts favored Johnson. Kennedy knew that having LBJ on the ticket would help him greatly in the South and that, if he were elected, Johnson's extraordinary legislative skills might assist him in enacting his program. The possibility of taking the second spot was broached with LBJ, and sure enough, he was receptive.

Bill Moyers was with Johnson the day JFK offered him the vice presidency, sleeping in the bathroom of the Johnsons' hotel suite when he heard the phone ring. "I thought I would get to the phone first in the hotel room," he recalls, "but Lady Bird picked it up. And I heard her as I came in the door saying 'Lyndon, it's Jack . . . Senator Kennedy.' LBJ woke up, listened to the voice, hung up and said, 'He wants to come see me.' And Lady Bird said, 'I hope you won't do it.'" Moyers opened the door for Kennedy when he arrived a short time later, but he retreated to his assigned bathroom while the two politicians talked. Although he could not hear anything that was said, Moyers is convinced that JFK knew exactly what he was doing and had no qualms about choosing Johnson as a running mate. "When [Kennedy] left that room, I was sure that he had communicated to Johnson that he really wanted him to run, and that LBJ was going to do it."[73]*

---

* Incidentally, Moyers wrote me that his unusual location was a product of Johnson's organization of his suite: "LBJ had asked me to move in for the duration of the convention; my cot was in that bathroom, along with my clothes bag, my toiletries, and some reading material; when I slept, I slept there—usually a couple of hours at night. LBJ didn't 'order' me to stay in the bathroom so that I could eavesdrop on [John or Bobby] Kennedy; I retreated to it out of protocol anytime he wanted a private conversation with a visitor, as he most certainly did when first Jack Kennedy and then Bobby came to see him. It would have been easy in either case for me to eavesdrop, but I didn't do so; I shut the door and because of the L-shaped configuration of the suite—the bathroom was in the foyer and LBJ and the guests were well around a corner and across on the far side of the living room—I couldn't hear the conversations. There have been many moments since when I regretted not eavesdropping, but I didn't,

Johnson thought his nomination was a done deal as word spread. Then JFK had second thoughts the very same day: What if his choice, a conservative Southerner, caused a split in the party? RFK and close aides Kenny O'Donnell and Ralph Dungan protested the possible choice. In order to line up liberal votes, they had promised to keep LBJ off the ticket. JFK also got an earful from labor leaders, who were angry with Johnson for supporting the Landrum-Griffin Act, a law they viewed as harmful to unions.

Kennedy dispatched Bobby to warn Johnson about the brewing revolt inside the party. Bobby offered Johnson the party chairmanship as an alternative, but LBJ, blinded by tears, steadfastly refused. He wanted the vice presidency; Johnson was willing to give up real power in the Senate in order to "get in line" for the presidency. "Well, then that's fine," replied an unhappy Bobby. "He wants you to be vice president if you want to be vice president"—not exactly the enthusiastic embrace a prospective ticket mate usually gets. Johnson never forgave Bobby for trying to drop him, and this episode was apparently the beginning of their long mutual loathing.[74]

Whatever the internal turmoil behind Johnson's selection as the vice presidential nominee, it turned out to be one key to a close victory in the fall. A Northern Yankee, Kennedy could not have been elected without Southern electoral votes that Johnson added in Texas and probably other closely contested states below the Mason-Dixon Line. The implications of JFK's decision would reverberate well beyond the election, of course. American history would have taken a different path, for good or ill, if one of the other possibilities had joined the ticket. Either Richard Nixon would have become president eight years before he actually did, or a Democratic president very unlike LBJ would have succeeded an assassinated Kennedy (assuming the murder would still have occurred). This alternate universe is fascinating to contemplate but essentially unknowable.

The world we do know proceeded from Johnson's selection to JFK's acceptance speech at the convention. At Bobby Kennedy's suggestion, the Los Angeles Coliseum was chosen as the site of the address instead of the convention hall, since the one-hundred-thousand-seat stadium could hold more people and would inject additional excitement into the closing hours. RFK was sold on the idea by a twenty-nine-year-old Los Angeles councilwoman, Rosalind Wyman, who had been instrumental in bringing the Brooklyn Dodgers to Los Angeles. When the younger Kennedy expressed concerns about filling the stadium, Wyman suggested that they close off half the structure, and Bobby agreed. As campaign manager, RFK looked for ways to enhance his

---

damn it, and had to rely instead on LBJ's debriefing of Lady Bird and me after each visitor had departed." Letter from Bill Moyers, May 29, 2012.

brother's image, and the coliseum speech was novel. What Bobby did not consider were the security implications. By selecting an open-air facility in front of thousands of unscreened people, Senator Kennedy would be vulnerable to attack by anyone who secured a ticket. The campaign made JFK even more vulnerable by having the candidate ride through the stadium in an open black convertible.[75*]

Fortunately, the address proceeded without incident. JFK impressed the stadium crowd as well as a much larger audience watching on TV with a dynamic presentation that provided the label for his eventual administration, the New Frontier. "For the problems are not all solved and the battles are not all won—and we stand today on the edge of a New Frontier—the frontier of the 1960s—a frontier of unknown opportunities and perils—a frontier of unfulfilled hopes and threats. Woodrow Wilson's New Freedom promised our nation a new political and economic framework. Franklin Roosevelt's New Deal promised security and succor to those in need. But the New Frontier of which I speak is not a set of promises—it is a set of challenges. It sums up not what I intend to *offer* the American people, but what I intend to *ask* of them. It appeals to their pride, not to their pocketbook—it holds out the promise of more sacrifice instead of more security."[76]

A young Nancy Pelosi, the future Speaker of the U.S. House of Representatives, was in the audience with her parents. Her father, a Kennedy Democrat and former mayor of Baltimore, had supported JFK early on. When Kennedy finished speaking, Nancy asked her father if they could go to "one of those [Los Angeles] restaurants that you read about in the paper." He took her to a ritzy eatery called Romanov's. "So we go in," she recalls, "and my father said, 'Boy! Did you find the most expensive restaurant in L.A.?" Just then, the door opened and Senator Kennedy waltzed in, followed by a huge entourage. "And he came right over," Pelosi says. "He knew how to play other politicians. He made it seem as if he had come to that restaurant to see my father. And after that, my father had no more concerns about the prices on the menu. He said, 'How did you find this place?,' 'This is such a great idea,' and 'I'm so glad we came here.'"[77]

---

* This was all too typical of the chances taken at the time not just by candidates for president, but by presidents themselves. Airtight security was almost never present, and a fatalistic, Pollyanna-like mantra of "nothing bad will happen" was the dominant philosophy of the age.

3

VICTORY WITHOUT
A MANDATE

WITH THE CONVENTION SAFELY behind him, Kennedy turned to the daunting task of convincing the American people to elect him their thirty-fifth president. Many needed no persuasion, and were already offering to help with the campaign. Young people in particular were attracted to Kennedy's youth and vigor. "I am a Chicago student, 16 years old," began a letter from one young man, "I may be too young to vote but I am not too young to be interested in politics. I live in the 45th ward 31st precinct and would do almost any work at home or in my precinct." Kennedy's speeches had caused him to think seriously about his country's future. "In days like these it is indeed (if I may quote) 'A time for greatness.' In the upcoming years the fate of all America . . . will hang more precariously than ever in our history on whoever is the upcoming president. For this position Mr. Kennedy is not a need but a *must*." A group of teenaged girls asked for permission to "start a Kennedy for President Club" in their hometown. They received the Kennedy blessing along with twenty-five JFK buttons. Another group of teenagers sent in a cheer they'd written for Jack: "Hurray for Kennedy! One, two, three, four, who are you going to vote for? Kennedy, that's who!"[1]

Scores of other songs, shouts, and slogan ideas poured into Kennedy's campaign offices during this period. A. V. Gallagher suggested "I'll Back Jack" or "K and J All the Way." Miss Joanne Hardman penned new lyrics to the *Notre Dame Victory March*: "Vote, vote for John Kennedy . . . He'll do the most for you and for me." Susan Jacobs, Janis Sherwin, and Terri Dee changed the title of "Dearie," a golden oldie that had once been a mainstay for Guy Lombardo, to "Kennedy."[2] Professional singers got in on the act as well. Frank Sinatra remade his hit song, "High Hopes," with new lyrics from the tune's originator, Sammy Cahn: "Everyone wants to back Jack, Jack is on the right track, 'Cause he's got high hopes, He's got high hopes, Nineteen Sixty's the year for his high hopes!" It was played frequently on the campaign trail at rallies, and became almost as ubiquitous in jukeboxes as the original.[3]

Nor were these outpourings of affection limited to young people and celebrities. Senior citizens responded favorably to Senator Kennedy's call for a national health insurance program for the aged. Ted Ruhig appreciated JFK's "forthright" and compassionate position on the issue, which he contrasted against "the pauper's oath approach of Mr. Nixon." Seventy-three-year-old Lewis Lincoln, a distant relative of the nation's sixteenth president, was equally direct. He called on seniors to ignore past party affiliations and vote Democratic. Otherwise, Lincoln warned, the "oldsters" wouldn't "get anything worth a whoop in better Social Security and medical care."[4]

The Kennedy campaign team developed a sophisticated strategy focused on the nine states that could deliver the most electoral votes (Massachusetts, New Jersey, New York, Pennsylvania, Ohio, Michigan, Illinois, California, and Texas). In New York the team made an end run around the regular Democratic organizations by establishing "Citizens for Kennedy." This new group allowed voters to back Jack without getting entangled in the New York Democratic Party's messy internecine war. JFK and Bobby also made sure that the Democratic National Committee worked hand in hand with the Kennedy campaign, something that had not always happened in previous presidential contests.[5]

Aware that new voters could determine the outcome of the election, Democratic leaders held eleven regional conferences on registering voters over an eight-day period. "Of the 107,000,000 Americans old enough to vote in 1960, approximately 40,000,000, it was estimated, had not bothered to register." Kennedy's campaign managers guessed that the majority of these eligible voters leaned left. Congressman Frank "Topper" Thompson (D-NJ), a colorful and vocal JFK backer from Trenton, was asked to spearhead the voter registration drive. Thompson's strategy bore fruit. On election day, the turnout exceeded the presidential election of 1956 by nearly seven million votes, although much of the increase may have been due to the perceived closeness of the 1960 contest.[6]

Lyndon Johnson was put in charge of JFK's strategy in the South. The Texas senator went on a whistle-stop train tour of Dixie aboard the *LBJ Special*. At each stop he twisted arms and warned Southerners not to stray from the party of their forebears. Kennedy made only a handful of speeches in areas of the South believed friendlier to a Yankee candidacy.[7]

A Gallup poll taken immediately after the political conventions showed Kennedy trailing fellow Irish American Nixon by six percentage points. JFK knew that his Catholic background was one reason he was behind, especially after Protestant leader Norman Vincent Peale and a group of conservative ministers called the Citizens for Religious Freedom convened at the Mayflower Hotel in Washington to discuss the "religious issue." Protestants were not the only voters concerned about JFK's religion. In September 1960,

Edward Bernays, a prominent member of New York's Jewish community, wrote to JFK campaign aide John Martin about the reservations of his fellow Jews: "I know that many Americans of Jewish background who might otherwise have voted the Democratic ticket are concerned about Kennedy's candidacy because he is a Catholic, and that they are intending to stay away from the polls and vote for no presidential candidate." Martin conceded the point. "I have just returned from campaigning," he wrote. "Everything I heard in New York—and in parts of Los Angeles—confirmed what you say."[8]

Kennedy fought back against the Peale group with withering witticisms. "We had an interesting convention at Los Angeles and we ended with a strong Democratic platform which we called 'The Rights of Man,'" he told a supportive crowd in New York. "The Republican platform has also been presented. I do not know its title, but it has been referred to as 'The Power of Positive Thinking'" (the title of Peale's popular self-help book). Kennedy's campaign workers also did their best to defend their candidate's religion. When a Baptist minister in Illinois was caught mailing anti-Catholic literature to voters, the Springfield office of "Citizens for Kennedy-Johnson" published the offending clergyman's name and address. Kennedy's official "Pennsylvania Memo" in October 1960 contained a number of sober warnings about the faith issue. "Governor [David] Lawrence strongly advises avoiding religion," wrote Martin. "Lawrence thinks we are OK in Philly and Pittsburgh—That Religious Feeling is Hurting Us in the Rural Areas—And So We Are Going to Whistlestop Tomorrow to Show Them We Are Nice Guys Without Horns." John Martin's other memos to JFK made frequent mention of the religious issue: "Jersey City—Briefing Sheet. Population 300,000. Hudson County. Heavily Democratic. Heavily Catholic. Local issue: Irrelevant (except Catholic)." He described Indiana as a pro-southern conservative backwater that "would like nothing better than to return to the 19th century . . . Many of its people are still anti-Catholic, pro-[Joseph] McCarthy, isolationist as to foreign policy . . . We are getting hurt badly by a strong and organized anti-Catholic campaign that feeds on the KKK hangover." Martin advised his boss to make only one passing reference to his religion during their stay in the Hoosier State—the "right of everyone to a job regardless of race or religious faith." Although confident that Michigan would prove friendlier, Martin warned that the campaign would be stopping in "some Dutch anti-Catholic Lutheran territory." The number one problem in California, he insisted, would be "anti-Catholic feeling in the valley, where Bible belt type farmers are numerous."[9]

By September Kennedy decided that he should try to reduce the impact of the religious issue by going into the lion's den. He accepted an invitation to speak at the Greater Houston Ministerial Association. The meeting had been arranged by the Reverend Herbert Meza, the group's program chairman and an associate pastor at Bellaire Presbyterian Church. Meza did not realize he was making history when he invited Kennedy to speak. His main motivation was simply to rekindle interest in the ministerial association. Meza also invited Nixon, but the vice president, not wanting to involve himself directly in his opponent's religious problem, politely declined. Lyndon Johnson asked if he could be introduced alongside Kennedy, but Meza—worried that the event had already become too political—rejected Johnson's request. LBJ was furious. "No damn little preacher is going to tell me what to do in Texas," he told an aide. When Johnson continued to press the issue, Meza threatened to step aside and make LBJ moderate the meeting, effectively ruining the occasion's potential impact as a "nonpolitical" forum. LBJ desisted and watched the speech on TV instead. But he never forgot or forgave Meza for snubbing him. Three full years later, when they met again in Texas, then-president Johnson refused to shake Meza's hand.[10] Actually, LBJ should have been grateful; he was lucky he had not caused the forum to be canceled or downgraded. This heavily covered event was critical in helping Kennedy overcome, barely, the religious prejudice that might have denied both JFK and Johnson their turns at the White House.

Sorensen recalled working on JFK's Houston speech: "My chief source of material was Kennedy's own previous statements on religion to the ASNE [American Society of News Editors], to the convention, to press conferences and to Look magazine." Sorensen and Kennedy realized that the Houston speech could determine the outcome of the election. While drafting the speech, Sorensen asked another Kennedy aide, Milton Gwirtzman, to find out how many Roman Catholics had died at the Alamo. When Gwirtzman could only come up with a list of names that sounded Catholic, Sorensen powerfully improvised: ". . . side by side with Bowie and Crockett died McCafferty and Bailey and Carey, but no one knows whether they were Catholics or not. For there was no religious test at the Alamo."[11]

The Unitarian Sorensen also asked a Catholic clergyman named John Courtney Murray for advice at the eleventh hour. Murray cannot remember what, if any, changes he may have suggested. "I told Sorensen at the time that it was unfair to ask me for an opinion just on hearing the speech on the phone, [and] he was standing by the side of a plane just about to take off for Houston," Murray later remarked. "My impression is that Sorensen wrote the speech himself."[12]

On September 12, 1960, Kennedy walked toward the podium in the ballroom of the Rice Hotel. He was visibly tense. Meza noticed that the senator's hands were shaking. Three hundred skeptical Protestant ministers glared at him. He knew that this speech could make or break his campaign. His nervousness fell away when he began speaking, and he ended up delivering a memorable plea for religious tolerance:

> I believe in an America where the separation of church and state is absolute—where no Catholic prelate would tell the president (should he be Catholic) how to act, and no Protestant minister would tell his parishioners for whom to vote—where no church or church school is granted any public funds or political preference . . . an America that is officially neither Catholic, Protestant nor Jewish—where no public official either requests or accepts instructions on public policy from . . . any . . . ecclesiastical source . . . where there is no Catholic vote, no anti-Catholic vote, no bloc voting of any kind . . . and where religious liberty is so indivisible that an act against one church is treated as an act against all.

Kennedy's next sentences made the newspapers the next morning, and the history books in the years that followed:

> I am not the Catholic candidate for president, I am the Democratic Party's candidate for president who happens also to be a Catholic. I do not speak for my church on public matters, and the church does not speak for me.[13]

After the speech, Kennedy patiently fielded questions from audience members who remained unconvinced. But he knew that he had already won the public relations battle. Several ministers conceded as much by coming forward to shake the candidate's hand once the speech had concluded. U.S. House Speaker Sam Rayburn, who had been watching the speech on TV, said, "By God, look at him—and listen to him! He's eating them blood raw. This young feller will be a great president!"[14]

In recent years, some conservative politicians, including Catholics, have criticized JFK for delivering a speech that they say "secularized" the presidency. Rick Santorum, a former Republican U.S. senator from Pennsylvania who unsuccessfully sought the 2012 GOP presidential nomination, said the Houston speech, once he read it many years later, made him "want to vomit." The Catholic Santorum argued that Kennedy created "a purely secular public square" in Houston that has since led to an increase in religious bigotry and scurrilous attacks on people of faith. Former Republican vice presidential nominee Sarah Palin, a nondenominational Christian, agreed. She found JFK's speech "defensive . . . in tone and content" and believes that it initiated an "unequivocal divorce" between religion and public service. Both politicians assert that JFK should have emphasized his faith.

Whatever the philosophical wisdom of that today, their advice then would have been deadly. In 1960, millions of Americans fervently embraced the mistaken idea that Catholic politicians were controlled by the Vatican. Kennedy would have only confirmed their suspicions if he had extended the discussion and elaborated on how his faith guided his political decisions. In order to win the election, he needed to sidestep the issue, not step in front of it, which is precisely what he did in Houston.[15]

Kennedy scored even more political points when he debated Vice President Nixon on national television. According to Ted Sorensen, JFK was "amazed" when the vice president agreed to four TV debates. "Nixon was apparently confident that having defeated Khrushchev [in the famous 1959 'Kitchen Debate' in Moscow], he could certainly defeat a young, comparatively unknown United States senator," Sorensen recalled. Eisenhower advised Nixon to avoid the debates "on the grounds that Nixon was much better known than Kennedy and therefore should not give Kennedy so much free exposure." Nixon ignored the advice. He had known Jack Kennedy for years and felt certain that he could derail the senator's campaign. Sorensen and Meyer "Mike" Feldman, another Kennedy campaign adviser, used note cards to train their man. "Mike had prepared a little blue card with Kennedy's position, Nixon's position, the positions of the two party platforms, and any votes or comments that either candidate had made," said Sorensen. Kennedy would either say "I know that one, go on to the next one" or request additional information. On the afternoon of the debate, JFK took a nap. "The story I like to tell is of when they delegated me to go wake him up," Sorensen recalled. "I opened the door and peeked in and there he was, lights on, sound asleep, covered in note cards."[16] Kennedy was also glowing with a healthy-looking tan, having practiced with Sorensen on the sun-splashed roof of the hotel.

Still sick from a stint in the hospital after a knee had become badly infected, Nixon refused to wear professional makeup for the debate. But he did allow an aide to slather "Lazy Shave" on his perpetual five o'clock shadow.[17] According to TV debate director Don Hewitt, Sorensen admitted that Kennedy had gone "behind closed doors and out of sight" to receive a "light coat" of makeup.[18]

Rejecting cosmetics wasn't Nixon's only mistake. He also agreed to discuss domestic issues during the first debate even though Republicans had traditionally struggled in this area. "Foreign affairs was my strong suit, and I wanted the larger audience for that debate," the vice president later revealed, blaming his aides for the error. "I thought more people would watch the first one, and that interest would diminish as the novelty of the confrontation wore off. Most of my advisers believed that interest would build as the campaign progressed, and that the last program, nearest election day, would be the most important one. I yielded to their judgment and agreed that in the negotiations to set up the debates I would agree to scheduling the domestic policy debate first and the foreign policy debate last."[19]

At half past eight on September 26, 1960, Howard K. Smith, a seasoned journalist working for CBS, stared into a camera in a Chicago TV studio and intoned, "Good evening. The television and radio stations of the United States and their affiliated stations are proud to provide facilities for a discussion of issues in the current political campaign by the two major candidates for the presidency. The candidates need no introduction." An estimated 70 million Americans, approximately equal to the almost 69 million who actually voted in the November election, were watching and listening.[20] Kennedy opened the debate by saying that America's image abroad depended on sound policies at home. Now was the time to get the country "moving again."[21]

The ailing Nixon leaned on the podium to ease his knee pain, and he came across as nervous, overly inclined to approve Kennedy's arguments, and unpresidential in appearance and approach. At one point, Nixon offered an extended "me-too" comment: "The things that Senator Kennedy has said many of us can agree with. There is no question but that we cannot discuss our internal affairs in the United States without recognizing that they have a tremendous bearing on our international position. There is no question but that this nation cannot stand still; because we are in a deadly competition, a competition not only with the men in the Kremlin, but the men in Peking. We're ahead in this competition, as Senator Kennedy, I think, has implied. But when you're in a race, the only way to stay ahead is to move ahead. And I subscribe completely to the spirit that Senator Kennedy has expressed tonight, the spirit that the United States should move ahead."[22]

In Nixon, Americans saw a physically unimposing man on their screens, dressed in a gray suit that faded into the set's background. The Republican was "half slouched, his 'Lazy Shave' powder faintly streaked with sweat, his eyes exaggerated hollows of blackness, his jaw, jowls, and face drooping with strain." Kennedy, on the other hand, looked healthy and confident. Questions about his youth and inexperience no longer seemed as relevant. The young man from Boston had shown that he could at least hold his own with the vice president of the United States, and maybe best him.[23]

Nixon's aides did their best to contain the damage. Herbert Klein, the vice president's campaign press secretary, blamed television for his boss's ghoulish appearance. "Mr. Nixon is in excellent health and looks good in person," he explained. Nixon's own mother didn't buy it. Shortly after the debates, Hannah Milhous Nixon phoned Rose Mary Woods, Nixon's secretary, to find out if her son was "feeling all right."[24] Ironically, JFK's mother, Rose, who had listened to the debate over the radio, thought that "Nixon was smoother."[25]

Rose's and Hannah's contradictory opinions were shared by many other Americans. According to a survey conducted by Sindlinger and Company, those who saw the debate on TV believed that Kennedy had won the debate; radio listeners arrived at the opposite conclusion. While there is no irrefutable polling or statistical evidence that the Kennedy-Nixon debates had a decisive impact on the election, or even that Kennedy "won" the first debate or the others, reporters following the campaign almost unanimously adopted that point of view. Campaign professionals on both sides cited anecdotes that supported the reporters' conclusions, and these informal assessments changed the tone of the coverage and perhaps the momentum of the campaign. Whether the pro-Kennedy assessment of the debates originated with the public or the press, there is little question that Kennedy received a perceptible boost. Television sets had replaced radios in many American homes by the time this campaign got under way. In 1960, 88 percent of U.S. households had one or more TV sets, an 11 percent jump from the previous decade.[26]

One debate effect was visible on the campaign trail. Suddenly, everyone wanted to catch a glimpse of America's first made-for-TV politician. "The size and enthusiasm of [Kennedy's] crowds increased immensely and immediately" after the first debate. On September 28, twenty thousand people greeted JFK's plane when it touched down in Erie, Pennsylvania, and he had been mobbed the day before by two hundred thousand Ohioans. Local police had trouble containing the huge crowds. In a precedent that would continue during the Kennedy presidency, Kenny O'Donnell had to "ask police officers not to push or pull Senator Kennedy while attempting to get him through crowds." O'Donnell explained that although the senator appreciated "the difficulties of officers [handling] crowds," he preferred that they "merely try to clear the way" rather than rush JFK past friendly voters. More than crowds were moved by the debate. Some skittish Southern Democratic governors were nudged off the fence because they sensed a winner. Ten of the eleven governors, all Democrats, who attended the Southern Governors' Conference in Hot Springs, Arkansas, signed a telegram congratulating Kennedy for his "superb handling of Mr. Nixon and the issues facing our country."[27]

Whatever the real political impact in 1960, the Kennedy-Nixon debates became mythical, and they are a sizable part of the Kennedy legacy. Every four years, the story of Kennedy's "triumph" leads the run-up to the presidential debating season, recycling the flickering images of those dynamic encounters. The contrast between JFK and Nixon on-screen still serves as a warning to politicians who are ill at ease on television. It is no accident that both LBJ and Nixon—two of the more media-awkward presidents—refused to participate in any TV debates in 1964, 1968, and 1972.

Jackie Kennedy generated as much excitement as her husband did. Cards and letters flooded into her office in the wake of her husband's TV appearances. Nancy Harrison, one of Jackie's secretaries, complained about the increased workload until she realized that she could send out "robot letters" containing standard responses like these:

"I am so glad you like my hair style and manner of dressing. A candidate's wife is no different from other women—she's pleased to know when people approve. Much more important, though, is the winning of this election, and I know you are doing all you can."

"I am enclosing our favorite recipe, as you requested."

"I'm so sorry, but it is impossible for me to send out my old clothes. I would never have enough clothes to fill the requests."[28]

Pregnant at the time with John Jr., Jackie's appearance also signaled to the public that JFK was a family man. As the world now knows, her husband cheated on her every chance he got—a fact some of the press knew at the time, but never reported. During the winter of 1960, Kennedy began a long affair with a beautiful brunette named Judith Campbell. At about the same time, Campbell also took up with the well-known Chicago mobster Sam Giancana. Kennedy pursued additional partners as well. During the Los Angeles convention, he rented a three-bedroom apartment so that he could be close to the "nearby home of a former diplomat's wife" and surprised Campbell by introducing her to a twenty-five-year-old beauty who had agreed to join them in a ménage à trois. When Campbell refused, Kennedy made sure that his newer friend got a ticket to the convention. The senator also hired prostitutes, apparently procured by close aides. Jackie was painfully aware of at least some of her husband's infidelities, but most of the time she dutifully played the role of a presidential politician's wife. Her motives can only be guessed at, but it was not an uncommon arrangement in a culture with very different gender norms than our own.[29]

The electorate and party activists were unknowing, luckily for John Kennedy. The carefully nurtured image of "the perfect family" encouraged the energetic efforts of housewives, who held Kennedy coffee klatches by the hundreds in their homes, and the babysitting skills of "Kennedy Girls," who watched children while parents voted.[30]

On the less wholesome side of the political tracks, the Kennedys believed the best defense for sleaze was a good offense. The journalist Jack Anderson, who sided with the Democratic ticket, investigated a secret, never-repaid $205,000 loan from Las Vegas mogul Howard Hughes to Donald Nixon, Vice President Nixon's brother. Drew Pearson, who was Anderson's editorial superior, preferred not to print the story late in the campaign, but Anderson was determined to make the information public—even if he lost control of the story. Anderson decided to tell a senior Nixon adviser that he was investigating the subject. The Nixon campaign then slipped a less damaging version to a GOP-leaning journalist working for the Scripps-Howard news service. But the Scripps-Howard headline gave an excuse to Anderson and Pearson to print a "correction" that included the unvarnished, damaging particulars. Remarkably, Anderson and Pearson even drafted follow-up statements for Lyndon Johnson and Texas Democratic congressman Jack Brooks calling for Senate hearings on the Nixon family's finances.[31]

Anderson had learned about the Hughes scandal from a Kennedy lawyer named James McInerney. When he visited McInerney's D.C. office one day, the attorney handed him confidential documents on the scandal. As the researcher Mark Feldstein assessed it: "How did JFK's campaign obtain this incriminating evidence? By paying the contemporary equivalent of $100,000 to a Los Angeles accountant named Phillip Reiner, one of Hughes' middlemen used to conceal Nixon's role in the deal. Reiner was a Democrat who recently had a falling out with his partners. With his attorney, Reiner had contacted Robert Kennedy, [JFK's] campaign manager. Soon after, a break-in occurred in the accountant's old office—and the Kennedys suddenly acquired a thick file filled with secret records documenting Nixon's shady deal. (Reiner's estranged partner filed a burglary report with police, but the crime was never solved.)" Twelve years before the Watergate break-in, the Kennedys proved that they were willing to break a few laws of their own so that they could win the White House.[32]

Unquestionably, Pearson's and Anderson's tactics would be rejected by any modern journalists who seek objectivity. Even in 1960, these actions were beyond the pale, and retrospectively they are an embarrassment for the two reporters. Yet many journalists at the time "liked Kennedy, agreed with his politics, and reveled in their acceptance by, and association with, the glamorous, dashing, wealthy, jet-setting Kennedys." Most were willing to overlook the clan's faults and write stories that burnished the family myth. David Halberstam, a reporter for the *New York Times*, called it the "gentlemen's agreement" among "The Good Journalists of Washington." According to Halberstam, these journalists believed that "the Kennedy Administration was one of excellence, that it was for good things and against bad things, and that when it did lesser things it was only in self-defense, and in order that it might do other good things." Those "lesser things" included campaign shenanigans.[33] Nixon had no such luxury: Imagine what would have happened had the press caught wind of similar dirty tricks by him.

Of course, the Nixon camp played its own dirty tricks in 1960. Thieves ransacked the offices of Dr. Eugene Cohen, the New York endocrinologist who was treating Kennedy's Addison's disease, and Dr. Janet Travell, JFK's personal physician.[34] Such political skulduggery was not uncommon in this era and was one reason why the public reaction to Watergate surprised Nixon. For the rest of his life, Nixon remained furious that JFK and others had gotten away with various ploys while his reputation had been permanently destroyed by a "third-rate burglary" (his description of the 1972 Watergate break-in).[35] This is not to equate prior campaign hijinks with the stunning scope of Watergate's perfidy; nonetheless, one can understand Nixon's reaction even while disagreeing with his argument suggesting equivalency.

Meanwhile, the campaign waged in public focused mainly on high-minded matters. Kennedy was on the road making tough statements about Cuba. On October 7, he told a Cincinnati crowd, "We must firmly resist further Communist encroachment in this hemisphere [by] encouraging those liberty-loving Cubans who are leading the resistance to Castro." Eight days later, he was in Johnstown, Pennsylvania, making a similar statement: "We must broadcast our story to Cuba. We must let those Cubans . . . who are not fighting for independence and wish to do so [know] that we are on their side." In New York City, he blasted the administration for mollycoddling Cuba, arguing that the United States "must attempt to strengthen the . . . democratic anti-Castro forces in exile, and in Cuba itself, who offer eventual hope of overthrowing Castro. Thus far these fighters for freedom have had virtually no support from our government."

Richard Nixon was stunned. In his mind, Kennedy had put the security of the country at risk in order to score political points. The vice president ordered an aide to call the White House to find out if Kennedy had been briefed by the CIA on the government's ongoing invasion planning. "He was told that Kennedy had been briefed." Today, it is not clear that he ever was, but JFK's comments did mislead anti-Castro Cubans (and perhaps the Pentagon) into believing that he would support a U.S. attack on Castro once he became president, the opposite of what happened in the 1961 Bay of Pigs invasion. On October 22, Nixon informed TV viewers that Kennedy's proposals on Cuba represented "the most dangerously irresponsible recommendations that he's made during the course of this campaign." U.S. interference in Cuba, warned Nixon, would violate the charters of the Organization of American States (OAS) and the United Nations and invite Soviet retaliation in Latin America. Actually, Nixon knew his own administration was planning an eventual invasion of Cuba, but he attacked Kennedy's statements anyway in order to protect what Nixon considered national security.[36]

Kennedy ignored the controversy and continued campaigning. Four days before the election, he flew to Norfolk, Virginia, home to one of the largest naval bases in the world, and rode in a red convertible from the airport to Granby High School. There he delivered a speech to more than twelve thousand rapturous supporters. It was the biggest political event that the city of Norfolk had ever seen. "No citizen can live in this section of Virginia without realizing there is a world of danger and opportunity surrounding us," he told the cheering multitude. "You must believe that the United States must go forward. You cannot possibly put your confidence in Democratic senators and Democratic congressmen and suddenly put in reverse and elect a Republican president. What sense does that make in the sixties? I come to you in these last four days. I come back where it all began, and I ask Virginia to give me her vote." Kennedy then flew across the state to Roanoke in the west, where many thousands turned out to greet him. Alvin Hudson, the Roanoke policeman responsible for JFK's security, made plans to escort the senator from the speaker's platform to a row of phone booths after the speech was over, but Kennedy refused to cooperate. "Instead of going back with me, he jumped over the wooden handrail that surrounded the speaker stand. He was my responsibility so I had to go with him. On the other side of the rail were about three or four banquet tables that had been arranged for the reporters. He jumped on top of one of these tables and the leg collapsed and we fell. On the way down, he grabbed the chain my whistle was on and ended up standing on it. It was under his foot and I had to ask him to get off my whistle." Hudson remembered that both candidate and crowd were amused by the incident.[37]

During the same week, Nixon campaigned in New York City with President Eisenhower. The political duo received a ticker tape parade and "shouts and cheers" from an estimated one to two million onlookers. Nixon had made poor use of Eisenhower, who was still remarkably popular—near 60 percent in the Gallup poll. Partly, the vice president wanted to prove to the country that he was his own man. Yet there was a hidden explanation. Ike's wife, Mamie, had telephoned Patricia Nixon earlier in the year to express concern over her husband's often-precarious health. It was clear that the First Lady would not welcome requests for strenuous campaign activities for the president. Nixon deferred to Mamie, not utilizing his best asset for most of the campaign. Meanwhile, President Eisenhower, unaware of his wife's action, was puzzled and hurt by Nixon's failure to ask him to do more. This comedy of errors had a fatal effect for Nixon, as Eisenhower might well have made the difference had he been sent to competitive states such as Illinois and Texas. As it was, Ike might have been the reason for the tightening polls at campaign's end. In mid-October, before Eisenhower's deployment, Kennedy had led Nixon by 51 to 45 percent, but three days before the election, after photos and film of Ike and Nixon together had dominated the news, Gallup showed Kennedy's lead had dwindled to a paper-thin 50.5 to 49.5 percent.[38]

BY NOVEMBER 5, JFK had visited 237 cities in forty-three states; Nixon had toured 168 cities in forty-nine states. The vice president ultimately kept his promise to visit all fifty states by squeezing in a trip to Alaska at the last minute. It was an extraordinarily foolish thing to do. If Nixon had focused his energy on the remaining battlegrounds, as Kennedy did, he might have carried more critical, very close states. By contrast, JFK could look back on a skillfully executed campaign that had transformed him from a little-known senator and presidential underdog into an apparent frontrunner who had united a party suffering from a post-FDR crisis of confidence. In the process, he had brought together the factions of the Democratic Party—to the extent that a young Catholic candidate could. To appease the left, he had openly proclaimed himself to be a liberal. "What do our opponents mean when they apply to us the label of 'liberal'?" he asked listeners at a liberal party dinner in New York.

> If by liberal they mean, as they want others to believe, someone who is soft on Communism, against local government, and unconcerned with the taxpayer's dollar, then the record of this party and its members demonstrates that we are not that kind of liberal. But if by liberal they mean someone who looks to the future instead of the past—someone who welcomes new ideas without rigid reactions—someone who cares about the welfare of the people, their health, their housing, their schools, their jobs, their civil rights and civil liberties—someone who believes that we can break through the stalemates and suspicions to find the road to peace—if that is what they mean by a liberal, then I am proud to say that I am a liberal.[39]

To win the confidence of Asian Americans, Kennedy dispatched an aide to address the Chinese National Businessmen's Organization. Lithuanian Americans were told that JFK would "smother" Soviet aggression in Eastern Europe. African Americans were impressed by his decision to phone Coretta Scott King when Dr. Martin Luther King, Jr., was incarcerated in Georgia. Young people were inspired by his talk of a Peace Corps, old people by his promise of Medicare, white Southerners by his choice of running mate.[40]

By and large, Kennedy had handled foreign policy issues with skill, despite Nixon's inherent advantages. His nuanced views on two small islands off the coast of China named Quemoy and Matsu deflected Nixon's criticism. The islands lie in the Taiwan Straits and in the 1950s and 1960s were considered strategically important to the defense of Taiwan. In summer 1959, the Chinese Communists held military exercises near the islands that were perceived as threatening. Hoping to convince the public that he would be tougher on Communism than Kennedy, Nixon accused the senator of "woolly thinking" for pointing out that the United States had no international agreement to defend the islands. But Kennedy finessed the dispute, allowing that the Asian islands would pose "a key decision for the next president . . . whenever the Chinese Communists decide . . . that they want to put us under pressure." At the same time, JFK's rhetoric on Communism and missile defense was as bellicose as Nixon's, if not more so. In any event, the Quemoy and Matsu issue vanished after the election, as is frequently the case with election controversies.[41]

ON ELECTION DAY, November 8, 1960, Kennedy voted at the West End Branch Library in Boston before flying to Hyannis Port to watch the election returns. He put on a sweater, lit a cigar, and settled in for a long night. Bobby's house on the Kennedy compound had been "converted into a communications and vote analysis center." On the ground floor of the house, telephones rang, Teletype machines spat out messages, and campaign workers scurried from one room to another. Upstairs, in one of the children's bedrooms, the pollster Lou Harris and an army of statisticians were crunching numbers and eyeballing data from previous elections.

The early results looked good. John Bailey, chairman of the Democratic National Committee, reported positive news from Connecticut. Philadelphia looked as if it would go for Kennedy: "The industrial centers of the Northeast, which had been hit hard by unemployment and economic stagnation, were turning in some of the highest pluralities for a Democrat since FDR in 1936." JFK's friends and relatives beamed with optimism. But the candidate remained guarded. In 1956 he had watched the vice presidential nomination slip through his fingers at the last minute. He would not relax until the entire country's vote had been counted. At one point during the evening, CBS-TV's IBM 7090 computer called the race for Nixon—then the network reversed itself and predicted a victory for Kennedy.[42] As the night wore on, it became apparent to everyone that the outcome was extremely close. In the wee hours, Ohio fell into Nixon's column, and no Democrat in the twentieth century except FDR in 1944 had ever been elected without it. Illinois was a complete toss-up, and Kennedy simply had to win the Land of Lincoln. Pennsylvania, Missouri, Minnesota, Michigan, and California were also on the razor's edge.[43]

Somehow, Kennedy grabbed a few hours of sleep once it was apparent that the election would not be decided until the next morning. By dawn's light on the eastern seaboard, as states still seesawed back and forth, the outline of Kennedy's Electoral College majority became apparent. At around nine A.M., Ted Sorensen reached JFK and congratulated his boss on becoming president-elect. "What happened in California?" Kennedy asked. Sorensen assured his boss that he had carried the Golden State. The networks said so, too. Actually, JFK lost California once the final rural votes trickled in. Nor had he won anything approaching a decisive victory. But at midmorning, with Illinois and Texas finally called in his favor by the slimmest of margins, John Kennedy could exhale and contemplate his move into the White House.[44]

Kennedy eventually learned that he had won the election by a mere 118,574 votes—a margin so tiny he was left without an effective mandate. (To make matters worse, by some calculations, JFK actually lost the popular vote to Nixon.)[45] But JFK's minimal victory was enhanced somewhat by the Electoral College, where he accumulated 303 votes to Nixon's 219. It may have been Kennedy's sizable electoral edge that deterred Nixon from seeking a recount in Illinois and Texas, where vote fraud was hardly unknown.[46] In Chicago, for example, where Mayor Richard J. Daley, Sr., ruled with an iron hand, JFK won with a massive majority of 319,000 votes. Statewide, Kennedy's plurality was a mere 8,858 votes out of more than 4.7 million cast. The Democrat also clinched Texas by just 46,257 votes out of more than 2.3 million votes cast. If Nixon had won Texas and Illinois, he would have been the thirty-fifth president of the United States. Nixon and many of his followers firmly believed that the Kennedys, Mayor Daley, and LBJ had stolen the 1960 election.[47]

In the days following the vote count, Republicans dispatched teams of investigators to ferret out cases of fraud. In Texas, they found some irregularities. In Fannin County, for example, there were 6,138 votes cast even though the county had only 4,895 registered voters. Three quarters of Fannin's votes had gone to Kennedy. "In one precinct of Angelina County, 86 people voted and the final tally was 147 for Kennedy, 24 for Nixon." GOP loyalists demanded a recount, but the Texas Election Board, controlled by Democrats, steadfastly refused. Illinois was an equally rich source of questionable votes. Earl Mazo, a reporter for the *New York Herald Tribune*, investigated the returns in Chicago. "There was a cemetery where the names on the tombstones were registered and voted," says Mazo. "I remember a house. It was completely gutted. There was nobody there. But there were 56 votes for Kennedy in that house." Mazo also found cases of GOP malfeasance in Illinois's southern counties. "In downstate Illinois, there was definitely fraud. The Republicans were having a good time, too. But they didn't have the votes to counterbalance Chicago. There was no purity on either side, except that the Republicans didn't have Daley in their corner—or Lyndon Johnson."[48]

From the vantage point of 2013, it is clear that some Kennedy supporters in Illinois and Texas stole votes. What we will never know is whether these votes would have made the difference in the election. Edmund F. Kallina, a professor of history at the University of Central Florida who researched the matter, acknowledges that "the counting of paper ballots in Chicago" was "unbelievably sloppy and inaccurate." But he also argues that partial recounts conducted in 1960 and 1961 demonstrate that fraudulent votes did not determine the outcome. "While there will never be a completely satisfactory account of the election in Illinois," Kallina argues, "Republican charges that the election was stolen must be presently regarded as unproven."[49]

Moreover, accusations of fraud were not enough to diminish the magnitude of the moment. On November 8, 1960, the American people—just enough of them—decided to give a forty-three-year-old Catholic the leadership of the free world. JFK's presidential résumé was thin by historical standards, and he was younger than a large majority of governors, senators, and representatives—not to mention all White House predecessors save Theodore Roosevelt. Kennedy was only the second person ever elected directly from the Senate to the White House.* People at home and around the world marveled at the election's astounding result. Journalist Joseph Alsop captured the mood of many Democrats when he wrote to Ted Sorensen, "No other choice that our people have had to make in my time has ever seemed to me so absolutely decisive. When you consider all the factors, it is a miracle that the right choice was made, even by the narrow margin."[50] And whether or not one believes John F. Kennedy was the right choice, it remains astonishing that the nation was willing to take such a leap into the unknown, to risk so much on a relatively untested politician.

---

* Warren G. Harding was the first and Barack Obama would be the third; in general, Americans prefer presidents who have executive rather than legislative experience.

4

THE TORCH IS PASSED

IT WAS A CROSS BETWEEN A CORONATION and a Hollywood extrava-
ganza. On the eve of the 1961 inauguration, singer Frank Sinatra and actor Peter
Lawford, the president-elect's brother-in-law and a member of Sinatra's "Rat
Pack," hosted a star-studded black-tie event at the Washington, D.C., Armory.
Ticket holders trudged through eight inches of snow to witness the spectacle.
Leonard Bernstein opened the evening with an original piece, "A Fanfare for
Inauguration," followed by a rousing rendition of John Philip Sousa's "The Stars
and Stripes Forever." Next, the entire cast, assisted by a number of college glee
clubs, came out on stage and sang a schmaltzy song entitled "Walkin' Down to
Washington."

> I'm walkin' down to Washington to shake hands with President Kennedy
> Walkin' down to Washington, like we used to do
> I'm walkin' down to Washington to shake hands with Lyndon Johnson
> Walkin' down to Washington, like we used to do[1]

When they had finished singing, the nation's man of the hour triumphantly
entered the arena, smiling and waving, his entourage in tow. Flashbulbs
popped and rapt well-wishers stretched out their hands. Bernstein's band
struck up "Anchors Aweigh," a tribute to John Kennedy's days as a PT boat
commander. From the presidential box, he listened to Mahalia Jackson sing
"The Star-Spangled Banner" and then laughed and clapped as Bette Davis,
Sidney Poitier, Laurence Olivier, Ella Fitzgerald, Gene Kelly, Alan King, Tony
Curtis, Nat King Cole, Jimmy Durante, and Milton Berle gave performances.[2]

The celebrations continued the next day, warming the biting chill of
winter in Washington. Congressmen, foreign dignitaries, artists, writers,
academics, and VIPs from all fifty states congregated on the east steps of the
Capitol to hear his inaugural address, which soared through the cold January
air like an eagle riding a thermal updraft: "Let the word go forth from this
time and place, to friend and foe alike, that the torch has been passed to a new
generation of Americans—born in this century, tempered by war, disciplined

by a hard and bitter peace, proud of our ancient heritage—and unwilling to witness or permit the slow undoing of those human rights to which this nation has always been committed, and to which we are committed today at home and around the world." The American people, declared the president, would "pay any price, bear any burden, meet any hardship, support any friend, oppose any foe, to assure the survival and the success of liberty." But they could only do so by serving their fellow citizens rather than their own parochial interests: "And so, my fellow Americans: Ask not what your country can do for you—ask what you can do for your country."[3] This line became an instant classic; it may be the sentence most associated with John F. Kennedy even today.

Far more memorable than most inaugural addresses, Kennedy's speech resonated with Americans, especially young people who were searching for purpose in their lives. Donna Shalala, the future secretary of Health and Human Services in the Clinton administration and president of the University of Miami, remembers watching it on a black-and-white TV in the lounge of her college dormitory. "Before I heard the speech I was thinking of being a journalist, a war correspondent as a matter of fact," Shalala says. Instead, she joined the Peace Corps before launching a successful career in education and public service. Gonzalo Barrientos was also in college when Kennedy took the oath. The president's inaugural address convinced him to focus on sociology, economics, and government instead of business. In 1974, Barrientos "became one of the first Mexican Americans elected to the Texas state legislature," where he remained for thirty-one years.[4]

Future House Speaker Nancy Pelosi attended the inauguration and remembers feeling overwhelmed when she heard the new president's speech. "It was so clear and it was so inspiring and so uplifting," she says. "His words were . . . I want to say, otherworldly. He was so enhanced as a person. Here was this lovely, young, brilliant, talented, politically astute person who was now the president of the United States. He was speaking for the ages. It was spectacular."[5]

Kennedy's inaugural address contains some of the most familiar words in our political lexicon: "Ask not . . ." "Let us never negotiate out of fear, but let us never fear to negotiate." "The torch has been passed to a new generation . . ." "So let us begin anew." Fifty years later, people are still talking and writing about it; young people who see it for the first time are still inspired. On January 20, 2011, top congressional leaders and White House officials gathered in the grand rotunda of the U.S. Capitol to hear it read aloud once more.[6]

Few know how much work went into the address. According to Ted Sorensen, JFK's primary wordsmith, no Kennedy speech had ever undergone so many drafts. "Each paragraph was reworded, reworked and reduced," Sorensen recalled. In 2011 Sorensen's former secretary, Gloria Sitrin, found one of those drafts—the earliest known copy, in fact—sitting in a dusty box in her garage. Thanks to her discovery, we are now aware of the existence of some awkward lines, including "our strength, like our dream, must be a seamless web" and "a Walpurgis Night dance of hideous destruction and death." Fortunately, they never made it into the final draft. More telling is a reference to racial discrimination that was deleted: "Our nation's most precious resource, our youth, are developed according to their race or funds, instead of their own capability." Kennedy feared the controversy this reference to civil rights might spark; his failure to embrace it in his life's most memorable speech is understandable but not admirable. Two of his advisers, Louis Martin and Harris Wofford, had to fight hard just to get Kennedy to add "at home" to the sentence on human rights—a small, opaque reference to the ongoing struggle for civil rights.[7]

After finishing the inaugural ceremonies, JFK did what new presidents always do: watch scores of floats and bands pass by from his reviewing stand near the White House. A half million people lined the route. That night, he attended a slew of official balls and galas, sneaking in brief sexual encounters at some places. One of his mistresses, a twenty-eight-year-old actress named Angie Dickinson, described sex with the president as "the most memorable fifteen seconds of my life." Later on, after the official schedule had been completed and Jackie had gone to bed, he stopped by the columnist Joseph Alsop's house for a nightcap. Alsop, who had been heating up leftover terrapin for "thirteen or fourteen people" when he heard the doorbell ring, was surprised to see the president of the United States, "standing there in the bright light with the snow behind" him. Alsop's guests giggled nervously as Kennedy made jokes about their host's taste in hors d'oeuvres. One young woman in attendance easily surrendered to Kennedy's advances. She wept after he left, "fearful that her relationship with the president was finished forever." The amazing part of this story is that JFK felt no inhibition about sowing wild oats in the home of a leading member of the journalistic establishment, and Alsop never reported a word of it.[8]

It was a fitting start of high points and low ones to a presidency that brought with it a welcome sense of style, humor, and haute couture, but also swinging-sixties titillation (or debauchery, depending on your point of view).[9] With the press turning two blind eyes, JFK's seemingly insatiable sexual desires led to brazen recklessness and predation—the unpleasant underbelly of a president who proclaimed high standards for others. Still, over the course of three years, the Kennedys managed to transform the sleepy village of Washington into a vibrant intellectual and cultural center, and the New Frontier had many attractive sides. JFK recruited "the best and the brightest" to government while Jackie worked tirelessly to give the American people a White House they could be proud of—and the First Lady was a huge part of the

Kennedy administration's public appeal. The generation that had been born during one world war and tested by another was eager to govern, and confident that their idealism and energy would triumph over all adversity.

But old and new challenges loomed on the horizon. Communism was on the march around the globe, trampling human rights and fomenting proletarian revolutions; the accelerating nuclear arms race could have easily ended in Armageddon; poverty persisted in America's remote mountain hollows and nearby urban neighborhoods; and the United States was at war with itself over the status of African Americans. If John Kennedy glimpsed the January-February 1961 "Special Inaugural" issue of the *Democratic Digest* with his picture on the cover, he might have seen an omen of the domestic conflict to come. "Join With Us in Celebrating Alabama's Confederate Centennial Celebration" invited an advertisement featuring a picture of the Confederacy's first and only president. "Re-enactment of the inauguration of President Jefferson Davis, as it happened 100 years ago, will climax Alabama's week-long Civil War Centennial Commemoration in Montgomery, birthplace of the Confederacy. Preceding this historic event will be a spectacular pageant and inauguration parade, a pilgrimage to ante bellum homes, a gigantic Old South Commemoration Ball, and many more colorful festivities that will reanimate the stirring days of 1861."[10] The ad also featured a congratulatory letter to JFK from Alabama's segregationist Democratic governor, John Patterson, who had supported Kennedy in 1960.[11]

AFRICAN AMERICANS IN Alabama and other Southern states were sick of living in the past.[12] On February 1, 1960, four black students from North Carolina Agricultural and Technical College challenged Greensboro's segregation laws by sitting at a "whites only" lunch counter in a local department store. Their protest touched off a wave of similar demonstrations across the South. Meanwhile in Washington, African diplomats were having trouble finding places to live because of their skin color. As chairman of the Senate Foreign Relations Subcommittee on Africa, Senator John F. Kennedy had recognized that the D.C. housing issue was affecting U.S. foreign policy. "I am very concerned about the unfortunate reflection which is cast on the United States by these events, particularly when they occur in the nation's capitol," he wrote Eisenhower's secretary of state, Christian Herter. "As a people and as a government we purport to welcome the new African nations to independence and the community of nations. We can hardly seem other than hypocritical if when the first African delegations come as representatives to the United Nations in New York and to open Embassies in Washington, they have difficulties in finding places to live where they will be welcome."[13]

Nonetheless, Kennedy seemed less concerned with making sure that his fellow citizens had equal access to housing. During the campaign, he had promised to end racial discrimination in federal housing with "the stroke of a pen." But the close results of the election had convinced him to keep his pen in his pocket. Kennedy interpreted his narrow margin of victory, and his dependence on Southern electoral votes, as a lack of a mandate to govern decisively on the contentious issue of civil rights. In addition, Kennedy had demonstrated no congressional coattails in November 1960; Democrats had lost twenty seats in the House of Representatives and two seats in the Senate. Worse, Southern Democrats controlled most key committees on Capitol Hill. Southerners controlled two thirds of the Senate's standing committees, while over on the House side, Southern congressmen held eleven of nineteen chairmanships.[14]

African Americans weren't sure what to make of their new president. Even though an estimated 68 percent had voted for Kennedy, they wondered how committed he was to the cause of civil rights.[15] Jackie Robinson, the sports legend who famously broke baseball's color barrier in the 1940s, was a Republican at the time, and blasted JFK even before he took office for "doing absolutely nothing for the Negroes in the country." But Robinson reacted favorably to Kennedy's early signals on civil rights once he was in office. "I believe I now understand and appreciate better your role in the continuing struggle to fulfill the American promise of equal opportunity for all," he wrote Kennedy in February 1961. "While I am very happy over your obviously fine start as our President, my concern over Civil Rights and my vigorous opposition to your election is one of sincerity. The direction you seem to be going indicates America is in for great leadership, and I will be most happy if my fears continue to be proven wrong." Robinson urged Kennedy to take swift action: "I would like to be patient Mr. President, but patience has caused us years in our struggle for human dignity. I will continue to hope and pray for your aggressive leadership but will not refuse to criticize if the feeling persist[s] that Civil Rights is not on the agenda for months to come."[16]

Yet civil rights was not a high priority for the new administration and Roy Wilkins, executive secretary of the NAACP, recognized it. Ten days after the election, Wilkins received word that the new president would not be pressing Congress to pass new legislation. He was disappointed, since Kennedy's timidity was at odds with his bold talk on some campaign occasions. Two months before he won, JFK had told the press that he would use the presidential bully pulpit "to get the broadly liberal Democratic plank [on racial equality] passed early in the next Congress." That plank stressed "equal access for all Americans to all areas of community life, including voting booths, school rooms, jobs, housing, and public facilities."[17]

Eventually, Kennedy's hand would be forced by public opinion, after the news media extensively covered civil rights demonstrations and the often-violent reaction to them in the South. In May 1961 activists known as "Freedom Riders" boarded buses in D.C. bound for New Orleans, and the plan was to challenge the South's segregation laws at various stops along the way. Robert Kennedy claimed that he didn't learn about the trip until after an angry mob in Anniston, Alabama, firebombed one of the buses. In Birmingham, police turned a blind eye while Ku Klux Klansmen savagely attacked the riders with bats and metal pipes. When the news broke, JFK was focused on an upcoming summit with the Soviets. He ordered his special assistant on civil rights, Harris Wofford, to "tell them to call it off." Wofford replied that he didn't think anyone could stop the riders. Both Kennedys preferred a battle in the courts to a battle in the streets, so RFK sent Justice Department aide John Seigenthaler to see Alabama's Governor Patterson, who promised to keep the peace. But it was too late; the situation in Alabama had already spun out of control. When the Freedom Riders reached Montgomery, they were ambushed by a bloodthirsty mob while the police looked the other way. Seigenthaler himself was knocked unconscious during the melee, while FBI agents watched from the sidelines and took notes.[18]

Vicious violence in the Deep South had the unintended effect of raising awareness of the Freedom Riders' peaceful protest. "For the Kennedy brothers, domestic affairs were an afterthought," observed Julian Bond, former chairman of the NAACP. "And civil rights movements were an afterthought beyond an afterthought. Now, all of a sudden, chaos has broken loose, attention is riveted, people are talking about this . . . The whole world is watching."[19]

In fairness, Bobby Kennedy cared more about civil rights than some of his official actions suggested. As a young law student at the University of Virginia in the early 1950s, he had pressured the college into allowing Ralph Bunche, an African American diplomat and Nobel Peace Prize winner, to speak before an integrated audience—a social taboo during Virginia's Jim Crow era. During a 2012 interview, RFK's son Max described the dangers his parents faced on the night before Bunche's address: "My mother says they were throwing things at the house all night; they were throwing rocks through the windows and they were throwing things that were on fire. And it was a really scary night in the house for my mother and for Dr. Bunche and for my father." Max believes that this experience helped convince his father of the need for social change: "[It was] a critical period in my father's growth when . . . [he was] beginning to look at the broader issues that [were] facing our country, but at a very communal level and at a place, quite frankly, where it was safe to do that."[20]

On Sunday, May 21, 1961, hundreds of civil rights activists joined Dr. Martin Luther King, Jr., at the First Baptist Church in Montgomery to show support for the Freedom Riders. The Kennedys had taken the precaution of sending a group of federal marshals to provide security. When an angry mob surrounded the church, the marshals used tear gas to keep people at bay until National Guardsmen could arrive to establish order and place the city under martial law. John Lewis, one of the young men inside the church at the time who became an influential congressman from Georgia decades later, credited JFK with saving his life. "Many of us probably would have been killed that night," Lewis believed.[21]

Max Kennedy noted that King mistrusted the Southern white marshals who had been sent to provide security, and he made his views known to the attorney general: "Dr. King got on the phone with my father and said, 'Listen, these marshals you've sent aren't worth a damn. They're all racists and they all want to kill me.' And my father said, 'Dr. King, if you didn't have those men there, you'd be as dead as Kelsey's nuts.' John Seigenthaler didn't know what 'Kelsey's nuts' were. He thought it was something kind of sexual which he'd never heard my father say in his life. [L]ater my brother Christopher talked to a Marine who said that they were the lug nuts on the jeeps that were very hard to loosen, and [the phrase] was supposed to be 'tight as Kelsey's nuts,' but my dad got it mixed up."[22]

Bobby Kennedy's "plan was to move the Freedom Riders out of Alabama as quickly as possible. 'I thought that people were going to be killed,' he said in 1964, 'and they had made their point. What was the purpose of continuing with it?' He called for a 'cooling-off' period. James Farmer [director of the Congress of Racial Equality] told a reporter, 'We had been cooling off for 100 years. If we got any cooler we'd be in a deep freeze.' Kennedy insisted the racial troubles would embarrass the president in his meeting with Khrushchev. Ralph Abernathy, King's chief deputy in the Southern Christian Leadership Conference, replied, 'Doesn't the attorney general know that we've been embarrassed all our lives?'"[23]

Mississippi officials threw the riders in jail when they reached Jackson. In public, JFK kept his distance, understanding that close association with civil rights demonstrators would hurt his agenda on Capitol Hill. But the Freedom Riders were hard for a president to ignore. While incarcerated they sang songs, lodged protests, and badgered their captors.[24]

For their part, some Kennedy administration officials wondered where the newfound activism was leading. Frustrated by the slow pace of change, some African Americans were turning to more radical figures such as Malcolm X and Elijah Muhammed. On April 19, Louis Martin, one of JFK's civil rights advisers and the only African American in his inner circle, sent a memo that was widely circulated within the administration on the growth of the Black Muslim movement. Martin assured his colleagues that most African Americans still believed that it was "possible to achieve first class citizenship" in the United States and that most thought of the Black Muslims as a "lunatic fringe." "It is inconceivable to me that such an anti-white separatist, pro-segregationist movement will ever win a dominant position in Negro life," Martin wrote. But he added that the growth of the movement should not surprise anyone who paid attention to "the uneasy state of race relations here coupled with developments in Africa." The best way to combat black extremism, he advised, was to give African Americans voting rights and equal access to jobs, housing, education, and public facilities.[25]

AT THAT TIME, Kennedy appeared far more interested in containing Communism than in promoting civil rights. Two of his early policy initiatives, the Peace Corps and the Alliance for Progress, were designed to lessen the influence of the Soviets and the Chinese in developing nations.[26] On March 1, he established the Peace Corps through an executive order and appointed R. Sargent Shriver, his brother-in-law, as the program's first director.[27] Shriver threw himself into the job, radiating "a sense of purpose that infused all who were drawn into his embryonic universe of peace and brotherhood. Dubious congressmen, a fretful Foreign Service, skeptical columnists, potential volunteers, and prospective host governments—all fell under the sway of his uncompromising idealism."[28]

Even some of the Peace Corps' harshest critics were eventually won over. When Senator Barry Goldwater first heard about the Corps, he thought it would serve as a sanctuary for beatniks and draft dodgers. Within a year, however, Goldwater had changed his mind. "I think the Peace Corps is beginning to remove the doubts from the doubters' minds. I have been impressed with the quality of the young men and women that have been going to work for it." Senator Prescott Bush, grandfather of President George W. Bush, was also impressed: "There were many who doubted whether the Peace Corps concept was feasible. Now, after a year of operation, there are few voices raised in criticism." Shriver forwarded these glowing reports to the White House. "Dear Mr. President," he wrote in March 1962. "When was the last time Russell Long defended a 'foreign aid' program? He has been a most unexpected but helpful booster." Shriver delighted in telling JFK about one particular incident. Senator J. William Fulbright was astonished when he heard that Congressman Howard W. Smith, the exceptionally conservative chairman of the House Rules committee, supported the Peace Corps. Fulbright raised an eyebrow and said, "Shriver, I'm getting suspicious about you."[29]

Kennedy unveiled his Alliance for Progress program—a Latin American version of the Marshall Plan—during a March 13, 1961, ceremony at the White House. The president promised to deliver health, education, work, land, and homes to Central and South Americans. Congress appropriated $500 million for the program right away and the following year allocated over $1 billion to Latin America. A river of Yanqui dollars flowed into Latin American coffers over the next decade.[30]

But Kennedy realized that money alone would not stop the spread of Communism in the region; force would sometimes be needed to protect national interests.[31] One use of force went particularly badly. In April 1961, in what turned out to be one of the worst decisions of his political career, Kennedy allowed fourteen hundred CIA-trained paramilitary men to launch an ill-fated invasion of Cuba at the Bay of Pigs.[32] He had been under pressure to do something to confront Fidel Castro since the day after his election, when JFK's transitional "Committee on National Security Policy" warned that a lack of "firm action" in Cuba would allow the country's Communists to consolidate power.[33] In late January, CIA officials ratcheted up the pressure by urging the president to launch an attack before Castro could fully align himself with the Soviet bloc and spread Communism throughout the Western Hemisphere. The attack, advocates claimed, would spark a homegrown uprising against Castro's government. Allen Dulles, director of the CIA, and Richard Bissell, deputy director of planning, assured the president that the invasion would be a slam dunk. Yet the scheme was so harebrained that some have since wondered whether top CIA and military officials pushed it on Kennedy in order to embarrass him, or force him to commit fully to overthrowing Castro once the poorly planned assault inevitably collapsed.

Most of Kennedy's military advisers supported the invasion. Just as important, the president thought that the operation had already received the scrutiny and blessing of his predecessor. In reality, Eisenhower had only approved the *training* of Cuban paramilitaries, not given the green light for a specific attack plan. While a distinct minority, a few people thought that the operation should be shelved. On February 11, 1961, JFK aide Arthur Schlesinger sent his boss a warning about the international consequences of a U.S.-sponsored attack on Cuba: "The result would be a wave of massive protest, agitation and sabotage throughout Latin America, Europe, Asia and Africa (not to speak of Canada and of certain quarters in the United States) . . . At one stroke, it would dissipate all the extraordinary good will which has been rising toward the new Administration throughout the world." Richard Goodwin (deputy assistant secretary of state for inter-American affairs), Chester Bowles (undersecretary of state), Dean Acheson (former secretary of state), and Senator Fulbright agreed with Schlesinger's assessment.[34] Fulbright denounced the

Bay of Pigs plan in the strongest possible terms. "To give this activity even covert support is of a piece with the hypocrisy and cynicism for which the United States is constantly denouncing the Soviet Union in the United Nations and elsewhere," he railed. "The point will not be lost on the rest of the world— nor on our own consciences." The senator counseled patience and reminded the president that the Castro regime was nothing more than "a thorn in the flesh" (not "a dagger in the heart") that could be removed without causing an international crisis.[35]

Even worse, Fidel Castro was informed about, and prepared for, the attack. By November 1960, Cuban and Russian intelligence realized the CIA was training anti-Castro exiles in Guatemala; and by early 1961, Soviet leaders knew that April 17 was the date selected for the invasion. A week before the assault, the *New York Times* reported that the Cuban government had reinforced military installations and deployed artillery and troops along the coast.[36]

Despite all the warning signs, Kennedy went ahead with the operation.[37] On April 15, eight aging B-26 bombers painted with Cuban Air Force insignia dropped bombs on three of Castro's air bases. Some Cuban T-33 jets survived, and they later helped repel the U.S.-backed paramilitary force. United Nations ambassador Adlai Stevenson, oblivious to what was actually happening, denied U.S. involvement before the U.N. General Assembly. When he learned the truth on April 16, he chided the CIA's Dulles and Secretary of State Dean Rusk for keeping him in the dark. Worried that the American role was about to be revealed to the world, Kennedy canceled a second airstrike scheduled for April 17 even though the CIA insisted it was essential if the invasion were to succeed. JFK also ordered the USS *Essex*—on patrol in the West Indies—to steer clear of the fighting. Without American military support, the invading brigade didn't stand a chance. Castro's T-33s destroyed six of the B-26s and two ships. One hundred fourteen exiles were cut down on the beach; 1,189 others were thrown in jail to await possible execution.[38]

A few days later, Kennedy called Eisenhower and asked the former president to meet him at Camp David to discuss the crisis. "I believe there is only one thing to do when you go into this kind of thing," Ike replied matter-of-factly, "It must be a success." He asked Kennedy why he hadn't provided air cover for the rebels. JFK answered that he had been worried about the Soviet response in Berlin. Eisenhower assured the president that the Communists only attacked when they detected weakness. "The failure of the Bay of Pigs will embolden the Soviets to do something that they would not otherwise do," he warned.[39] "Well," said Kennedy, "my advice was that we must try to keep our hands from showing in the affair." Eisenhower was stunned. "Mr. President, how could you expect the world to believe that we had nothing to do with it? Where did these people get the ships to go from Central America to Cuba? Where did they get the weapons?"[40]

The sad truth was that the inexperienced Kennedy had not paid enough attention to the details of the plan, deferred to some military and civilian aides too much, and failed to think through the consequences of his actions.[41] For example, advisers had assured him that the paramilitaries could retreat to the safety of Cuba's Escambray Mountains if the worst happened. However, the Escambray lay eighty miles from the invasion point over a treacherous stretch of swampland. No one had studied the map with sufficient care. The operation was poorly planned and sloppily executed.[42]

Kennedy loyalists tried to pin the blame for the defeat on everyone but the president. Eisenhower served as a convenient scapegoat for a brief time.[43] To his credit, JFK accepted full responsibility for the fiasco in short order. "There's an old saying," he told the press, "that victory has a hundred fathers and defeat is an orphan ... I am the responsible officer of the government and that is quite obvious." The American people appreciated the president's candor, and they rallied behind their leader at a time of crisis. By the end of April, Kennedy's approval ratings had soared above 80 percent.[44] Nevertheless, the incident caused considerable damage to America's reputation abroad and strengthened ties between Havana and Moscow.[45] Almost immediately, Castro issued an official declaration that Cuba was a Marxist-Leninist country.[46] The following year, Castro allowed the USSR to put nuclear missiles in Cuba, a decision that triggered the most serious crisis of the Cold War. The Bay of Pigs incident had occurred in Kennedy's first hundred days in office and badly tarnished his administration's reputation both in Washington and many foreign capitals. "How could I have been so stupid?" Kennedy was said to have muttered on more than one occasion.

There had been outside pressures on Kennedy to act precipitously. The president of Guatemala told Kennedy that he wanted the Cuban paramilitaries out of his country by the end of April.[47] Cuban expats wanted Castro's head on a platter without delay. No doubt President Kennedy was also motivated by a political need to project a tough-on-Communism image. He remembered the attacks on President Truman as insufficiently resolute against the Reds, and he wasn't going to yield that ground again to the Republicans.[48] Kennedy himself had criticized the Eisenhower administration during the campaign for showing weakness toward Cuba. For these reasons and more he had felt compelled to act.[49] But even this major blunder did not lessen the Kennedy administration's resolve to eliminate Castro. Shortly after the Bay of Pigs, the president approved Operation Mongoose, a program of secret military missions, sabotage, and assassination plots designed to topple the Castro regime. "The lesson Kennedy drew from the Bay of Pigs was not that he should talk to Castro, but that he should intensify his efforts to overthrow him."[50] JFK's unrelenting hostility toward Castro made it exceedingly difficult for any of his successors to reverse course—and none of them has done so in a fundamental way during the fifty-four years Fidel or his brother Raul have governed Cuba.

CUBA WAS ONLY a part of Kennedy's global efforts to contain the spread of Communism. In Asia, a carrot-and-stick approach was employed. Foreign aid to the region was combined with the dispatch of Green Berets to Vietnam and military supplies to Laos. Laos had been on the president's plate from the very beginning. Today, most Americans associate the Vietnam War with the Kennedy presidency, but in 1961, the conflict in Laos seemed like the larger challenge. The day before the inauguration, Eisenhower had told Kennedy that he might need to send troops to the country to prevent a Communist takeover and chain reaction in Asia. Arthur Schlesinger suggested that JFK may have "spent more time on Laos than on anything else" during the first sixty days of his administration. Laos was an artificial construct, a product of the 1954 Geneva Accords that had divided French Indochina into three separate countries, Cambodia, Vietnam, and Laos. Prince Souvanna Phouma—Laos's first prime minister—enjoyed the support of the Laotian people but alienated Washington by trying to form a coalition government with the Pathet Lao, the local Communist group led by his half brother.

Haunted by the prospect of a future "domino effect" in Asia, Eisenhower had ordered the CIA to begin looking for ways to replace Souvanna. In 1958 a staunch anticommunist, Phoui Sananikone, seized power and blacklisted the Pathet Lao, which immediately triggered a civil war. When it became clear that Phoui's army was no match for the Pathet Lao, the CIA supported a coup that brought a pro-American general, Phoumi Nosavan, to power. Phoumi's ham-fisted policies divided the country even further. This opened the door to Soviet intervention, and Laos was soon flooded with Russian-made weapons. Kennedy's advisers urged the dispatch of troops to Laos, but the president resisted; the Bay of Pigs debacle had made him skeptical of Pentagon recommendations.[51] That skepticism deepened when Joint Chiefs chairman Lyman Lemnitzer said that he could "guarantee victory" in Laos if he were "given the right to use nuclear weapons." Instead, JFK decided to bluff Moscow by mobilizing his warships and troops in Asia. He also sent Secretary Rusk and Ambassador-at-Large W. Averell Harriman to Geneva to negotiate an agreement.[52]

In the midst of all this foreign intrigue, President Kennedy arrived in Canada for his first international trip in mid-May. After addressing the Canadian

Parliament, Kennedy joined Prime Minister John Diefenbaker for a tree planting ceremony at Government House. As soon as his spade hit the soil, the president felt a sharp twinge in his back. His physician described the pain that followed as "something like a steady toothache." The muscles between Kennedy's lumbar vertebrae and sacrum went into spasms and he began receiving injections of novocaine. When he got back to Washington, he was taken off Air Force One with a forklift and hobbled across the tarmac on a pair of crutches. "Remarkably, all during this period and until the *New York Times* published a fairly explicit account on June 9, the President's condition was known only to his doctors. With a round of delicate European visits coming up . . . not a hint of his indisposition went beyond the Oval Office."[53]

His ailment notwithstanding, Kennedy began an emphasis on the space program as a way to keep pace with the Soviets. On May 25, shortly before leaving for Europe, he outlined a bold new vision for America's space program. In the wake of cosmonaut Yuri Gagarin's triumphant orbit around the earth, the president told Congress that the nation should "commit itself to achieving the goal, before this decade is out, of landing a man on the moon and returning him safely to the earth." "No single space project in this period," he added, "will be more impressive to mankind, or more important for the long-range exploration of space; and none will be so difficult or expensive to accomplish." Kennedy's larger goal was to show the world that the United States was still the global leader in science, since developing nations might want to be aligned with the side demonstrating technological superiority. Or, as Vice President Johnson put it: "In the eyes of the world, first in space means first, period; second in space is second in everything." Furthermore, the goal of landing a man on the moon meshed nicely with Kennedy's futuristic, adventuresome vision for the New Frontier, one that held special appeal for young people.[54]

No one knew until many years later that Kennedy had first suggested sending U.S. astronauts to Mars instead of the moon, or that Robert Seamans, Jr., NASA's associate administrator, was the person who talked him out of it. "Bob told me the story of working three days and nights [putting] together . . . the case for [going] to the moon," says Chuck Vest, one of Seamans's former colleagues. "Suppose the president had gotten up in this inspirational speech and set a goal that was not only audacious, but couldn't be accomplished? The goal had to be right and Bob played a . . . major role in doing that."[55]*

---

* The space race is a useful reminder that the rivalry between the two superpowers wasn't completely destructive, with all by-products generating doom and gloom. The Cold War produced some social dividends, and the contest for space exploration yielded scientific breakthroughs

Kennedy's daring moon goal probably would have fallen flat if the Soviets hadn't taken the lead in space. Dan Fenn, who worked as a Kennedy aide before becoming the initial director of the JFK Library, believes that Cold War considerations came first in the president's mind. "Kennedy said, 'Look—I don't care that much about space,'" Fenn says. "'If we're going to spend a billion dollars, I'd rather spend it looking for a cure for cancer. But given the competition with the Soviets, that's what I care about and that's why I want to do this.'" Even so, Kennedy had second thoughts as his term progressed. "Why should we spend that kind of dough to put a man on the moon?" he asked a surprised NASA administrator James Webb in September 1963. Kennedy was looking for ways to save money and even approached Khrushchev about a Soviet-American partnership to reach the moon. When Khrushchev responded favorably, JFK ordered Webb to make it happen. But the president died before the head of NASA could carry out his orders.[56] If JFK had lived and Russian cosmonauts had walked on the moon alongside U.S. astronauts, Kennedy's legacy would be quite different than it is.[57]

In any case, the moon speech gave Kennedy added confidence as he departed for Europe—and so did the powerful drugs he was taking. Without telling anyone, the president had arranged a separate flight for a physician named Max Jacobson (aka Dr. Feelgood), who had been giving him "amphetamines and back injections of painkillers" for months. Jacobson, a borderline quack who had made a name for himself prescribing "speed" to celebrities, was also giving Jackie narcotics for postpartum depression.[58] Kennedy had started seeing the New York doctor the previous year when he had needed relief from campaign-related aches and pains. After the election, the president kept Jacobson on the payroll; the doctor's services helped preserve his image as a healthy, robust leader. Kennedy was also receiving medicines from his personal physician, Dr. Janet Travell, who injected her boss's back with two or three procaine shots each day. It is anyone's guess how much these drugs affected Kennedy's mood and judgment, but it is impossible to argue they had no effect whatsoever.[59]

On May 31, 1961, Air Force One touched down at Orly Airport in Paris. President Kennedy needed to reassure President Charles de Gaulle of his commitment to France's security. After a series of preliminary meetings, JFK rode with de Gaulle in a "big open car . . . up the Champs Elysées" to the Arc de Triomphe, where, in a touching state ceremony, he rekindled the eternal flame at the Tomb of the Unknown Soldier. Mrs. Kennedy absorbed the

---

that have made our lives easier. Computer technology received an early boost from the space race, as well as devices as diverse as aerodynamic golf balls, comfortable running shoes, scratch-resistant lenses, and machines that check blood pressure, to mention just a few.

somber images and quiet dignity of the occasion; it was a poignant way to pay tribute to fallen heroes.

De Gaulle and the people of France were smitten with the beautiful First Lady. Mrs. Kennedy's command of their language, Gallic pedigree, and fashion sense (including frequent choice of Oleg Cassini outfits) made her perhaps the most celebrated American to visit Paris since Ben Franklin and Thomas Jefferson had walked the city's streets nearly two centuries earlier. Enraptured Parisians lined the Kennedys' motor route shouting "Vive Jacqui!" Like the quaintly dressed Franklin, Jackie Kennedy knew how to use clothing to her advantage—especially in a time when prominent women were judged as much by their appearance as their abilities.[60] She arrived for a dinner at the Elysée Palace wearing a "pink-and-white straw-lace straight-line dress" that turned heads. The president acknowledged his wife's irresistible appeal during the toasts: "My preparation for the presidency did not include acquiring firsthand knowledge of France through diplomatic experience—I acquired it through marriage instead." At a subsequent press luncheon, JFK delivered an even more memorable line regarding Jackie's je ne sais quoi: "I do not think it altogether inappropriate to introduce myself to this audience. I am the man who accompanied Jacqueline Kennedy to Paris, and I have enjoyed it." That night at Versailles, Jackie flattered her hosts by wearing another French couture creation, an evening gown and coat designed by Hubert de Givenchy.[61]

The president had his own small triumphs as well, especially when he employed his wit. During a ceremony at the Hôtel de Ville (Paris's city hall), he relayed an amusing story about Pierre L'Enfant. The French architect had presented a bill for $90,000 to Congress for designing the city of Washington, but he received only $3,000. Quipped the president, no doubt referring to his wife's sizable clothing expenditures: "Some have been unkind enough to suggest that the dress designers of Paris have been collecting his bill ever since." Parisians swooned over Kennedy's charm and good looks, describing him as "formidable," an adjective they "usually reserved for their own leader." The host of the event told an American reporter, "Your president, he is very good. He marches very quickly, that young man."[62]

Kennedy enjoyed the adulation, but knew that he would soon be dealing with a much tougher audience in Vienna. Soviet premier Nikita Khrushchev had agreed to meet Kennedy for the first time on June 3, 1961. The Bay of Pigs fiasco had made JFK look weak and Khrushchev would try to test him, especially on Berlin. Was the Soviet leader willing to risk a war over the city? De Gaulle didn't think so. Khrushchev was bluffing, he said, and the president should stick to his guns.[63]

Kennedy wasn't so sure. After all, Berlin was the Cold War's preeminent hot spot and a major embarrassment for the Soviets. At the end of World War

II, the Allies had divided the city (as well as the whole of Germany) into four occupation zones controlled by American, French, British, and Russian forces. Unfortunately for NATO, Berlin lay 110 miles inside Communist East Germany, making it difficult to defend. In 1948, the Soviets had closed off the highways, railroads, and waterways leading into the city with the hope of seizing control. Harry Truman responded by airlifting two million tons of supplies to West Berlin and putting troops and bombers on standby. This show of force convinced the Soviets to back down, but they had never abandoned the dream of seeing the city united under a Communist dictatorship. The East German people grew to loathe the Soviet system; by 1961, thousands of them were pouring across the border each month in search of jobs and freedom. Khrushchev was under pressure to stop the exodus before Walter Ulbricht's Communist government collapsed. He thought that the best way might be to sign a peace treaty with East Germany, which in turn—as a supposedly independent state—could then expel the Western allies from Berlin and absorb the city. Such an agreement would also keep Germany from reuniting, a primary goal for Russia, having lost more than twenty million people to German aggression during the war.[64]

On June 3, 1961, Kennedy shook hands with Khrushchev on the steps of the American embassy in Vienna. The president certainly felt good since, in preparation for the meeting, he had instructed Jacobson to inject him with painkillers. When the press corps asked for additional pictures, he smiled and said, "Tell the chairman that it's all right with me if it's all right with him." Khrushchev grinned and struck a pose. Behind closed doors, however, things quickly turned ugly. When Kennedy suggested that the two leaders work together to maintain the geopolitical status quo, Khrushchev lectured the young president on the inevitable triumph of Communism. "Ideas have never been destroyed and this is proven in the whole course of human development," he railed. "The Soviet Union supports its ideas and holds them in high esteem. It cannot guarantee that these ideas will stop at its borders." When Kennedy warned about the dangers of miscalculation and war, Khrushchev told a story about a man who kept trying to control his son after he'd already grown up. One day the son simply refused to take any more instructions from his aging father. The parallels were obvious. "We have grown up," said the Soviet chairman. "You're an old country. We're a young country." Khrushchev threw verbal punches the rest of the afternoon. He got JFK to admit that the Cuban operation had been a "mistake" and pointed out the hypocrisy of opposing Castro while supporting right-wing dictators like Francisco Franco in Spain. He also lambasted the United States for supporting the "old colonial powers of Western Europe." "The United States itself rose against the British," he lectured, "but now the U.S. has changed its position and it is against other people following suit." The sole bright spot in the afternoon came when Khrushchev agreed to support a neutral government in Laos. Kennedy's military mobilization had convinced Khrushchev that the United States was planning to invade the country, so in the Soviet's mind, neutrality was a better alternative. This lone concession was not enough to console JFK, who hung his head in dismay at the end of the day. "He treated me like a little boy," the president complained. "Like a little boy."[65]

Jackie did all she could to salvage the situation. At a state dinner that night at Schönbrunn Palace, she wore a shimmering pink-silver gown which accentuated her shapely figure (Oleg Cassini thought that she looked like a "mermaid"). Khrushchev, like de Gaulle, was far more taken with Mrs. Kennedy than with her husband. His own spouse, Nina, was wearing a frumpy business suit without any makeup—a symbolic gesture intended to promote Soviet values and expose the West's decadence. When asked by one of the reporters if he would like to shake hands with JFK, Khrushchev gestured toward Jackie: "I'd like to shake *her* hand first." Eddy Gilmore captured the mood of the event in an article penned for the *Washington Post*: "Jackie Kennedy waltzed through Vienna today in an elegant triumph that included even Soviet Premier Nikita S. Khrushchev. Meeting her for the first time, the tough and often belligerent Communist leader looked like a smitten school boy when the ice thaws along the Volga in springtime." Sensing her advantage, Mrs. Kennedy lavished attention on the Soviet leader at dinner, asking him friendly questions about his homeland. When Khrushchev launched into a tedious monologue on the wonders of the Soviet educational system, Jackie said, "Oh, Mr. Chairman, don't bore me with statistics." Khrushchev "suddenly laughed and became for a moment almost cozy."

In another part of the city, Kennedy's advisers were reviewing the minutes of the day's sessions and wringing their hands—the president had been soundly thrashed. George Kennan, the former ambassador to Moscow, thought that Kennedy had come across as a tongue-tied rookie. Paul Nitze, assistant secretary of defense, compared Kennedy's performance to a meaningless dance routine. The Soviets were even more unimpressed. Khrushchev was beginning to think that his inexperienced opponent might be a flaccid American intellectual.[66]

The sparring match between the leaders of East and West continued the next day. When the discussion turned to a ban on nuclear testing, Khrushchev scoffed at the idea of giving United Nations inspectors free reign on Soviet soil. He viewed the international assembly as a tool of capitalist oppression. One needed to look no further than the Congo for proof, he argued. U.N. troops helped topple Patrice Lumumba, the Republic of Congo's first prime minister and a Soviet ally, an action that had famously prompted Khrushchev to pound his shoe on a desk at the U.N. in protest. Better to have a "troika" consisting of one capitalist, one Communist, and one neutral observer manage the inspections. Now it was Kennedy's turn to scoff. Such an arrangement would give the Soviets an unfair advantage, he complained.

When Khrushchev pressed for a general disarmament agreement instead of a single test ban treaty, Kennedy realized that the discussions were leading nowhere and changed the subject. Talk turned to Berlin, and the Soviet chairman grew visibly agitated, describing the West's part of the city as "the bone in the Soviet throat." Kennedy had none of it, and insisted that the United States would defend West Berlin at all costs. Khrushchev bellowed, "If the U.S. wants to start a war over Germany, let it be so." The Soviet Union would sign a peace treaty with East Germany by the end of the year, starting the process of West Berlin's absorption, and it was up to the United States to decide whether that meant war. Kennedy didn't flinch: "Then, Mr. Chairman, there will be war. It will be a cold winter." The Berlin crisis had begun.[67]

It was one of the most dangerous moments of the Cold War. A single misstep on either side could have plunged the earth into nuclear winter, and this thought weighed on Kennedy. According to the journalist James Reston, the president appeared "shaken and angry." Close aide Kenny O'Donnell could see that JFK was haunted by the prospect of a nuclear exchange.[68] "All wars start from stupidity," JFK said on the flight back to Washington. "God knows I'm not an isolationist, but it seems particularly stupid to risk killing a million Americans over an argument about access rights on an Autobahn in the Soviet zone of Germany, or because the Germans want Germany reunified. If I'm going to threaten Russia with a nuclear war, it will have to be for much bigger and more important reasons than that. Before I back Khrushchev against the wall and put him to a final test, the freedom of Western Europe will have to be at stake."[69]

On June 6, 1961, the president appeared on television and briefed the American people on his trip to Vienna. "Mr. Khrushchev and I had a very full and frank exchange of views on the major issues that now divide our two countries. I will tell you now that it was a very sober two days. There was no discourtesy, no loss of temper, no threats or ultimatums by either side." Kennedy was less than fully truthful, of course. Khrushchev's announcement that he would sign a treaty with East Germany by December was a crystal-clear ultimatum, but the president did not want to trigger panic. The Vienna talks had been "useful," he said, and the "somber mood that they conveyed was not cause for elation or relaxation, nor was it cause for undue pessimism or fear." Instead, they had "simply demonstrated how much work we in the Free World have to do and how long and hard a struggle must be our fate as Americans in this generation as the chief defenders of the cause of liberty." Behind the scenes, though, airy discussions about liberty took a back seat to preparations for a Berlin crisis. Bobby Kennedy thought that there was a "one-in-five chance of war" during this period. Dean Acheson, former secretary of state, advised the president to draw a line in the sand for the Russians. "Until this conflict of wills is resolved," he wrote in a top secret memo, "an attempt to solve the Berlin issue by negotiation is worse than a waste of time and energy. It is dangerous." Acheson went on to describe Khrushchev as a capricious despot who could not be "persuaded by eloquence or logic, or cajoled by friendliness." It was time for the American eagle to show its talons, and the Joint Chiefs of Staff agreed. In the parlance of the time, West Berliners were better off dead than red. Besides, most American policymakers reasoned, the Soviets would back down in the face of American military superiority.[70]

Kennedy still lacked a clear strategic policy on Berlin, and time was running out. He needed to devise a way to unite the American people and send the Soviets a firm message about the West's determination to defend democratic Germany, but at the same time provide Khrushchev with an escape hatch. Kennedy scheduled a nationally televised address to the nation on July 25, even as his advisers strongly disagreed about the right approach. According to Sorensen, "Few presidents had ever worked harder to get the right words, establish the right mood, and send the right signals. No president had ever believed more was at stake."[71]

Some of Kennedy's men had even worked on a plan to launch a preemptive nuclear strike against the Soviet Union. In early July, a young Harvard professor and government consultant who would rocket to fame in the Nixon administration, Henry Kissinger, sent JFK's national security adviser, McGeorge Bundy, a memo on the problem of the president's limited options in Berlin. At the time, U.S. policy called for massive retaliation in the event of an attack, which meant firing every single nuclear weapon at every available target, "no matter how limited the cause of the war might be." Kissinger thought that it might be possible to wage a limited nuclear war instead. He discussed the idea with Carl Kaysen and Henry Rowen, two fellow intellectuals who were working on defense issues for the administration. Kaysen and Rowen began exploring alternatives to the nuclear doomsday scenario.[72]

By the time of his speech, Kennedy had settled on a somewhat bellicose approach to Berlin. "Seven weeks ago tonight I returned from Europe to report on my meeting with Premier Khrushchev and the others," he began, his eyes flitting between his notes and the camera. "In Berlin, as you recall, [Khrushchev] intends to bring to an end, through a stroke of the pen, first our legal rights to be in West Berlin—and secondly our ability to make good on our commitment to the two million free people of that city. That we cannot permit." The president warned about the sacrifices that would be required to protect West Berlin. "In the days and months ahead, I shall not hesitate to ask the Congress for additional measures, or exercise any of the executive powers that I possess to meet this threat to peace. Everything essential to the security of freedom must be done; and if that should require more men, or more taxes, or more controls, or other new powers, I shall not hesitate to ask them." In the short term, he would need an extra $3.2 billion, additional soldiers, sailors, and airmen that would require a massive expansion of the draft, authority to activate the reserves, and more "non-nuclear weapons, ammunition, and equipment."

Kennedy's call for public sacrifice echoed the themes that he had outlined in his inaugural address ("... we shall pay any price, bear any burden, meet any hardship . . . to assure the survival and the success of liberty"). He added that he was "well aware of the fact that many American families will bear the burden of these requests." Jobs and educations would be interrupted; "husbands and sons will be called away; incomes in some cases will be reduced. But these are burdens which must be borne if freedom is to be defended—Americans have willingly borne them before—and they will not flinch from the task now."

Contemporary Americans may be stunned to read these words. In recent years, presidents have often avoided asking citizens to make sacrifices even in wartime. Taxes must never be raised, nor expenditures reduced in other areas to support an emergency priority. Nor can citizens be expected to serve in the military; that essential element of national defense is provided only by a relative handful of volunteers. Shortly after the 9/11 attacks, for example, President George W. Bush called neither for a military draft nor even for a "homeland security and war on terrorism" tax that most Americans would willingly have paid. Instead, he told Americans to "get down to Disney World" and to "enjoy life, the way we want it to be enjoyed."[73] Wars in Afghanistan and Iraq were put on the national credit card and added to a burgeoning debt, while taxes were simultaneously reduced further. In 1961, however, most Americans were willing to put the country's best interests ahead of their own. The Great Depression and World War II generations were used to, and expected to make, sacrifices in order to secure their nation domestically and internationally.

Part of Kennedy's speech, however, sent a chill down the spines of Americans: "In the event of an attack, the lives of those families which are not hit in a nuclear blast and fire can still be saved—if they can be warned to take shelter and if that shelter is available. We owe that kind of insurance to our families—and to our country." It was a message intended to convince Congress to spend more money on civil defense.

Kennedy also presented the Soviets with their escape hatch: "We recognize the Soviet Union's historical concern about their security in Central and

Eastern Europe, after a series of ravaging invasions, and we believe arrangements can be worked out which will help to meet those concerns, and make it possible for both security and freedom to exist in this troubled area." The president expressed his willingness to seek a solution through "quiet exploratory talks" or either "formal or informal meetings." He hoped that "military considerations" would not "dominate the thinking of either East or West." Nevertheless, Kennedy appeared to accept de Gaulle's assertion that Khrushchev was bluffing, and left it to Moscow to decide whether there would be war or peace. Kennedy closed with an appeal for backing from his fellow citizens: "In meeting my responsibilities in these coming months as president, I need your good will, and your support—and above all, your prayers."[74]

By and large, the press interpreted the speech as hard line and downplayed the president's peace overtures. As expected, the public rallied around their commander in chief while lawmakers approved funding for virtually all of Kennedy's specific requests.[75]

JFK still hoped to avoid a fight. What he had intentionally left out of the speech was just as important as what he had included in it. When the Warsaw Pact Council convened in early August 1961, East German Communist leader Walter Ulbricht pointed out that Kennedy had limited his comments "to the protection of West Berlin—thus signaling NATO's intention of doing nothing as long as the East did not encroach on its rights." Ulbricht therefore proposed closing the border between East and West Berlin, a plan known as "Operation Chinese Wall" that had been tossed around in Communist circles for several years. Khrushchev approved the scheme, and in the early hours of August 13, East German troops began building the infamous, 103-mile-long Berlin Wall, running through the center of the city and dividing the eastern and western sectors. West Germans were shocked and demanded a forceful response, but Kennedy kept his cool. The press photographed a smiling Kennedy sailing around Nantucket Sound—not the image of a chief executive in crisis mode. JFK knew that a wall was better than a war. Besides, the Communists were showing the world how pathetic their system really was; only failed regimes build fences to keep people in.

Still, the president had to reassure West Germany of America's commitment to its security. He dispatched a "small battle group of fifteen hundred military men to travel on trucks down the autobahn through East Germany to West Berlin"; the troops received a warm welcome as they rolled through the city's shopping district. Kennedy also sent General Lucius Clay—the hero of the 1948 Berlin airlift—and Vice President Johnson to meet with Mayor Willy Brandt and boost Berlin's spirits. The strategy worked. Johnson "rode to the city center in an open car cheered by 100,000 spectators lining the roads. Stopping the car repeatedly, he plunged into the appreciative crowds, shaking hands, distributing ball point pens, and responding with visible emotion to the displays of enthusiasm." From a security standpoint, it was a risky move, but it convinced the besieged residents of West Berlin that they had a friend in the White House.[76]

Tensions over Berlin gradually eased during the month of September. Kennedy spoke about the dangers of nuclear war before the United Nations and began a friendly correspondence with Khrushchev. At the same time, the defense analysts Kaysen and Rowen produced a thirty-three-page memo entitled "Strategic Air Planning and Berlin" that Kaysen sent to General Maxwell Taylor, one of Kennedy's primary military advisers, questioning the wisdom of using the full U.S. nuclear arsenal (more than 5,500 weapons) no matter the scale of the conflict. Instead, it recommended pinpoint strikes against Soviet air bases and missile sites that would bring a quick and relatively bloodless victory. In short, Kaysen and Rowen were proposing "a plan to wage *rational* nuclear war." Kennedy, who read at least a summary of the memo, remained wary and asked probing questions. How could the president maintain control once the war began? And wasn't there a danger of using more bombs than were necessary? He revisited these questions during an October 10 security meeting when Paul Nitze, assistant secretary of defense for international security affairs, presented him with a four-point plan for dealing with any new crisis in Berlin. Point four of Nitze's report echoed Kaysen's recommendations: the United States might be able to achieve its objectives by waging a limited nuclear war. Kennedy again asked how he could keep a limited war from turning into a holocaust. His advisers could not give him a good answer. Secretary of Defense McNamara thought that "neither side could be sure of winning by striking first." Secretary of State Rusk said that "the first side to use nuclear weapons will carry a very grave responsibility and endure heavy consequences before the rest of the world." Yet Nitze still believed that the United States could win a nuclear war and warned about the consequences of allowing the Soviets to strike first.[77]

Kennedy left the matter unresolved, but he decided to send Moscow a strong message about the West's military prowess. He authorized Roswell Gilpatric, the deputy secretary of defense, to boast in public about America's nuclear superiority. It was a very different approach from the one he had adopted during the campaign about the alleged "missile gap" with the Soviet Union. Whether then-Senator Kennedy really believed that the gap existed remains a source of debate among historians.[78] In any case, his campaign statements on the issue were erroneous. As president, he acknowledged as much by allowing Gilpatric to publicly trumpet America's sizable nuclear advantage.

At a dinner in Hot Springs, Virginia, Gilpatric told a roomful of businessmen that the United States possessed "a nuclear retaliatory force of such lethal power that an enemy move which brought it into play would be an act of self-destruction on his part." The deputy secretary backed up his assertion with specifics, citing the "six hundred heavy bombers and many more medium bombers," "six Polaris submarines . . . carrying . . . ninety-six missiles," and "carrier strike forces and land-based theater forces" that could utterly destroy any enemy. And to remove all doubt, he made it clear who that enemy was: "In short, we have a second strike capability which is at least as extensive as what the Soviets can deliver by striking first. Therefore, we are confident that the Soviets will not provoke a major nuclear conflict." Gilpatric's comments angered Khrushchev, who was also upset over Kennedy's decision to deploy Jupiter missiles to Turkey.[79] In order to close the gap and create a bargaining chip for Berlin, Khrushchev deployed nuclear missiles to Cuba the following year. The end of one crisis thus planted the seeds for the next, a far worse one that would bring the world to the brink of Armageddon. Moreover, Khrushchev ended the Soviet ban on atmospheric nuclear tests and allowed Russian tanks in East Berlin to take aim at American tanks positioned on the other end of the Friedrichstrasse. Kennedy's braggadocio had backfired; the Soviets were more determined than ever to challenge America's strength.[80]

On January 11, 1962, the president reviewed the accomplishments of his first year in office during his State of the Union address.[81] The Alliance for Progress, he said, had brought hope and a renewed faith in the United States to Latin America. More money would be needed for the Alliance in the coming year to fend off the challenge of Communism. The Peace Corps had expanded into fourteen countries and given the world "a glimpse of the best that is in our country." The organization's main problem was that it could not keep up with global demand for volunteers. And by helping people, the president said, the United States was also helping the cause of freedom. In Laos, that meant supporting a neutral government composed of the nation's various factions, including the Communist Pathet Lao. Kennedy acknowledged that there was still work to be done in Laos to achieve a final peace settlement but asserted that "the spread of war—which might have involved this country also—and a Communist occupation have thus far been prevented." Moreover, peace in Laos would help ease tensions in Vietnam, "where the foe is increasing his tactics of terror—where our own efforts have been stepped up—and where the local government has initiated new programs and reforms to broaden the base of resistance." The U.S. government would continue to help South Vietnam resist Communist aggression. It would do the same for the people of West Berlin.

Black Americans, he asserted, deserved equal employment opportunities, "the right to vote, the right to travel without hindrance across state lines, and the right to free public education." "As we approach the one hundredth anniversary, next January, of the Emancipation Proclamation," the president intoned, "let the acts of every branch of the government—and every citizen— portray that 'righteousness does exalt a nation.'" Nonetheless, Kennedy had avoided making the truly tough decisions on civil rights; the events of 1962 would force him to move farther down freedom road.[82]

Hoping to put the Bay of Pigs embarrassment behind him, Kennedy avoided mentioning Cuba in his speech. Instead, he relied on the soaring rhetoric that had inspired the nation and helped him win the White House. Like presidents who had preceded him, Kennedy believed that America had a special role to play in nurturing and protecting liberty: "A year ago, in assuming the tasks of the presidency, I said that few generations, in all history, had been granted the role of being the great defender of freedom in its hour of maximum danger. This is our good fortune; and I welcome it now as I did a year ago. For it is the fate of this generation—of you in the Congress and of me as president—to live with a struggle we did not start, in a world we did not make. But the pressures of life are not always distributed by choice. And while no nation has ever faced such a challenge, no nation has ever been so ready to seize the burden and the glory of freedom."[83]

5

STEEL AT HOME
AND ABROAD

ON MARCH 13, 1962, Secretary of Labor Arthur Goldberg briefed the president on the status of a contract dispute between workers and executives at the United States Steel Corporation. "I have spoken privately with both parties," Goldberg wrote, "and at my request they are meeting privately to determine if an agreement in principle can be concluded before the formal negotiations resume on Wednesday." A week later, the secretary reported that there were still unresolved "differences" but that the two sides were "not too far apart." The breakthrough came on March 31 when David McDonald, president of the United Steelworkers union, agreed to a ten-cent increase in wages and benefits for his members, a modest amount well within the government's wage and price guidelines. In return, Roger Blough, the chairman of U.S. Steel, tacitly agreed (though never explicitly) to hold the line on prices. Kennedy was delighted; Blough's and McDonald's selflessness would help keep America's factories humming and check inflation. The president praised his secretary of labor—a former steelworkers union lawyer—for brokering the deal. "Terrific, Arthur. Terrific job," he gushed after learning about the agreement. Goldberg predicted that the settlement would lead to "comparable settlements in iron ore, aluminum can manufacturing, and steel fabricating."[1]

On April 10, 1962, JFK "was surprised to note that his appointment calendar included a 5:45 P.M. appointment for Roger Blough." He phoned Goldberg, who told the president that he didn't know what Blough wanted. The suspense ended when the steel executive waltzed into the Oval Office at the appointed hour and handed the president a copy of a press release announcing a $6 per ton increase in U.S. Steel prices. JFK's initial shock over the announcement quickly changed to anger. "You have made a terrible mistake," he told Blough. "You double-crossed me." White House aide Kenny O'Donnell had seen the president equally furious on only one other occasion, when a scheduling mix-up during the campaign had put him in the wrong state at the wrong time. The president's wrath surprised Blough, who explained that he "had never said he would not raise prices." After the chairman left, Kennedy summoned Goldberg to the Oval Office. The president paced the floor, venting his spleen: "He fucked me. They fucked us and we've got to try to fuck them." The labor secretary offered to quit, but JFK insisted that he stay. Next, the president phoned McDonald and explained what had happened: "Dave, you've been screwed and I've been screwed," he said. He had put his personal prestige on the line in order to stabilize steel prices and received a slap in the face in return. Blough was putting his bottom line ahead of his country's best interests. "My father always told me that all businessmen were sons-of-bitches," he remarked, "but I never believed it till now."[2] When the comment leaked to *Newsweek*, Kennedy denied that he had meant all businessmen. "His father had referred only to steel men, he protested." Nevertheless, Kennedy was determined to fight. If Blough wanted a war, then the president would give him one.[3]

The next day, as other steel companies began raising their own prices, Kennedy held a press conference and told the assembled journalists that the industry's actions represented "a wholly unjustifiable and irresponsible defiance of the public interest." "In this serious hour in our nation's history," he lectured, "when we are confronted with grave crises in Berlin and Southeast Asia, when we are devoting our energies to economic recovery and stability, when we are asking reservists to leave their homes and families for months on end and servicemen to risk their lives—and four were killed in the last two days in Vietnam—and asking union members to hold down their wage requests at a time when restraint and sacrifice are being asked of every citizen, the American people will find it hard, as I do, to accept a situation in which a tiny handful of steel executives whose pursuit of private power and profit exceeds their sense of public responsibility can show such utter contempt for the interests of 185 million Americans." It was the most forceful presidential assault on a private company since Teddy Roosevelt had ordered the dissolution of the Northern Securities Company sixty years earlier.[4] Kennedy warned that the steel price hike would "increase the cost of homes, autos, appliances, and most other items for every American family." Rather than let that happen, he had instructed the Justice Department, the Federal Trade Commission, and the Defense Department to take action.[5]

The Pentagon canceled its contracts with U.S. Steel. When Secretary of Defense Robert McNamara discovered that a $5.5 million steel plate order had been split between Blough's company and a smaller firm called Lukens Steel, he turned over the entire order to Lukens. At the Justice Department, Robert Kennedy skirted the edges of legal and ethical behavior by ordering his underlings to harass the offending steel executives and their allies. FBI agents stormed into corporate offices and subpoenaed corporate and personal records. One agent "phoned [an Associated Press] journalist at 3:00 A.M. and insisted on interviewing him an hour later at his house about a story he had written on the steel companies." Once the steel executives assessed the situation and realized that the federal government had the power to audit their books and rescind their tax depreciation allowances at any time, they caved.[6] One by one, the companies fell in line and withdrew their price increases. The president appeared to have jawboned an entire industry into submission in only three days.[7] Not every observer agreed that JFK bested the executives; some thought that market considerations (i.e., low steel prices) were the real reason the crisis ended when it did.*

Kennedy's critics had a field day. The *New York Herald Tribune* published a political cartoon showing Pierre Salinger, the White House press secretary, telling JFK, "Mr. Khrushchev said he liked your style in the steel crisis." Another cartoon showed two executives in a private club with a caption that read, "My father always told me that all presidents were sons-of-bitches." Conservative businessmen wore buttons identifying themselves as members of the "S.O.B. (Sons of Business) Club." Senator Barry Goldwater accused Kennedy of trying to bring socialism to the United States. The din of criticism grew even louder in late May when the stock market tumbled. Shares trading on the New York Stock Exchange on May 28 lost more than $20 billion in value. It was the worst day on Wall Street since the infamous 1929 crash that had ushered in the Great Depression. Kennedy's critics claimed that his attack on the steel industry had precipitated the crisis by undermining public confidence in the American economy. The president's supporters scoffed, arguing that he had been acting "in the progressive tradition of strong presidents since Jackson" and that his handling of the steel crisis had nothing to do with the temporary drop in stock prices.[8]

While insisting he had done the right thing, JFK worked hard to overcome the criticism and improve his standing in the business community. He invited prominent business leaders to black-tie dinners at the White House and forged closer ties with the conservative Business Council. In July he approved new depreciation allowances for machinery and equipment, a tax favor for business. In October Congress passed his investment tax credit bill, which provided industry with a 7 percent tax credit on new investments. Kennedy also pushed for a general tax cut, telling the American people that federal tax policy represented "the single most important fiscal weapon available to strengthen the national economy." "The right kind of tax cut at the right time is the most effective measure that this government could take to spur our economy forward," he announced on TV. "For the facts of the matter are that our present tax system is a drag on economic recovery and economic

---

* See Grant McConnell, *Steel and the Presidency* (New York: W. W. Norton, 1963).

growth, biting heavily into the purchasing power of every taxpayer and every consumer."[9]

This statement was controversial in 1962. Today, tax cuts of various kinds are a popular and oft-used fiscal tool, especially prized by Republicans but also employed frequently by Democrats, regardless of the impact on the federal budget deficit. But in the early 1960s, many people, including a sizable proportion of Republicans, opposed lowering the tax rate too much because that action could produce higher national indebtedness as well as runaway inflation. At the same time, tax rates were far higher than they are today. In the early 1960s, people who made $4,000 paid a 20 percent tax, while those with incomes of $400,000 and over paid as much as 91 percent in taxes—at least theoretically, since there were many tax shelters and dodges for the well-off, just as there continue to be in this century. Under Kennedy's plan, tax rates would be lowered to 14 percent for small incomes and 65 percent for large ones.[10]

Kennedy's support for tax cuts stemmed in part from his conversion to Keynesian economics.[11] John Maynard Keynes, a British economist who taught at Cambridge earlier in the twentieth century, believed that governments could moderate the effects of economic downturns by cutting taxes and running temporary deficits. On June 11, 1962, the president explained the reasons for his newfound Keynesian faith at Yale's graduation ceremony: "The myth persists that federal deficits create inflation and budget surpluses prevent it. Yet sizable budget surpluses after the war did not prevent inflation, and persistent deficits for the last several years have not upset our basic price stability. Obviously deficits are sometimes dangerous—and so are surpluses. But honest assessment plainly requires a more sophisticated view than the old and automatic cliché that deficits automatically bring inflation." The president believed that past economic shibboleths were insufficient to meet the economic demands of the 1960s, and this potential abandonment of traditional principles caused consternation in parts of the establishment. According to Arthur Schlesinger, the "old Elis [Yalies] had listened" to the president's words "with acute discomfort" while the deficit-averse business community regarded it as almost blasphemous.

In response to the criticism, Kennedy tweaked his plan, but he was determined to achieve an across-the-board tax cut. The House of Representatives passed the administration's tax cut bill two months before JFK made his final trip to Dallas, and it likely would have cleared the Senate in 1964 if the president had lived. Lyndon Johnson was able to shepherd a variation of the bill through Congress that trimmed tax withholding rates, increased the child care expenses deduction, and dropped the tax rate on marginal incomes over $400,000 from 91 to 70 percent. The latter was a significant reduction in taxes for the wealthiest Americans, engineered by a Democratic president and Congress.[12]

Kennedy's tax cut proposal was radical for its time and is one of JFK's least remembered yet most lasting initiatives. Modern proponents of supply-side economics, many of them Republicans, have frequently invoked the Kennedy viewpoint over the years in an attempt to disarm their critics. For example, in 2010, the Massachusetts Republican senatorial candidate Scott Brown ran a television ad that included an excerpt from Kennedy's tax cut speech. The image gradually dissolved into a picture of Brown, who shared the tax cut outlook of the Bay State's political patron saint. It was considered a turning point in Brown's successful upset victory in capturing the Senate seat of the late Edward Kennedy.[13]

WHILE FEW RECALL the tax cut proposal of 1962, no one will ever forget the most serious confrontation of the Cold War, the Cuban Missile Crisis. On the morning of Tuesday, October 16, 1962, JFK was still in bed reading newspapers when his national security adviser, McGeorge Bundy, arrived with urgent news: A U-2 spy plane flying over Cuba two days earlier had detected Soviet medium-range missiles that could be fitted with nuclear warheads and fired on U.S. cities.[14] The president was genuinely stunned—were the Russians trying to start a nuclear war? None of his Kremlinologists had anticipated the move, and in September JFK had made it clear that if Khrushchev tried to supply Cuba with offensive (rather than just defensive) weapons, the "gravest issues would arise." How could the Soviet leader engineer a provocation so threatening it was certain to invite the most serious possible response from the United States? Kennedy told Bundy to schedule an 11:45 A.M. meeting with his top intelligence, military, and foreign policy advisers. A dozen or so men joined the president in the cabinet room at the appointed hour to decide how to respond. (The press would later dub the group Ex Comm, short for the Executive Committee of the National Security Council.) For once, a hackneyed phrase proved completely true: The fate of the world hung in the balance.[15]

As the meeting began, JFK switched on a secret taping system that he had ordered installed in the cabinet room over the summer. A devoted student of history, the president knew that future generations of scholars would want a record of the group's conversations—and no doubt he himself saw immediate and long-term personal uses for these transcripts, from holding his advisers accountable to writing his memoirs.

Arthur Lundahl, head of the National Photographic Interpretation Center, began the meeting:

"This is the result of the photography taken Sunday, sir."

"How do you know this is a medium-range ballistic missile?" asked Kennedy, who thought that the tiny images on the photos resembled "little footballs on a football field" instead of Russian weapons.

"The length, sir."

"The what? The length?"

"The length of it. Yes."

Lundahl then introduced Sidney Graybeal ("our missile man") who showed the president pictures of "similar weapons systems taken during Soviet military parades."

"Is this ready to be fired?" asked Kennedy.

"No, sir," answered Graybeal.

Actually, no one knew for sure whether any missiles were operational. Bundy wondered if there weren't other sites on the island that might be more advanced, since the U-2 had photographed only a small portion of western Cuba. Kennedy immediately ordered additional reconnaissance flights to get as much good information as possible before he made any decisions. At the moment, though, Kennedy wondered how he could avoid launching an attack, even if only a surgical air strike against the missile sites. He asked his advisers to weigh in on Khrushchev's game plan. General Maxwell Taylor, chairman of the Joint Chiefs of Staff, seconded the president's suggestion that the Soviets might be trying to compensate for a perceived American advantage in the nuclear balance of terror. Short-range missiles in Cuba were a cheap, effective way to deliver a heavy payload against U.S. targets. Secretary of State Dean Rusk added that Khrushchev could also be trying to use Cuba as a bargaining chip for Berlin. If the United States launched a preemptive strike against Castro, the Soviet chairman would have an excuse to send tanks into West Berlin. Kennedy listened to the chatter a while longer, then told the group to reconvene at 6:30 P.M., commanding in the meantime that everyone should leak nothing and project an air of normality.[16]

That night, Taylor told the president that surgical airstrikes might not be able to eliminate all of the missile sites. Secretary McNamara suggested a naval blockade instead of pinpoint attacks. At first Kennedy did not like the idea, in part because of his disagreement with McNamara over the situation's overall strategic importance. The secretary of defense remained skeptical that Russian missiles in Cuba would be enough to topple America's nuclear advantage; JFK was more concerned with Khrushchev's newfound diplomatic clout. Once the weapons were operational, the president reasoned, the Communists could ride roughshod over Latin America's fragile democracies and maybe even blackmail the United States into making concessions on Berlin. In addition, an unchecked military buildup in Cuba would strengthen Castro.

But what was the appropriate response? No one could say for sure, and the president ended the meeting having more questions than answers.[17]

The next day, Kennedy tried to maintain the appearance of normality by following his preset schedule. He met with the West German foreign secretary at ten A.M. and attended a luncheon at the Libyan embassy. On the way to the luncheon, he ordered his driver to stop at St. Matthew's Cathedral. "We're going in here to say a prayer," he told an aide. "Right now we need all the prayers we can get." That afternoon, he flew to Connecticut to campaign for Abraham Ribicoff, the former secretary of the Department of Health, Education, and Welfare who was running for a Senate seat. Meanwhile, the president's advisers were huddled in near-constant meetings. By this time, U.N. ambassador Adlai Stevenson and former secretary of state Dean Acheson had joined the discussion. Stevenson wanted the president to exhaust the diplomatic route before unleashing the military; Acheson, on the other hand, thought that the United States would lose face if it didn't respond forcefully. Curtis LeMay, the hawkish Air Force chief of staff and architect of the incendiary air raids against Japanese cities during World War II, agreed with Acheson and began drafting plans for air sorties against Cuba.[18]

A day later, Ex Comm received new intelligence showing the installation of intermediate-range missiles in Cuba that could reach eastern and southern sections of the United States. Dean Rusk worried about Russian missile bases popping "out like measles all over the world." Maxwell Taylor and the Joint Chiefs now recommended a full-scale invasion of Cuba. Undersecretary of State George Ball and Robert McNamara discussed the consequences of a military response, and their conversation indicates an unannounced strike, which would have increased the odds of taking out all of the missile sites, was still under consideration. "If there is a strike without a preliminary discussion with Khrushchev, how many Soviet citizens [manning the sites] will be killed, I don't know, there could be several hundred, perhaps at a minimum," the secretary of defense mused. "We're using napalm, 750-pound bombs . . . This is an extensive strike we're talking about." And then how would Khrushchev respond? "It seems to me," Ball added, "it just must be a strong response and I think we should expect that. And therefore the question really is, 'Are we willing to pay some kind of a rather substantial price to eliminate these missiles?' I think the price is going to be high. It may still be worth paying to eliminate the missiles, but I think we must assume that it's going to be high." The president agreed that America "needed to take some action," but nothing that would trigger a "nuclear exchange" with Russia, a scenario he described as "the final failure." Kennedy returned to the idea of a blockade: Would it require a declaration of war? And what should the United States do about the missiles that were already in Cuba?[19]

Later that day, again in an effort to project nonchalance, Kennedy kept a prearranged appointment with Soviet foreign minister Andrei Gromyko to discuss the Berlin question. Gromyko had no idea that Kennedy knew about the missiles, and the president kept his cards hidden. The Soviet minister said that Castro was worried about an American invasion and claimed that the USSR had supplied him with weapons for defensive purposes only; poker-faced and baldly lying, Gromyko promised that no offensive weapons had been or would be introduced into Cuba. The president responded by reading an excerpt from his September 13 speech, which warned the Soviets against arming Cuba with offensive weapons. The inscrutable Gromyko sat in stony silence. After the meeting, Kennedy told Robert Lovett, a former secretary of defense during the Truman administration, that he had been sorely tempted to show the Russian the photographs of the missiles sitting in his desk drawer.[20]

That evening, the blockade option gained traction. Most of the Ex Comm members now favored it, and Kennedy liked the idea of taking a gradual first step, one that would give Khrushchev time to back down. As a result, the president ordered the military to begin working on the blockade specifics, while retaining a backup plan for outright invasion of Cuba. The next morning, he held a meeting with the Joint Chiefs, who were still pressing for a full-blown attack. "I think that a blockade, and political talk, would be considered by a lot of our friends and neutrals as being a pretty weak response to this," said Curtis LeMay, "and I'm sure a lot of our own citizens would feel that way, too. In other words, you're in a pretty bad fix at the present time."[21] LeMay's blunt comment annoyed Kennedy. "What did you say?" he asked. When LeMay repeated it, the president chuckled and said, "You're in there with me."[22]

Weary of the vacillation and bickering among his advisers, JFK instructed his brother Bobby and Ted Sorensen to work toward a consensus; he wanted to make a final decision over the weekend but was leaving on a brief campaign trip to Illinois. In the president's absence, the members of Ex Comm assembled an acceptable compromise, one that combined a blockade with plans for air strikes. Fabricating a head cold to the press, JFK cut short the campaign stumping and came back to the White House on Saturday to hear a new idea pushed by Adlai Stevenson: Why not swap Guantánamo and the NATO missiles in Turkey and Italy for the missiles in Cuba? Kennedy politely declined to engage in such high-stakes horse trading. The United States, insisted the president, could not reward the Soviets for their duplicitous behavior. Then the president was presented with two final options: He could authorize an air strike, which would likely lead to a general invasion of Cuba, or he could start the confrontation with a naval blockade of the island nation and progress from there as needed. Roswell Gilpatric, deputy secretary of defense, helped nudge Kennedy toward the safer choice: "Essentially, Mr. President, this is a choice between limited action and unlimited action, and most of us think that it's better to start with limited action." The president agreed.[23]

It was finally time to go public, to let America and the world know of the extreme danger existing at the moment. On Monday, October 22, 1962, a cryptic announcement from Pierre Salinger, the president's press secretary, had alerted the country that the president would deliver a nationally televised address at seven o'clock that evening concerning a matter of the "highest national urgency." At the appointed hour, Americans huddled around their radios and television sets.

"Good evening, my fellow citizens," Kennedy began. "This government, as promised, has maintained the closest surveillance of the Soviet military buildup on the island of Cuba. Within the past week, unmistakable evidence has established the fact that a series of offensive missile sites is now in preparation on that imprisoned island. The purpose of these bases can be none other than to provide a nuclear strike capability against the Western Hemisphere." After explaining the danger posed to U.S., Canadian, and Latin American cities, the president accused the Soviets of promulgating lies. In September they had said that the weapons in Cuba were for defensive purposes only and the USSR never deployed ground-to-ground missiles to other countries. He also mentioned his meeting with Gromyko. Next, the president explained why missiles in Cuba mattered: "We no longer live in a world where only the actual firing of weapons represents a sufficient challenge to a nation's security to constitute maximum peril. Nuclear weapons are so destructive and ballistic missiles are so swift, that any substantially increased possibility of their use or any sudden change in their deployment may well be regarded as a definite threat to peace." And rather than accept that threat, he said, the United States would begin a "quarantine" of Cuba; the word "blockade" was not employed since it had graver diplomatic implications. In addition, the military was placed on heightened alert, the U.S. base at Guantánamo Bay, Cuba, was reinforced, and the United Nations was asked to pressure the USSR. Kennedy called upon Khrushchev "to halt and eliminate this clandestine, reckless, and provocative threat to world peace and to stable relations," noting that the United States would regard a nuclear attack from Cuban territory on any country in the Western Hemisphere as an attack by Russia itself, which would trigger "a full retaliatory response upon the Soviet Union." The president also declared that he was prepared to check any aggressive action by the Soviets "anywhere in the world," especially West Berlin. "Our goal is not the victory of might," he concluded, "but the vindication of right—not peace at the expense of freedom, but both peace and freedom, here in this hemisphere and, we hope, around the world. God willing, that goal will be achieved."[24]

Bobby Kennedy later remembered the mood in the White House after the president's speech: "We went to bed that night filled with concern and trepidation, but filled also with a sense of pride in the strength, the purposefulness, and the courage of the president of the United States." While he hoped otherwise, JFK feared his speech might prompt an immediate Soviet military response. When Tuesday morning dawned and the world was still intact, the president and his advisers exhaled slightly. So did the American people. A Gallup poll taken after the speech showed that 84 percent of the respondents supported the quarantine, even though one in five thought that it would lead to World War III. Tens of thousands of telegrams poured into the White House favoring the president's position by a ten-to-one ratio. Americans were speaking nearly with one voice, and it demanded the removal of the missiles in Cuba.[25]

The quarantine went into effect at 10:00 A.M. on Wednesday, October 24, 1962. By then, sixty-three ships, including a number of Latin American vessels, were patrolling the waters around Cuba.[26] Scores of other ships, airplanes, and troops were on standby, awaiting orders from the president to attack. A few minutes after ten o'clock, McNamara relayed a message from the Navy—two Soviet ships, the *Kimovsk* and the *Yuri Gagarin*, were maintaining a steady course toward Cuba and would reach the quarantine line in roughly two hours. Immediately afterward, word came that a Russian sub had been spotted between the two vessels. The Pentagon ordered Strategic Air Command to prepare for a nuclear war. Potentially millions of people would die if the Russian ships failed to turn around. The intense stress pushed the president almost to the breaking point. He and his brother Robert stared at each other, wondering if their decision had doomed the planet. Bobby reported experiencing morbid flashbacks to the demise of his brother Joe, Jack's brush with death, and Jackie's miscarriages. People in the room were talking, but he said he couldn't hear what they were saying.[27]

At 10:25 A.M. CIA director John McCone broke the tension by reporting that several of the inbound Soviets vessels had stopped short of the quarantine line. Word came a few minutes later that additional ships were returning to Russia. "We're eyeball to eyeball and I think the other fellow just blinked," whispered Dean Rusk. Actually, unbeknownst to the White House, Khrushchev had ordered his vessels to turn back more than a full day earlier, and they were farther from the quarantine line than U.S. reports suggested. Still, Rusk was right—the Soviets had blinked; for the first time since the crisis began, events were moving away from war.[28]

The crisis was far from over, however, and could not end while Soviet missiles remained in Cuba. On Thursday afternoon at the U.N., Adlai Stevenson ripped into the Soviet ambassador: "Do you, Ambassador Zorin, deny that the USSR has placed and is placing medium- and intermediate-range missiles and sites in Cuba? Yes or no? Do not wait for the translation. Yes or no?" When the Russian replied that he was not in an American courtroom and would answer in due course, Stevenson said, "You are in the courtroom of world opinion right now," and added that he was prepared to wait for Zorin's answer "until hell freezes over." Kennedy, watching the drama unfold on television, appreciated Stevenson's rhetorical flourish. "Too bad he didn't show some of this steam in the 1956 campaign," he chuckled.[29]

On Friday, October 26, a group of elite policymakers drawn from the National Security Council decided to recall three of the team's saboteurs that were already on their way to Cuba as part of Operation Mongoose's effort to topple Castro. Adding chaos to crisis was unwise, they reasoned. That same day, the State Department received a letter from Khrushchev addressed to the president. The informal tone convinced Llewellyn Thompson, the U.S. ambassador to Russia, that the chairman had written it without any input from his advisers. Worried about the prospect of a nuclear war, Khrushchev offered to withdraw the missiles in exchange for a U.S. pledge not to invade Cuba. He sent a similar message through Aleksandr Fomin, the KGB station chief in Washington.*

Kennedy remained appropriately skeptical, given the earlier duplicity by the Soviet regime. His suspicions hardened the next day when the Soviets released a second statement, adding a new condition for peace: the withdrawal of American missiles in Turkey. The members of Ex Comm were uncertain about the proper response, but Robert Kennedy suggested that they simply ignore the second statement and respond to Khrushchev's original letter. JFK liked the idea and ordered Sorensen to draft a reply. He also dispatched his brother to meet with Anatoly Dobrynin, the Soviet ambassador to the United States. At the same time, Kennedy was coming under increased pressure from his military advisers to launch an attack. At four P.M. he learned that a Soviet surface-to-air missile had killed a U-2 pilot, Major Rudolf Anderson, overflying Cuba earlier that day. The Joint Chiefs demanded an eye for an eye, but the president refused. Khrushchev needed time to mull over his proposal, and a military response of any kind might short-circuit the only real chance to avert nuclear war. Moreover, the Bay of Pigs crisis had taught Kennedy that his generals could be very wrong.[30]

At 7:45 P.M., Robert Kennedy received Ambassador Dobrynin in his office

---

* Fomin communicated with the State Department not directly but by using an intermediary, the television journalist John Scali. This was an era when reporters could sometimes play an inside game without professional retribution.

at the Justice Department. "I want to lay out the current alarming situation the way the president sees it," the attorney general explained. The downing of the U-2 plane meant that there was "now strong pressure on the president to give an order to respond with fire if fired upon" that could easily spark a "chain reaction."[31] RFK then summarized the main points of the president's response to Khrushchev's October 26 letter: if the Soviets dismantled their missiles, the United States would lift its embargo and promise not to invade Cuba. When Dobrynin asked about the missiles in Turkey, RFK assured him that the issue was negotiable, although the president could not publicly announce any such deal for fear of undermining the NATO alliance. Instead, President Kennedy would order the dismantling of the missiles in a few months, after the crisis had passed.[32]

When Khrushchev learned about the meeting, he wasted no time in accepting Kennedy's terms. The Soviet leader further ordered an immediate radio broadcast of his decision so the news would be received and confirmed by Washington before events could spiral further out of control on either side. JFK was inclined to believe the crisis was over but some of his military advisers disagreed. They were convinced that the Soviets were employing a clever delaying tactic and urged the president to attack. Yet after the Bay of Pigs, Kennedy had learned caution—that discretion truly was the better part of valor. In a nod to their concerns, though, the president promised he would maintain the Cuban quarantine until all of the missiles were removed.[33]

Negotiations with the Soviets continued over the next few weeks about nagging details. Washington wanted Moscow to remove its IL-28 airplanes, which had the capability to drop nuclear bombs on American cities; allow on-site verification of the dismantling process; and provide safeguards against the reintroduction of offensive weapons. The Kremlin balked at first, insisting that it had already fulfilled its bargain, but eventually conceded on all points. In response, Kennedy was able to announce an end to the quarantine on November 20, 1962.[34]

Although decades have elapsed since the Cuban Missile Crisis, it continues to fascinate—and haunt—us. Without question, it was the most perilous moment of the Cold War, and, one could argue further, the most dangerous moment in the history of mankind. A nuclear exchange with Russia would have made the carnage of Hiroshima and Nagasaki appear minor. Fifty years on, what lessons should we draw? Perhaps above all, governments should remember that peace can be achieved even when hope for peace appears forlorn. Shrewd leaders must understand, as Kennedy did, how to combine the threat of military force with face-saving diplomatic options that rational regimes (where they exist) will normally prefer to their own destruction. Military options usually are enticing because they offer the promise of quick and total victory, yet the promise often turns out to be an illusion. In the case of Cuba, the president's generals preferred to destroy the missile sites, which would have solved the immediate threat while creating a far greater one—all-out war. President Kennedy's intelligence, patience, and probing questions during the crisis validated the wisdom of the Founders' decision to put military leaders under civilian control. A less thoughtful or cautious commander in chief might have given in to his generals' pleadings. Kennedy's wisdom and sober judgment in October 1962 have justifiably been praised by historians, and this was probably his finest moment as president. The costly lessons learned at the Bay of Pigs paid off for the president and the world.

Not incidentally, the harrowing events of "the missiles of October" prodded President Kennedy to reevaluate his policies. Could some longer-term good come from this near-death experience? Was common ground between East and West more possible than he had yet conceded? Might the United States and the Soviet Union work together to limit the proliferation of nuclear weapons? As we will see, Kennedy would emphasize these themes in his final year in the White House.

In the meantime, Kennedy had a different kind of confrontation at home to manage. In June 1962, the U.S. Fifth Circuit Court of Appeals ordered the University of Mississippi to admit James Meredith, a black Air Force veteran who believed that God had chosen him to challenge the state's segregation laws.[35] Mississippi governor Ross Barnett, a Democrat, rejected the federal court's order and told his constituents that he "would not surrender to the evil and illegal forces of tyranny." The Kennedys, embracing their constitutional responsibilities, urged Barnett to obey the law. But the governor proved to be stubborn; he knew that racial integration was the third rail of Mississippi politics and that if he bowed to Washington's will, his constituents would punish him and his party at the polls. Instead of complying with the court's order, Barnett physically blocked Meredith from registering while giving a states' rights oration explaining his resistance.

The Kennedys made several attempts to negotiate with the governor and thought that they had found a reasonable solution: If Barnett maintained law and order, they would keep their troops on the sidelines. But the brothers knew better than to fully trust the governor and took additional safety precautions. Following established law, President Kennedy seized control of the Mississippi National Guard and dispatched federal marshals to protect Meredith. He also went on television to remind Americans that the United States was "founded on the principle that observance of the law is the eternal safeguard of liberty and defiance of the law is the surest road to tyranny." At the same time, Kennedy attempted to console white Southerners, most of whom were fellow Democrats. "I recognize that the present period of transition and adjustment in our nation's Southland is a hard one for many people," he said. "Neither Mississippi nor any other Southern state deserves to be charged with all the accumulated wrongs of the last one hundred years of race relations. To the extent that there has been failure, the responsibility for that failure must be shared by us all, by every state, by every citizen." He went on to remind Mississippians of their accomplishments "on the field of battle and on the gridiron" and urged calm. "The eyes of the nation and of all the world are upon you and upon all of us," said the president. "And the honor of your university and state are in the balance. I am certain that the great majority of the students will uphold that honor."[36]

Alas and inevitably, many did not, and on the evening of September 30, 1962, Mississippi's campus became a war zone. An enraged mob of thousands hurled bricks and bottles at Meredith's dormitory while angry shouts and gunshots echoed through the humid night. Governor Barnett withdrew his state troopers and let the federal marshals fend for themselves. Two people died and hundreds of others were injured, including twenty-seven marshals who suffered bullet wounds. Kennedy finally ordered federal troops to the scene, though they arrived too late to repel the initial waves of violence. It certainly had not unfolded the way the president and attorney general had envisioned, and they were criticized—and were critical of themselves—for poor planning.

James Meredith blamed "the lack of clear authority" in Washington for the fiasco. But he also remained optimistic that the civil rights movement would ultimately triumph. A year after the riot, having finished his degree, Meredith waxed optimistic in a letter addressed to the attorney general. "Today regardless of all other considerations, I am a graduate of the University of Mississippi. For this I am proud of my country—the United States of America." He was also proud of the marshals who had risked their lives for his safety. "If I had no other measure by which to evaluate the trend of the American mind than the United States marshals with which I came in contact during my stay at the University of Mississippi, I would be very much encouraged. The marshals, many of whom were Southerners themselves, in addition to their security duties, were a constant reminder to me that white Americans could and would respect the rights of other Americans."[37]

The Kennedys weren't as optimistic as Meredith about race relations. By the fall of 1962, they were worried about pushing too hard and fast on civil rights, and the bloodshed in Oxford had shown them what might happen if they did.[38] President Kennedy refused to ask Congress for a strong civil rights bill and waited until the midterm elections were safely behind him before signing an executive order banning discrimination in federally funded housing—a promise he had made long ago. Civil rights leaders were growing restless and angry: why was the president dragging his feet when the movement was at a critical moment? After all, Kennedy possessed a great deal of political capital in 1962. His handling of the Cuban Missile Crisis in October had pushed his approval ratings much higher (74 percent job approval according to the Gallup poll) and allowed Democrats to gain seats in the Senate while losing only four seats in the House in November. This was a far better showing than the president's party usually posted in midterm elections.[39]

Instead of putting the full power of the White House behind comprehensive civil rights legislation, though, Kennedy opted for a piecemeal voting rights bill, which he introduced in February 1963. Mainly, the bill declared that a sixth grade education would be sufficient, in and of itself, to prove literacy, so that anyone with this level of schooling could avoid the infamous Southern registrar's trick of requiring blacks to read aloud and interpret the Constitution before they could be enrolled as voters. As disappointing as the president's proposal was to civil rights activists, in Kennedy's mind the country was not ready for an omnibus bill. The Kennedy administration certainly wasn't ready, and the president told an aide that the conservatives on Capitol Hill would "piss all over" him if he pressed too hard on civil rights. Kennedy also continued to appoint segregationist judges and refused a request from the Civil Rights Commission to withhold federal funds from Mississippi until the state complied with court orders.

The president's timidity irked Martin Luther King, Jr. In the early spring of 1963, King published an article in *The Nation* containing a number of tough criticisms of Kennedy. "The Administration sought to demonstrate to Negroes that it has concern for them," he explained, "while at the same time it has striven to avoid inflaming the opposition. The most cynical view holds that it wants the votes of both and is paralyzed by the conflicting needs of each." Unwilling to wait for Kennedy to initiate civil rights action, King made plans to provoke an incident in Birmingham, Alabama, often termed the most segregated city in America. In April, King and colleagues held mass meetings and demonstrations in the streets and boycotted the city's businesses. When an Alabama court issued an injunction against the protests, King ignored the order and was promptly arrested. His famous "Letter from a Birmingham Jail," which was written to white clergy who were uncomfortable with his tactics, could just as easily have been addressed to John F. Kennedy. "I must confess that over the past few years I have been gravely disappointed with the white moderate," King wrote. "I have almost reached the regrettable conclusion that the Negro's great stumbling block in his stride toward freedom is not the White Citizen's Counciler or the Ku Klux Klanner, but the white moderate, who is more devoted to 'order' than to justice." JFK had been stressing law and order for over two years, and urged blacks to take their grievances to court, not to the streets. But Kennedy's cautious pragmatism, which had served him well in many respects, did not mesh with the spirit of the civil rights movement. African Americans wanted major changes right away; they were unwilling to sit in the back of the bus any longer.[40]

Eugene "Bull" Connor, Birmingham's commissioner of public safety, and the Birmingham police preferred the racist status quo and decided to arrest King's followers for even the smallest legal infractions. By early May, violent cruelty had replaced arrest. When a crowd of protesters, including young children and high school students, marched in defiance of a city ban, Connor's henchmen used German shepherds and pressure hoses to mow them down. The television images were flashed across the world; President Kennedy saw the pictures the next morning in the *New York Times* and told an aide they made him "sick." Baseball great (and Republican) Jackie Robinson again blasted JFK for sitting on the fence. "The revolution that is taking place in this country cannot be squelched by police dogs or high power hoses," he observed. "I must state bluntly that there will be grave doubts as to the sincerity of your administration unless you face this issue in the forthright manner with which you handled the steel industry and the Cuban situation. The eyes of the world are on America and Americans of both races are looking to you."

In his heart, Kennedy must have known that Robinson was right. He sent Burke Marshall, an assistant attorney general, to Birmingham to negotiate a truce. Marshall found Birmingham's white residents circling the wagons. In their eyes, King and his followers were outside agitators who were stirring up the local black population. Marshall Haynes, the vice president of a real estate and insurance company in Birmingham, probably spoke for many of his fellow whites in a letter addressed to Marshall:

> In your interview it seems you made a statement that no official of the community had offered to meet with the Reverend Martin Luther King or the Reverend Fred Shuttlesworth [King's co-organizer]. I honestly do not see how any government official or business group or church group in the Birmingham area could with good conscience sit down with this element and discuss Birmingham problems. In the past several months there have been some community meetings in this area to which substantial Negro citizens have been invited and have attended; but Mr. King and his associates have made and are continuing to make a real effort to brand most of the local leadership "Uncle Toms" and to associate them with a moderate approach on integration.

Marshall forwarded the letter to RFK, adding "This shows how far we are from any understanding or tolerance." By then, however, the Justice

Department had already brokered a fragile compromise. Unwilling to endure a permanent loss of profits, Birmingham's business leaders agreed to gradually desegregate the city's schools, lunch counters, and department stores.[41]

But not every Alabamian was ready to surrender so easily. Bombs exploded in front of a black-owned hotel and Martin Luther King's brother's house. In response, blacks attacked the city's police and firemen. At the same time, Governor George Wallace vowed to block the integration of the University of Alabama. The South was descending into a second civil war, this one undeniably about race. In late May JFK met with his civil rights advisers, who suggested that he urge black and white Southerners to convene jointly for a series of peace conferences. "The people in the South haven't done anything about integration for a hundred years," the president replied, "and when an outsider intervenes, they tell him to get out—they'll take care of it themselves, which they won't."[42] At last Kennedy jumped off the fence and fully into the fray, deciding to propose a comprehensive civil rights bill. Wallace's stand in the schoolhouse door gave the president enough political cover to take his own stand.[43]

On June 11, 1963, regular programming on all networks was interrupted for a special address from the president. "Good evening, my fellow citizens," he began. "This afternoon, following a series of threats and defiant statements, the presence of Alabama National Guardsmen was required on the University of Alabama to carry out the final and unequivocal order of the United States District Court of the Northern District of Alabama. That order called for the admission of two clearly qualified young Alabama residents who happened to have been born Negro." JFK praised the students at the University of Alabama for their restraint, and then addressed the larger issue: "I hope that every American, regardless of where he lives, will stop and examine his conscience about this and other related incidents," reminding his audience that the United States had been "founded by men of many nations and backgrounds." "We are confronted primarily with a moral issue. It is as old as the Scriptures and is as clear as the American Constitution." Black Americans, he said, were citizens of the United States, and as such were entitled to the same rights and privileges that every other citizen enjoyed. How many white citizens, he asked, would be satisfied if they couldn't vote for their elected officials, send their kids to the best schools, or eat lunch in certain restaurants? The crisis could not be solved through "talk," "token moves," "repressive police action," or "demonstrations in the streets." Instead, Congress needed to desegregate the country's schools, provide additional protections for black voters, and "enact legislation giving all Americans the right to be served" in public facilities. "This is one country," the president declared. "It has become one country because all of us and all the people who came here had an equal chance to develop their talents." It was finally time to give black families the same chance.[44]

JFK adviser Louis Martin, who had been instrumental in persuading candidate Kennedy to call Coretta Scott King after her husband had been jailed, called the speech "the most forthright statement ever made on civil rights." "I told the president the wonderful reaction to his speech among Negroes," Martin recorded in his diary. "He asked me to read telegrams of protests from 'nuts & [kooks].' Then he asked Mrs. Lincoln [JFK's secretary] to bring in congratulatory telegrams which I also scanned." Kennedy's speech reflected his maturity on the civil rights issue. Born into a white-run world where blacks were almost entirely powerless servants in the background, he had not given much thought to the problems of dark-skinned Americans for most of his life, and as president only when their difficulties crowded inescapably onto his plate. However belatedly, Kennedy came to understand the immorality and injustice of America's deeply rooted racism and the legally and culturally sanctioned discrimination that enabled it.

The day after Kennedy's speech, a white supremacist named Byron De La Beckwith shot and killed a thirty-seven-year-old civil rights leader, Medgar Evers, who was walking up the driveway to his own home when struck down. His murder was witnessed by his two young children. On June 13, JFK wrote a letter to Evers's widow that in some ways would apply to the president himself in six months: "Although comforting thoughts are difficult at a time like this, surely there can be some solace in the realization of the justice of the cause for which your husband gave his life. Achievement of the goals he did so much to promote will enable his children and the generations to follow to share fully and equally in the benefits and advantages our nation has to offer." In the margins of the letter, he scrawled a handwritten message: "Mrs. Kennedy joins me in extending her deepest sympathy." Six days later, President Kennedy sent to Congress a civil rights bill that was more thorough than anything Lincoln ever contemplated. It banned segregated public accommodations and gave the Justice Department additional power to deal with school districts that were defying *Brown v. Board of Education*, the 1954 Supreme Court decision requiring public schools to integrate.[45]

With hope of pressuring Congress on the bill, civil rights leaders organized a march on Washington. The Kennedy brothers opposed the idea. They thought that a massive demonstration at such a delicate time would actually undermine congressional support and maybe even lead to violence. On June 23, 1963, Lawrence Spivak, host of NBC's *Meet the Press*, asked Bobby Kennedy if he thought that a march on Washington would "hurt" the cause of civil rights or "help get civil rights legislation through." Bobby said that he didn't think that the president's bill "should be discussed under an aura of pressure" and called the announcement of a march "premature." But he also expressed support for the people's "right to petition" and said that black citizens "as well as others" had the right "to make their views known."

Privately, RFK expressed contempt for the march and some of its organizers. During a Georgetown dinner party, he asked Marietta Tree, a U.S. delegate to the United Nations, if she were in town "for that old black fairy's anti-Kennedy demonstration." The "old black fairy" to whom he was referring was Bayard Rustin, one of the march's organizers and a former member of the Young Communist League who had once been arrested on a sodomy charge. When Tree tried to change the subject to Martin Luther King, Bobby said, "He's not a serious person. If the country knew what we know about King's goings-on, he'd be finished." Kennedy was referring to King's extramarital sexual activities, which the FBI had learned about while ostensibly hunting for Communists inside of his organization. The hypocritical dimension of Kennedy's comment, given JFK's near-constant philandering and RFK's knowledge of it, is obvious. The president eventually endorsed the march, but on his own terms. He and Bobby reserved the right to censor speeches that they thought were too inflammatory or critical of the White House. The brothers pressured John Lewis, the twenty-three-year-old president of the Student Non-Violent Coordinating Committee, into watering down a passage in his speech that was critical of the Kennedy civil rights bill.[46] They also convinced King and his associates to move the event from Capitol Hill to the Lincoln Memorial. While the shift in locale was intended to get the demonstrators away from Congress, the Lincoln Memorial provided King with the perfect backdrop for his speech.[47]

On August 28, hundreds of thousands of people gathered on the National Mall for the "Great March for Jobs and Freedom." The atmosphere was festive.[48] High school groups sang and clapped their hands; well-dressed men and women, including many white and black college students, carried signs and shouted slogans; Joan Baez, Bob Dylan, Harry Belafonte, and other celebrities entertained the crowd. In the late afternoon, under Lincoln's watchful gaze, King delivered for the ages his "I have a dream" speech, which, according to historian Robert Dallek, "genuinely impressed and moved" Kennedy. But the president knew that the fight for reform would involve more than just organizing a march or delivering a brilliant speech. He tried to lower expectations among civil rights leaders by describing the tough road that lay ahead. When one of the march organizers encouraged him to take his case directly to the people, JFK pointed to the political costs of such a move. Republicans, he said, would make inroads among disgruntled white voters by saying that the president was forcing them to accept a radical left-wing agenda. (Richard Nixon's "Southern strategy," employed in 1968, demonstrated that Kennedy's political instincts were correct.) Instead, President Kennedy said, leaders should pressure the GOP to jump on the civil rights bandwagon.[49]

In mid-September, a bomb exploded in front of the Sixteenth Street Baptist Church in Birmingham, killing four black children including Addie Mae Collins, sister of Sarah Collins Rudolph. "Our city was known as the 'Magic City' but it became the 'Tragic City.' There were so many bombs going off there," explained Rudolph, who had arrived at the church moments earlier with her sister. "BOOM! All I could say was 'Jesus.' It scared me so bad . . . The debris came in and I was blinded instantly from the glass of the stained-glass window. I stayed in the hospital about two months. They removed twenty-two pieces of glass out of my whole face, and [removed] my right eye."

African American leaders urged the president to seize control of Birmingham. JFK refused and told them to remain patient while his civil rights bill wended its way through Congress. He hoped that the bill would buy much-needed time for the country to adjust to the realities of a less racially driven society. He was also optimistic about his chances for reelection, guessing that "local candidates would be hurt more than the national ticket—that passage of the bill would cool tempers off and let other issues rise—and that the explosive costs of inaction would have been greater than those of any action he had taken." But the bill's progress ground to a halt on Capitol Hill with many Southern Democrats determined to stop it. By the time JFK left for Dallas, it seemed unlikely that his legacy would include a new civil rights law, at least during his first term. Election years were not usually characterized by enactment of hugely controversial legislation.[50]

6

EUROPE, SPACE, AND SOUTHEAST ASIA

DURING THE SUMMER OF 1963, even while the civil rights issue was paramount, the president began to rethink America's Cold War objectives. The Cuban Missile Crisis gave him a greater appreciation for the precariousness of life in the nuclear age. He wanted to reduce tensions between the superpowers before it was too late. In June, on the day before his nationally televised civil rights address, Kennedy outlined his new vision for "world peace" in a graduation speech at American University in Washington. "What kind of peace do we seek?" he asked. "Not a Pax Americana enforced on the world by American weapons of war. Not the peace of the grave or the security of the slave. I am talking about genuine peace, the kind of peace that makes life on earth worth living, the kind that enables men and nations to grow and to hope and to build a better life for their children—not merely peace for Americans but peace for all men and women—not merely peace in our time but peace for all time."

After reminding his listeners of the futility of "total war" in the nuclear age, JFK challenged Americans to examine their own prejudices and assumptions. "First: let us examine our attitude toward peace itself," he said. "Too many of us think it is impossible. Too many think it unreal. But that is a dangerous, defeatist belief. It leads to the conclusion that war is inevitable—that mankind is doomed—that we are gripped by forces we cannot control." Kennedy captured the cynicism of the age, perhaps a lingering aftereffect of the Cuban Missile Crisis. Though relieved that disaster had been averted, many Americans also embraced Epicurean fatalism, a philosophy that we should "eat, drink, and be merry, for tomorrow we die." Kennedy wanted Americans to feel hopeful about the future. Further, as a World War II veteran, he knew that there was no glory in war. He had seen men die in combat and wanted to spare his children and grandchildren similar horrors. Since war was a "man-made" problem, he said, it could be eliminated by men, since "no problem of human destiny is beyond human beings." (Barack Obama chose these words to be stitched into the presidential carpet in the

Oval Office.) Although JFK acknowledged that there were enormous differences between the United States and the USSR, he believed that the two nations could work together to find common ground. "And if we cannot end now our differences, at least we can help make the world safe for diversity. For, in the final analysis, our most basic common link is that we all inhabit this small planet. We all breathe the same air. We all cherish our children's future. And we are all mortal."[1]

Nikita Khrushchev called it "the greatest speech by any American president since Roosevelt." The frigid relationship between Moscow and Washington had begun to thaw. A nuclear test ban treaty, which had been discussed off and on for years, seemed possible. While Soviet and American diplomats prepared to hammer out the details of the treaty in the summer, Kennedy departed for Europe. He had originally planned to go to West Germany alone, but added Italy and England to the itinerary for political reasons and Ireland for personal ones. During what turned out to be the final months of his presidency, Kennedy became intrigued with his Celtic heritage and all things Irish. In preparation for the trip, the president "read Irish histories, traced the lineage of the Kennedys and the Fitzgeralds, studied the writings of John Boyle O'Reilly and the exploits of the Irish Brigade in the American Civil War, and arranged with the successors of that brigade, the New York Fighting 69th Irish National Guard regiment, to present one of its flags from the battles of Fredericksburg, Chancellorsville, and Gettysburg to the Republic of Ireland." Feelings on the other side of the Atlantic were equally warm, so much so that Bono, the lead singer of the rock group U2, has said that his home country's fascination with America "got out of hand" in the early 1960s and that the Irish "saw the Kennedys as our own royal family out on loan to America." When O'Donnell told his boss that a trip to Ireland would be "a waste of time," JFK responded, "Kenny, let me remind you of something—I am the president of the United States, not you. When I say I want to go to Ireland, it means that I'm going to Ireland. Make the arrangements." Kennedy wanted an uplifting vacation and thought that a quick trip to the Emerald Isle would provide the perfect escape.[2]

But first, he needed to keep his promise to visit West Germany, and the trip turned truly historic. An estimated three fourths of the population of West Berlin flooded the streets of their city to see JFK. After touring the wall that had been built to keep East and West apart, Kennedy delivered a brilliant speech that most Americans and Germans alive at the time recall to this day. "Two thousand years ago," he said, "the proudest boast was 'Civis Romanus sum.' Today, in the world of freedom, the proudest boast is 'Ich bin ein Berliner.'" West Berliners roared their approval. He was their president as much as anyone else's, the guarantor of their rights and freedoms. Next, JFK took pot shots at the Communists as severe as anything ever uttered by Ronald Reagan:

> There are many people in the world who really don't understand or say they don't, what is the great issue between the free world and the Communist world. Let them come to Berlin. There are some who say that Communism is the wave of the future. Let them come to Berlin. And there are some who say in Europe and elsewhere we can work with the Communists. Let them come to Berlin. And there are even a few who say that it is true that Communism is an evil system, but it permits us to make economic progress. *Lass' sie nach Berlin kommen* [Let them come to Berlin].

Speaking into a bank of microphones, the wind blowing through his thick thatch of auburn hair, Kennedy closed with a proverb and a prediction: "Freedom is indivisible, and when one man is enslaved, all are not free. When all are free, then we can look forward to that day when this city will be joined as one and this country and this great continent of Europe in a peaceful and hopeful globe. When that day finally comes, as it will, the people of West Berlin can take sober satisfaction in the fact that they were in the front lines for almost two decades." It was one of the high points of his presidency. Like his eventual successor Ronald Reagan, John Kennedy knew that Communism was a bankrupt system and that it was only a matter of time before it vanished from the earth.[3]*

At the time, however, JFK's advisers were worried that the speech might have torpedoed the test ban treaty. Kennedy went into damage control mode and delivered a dovish speech later that day at the Free University of Berlin. As Kenny O'Donnell later recapped it, "Fortunately, Nikita Khrushchev, who might have remembered a few ill-timed emotional outbursts of his own, decided to ignore the City Hall speech and to accept the Free University speech, and went ahead with his endorsement of the atmospheric test ban treaty."[4]

It is also worth noting that the majesty of a presidential speech such as Kennedy's in Berlin benefited from both the drama of the Cold War and the American media's belief in that era that it was unpatriotic to point out small flaws in a president's rhetoric. The famous phrase "Ich bin ein Berliner" liter-

---

* In 1989, East and West Berliners tore down the wall that had kept them separated for so long, and to this day, residents of Berlin still celebrate the Kennedy speech that lifted their spirits during a dark time in their history. For the fortieth anniversary of the speech, they gathered in front of the Rathaus Schöneberg (city hall) in John-F.-Kennedy-Platz to hear the president's speech rebroadcast over giant loudspeakers.

ally translates as "I am a jelly doughnut." Such a slip today would dominate the cable news networks and blogosphere for days, wiping out the emotional impact of such an address. But JFK's German hosts, and the accommodating White House press corps, appreciated Kennedy's effort and let the mistake slide.[5]

FROM BERLIN, KENNEDY flew to Ireland. He was struck by how quiet it was when he landed at Dublin Airport. "Maybe we got our schedules mixed up here," he said jokingly. Irish leaders later claimed that people were in awe; they could scarcely believe that one of their own was the leader of the free world. From the airport, JFK rode in an "open Lincoln, a vintage model from the Eisenhower era flown in from Berlin earlier in the day, for the ten-mile ride by motorcade into Dublin." As the car wended its way along a road lined with well-wishers, Kennedy stood up so that they could get a better look at him. "The thought occurred to the Irish president [Eamon de Valera], he remembered a few years later, 'what an easy target he would have been.' Kennedy's security detail was concerned about the exposure, but de Valera took comfort in the tremendous outpouring the Irish were giving Kennedy." He did not believe that the president was in any danger.[6]

JFK received a hero's welcome all across Ireland. The residents of New Ross (the point from which Kennedy's great-grandfather, Patrick, had sailed for America 115 years earlier) hung banners reading WELCOME HOME, MR. PRESIDENT. "When my great-grandfather left here to become a cooper in East Boston," he told the crowd, "he carried nothing with him except two things: a strong religious faith and a strong desire for liberty. I am glad to say that all of his great-grandchildren have valued that inheritance. If he hadn't left, I would be working over at the Albatross Company [a nearby fertilizer plant], or perhaps for John V. Kelly [a local pub owner]." The crowd exploded with laughter.[7]

From New Ross, Kennedy drove to his family's ancestral homeland at Dunganstown, where he was entertained by a slew of relatives. When a cousin named Jim Kennedy poured him a large Irish whiskey, the president surreptitiously handed it to an aide, who dutifully gulped it down.

The president also attended a memorial service for the executed leaders of the 1916 Easter Uprising and watched in awe as cadets from the Military College at the Curragh performed a flawless drill. It turned out to be his favorite part of the trip. He later told his sisters that he wished he "had a film of that drill so that we could do something like it at the Tomb of the Unknown Soldier." Jackie made a mental note of the president's comments.[8]

John Kennedy fell in love with the people of Ireland. He left with a heavy heart and promised to return. "This is not the land of my birth," he said, "but it is the land for which I hold the greatest affection, and I certainly will come back in the springtime." When Sean Lemass, the Irish prime minister, visited the United States in October, JFK lent him Air Force One—an honor he had never bestowed on any other world leader.[9]

The Irish weren't the only ones who gave JFK a warm welcome. Italians were almost as excited about shaking hands with the Catholic president of the United States. When Kennedy's convertible rolled through the streets of Naples, a frenzied crowd blocked its progress; thousands of people were "screaming" and "swarming all over. It was the noisiest demonstration of the entire European tour." For Kennedy's security detail, the trip was nerve-wracking. Two days earlier in Rome, the Italians had reneged on an agreement to allow Secret Service agents to flank Kennedy's vehicle (they had been elbowed out by Italian motorcycle cops). Now, Jerry Blaine and Dave Grant—two of the men assigned to protect the president—found themselves seated on the trunk of an Italian car fending off overzealous Neapolitans. "There were no handrails like they had on President Kennedy's limousine, and they found themselves throwing people off the car while trying to stay aboard the rounded trunk. People were weaving in between the motorcycles and one by one the riders became engulfed by the crowd. At one point Blaine felt his sleeve rip and his watch fall to the ground as he shoved people away. The agents felt as if they were fighting for their own lives." Fortunately, the president made it through the ordeal without a scratch.[10] As in Ireland and elsewhere, only luck prevented a tragedy. Another obvious warning about inadequate presidential security was ignored.

Kennedy also paid his respects to Pope Paul VI by making a brief stop at the Vatican. It was the last destination on what turned out to be the last of the nine international journeys during his presidency, many of them multicountry tours.[11] The press speculated on whether the president would kneel and kiss the pope's ring—a standard practice among Catholics—but JFK knew better than to provoke the wrath of Protestant voters. "Norman Vincent Peale would love that," he quipped, "And it would get me a lot of votes in South Carolina."[12] The ring went unkissed.

THE PRESIDENT FOUND a crowded in-box the next day when he returned to the Oval Office. Not only had his civil rights bill stalled on Capitol Hill, but the situation in Vietnam was rapidly deteriorating. When JFK took office, eight hundred American military personnel were stationed in South Vietnam; he had increased the number to sixteen thousand in only two years. The president saw Vietnam as a test case for his "flexible response" doctrine, which relied on a variety of methods to stop the spread of Communism. Eisenhower had been wary of American involvement in Vietnam, having watched the French get bogged down in Southeast Asia and then withdraw in humiliation in 1954. Kennedy was also cautious—he had refused a 1961 Pentagon recommendation to commit two hundred thousand U.S. troops to Vietnam—but he had talked tough as a cold warrior, and did not want to see any country fall to Communism on his watch. Still, gradually, the U.S. troop "advisers" had been drawn surreptitiously into direct fighting; the recipe for much deeper involvement was being concocted. In actions that some liberals have long forgotten, Kennedy ordered Green Berets to use counterinsurgency tactics against Communist guerrillas; he approved the use of napalm, a jellied gasoline that sticks to the skin as it burns, as well as Agent Orange, a defoliant that causes birth defects; and he provided Ngo Dinh Diem, the authoritarian ruler of South Vietnam, with guns and money.[13]

But by the autumn of 1963, Kennedy realized that his Vietnam strategy was not working. The previous December, Democrat Mike Mansfield, the Senate majority leader, returned from Indochina with a gloomy report—the United States was getting sucked into a tar pit, just as the French had a decade earlier. In addition, "Diem had resisted American combat troops. He did not want the U.S. to take over his war and his country. Moreover, he continued to defy the Kennedy administration's insistence that he make internal reforms." The mostly Buddhist South Vietnamese distrusted and disliked Diem, a Roman Catholic who had once lived in New Jersey. The previous May, during a ceremony celebrating the birth of the Buddha, Diem's troops had opened fire and killed nine worshippers. Monks began setting themselves on fire in protest. Diem's sister-in-law, a ruthless aristocrat named Madame Nhu, smiled when she heard the news. "Using the Vietnamese word for monk, she called it 'barbecue á bonze,' and offered to provide gas and matches to any monks or American reporters who would do the same thing."[14]

Despite U.S. warnings and protests, Diem continued to clamp down on dissenters. His troops raided Buddhist pagodas, desecrated religious statues and holy relics, and threw monks and nuns in prison. For many South Vietnamese, Communism began to look like the lesser of two evils. Aware that the situation was spiraling out of control, JFK made a shrewd political move: he replaced Ambassador Frederick "Fritz" Nolting with his old Bay State rival, Henry Cabot Lodge, Jr., who had lost his U.S. Senate reelection bid to Kennedy in 1952 and later served as Richard Nixon's running mate in 1960. JFK knew that having a Republican plenipotentiary would provide him with useful political cover if the worst-case scenario unfolded in Vietnam. He also genuinely liked and respected Lodge, a seasoned diplomat who spoke fluent French. Lodge's appointment came at a time when the administration understood that

Diem's days were numbered. Rumors of a revolt against Diem circulated freely on the streets of Saigon.

Diem's stubborn refusal to embrace reform convinced JFK to support his ouster.[15] Kennedy could not let Vietnam fall to the Communists, especially right before the 1964 election. He remembered the severe criticism that Harry Truman had received for letting Mao Zedong's forces overrun China and, after considerable debate, "agreed to a U.S.-backed coup." At the same time, he reserved the right to change his mind up to the last minute. On August 30, 1963, Lodge sent a top secret cable to Washington intended for the president's eyes only: "I fully understand that you have the right and responsibility to change course at any time," he wrote. "Of course I will always respect that right. To be successful, this operation must be essentially a Vietnamese affair with a momentum of its own. Should this happen you may not be able to control it, i.e. the 'go signal' may be given by the generals."[16]

Roger Hilsman, assistant secretary of state for Far Eastern affairs, sent his own top secret memo to Rusk about how the administration should respond when the putsch came. "We should encourage the coup group to fight the battle to the end and destroy the [presidential palace] if necessary to gain victory," he wrote, adding that if Diem's family were taken alive, they "should be banished to France or any other European country willing to receive them." As for the leader himself, he "should be treated as the generals wish."[17]

On November 1, 1963, twenty-one days before the president went to Dallas, soldiers surrounded Diem's palace. The Vietnamese leader immediately phoned Lodge. "Some units have made a rebellion and I want to know what is the attitude of the United States?" he asked. "I do not feel well enough informed to be able to tell you," the ambassador replied coyly. "I have heard the shooting, but am not acquainted with all of the facts. Also it is four thirty A.M. in Washington and the U.S. government cannot possibly have a view." Diem couldn't believe his ears—Washington must have some sort of position! Lodge remained evasive and "told Diem to phone him if he could do anything for his personal safety."

The South Vietnamese president was brutally executed the next day, along with his brother. When JFK heard the news, he "leaped to his feet and rushed from the room with . . . a look of shock and dismay," recalled Maxwell Taylor. Another aide remembered JFK blaming the CIA for Diem's murder. "I've got to do something about those bastards," he said. "They should be stripped of their exorbitant power." In the months leading up to the assassination, Kennedy had tried to warn Diem that his life was in danger. He sent a trusted friend, Torby Macdonald, to Saigon to plead with the South Vietnamese president to purge his government of corrupt officials and "take refuge in the American embassy." Diem had stubbornly refused. On November 4, the president recorded what amounted to a personal confession of his role in the assassination. "We must bear a good deal of responsibility for it," he admitted. "The way he was killed . . . made it particularly abhorrent."[18]

When the coup occurred, Kennedy was still unsure about the right road to take on Vietnam. He had inherited the problem from Eisenhower and arguably made it worse by sending additional military advisers to Saigon. His unwillingness to set firm policy stemmed in part from the conflicting reports he was receiving. When one general and a State Department employee who had both visited Vietnam gave him opposing accounts of the war's progress, JFK joked, "You both went to the same country?"[19]

At this early stage, few in power or in the general public understood the dangers of Vietnam, or how events were inexorably drawing the United States into an explosive civil war. In the spring of 1962, when a reporter asked him what he planned to do about mounting casualties in Vietnam (a quartet of sergeants had recently died), Kennedy called the conflict "a very hazardous operation, in the same sense that World War II, World War I, Korea" had been when "a good many thousands and hundreds of thousands of Americans" had perished. "So that these four sergeants are in that long roll. But we cannot desist in Vietnam." During his 1963 State of the Union address, Kennedy claimed that the "spearpoint of aggression" in Vietnam had been "blunted." The address Kennedy was supposed to deliver at the Dallas Trade Mart on the day he died contained an equally firm message: "Our security and strength, in the last analysis, directly depend on the security and strength of others, and that is why our military and economic assistance plays such a key role in enabling those who live on the periphery of the Communist world to maintain their independence of choice. Our assistance to these nations can be painful, risky and costly, as is true in Southeast Asia today. But we dare not weary of the task."[20]

In public, then, President Kennedy had been consistent and resolute, for the most part, about American involvement in Vietnam. In private, at least as his closest associates told it later, he remained skeptical about U.S. intervention in the region. "They keep telling me to send combat units over there," he said with regard to his generals' demands for additional troops. "That means sending draftees, along with regular Army advisers, into Vietnam. I'll never send draftees over there to fight."[21]

However, JFK never made his doubts clear on the record, never outlined precisely his intentions for Vietnam, leaving his successor the ability to follow his own path while claiming it was Kennedy's. Undeniably, there were contradictions in JFK's Vietnam record; he said one thing but did another. In October 1963, President Kennedy announced that the United States would withdraw one thousand military personnel by the end of the year. At first glance, this announcement seems to indicate that Kennedy was ready to wind down some operations in Vietnam. But months earlier, a British counterinsurgency expert, Robert K. G. Thompson, had told him that withdrawing a thousand men "would show that (1) [the Republic of Vietnam] is winning; (2) take steam out of anti-Diemists; and (3) dramatically illustrate honesty of U.S. intentions." Point two became moot after Diem's death, but Kennedy knew that points one and three could still affect the outcome of the 1964 election. Although most voters at the time could not have found Vietnam on a map, some political opponents—and friends, too—began to criticize the administration for its handling of the war. The Republican National Committee demanded that the president give "a full report to the American people" on the situation in Vietnam, even while adding that it was "firmly behind any policy which will block the Communist conquest of Southeast Asia." In April 1962, a group of academics, businessmen, theologians, and journalists had published "an open letter to President John F. Kennedy against U.S. military intervention in South Vietnam." "Frankly, we believe that the United States intervention in South Vietnam constitutes a violation of international law, of United Nations principles, and of America's own highest ideals," the group argued. "We urge, Mr. President, that you bring this intervention to an immediate end and that you initiate a special international conference to work out a peaceful solution to the crisis in Vietnam, as you have endeavored to do in Laos." Signatories included Roland Bainton, a Yale divinity professor and author of a well-known book on Martin Luther, and Linus Pauling, a Nobel Prize–winning physicist. The group published a second, similar letter the following year.[22]

Kennedy did not respond to the appeals. But on November 21, the day he departed for Texas, he told an aide to put together "an in-depth study of every possible option we've got in Vietnam, including how to get out of there." He wanted to review the "whole thing from the bottom to the top."[23]

What would have happened if JFK had lived? Though pro-Kennedy advocates and anti-Kennedy detractors have attempted to project a future agreeable to their own perspectives, there is no inarguable answer. As the historian Stephen Rabe notes, Kennedy "would have faced the same crisis that President Johnson encountered in 1964–1965. Communist forces would win the war in South Vietnam if the United States did not use its military might to stop them." JFK's life lessons, before and during his presidency, had taught him not to accept anything short of victory, and so in all likelihood he would have avoided a hasty retreat.[24] And he might have accelerated troop deployments in the run-up to the 1964 election. The conservative Barry Goldwater, destined to be the Republican presidential nominee whether or not Kennedy had lived, would have insisted on toughness, and Kennedy would not have wanted to give his opponent an opening. On the other hand, a number of prominent Kennedy administration officials, most notably Robert Kennedy but many others, too, changed their minds about the Vietnam War when the carnage mounted and it became likely that the war was unwinnable. They would probably have advised the president in a second term to negotiate a settlement or at least keep the Southeast Asian engagement modest.

John Kennedy had far more international and foreign policy experience than Lyndon Johnson, a classic domestic policy politician. Kennedy had seen the horror of war close up, in PT 109 and when his brother Joe died in a plane crash; Johnson had never seen real combat. JFK also had searing, unpleasant experiences involving the competency and prejudices of his generals and the CIA during the Bay of Pigs, the Cuban Missile Crisis, and other events—an education LBJ apparently missed or ignored. No one will ever know for sure, but the weight of evidence, looking at the whole of Kennedy's career, would argue against his committing more than a half million troops to the fight in Vietnam, or doing so in such a foolishly slow manner as Johnson chose (which allowed the enemy to keep up). Having seen how difficult it could be to manage a tiny secret war against Cuba—just ninety miles from U.S. shores—would JFK have bet his entire presidency on a major Cold War confrontation in Vietnam, six thousand miles away? It is hard to believe that the Kennedy image makers, especially Bobby, would have permitted JFK to be burned in effigy all over the country, letting the intelligentsia JFK admired and considered himself a part of slip away because of the Vietnam draft. University communities and well-educated elites were a key part of Kennedy's political base, and good politicians always try hard to avoid alienating their base. Further, the Cuban Missile Crisis shows how clever and resourceful Kennedy could be under pressure. At a minimum, we can say that during his final weeks in office, JFK was reconsidering his Vietnam policy and refused to take any options off the table.[25]

KENNEDY'S FINAL DAYS also paint a picture of a man who craved excitement. Perhaps because two of his siblings, Joe and Kathleen, had died young and the president himself had repeatedly faced death—as a youth, in World War II, and after a back operation in the 1950s—JFK seemed unusually conscious that his time on earth was fleeting. Kennedy could be humorously morbid, joking about the best ways to die (war and poisoning were his choices) and how short his life would be (he once guessed he would make it to forty-five, only a year off the final mark).[26] He strove to secure a place in the history books before it was too late. Friend and foe alike agree that John Kennedy seized every moment, embraced every challenge, and lived life to its absolute fullest. This restless ambition sometimes produced great blessings for the nation. In September 1963 the Senate approved his Atmospheric Test Ban Treaty; never again would the Soviet Union or the United States detonate nuclear devices above ground. According to Ted Sorensen, "No other single accomplishment in the White House ever gave him greater satisfaction." The treaty helped preserve the environment and also reduced tensions between the two superpowers, while paving the way for future Cold War agreements.

Moreover, JFK convinced the country that, however huge the obstacles, it could land a man on the moon. Twenty-four hours before he died, Kennedy spoke at the Aerospace Medical Health Center in San Antonio, where he encouraged his fellow citizens to keep their eyes on the heavens:

> We have a long way to go. Many weeks and months and years of long, tedious work lie ahead. There will be setbacks and frustrations and disappointments. There will be, as there always are, pressures in this country to do less in this area as in so many others, and temptations to do something else that is perhaps easier. But this research here must go on. This space effort must go on. The conquest of space must and will go ahead. That much we know. That much we can say with confidence and conviction.

Other, small achievements toward the conclusion of the Kennedy presidency are often overlooked but deserve mention. After standing up to Soviet aggression in Cuba, Kennedy offered his enemy an olive branch when the threat diminished. In October 1963 he authorized the sale of American wheat to the Soviets in order to help them cope with a poor harvest. The same month, while Congress debated his civil rights bill, the President's Commission on the Status of Women issued its final report. In response, JFK created the Interdepartmental Committee on the Status of Women and the Citizens' Advisory Council on the Status of Women. Both committees "provided ongoing leadership" on gender issues which, according to some Kennedy advocates, helped usher in the modern women's rights movement.[27] Kennedy's New Frontier agenda also included the Equal Pay Act, signed by JFK in June 1963, which claimed to eliminate pay inequities based on gender. In practice, it had little effect in most economic sectors until strengthened by court decisions in the 1970s and further congressional action in subsequent administrations.[28] Otherwise, Kennedy produced few advances for women in politics or government. His cabinet, for example, did not include a single woman, and he was certainly no feminist in his professional or private life. Offsetting his accomplishments, JFK had a much darker side. The same internal fire that fueled his political success could also burn out of control. A ten-year-old John Kennedy had once noted in a letter to his father (requesting an allowance increase) that he had "put away childish things."[29] He achieved that goal in many areas of life, but not in his irresponsible relationships with young, beautiful women. In July 1963 FBI director J. Edgar Hoover informed Bobby Kennedy that he knew about the president's past relationship with an alleged East German spy named Ellen Rometsch. The wife of an army officer who had been assigned to the West German embassy, Rometsch supplemented her income by turning tricks for Washington's best and brightest. Her pimp was a high-profile Senate aide named Bobby Baker, who had close ties to Lyndon Johnson. In late August 1963, Rometsch was flown back to Germany on a U.S. Air Force transport plane at the behest of the State Department. According to author Seymour Hersh, she was accompanied by La-Vern Duffy, one of Bobby Kennedy's colleagues from his days on the McClellan Committee. Records related to Rometsch's deportation have either vanished or were never created in the first place.[30]

As the Rometsch case demonstrates, Kennedy's unrestrained sexual appetite threatened his personal and political safety. It also alienated some of the men who were assigned to protect him. Larry Newman remembered the "morale problems" that the president's indiscretions caused among his fellow Secret Service agents. "You were on the most elite assignment in the Secret Service, and you were there watching an elevator or a door because the president was inside with two hookers," said Newman. "It just didn't compute. Your neighbors and everybody thought you were risking your life, and you were actually out there to see that he's not disturbed while he's having an interlude in the shower with two gals from Twelfth Avenue." Newman also remembered joking with his colleagues about which one of them would testify on Capitol Hill if and when "the president received harm or was killed in the room by these two women." Kennedy had affairs with scores of other women, including two White House interns nicknamed "Fiddle" and "Faddle," Pamela Turnure (Jackie's personal secretary, whom JFK had conveniently encouraged her to hire), and Mary Meyer, a prominent Georgetown artist who was the "niece of Gifford Pinchot, the conservationist and Teddy Roosevelt's chief forester."[31] JFK probably also had an affair with Marilyn Monroe. Although Kennedy's strongest supporters have denied the relationship, pointing out there is no absolute proof, the behavior fit the president's pattern, and he had opportunities to pursue it. Both Kennedy and Monroe discussed the encounters with friends, and they were in at least one secluded place together.[32]

The well-supported story of Mimi Alford, a nineteen-year-old White

House intern at the time of her involvement with JFK, is impossible to over-look.[33]* Initiated into JFK's sexual world just four days into her internship, Alford lost her virginity to Kennedy as he conducted what can only be called a deeply inappropriate affair with a young charge; it even included a Kennedy-directed episode of oral sex with aide Dave Powers while Kennedy watched. This behavior, barely hidden from others within the White House and in-volving government resources to shuttle Alford to and from the traveling president, has caused some to question Kennedy's basic fitness for the highest office. Many have tried to reconcile JFK's high-minded, skilled public per-sona with his sleazy, reckless private self. It is simply impossible to match up the two sides rationally, and it is certainly inadequate to say that the rules of his time or a sometimes empty marriage permitted or justified these esca-pades. Any private citizen with modest responsibilities would be condemned for them, and as president, JFK risked his White House tenure, the welfare of his party, his policy goals, and everyone he supposedly held dear.[34]

Jackie was European in outlook, and while aware of some of her husband's philandering, she apparently tried to tolerate it as Continental wives had done for centuries. The late Robert Pierpoint, the White House correspondent for CBS television during the Kennedy years, once recalled an episode that re-vealed Mrs. Kennedy's matter-of-fact acceptance of JFK's bold unfaithfulness:

> I was sitting in the White House press room one day shortly after noon. And through the corridor came a French magazine correspon-dent who worked for *Paris Match* and he said, "Bob, I've just had a very unusual experience. I have to tell somebody about it." He was somewhat agitated and said that he had been invited to have lunch with Jackie upstairs in the private area and the president joined them, and then after lunch the president said, "Jackie, why don't you show our friend around?" She did, and brought him over to the west wing. Between the cabinet room and the Oval Office there is a small room where the secretaries sit. As she ushered him into that room she said in French, "And there is the woman that my husband is sup-posed to be sleeping with." He was quite upset and didn't know what to answer; it was kind of embarrassing for him.[35]

Although the president's infidelities often put a terrific strain on his mar-riage, he and Jackie appeared to reconcile after their infant son Patrick Bou-vier died in August 1963. Born with a severe lung problem, Patrick survived

---

* Alford had refused to talk for years, but in 2011, at age sixty-nine, she published a book about her relationship with the president.

for only two days. Afterward, a close friend saw the president—deeply distraught and openly weeping after his son's death—holding Jackie in his arms, "something nobody ever saw at the time because they were very private people." That autumn, close observers said they detected renewed affection in this most enigmatic of public-private couples. Though anyone would be skeptical, given long past practice, perhaps JFK's views and behavior were changing in this realm as well. There would not be enough time to find out.

On October 28, 1963, the family attended a public worship service together for the first time at a church in Middleburg, Virginia, called St. Stephen the Martyr.[36] Never an especially religious person—despite his strong public and political identification with the Roman Catholic Church—Kennedy might have contemplated the life of the man for whom the church was named: Stephen was murdered for defying the religious orthodoxy of his day. The president had always respected courage and admired people who were willing to sacrifice their careers and lives for their principles. While in the White House, Kennedy had shown courage in challenging the steel industry, the Soviet Union, his generals, and eventually, segregationists. President Kennedy was no saint like Stephen, but he had shown and earned grace during the better part of three tumultuous years in power. Three weeks after the worship service, he would proceed to his own martyrdom.[37]

7

ECHOES FROM
DEALEY PLAZA

WINSTON CHURCHILL'S DICTUM ABOUT Russia fully applies to the murder of John F. Kennedy: It is a riddle wrapped in a mystery inside an enigma. The intrigue is part of the lasting Kennedy legacy. In fact, as cynical as it may sound, the assassination has taken a short presidency and made it the stuff of legend. The gnawing sense of incompleteness, the intense emotions of regret and grief felt simultaneously by almost everyone, and the overwhelming melancholia of unfulfilled dreams obliterated John Kennedy's faults. They created in the slain president the image of a secular saint that has proven impervious to all sorts of lurid revelations over a half century.

Eerily, JFK foresaw the advantages of an early death. Much given to speculation about his possible assassination—he brought the subject up frequently with family and friends—Kennedy said to Jackie after his triumph in the Cuban Missile Crisis, "If anyone's going to kill me, it should happen now." The comment was made after a historian's lecture on Abraham Lincoln, where Kennedy had asked, 'If Lincoln had lived, would his reputation be as great?" The historian's answer was obvious—no, because Lincoln would have had to struggle with the titanic problems of post–Civil War reconstruction. Instinctively, Kennedy understood that it is better for a leader to leave the stage in both a moment of triumph and the tragedy of too short a time than to face the inevitable, wearing controversies of many years' leadership, being ushered out of office to a chorus of critical evaluations about his shortcomings. Such is the fate of most presidents.[1]

In any event, it is impossible to understand the Kennedy legacy without understanding the assassination—the sequence of events, as well as what most Americans *think* happened and why. Millions have never been, and will never be, satisfied with the official findings of two separate government inquiries—not least because the inquiries came to opposite conclusions on the critical question of conspiracy. The assassination dictated that JFK would not have the time to create a full record and make his whole claim on history. For fifty years the unfinished record of the man and his presidency has stirred Americans as they mourned an unconscionable loss and wondered what might have been. This "ghost legacy" is as powerful as the real one.

FOUR DAYS AFTER JFK was laid to rest in Arlington Cemetery, President Lyndon Johnson asked the Chief Justice of the United States to head a federal probe into the assassination. Earl Warren initially refused. He did not think that Supreme Court justices should be saddled with additional responsibilities when they already had a crowded docket; why not ask a retired judge to spearhead the investigation instead? Undeterred, LBJ summoned Warren to the Oval Office. The Chief Justice later recalled their meeting:

> [T]he president told me how serious the situation was. He said there had been wild rumors, and that there was the international situation to think of. He said he had just talked to [Secretary of State] Dean Rusk, who was concerned, and he also mentioned the head of the Atomic Energy Commission, who had told him how many millions of people would be killed in an atomic war. The only way to dispel these rumors, he said, was to have an independent and responsible commission, and that there was no one to head it except the highest judicial officer in the country . . . He said that if the public became aroused against Castro and Khrushchev there might be war. "You've been in uniform before," he said, "and if I asked you, you would put on the uniform again for your country." I said, "Of course." "This is more important than that," he said. "If you're putting it like that," I said, "I can't say no."[2]

LBJ signed an executive order later that day that created "a Commission to ascertain, evaluate, and report upon the facts relating to the assassination of the late President John F. Kennedy and the subsequent violent death of the man charged with the assassination." The other members of what became known as the Warren Commission were Democratic congressman Hale Boggs, Senator Richard B. Russell, Republican congressman and future president Gerald R. Ford, Senator John Sherman Cooper, former CIA director Allen Dulles, and John J. McCloy, FDR's assistant secretary of war. (Three of the four congressional members, Russell, Boggs, and Cooper, only reluctantly supported all the conclusions and would later criticize parts of the commission's final report; alone among the congressional members, Ford was an enthusiastic backer.)[3] Among the staff hired by the commission was a future United States senator, Arlen Specter, who served as an assistant counsel.[4]

The Warren Commission was doomed from the start, because Washington's power brokers, led by the new president himself, were far more interested in preserving domestic tranquility than in finding the full truth. They wanted a report that would first calm citizens' jangled nerves by reassuring them that a lone nut named Lee Harvey Oswald had acted completely on his own. Conspiratorial chatter, so the reasoning went, would only undermine public trust in government and perhaps even lead to war. Just thirteen months earlier, the United States had narrowly avoided a nuclear conflagration with Russia, and the Cold War was still freezing. The public was suspicious of Russia, Cuba, and more. In the immediate aftermath of the assassination, 62 percent of the American people believed that their president had been killed in a conspiracy. Official Washington had to respond.[5]

On the Monday after the assassination, while most Americans were watching JFK's funeral services on television, Nicholas Katzenbach, deputy attorney general, sent a memo to Bill Moyers, then an LBJ aide, that stressed two points: "1. The public must be satisfied that Oswald [who had been killed the previous day] was the assassin; that he did not have confederates who are still at large; and that the evidence was such that he would have been convicted at trial. 2. Speculation about Oswald's motivation ought to be cut off, and we should have some basis for rebutting thought that this was a Communist conspiracy or (as the Iron Curtain press is saying) a right-wing conspiracy to blame it on the Communists."[6]

It was impossible for anyone to know, seventy-two hours after the assassination, exactly what had transpired in Dallas, much less that Oswald was the lone assassin and would have been convicted at a trial. Moreover, this memo puts far more emphasis on public relations, and on pushing a preconceived, sanitized notion of the murder of the president, than it does on an honest effort to uncover all the facts. In Katzenbach's defense, his primary motive might have been to tamp down rumors of a conspiracy before they overtook the facts, which was not unreasonable. And this same course of action was recommended by others besides Katzenbach. FBI director J. Edgar Hoover told another of LBJ's aides, "The thing I am most concerned about . . . is having something issued so we can convince the public that Oswald is the real assassin."[7]

Hoover had good reasons to be concerned. While presidential protection was the province of the Secret Service and not the FBI, his agency had also failed to notice disturbing signals from Oswald, a known Communist sympathizer who had defected to the Soviet Union for a time and had a history of instability and violent tendencies.[8] In the weeks leading up to the assassination, James Hosty, an FBI agent working in the Dallas field office, had twice visited the house where Marina Oswald lived and Lee Oswald visited. Hosty questioned Marina but had not been able to find Lee on either occasion—

though Hosty was told a critical piece of information, that Oswald was working at the Texas School Book Depository. When Lee learned about Hosty's visits, he flew into a rage and stormed into the Dallas FBI office, demanding to see Hosty. A receptionist told Oswald that the agent was at lunch, so Oswald left a note that apparently said, "If you have anything you want to learn about me, come talk to me directly. If you don't cease bothering my wife, I will take appropriate action and report this to the proper authorities." We have to take Hosty's word for this because his boss, Gordon Shanklin, ordered him to destroy the note in the wake of Oswald's death. An FBI supervisor ordered the destruction of significant material evidence in the murder investigation of President Kennedy. This story, like so many others, was missed by the Warren Commission. Many years later, Hosty was temporarily suspended when it became apparent he had misled the commission, but Hosty was a small cog in a giant bureaucratic machine that often cared more about good press than truth. Hosty took aim at J. Edgar Hoover in his 1996 book, *Assignment: Oswald*, noting that he (Hosty) "came to understand that one of our jobs was to protect the bureau's image at all costs, even if it ran roughshod over individuals or principles."[9]

In what critics charged—accurately or not—was yet another attempt to protect the FBI's reputation, Hoover launched his own selective investigation into the Kennedy murder and, at LBJ's behest, sent the Warren Commission a copy of the bureau's final report less than a month after the assassination.[10] It concluded that Oswald had been the lone gunman and that no conspiracy existed. The report also "determined" that Oswald had fired three shots from the Texas School Book Depository—the first, it said, had hit JFK in the back, the second had injured Governor Connally, and the third had shattered the president's skull. Many assassination researchers over the decades have disputed Oswald's role, while others have supported the FBI's assertion in this regard, but the bureau's rushed conclusion about the three bullets is almost universally regarded as wrong today. Interestingly, although the Warren Commission "asked that the bureau's report not be made public until it had a chance to review it," newspapers quickly printed that the FBI had effectively quashed rumors of a conspiracy.[11]

With the flawed FBI report as its starting point, the Warren Commission launched its own rushed investigation of the JFK assassination beginning in February 1964. Acting on President Johnson's instructions, Earl Warren urged the commission to complete its work before July, when the presidential campaign would likely heat up. Over the next six months, the commission recorded the testimony of 552 people, "examined thousands of documents," and held fifty-one sessions. Commission members skipped many of the meetings. Senator Russell, for example, attended only five of the fifty-one; John

McCloy showed up for sixteen. The hard work was assigned to assistants like Arlen Specter, who invented the "single bullet theory" to reconcile apparently indisputable facts that emerged in the course of the Warren investigation, including the reality that Oswald or any marksman needed a certain number of seconds to fire a Mannlicher-Carcano rifle repeatedly within the elapsed time of the shooting.[12] Specter and his colleagues had screened the publicly unseen amateur home movie shot by businessman Abraham Zapruder in Dealey Plaza, which cast grave doubts on the validity of the FBI report.[13] It showed Governor Connally groaning in agony less than two seconds after Kennedy was shot in the back. The commission realized that no marksman, however skilled, could fire two shots within two seconds from a bolt-action rifle. Specter's single bullet theory—which asserted that the bullet striking JFK's back continued on, cleanly, through Kennedy's throat to cause all of Connally's wounds—neatly resolved the dilemma.

Other Warren Commission staffers investigated the Jack Ruby case and concluded that Ruby had impulsively killed Oswald in a fit of pique. Other pieces of the assassination puzzle were similarly assembled into the overall pattern—some easily and others with difficulty. The time pressures guaranteed that all of the evidence would not be gathered and sifted, and many key witnesses were not even interviewed. Gerald Ford was so anxious to close the case that he changed the description of the president's back wound so that it would comply with Specter's single bullet theory.[14] Ford would later insist that he was simply trying to make the report "more precise." But confidential files released in 2008 show that Ford had also opened a back channel to the FBI at the beginning of the investigation. At a December 1963 meeting, he told the assistant director of the FBI, Cartha "Deke" DeLoach, that two members of the commission did not believe that JFK had been shot from the sixth floor of the School Book Depository. Ford assured DeLoach that these members' dissenting views "of course would represent no problem." He also promised to keep the FBI informed on the inner workings of the investigation.[15] Until his death, Ford insisted publicly and privately that the Warren Commission was right and that he had never seen any evidence to dissuade him.[16]

Commission member and former CIA director Allen Dulles coached at least one CIA official on how to handle the commission's inquiries. On April 11, 1964, Dulles met with Agent David E. Murphy to discuss the allegations surrounding Oswald's true affiliations: had Oswald been recruited by the CIA or the KGB, as some were claiming? Dulles advised Murphy to deny both charges categorically in order to end the debate quickly. Dulles also knew about the CIA-sponsored assassination attempts on Castro, about which the commission was never told. Of course, it is possible that Dulles was simply trying to protect the agency he loved, but his witness tampering and refusal to share critical information with fellow commissioners casts further doubt on the investigation.[17]

On September 24, 1964, the Warren Commission presented its final report to the president of the United States. Johnson released a letter of appreciation later that day: "The commission, I know, has been guided throughout by a determination to find and tell the whole truth of these terrible events. This is our obligation to the good name of the United States of America and to all men everywhere who respect our nation—and above all to the memory of President Kennedy."

Like the FBI, the Warren Commission concluded that Oswald and Ruby had committed their crimes without help or encouragement from anybody else. While some prominent journalists such as CBS's Walter Cronkite were privately skeptical, news organizations generally did not question the findings. This was an era very different from today, when columnists and publishers were often the government's lapdogs.[18] In editorials, the nation's newspapers were overwhelmingly deferential. For example, Marquis Childs, a syndicated columnist, described the report as "a monument to patient sifting and analysis of fact, rumor, suspicion and wild conjecture." Childs also reminded his readers that no one had "come forward with any solid evidence that others participated with Oswald in the crime."[19]

Childs's views were in the majority at first. Most Americans initially accepted the conclusions of the Warren Report. After it was released, only 31 percent of the public still believed that JFK had been the victim of a conspiracy, exactly half of what the percentage had been in the immediate aftermath of the assassination. Remarkably, although it would not be known for many years, Senator Russell and the new president of the United States were two of the remaining skeptics, as they admitted during a recorded phone conversation:

> JOHNSON: Well, what difference does it make which bullet got Connally?
> RUSSELL: Well, it don't make much difference. But . . . the commission believes that the same bullet that hit Kennedy hit Connally. Well, I don't believe it!
> JOHNSON: I don't either.[20]

Ironically, in its rush to tamp down the rumors surrounding the assassination, the Warren Commission guaranteed the perpetuation of conspiracy theories for years to come. In the early 1960s, the public was thought incapable of handling the truth. Rather, it had to be spoon-fed a convenient, calming version of events. Americans were never told about the government's efforts to murder Fidel Castro and other world leaders, which many might have seen as sufficient motive for a revenge killing. Nor did the public know about Washington's relationships with the Mafia, Oswald's full history, or many other things that might have had a direct bearing on the events of November 22, 1963.

Instead, the Warren Commission gave everyone a sanitized, abbreviated version of the assassination. The public was condescendingly told to accept the official account without subversive, unpatriotic questioning. The commission laid the groundwork for the cynicism that became deeply rooted in the late 1960s and the 1970s—a profound distrust of the "official" government story about anything. Instead of being viewed as authoritative, government pronouncements became mocked as deceitful propaganda from the Ministry of Truth. The pattern became unmistakable. Assassinations, which became frighteningly common, were always carried out by lone gunmen, according to the government. The bloody Vietnam conflict, sold by Washington as a winnable war against international Communism, unfolded in a fog of deception, with leaders knowing privately that the war was likely to be lost. The Watergate scandal and resulting investigations revealed the treachery of many at the top as nothing had done before. The effective suspension of the Bill of Rights by the CIA and the FBI became apparent. The Warren Commission was their prologue, the first damaging government whitewash of the 1960s. In the movie *Men in Black*, Tommy Lee Jones's character explains to his partner that the MIB division is above the law, and its purpose is to protect the public from knowing that Earth is constantly threatened by alien life forms. "There's always an Arquillian battle cruiser or a Korilian death ray or an intergalactic plague that is about to wipe out life on this miserable planet," Jones says. "The only way these people get on with their happy lives is they do not know about it." This is not so far removed from the motivation that spawned and shaped the Warren Commission.[21]

The inadequacies of the Warren Commission left the door wide open for conspiracy theories of all sorts, and they have flourished in the half century since November 22, 1963. The proportion of Americans who believe in a JFK assassination conspiracy has skyrocketed. In 2003 an ABC News poll showed that a whopping 70 percent of Americans reject the Warren Commission's basic finding of a lone gunman.[22] The same survey found that 68 percent think Washington orchestrated a cover-up.[23] This number is not merely composed of the predictable antiestablishment crowd from the hinterlands; Americans who are suspicious of the Warren Report include representatives of the Beltway powerful. Former House Speaker Nancy Pelosi says that she "read the Warren Commission report, every analysis of it, every challenge to it as time passed . . . I even took the opportunity to ask Senator Specter about it."[24]

Countless books, television specials, newspaper articles, and Internet sites claim to know the truth about the assassination. The Mafia, the CIA, anti-Castro Cubans, pro-Castro Cubans, LBJ, the Secret Service, the Soviets, Texas oil millionaires—all have been implicated. Kennedy scholar William Lester recently unearthed a letter from JFK to the CIA, written ten days before the assassination, requesting information on UFOs. The *Daily Mail* in Great Britain asked, "Was JFK killed because of his interest in aliens?"[25]

Americans are understandably confused by the flood of contradictory information and disinformation. Many have thrown up their hands in despair and decided we will never know the truth about the events in Dallas. Even some honest experts who have devoted many years of their life to studying the Kennedy assassination are puzzled. They keep putting the pieces together, but always find some that don't fit. Dallas's own Jerry Dealey, a lifelong assassination researcher and descendant of Dealey Plaza's namesake, can rattle off every detail of that day. At the end of a long tour of key Dallas sites and an intense discussion, Dealey sighed, then admitted, "I know everything about the assassination, except what really happened."[26]

AND YET WE do understand a good part of the story. For example, any fair-minded observer can conclude that both the Dallas police and, far more important, the federal government botched the most important murder investigation of the twentieth century. Anyone who had watched a few episodes of *Perry Mason* by 1963 knew that the authorities were supposed to cordon off the crime scene and restrict the handling of evidence, even for everyday crimes. Yet in response to the shooting of the president of the United States, the Dallas police kept Elm Street open and allowed the general public to roam freely across Dealey Plaza, taking pictures and potentially hunting for souvenirs. Billy Harper, a young medical college student, found a piece of JFK's skull lying in the grass between Elm and Main Streets. (Fortunately, Harper reported his gruesome discovery to the authorities.) The Dallas police removed a bag that Oswald had allegedly used to conceal his rifle before it could be photographed. The cartridge cases found on the sixth floor of the Book Depository were carelessly tossed into a single envelope without identifying the precise location where each was picked up.

And why was the chief suspect in the president's murder paraded in front of the press? Journalists in 1963 were sometimes allowed to interview murder suspects before they went to trial, but this wasn't a garden variety homicide. A good many people swarming police headquarters in the forty-eight hours after the assassination were not required to show press credentials. Any determined person could have smuggled in a gun and shot Oswald. While carried out openly at the request of the news media to prove Oswald wasn't being mistreated (as rampant rumors had wrongly suggested), the accused assassin's transfer from the city to county jail in a crowded basement was just one of many opportunities for the disaster that happened on Sunday, November 24.[27] Some Dallas police officers and supervisors seemed more like Keystone Kops than well-trained law enforcement professionals.[28]

A police division in a midsized city might be excused some inability to handle unexpected world-class mayhem. The White House and its investigatory agencies had no such defense in the months following the assassination. The new president made it clear from the start that he wanted a short, superficial inquiry that neatly buttoned up the messy matter of how he had become chief executive. The FBI and the CIA appeared to be more determined to cover their tracks and make sure they weren't blamed for missteps than to get to the bottom of what happened in Dallas.

The Warren Commission became the focus of these hidden agendas, and the resulting commission blunders undermined its claim to have conducted a thorough inquiry. Chief among them was the failure to interview significant eyewitnesses. On the morning of the assassination, Bill and Gayle Newman and their two boys, Billy and Clayton, were waiting at Love Field for Air Force One to arrive. But the size of the crowd convinced Bill to take the family downtown to watch the parade instead. They found a good viewing spot on a patch of grass inside Dealey Plaza at the end of the long motorcade route (soon to be renamed forever "the grassy knoll"). Bill could hear crowds cheering in the distance as the motorcade grew closer. He remembers seeing a well-dressed man, Abraham Zapruder, standing on a concrete pedestal holding a movie camera. When the president's car turned onto Elm Street and drove down the center lane, Bill heard two loud booms. "I thought somebody had thrown a couple of firecrackers or something beside the president's car," he told an interviewer, "and I can remember the thought of, you know, that's a pretty poor joke, somebody to do something like that." Bill realized that it was no prank when he saw the president come up out of his seat with his arms in the air. He also noticed that Governor Connally's eyes were "protruding" and that his shirt was covered in blood. When the presidential limousine pulled directly in front of the Newmans, who were standing on the curb, they heard a third shot. "And I saw the side of the president's head blow off and saw the flash of white and the red," Bill recalls, "and he went across the seat . . . into Mrs. Kennedy's arms. And she hollered out, 'Oh my God, no! They've shot Jack!' " Bill and Gayle instinctively threw themselves on top of their children to shield them from danger. When they were certain that the threat had passed, they got up and began climbing the grassy knoll. Gayle could see a crowd of people "rushing towards the railroad tracks behind the concrete wall." Bill noticed some men running in the same direction who were carrying what he thinks might have been Thompson submachine guns. To this day, he is not sure if the men he saw were FBI or Secret Service or other law enforcement officers, but he believes that they jumped off one of the cars in the presidential motorcade and ran toward the rail yard (not the School Book Depository) in search of the assassin.[29] Bill and Gayle were curious to see what was happening on the other side of the fence, but they were buttonholed by two reporters from WFAA-TV who wanted to interview them.* A short time later, the Newmans found themselves sitting inside WFAA's main studio fielding questions from the station's program director, Jay Watson. "You . . . think the shot came from up on top of the viaduct [the so-called triple underpass at Dealey Plaza] toward the president, is that correct?" asked Watson. "Yes, sir," Bill replied before correcting himself, "no, not on the viaduct itself, but up on top of the hill, a little mound of ground with a garden."[30] Gayle Newman told Watson that she heard three shots—the first caused Kennedy to rise "up in his seat"; the second caused Governor Connally to grab "his stomach" and topple "over to the side"; and the third hit the president in the head.[31]

The Warren Commission concluded that only two bullets struck Kennedy and Connally. Although the Newmans gave statements to the sheriff's office and were visited by two FBI agents on the Sunday after the assassination, the two witnesses closest to the limousine at the time of Kennedy's murder, and positioned perfectly to take in the entire scene of the crime, were never formally interviewed by the Warren Commission. "I'm really surprised that they did not interview us," Bill Newman said, "but I guess they didn't see the need to." He admits that it may have been because the family could not confirm the preferred theory, that the shots had come from the Book Depository.[32] One of the country's acknowledged experts on the assassination, Gary Mack, who has personally interviewed many of those connected to the events in Dallas in his role as curator of the Sixth Floor Museum (located in the old School Book Depository), estimates that "about fifty people thought *at least one of the shots* came from [JFK's] front [and] not the Depository."[33]

The Warren Commission also overlooked H. B. McLain, a Dallas motorcycle cop who was part of the presidential motorcade. McLain was on

---

* Live television reporting has always been a dangerous business, and inaccurate information was aired almost immediately on November 22. In the first minutes after he began his CBS broadcast, Walter Cronkite actually suggested that the Newmans could be the assassins. (They were not named, but Cronkite said Secret Service agents and others had surrounded them on the grassy knoll.) See "Two Hours of Uncut 11/22/63 CBS-TV Coverage, Starting at 1:30 P.M.," YouTube, http://www.youtube.com/watch?v=t_Ry9-bpixM [accessed April 23, 2013.]

Houston Street when he heard a single shot and saw pigeons flying off the roof of the Depository. At first he assumed it was someone in the building firing a gun to scare off the birds. That is, until he heard Dallas police chief Jesse Curry's voice come over the radio. "Chief said, 'go to Parkland Hospital,'" McLain recalls, "And it was already set up if anything went wrong . . . So when he said 'go to Parkland,' we went to Parkland." When he arrived at the hospital, he found a nearly immobilized Mrs. Kennedy, in a state of shock, sitting in the back of the presidential limousine:

> When the president's car pulled in, I pulled in beside of it. And she was laid over his head. And she wouldn't raise up to take his body out of the car. And I finally reached over and caught her by the shoulder. And I said, 'Come on. Let them take him inside.' She didn't make a sound. And I walked her inside, turned around and come back out.

McLain says he did not linger long inside the hospital because, "I just knew I didn't have no business in there." That the Warren Commission would fail to interview someone so well placed in the motorcade—a law enforcement official who had carefully noted key details and closely observed the as-yet-undisturbed crime scene in the limousine before almost anyone else—is difficult to understand. It is true that McLain failed to fill out a police report on his actions that day, as requested by his Dallas department, but the Warren Commission had a list of the officers in the motorcade—where McLain was prominently positioned. Aggressive investigators would have contacted him.

Underlining the Warren Commission's error, H. B. McLain would later become a significant figure during the reopening of the assassination investigation in the 1970s. McLain was linked to the now-famous "Dictabelt recording." In the early 1960s, police departments routinely recorded conversations between officers and headquarters on Dictaphone brand dictation devices. In 1978 the House Select Committee on Assassinations (HSCA), tasked with reinvestigating the deaths of JFK and Martin Luther King, Jr., learned that a Dallas police officer with a radio microphone stuck in the "on" position might have inadvertently helped to record the key minutes of the assassination—potentially a match for the soundless Zapruder film. The Dictabelt contained sounds that acoustic experts identified as gunshots. The committee then examined photographic evidence and determined that McLain had been the officer with the stuck microphone. McLain himself always denied this claim and wondered how he could have heard Chief Curry's voice if his mike had been stuck in the "on" position. Of course, it is possible the microphone was stuck for a while, and the jostling of the travelling cycle "unstuck" it.[34]

In any event, the recording presumably came from McLain or one of the other motorcycle policemen in the motorcade, and the Dictabelt recording caused the HSCA to rewrite history. Based largely on this extraordinary piece of evidence, indicating that too many shots had been fired from too many locations for the assassination to have been the work of Oswald alone, the HSCA decided that the Warren Report was wrong, and concluded instead that JFK had probably been killed by more than one person—the definition of a conspiracy. We will return to the Dictabelt later.

The Newmans and H. B. McLain were among dozens of well-placed witnesses never interviewed by the Warren Commission. When asked why the commission ignored her, grassy knoll onlooker Marilyn Sitzman gave a pithy reply: "Because it was [the 1960s], I was female and I was young. And I was irrelevant." In reality, Sitzman was an important eyewitness. Her boss, Abraham Zapruder, the owner of a Dallas clothing business, brought his 8-millimeter camera to the parade so that he could capture Kennedy's visit on film. Sitzman steadied Zapruder, who had vertigo, as he stood on a wall on the grassy knoll and filmed JFK during the final moments of his life. When the shots rang out, she kept her boss in place so he could record some of the most infamous seconds in history. Thanks to Sitzman's presence of mind, we have reasonably clear footage of the president's assassination.*

Sitzman remembered hearing shots coming from the School Book Depository, but she did not turn her head. "We kept our attention on what was happening exactly in front of us," she recalled, "and if you look at his film, there's very little jumping. It's very steady considering what was going on, and that's why I'm saying the sound we heard . . . the third sound still sounded a distance [away] because if it had been as close as everybody's trying to tell us, you know, twenty feet behind us [over the picket fence] . . . we would have jumped sky high." This is an important firsthand account that argues against a grassy knoll or picket fence shooter.† Zapruder and Sitzman could not have kept the camera steady if a second gunman had been firing in very close proximity. In that case, as Sitzman said, "That film would have been bounced all over the place."

Of course, in the Kennedy assassination mystery, few things are clear-cut and definitive. Sitzman, who passed away in 1993, also believed that the second gunman could have been using a silencer. "I have no qualms saying that I'm almost sure that there was someone behind the fence or in that area up

---

* You can see the footage for yourself at http://emuseum.jfk.org/view/objects/asitem /items@:32274.
† The picket fence is actually a stockade fence without the openings of a picket fence, but almost everyone refers to this element of Dealey Plaza as "the picket fence," so we will, too.

there [near the fence]," she asserted, "but I'm just as sure that they had silencers because there was no sound." Over the years, Sitzman was occasionally approached by researchers who she claimed were trying to coach her. Mark Lane, author of the conspiratorial bestseller *Rush to Judgment*, conducted a phone interview with her as he was finishing his manuscript. "Last words he said were, 'Now, you did hear those six shots behind you?'" she recalled. "I said, 'No, I never heard anything behind me.' 'Oh.' You know, I never heard from that man again." In addition, she described Oliver Stone's movie *JFK* as a "comic book type thing" even while acknowledging that it contains a number of truths.[35]

The Warren Commission should also have interviewed Elsie Dorman and Robert Croft, two amateur photographers who captured images of the president's motorcade as it drove through Dealey Plaza. Dorman filmed JFK from the fourth floor of the School Book Depository with "her husband's Kodak Brownie, Model 2 home movie camera." Although Dorman's footage is brief and shaky (she did not have any experience operating a movie camera), it clearly shows the president's car as well as people who were standing in vital Dealey Plaza spots. Robert Croft captured photos of JFK seconds before he died. In recent years, Dorman's and Croft's images have provided valuable clues to assassination researchers. The Dorman film helped one investigator discredit a story by the reporter Travis Lynn, who claimed he had left a tape recorder in Dealey Plaza on November 22. Dorman's film shows that there was no equipment anywhere near that location. Croft's still photos convinced the HSCA that Kennedy's suit jacket was bunched up at the neck at the time of his death—a key piece of evidence that might explain why the holes in his shirt and jacket weren't logically aligned with the bullet hole in his back.[36]

No one from the commission talked to Jim and Patricia Towner and their daughter Tina, either.[37] The Towners were taking film and photos in Dealey Plaza seconds before the assassination. While talking to a policeman and waiting for the motorcade, Jim Towner noticed a man in a "white coat" peering out of the sixth floor window of the School Book Depository. "And I didn't know who it was," he recalled. "And I told the patrolman, I said, 'That nut. He doesn't know that he can come down and watch it from the street.'" The policeman didn't bat an eye. Plenty of other people were hanging out of their office windows, he replied nonchalantly. Jim conceded the point and forgot about the man in the window, who was presumably Lee Oswald.

As the presidential motorcade passed, the Towners began walking back toward their car, parked near the railroad tracks on the other side of the picket fence, when they heard a loud popping noise. "Oh mercy, some fool is shooting firecrackers," said Mrs. Towner. "That's no firecracker," replied Jim, who had served in the military and was familiar with gunfire. "That's a thirty-[aught]-six rifle." He heard a total of three shots, which he thought had come from the Book Depository. Swept up in the nervous energy of the moment, he followed a crowd of "spectators" and "policemen" behind the picket fence and into the railroad yard, where he encountered "a white-uniformed black man with a cap" standing on the back of a Pullman dining car. "Did you see anybody coming this way?" someone in the crowd hollered. "No sir, I haven't seen anybody back here," said the porter, "and I've been back here watching the whole thing." Jim then proceeded to the grassy knoll, where he came across a man who was "shaking and crying." "Oh, he's dead. He's dead," the unidentified man sobbed. "The whole side of his head blew off."

Although the FBI eventually requisitioned the Towners' film and photos, no one from the bureau or the Warren Commission ever interviewed the family, even though they had important firsthand observations about several critical aspects of the assassination. "Well, I thought it was pretty stupid," Jim Towner commented in 1996 about the failure to reach out to the porter or his own family.[38] The porter, Carl Desroe, was not identified or interviewed by the commission, and before his death, he shared his story only with his pastor, Bishop Mark Herbener. Bishop Herbener was the first to identify Desroe in 2006. Desroe and his wife had been on the overpass before Kennedy's motorcade approached, but had been ordered off by unknown "officials." Desroe's wife, Amelia, told Herbener, "I saw some things . . . I'm afraid to tell anybody. I'll never tell anybody. I'm afraid for my life." Herbener knew the couple well. Desroe was the personal porter to the president of Katy Railroad. As for Amelia, Herbener said, "What she saw or thinks she saw, I have no idea. She wasn't a screwball. She was a pretty genuine person." Both Desroes are long deceased.[39]

These credible accounts show that the Warren Commission missed key witnesses who might have been able to clear up some of the confusion emerging from that day. But for whatever reason, the commission appears to have been particularly uninterested in strategically placed onlookers who believed that shots came from the picket fence area. Mary Woodward, Maggie Brown, Aurelia Lorenzo, and Anne Donaldson all worked for the *Dallas Morning News* in 1963 and all of them were standing on the north curb of Elm Street. They told the press that they heard shots coming from behind them, "a little to our right," and none ever heard from the Warren Commission. Neither did A. J. Millican, who had been standing near Woodward and her colleagues when he heard what he said were a total of eight shots coming from various directions, including two "from the arcade between the bookstore and the underpass" and three more "from the same direction, only farther back." John and Faye Chism also believed they heard shots coming from behind them; they were ignored.[40]

Nor did the Warren Commission thoroughly investigate a story told by Victoria Adams, a young woman who watched the president die from the fourth floor of the Texas School Book Depository. Adams said that after the shots were fired, she fled down the Depository's back stairwell, supposedly the same stairwell that Oswald used to make his escape from the sixth floor. Adams testified that she did not see or hear Oswald in the stairwell immediately after the assassination. The staff of the Warren Commission seemed to view Adams not as a vital witness but as a threat to their preferred timeline of events, and they alternately ignored and defamed her.[41]

Had the Warren Commission enlisted Dallas police and citizens to identify more of those present in the Plaza and Depository while their memories were fresh, they might have secured many more reliable accounts from every perspective that could have enabled the commission and the public to weigh the preponderance of the evidence. One result of a contemporaneous and vigorous search for witnesses in 1963 and 1964 would have been to diminish the credibility of some individuals who turned up years later with dramatic but questionable narratives about the assassination.

Gordon Arnold, like Jim Towner, said that he saw a man on the grassy knoll who was shaking and crying. In Arnold's version of the story, however, the weeping man pointed a gun at him and demanded his camera. "And he used some expletives to explain to me that he was going to have the camera, and I pitched it to him," he recalled. After ripping out the film, the man tossed the empty camera back to Arnold before he (and another unidentified person accompanying him) disappeared behind the picket fence. Arnold says that the crying man was wearing yellow-tinted shooter's goggles and what "looked like a Dallas police officer's uniform." He also claims that he heard shots whistling over his head that had originated from behind the picket fence, which caused him to lie flat on the ground. "It's not a noise," Arnold said in 1989, "You feel something go past you . . . You'll hear a noise following behind it, and to me, I knew I was dead because that was a bullet that just went over me." However, Arnold did not come forward until fifteen years after the assassination, in 1978. His son and widow confirmed in 2006 that they had heard him recount this story over the years, but families are sometimes told tall tales by a loved one. One anticonspiracy author, Gerald Posner, has claimed that Arnold is not visible in any photos, and that he probably wasn't present at all in Dealey Plaza.[42] But others who have closely studied the Arnold case strongly disagree. It is impossible to know for certain, but some aspects of Arnold's story match verified eyewitness anecdotes that Arnold could not have known about simply by reading published reports.[43]

Like Arnold, other apparent witnesses with blood-chilling tales popped up years later. A deaf-mute named Ed Hoffman claimed that he saw shady characters behind the picket fence on the day of the assassination. Hoping to catch a glimpse of the president, Hoffman positioned himself on the shoulder of Stemmons Freeway, "two hundred yards west of the parking lot behind the picket fence at an elevation of about the height of the first floor of the Texas School Book Depository." From this vantage point, he supposedly saw a man with a rifle running along the back side of the fence dressed in a suit, tie, and overcoat. According to Hoffman, the man tossed his rifle to a second man wearing a railroad worker's uniform; the second man hastily disassembled the weapon and crammed it into what looked like a railroad brakeman's tool bag. Both men then disappeared. Hoffman insists that he tried to report what he had seen to the authorities, but his communications handicap hindered him, and police never followed up on his story. Hoffman did not go public with his account until 1967. Are his observations accurate or did he invent them? Again, one cannot say for certain and experts on the assassination disagree, but Hoffman—who has been prominently featured in TV shows questioning the Warren Commission—has altered his tale when challenged, and his reported line of sight may not fit what he said he witnessed.[44]

Other late-emerging accounts seem largely unsubstantiated and highly improbable, but at this late date it is difficult to separate truth from fiction. Ken Duvall, a truck driver who occasionally made deliveries to the Book Depository, described a man in the grassy knoll area who was, or resembled, a railroad worker. Duvall says that he was sitting on the front steps of the Depository on the day of the assassination when he noticed a suspicious-looking vehicle. "[T]here was a black car, on our left side, parked parallel with the School Book Depository . . . When Kennedy's [car] came down Main Street to turn right, to come up to the School Book Depository . . . this guy was sitting here in the black car, he was waiting for [Kennedy] and them to turn right. And when he did, well he came up right by us—we're sitting on the third step—and we look down in the car, and . . . he has a pair of coveralls on, and he went down to the building there at the end of the [picket] fence, and got out, and was holding something under his coveralls." Duvall believes that the object was a rifle. "And it evidently had a silencer," he says, "because nobody . . . heard the [man's] shot." Duvall also says that he encountered Lee Oswald in a lunchroom on the second floor of the Book Depository thirty minutes before the presidential motorcade arrived. "We're gonna go out here and watch the president come by, you gonna go see him?" he supposedly asked Oswald. "Yeah, I'm gonna go see him." Duvall accepts the Warren Commission's conclusion that Oswald shot JFK from the Depository, but he thinks the fatal head wound was caused by the mystery man wearing coveralls.[45] Contrary to Duvall's account, though, no films or photos show a black car in the location he described, and no one who had wanted to catch a glimpse of Kennedy's limousine would have been sitting on the steps of the Depository behind a crowd of standing spectators.

Victoria Rodriguez's story seems equally suspect, both because of its very tardy telling and the lack of confirming testimony from others on scene. In 2010—forty-seven years after the assassination—Rodriguez came forward with an elaborate story about three suspicious-looking men who she says were milling around behind the picket fence right before the assassination. Rodriguez was thirteen years old in 1963. On November 22, she and several of her schoolmates were in a car parked near the Book Depository waiting for their chaperone, who was chatting with another adult. That's when she says she saw a man in a cap and coveralls who looked "like one of those Saturday . . . matinee kind of characters that you would immediately identify as a railroad man." He was standing on the railroad bridge overlooking Dealey Plaza. One of Rodriguez's friends insisted that the man wasn't supposed to be on the bridge. When someone asked why, the girl replied, "Because my father is a manager in that railroad yard over there . . . and he told us at breakfast this morning that we could not go over there because government men had come and said that . . . not even any of the employees could be up on the bridges or anywhere where they had any kind of sightline to the motorcade route."[46] Rodriguez claims that the railroad man signaled to a second man who was lurking near a tree, and that the second man was dressed in a bomber jacket, a "hunter's plaid shirt," casual slacks, and a bolo tie. A third man arrived shortly afterwards in "a blue . . . nondescript Chevrolet." He was in his twenties, Rodriguez says, and was wearing a dark blue outfit that looked like a gas station attendant's uniform (she has since nicknamed these three men "tall-blue," "railroad-man," and "bolo-tie"). Tall-blue was wearing a blank name patch on his uniform. She heard him say, "I'm sorry I was held up, you know I couldn't help it." "[A]nd so anyway as bolo-tie comes up he looks over at me," Rodriguez recalls, "and he gives me a calculating glance . . . to kind of assess the threat . . . and I of course quickly . . . looked away, but I knew my timing and I looked back at them. When they came up and [tall-blue] was apologizing [but] bolo-tie shushed him immediately." Bolo-tie supposedly said, "We don't have time for that now" before speaking in hushed tones. Rodriguez then saw bolo-tie hand tall-blue a package in a strange spinning motion that reminded her of a marching band maneuver. After that, both men got in their cars and drove away, while railroad-man hustled down the track "lickity split" and disappeared. Although suspicious, Rodriguez says she put the incident out of her mind until she saw a young man in a sporting goods store one day buying a firearm. Right then, she says, a lightbulb went off. "[A]nd here was this package-looking thing, the same dimensions, the same shape, about as long as a man's thigh, and flat rectangular ... And bam, it put me right there looking at that package change hands with these fellows." Rodriguez says she suddenly realized that bolo-tie had given tall-blue a rifle.[47]

There is no shortage of strange tales from Dealey Plaza, some told by law enforcement personnel who were present for the assassination or its aftermath. For example, Deputy Sheriff Roger Craig claims that he was standing in front of the courthouse on Main Street when he heard the shots. Trained to respond in a crisis, Craig made the short trip over to Dealey Plaza. While questioning witnesses and searching for clues, he heard someone whistle. "I turned and saw a white male in his twenties running down the grassy knoll from the direction of the Texas School Book Depository building," he later recalled. "A light green Rambler station wagon was coming slowly west on Elm Street.[48] The driver of the station wagon was a husky looking Latin, with dark wavy hair, wearing a tan windbreaker type jacket. He was looking up at the man running toward him. He pulled over to the north curb and picked up the man coming down the hill." Craig says that heavy traffic prevented him from stopping the vehicle and that it sped away traveling west on Elm Street. He says he then walked over to the Depository and asked to speak with someone in charge. A man in a gray suit identified himself as a Secret Service agent. At first, the man seemed uninterested in Craig's story, but then started taking notes when Craig mentioned the station wagon. Later that day, Craig stopped by Dallas police headquarters. When he saw Lee Oswald, he identified him as the man he had seen running down the grassy knoll. Craig also says that he asked Oswald about the Rambler. "That station wagon belongs to Mrs. Paine," Oswald supposedly replied, "Don't try to drag her into this."[49] Oswald then allegedly added, "Everybody will know who I am now." Dallas police captain Fritz did not believe Craig's story and said that the officer never set foot inside Oswald's interrogation room and therefore had no opportunity for a conversation. Whose testimony should we believe?[50] Although there are problems with Craig's account, where you stand on this one, like so many other aspects of November 22, depends on where you sit—with the lone gunman conclusion or a conspiracy theory.

One aspect of Craig's testimony is especially noteworthy: his alleged encounter with a Secret Service agent. Other witnesses, many reliable, claim to have seen or talked to one or more Secret Service agents in Dealey Plaza that day. But the Secret Service—whose agents are trained to stay with the president and other protectees in the event of an emergency—has always insisted that none of its employees was on the ground at Dealey Plaza in the immediate aftermath of the shooting. The Warren Commission confirmed this fact by tracing the movements of all agents assigned to the Dallas motorcade.[51] However, Dallas officer Joe Marshall Smith was one of the first policemen to climb the grassy knoll to the parking lot behind the picket fence.[52] Told by a witness that the shots had come from the bushes, Smith drew his revolver. "He was beginning to feel, as he put it, 'damn silly' when he came across a man standing by a car. The man reacted quickly to the sight of Smith and an accompanying deputy. As Smith remembered it, 'The man, this character, produces credentials from his hip pocket which showed him to be Secret Service. I have seen those credentials before, and they satisfied me and the deputy sheriff [who was with Smith]. So I immediately accepted that and let him go and continued our search around the cars.'"[53] According to Smith, the man was wearing casual clothes and had grime under his fingernails. Gordon Arnold also reported the law enforcement officer who took his camera film was a man with dirty fingernails. Without any explanation or additional investigation,[54] the Warren Commission accepted the Secret Service's recommendation that it disregard Smith's story.[55] Smith was a dependable, low-key officer, and no one has suggested he was given to embellishment. This is one of the nagging examples of credible testimony that makes a reasonable person question the conclusions of the Warren Commission. Who was the individual with Secret Service credentials, when those who should know insist no real Secret Service agents could have been at that location?[56] Perhaps more disturbing was the official handling of Smith's statement. It suggests an ostrichlike approach to the evidence: Clues that may have strengthened the case for conspiracy were set aside or downplayed by the commission.

Robert Blakey, the former chief counsel and staff director of the House Select Committee on Assassinations, believes that Smith was telling the truth. "He met somebody coming, and the guy identified himself as a Secret Service agent. There were no Secret Service agents up there. And when they got behind the picket fence, it had been raining that day, and the ground was damp. There were footprints where the person [on] the grassy knoll was supposed to [have been] and . . . he had wiped mud off his feet [on] one of the cars that was there. This is testimony that's consistent with somebody being there." In addition, Blakey theorizes that the person behind the fence might have been a Mafia hit man sent to kill Oswald after he assassinated the president. "It's a standard mob format," he says. "Somebody always kills the assassin. And then you kill the people who killed the assassin."[57]

In addition to Smith, another completely believable eyewitness is Pierce Allman, the program director for WFAA radio. Allman chose the critical corner of Elm and Houston to observe the motorcade. Just seconds before the shots, Kennedy passed within a few feet of him, and Allman reports having shouted, "Welcome to Dallas, Mr. President," among the last words the president likely heard. Allman was also one of the first to reach the Newmans as they lay sprawled across the lower grassy knoll, asking them, "Are you all right?" And then Allman's journalistic instincts came to the fore, and he realized he needed to find a telephone. The Depository was logically the closest place, and at the door he asked a young man who was exiting the building where he could make a call. The man helpfully pointed out a place inside. That man was Lee Oswald as he was leaving the Depository. Oswald told police about the encounter with Allman as he attempted to account for his whereabouts after the shooting. The Secret Service eventually figured out it was Allman and discussed the incident with him later. Allman told them the timing and gave a general description of Oswald—but he also told them something interesting. After Allman had been on the telephone in the Depository for a few minutes, a man identifying himself as belonging to "Army Intelligence" told Allman to hang up the phone and leave. The Secret Service told Allman he must have been mistaken because no one from Army Intelligence was on the scene. But Allman is certain of what he heard. The man may have been James Powell, a specialist from the Army Intelligence Corps, who was at Love Field and then the corner of Elm and Houston to observe the motorcade, apparently as just an interested bystander. Powell snapped a photo of the Depository about thirty seconds after the shooting, when a bystander pointed to it as the source of some or all of the shots.[58]

Another eyewitness, Malcolm Summers, claims to have seen a strange man on the grassy knoll. Summers says he was standing in the middle of Dealey Plaza, opposite the knoll, when he saw the president struck by a bullet. A motorcycle cop who had been escorting the motorcade immediately threw down his bike and stood directly in front of Summers. "[He] looked straight in my direction like he was going to pull his gun," the Dallas native remembered. "[H]e was looking at me, and I knew he wasn't looking at me, but I mean, in my direction. I thought, well, somebody behind me was doing the firing, and because I thought that . . . I fell down, I hit the ground." Summers eventually got up and followed a crowd across the street toward the picket fence. There he encountered a clean-shaven, well-dressed man with a coat over his arm. Summers spotted a gun underneath the man's coat. "You better not come up here," the man warned. "You could get shot."[59] Declining to argue with an armed man, Summers retreated back across the street to his office on Houston Street. A short time later, he departed work. "When I was leaving, I noticed . . . three Spanish-looking guys jump in their car, and they were leaving from the front of the post office where they were parked," Summers recalled, adding that the three men seemed like they were "in a hurry" and "left at a great speed." They drove in the direction of Oak Cliff, a neighborhood suburb of Dallas. Summers says he did not think much of the incident until he later learned that Lee Harvey Oswald had allegedly headed for Oak

Cliff, Officer J. D. Tippit was shot there, and Jack Ruby had once lived in the neighborhood.[60]

The armed man Summers saw on the grassy knoll might have been a co-conspirator in the president's death, or he just as easily could have been a Dallas County sheriff. In 1963 the sheriff's office stood on the corner of Main and Houston Streets. Houston connects Main with Elm, and thus was very near Dealey Plaza. Law enforcement personnel apparently poured out of the building after the shots were fired. The "Spanish-looking guys" could have been anti-Castro Cubans who had taken part in the assassination as revenge for the Bay of Pigs and were on their way to meet Oswald or Ruby—or the whole episode could have been innocent and unrelated to JFK's killing. Even though Summers gave a prompt statement to the sheriff's office and the Secret Service interviewed him on two separate occasions, the authorities apparently made no comprehensive efforts to identify the men Summers saw while the trail was hot.[61]

Then there is the seemingly trustworthy account of Earlene Roberts, the woman who ran the Dallas boarding house where Oswald stayed most of the time, and who told the Warren Commission that she had been watching television in the living room at around one P.M. on November 22 when Oswald rushed in and went straight to his room. That is when Roberts supposedly saw a police cruiser:

> WARREN COMMISSION STAFFER: Did this police car stop directly in front of your house?
> MRS. ROBERTS: Yes—it stopped directly in front of my house and it just [went] "tip-tip" [the sound of the horn being tapped twice] and that's the way Officer Alexander and Charles Burnely would do when they stopped, and I went to the door and looked and saw it wasn't their [squad car] number.[62]

Why did an unidentified police car honk twice in front of Oswald's boarding house while he was inside, just after the assassination? Was it a prearranged signal from his coconspirators or handlers, or just another coincidence? Is it possible that Roberts's police friends were riding in a different cruiser that day and drove off when they were ordered by radio to another location? Or is conspiracy author James Douglass right to conjecture that "the horn signal to Oswald came from two uniformed men in a counterfeit police car" who were part of a clandestine group of assassins?[63] Douglass's assertion seems fantastic, yet so many peculiar things happened that cruel day in Dallas—things that were unexplained and, unfortunately, unexplored at a time when they might have been clarified.

Dallas officer Marvin Wise told another odd but ultimately truthful story that has been elucidated only in recent years. Shortly after the shots were fired, Wise learned that three men (later known as "the three tramps") had been seen climbing into a boxcar in the rail yard behind the Book Depository. By acting quickly, he managed to apprehend the suspects before they could escape and turned them over to the Dallas County sheriff's office.[64] Photos taken in November 1963 (which were not made available to the public until the 1970s) as well as police records released in 1989 show that a trio of men were taken into custody but released a short time later. For years, conspiracy theorists claimed that one of the men was Charles Harrelson, the father of actor Woody Harrelson.[65] Frank Sturgis and Howard Hunt, both key figures in the 1972 Watergate break-in at the Democratic National Committee headquarters, were also named from time to time as suspected members of the "tramp" group (they were not). But the least convincing source for the Harrelson-did-it theory was Harrelson himself. Harrelson had ties to organized crime and was convicted in 1982 of murdering a federal judge in Texas. Looking for a way out of a long jail sentence, the newly arrested and cocaine-high Harrelson "confessed" to being part of a team of Kennedy assassins and offered the prosecutors a deal: He would identify the other team members if he could walk free. The authorities were not foolish enough to buy Harrelson's story, and he later admitted he invented it. In 1989 the Dallas Police finally released files that showed the "three tramps" were actually unfortunate unknowns named Gus Abrams, Harold Doyle, and John Gedney—drifters who just happened to be in the wrong place at the wrong time.[66]*

While some of the witness accounts are disquieting because of their implications for possible conspiracy, there are also pro-conspiracy testimonies that are as doubtful as Harrelson's and Hunt's assertions. Jean Hill is one Dealey Plaza witness who saw her opportunities and took them, making it up as she went along and fooling many. Hill and her friend Mary Moorman were standing in the center of Dealey Plaza (opposite the grassy knoll) when they saw Kennedy's motorcade pass by. "Hey, Mr. President," Hill shouted, "we want to take your picture." When she heard the shots ring out, Moorman urged her friend to take cover. But Hill says that she was oblivious to the danger and kept her eyes focused on the surrounding area. "I looked up and saw a flash of light, a puff of smoke from the knoll," she said, "And I knew a shot

---

* On his deathbed, E. Howard Hunt told his son, on videotape no less, that he had been one of the tramps, and this dramatic "revelation" has been widely circulated. Perhaps he was seeking one last historically significant dose of villainy for his obituary, or maybe he was playing a final macabre trick. But Hunt had not been one of the Dallas tramps, proving once and for all that deathbed confessions are not always truthful.

had come from there and I kept looking . . ." Hill maintained she saw a man in a brown hat and overcoat "walking faster than . . . normal" from the Book Depository toward the rail yard. His name? According to Hill, it was Jack Ruby. Suspicious, Hill followed Ruby (she says she didn't know his name at the time), and that's when she reported being stopped by another man who flashed a badge and identified himself as a Secret Service agent. He allegedly confiscated a set of Polaroid pictures that Hill had been holding for Moorman. "You are coming with me," the man supposedly told her. Hill says that when she refused, the man put her neck in a Vulcan death grip and was soon joined by another man, who helped escort her to a room on "about the fourth or fifth floor in the Courts Building." Other shadowy figures in the room asked her how many shots she had heard. "Four to six," Hill replied. No, she had only heard three, they insisted. Hill also claimed to have seen a patrolman on the grassy knoll holding a rifle instead of a standard issue police shotgun.

However, in her original police statement on November 22, Hill said that she was turned back by officers when she got to the grassy knoll and that a "Mr. Featherstone" escorted her to the Dallas County sheriff's office. Jim Featherston, a reporter for the *Dallas Times Herald*, and Mary Moorman both confirmed this initial version of Hill's experience. Hill also gave a widely seen interview to a local TV station shortly after the assassination, but did not mention the flash of light, the puff of smoke, the man in the brown overcoat, the men on the grassy knoll, or the interrogation in the Courts Building. Therefore, we can reasonably assume that Hill, now deceased, fabricated parts of her story.

In 2011, Mary Moorman gave her most extensive interview since the assassination. Moorman, not Hill, took the most famous still photograph of the moment the fatal bullet struck John Kennedy—a photo that may or may not show a man in a uniform behind the picket fence, and an apparent puff of white smoke that may or may not have been the aftermath of a gunshot. More recently, Moorman told me that she does not recall seeing anything out of the ordinary behind the fence, and she is not at all convinced that her famous photograph reveals a second shooter.[67] Interestingly, Moorman's sightline positioning and exceptionally important snapshot won her an actual invitation to give testimony to the Warren Commission staff, but she injured her ankle and asked for a postponement. She never heard from the commission again, despite having taken the photo that is perhaps the most revealing supplement to the Zapruder film.[68]

Jean Hill's creativity may only be outdone by a U.S. Air Force sergeant named Robert Vinson. Vinson says that he boarded a C-54 cargo plane at Andrews Air Force Base on November 22 that he assumed, or was told, was traveling to Denver. Vinson and his wife lived in Colorado at the time. The sergeant says that the aircraft "bore no military markings or serial numbers" and that two men wearing "olive drab coveralls" (also with "no markings") got on board with him. Instead of flying to Colorado, though, the plane "landed abruptly in a rough, sandy area alongside the Trinity River" in Dallas at three P.M. CST and picked up two men—a Latino and a Caucasian man Vinson identified as a Lee Harvey Oswald look-alike. The plane then took off and landed at Roswell Air Force Base in New Mexico. From there, Vinson says, he hopped a bus to Colorado. Beyond a complete lack of corroborating evidence, Vinson's story contains at least one major flaw: The section of the Trinity River that cuts through Dallas is bordered by two major roadways, the Stemmons Freeway and Industrial Boulevard. Therefore, it seems somewhat unlikely that a C-54, a propeller plane with a wingspan of 117 feet, could have made a safe sand landing next to dual thoroughfares in the middle of the afternoon without anyone's noticing, especially on a day when police and reporters were swarming.[69]

Why would Vinson make up such a story? In his case and others, no one can say with certainty, but a desire for money or attention—often granted to almost anyone who has "new information" or a novel theory about the assassination—might be one reason. More than a few have cashed in over the previous half century. While there are many legitimate researchers who have spent much of their own time and money to investigate the assassination, there are others who have sought treasure from the tragedy.

Occasionally, a central figure in the November 22 saga will shift his or her story. Motives can only be guessed at, but the conspiracy pot is usually stirred as a result. One need look no further than Lee Harvey Oswald's widow, Marina, who remarried two years after the assassination to a Texas Instruments employee, Kenneth Jess Porter, and is still living in the suburbs of Dallas.[70] Marina told the Warren Commission that she believed her first husband shot JFK, but she later recanted—without any specific evidence being presented to support her change.[71] Retired Dallas policeman Jim Leavelle, best remembered as the detective in a beige cowboy hat standing next to Oswald as Ruby pulled the trigger, has had meals from time to time with Marina and her husband, and also with Lee's brother, Robert Oswald.[72]

This previously undisclosed bond will startle most people. It seems odd but it is compelling. After all, these individuals had their lives forever and involuntarily transformed by the actions of Lee Oswald, and together they were caught up in a maelstrom only the participants could fully comprehend. At one such dinner years after the assassination, Leavelle remembers that Marina was "sounding him out" to see if he had changed or would change his opinion about Oswald's guilt. The crusty, plain-spoken Leavelle thinks that assassination researchers had told Oswald's widow that, " '[Lee] didn't shoot anybody, he was a patsy, somebody else done the shooting and they were putting it on [Lee].'[73] And then so I said, 'Well, that's hogwash, of course. It just didn't happen that way.' "[74] In time, Marina Oswald Porter not only changed her story but began insisting on payment for interviews. Henry Hurt, a seasoned reporter who penned stories for *Readers' Digest* and wrote a bestseller on the Kennedy assassination, said, "Every time I talked to her, it was off the record because we wouldn't pay. [Once] we talked theoretically and I said, 'Well, what would you give me for [several thousand dollars]?' She replied, 'I'll just say anything you want for that much.' " Hurt researched the Kennedy murder for many years, and kept up with Oswald's widow. "Marina told her story forty different ways," he reports.[75]

Another Oswald who frequently changed her story and demanded money for interviews was Lee's mother, Marguerite. On the day of the assassination, she called the *Fort Worth Star Telegram* looking for a ride into Dallas. CBS's Bob Schieffer was then a cub reporter for the *Star Telegram* and just happened to pick up the phone when Marguerite called. "And I said, 'Lady, we're not running a taxi service here. Besides, the president's been shot,' " Schieffer recalls. "So she says, 'Yes, I heard it on the radio, I think my son is the one they have arrested.' Well, I immediately dropped this business about not running a taxi service and I said, 'Where are you? I'll come out and get you.' " Schieffer quickly roped in a co-worker and his car, and they chauffeured Marguerite from Fort Worth to Dallas police headquarters. "I interviewed her on the way, and it was obviously the biggest story I'd ever gotten. She was truly an evil person. She was a lunatic. She was obsessed with money. She had actually worked for a time as a governess or au pair for the publisher of the *Star Telegram*, Amon Carter, Jr., and Mrs. Carter had let her go because she had tried to extort money from the children, trying to get their allowance money, selling them little carved soap [figures] and things like that. I mean she was truly obsessed and on the way to Dallas she kept saying to me that everybody will be sympathetic to [her son's] wife and 'nobody will remember momma' and 'I'll die, I won't have any means of income and what's going to happen to me?' And the things that she was saying were so harsh that I didn't put some of them in the paper." In the years that followed, Schieffer says, Marguerite occasionally contacted him to see if CBS would pay her for an interview. "And I said, 'No, we don't do that.' And she would say, 'Well, I really need some money and I know some things.' Well, she didn't know anything by that time. I guess she got paid for a couple of interviews and she basically lived out her life selling [her son's] clothes and things of that nature to souvenir hunters [until] she finally passed away."[76]

Exposure to the truth about Oswald's very unusual mother, upbringing, and life make it easier to understand why Oswald may have undertaken the assassination—although the word "why" presumes an underlying rationality that might not have existed in this deeply troubled individual. Thus, the glaring inadequacies of the Warren Commission inquiry do not automatically mean that the commission erred in fingering Oswald as the lone gunman.[77] Much testimony supports the commission viewpoint. Tom Dillard, a photographer for the *Dallas Morning News* in 1963, has long accepted the conclusions of the Warren Commission report. On the day of the parade, he had hoped to be able to ride directly in front of the president's limousine on a flatbed truck, but the Secret Service, concerned about evacuating Kennedy in an emergency, nixed the idea. Instead, Dillard was placed in a convertible several cars behind the presidential limousine. Dillard was on Houston Street, passing the Dallas County sheriff's office, when he heard the shots. He dismissed the first one as a "torpedo" (a large firecracker that can explode underwater). But when he heard the second shot, he realized it was rifle fire. At the third shot, Dillard says he exclaimed, "My God, they've killed him."

Bob Jackson, a photographer for the *Dallas Times Herald* who was in the car with Dillard, said, "There's a guy with a rifle up in that window." "I said, 'Where?'" Dillard recalled during a 1993 interview, "Bob says, 'In that window up on that building right there' . . . And by that time, I shot a picture with the wide-angle camera." His photo captured Bonnie Ray Williams and Harold Norman peering out of the fifth floor corner window of the Book Depository; above their heads can be seen some of the boxes from the "sniper's nest"—but no Oswald. Dillard has lost sleep over the years thinking about what might have been. If he had only "shot it a little quicker," he might have captured Oswald in the window. But Dillard firmly believes the shots came from the Depository's sixth floor window.[78] Mal Couch, a WFAA-TV cameraman, was also in the car with Dillard. He confirmed that Jackson said he saw a rifleman in the Book Depository. "And I looked up in the window and saw about a foot of the rifle going back in the window."[79]

Just after the shots, Couch and the other journalists ordered the driver to stop their car, and they jumped out. As Couch moved down the street toward the grassy knoll, he noted that "There were guys there, and I'm sure they were Secret Service men or FBI . . . And one of them reached down, and he picked up something. And I walked past him. It was a piece of brain matter that had been in the street." According to Couch, the man was dressed in a gray suit or a coat and tie and simply walked away with what appeared to be a piece of Kennedy's brain or skull that was "probably around three or four inches long."

No one has ever conclusively identified this individual. However, it is possible he was the person who handed Dallas County deputy Seymour Weitzman a skull fragment.[80] Weitzman testified to the Warren Commission that, within ten minutes of the assassination, "[S]omebody brought me a piece of what he thought to be a firecracker . . . but I turned it over to one of the Secret Service men and I told them it should go to the lab because it looked to me like human bone. I later found out it was supposedly a portion of the president's skull."[81]

Weitzman himself had been standing at the corner of Main and Houston, just a few dozen yards from the presidential limousine when the shots were fired. As befits his law enforcement training, he ran toward the limo in time to see it speed away, then immediately scaled the wall at the top of the grassy knoll, next to the picket fence, because that's where a bystander told him the shots had come from. He saw the rail yards behind the knoll before just about anyone, and reported to the Warren Commission, "We noticed numerous kinds of footprints that did not make sense because they were going [in] different directions." The commission interrogator asked Weitzman, "Were there other people there besides you?" "Yes, sir, other officers, Secret Service as well." Here is more reliable testimony that Secret Service officers, or people impersonating them, were present in Dealey Plaza at the time of, or immediately after, the shooting. The Warren Commission staff did not further question Weitzman about this, asked him for no names, and never bothered to reconcile Weitzman's testimony (and the statements of others we have cited) with the commission's firm conclusion that no Secret Service personnel were present in Dealey Plaza.[82]

AS THESE CONFLICTING examples demonstrate, it is difficult to separate fact from fiction when dealing with eyewitness accounts of events on November 22, 1963. Human beings notice different things during a crisis, and they see only a small part of the whole. They also tend to confuse media reports and the stories of other eyewitnesses with what they actually saw or heard.[83] And of course, some people will make wild statements to garner attention. The result is a hodgepodge of truths, half-truths, blatant falsehoods, and sensational embellishments. Decades after the assassination, people pop up who claim to have been in Dealey Plaza or on the grassy knoll at precisely the moment of the assassination.[84] Because the local police and then the Warren Commission did not catalog and contact many key Dealey Plaza witnesses, it is very difficult to verify or disprove new accounts. Maybe the individuals coming forward are honest, or perhaps they wanted to be at a seismic historical event so badly that they invented a personal association. Retired Dallas officer Leavelle notes that if everyone who claims to have been on the grassy knoll on November 22 had actually been there, "You couldn't put them in the Rose Bowl."[85]

One theory that explains all, or even a preponderance, of the testimony is impossible to achieve—unless one approaches the explosive subject with a predetermined answer. This has been the path chosen by most authors and filmmakers. Naturally, potentially fallible judgments must be made by any researcher. Some witnesses' statements ring true. Others are a mixture of accurate and inaccurate observations by people sincerely trying to recall the most dramatic moments of their lives—a few seconds of chaos in a large, noisy crowd, with only fragments recollected about what happened before and after the shots. The memories have also been infected by an avalanche of news coverage that continued for years, as well as hundreds of personal conversations about this seminal event with family and friends. Inevitably, some witnesses have been mistaken, and a few have made up their versions. One thing is certain: They cannot all be right, given the inherent contradictions.

A fair investigation can only reach a truthful conclusion once all the relevant testimony has been considered and compared. That the Warren Commission failed to do so is obvious to any unbiased investigator. In the days, weeks, and months following November 22, the trail was hot and memories were at their sharpest. The commission had the strong backing of Congress and the country, and whatever money and staff were needed to produce a thorough report would have been forthcoming. While impatient, the public would have been willing to give the investigators the time they required to produce complete answers. Instead, many critical witnesses were overlooked, many paths were not taken and tips not pursued, and a political schedule—not an investigator's timetable—determined the release date. Those responsible for these decisions would say the nation needed to move on. Yet the irony of the commission's rushed and predigested report is that the nation was caught in a time warp for years. Instead of shutting the door on cynical and destructive assassination speculation, the Warren Commission maximized the opportunities for it.

8

11/22/63: QUESTIONS, ANSWERS, MYSTERIES

HUGH AYNESWORTH, A JOURNALIST WHO covered the Kennedy assassination for the *Dallas Morning News* and has followed the attendant controversies for decades, is unable to reconcile all the disparate accounts of the chaotic assassination scene, yet he's skeptical that they add up to a conspiracy. "There's never been a homicide investigated to this extent in the history of the world," Aynesworth remarked. "There are people who believe this, believe that, want to believe it, need to believe it. But it isn't there." Like many, Aynesworth initially thought that the Russians might have been behind 11/22.[1] But today he is convinced that Oswald acted alone, and he suspects that a domestic argument between Oswald and his wife could have been the tipping point that sent him over the edge.[2] "She [Marina] ridiculed him constantly," says Aynesworth. "And rightfully so, I would say. Here's a guy that would spend money on having things printed up for the Fair Play for Cuba Committee and would run around here, there, and everywhere spending money that he didn't have, living off neighbors, living in wretched places, not eating well. I would have been pissed at him, too." Aynesworth is astonished that his fellow Americans continue to believe in an 11/22 conspiracy. "It's just weird," he says.[3]

Maybe Hugh Aynesworth and others who believe as he does are right; maybe there was no conspiracy. Maybe Oswald committed the crime of the century without any help. But fifty years later, some things still do not add up, and it is unlikely this murder will ever be solved to the satisfaction of many, if not most, Americans. I do not presume to know for certain what happened on November 22, 1963, and we are long past the point when all the mysteries can be cleared up. But what is still possible after the passage of fifty years is to present the evidence most acknowledge to be true, and from there to offer the most reasonable explanations that can be mustered—and also eliminate the least plausible hypotheses. Naturally, not all the questions in this untidy murder can be answered fully. There are leftover paradoxes galore.

* * *

AN UNDERSTANDING OF Lee Harvey Oswald is essential to unraveling the events that unfolded on November 22. He was born on October 18, 1939, in New Orleans and endured a tumultuous childhood. He never knew his father, Robert Oswald, Sr., who had died of a heart attack before Lee was born. As Lee's brother Robert once commented, their mother made it quite clear on numerous occasions that her children were a burden to her.[4] At one point, Oswald's mother, Marguerite, decided that she could no longer work and rear children at the same time, and so she placed Lee and his two brothers in an orphanage. One sibling was Lee's half brother from Marguerite's first unsuccessful marriage, in the mid-1930s. In 1944 she moved the family to Dallas and married for a third time the next year, to Edwin Ekdahl. The marriage quickly fell apart, however, and Marguerite returned to New Orleans. A few years later, she took Lee to New York City.

As the Warren Commission noted, "The ensuing year and one-half in New York was marked by Lee's refusals to attend school and by emotional and psychological problems of a seemingly serious nature." He was sent to Youth House, a public treatment facility for juvenile delinquents. A social worker there described Lee as an "emotionally starved, affectionless youngster" who liked to keep to himself. When he continued to get in trouble at school, a New York court recommended that he receive additional psychotherapy. But before that could happen, Marguerite abruptly moved the family back to New Orleans in 1954. Oswald soon dropped out of school and worked a series of odd jobs. "It was during this period that he started to read Communist literature," reported the Warren Commission. "Occasionally, in conversations with others, he praised Communism and expressed to his fellow employees a desire to join the Communist Party. At about this time, when he was not yet seventeen, he wrote to the Socialist Party of America, professing his belief in Marxism." Oswald briefly returned to school when his mother moved to Fort Worth, but he left for good and joined the Marine Corps in October 1956.[5]

Oswald had a checkered career in the Marines. Two months after he enlisted, he shot a score of 212 with an M-1 rifle, a full "two points over the score required for a 'sharpshooter' qualification, the second highest in the Marine Corps."[6] In 1957 he received radar and aircraft surveillance training before receiving a transfer to a Marine air base in Atsugi, Japan (close to Tokyo). At the time, Atsugi served as an operational base for the U-2 spy plane, America's most sophisticated military aircraft. The U-2 could take pictures, jam enemy radar, and avoid missiles by flying at an eye-popping altitude of 90,000 feet. Oswald worked in a radar unit that kept track of U-2 flights, though he did not have direct access to the plane itself. He had barely gotten settled in Japan when he learned that he was being sent to the Philippines for additional training. Upset by the news, Oswald shot himself in the arm with a .22-caliber

pistol. He was sent to the Philippines anyway and court-martialed for possession of an illegal firearm. The military fined Oswald and sentenced him to
twenty days of hard labor.

Oswald's military career went further downhill after that. In June 1958 he
poured a drink over the head of a sergeant whom he blamed for assigning
him extra kitchen duties. This led to a second court martial and twenty-eight
days in the brig at hard labor. Oswald was then transferred to a Marine base
located near El Toro, California. All the while, he was growing more and
more interested in Communism. At the El Toro base, Oswald immersed himself in the Russian language by reading Russian books and blaring Russian
records—much to the chagrin of his fellow Marines. He also tried and failed
to pass a Marine proficiency exam in spoken and written Russian. He preached
the merits of socialism so often that some of his acquaintances began referring
to him as "Comrade Oswaldskovich," a nickname that Oswald relished. He
and another Marine, Nelson Delgado, spoke in glowing terms about the
revolution in Cuba and toyed with the idea of traveling to Havana to join
the fight.[7]

Delgado advised Oswald to write to the Cuban embassy in Washington,
and Oswald would later say that he got in touch with Cuban diplomats. Delgado began noticing letters addressed to Oswald that were affixed with the
Cuban official seal and heard his friend say that he had visited the Cuban
consulate in Los Angeles. One night, Delgado saw Oswald at the front gates
of the El Toro base talking to a stranger, possibly Cuban (in Delgado's estima-
tion), wearing an overcoat. Delgado also claimed that Oswald asked him to
put a duffel bag in a locker at the Los Angeles bus station. Intrigued by his
friend's request, Delgado rummaged through the duffel bag and found pictures of U.S. fighter jets, raising the question of whether Oswald was spying
for the Cuban government.[8]

Why the U.S. Marine Corps allowed Oswald to promulgate Communist
propaganda among its soldiers at the height of the Cold War, when anticommunist witch hunts were all the rage, is puzzling to say the least. A captain
named Robert Block seems to be the only one who confronted Oswald about
his leftist leanings after Block found out that the private was reading magazines such as *The Worker*. Oswald told Block that he was simply trying to
learn more about the enemy, a flimsy excuse the captain reluctantly accepted.
In August 1959 Oswald applied for a hardship discharge, claiming that his
mother had injured herself at work and needed his support; in reality, Marguerite was fine. At the same time, he applied for a passport, listing Switzerland, Finland, England, France, Germany, Russia, Cuba, and the Dominican
Republic as the places he intended to visit. Both applications were approved.
Oswald told the passport office that he planned on attending Albert Sch-

weitzer College in Switzerland and Turku University in Finland. Oswald's application to Schweitzer shows his manipulative character. In the "remarks" section, he wrote, "Please inform me of the amount of the deposit (if required) so I can forward it and confirm my reservation, and show my sincerity of purpose. Thank you." Oswald could not have been more insincere. He had no intention of enrolling at Schweitzer. This was his way of getting to Europe so that he could defect to the Soviet Union.[9]

In September 1959, Oswald took a bus to Forth Worth to visit his mother. Marguerite was surprised when her son told her that he was leaving to sail to Europe in order to take a job with an import-export business. She did not know that her son had decided to defect. By appearances, at least, Oswald was convinced that Communism was the wave of the future and that the Soviets might recognize his talents and put him in charge of something important. On September 20, 1959, Oswald boarded a freighter bound for France. From there he traveled to England and then to Helsinki, Finland, where he rented rooms in two pricey hotels, the Torni and the Klaus Kurki. On October 12, Oswald applied for a tourist visa at the local Soviet consulate. His application was approved two days later and he left for Moscow. At the time, friends said Oswald was careful with his money. It seems strange that he could have afforded meals, first-class hotels, and airfare on a Marine private's salary, suggesting either that he had saved up the cash or someone else was covering his expenses.[10]

The CIA claims that it first became aware of Oswald when he tried to renounce his citizenship at the U.S. embassy in Moscow on October 31, 1959. "I've thought this thing over very carefully and I know what I'm doing," he told the consul. "I was just discharged from the Marine Corps on September eleventh and I have been planning to do this for two years." Oswald went on to explain that he had been a radar operator for the Marines and that he planned on sharing what he knew with Soviet officials. When the consul informed the ex-Marine that he needed to wait a few days before he could fill out the necessary paperwork, Oswald left in a huff and never went back. Embassy staff immediately cabled the CIA at Langley about the incident.[11]

The news didn't stay confidential for long. The following day, the *Washington Post* ran a story entitled "Ex-Marine Asks Soviet Citizenship," which quoted Oswald as saying that he would "never return to the United States for any reason." The paper also reported that Oswald was the "third American to have sought to renounce his citizenship and stay in Russia in recent months." The other two defectors were Nichols Petrulli, a sheet metal worker from Valley Stream, New York, and Robert Webster, a plastics expert from Cleveland, Ohio, who had gone to Moscow in connection with the American National Exhibition—the site where Vice President Richard Nixon and Soviet premier

Nikita Khrushchev engaged in their famous "kitchen debate" during a Nixon trip to the USSR.[12]

The article did not mention that Oswald's request for Soviet citizenship had already been denied—or that Oswald had melodramatically attempted suicide shortly after receiving the news. On October 21, 1959, Oswald wrote in his diary, "I am shocked!! My dreams! . . . I have waited for 2 year[s] to be accepted. My fondes[t] dreams are shattered because of a petty [Soviet] official . . . I decide to end it. Soak fist in cold water to numb the pain, Th[e]n slash my left wrist. Th[e]n plaug [plunge] wrist into bathtub of hot water . . . Somewhere, a violin plays, as I watch my life whirl away. I think to myself 'How easy to Die' and 'A Sweet Death, (to violins) . . .'" This had all the markings of a genuine try at suicide, which lends credence to those who say Oswald was not put up to the defection by the U.S. government. (The CIA might have wanted to plant an agent who could provide the Soviets with misinformation about the U-2 spy plane.) Oswald could have succeeded in killing himself had an Intourist guide (basically, a Soviet minder) not found him lying in a pool of his own blood. He was rushed to nearby Botkinskaya Hospital, where he received blood transfusions and a psychiatric evaluation. According to a Soviet official who defected to the United States, Yuri Nosenko, two Russian psychiatrists diagnosed Oswald as "mentally unstable." Nosenko supposedly handled Oswald's case for the KGB.[13]

Nosenko claimed that the KGB dismissed Oswald as disturbed and deranged and then left him alone after the diagnosis, but this explanation is dubious. Why the authorities would willingly take on a problem like Oswald—an individual they had diagnosed as unstable—when they could easily have had him delivered to the U.S. embassy begs an answer. As it developed, Oswald did not formally defect, since he never filled out the paperwork to renounce his American citizenship; instead, he was granted temporary residence in the USSR, with guaranteed employment and housing.[14] However, if he was worth the trouble to accept and settle in the Soviet Union, the KGB would hardly have ignored a Marine who had worked with U-2 planes. The Nosenko story seems even less plausible when the events of May 1, 1960, are taken into account. On that day, the Soviets shot down a U-2 flying over their airspace and captured a U.S. Air Force pilot, Francis Gary Powers. At first, the United States pretended that Powers had been collecting weather data. But when Khrushchev produced damning evidence that showed otherwise, President Eisenhower admitted that the government had lied and the U-2 had been sent to spy on the Russians.

Oswald was living in the Soviet Union at the time, and he could have provided the Soviets with information that helped them target the plane. Gary Powers certainly thought he had. In his later years, Powers theorized that intelligence provided by Oswald had helped the Soviets figure out how to use their missiles at higher altitudes. Powers's son, Gary Powers, Jr., has continued his father's quest for an answer: "It makes sense Oswald . . . would have given the Soviets information on the U-2. He was privy to the altitudes the U-2s were flying. And it's interesting that he defected in 1959. Dad was shot down in May of 1960. The Soviets were starting to improve their SA-1 and SA-2 missiles during that time frame." Powers's plane was downed by an SA-2, also known as an S-75 Dvina.[15]

The younger Powers remembers a story his father told about his time in captivity. "There was some guy dressed in a Russian uniform that looked American and spoke with an American accent," he says. "He would have been considered an American for all intents and purposes if he had been in the States. But he was dumber—my dad would have said 'dumber than a doorknob'—asking the wrong questions, and just didn't know what to ask." Powers Sr. came to believe that person was Lee Oswald. When Captain Powers returned home—he regained his freedom in a spy swap in February 1962—he went to the family farm in Pound, Virginia. While watching television one day in 1962 or 1963, prior to JFK's assassination, Powers saw a news story on Oswald. "My dad got very agitated and said, 'I've got to tell someone about him.' That's what I've heard from my Aunt Joanne."[16] Powers does not know if his father followed through.[17]

The Gary Powers saga leads to a logical question: Did Oswald cooperate with, or work for, the Soviet authorities during his time in the USSR? According to Nosenko, the answer is no. "The KGB didn't want Oswald from day one," he insisted during a 1992 interview. And yet Soviet officials were willing to provide Oswald with an identity card, a rent-free apartment, and a job at a radio and television factory in Minsk. He was living better than most Soviet citizens, who were paid low salaries and forced to live in ramshackle housing. Oswald's extra income also made him a more attractive marriage prospect, and in April 1961, he wed a young pharmacology student named Marina Prusakova. The couple had met at a trade union dance held at the Palace of Culture in Minsk. Oswald's accent convinced Marina that he was from one of the Baltic states.[18]

When the former Marine fell ill, she visited him in the hospital. They married less than two months after they met. Marina's uncle (also her guardian) was a high-ranking member of the Communist Party and a lieutenant colonel in the MVD, the Soviet Ministry of Internal Affairs.

On the surface, Oswald seemed to have a good life in the USSR—a beautiful wife, a decent job, and privileges above the average. In reality, ever the malcontent, Oswald was chafing under the Soviet system. In the late summer of 1961, he made the following entry in his diary:

> As my Russian improves I become increasingly conscious of just what sort of a society I live in. Mass gymnastics, compulsory after-work meeting, usually political information meeting. Compulsory attendance at lectures and the sending of the entire shop collective (except me) to pick potatoes on a Sunday, at a state collective farm: A "patriotic duty" to bring in the harvest. The opinions of the workers (unvoiced) are that it's a great pain in the neck . . . [Misspellings corrected here].

Convinced that the Soviets had perverted the teachings of Karl Marx, Oswald began searching for a way to get back to the United States, the nation he had loudly denounced a couple of years earlier. He contacted the U.S. embassy in Moscow and explained that his decision to defect had been a big mistake. He also encouraged Marina to apply for a visa. Lee and Marina's applications were approved in a little over a year by both American and Soviet officials. The State Department helpfully provided him with a loan to cover his travel expenses.[19] In June 1962, the family arrived in the United States.[20] Thus, an ex-Marine defector—in those days, they were openly referred to as traitors—who might have provided the Soviets with vital information about U.S. military assets received relatively easy clearance back into the United States, with financial help from the taxpayers. Not surprisingly, some people find this suspicious and wonder whether Oswald was sent back to the United States for a reason—by either superpower. The CIA says that it did not keep track of Oswald while he was in the USSR because its spies were busy working other cases. But the agency admits that it did "read the FBI reports on him" and "watched as the State Department did its job of screening him for repatriation."[21]

It is also possible that Oswald was part of a top secret "fake defector" program. The CIA has never admitted that such a program existed, but congressional documents show that one of Langley's operatives who went by the pseudonym "Thomas Casasin" had at one time "run an agent into the USSR."[22] "Casasin" acknowledged an awareness of Oswald's defection to the Soviet Union and his job at a radio factory in Minsk, but he said no more than that. We may never know whether the agency ever approached Oswald, in or out of Russia, but this little-known anecdote adds a modicum of credibility to the idea that the CIA may have had designs on Oswald at some point before, during, or after his defection.[23]

The FBI began tracking Oswald ten days after his defection "to evaluate him as a security risk in the event [that] he returned" to the United States. When the Oswalds arrived in Texas, the bureau decided to interview Lee to find out if he had ever been approached by the KGB. Oswald said no, but also refused to take a lie detector test. Apparently satisfied despite the lack of full cooperation from Oswald, the FBI put the Oswald case on the back burner. The CIA claims that it never debriefed the former Marine, even though he had once bragged about sharing military secrets with the KGB.[24] Only a handful of Americans were recorded as defecting to the Soviet Union during the 1950s and early 1960s. This was an extraordinarily rare event, and the overall lack of urgent interest in Oswald's case by the FBI and especially the CIA is remarkable, assuming it is true.

LAW ENFORCEMENT AGENCIES and assassination researchers have focused on Oswald's connections since he was arrested in 1963. There is no absolute proof of any conspiratorial association—whether with the CIA, FBI, Mafia, or Communists—but there are hints that Oswald could potentially have been in league with one or more groups.

Since the 1970s the public has known of the Kennedy administration's energetic, highly classified efforts to overthrow Fidel Castro. The Marxist dictator of Cuba had seized power from a corrupt despot, Fulgencio Batista, in 1959. During the Batista years, powerful crime figures from the United States turned Cuba into the Las Vegas of the Caribbean. They set up casinos and brothels, bribed Cuban officials, and used the country as an entrepôt for the narcotics trade. Most Cubans were disgusted with Batista's crime and vice, and many rejoiced when Castro came to power. Others fled to the United States, especially south Florida, and immediately began plotting to overthrow the new left-wing dictator, who declared his regime socialist and chose to associate it with the Soviet Union.

At the height of the Cold War, most Americans were instinctively anti-Castro, recognizing the dangers of a Communist state just ninety miles from America's southernmost shore. The military and CIA had begun extensive planning to oust Castro during the Eisenhower administration, and one of President Kennedy's first major decisions was to go forward with the U.S.-backed invasion of Cuban exiles in April 1961. After the Bay of Pigs, a chastened JFK and his brother Robert became obsessed with deposing Castro. RFK created a major program of subterfuge and disruption known as Operation Mongoose to bring about Castro's downfall, and the Kennedys authorized the CIA to do whatever was necessary to engineer a coup d'état in Cuba. This led to serious assassination efforts but also cartoonish schemes such as exploding cigars since Castro was addicted to the tobacco leaf. The CIA even worked with Mafia chieftains to arrange for Castro's demise; political bedfellows were rarely stranger, but La Cosa Nostra (another name for the Mafia)[25] had lost many millions of dollars when Batista fell. The Cuban expatriates in south Florida were willing partners, too.[26]

Meanwhile, despite his disillusionment with the Soviet Union and return to the United States, Oswald made contact with the local Russian diaspora in Fort Worth, Texas. Oswald had personal reasons for doing so. Marina was homesick and did not speak much English, and Lee was now used to Slavic people and their ways. Soon Oswald became friends with a peripatetic baron named George de Mohrenschildt, whose life sounds like something out of a James Bond novel. His father, a wealthy Russian nobleman, managed to escape from a Soviet prison where he was sent after denouncing the Bolshevik Revolution. He then moved his family from Minsk to a posh estate in Poland, where George spent his youth. While still in his twenties, George left Europe to tour the United States and managed to become friendly with some of America's East Coast elites, including a family named Bouvier, whose daughter Jacqueline would one day become First Lady, and another family named Bush. George H. W. Bush's nephew roomed with de Mohrenschildt at Phillips Academy.[27]

In the years that followed, de Mohrenschildt became involved in intelligence operations. During World War II he gathered information on pro-German activity in the United States for the French government; there are allegations that he was spying for the Nazis at the same time, but these have never been proven. In 1942 he shared a house with a senior naval officer and a British intelligence agent in Washington and offered his services to the Office of Strategic Services (the predecessor to the CIA), which turned him down because of the double-agent rumor. During the 1950s, de Mohrenschildt worked for the International Cooperation Administration, a CIA-sponsored subsidiary of the Agency for International Development. In the early 1960s, while touring Central America and the Caribbean, he was photographed with the American ambassador to Costa Rica. In addition, de Mohrenschildt and his wife visited Guatemala, which was a strategic launching site for CIA-backed Cuban exiles during the Bay of Pigs.

Some think the CIA, which at times almost certainly had some sort of relationship with de Mohrenschildt, used him to make contact with Oswald. The baron himself, however, denied the connection, insisting that no "government would be stupid enough to trust Lee with anything important."[28] The full truth is especially elusive, but de Mohrenschildt's acquaintance with Lee Oswald is curious. For someone dismissed as an obvious loser of little consequence, Oswald kept popping up in the company of well-connected individuals such as de Mohrenschildt.[29]

De Mohrenschildt introduced Oswald to Michael and Ruth Paine, two political leftists who were out of place in Texas's conservative milieu. Although separated, the Paines took an interest in Marina and Lee and began inviting them to social functions.[30] Michael Paine worked as an engineer for Bell Helicopter, a job that required a security clearance; his stepfather, Arthur Young, had designed the first Bell helicopter. His estranged wife was a Quaker pacifist who had reached out to Dallas's Russian community in order to practice her language skills. The Paines were initially enthusiastic about their relationship with the Oswalds. Michael was keen to meet an American defector perhaps because his father was a devoted Trotskyite. Ruth was excited about conversing in Russian with a native speaker.

But the Paines soon realized the Oswalds were a family in crisis. Lee had a hard time keeping a job, and Marina began complaining to Ruth about her husband's meager salary and low sex drive. Even worse, it became apparent that Oswald mistreated his wife to the point of physical abuse. Ruth felt sorry for Marina and did all she could to help.[31]

In early 1963 the mercurial Oswald went on a gun-buying spree. Using an alias (A. Hidell), he ordered a .38 Smith & Wesson revolver from a Los Angeles mail order company and a 6.5-millimeter Mannlicher-Carcano rifle from another mail order outfit in Chicago. Both guns arrived in March. One sunny afternoon, Oswald asked his wife to take a picture of him with his weapons. Although bemused and a little frightened by the request, Marina agreed and snapped at least three photos that have since become iconic images.[32] Oswald is dressed in black, holding the rifle in one hand and two left-wing magazines in the other with the Smith & Wesson hanging from his hip. Over the years, conspiracy theorists have claimed that the photos were faked by someone attempting to frame Oswald. But in the late 1970s, the House Select Committee on Assassinations, assisted by photography experts, verified their legitimacy. By any measure, this is a disturbing picture: a troubled man who had perhaps already decided to promote his ideology, as Mao had argued, with the power that comes from the barrel of a gun.[33]

The same week that Oswald asked Marina to take the photograph, he learned that he had been fired from his job at Jaggers-Chiles-Stovall, a Dallas cartography company that occasionally did classified work for the U.S. government. Unemployed, unhappily married, and at odds with American society and values, Oswald decided to act in dramatic fashion. On April 10, 1963, he left his apartment shortly after dinner without telling his wife where he was going. When he failed to return at a reasonable hour, Marina went to his room and found a note that contained a list of grim instructions.

"Send the information as to what has happened to me to the [Soviet] Embassy and include newspaper clippings," the note read. "I believe that the Embassy will come quickly to your assistance on learning everything." The note also said that she could "throw out" or give away his clothing, but requested that she hang on to his "personal papers." Oswald had decided to end his life in a blaze of glory: "If I am alive and taken prisoner, the city jail is located . . .

right in the beginning of the city after crossing the bridge." Where had he gone? Marina told the Warren Commission that Lee came home that night looking "very pale." "And he told me not to ask him any questions," she testified. "He only told me he had shot at General Walker."[34]

Major General Edwin A. Walker was a member of the extremist John Birch Society, which had declared at one point that President Eisenhower, the supreme allied commander during World War II, was a "Communist" or a "stooge."[35] Walker had retired from the army after being accused of indoctrinating his troops with right-wing propaganda. After leaving the military, he moved to Dallas and settled in a large house in an upscale area. In the spring of 1962, he challenged Governor John Connally in the Democratic gubernatorial primary and received around 10 percent of the vote. Not to put too fine a point on it, Walker was a racist and arch-segregationist, and he called for thousands of civilian volunteers to march on Oxford when the African American James Meredith tried to enroll at the University of Mississippi in the fall of 1962. In the wake of the violence at Ole Miss, he was arrested and charged with instigating a riot. The authorities eventually released Walker on a $50,000 bond.

Volkmar Schmidt, a friend of George de Mohrenschildt's who also associated with the Russian expatriates, believes a conversation he had with Lee Oswald one night may have convinced him to take a potshot at Walker and later, JFK. Schmidt says that an academic acquaintance had told him that showing empathy toward troubled individuals sometimes brought them back to reality. Schmidt says he employed this tactic during a conversation with Oswald because he considered him to be a "very disturbed man" and "totally desperate." "When I heard how hateful he was towards Kennedy and Cuba . . . I tried to say 'hey, there's something much more real to be concerned about, because I don't know about Castro, but I know about this Walker, he's kind of a Nazi, yeah?'" Schmidt said during a 1995 interview.[36] "Not so bad as those Nazis in Germany, but I had specifically mentioned to . . . Oswald that Walker had given a speech to the students at the Mississippi campus and those guys went off and killed a couple of journalists." Schmidt says that he encouraged Oswald to "think about" the Walker incident and the importance of bringing "justice to the minorities" in a "constructive" fashion. Schmidt thinks Oswald may have decided then and there to assassinate Walker: "Actually, a few days after I talked with him, he bought his weapons," Schmidt says.[37]

On April 10, 1963, the available evidence suggests that Oswald used his Mannlicher-Carcano rifle to shoot at Walker while the general was sitting at his desk at home. Aiming from a nearby parking lot, Oswald fired a bullet that passed through a wooden window cross strip as well as a masonry wall, and it fell harmlessly onto some papers. Marina testified that Lee wasn't sure if he had hit Walker and seemed disappointed the next day when he learned from newspapers that the general was unharmed. Some assassination researchers do not believe that Oswald ever attempted to kill Walker. Mark Lane, for example, points to a photograph of Walker's house, later found in Oswald's belongings, which allegedly changed over the course of the JFK investigation. Marina said that when she first saw the photograph, it included an image of a license plate that was later covered over with a "black spot," which raises the question of whether the FBI, which at one point gained possession of the photo, tried to hide the identity of the true assassin.[38] In the unlikely event the FBI undertook such a deception, we would be forced to discount a good deal of Marina's other testimony about the Walker matter—much of it compelling and accompanied by circumstantial evidence such as Oswald's note to his wife.[39] Marina claimed that Oswald had told her that, contrary to Volkmar Schmidt's belief that he had planted the idea in Lee's mind, he (Lee) had been planning the Walker murder for two months and that he had waited until a church next door to Walker held services so that his comings and goings would attract less attention. Further, while the FBI could not absolutely say that the bullet found in Walker's home came from Oswald's rifle, the grooves on the bullet were consistent with Oswald's rifle.[40]

Marina shared a second tale with the Warren Commission that is quite revealing. Several days after the Walker incident, she said, Lee was reading the morning newspaper when he suddenly decided to change into a "good suit." When Marina saw him tucking a pistol into his belt, she asked him where he was going. "Nixon is coming," Lee replied, indicating that the former vice president was going to be in Dallas. "I want to go and have a look." Marina immediately called her husband into the bathroom and tearfully "told him that he shouldn't do this, that he had promised me." "I remember that I held him. We actually struggled for several minutes and then he quieted down. I remember that I told him that if he goes out it would be better for him to kill me than to go out."[41] Actually, Nixon was not in Dallas, and the reasons for Oswald's bizarre behavior remain unclear. Marina guessed he staged the incident to torment her.

This episode suggests again that Oswald had entered a violence-prone phase, with his deep-seated personal anger being directed at political figures from General Walker to former vice president Nixon. These were two conservatives, while Kennedy was—in the context of the times—a moderate to liberal Democrat, and possibly more acceptable to Oswald ideologically, though the Kennedy administration's posture toward Castro may have negated any advantage JFK had. Over the next six months, it is not much of a stretch to imagine that Oswald's inner fury about the course of his life, and the threatening resentment he was manifesting toward those in positions of influence, could have expanded to include anyone at society's pinnacle, certainly a president.[42]

It is difficult to get a good read on Oswald's views and state of mind, especially in his final months, because he mainly kept to himself. Wesley Buell Frazier, Oswald's co-worker at the Book Depository and car pool companion, never noticed anything unusual about his friend's behavior at the office. "Lee was a very professional guy," Frazier told me. "[But] he wasn't the type of person to come up and initiate a conversation. If you asked him something, he would answer you. The only time he would initiate something at work was when he was reading the invoice and he wasn't quite sure about the book or where it was. Then he'd come ask me." Frazier also noted that some coworkers made fun of Oswald's chilly demeanor, and that his occasional attempts to fit in, by playing cards or the like, often fell flat.[43]

The Nixon incident and the attempt on Walker's life, however, are two of the most convincing indicators that Oswald was capable of considering or trying to carry out high-level political murder. Yet such a conclusion does not address the larger concern about possible accomplices for Oswald from governmental agencies and nongovernmental organizations in more than one city. New Orleans, as well as Dallas, has provided tales of JFK assassination conspiracies. Not long after the attempted Walker murder, Oswald traveled to the Crescent City, planning to move his family there. While looking for a job and residence in New Orleans, Oswald moved in with his uncle, Charles "Dutz" Murret, a small-time hustler and bookie for Carlos Marcello, New Orleans's premier Mafia boss. According to an FBI informant (a businessman code-named SV T-1), Oswald received money from a man who was later identified as Joseph Poretto, one of Marcello's chief lieutenants. Had the informant misidentified, or correctly recognized, Poretto and Oswald? Was SV T-1 even telling the truth?[44] Murret testified before the Warren Commission that he was the only one who had lent his nephew money. In any case, we know that Oswald had enough to rent a $65-per-month apartment shortly after arriving in New Orleans. He also found a job at the William B. Reily Coffee Co., which paid him $1.50 per hour to grease the fittings on its machinery.

In early May, Marina and the Oswalds' infant daughter joined Lee. Ruth Paine drove them down from Dallas in her station wagon. After Paine left, Oswald wrote to the national headquarters of the Fair Play for Cuba Committee, a pro-Castro organization, requesting permission to set up an FPCC chapter in New Orleans. Too impatient to wait for an answer, Oswald went to a local print shop and ordered a thousand handbills with the words "Hands

Off Cuba! Join the Fair Play for Cuba Committee, New Orleans Charter Member Branch" printed on them. Oswald first distributed his handbills on June 16, 1963, but stopped after a policeman ordered him to move on. As his activities continued later in the summer, Oswald became a minor news curiosity in New Orleans, was filmed by New Orleans TV news, and even debated U.S.–Cuba policy on a local radio show.[45]

But gradually, continuing a pattern seen before, Oswald lost interest in the FPCC and his life in the Big Easy. He was unable to hold onto his job at the Reily Coffee Company for long; according to his supervisor, Oswald frequently played hooky at a nearby service station called the Crescent City Garage. In 1978, fifteen years after JFK's assassination, the garage's owner, Adrian Alba, came forward with an account about a man he believed was an FBI agent from Washington. According to Alba, the man flashed bureau credentials and requisitioned a green Studebaker. Alba's garage maintained some of the FBI's unmarked cars. The next day, Alba claimed he saw the Studebaker pull up in front of the coffee company. "Lee Oswald went across the sidewalk," Alba testified, "He bent down as if to look in the window and was handed what appeared to be a good-sized envelope, a white envelope. He turned and bent as if to hold the envelope to his abdomen, and I think he put it under his shirt. Oswald then went back into the building, and the car drove off." Alba also said that the man met Oswald a second time and returned the Studebaker a few days later. When asked why he hadn't come forward with the information earlier, Alba said that he had forgotten about it until he saw a television commercial one day that featured a man leaning in a car window.[46]

Alba's tardy yarn could be easily dismissed, save for the considerable evidence linking Oswald to the FBI and other secretive organizations. In late July 1963, having lost his coffee job and learning that the Marines had rejected his request to have his honorable discharge reinstated, Oswald resumed his role as a New Orleans street preacher for Fidel Castro.[47] At the same time, he made an attempt to infiltrate the enemy camp by posing as an anti-Castro activist. On August 5, 1963, Oswald walked into a store owned by an anti-Castro militant, Carlos Bringuier, and claimed to be a former Marine willing to train anti-Castro Cubans for combat. The next day, Oswald gave Bringuier a copy of a Marine Corps manual as proof of his credentials. A few days later, however, Bringuier learned from a friend about Oswald's previous role in handing out pro-Castro leaflets. Enraged by the deception, Bringuier immediately left his shop and went to confront Oswald. The two men caused a scene on a city sidewalk that drew a crowd. Oswald and Bringuier (and two of Bringuier's fellow Cubans) were arrested for disorderly conduct.

While still in jail, Oswald demanded to speak with the FBI. In what many say is a suspicious response, the agency granted his request and, within a matter of hours, sent Special Agent John Quigley to see him. How Oswald was able to summon an FBI agent and whether he had a "special relationship" with the agency, as some have suggested, are unanswerable questions. Perhaps Quigley was merely conducting a routine interview with a person he knew had defected to the Soviet Union (the FBI admits it kept an extensive file on Oswald prior to 11/22). Though it is much more of a stretch, some JFK assassination conspiracy backers think the confrontation with Bringuier could have been an orchestrated ruse designed to shore up Oswald's Communist bona fides before he murdered Kennedy. The narrative becomes even more complicated because of Bringuier's CIA-tinged background. Bringuier was the New Orleans representative of the Directorio Revolucionario Estudiantil (DRE for short), an anti-Castro student group with ties to the CIA.[48]

Perhaps one could make the argument that Lee Oswald, in an attempt to live up to his imagined importance, sought out exciting figures in society's shadows. Maybe also, by coincidence, the CIA and FBI had a presence everywhere Oswald happened to be in the early 1960s. It could be that Oswald was just a Forrest Gump–like character who popped up at interesting moments wherever he happened to live. But just as conceivably, whether related to the Kennedy assassination or not, Oswald actually had secretive contacts with the CIA, the FBI, or both.[49]

Consider the address found on some of Oswald's pro-Castro literature—544 Camp Street. According to assassination researcher Jim Marrs, "It was at 544 Camp Street in an old, three-story office building that the paths of Lee Harvey Oswald, the FBI, the CIA, anti-Castro Cubans, and organized crime figures all crossed." The Cuban Revolutionary Council (CRC), another anti-Castro organization sponsored by the CIA, rented an office at 544 Camp Street right before Oswald moved back to New Orleans. Guy Banister, a former FBI agent who kept files on New Orleans's left-wing organizations, rented space at the same location. According to Delphine Roberts, Banister's secretary and mistress, Oswald met with her boss on several occasions in New Orleans. "He seemed to be on familiar terms with Banister and with the office," she said. "As I understood it he had the use of an office on the second floor, above the main office where we worked. I was not greatly surprised when I learned he was going up and down, back and forth. Then, several times, Mr. Banister brought me upstairs, and in the office above I saw various writings stuck up on the wall pertaining to . . . Fair Play for Cuba." Roberts may or may not be revealing the full story. She has previously received money for this information and once told an interviewer that she did not consistently tell "all the truth." Yet there are other witnesses who say that Banister and Oswald knew each other. For example, William Gaudet, "a CIA asset in

New Orleans of many years," told the House Select Committee on Assassinations that he saw Banister and Oswald chatting on a street corner.[50]

Also stirring Oswald conspiracy talk is Guy Banister's alleged links to an enigmatic, bizarre figure, David Ferrie, a pilot suffering from bipolar disorder who lost his job at Eastern Airlines after being accused of molesting a fifteen-year-old boy. Afflicted with a rare medical condition that causes severe hair loss, Ferrie was sometimes seen wearing a red wig and fake eyebrows. A staunch anticommunist, he trained anti-Castro Cuban exiles for raids against Castro and sometimes even flew missions into Cuba. His anticommunist activities in New Orleans apparently brought him into contact with Guy Banister, Carlos Marcello, and William Gaudet. Ferrie supposedly bought weapons from mob boss Marcello and turned them over to Banister and CIA asset Gaudet, who in turn passed them on to Cuban exiles.

Robert Morrow, the author of a heavily criticized autobiography entitled *First Hand Knowledge*, claims that he and Ferrie flew to Cuba in 1961 looking for Soviet missile sites. The following year, says Morrow, when Kennedy refused to invade Cuba during the missile crisis, the CIA and anti-Castro Cubans began plotting his assassination, and the mob provided financing for the operation. Morrow also says that the CIA ordered him to buy Mannlicher-Carcano rifles from a surplus store in Maryland that he was told would be used to assassinate a South American dictator. He allegedly gave three of the rifles to David Ferrie. The Dallas police found a Carcano rifle on the sixth floor of the Texas School Book Depository. Did Ferrie give Oswald one of Morrow's rifles? The claim does not hold up to scrutiny. Morrow says that he purchased 7.35-millimeter rifles, while the weapon found at the Book Depository was a 6.5-millimeter Carcano. To date, Morrow has not produced any documents verifying his story. Robert Blakey, chief counsel and staff director of the House Select Committee on Assassinations, puts little stock in Morrow's version of events. "It's established beyond all reasonable doubt," insists Blakey, "that the Cubans were connected to the mob, and the mob was connected to the CIA, but the president that they were trying to assassinate was Castro, not Kennedy."[51]

On the other hand, it is a well-established fact that Ferrie and Oswald crossed paths on at least one occasion. In 1993 a photograph surfaced showing a teenaged Oswald and a middle-aged Ferrie together at a 1955 Civil Air Patrol cookout.[52] Soon after the Kennedy assassination, Ferrie denied ever knowing Oswald, and the FBI and Warren Commission accepted his statement at face value. In the late 1960s, however, New Orleans district attorney Jim Garrison interviewed six people who said that they had seen Ferrie and Oswald together at a voter registration office in Clinton, Mississippi. According to these witnesses, Oswald and Ferrie and an unknown third man showed up at the office in September 1963 driving a black Cadillac. The three men were memorable since there were few white faces at the registration drive sponsored by the Congress of Racial Equality (CORE), and witnesses testified that one of the men was wearing a curious wig and fake eyebrows. According to Henry Palmer, Clinton's registrar, Lee Oswald handed him a Navy ID card and tried to register to vote, but Palmer turned down the request on the grounds that Oswald had not lived in the area long enough. Oswald thanked Palmer before leaving with the two men. Garrison was known for questionable tactics and highly criticized for his conduct before and during the trial.[53] Did he coach these witnesses into telling a lie, or had they actually encountered Oswald et al. two months before the assassination?[54] If Oswald and Ferrie really were together in Clinton, then it suggests a closer relationship that the Warren Commission should have examined.

Assassination researchers frequently encounter chronicles that seem promising on the surface but end up leading nowhere or raising a host of unanswerable questions. One of them involves Silvia and Annie Odio, who believe they saw Oswald in the company of anti-Castro Cubans two months before the assassination. The Odio sisters claim that during the last week of September 1963, three men—one Caucasian and two Latinos—visited Silvia's apartment in Dallas. "The taller, more vocal man gave his 'war name,' or Cuban underground alias, as 'Leopoldo.' Silvia recalled the name of the shorter, stockier man with glasses as 'Angelo' or 'Angel.' The third man, their 'gringo American' friend, said little." The two Latino men said that they were members of the Cuban resistance movement and that they were friends with the girls' father, Amador Odio, another anti-Castro activist who was then being held in a Cuban prison. According to Silvia, Leopoldo introduced his white companion as "Leon Oswald" and asked for help in raising money for an organization known as JURE (Junta Revolucionaria Cubana). When Silvia gave a cagey reply, the men departed. A day or two later, she says, Leopoldo called her and asked what she thought of the American. "I don't think anything," Silvia supposedly replied. "You know, our idea is to introduce him to the underground in Cuba because he is great, he is kind of nuts," Leopoldo continued. "He told us we don't have any guts, 'you Cubans,' because President Kennedy should have been assassinated after the Bay of Pigs, and some Cubans should have done that . . ." Unnerved by the conversation, Silvia says she abruptly ended it and never heard from Leopoldo again. After the assassination, however, she said she recognized Lee Oswald as the white man who had visited her apartment.

The House Select Committee on Assassinations concluded that Silvia's testimony was "essentially credible" and the Caucasian male she saw could have been Oswald. But as usual, it is not a perfect story. Annie Odio says that she did not hear the white man introduced as Leon Oswald. Silvia Odio also wavered when the Warren Commission showed her a photo of Oswald. "I think this man was the one that was in my apartment," she said. "I am not too sure of that picture."[55] Unlike the House Committee, the Warren Commission concluded that Oswald could not have been in the Odio household on the night in question because it was believed Oswald was in Mexico City at the time—although this assumption is disputed by some researchers, a few of whom insist it wasn't even Oswald who appeared in Mexico City.

There is considerable evidence that Oswald did indeed go to Mexico. Just two months before the assassination, Oswald's life was once again in shambles. He and Marina had decided to separate (she moved back in with Ruth Paine), and he was unemployed. The job at the coffee company, for all its shortcomings, had at least put bread on the table for a while. Oswald had become a desperate man. The Warren Commission said he went looking for aid at the Cuban embassy in Mexico City.[56] Silvia Duran, a Mexican national who spoke English, worked as a secretary at the embassy and remembered the day (Friday, September 27, 1963) that Oswald walked in the front door. He told her that he was on his way to the Soviet Union, wanted to spend a few weeks in Cuba beforehand, and needed to obtain a transit visa.[57] Oswald showed her his American Communist Party and Fair Play for Cuba Committee membership cards, documents from his time in the Soviet Union, and a newspaper clipping of his arrest in New Orleans. Duran informed Oswald that he would still need to fill out an application and submit passport-sized photographs before he would be granted a visa. Oswald left in a huff but returned an hour later with the photos. He then demanded that the embassy immediately issue him a visa. Duran suggested that he talk to the Soviet embassy—if the Soviets gave him permission to visit the USSR, she said, the Cuban government could expedite his request.

Enraged by the delay, Oswald caused a scene that brought the Cuban consul, Eusebio Azcue, out of his office. After a brief shouting match, Azcue asked Oswald to leave. Undeterred, Oswald made the short trip over to the Russian embassy two blocks away and demanded a Soviet visa. When told that it would take at least four months to process his request, the former Marine shouted, "This won't do for me! This is not my case! For me, it's all going to end in tragedy!" He was escorted off the premises, but returned the next day. During an interview with one Soviet official, Oswald claimed that the FBI was after him and that he carried a gun for protection. The official was startled when Oswald suddenly produced a .38-caliber revolver and waved it in the air. "See?" said Oswald, "This is what I must now carry to protect my life." The official was able to seize the revolver and remove its bullets. When Oswald learned that his request for a quick visa had been turned down, he became depressed. He retreated from the Soviet embassy but decided to press the Cubans one last time. After becoming embroiled in another heated argument with Azcue, Oswald left the Cuban embassy and never returned.[58]

Without question, someone showed up in the Cuban and Russian embassies claiming to be Lee Oswald, but was he actually an Oswald impostor? The CIA may have the answer. In 1963, unsurprisingly, the agency had self-operating surveillance cameras that took photographs of persons coming in and out of the Cuban and Soviet embassies. On October 9, 1963, the Mexico City CIA station received word from "a sensitive source" that a man named Lee Oswald had been in contact with the local Soviet consulate. According to the CIA, the name "Oswald" meant nothing to the Mexico City station, but it forwarded the report to the CIA's Langley headquarters anyway. Langley checked its files and cabled a perfunctory reply that contained only the basic facts of the Oswald case—he had defected to Russia, married a Soviet woman, and returned to the United States after realizing that he had made a mistake.[59] On October 10, a memo went out to the FBI, the Immigration and Naturalization Service, the State Department, and the Navy that described Oswald as a six-foot-tall thirty-five-year-old with an athletic build and a receding hairline. The real-life Oswald was a thin, undernourished twenty-three-year-old who was no taller than five feet nine.[60] Supposedly, the bogus description was the result of a clerical error: An agent in Mexico City had mistakenly attached Oswald's name to a photograph of another man.[61]* CIA's casual handling of the Oswald case and misleading cables convinced the FBI to remove Oswald's name from a security watch list.[62]

Perhaps the CIA's explanation should be accepted. After all, federal bureaucrats routinely make slipups, put innocent people on no-fly lists, misplace Social Security records, and the like. But the more one studies the possible relationship of Oswald to the CIA, the more legitimate doubts spring forth. First, the CIA was never able to produce an actual photo of Oswald coming in or out of the Soviet or Cuban embassies. The agency's official explanation is that its cameras were not designed to take pictures around the clock and that Oswald must have visited the embassies in between photo sessions. This account is confounding. Oswald went in and out of the two embassies under surveillance at least five times at widely varying hours, and yet we are asked to believe the spy cameras were not able to capture a single image of him. Espionage in the early 1960s wasn't the science that James Bond thrillers would lead us to assume, but automatic cameras were neither rare

* This individual, whose picture is shown on page _____, has never been identified.

1935. Young Jack Kennedy led an exceptionally privileged and worldly life, born of money and position. Here, JFK and his sisters Patricia (left) and Eunice (right) were photographed in the hills above Cannes, France, on vacation with their parents.

1944. John Kennedy's service in World War II was a central part of his biography in running for political office. Here, he shakes hands with Captain Conklin, Commandant, Chelsea Naval Hospital in Boston, after being presented with a medal for heroism, June 12, 1944.

1948. Some of the Kennedy family at Thanksgiving in Hyannis Port, Massachusetts. From left: John F. Kennedy, sister Jean Ann, mother Rose , father Joseph, Sr., sister Patricia, brother Robert, sister Eunice, and brother Edward Kennedy (squatting).

1951. Television quickly recognized the potential star power of young John F. Kennedy. Here, JFK appears on an early edition of NBC's *Meet the Press*, December 2, 1951. Left to right are interviewer Ernest K. Lindley, May Craig, James Reston, Lawrence Spivak, moderator Martha Rountree, and Congressman Kennedy in his third House term.

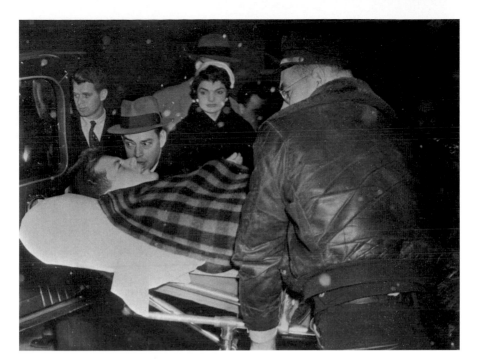

1954. During the 1950s, Kennedy was operated on twice for spinal problems and came close to death once during the recovery. Here, Senator Kennedy is being lifted into an ambulance after surgery in a New York hospital, accompanied by Mrs. Kennedy and brother Robert, to begin convalescing at his family's Palm Beach home for several months.

1957. Robert Kennedy was a close adviser to his brother throughout JFK's political career. Here, RFK, counsel for the Senate Permanent Subcommittee investigating labor racketeering, huddles with Senator Kennedy, a member of the committee, on February 26, 1957.

1959. John Kennedy and Richard Nixon, young World War II veterans in Congress, had been genuine friends early in their political careers. In this photo from June 19, 1959, Vice President Nixon shakes hands with Senator and Mrs. Kennedy as they each change planes at Chicago's Midway airport. By this time, both men realized they might be running against one another the following year.

1960. William C. Battle, son of Virginia governor John Battle, served with JFK in the Pacific during World War II and later helped manage his campaign in West Virginia. Here Battle and Kennedy are shown disembarking from the senator's private plane during the crucial Mountain State primary.

1960. Now the official Democratic nominee for president, Senator Kennedy rides in an open convertible into the Los Angeles Memorial Coliseum on the last day of the party's national convention, July 15, 1960. He delivered his acceptance address before a crowd estimated to be as many as eighty thousand.

1960. John Kennedy almost certainly would not have defeated Richard Nixon without his superior performance in the four televised presidential debates in the fall of 1960. Here, moderator Howard K. Smith is looking up at a wan Vice President Nixon, who had been ill, while a tanned, rested Senator Kennedy takes notes during the first debate on September 26. The debates were a first of their kind.

1960. Senator Kennedy protests as a policeman hauls away an unidentified admirer who wanted to shake hands with him in Grand Rapids, Michigan, on October 14, 1960. (At Kennedy's insistence, the woman was later allowed to meet him.) The throng surrounding Kennedy's car was a security nightmare.

1961. Despite bitter cold and heavy snow the previous evening, Kennedy's inauguration drew large crowds. They were rewarded with one of the most inspiring inaugural addresses in the nation's history, after the oath of office was administered by Chief Justice Earl Warren, 1961.

1961. The spread of Communism in Southeast Asia was an unavoidable focus for the Kennedy Administration. Here, at a news conference on March 23, 1961, President Kennedy points to a map showing the progress of the Communists into Laos, Vietnam's neighbor.

1961. Kennedy's infidelities put great strain on his marriage, but nonetheless he and Jackie appeared to have a deep reservoir of affection for one another. Here, President Kennedy fixes Jackie's wind-blown hair as they ride in a convertible between Blair House and the White House in May 1961.

1961. On May 31, 1961, President de Gaulle of France welcomed First Lady Jackie Kennedy to the Elysée Palace. Madame de Gaulle and President Kennedy stand to the side. The French were taken with Mrs. Kennedy's beauty, style, and impeccable French. The President commented to a press lunch in Paris that he had become "the man who accompanied Jacqueline Kennedy to Paris."

1962. President Kennedy looks on as Jackie speaks in Spanish to the soldiers of the Bay of Pigs Brigade from an open car. Miami, Florida, December 29, 1962.

1962. The Kennedy family captivated much of America and was a source of comedic inspiration for some. This popular long-playing album, *The First Family*, was distributed widely in 1962 and starred Vaughn Meader as the voice of President Kennedy. His career as a JFK imitator ended on the day the president was shot.

963. Only in his last months in office did President Kennedy move decisively to secure fundamental liberties for African Americans via legislation. On New Year's Day 1963, JFK met with various ivil rights and labor leaders, including Dr. Martin Luther King, Jr. (who was being wiretapped by he FBI with the knowledge of Attorney General Robert Kennedy).

1963. President Kennedy's nonchalance and fashion sense transformed him into a cultural icon. Here the commander in chief jokes with two military officers on the aircraft carrier USS *Oriskany* during a naval exercise off San Diego on the anniversary of D-Day, June 6, 1963.

1963. An emotional high point for the president was his visit to the land of his ancestors, Ireland in June 1963. Enormous crowds followed him everywhere, but in this intimate setting, JFK has te with distant relatives, the Ryan family of Duganstown.

963. President Kennedy's motorcade was actually at a halt leaving the Quirinal Palace, home of
aly's president in Rome. JFK would have been an easy target for any sniper in this circumstance.
wo Secret Service agents are riding on the back of the limousine, in position to protect the president
uickly if needed. In Dallas, no agents rode on the back of the car.

1963. President Kennedy met Pope Paul VI in Vatican City on July 2, 1963. The pope had been
1 office for less than two weeks, having just succeeded the late pope John XXIII. Because of con-
inuing sensitivity about Protestant claims of excessive papal influence on the Catholic Kennedy, the
resident did not kiss the pope's ring, as is customary. This did not sit well with some in the papal
ircle, but it was a reasonable precaution with the reelection campaign pending in 1964.

1963. President Kennedy took a gamble in pledging that Americans would beat the Russians and land on the moon by the end of the 1960s, but his space program inspired the nation—and achieved its goal. In his last week, on November 16, 1963, the president flew to Cape Canaveral, Florida (soon to be renamed Cape Kennedy), to be briefed concerning the plans to build the giant Saturn rocket that would eventually power the astronauts to the Moon.

1963. President Kennedy's last speech, delivered outside the Texas Hotel in Fort Worth on the morning of November 22, 1963. Right to left behind JFK are Vice President Lyndon Johnson and Governor John Connally, who would be badly wounded in the presidential car. To Connally's right is U.S. Senator Ralph Yarborough (D-Texas), whose political feud with LBJ and Connally—and the need to calm it—was one of the motivations behind JFK's Texas trip.

WESTERN UNION

```
431P PST NOV 21 63 LB283 0E369
SPF360 LE238 OB381 PB440  O P WB242 RX GOVT PD
THE WHITE HOUSE WUX WASHINGTON DC 21 618P EST
THOMAS W SARNOFF, REPORT DELIVERY
FIRST ANNUAL BROTHERHOOD TESTIMONIAL DINNER LE GRAND TRIANON
   BEVERLY WILSHIRE HOTEL , CARE ASST MGR ON DUTY
   BEVERLY CALIF
```

ON THE OCCASION OF YOUR FIRST ANNUAL BROTHERHOOD TESTIMONIAL
DINNER I AM DELIGHTED TO JOIN THE MEMBERS OF THE BROADCASTING
AND MOTION PICTURE INDUSTRIES IN THIS TRIBUTE TO DANNY KAYE.
THAT YOU HAVE SINGLED OUT DANNY KAYE-- KNOWN AND ADMIRED THROUGHOUT
THE WORLD FOR HIS WORK ON BEHALF OF UNICEF FOR YOUR FIRST AWARD
IS MOST APPROPRIATE. DANNY KAYE HAS GIVEN GENEROUSLY OF HIS
TALENTS TO ALL PEOPLES OF THE WORLD, PARTICULARLY TO CHILDREN,
AND I AM HAPPY TO EXTEND TO HIM MY CONGRATULATIONS AND WARM
BEST WISHES.

1270 (1-51)

1963. This Western Union telegram, sent at 6:18 pm on November 21, 1963, sent President Kennedy's congratulations to actor Danny Kaye for his work with UNICEF. It is one of the last written messages from JFK before he was assassinated the next day.

WESTERN UNION

2/0FWB242

THE WHITE HOUSE HAS RECENTLY FELT THE ABSENCE OF ITS MOST CONSTANT
WATCH-DOG, SANDER VANOCUR, AND IT IS ENCOURAGING TO KNOW THAT
MR SARNOFF IS EXERCISING HIS EXECUTIVE PREROGATIVE IN PUTTING
HIM TO WORK AGAIN THIS EVENING. I HOPE THAT HIS TALENTS AS
AN ENTERTAINER IN BEVERLY HILLS WILL NOT PERMANENTLY IMPROVERISH
US OF HIS NEWS SENSE IN WASHINGTON.
   TO ALL OF YOUR MEMBERS WHO ARE JOINED IN A COMMON CONCERN
FOR THE HUMAN RIGHTS AND OPPORTUNITIES OF ALL AMERICANS, I
EXTEND EVERY GOOD WISH
   JOHN F KENNEDY 431P
(7).

963. Telegram to Danny Kaye (page 2).

1963. Lee Harvey Oswald had long been a troubled individual, perpetually dissatisfied with his lot in life but incapable of changing it. In this famous photo taken by his wife, Oswald posed with a revolver, rifle, and two left wing magazines on March 31, 1963. Over the years, some critics have charged that the photo was doctored, but a congressional committee validated its authenticity in the late 1970s.

Comm. Exh. 237

1963. This person was photographed coming in and out of the Soviet Embassy at about the same time as Oswald's September 1963 trip to Mexico City. Some claim he was an agent of the eventual assassins, sent to impersonate Oswald. Others say he was a KGB scientist named Yuriy Moskale. He has never been conclusively identified.

1963. The Kennedys arrive in Dallas at Love Field, late in the morning on November 22, 1963. "You can see the president's suntan from here," said an on-air local TV newsman.

963. Not everyone at Dallas's Love Field was friendly to the Kennedys. Among those waiting for he presidential couple on November 22 were sign-carrying protestors, including one urging people o VOTE WHITE.

1963. The casual security in Dallas on November 22 is demonstrated by this photo of the presidential car, slowed to a crawl by traffic and crowds. President Kennedy waves to people riding in a sidelined bus on Main Street, just blocks from Dealey Plaza.

1963. This revealing, little-seen photograph shows the Kennedys and the Connallys riding in the presidential car through Dallas. President Kennedy is squeezed in the back seat; Governor Connally is sitting on the jump seat about a half foot lower and slightly to the left of JFK. This positioning is critical in understanding the eventual bullet trajectories.

nor complicated at that time—and these were the top priority diplomatic missions maintained by America's foremost enemies.

The story becomes stranger still when considering Daniel Watson's testimony before the House Select Committee on Assassinations. Watson was the deputy chief of the Mexico City CIA station between 1967 and 1969. He told the House Committee that Winston Scott, Mexico City's station chief in the early 1960s, "had a personal private safe in which he maintained especially sensitive materials." When Scott died in 1971, James Angleton, the controversial director of the CIA's top level counterintelligence unit,[63] personally flew to Mexico City in order to clean out Scott's safe. Although the House Committee staff were able to inspect what they were told were the safe's contents seven years after Angleton's trip (and did not find anything incriminating in what they were given), it is highly unusual, to say the least, for someone of Angleton's influence to fly abroad to clean out a station chief's safe.[64]

Also, it is becoming increasingly clear that the CIA had pertinent records on Oswald at the highest levels by the fall of 1963—information well beyond what the bare-bones memo sent to the Mexico City station suggested the CIA knew about Oswald. According to Jefferson Morley, a former *Washington Post* reporter who has spent years investigating the CIA, agency officials "were deliberately concealing from Win Scott all they knew about Lee Harvey Oswald." Morley and another researcher, the University of Maryland history professor John Newman, who once worked as a military intelligence officer, have spent countless hours piecing together the CIA's paper trail. They interviewed Jane Roman, the CIA officer who had originally signed off on the bland 1963 cable to Mexico City. After showing Roman several routing slips that proved three FBI reports on Oswald had circulated through Langley's offices in 1962 and 1963, Newman asked, "Is this the mark of a person's file who's dull and uninteresting?" "No, we're really trying to zero in on somebody here [Oswald]," Roman admitted. The reports included information on Oswald's interview with the FBI—when he refused to take a lie detector test, his activities on behalf of the Fair Play for Cuba Committee, and his scuffle with Bringuier and the two other DRE Cubans on the streets of New Orleans. None of this information made it into the memo to Mexico, which was approved by several top CIA officials including Tom Karamessines, the former Athens station chief, and William Hood, chief of covert operations for the Western Hemisphere.[65]

Other documents seem to have vanished into thin air. Agent Raymond Rocca remembered at least one other Oswald-related cable that came in to Langley from Mexico City that has since gone missing. In 1978, when the House Select Committee on Assassinations showed the agent a cable dated October 9, 1963, Rocca said, "It is my impression that there were earlier cables, that there was an earlier cable."[66]

In addition, CIA officials undeniably withheld important information on Oswald from the Warren Commission. Under a top secret program known as HT/LINGUAL, agents intercepted Oswald's correspondence during his time in the Soviet Union. When members of the Warren Commission inquired about a letter Marguerite sent to her son in 1961 (which was intercepted and read by Langley), they were told that the letter contained "no information of real significance." CIA's own documents, however, show that the letter was passed along to at least one high-ranking official with the message, "This item will be of interest to Mrs. Egerter, CI/SIG, and also to the FBI." "CI/SIG" refers to CIA's Special Investigations Group, which was part of the agency's counterintelligence division.[67]

The pieces of the Oswald puzzle stamped CIA may be ill-fitting, but they could reasonably create a portrait of covert action. CIA headquarters might have found a good use for Oswald and would not have wanted to share how much they knew about this particular asset with lower-level employees or foreign country stations.[68] This reasonable interpretation of the evidence does not require a belief that a "rogue element" near the top of the CIA was preparing Oswald to assassinate Kennedy. It is more likely that the agency could have viewed Oswald as a malleable potential low-level operative with an unusual combination of background experiences and contacts, including firsthand knowledge of the Soviet Union, pro-Castro elements, and anti-Castro Cubans. At the least, despite his hotheaded nature, he could infiltrate and report about targeted groups. Oswald's shady past, shaky economic situation, and seditious political views meant that the CIA held all the cards. Oswald was needy for money and attention, and he had an insatiable desire to feel important. After Kennedy's assassination, the leadership of the CIA would have had the same motive as J. Edgar Hoover did at the FBI, to cover its tracks lest it be blamed for failing to spot and stop a potential presidential killer in its midst. To this day, the CIA remains tight-lipped about what it knew about Oswald, so much that journalist Morley has been forced to sue to gain access to potentially revealing CIA documents.

At the center of the CIA-Oswald puzzle is a deceased prominent figure in the agency, George Joannides. In the early 1960s, Joannides ran the psychological warfare branch at the CIA station in Miami, where he worked closely with the Directorio Revolucionario Estudiantil (DRE)—the same group Oswald crossed paths with in New Orleans. The CIA's own records show that Joannides paid DRE $18,000 to $25,000 a month while assisting the group in planning its operations. In addition, Joannides traveled to the other key Oswald city, New Orleans, on CIA business in 1963 and '64, although the details are unknown. At the time, DRE did everything it could to brand Oswald as a

Communist.[69] After the scuffle in New Orleans, Carlos Bringuier challenged Oswald to a radio debate and forwarded a tape of the debate to Joannides. In the immediate aftermath of the assassination, DRE released incriminating documents that helped shape public opinion about Oswald. When Jeff Morley asked to see Joannides's reports, the CIA told him they never existed. "When a CIA case officer is running a group like that," the reporter says, "the standard operating procedure was to file what was called a monthly progress report. I've spoken to probably ten former CIA people and asked them, 'Is it possible that he [Joannides] didn't report about this group? And every person I talked to said, 'No, it's not possible. He reported on that group.'" Morley also wonders about Joannides's relationship with Karamessines, a fellow Greek American who approved the boilerplate message that went to Mexico City. All this leads to speculation that in the months leading up to the assassination, Karamessines and Joannides may have been grooming Oswald for an operation that involved DRE.

It is damning that the CIA withheld all information from the Warren Commission about Joannides's Cuban efforts as well as the agency's intense work to overthrow Fidel Castro—an undeniable possible motive for a counterassassination move against a U.S. president. This directly subverted the stated goals of the Warren Commission and denied to it the opportunity to more fully explain the events of November 22. In the 1960s, though, the CIA may have had the backing of President Johnson in its subterfuge. The Cold War was raging, and LBJ feared the American people would favor military retaliation if they suspected that Cuba or Russia was behind the assassination.[70] What is far worse is that the CIA continued to refuse to provide this critical information when a new investigation of JFK's murder was organized in the mid-1970s, at a time when political conditions were very different and retaliatory war would have been unthinkable after the Vietnam debacle. Both the public and the Congress were demanding to know the full truth after more than a decade of deceit. However, the House Select Committee on Assassinations had no more luck in prying the truth out of the CIA in the seventies than the Warren Commission had in the sixties. The only reason we know anything at all about Joannides's connection to DRE is because of the Assassination Records Review Board, a federal panel assembled in response to Oliver Stone's 1991 movie JFK. Stone's incendiary charges of a CIA-led conspiracy to murder the president—however exaggerated or imagined they might have been—generated fierce demands from politicians and citizens for answers at long last.[71]

"At long last" is a relative term with the CIA. More than twenty years later, we are still awaiting the release of key documents from the agency on matters related to November 22. In 2005 the widely respected chief counsel to the House Select Committee on Assassinations, Robert Blakey, told a room full of assassination researchers in Bethesda, Maryland, that the CIA "set [him] up" in the late 1970s. Blakey revealed that the CIA called George Joannides out of retirement to serve as its liaison with the House Committee to "help it find and review CIA documents during its investigation." This was despite Blakey's agreement with the CIA that no one who had any connection to Oswald or assassination-related matters would be a part of the House Committee's investigation. In 2011 Blakey went further in an interview for this book: "Of course they [the CIA] lied to us. There's a federal statute that says what they did was a felony. Obstruction of a congressional investigation is a felony. They signed an agreement pledging full cooperation, and they broke the contract." "The CIA duped Blakey, and he admits it," commented the reporter Jefferson Morley. "This shows bad faith and [the CIA's] intent to hide something. That's why I don't give them the benefit of the doubt, because they had the chance to come clean [during the House investigation], and instead they created a mechanism where this whole thing would stay hidden for another forty years," until documents are finally released in 2017—assuming they still exist, have not been altered, or are not so heavily redacted as to be useless.[72]

It is even more outrageous than Morley suggests. Neither Joannides nor anyone else at the CIA ever told the House Committee that Joannides had worked with DRE in Miami and therefore had a clear conflict of interest. No one ever told the committee that within hours of Kennedy's assassination, Joannides gave the green light to Cuban exiles in Miami to unleash a propaganda campaign linking Oswald to Castro, which affected newspaper coverage.[73] In addition, according to Blakey, Joannides "frequently blocked the efforts of the House panel's young researchers" when they tried to gain access to relevant CIA files. At the time, Blakey heeded the agency's request that he tighten the reins on his aggressive aides, a decision he now regrets. In a stunning evaluation that speaks volumes about the CIA's suspicious lack of candor throughout decades of investigation, Blakey flatly asserted, "I have no confidence in anything the agency told me."[74] He added, "Many have told me that the culture of the agency is one of prevarication and dissimulation and that you cannot trust it or its people. Period. End of story. I am now in that camp."[75] CIA officials insist that they have been telling the truth all along and in 1981 awarded Joannides the Career Intelligence Medal, one of the agency's highest honors.[76]

Americans who have followed the CIA's postwar history instinctively suspect Blakey is correct. The paranoia of the nuclear age and the genuine threat posed by foreign enemies gave the CIA enormous and often little-supervised power.[77] A Senate investigation headed by Idaho Democrat Frank Church in the 1970s revealed that even presidents did not have full control over what went on at the agency.[78] A decade before the Church Committee convened— just a month after the assassination, in fact—former president Harry Truman, the man who oversaw the creation of the CIA, published a knowing editorial in the *Washington Post* on the agency's lack of accountability. "For some time I have been disturbed by the way CIA has been diverted from its original assignment," Truman revealed. "It has become an operational and at times a policy-making arm of the government. This has led to trouble and may have compounded our difficulties in several explosive areas. I never had any thought that when I set up the CIA that it would be injected into peacetime cloak and dagger operations."[79] In a dangerous world, then and now, few serious people question the need for some kinds of counterintelligence and espionage. The CIA has proved its worth countless times, such as in the impressive operation in 2011 to find and kill Osama bin Laden. But Truman's wise words, and the CIA's actions before and after President Kennedy's assassination, are a reminder of the urgent need for close supervision, unceasing vigilance, and in some cases, complete transparency—even from a secret spy division of government.[80]

Another peculiar story involving the CIA and Oswald concerns audiotapes made during Lee Oswald's trip to Mexico City. During the Cold War, American and Soviet intelligence agents routinely bugged each other's telephones, and the CIA in Mexico City had tapped the phones at the Cuban and Soviet embassies. The CIA maintains that it does not have any original recordings of the calls Oswald made to the Soviet embassy because it routinely erased low-priority conversations and then reused the tapes.[81] Yet at least a couple of the "low-priority" calls involving Oswald (or an individual identified as Oswald) were important enough for the CIA to transcribe. On September 28, 1963, at 11:51 A.M., the CIA eavesdropped on a call made to the Soviet embassy in which Oswald tried to expedite his exit back to a Communist state. The American transcribers were native Russian speakers who described Oswald's attempt at the language as "terrible, hardly recognizable."[82] Yet Oswald had studied Russian, spoke it at home, and lived in the Soviet Union for several years. On October 1, Oswald supposedly made another call to the Russian embassy. The same native Russian transcribers (Boris and Anna Tarasoff) testified that the male voice heard on the September 28 and October 1 tapes are from the same person, whether Oswald or someone else. In the wake of the assassination, FBI agents who listened to the tapes were convinced that the voice was not Oswald's. These agents also saw the CIA's photograph of "Oswald" and knew immediately the picture was not of the same man arrested in Dallas. On November 23, 1963, J. Edgar Hoover called the Oval Office:

JOHNSON: Have you established any more about the [Oswald] visit to the Soviet Embassy in Mexico in September?

HOOVER: No, that's one angle that's very confusing for this reason. We have up here the tape and the photograph of the man who was at the Soviet Embassy, using Oswald's name. That picture and the tape do not correspond to this man's voice, nor to his appearance. In other words, it appears there was a second person who was at the Soviet Embassy.[83]

Thus, the director of the FBI flatly contradicted the claim of the CIA that no tapes of the September 1963 events in Mexico City were preserved. J. Edgar Hoover unmistakably acknowledged the existence of at least one tape, and that FBI personnel had listened to it, determining that the voice (and photograph) were not Oswald's. (Hoover's assertion is backed up by two attorneys for the Warren Commission, who say a representative of the CIA played the tapes for them in early 1964.) So who was impersonating Oswald on the phone in Mexico City? Was this a CIA agent fishing for more information about Oswald's intentions? Was it a CIA attempt to further tie Oswald to the Communists prior to an attempt on President Kennedy's life? Or is it something else entirely? In addition, what actually happened to the tapes of Oswald or his impersonator? When were they lost or destroyed, and by whom?

It would also be very useful to know more about the LBJ-Hoover chat, and where it led, but (foreshadowing the infamous 18½-minute gap in a key tape of President Nixon during the Watergate scandal[84]) there is a 14-minute gap in the tape of the conversation. In 1999, the researcher Rex Bradford requested this significant tape from the LBJ Library in Austin, Texas. "And then something very funny happened," Bradford says. "[The librarian] said, 'Well, you know, that tape is very poor quality, hard to listen to, you see, he was using his vice presidential taping equipment, you don't really want that tape.' And I said, '. . . I have audio engineering friends, we can probably do something.'" Bradford says that after the librarian reluctantly sent him the cassette tape, he played it and heard "fourteen minutes of pure hiss" in the middle of the conversation, as though that portion had been erased. Bradford is skeptical of the librarian's explanation because the other phone calls on the tape, presumably recorded with the same vice presidential equipment, were "just fine."[85]

Other tapes related to the assassination have disappeared altogether or had significant portions erased under mysterious circumstances. Anne Goodpasture, a CIA operative who worked with Win Scott (Mexico City's station chief), told a reporter in 2005 that she thought Scott had made a copy of Oswald's taped conversation with Soviet embassy officials and "squirreled it away in his safe." A subsequent lawsuit filed by Scott's son Michael revealed that his father's safe did indeed contain audiotapes, which further highlights James Angleton's personal visit to Mexico City to clean out Scott's safe shortly after he died, taking the contents with him back to D.C. It was the last anyone outside the CIA would see or hear of that tape—vital evidence that also has significant historical value. The question is why. What was Angleton trying to conceal?[86]

9

ROUNDING UP THE USUAL SUSPECTS: THE ASSASSINATION'S PUZZLE PALACE

THE FBI AND THE CIA ARE AT THE HEART of many conspiracy theories about JFK's killing. Researchers tend to be harsh, and some assume the absolute worst about Hoover and key leaders inside the CIA—direct involvement in JFK's assassination—without providing ironclad proof of the most serious allegations. There is no question, however, that both agencies were trying to cover their tracks to avoid blame; insiders quickly picked this up. Shortly after November 22, John Whitten, a CIA agent who ran covert operations in Mexico and Central America, was put in charge of the CIA's internal investigation of Oswald, a job that required close contact with FBI officials. In December 1963, the agent caught a glimpse of the early FBI report on the assassination, the same one that served as the starting point for the Warren Commission. Whitten was shocked when he realized that both the FBI and CIA had been purposely withholding critical information from him. When Whitten complained to his superiors, he was "told that his services would no longer be needed" and "was sent back to his Latin American duties." Apparently, Whitten was taken off the case by James Angleton, CIA's director of counterintelligence.[1]

But a cover-up to avoid culpability for missing signs of an impending assassination, or having worked with the assassin in some undercover capacity prior to November 22, is very different from the institutional orchestration of the murder of a U.S. president. Author Mark North has accused Hoover, in effect, of being a silent accomplice to the assassination. In his book *Act of Treason*, North argues that the FBI director knew about a Mafia plot to kill JFK but did nothing about it for two reasons. First, Hoover thought of Kennedy as "an indecisive, immoral liberal who, if left in place, would destroy the nation." The irony, given Hoover's unconventional private life, must be noted. And second, because "JFK had made it known that he intended, by the end of his first term in office, to retire [Hoover] and replace him with a man of his own, more liberal political philosophy." This argument is weak. While Kennedy would no doubt have preferred someone other than Hoover as FBI director, Hoover had cleverly accumulated evidence of JFK's infidelities and had made certain the Kennedys were aware of his proofs—which provided an unusual form of job security.

In any event, North claims that the "overwhelming body of evidence" points to the New Orleans mob boss Carlos Marcello as the person who masterminded the assassination. By the fall of 1962, Marcello was facing a federal indictment, possible deportation, and relentless attacks from Bobby Kennedy's Justice Department. He "realized that by placing the presidency in the hands of Lyndon Johnson" he could possibly "remedy the situation." It was "common knowledge," says North, that LBJ had "no interest in pursuing the Mafia." Before the Kennedys came to power, the FBI director had sometimes turned a blind eye to mob activity. During World War II, for example, the federal government essentially subcontracted the security of New York's waterfront district to a Mafia thug, Charles "Lucky" Luciano. The deal was simple: if Luciano's henchmen kept an eye out for German and Japanese saboteurs, then Hoover's G-men would not examine their business activities too closely.[2] In Hoover's eyes, the Communists and their "useful idiots" in the United States were a greater threat than "patriotic" Mafia bosses.[3]

FBI informers and pre–November 22 eavesdropping had yielded a couple of clues that mob godfathers had drawn a bead on JFK. The assassination researcher Lamar Waldron has asserted, "In autumn 1962, according to one of his former associates, [Carlos] Marcello met with three men on the mobster's 3,000-acre estate outside New Orleans." During this meeting, the conversation turned toward the Kennedys. Marcello detested RFK, who was working to dismantle his business operations and had even secured his deportation to Guatemala. He "referred to President Kennedy as a dog, with his brother Robert being the tail. 'The dog,' he said, 'will keep biting you if you only cut off its tail.'" In other words, Marcello believed he needed to kill JFK in order to neutralize Bobby.[4]

Marcello is not the only Mafia chieftain to be implicated by assassination researchers. Santo Trafficante, a mob boss whose fiefdom was southern Florida, supposedly made a similar threat during a conversation with a Cuban exile, Jose Aleman. According to Aleman, Trafficante complained that the Kennedy brothers were "not honest. They took graft and they did not keep a bargain . . . Mark my word, this man Kennedy is in trouble, and he will get what is coming to him." When Aleman remarked that JFK would probably win a second term, Trafficante allegedly replied, "You don't understand me. Kennedy's not going to make it to the election. He is going to be hit."[5]

The lack of swift and decisive action once these threats became known to the FBI is disturbing. But it pales by comparison with the bureau's casual attitude toward Lee Harvey Oswald. How could Oswald have escaped identification as a real and present danger, given his unusual history as a turncoat and agitator? In the entire United States there lived only a handful of former defectors to Communist states; in Texas, exactly one, Lee Oswald. Make no mistake—the FBI knew that Oswald was in the Lone Star State. By October 1963, the bureau also "knew him as a possibly deranged Marxist who supported the Cuban revolution, who was capable of violence, and who had been in recent contact with Soviet intelligence officers." Hoover's G-men also knew where Oswald worked, and one might think this relevant fact would have occurred to an alert bureau matching up potential assassins with presidential motorcade routes. The FBI certainly realized this after the fact. Agent James Hosty had been tracking Oswald for months and, under orders, destroyed evidence after the assassination to cover the bureau's tracks. "We failed in carrying through some of the most salient aspects of the Oswald investigation," Hoover later admitted. "It ought to be a lesson to us all, but I doubt if some even realize it now." The magnitude of the FBI's mistake should not be understated. Hoover himself termed it "gross incompetency" and it resulted in the decapitation of the elected U.S. government.[6] However, incompetency does not equal complicity in the murder of a president. The evidence, fairly sifted, does not justify such speculation.

THE FEDERAL BUREAU of Investigation and the Central Intelligence Agency are frequently lumped together in the public's mind as secretive organizations. But their missions and methods are different, and that distinction applies to any study of the Kennedy assassination. In matters pertaining to November 22, the CIA's role was utterly unique—a subtle, ambiguous, murky tale that befits the nature of the agency. It is highly unlikely that the CIA had any institutional role in John Kennedy's murder, nor were the vast majority of its personnel trying to cover up the real facts. In truth, the agency spent considerable resources in diligently checking out all manner of rumors and reports. On November 24, 1963, for example, the U.S. naval attaché in Canberra, Australia, reported a telephone call from "an anonymous individual who had described himself as a Polish chauffeur for the Soviet Embassy in that city. This individual, while discussing several matters of intelligence interest, touched on the possibility that the Soviet government had financed the assassination of President Kennedy." The Navy office had received a similar call the previous year, before Dallas. Australian authorities shrugged off the incident, but the CIA launched a full inquiry and sent reports to the White

House, the State Department, the Secret Service, and the FBI. A few days later, the agency also received information from the Dutch Foreign Office that hinted at Cuban Communist involvement in Kennedy's murder. When a Dutch official had mentioned the Bay of Pigs fiasco during a November 7, 1963, reception at the Soviet embassy, Ricardo Santos, a senior official of the Cuban embassy in the country, allegedly replied, "Just wait and you will see what we can do. It will happen soon." When the Dutch official asked for specifics, Santos merely said, "Just wait, just wait."[7]

The CIA also investigated a letter sent to the U.S. embassy in Stockholm, Sweden, dated November 25, 1963, which claimed that Chinese Communists had indoctrinated Oswald during his stay in the Soviet Union. According to the letter's author, the Chinese had hired Oswald to pose as a Castro sympathizer so that the United States would bomb Cuba once Oswald had killed the president. This attack would in turn force the Soviets to retaliate against the Americans and simultaneously share their nuclear secrets with the "Red Chinese." Once the Communist bloc won the war, the Chinese would assassinate Soviet premier Khrushchev and take over the world.

The Stockholm embassy considered the letter a "crank"—after all, if the writer had known all this he would have been one of the world's best-informed people, and would not likely have had to resort to an anonymous letter to an out-of-the-way embassy. Nonetheless, the CIA had the missive forwarded to Langley for analysis.

The CIA chased other phantoms. The Berlin station interviewed a Moroccan student named Mohammed Reggab who claimed that he had known Marina Oswald in 1961 and kept a picture and letter from her at his house in Casablanca. The CIA gave Reggab a polygraph test and decided that he was lying. Another dead end involved a twenty-four-year-old Army private named Eugene Dinkin. On the very same day he was scheduled to receive a psychiatric evaluation, Dinkin went AWOL from his unit in Metz, France, and entered Switzerland using a fake ID and "forged travel orders." On November 6 and 7, "he appeared in the press room of the United Nations office in Geneva and told reporters he was being persecuted. He also wished to alert the world to the U.S. government's 'propaganda campaign.'" More important, at least one reporter thought she heard Dinkin say that "they" were plotting against JFK and that "something" big would happen in Texas. The CIA investigated Dinkin's story, but could not find any evidence linking him to the Kennedy murder.[8]

Between October 1963 and September 1964, CIA employees were diverted from other duties to investigate scores of allegations that led nowhere. Did the Soviets take advantage of the confusion to launch a disinformation campaign blaming right-wing, anticommunist elements for Kennedy's murder? It is certainly possible and would have served their interests. On November 26, 1963, a CIA agent with the code name of W/1 met with a Soviet spy known only as M in a busy café on the Rue Marcelin Berthelot in Paris. W/1's mission was to gauge the Soviet reaction to Kennedy's assassination and find out what they knew about Oswald. M pointed out that Kennedy had been opposed by a number of powerful right-wing organizations, thereby implying that one of these groups had likely planned the president's murder. In addition, M predicted that the U.S. investigation of the assassination would turn up nothing since "the Dallas police had silenced Oswald." When W/1 asked about Oswald's time in the Soviet Union, M denied ever knowing the ex-Marine and insisted—obviously incorrectly—that foreigners were not allowed to work in the USSR.

The historian Max Holland believes that Soviet disinformation of this sort helped spark the most famous anti–Warren Commission event of the 1960s, later to be memorialized inaccurately in Oliver Stone's movie *JFK*. New Orleans's flamboyant district attorney, Jim Garrison, held a show trial in 1969 to find President Kennedy's real killers. Garrison charged a local businessman, Clay Shaw, with JFK's murder, but in Garrison's concoction, the murder conspiracy was much wider, taking in a good portion of the U.S. government, especially the CIA. Max Holland uncovered a 1967 article in an Italian newspaper, *Paese Sera*, that claimed Clay Shaw had served on the board of a dummy corporation in Rome (Centro Mondiale Commerciale, or CMC) that funneled cash to CIA operatives. The story was totally false, but Holland says that it helped convince Garrison that he was on to something big. Twenty years later, the same bogus story made it into Stone's movie. During a scene in the district attorney's office, Garrison (played by Kevin Costner) confronts Shaw (Tommy Lee Jones) while holding a copy of the article:

> GARRISON: Mr. Shaw, this is [an] Italian newspaper article saying that you were a member of the board of Centro Mondiale Commerciale in Italy—that this company was a creature of the CIA for the transfer of funds in Italy for illegal political espionage activity. [The article] says that this company was expelled from Italy for those activities.
>
> SHAW: I'm well aware of that asinine article. I'm thinking very seriously of suing that rag of a newspaper . . .
>
> GARRISON: Mr. Shaw, [have] you ever been a contract agent for the Central Intelligence Agency?

Shaw had worked with the CIA as a paid informant, but only for a brief period in the 1950s. Yet Stone portrayed Shaw as one of Langley's top operatives. After the collapse of the USSR in the early 1990s, Holland found a telling document in the Soviet archives entitled "Disinformation Operations of the KGB through *Paese Sera.*" According to the document, "Department A of the First Chief Directorate" began "a series of disinformation operations" in 1967 that included feeding phony stories to an "emplacement" in New York. Holland dug through old newspapers until he found the CMC story reprinted in a New York–based weekly called the *National Guardian*. Logically, the KGB's goal was not just to point an accusing finger at its right-wing enemies but also to keep public suspicion away from the Soviets while the American people sought a fuller answer to the Kennedy murder mystery.[9]

LONG BEFORE OLIVER Stone turned his prodigious talents to the Kennedy murder, the KGB and the Soviet leadership were worrying about the public framing of the assassination, given Oswald's defection to the USSR. Yet much of the informed speculation from the very beginning pointed to JFK's domestic enemies, not his foreign adversaries. Those believing this conjecture included some of the Kennedy family. In late November 1963, Robert Kennedy arranged a meeting in Russia between an artist friend of his, William Walton, and a Soviet defense attaché, Georgi Bolshakov, who had helped the Kennedys during the Cuban Missile Crisis by serving as a diplomatic back channel to the Kremlin. Walton and Bolshakov met at a restaurant in Moscow called the Sovietskaya. "Bolshakov, who had himself been deeply moved by [the] assassination, listened intently as Walton explained that the Kennedys believed there was a large political conspiracy behind Oswald's rifle. Despite Oswald's connections to the Communist world, the Kennedys believed that the president was felled by domestic opponents."[10]

Some of JFK's aides long believed much the same. During a dinner at Jimmy's Harborside Restaurant in Boston five years after the president's death, Kenny O'Donnell told the future Speaker of the House, Tip O'Neill, that he had heard two shots come from behind the picket fence on November 22. O'Donnell was in a car closely following the presidential limo when JFK was killed. "That's not what you told the Warren Commission," O'Neill replied. O'Donnell admitted as much and explained why. "I told the FBI what I had heard but they said it couldn't have happened that way and that I must have been imagining things. So I testified the way they wanted me to. I just didn't want to stir up any more pain and trouble for the family." Dave Powers, another close JFK adviser sitting next to O'Donnell in the car, attended the same dinner with O'Neill. Powers confirmed O'Donnell's recollection, claiming he had also heard two shots from the grassy knoll.[11]

For a long time, Ted Sorensen, JFK's loyal wordsmith, accepted the conclusions of the Warren report. In his bestseller *Kennedy* (first published in 1965), Sorensen wrote, "Personally I accept the conclusion that no plot or political motive was involved, despite the fact that this makes the deed all the more difficult to accept." But toward the end of his life, Sorensen had second thoughts. Encouraging a read of James Douglass's *JFK and the Unspeakable*, Sorensen said, "I endorse no conspiracy books, but that one made an impression. Its thesis is that Kennedy was killed by those opposed to his switch toward peace regarding the Soviets, the Cubans, and the North Vietnamese. That has a credible ring to it but lacks hard evidence including names that could stand up in [a] courtroom."[12]

Strangely, President Kennedy himself had considered the possibility of a military and intelligence community coup d'état. "It's possible," he told Red Fay, one of his closest confidants, in the summer of 1962. "It could happen in this country, but the conditions would have to be just right. If, for example, the country had a young president, and he had a Bay of Pigs, there would be a certain uneasiness. Maybe the military would do a little criticizing behind his back, but this would be written off as the usual military dissatisfaction with civilian control. Then if there were another Bay of Pigs, the reaction of the country would be, 'Is he too young and inexperienced?' The military would almost feel that it was their patriotic obligation to stand ready to preserve the integrity of the nation, and only God knows just what segment of democracy they would be defending if they overthrew the elected establishment."[13]

Given the lack of hard evidence, to accuse any arm or agency of the federal government of orchestrating Kennedy's assassination is both irresponsible and disingenuous. At the same time, it is impossible to rule out the possibility that a small, secret cabal of CIA hard-liners, angry about Kennedy's handling of Cuba and sensing a leftward turn on negotiations with the Soviets and the prosecution of the war in Vietnam, took matters into their own hands lest the United States go soft on Communism.[14] There are plenty of historical parallels. In 44 B.C., twenty-three Roman senators stabbed Julius Caesar to death because they considered him a tyrant. In 1865, a handful of Southern nationalists hatched a successful plot against Abraham Lincoln for similar reasons. In 1914, members of a secret Serbian sect known as the "Black Hand" murdered Archduke Franz Ferdinand and his wife, Duchess Sophie, precipitating World War I. In the early 1960s, the CIA tried to assassinate Fidel Castro at least eight times, and the Cuban regime claims the attempts numbered closer to six hundred. The idea that a rogue element within the CIA, operating as an impregnable cell, could have assassinated Kennedy is not a mere flight of fancy. After all, during the Cold War, top CIA officials often ran clandestine operations without much or any oversight, and conducted disinformation campaigns that covered their tracks well.[15]

THOSE WHO LIVED through the tumult following the Kennedy assassination remember that few initially mentioned the CIA as a possible culprit. No one except for a tiny elite group of insiders knew of the CIA's efforts to kill Fidel Castro, or of some CIA higher-ups' views of President Kennedy. It would have been considered unpatriotic at the time to suggest seriously the possibility of CIA involvement—although a few years later, President Johnson expressed a belief in private in 1967 that the CIA had had a role in Kennedy's death.[16] The Communists, on the other hand, were juicy targets right from the beginning. Since Oswald had embraced Marxism, defected to the USSR, and handed out flyers for Fidel Castro, many Americans thought it reasonable to assume that the Soviets or Cubans could have been behind JFK's murder.

Once Oswald was arrested, his Marxist past became known within hours, and an incident in the Dallas district attorney's office nearly lit the fuse on a confrontation with the Soviet bloc. Assistant D.A. Bill Alexander searched Oswald's apartment, which was cluttered with books and letters making clear his ideological affiliation. By ten P.M. on November 22, Alexander was composing Oswald's indictment when a Dallas reporter called and Alexander answered the phone. The reporter wanted to know about Oswald. "I told him [Oswald] was a Communist," said Alexander. The reporter replied that he would need something more substantial than Alexander's word. "All right, how about if the indictment reads, 'Oswald did then and there with malice aforethought kill John Kennedy, president of the United States, in furtherance of a Communist conspiracy'?" The reporter was well pleased: "Yeah, I can run with that." Washington was not as pleased once word reached senior officials there. Clark Clifford, a high-level adviser to Presidents Truman and now Johnson (later LBJ's defense secretary), called district attorney Henry Wade, Alexander's boss, to protest vigorously. "What the hell is Alexander trying to do, start World War III?" thundered Clifford. The "Communist conspiracy" clause was quickly dropped from both the indictment and the newspaper.[17]

Nonetheless, Lyndon Johnson feared precisely this scenario: that the public would conclude the Communists were behind JFK's murder, inevitably sparking a demand for nuclear retaliation—which in turn was a powerful motive for pinning it all on Oswald as a lunatic gunman. The irony is that, again completely in private, LBJ often told aides and reporters that Castro was responsible for Kennedy's murder and thus Johnson's own presidency.

(As noted above, Johnson had also confidentially suggested that the CIA had an undefined role in the events of November 22.)[18] Among LBJ assistants who have confirmed the president's Castro allegations is Joseph Califano, later President Carter's secretary of health, education, and welfare.[19] During a confidential interview with ABC journalist Howard K. Smith in October 1968, Johnson said, "I'll tell you something about Kennedy's murder that will rock you . . . Kennedy was trying to get Castro, but Castro got to him first." Smith said that he was "rocked all night" by Johnson's shocking statement, but that the president never gave him any additional details.[20] LBJ told Leo Janos of *Time* magazine that Kennedy "had been operating a damned Murder, Inc. in the Caribbean." Even Earl Warren had suspicions about Cuba and considered the Communist nation "one of the principal suspects."[21] As author Henry Hurt points out, Castro "possessed the motive, means, and opportunity" to kill Kennedy, especially since the dictator had successfully infiltrated the Cuban exile community with an army of undercover agents.[22] Castro cast suspicion on himself by delivering a vitriolic speech in Brazil a few weeks before the assassination. "United States leaders should think that if they are aiding terrorist plans to eliminate Cuban leaders," he warned, "they themselves will not be safe."[23] Of course, the Cuban dictator knew what Americans did not: He was a constant CIA target.

Did Johnson really have proof that Castro was responsible for Kennedy's murder? A mysterious meeting held in Mexico City among high-ranking federal officials offers tantalizing clues. Shortly after the assassination, U.S. ambassador Thomas Mann convened with FBI agents Larry Keenan and Clark Anderson, CIA station chief Winston Scott, and CIA agent David Atlee Phillips in Mann's office. When Mann suggested that Cuban and Russian Communists might have planned November 22, Keenan assured him that it was an open-and-shut case—an emotionally disturbed Marxist named Lee Oswald had acted completely on his own. Mann was flabbergasted. "I hadn't reached any conclusion," he would say later, "and that's why it surprised me so much. That was the only time it ever happened to me—'We don't want to hear any more about that case—and tell the Mexican government not to do any more about it . . . We just want to hush it up.'"[24]

Brian Latell, a former CIA agent and Cuba expert, recently published a book that raises new questions about Castro's possible links to November 22. In 2007 Latell was granted permission to interview Florentino Aspillaga, a high-level Cuban defector who worked for Castro's intelligence service in the early 1960s. Aspillaga told Latell that on the morning of the assassination, four hours before Kennedy died, he received orders to monitor radio signals coming from Texas. Aspillaga explained that the unusual directive caught him off guard since he was normally told to monitor CIA radio traffic. Separately, Latell discovered that Oswald may have bluntly threatened to kill Kennedy during his visit to the Cuban consulate in September 1963, and that Castro was quickly informed of Oswald's vow. Yet Castro did not send any warnings through his channels to Washington. None of this is conclusive. Perhaps on November 22, Castro and his henchmen may have wanted to know if Kennedy would address Cuba again in his scheduled speeches; just a few days earlier in Tampa and Miami, JFK had bashed Castro at length.[25] And it may be that the Cubans dismissed Oswald's rant as unserious. It may also be true that Castro, having been targeted so often by the CIA for assassination, felt no special obligation to alert the American authorities about a threat on Kennedy's life.[26]

We cannot really know what role Cuba might have played unless investigators gain unfettered access to Castro government documents, assuming they exist and have not been altered. Still, the best available evidence casts doubt that Castro was actively involved in Kennedy's murder, and nothing Latell has uncovered proves otherwise. While it is always possible that Castro's reaction to the news of Kennedy's death was feigned, he did not seem like a man who had been embroiled in a plot or had advance knowledge. The Cuban dictator appeared "shocked and saddened" by the announcement and said over and over again, "Es una mala noticia" ("This is bad news"). Also, shortly before the assassination, Castro told the French journalist Jean Daniel that Kennedy had a chance of becoming "the greatest president of the United States, the leader who may at last understand that there can be coexistence between capitalists and socialists." In the end, the CIA was officially unable to establish any links between Cuba and JFK's death. On March 3, 1964, a CIA operative sent Langley the details of an interview he had conducted with a Cuban official who claimed that "Castro felt that it was possible that . . . Kennedy would have gone on ultimately to negotiate with Cuba," not because of "love for Cuba" but rather "for practical reasons." Moreover, he had heard Castro denouncing LBJ "in harsh terms," hardly the reaction expected if Castro had wanted to replace JFK with LBJ—and there was no reason prior to November 22 for Castro to believe that Johnson would be better on Cuba policy than Kennedy had been.

In 1978 Castro himself told the House Select Committee on Assassinations that killing Kennedy would have been an "insane" thing for him to do. "That would have been the most perfect pretext for the United States to invade our country which is what I have tried to prevent for all these years."[27] Rather, Castro pointed an accusing finger at his own enemies in the United States, CIA-trained anti-Castro Cuban exiles. Fabian Escalante, the former head of Cuba's Department of State Security, says that the exiles "had planned to kill Kennedy twice in November 1963, because they felt the U.S. president had

done too little to topple the [Castro] government on the Caribbean island."
According to Escalante, the exiles hoped that Kennedy's death would trigger
a U.S. invasion of Cuba.[28]

Edward Martino's peculiar story about his father, John, lends some credibility to Escalante's claim. John Martino, who had Mafia connections, spent three years in one of Castro's prisons, and he emerged from that ordeal fiercely anticommunist. Martino traveled to Dallas twice in the autumn of 1963 and, on the day of the assassination, ordered his son to stay home from school and monitor the news. At lunchtime, when his son alerted him that Kennedy had been shot, the elder Martino appeared tense but unsurprised and spent many hours on the telephone, doing his part to blame Fidel Castro. In later years, John Martino claimed that he was a low-level operative in a plot to kill Kennedy that had been masterminded by anti-Castro Cubans and the Mafia, possibly with some CIA involvement. Martino told friends that Oswald had been manipulated by the anti-Castro group to assassinate Kennedy in order to trigger a U.S. invasion of Cuba.[29]

For their part, the Soviets had unfettered access to Lee Oswald for years and could have recruited him or created a brainwashed "Manchurian candidate" assassin.[30] However, common sense and the existing evidence lead to a conclusion similar to the Cubans. A few months before he died, JFK signed the Limited Nuclear Test Ban Treaty with the Soviet Union, abolishing aboveground nuclear weapons tests. The treaty represented a breakthrough in arms control between the superpowers and opened the door to further agreements that could have lessened Cold War tensions and saved both nations billions in defense expenditures. Since Khrushchev was putting his country on a path toward detente, and saw that Kennedy was doing the same, why would he risk war by authorizing the murder of his negotiating partner? He had come to understand what the consequences of nuclear war would be. In July 1963 Khrushchev told his fellow Communists that "only madmen" believed that the USSR could triumph in a nuclear war. "A million workers would be destroyed for each capitalist," said the Soviet premier. "There are people who see things differently. Let them. History will teach them."

In the months following the assassination, Khrushchev became convinced that a conspiracy of some sort, possibly organized by U.S. "reactionaries" had brought about Kennedy's murder. The Soviet chairman did not believe that Oswald acted alone and expressed doubt to one prominent journalist, Drew Pearson, that "the American security services were this inept." "What really happened?" he asked, and his suspicions were echoed by his wife, Nina, in May 1964.[31] Sergei Khrushchev, the son of the Soviet premier, who now lives and teaches in the United States, remembers: "First of all, my father had no idea how [the assassination] happened and what happened. He tried to figure it out from [the] KGB, and of course [the] KGB said they were never involved with this. He knew it was not Soviets and he thought it was not Cubans, but he didn't have control over Soviets completely." A rogue group of Soviet hard-liners or a secret KGB cabal similar to the one alleged by some to have existed within the CIA could have planned the president's murder, but theories with-out a shred of hard evidence must eventually be set aside.[32]

During a 1999 summit in Cologne, Germany, Russian president Boris Yelt-sin presented President Bill Clinton with a surprise gift, "a report on declassi-fied Russian information relating to the assassination of President John Kennedy." Although the account contained some intriguing materials, such as a handwritten note from Oswald to the Supreme Soviet asking for asylum and citizenship, it "did not alter Washington's conclusion regarding KGB re-cruitment of Oswald" or "even shed much new light on what was already known about Oswald's time in the Soviet Union."[33]

So if Oswald was not a Soviet agent, could he have been a hit man for the mob?[34] Certainly, the American public has been conditioned by the media and Hollywood to believe that the Mafia is a well-oiled killing machine that can take down anyone. In the movie *The Godfather, Part II* (1974), mob boss Michael Corleone (Al Pacino) has this famous exchange with his half-brother, Tom Hagen (Robert Duvall) about plans to kill another top mobster:

> HAGEN: It would be like trying to kill the president. There's no way we can get to him.
> CORLEONE: Tom, you know you surprise me. If anything in this life is certain, if history has taught us anything, it's that you can kill *anybody.*[35]

The first two *Godfather* movies were released in the 1970s, just as the pub-lic, and the House Select Committee on Assassinations, were reconsidering the Warren Commission's findings.[36]

Many Mafia kingpins loathed the Kennedys, mainly because RFK went after organized crime with a vengeance once he became attorney general.[37] He raised the number of mob convictions from 35 in 1960 to 288 in 1963. Did Bobby's aggressive tactics represent a betrayal of a deal between Joseph P. Ken-nedy, Sr., and the mob? The father's ties to organized crime allegedly dated back to his days as a bootlegger during Prohibition.[38] Shortly before the 1960 election, Joseph Kennedy was said to have promised Chicago mafioso Sam Giancana access to the White House in return for intervening with another mobster, Frank Costello, who had threatened to kill him over a property dispute. The elder Kennedy was said to have told Giancana, "You help me now, Sam, and I'll see to it . . . that you . . . can sit in the goddamned Oval Office if you want. That you'll have the president's ear."[39] According to some published sources, Giancana agreed to the deal and convinced Costello to take the ambassador off his hit list. Even before this incident, Giancana had apparently helped JFK by distributing the Kennedy patriarch's cash to buy endorsements and votes during the critical West Virginia Democratic primary election in May 1960. And when JFK began having an affair with a black-haired beauty named Judith Campbell while he was still a U.S. senator, Giancana slept with her as well, reportedly so that he would eventually have a direct link to the White House.

The intermediary for the Kennedy-Giancana joint ventures was Frank Sinatra, an avid Kennedy supporter until their falling-out during JFK's presidency.[40] Sinatra introduced Senator Kennedy to Judy Campbell in Las Vegas. Moreover, as Sinatra's daughter Tina informed CBS's *60 Minutes*, her father called Giancana and acted as the go-between for the West Virginia primary shenanigans. When the Kennedys turned on Giancana once they were in the White House, Sinatra had to work hard to deflect the mobster's wrath at Sinatra on account of the Kennedys' unfaithfulness. In atonement, the singer played at Giancana's club, the Villa Venice, with his "Rat Pack" of fellow entertainers, for eight nights in a row.[41] Sinatra worked his way back into Giancana's good graces, but the Kennedys never did.[42]

If Giancana followed through, he might have worked with fellow Mafia don Carlos Marcello, who had been deported by RFK and was, if anything, even angrier than Giancana with the Kennedys. In 1979 the New Orleans–based Marcello told an undercover FBI agent that he had known Dutz Murret (Oswald's uncle) and that Oswald had worked as a runner for Murret's bookmaking operation. Marcello supposedly knew David Ferrie as well. Ferrie had been hired as a researcher by Marcello's attorney, G. Wray Gill. When Ferrie wasn't researching cases for Gill, he did part-time investigative work for Guy Banister, another Marcello employee. Oswald's Marxist political views might have made him a suitable triggerman. Once the hit went down, federal law enforcement agencies and the public would blame Communists, not mobsters. Perhaps Marcello approached Oswald indirectly, through an intermediary posing as a Castro supporter. Some assassination buffs contend that the man who appeared at the Cuban embassy in Mexico City and was misidentified as Oswald was an impostor dispatched by the mob so that the real Oswald would be contemporaneously linked with Cuban and Soviet Communists.[43]

The HSCA's Robert Blakey believes that Marcello and Santo Trafficante, the mob don of southern Florida, were the brains behind the Kennedy murder. As proof, Blakey points to the confessions that Marcello and Trafficante made shortly before they passed away. In 1985, an FBI prison snitch named Jack Van Laningham heard Marcello say, "Yeah, I had the little son of a bitch [JFK] killed, and I would do it again; he was a thorn in my side. I wish I could have done it myself." Marcello also told Van Laningham that he had been introduced to Lee Oswald by a man named "Ferris" (possibly David Ferrie) and that he, Marcello, had personally helped Jack Ruby get "set . . . up in the bar business." From his deathbed, Santo Trafficante told his lawyer, Frank Ragano, that he and Marcello had masterminded the assassination. Ragano published this story in his autobiography, *Mob Lawyer*. But Ragano apparently added this explosive revelation to his autobiography while he was trying to sell the manuscript—and just three weeks after the release of *JFK*, convenient timing so that he could capitalize on the movie sensation.[44]

Jimmy Hoffa, the corrupt president of the Teamsters Union, must also be included on a list of crime figures with strong motives to kill John F. Kennedy. Hoffa and Bobby Kennedy had a hatred for one another that would melt steel, stemming from the McClellan Committee hearings in 1957, when RFK served as counsel and grilled Hoffa in an unrelenting manner. Still enraged by Hoffa's smug answers to his inquiries, Bobby as attorney general set up a special "Get Hoffa" unit within the Justice Department. He was determined to destroy Hoffa no matter the cost. The usual union ties with Democrats did not come into play, since the Teamsters often supported Republican candidates. Hoffa grew deeply frustrated with the increased pressure from Washington and began making threats against the attorney general. According to a government informant, Hoffa discussed two "separate murder plans aimed at Robert Kennedy." The first involved blowing up RFK's estate in Virginia, Hickory Hill. The second is eerily familiar: Hoffa thought RFK could be "shot to death from a distance away; a single gunman could be enlisted to carry it out—someone without any traceable connection to Hoffa and the Teamsters; a high-powered rifle with a telescopic sight would be the assassination weapon." Hoffa also thought that the South would be the ideal location for the hit since the authorities would likely blame it on segregationists.

Did Hoffa implement this plan, but change the target to JFK instead of RFK?[45] Or maybe the mob and a rogue group of CIA agents worked together to kill Kennedy. There was no hesitation by the CIA in reaching out to mobsters when they could be helpful, as they had done in planning assassination attempts against Castro. During the winter and spring of 1961, Robert Maheu, an FBI agent acting on behalf of the CIA, held meetings in Miami with crime kingpins Sam Giancana, Johnny Roselli, and Santo Trafficante. Maheu told them that if the mob wanted to murder Castro in order to reclaim their assets in Havana, the U.S. government would be glad to lend a hand. This foul relationship continued for years, even after senior administration officials thought it had ended, and the CIA continued to work with the Mafia to find ways to eliminate Castro. For example, CIA agent William Harvey delivered poison pills to Johnny Roselli, meant for Castro, even after CIA headquarters had told Attorney General Kennedy that the agency had severed its ties with gangsters.[46]

The counterargument to the Mafia theory is that even for the mob, a presidential assassination is potentially pulling the pin on a nuclear grenade. Presidents and attorneys general come and go, just like police crackdowns at the local level. Far better to wait the Kennedys out than to risk the wrath of a provoked public that would have demanded full retribution for the death of its president. Emotion and fury might have gotten the better of the godfathers' judgment, yet most organized crime experts do not believe that any of the bosses would have been willing to take such a risk. Ralph Salerno, who served as a consultant to the House Select Committee on Assassinations and the Department of Justice, tried hard to find evidence of mob involvement in JFK's death. He told an ABC reporter, "I felt it would have raised the hackles of the entire nation against organized crime so I would have loved to have found something. But I didn't find that." Salerno has expressed great respect for his former HSCA colleague Robert Blakey, but he disagrees with Blakey's conclusion about Mafia involvement. Perhaps reflecting that lack of consensus, the House committee's final report uses a bit of ambiguous language. While acknowledging that "the national syndicate of organized crime, as a group, was not involved in the assassination of President Kennedy," it says that "the available evidence does not preclude the possibility that individual members may have been involved."[47]

Bill Roemer, who helped the FBI dismantle mob operations in Chicago, is less wishy-washy. "I spent thousands and thousands of hours listening to surveillance tapes on the top mobsters in the country," he says. "[W]hen the assassination of the president happened, they discussed it relentlessly, but there was never any sign they had anything to do with it." Both Salerno's and Roemer's statements are compelling. These organized crime fighters, despite a strong desire to expose the mob's sinister nature, could not find substantial evidence linking the Mafia to Kennedy's death. This balances somewhat Robert Blakey's strong, informed opinion that organized crime is the premier suspect.[48]

IF MOB BOSSES were orchestrating the Kennedy assassination, they needed small-time flunkies to carry out the murder. And thus we come to the checkered career of Lee Oswald's killer, Jack Ruby, whose deadly act is one of the few connected to the Kennedy assassination that is undisputed. It was, after all, a nationally televised murder—the nation's first-ever live TV homicide.

Jacob Rubenstein was born into a dysfunctional Polish Jewish family in 1911. As a child, he witnessed frequent fights between his alcoholic father and mentally ill mother. When the couple's marriage ended in 1921, Rubenstein and his seven siblings were sent to live in foster homes. The divorce affected Rubenstein deeply and he soon began acting out; a psychiatric report labeled him as a "quick tempered" and "disobedient" young man.[49]

Jack quit school in the eighth grade and finished his education on the streets of Chicago. At one point, he earned money by running errands for Al Capone, the Windy City's most notorious Mafia chief. During the Great Depression, Rubenstein scalped baseball tickets, sold busts of FDR, and worked as a singing waiter in order to make ends meet. In 1937 he took a job as a secretary for Chicago's Scrap Iron and Junk Handlers Union, which brought him into contact with criminal elements. When his boss, a rogue named John Martin, shot the founder of the scrap iron union over a financial dispute, Rubenstein was questioned by police but found innocent of any wrongdoing. "Martin was replaced and the reorganized union was dominated by its secretary-treasurer, Paul J. Dorfman, a man with longstanding connections to Chicago racketeers."[50]

During World War II, Rubenstein served in the Air Force. When the war ended, he set up a small business in Chicago with his brothers and shortened his name to "Ruby"; bowing to the anti-Semitism of the day, he thought Ruby sounded "more American." When the business failed, he relocated to Dallas and established a series of nightclubs, most of which went bankrupt. Accustomed to using violence to settle disputes, Ruby would sometimes punch or pistol-whip customers who got out of line. And yet he never got into any real trouble with the Dallas police. Partly, this was due to Ruby's untiring efforts to make friends with members of the department. Some officers even patronized his clubs and were treated well. This form of petty corruption was tolerated and even accepted by the department. As a result, the Warren Commission found that "Ruby's police friendships were far more widespread than those of the average citizen." As he was being wrestled to the ground after shooting Oswald, Ruby told the arresting officers, "I am Jack Ruby. You all know me." They certainly did.[51]

Some individuals in organized crime also knew Jack Ruby. Irwin Weiner, one of Jimmy Hoffa's closest associates, described the Chicago native as "a friend of mine." FBI records show that Ruby phoned Weiner on October 26, 1963. "He called me," Weiner admitted. "I talked to him. What I talked to him about was my own business. And I just don't want to, don't feel that I should discuss it with anyone. It has no relation, it has no bearing on anything."[52]

Ruby made other possibly suspicious phone calls in the weeks leading up to the assassination. For example, on November 7, 1963, Ruby spoke with

Barney Baker, a Hoffa associate whom RFK once called a "roving organizer and ambassador of violence." He talked to Baker on at least two other occasions during the same month, though no one knows for sure what they discussed. Ruby also made calls to Russell Mathews (a drug dealer who knew Carlos Marcello), Nofio Pecora (another Marcello lieutenant), Michael Shore (a record company executive with ties to the West Coast Mafia), Lenny Patrick ("a notorious member of Chicago's outfit"), and other disreputable characters. Ruby later insisted that he was simply trying to get advice from these men on how to handle the American Guild of Variety Artists, a Mafia-controlled union that represented strippers and nightclub entertainers.[53]

As in so many other areas, the Warren Commission was slapdash and did not thoroughly investigate Ruby's mob connections. That did not prevent the commission in its final report from stating categorically:

> Based on its evaluation of the record . . . the Commission believes that the evidence does not establish a significant link between Ruby and organized crime. Both State and Federal officials have indicated that Ruby was not affiliated with organized criminal activity. And numerous persons have reported that Ruby was not connected with such activity.[54]

Fifty years on, it is clear that the Warren Commission was wrong, and that Ruby knew scores of mob figures, including David Yaras, a man whom the Justice Department considered a close associate of Sam Giancana's. Ruby and Yaras had become acquainted in the late 1930s or early 1940s. Yaras described his friend as a silver-tongued "Romeo" who was good at "picking up girls."[55]

Ruby also was acquainted with Joseph Campisi, "a close associate of Dallas mob boss Joseph Civello" and Frank Caracci, one of Carlos Marcello's lieutenants. Campisi visited Ruby in jail a few days after he shot Oswald; Caracci and Ruby talked on the phone several times during the summer and fall of 1963 and met in person at least once. Ruby knew plenty of other mobsters, including Johnny Roselli (the same Roselli who met with the FBI's Robert Maheu in Miami) and Lewis McWillie, another one of Sam Giancana's associates.[56]

Chuck Giancana is convinced that his brother not only knew Ruby, but also ordered the hit on Oswald. According to Chuck, Sam used Jack to open "a seedy night spot that the Chicago [mob] syndicate would slowly transform into a jumping strip joint, offering clientele everything from bookmaking to prostitutes." The job required someone who could deliver envelopes full of cash to local law enforcement personnel, and perhaps Ruby cultivated close ties with Dallas police officers so that it would be easier to bribe them on be-half of Giancana.[57]

The FBI was aware of Ruby's Mafia ties and tried to recruit him as an in-formant. In 1959 agent Charles Flynn approached Ruby nine times asking for information on gambling operations, drug networks, and organized crime in the Dallas area. But Ruby never divulged any useful information, and the FBI eventually ceased all contact with him.

And then there is Ruby's apparent connection to Cuba. According to a former associate, James Beard, Ruby periodically delivered guns and ammu-nition to pro-Castro Cubans. Beard says that he "personally saw many boxes of new guns, including automatic rifles and handguns" onboard a boat pi-loted by Ruby. At the time, the mob was hedging its bets by supplying weap-ons to Castro's friends and foes alike, hoping to win favor with whichever side ultimately triumphed. (Mobsters turned against Castro only after he seized power and began cracking down on their nefarious activities.) A Texas gun-runner named Robert McKeown says that Ruby got in touch with him in 1959 about transporting a number of jeeps to Castro's army. McKeown gathered that Ruby was working for Santo Trafficante, the godfather in south Florida, and says that the nightclub owner asked for help in "getting some people out of Cuba" for "a man in Las Vegas."[58]

Even the Warren Commission admitted that Ruby traveled to Cuba in 1959. Whether the commission coaxed the whole truth out of Ruby is another matter. "I want to tell the truth, and I can't tell it here," Ruby told Earl Warren in June 1964 from his Dallas jail cell. "Unless you get me to Washington, you can't get a fair shake out of me." Ruby insisted that his life was in danger if he stayed in Dallas, but Warren refused to transfer him. Ruby also reportedly told a friend who came to see him in jail, "Now they're going to find out about Cuba, they're going to find out about the guns, find out about New Orleans, find out about everything."[59]

Persistent reports have also suggested that Jack Ruby and Lee Oswald knew each other. If true, this would add spice to accusations of a possible conspiracy. Yet these assertions have tended to fall apart upon close examina-tion. Beverly Oliver, a Dallas woman who claimed she was in Dealey Plaza on November 22, declared that Ruby had introduced her to "Lee Oswald of the CIA" before the assassination.[60] But it is doubtful that Oliver was present in Dealey Plaza, and her yarn changed a good deal over the years. The House Select Committee on Assassinations, after interviewing her in executive ses-sion, did not consider her legitimate.[61] A Dallas waitress, Mary Lawrence, reported that Ruby and Oswald ate a late-night meal at her restaurant. Yet Lawrence said "Oswald" had a small scar near his mouth, which Oswald lacked but Larry Crafard, a close friend of Ruby's who resembled Oswald, did indeed have.[62]

Some of Ruby's employees at the Carousel Club alleged that Oswald was often at the club, drinking and reveling with strippers. This contradicts testimony from Oswald's landlady and other rooming house tenants that Oswald was regularly home by six P.M. Dallas policeman Jim Leavelle investigated some of these reports, but he found them groundless: "If Oswald had any redeeming qualities, [they were that] he didn't drink alcohol and hang around clubs... People would say, 'Oswald was up there in Ruby's club drinking and all this stuff, and so-and-so saw it.' And I'd go to so-and-so and he'd say, 'well, I didn't really see him but my friend George over there, he saw him.' And I'd go to George—and he didn't see Oswald, but his friend Frank did. And I never could get to the end of the damn line. There wasn't nothing to it."[63]

No single aspect of the Kennedy assassination has done more to perpetuate conspiracy theories than the cold-blooded execution of Lee Harvey Oswald. Americans already in shock over the president's brutal death were further numbed as they watched a new killing happen on television. For almost everyone, the quick elimination of the accused assassin seemed frighteningly convenient. The government and the news media kept a great deal from the public in those days, but that didn't mean people couldn't reason for themselves. In millions of homes throughout America, people uttered versions of what my father exclaimed seconds after Ruby shot Oswald: "*They* want to shut him up." Not "he," but "they." As Nancy Pelosi put it, "As soon as I saw Jack Ruby shoot Oswald, I thought, 'Of course! That's what they do to somebody who kills somebody—kill him so that he can't talk.'"[64] In my large extended family, gathering for a sad Thanksgiving less than a week after the events in Dallas, every single relative expressed a belief in a conspiracy, most because of Oswald's elimination. Whether true or not, Americans sensed that large, evil, unseen forces were at work, and this gnawing suspicion added immensely to the disquiet of the time.

Once again, given an inadequate investigation when the trail was hot and after the passage of a half century, it is impossible to say with certainty whether Ruby was another "lone gunman" or part of a conspiracy. Ruby's own contemporaneous comments lead us in two different directions. He told police that he had shot a smirking Oswald in a fit of pique so that Mrs. Kennedy would not have to return to Dallas and go through a trial "for this son-of-a-bitch." Detective Barnard Clardy told the Warren Commission that he heard Ruby say, "If I had planned this I couldn't have had my timing better," and that "It was one chance in a million." In addition, right after he was arrested, Ruby told Bill Alexander, Dallas's assistant district attorney, that he was "proud that he killed the man who killed the president because it showed that Jews have guts." "He thought that he would be a hero," Alexander told me. "He said, 'you guys [the police] couldn't do it.'"[65]

There is also testimony that Ruby became deeply upset about JFK's death. He might have been acting, but his emotions appeared genuine to those who knew him best. Ruby's sister, Eva Grant, put Jack's demeanor over the weekend this way: "He was sick to his stomach . . . He looked terrible . . . He looked [like] a broken man [and said], 'I never felt so bad in all my life even when Ma and Pa died . . . someone tore my heart out.'"[66]

Did Ruby, a self-professed admirer of the Kennedys, at least after the assassination, act on impulse when he shot Oswald? Or had he been hired to silence a patsy who might squeal to the police?

Unfortunately, Ruby's trial was almost perfunctory and did not address these questions, and a Texas jury sentenced him to death for his crime. (The conviction was later overturned by an appeals court.) Jim Cunningham, a retired Texas Instruments engineer and one of the last surviving members of Jack Ruby's jury, says that Melvin Belli, Ruby's celebrity attorney from California, didn't understand the Texas system and put on a poor case. But the key factor in the jury's decision was Ruby's own actions. While Cunningham was one of three jurors who at first voted against the death penalty, and considered a lesser penalty such as "murder without malice," he joined all his colleagues in a vote for capital punishment in the end: "If [Ruby] had no malice, why was he in the basement of the police station with a gun? . . . Ruby had a temper and finally it got him into so much trouble he couldn't get out of it."[67]

For some Americans who lived at the time, Ruby was a folk hero who had avenged the murder of their president and spared the country a lengthy, expensive trial. When he was diagnosed with cancer in 1966, Ruby received a flood of sympathy cards and letters from admirers. Most expressed gratitude for Oswald's murder. Ruby may not have been able to appreciate them at the time—nor to give any deathbed confessions—because his mind and body were rapidly deteriorating. Ruby began to experience paranoid delusions. "He raved again and again that Jews were being tortured and killed because Gentiles wanted revenge for his crime. He shouted that he could hear screams from the jail cellar, machine guns in the street." He also gave visitors pieces of paper with phone numbers on them, explaining, "These people have been murdered. They're all out to get the Jews, and these people won't answer the phone because they're dead."

At saner moments, Ruby seemed determined to dispel rumors that he had been part of a conspiracy. "The ironic part of this is, I had made an illegal turn behind a bus to the parking lot" near the jail, he said from his hospital bed. "Had I gone the way I was supposed to go—straight down Main Street—I would've never met this fate, because the difference in meeting this fate was thirty seconds one way or the other." Earl Ruby told the press that his brother wanted to take another lie detector test (he had already taken two) "so that people will be convinced that there was no plan on his part, or conspiracy of any kind." A month before he died, Ruby said, "There is nothing to hide. There was no one else."[68]

The best evidence that Ruby's encounter with destiny may have been accidental is derived from his actions on the day of the Oswald shooting. Ruby was in downtown Dallas Sunday morning, November 24, in order to send money to one of his strippers who had requested urgent help. We know Ruby was in the Western Union office, not far from the Dallas jail, at 11:17 A.M., since his money order was stamped at that exact time—and all Western Union clocks were carefully synchronized each morning. Oswald had been scheduled to be transferred from the city jail to the Dallas County jail sometime after ten A.M., and if Oswald had been moved shortly after ten, he and Ruby would have never crossed paths.[69] Instead, at the last minute, a postal inspector had a few questions for Oswald, and Oswald himself unexpectedly requested a change of clothing upstairs in the interrogation room, which delayed his transfer—just enough time to permit Ruby to make the journey to the police basement entrance, gain admission to the media spectacle (apparently from either a friendly or an inattentive policeman), and find a suitable perch for close observation. If Ruby had been under orders to kill Oswald, he would never have cut the timing so close, and he would not have run a trivial errand in advance. Nor would he have brought his dog, Sheba—his companion animals were like children to him—and left her locked up in his car while he undertook a high-profile shooting that meant he would certainly be arrested and might even be killed via police counterfire. Finally, murdering Oswald would not have protected the plotters of November 22. Ruby would know who put him up to his part in the cover-up, and would talk sooner or later. Wouldn't Ruby have had to be eliminated eventually, too—and then the person who killed Ruby, and on and on? Ironically, the episode most Americans cite as having convinced them of a JFK assassination conspiracy may be the easiest to debunk, simply by following the details of Ruby's day and the illogic of this particular alleged "silencing."

An alternate explanation that places Ruby inside a mob conspiracy to kill JFK is offered by HSCA counsel Robert Blakey: "Did [Ruby] get [Oswald] that day [November 24] serendipitously? Or did he get him that day with a connection with some of the crooked cops in the Dallas police? And they were crooked. And they were connected to the organized crime in town—not the whole police department, but substantial numbers of them. I don't know how

[Ruby] got in [to the police basement] for sure. There's some suspicion that he was let in. Even if he got in serendipitously, he still got in. He was stalking [Oswald]. If he hadn't got him today, he'd have got him tomorrow."[70] Adding some credence to this view are Ruby's actions on Friday evening, November 22. Ruby got all the way to the door of Captain Fritz's office, where Oswald was being interrogated, and actually opened it several inches before he was stopped by two policemen.[71] Was Friday's bold move Ruby's first attempt to get Oswald? Blakey's argument about Ruby is plausible, but on balance, it is less convincing than the coincidental theory.

Whatever his motivations, Jack Ruby was no hero. He robbed America of a fuller explanation of the Kennedy assassination. In time, it is highly probable Lee Oswald would have provided a great deal of information, either about his own objectives or the existence of a wider conspiracy. The year 1963 preceded significant Supreme Court decisions that enhanced the constitutional guarantees possessed by accused criminals, and police departments were often not terribly fussy about the rights of those in custody. When I asked Bill Alexander, one of Oswald's ranking interrogators for the short time he was in the Dallas jail, what would have happened if Oswald had lived, he reminded me that they were gathering incriminating evidence from many sources and Oswald's own writings. They had already surprised Oswald with what they knew about him (his rifle purchase, the staged photograph with the gun, and other details). By Monday, Alexander felt, they would have had enough hard proof to make him crack. And if he didn't, would the police have gotten a bit rough with Oswald behind closed doors? "Oh, surely not!" quipped Alexander in mock horror. "We would have [just] made him understand we [meant business]."[72]

EXAMINING THE PHYSICAL EVIDENCE: OLD AND NEW CONTROVERSIES

HARD PROOF IS OFTEN LACKING to support plausible conjecture, semi-reliable hearsay, and logical guesswork. Unfortunately, contrary to what the experts say on TV crime shows, the same is true for some of the physical evidence. Where you stand on that evidence depends on where you sat on November 22, 1963, or shortly thereafter. Take the medical findings and judgments of those who saw President Kennedy right after his fatal shooting.

President Kennedy arrived at Parkland Hospital within a few minutes of the shooting, at around 12:35 P.M. Hospital staff gave him the designation "No. 24740, Kennedy, John F."[1] When Dr. Charles Carrico received Kennedy in Trauma Room One, he knew the situation was extremely grim, and noted JFK's color as blue-white or ashen, an indication of poor blood circulation. Dr. Carrico also noticed that the president was having trouble breathing and "had no palpable pulse." In addition, Kennedy's eyes were wide open and unresponsive to light. As Dr. Carrico was making these observations, Trauma Room One began to fill with medical personnel. With the assistance of other doctors and a senior nurse, Dr. Carrico opened the president's shirt and put an ear to Kennedy's chest. Carrico detected a faint heartbeat, so the assembled physicians began working to restore the president's breathing.[2]

While inserting a breathing tube down the president's throat, Carrico noticed a small wound in the front of his neck. He described it as "rather round" without "jagged edges or stellate [starlike] lacerations." Carrico made these observations as he was connecting the breathing tube to a respirator machine.[3]

At this point, Dr. Malcolm O. Perry and other doctors arrived, and Perry assumed control over the effort to resuscitate the president.[4] Perry noted a wound "in the lower part of the neck below the Adams apple," which he described as "a small, roughly circular wound of perhaps 5mm in diameter from which blood was exuding slowly."[5] Since it seemed obvious that the president was losing oxygen through this hole, Perry decided to perform a tracheotomy. Using a scalpel, he made a "transverse incision right through the wound in the neck." Dr. Robert McClelland, one of the teaching faculty at Parkland, assisted with this procedure. Perry also asked another doctor to insert a tube in the president's chest in order to drain excess blood and air.[6]

Dr. Kemp Clark, Parkland's chief neurosurgeon, inspected the president's massive head injury. Clark could see "a large, gaping wound in the right rear part of the head, with substantial damage and exposure of brain tissue, and a considerable loss of blood." Although he "did not see any other hole or wound on the president's head," Clark later admitted that the massive amount of blood and thick hair could have concealed the full extent of the president's injuries. Finally unable to detect any pulse, the physician began performing external cardiac massage.[7]

Dr. Marion T. Jenkins, one of Parkland's anesthesiologists, later said that at this point, after "Dr. Clark had begun closed chest cardiac massage," he became "aware of the magnitude of the wound, because, with each compression of the chest, there was a great rush of blood from the skull wound. Part of the brain was herniated [i.e., the brain projected through the blasted-out cranial cavity]; I really think part of the cerebellum, as I recognized it, was herniated from the wound; there was part of the brain tissue, broken fragments of the brain tissue on the drapes of the cart on which the president lay."[8] As the physicians worked desperately to save the president's life, Mrs. Kennedy forced her way into the operating room cupping a sizable piece of her husband's brain that she had retrieved from the trunk of the limousine—an action captured in famous photos and the Zapruder film of the awful instants after the shots were fired.[9] Jenkins described the horrific scene: "Jacqueline Kennedy was circling the room, walking behind my back. The Secret Service could not keep her out of the room. She looked shell-shocked. As she circled and circled, I noticed that her hands were cupped in front of her, as if she were cradling something. As she passed by, she nudged me with an elbow and handed me what she had been nursing in her hands—a large chunk of her husband's brain tissues. I quickly handed it to a nurse."[10]

But it was much too late for miracles. The president had been brain-dead from the moment his skull exploded under fire at 12:30 P.M. The time of John Fitzgerald Kennedy's death was somewhat arbitrarily fixed by the doctors as being 1:00 P.M. CST. Dr. Clark signed the death certificate, citing a gunshot wound to the head as the cause of death.[11]

Years later, one of the attending doctors told an interviewer that "as soon as we realized we had nothing medical [left] to do, we all backed off from the man with a reverence that one has for one's president. And we did not continue to be doctors from that point on. We became citizens again, and there were probably more tears shed in that room than in the surrounding hundred miles." Most of the doctors quietly left the room, with a couple staying behind to remove tubing and medical equipment from the president's body.[12]

Assistant Press Secretary Malcolm Kilduff had accompanied Kennedy to Dallas in lieu of Press Secretary Pierre Salinger, who was on a mission abroad with cabinet members. It was left to Kilduff to make the official announcement of the president's death to journalists gathered in the hospital. "His eyes red-rimmed, his voice barely controlled, [Kilduff] said: 'President John F. Kennedy died at approximately one P.M. central standard time here in Dallas. He died of a gunshot wound in the brain.'"[13]

When Kilduff had finished speaking, Drs. Perry and Clark gave an impromptu press conference. Perry told reporters that he had located "an entrance wound in the front of the throat" that had likely been caused by a bullet moving toward the president.[14] Months later, he would describe this wound to the Warren Commission as "roughly circular." When asked whether it was an exit or entry wound, Perry told the commission that "it could have been either."[15] By contrast, in his 1992 book, *JFK: Conspiracy of Silence*, Dr. Charles Crenshaw claimed that he had "identified a small opening about the diameter of a pencil" in the middle of the president's throat, and he remained convinced that it was "an entry bullet hole. There was no doubt in my mind about that wound. I had seen dozens of them in the emergency room."[16] If Crenshaw is correct, this bullet could not possibly have caused Governor Connally's wounds, since it was coming from Kennedy's front and not his back.[17] Other doctors who certifiably were in Trauma Room One insist that Dr. Crenshaw did not treat President Kennedy or was in no position to observe anything significant.[18]

Perry also told the press on November 22 that he could not identify the entry point for the bullet that had shattered the president's skull. This statement was corroborated by Dr. Clark, who said that "the head wound could have been either the exit wound from the neck or it could have been a tangential wound, as it was simply a large, gaping loss of tissue."[19]

Given the nature of the resuscitation efforts and the confusion of the day, none of the physicians in Trauma Room One could have conducted a thorough examination of the president's head wound. Yet a physician who spent considerable time in the room holding the president's shattered head and looking directly at the cranial wound for many minutes was Dr. Robert McClelland. One of the few surviving occupants of Trauma Room One on November 22, he told me that not only was "a third to a half of the president's brain" shot away, but while the other doctors were working feverishly to revive Kennedy, "the right half of [Kennedy's] cerebellum fell out of the hole in his skull cavity."[20]

To McClelland, from those awful minutes at Parkland onward, the wound in the back of Kennedy's head seemed like an exit wound. During testimony to the Warren Commission, McClelland did admit, when questioned, that he had only "partially" examined the president's head wound.[21] Yet in 2011, McClelland recalled that years of reflection had led him to a definite conclusion: The opening he saw in the back of the president's skull was most certainly an exit wound, consistent with a shot from the picket fence area. McClelland's medical opinion is that the bullet entered JFK's forehead around the hairline and blew out the right side and back of his skull. McClelland believes that his initial interpretation of the president's wound is consistent with Kennedy's violent motion backward and then to the left in the Zapruder film, which he first saw years after he formed a judgment based on the skull wound by itself.

A widely respected medical professional, McClelland not only attended JFK but operated on the wounded Governor Connally, Lee Oswald after he was shot, and several years later, Abraham Zapruder, who was suffering from gastric cancer.[22] People who have known McClelland throughout his professional life vouch for him enthusiastically. He is not bombastic, but quiet and authoritative. In the aftermath of the assassination, he was flown to Washington to examine autopsy photos, and he is sure that the one showing the small bullet hole in the back of the skull was forged or altered. The shot came from the front, McClelland insists. He even kept the shirt he was wearing on November 22. It is soaked in JFK's dried blood and brain matter, which drained onto McClelland as he performed his gruesome task. He has preserved the shirt in a plastic bag since that day. (See the photo on page 2 of the second insert.)[23] All this being true, his admired professionalism and strong impressions from November 22 do not make McClelland's view of the head wound unassailable. This was his notion or inkling, but no X-rays had yet been taken.

Not long after Kennedy expired, the White House staff and Secret Service, with Mrs. Kennedy at their side, began wheeling JFK's body out of Parkland Hospital. Earl Rose, Dallas County's medical examiner, tried to stop them. "I was trying to explain . . . that Texas law applied in the . . . case of the death of the president, and that the law required an autopsy to be performed in Texas." Kennedy's aides refused to comply, and the situation became tense, with armed agents determined to get the president's body back aboard Air Force One and eventually to an official autopsy at Bethesda Naval Hospital in Maryland. Voices were raised, and given the circumstances, Rose had to relent or be run over. The law was actually on Rose's side. Remarkably, the killing of a president was not yet a federal crime in 1963. JFK's homicide had occurred in Dallas and as such fell under the jurisdiction of Texas authorities. Rose always insisted that the autopsy should have been performed in Dallas.

"People are governed by rules and in a time of crisis it is even more important to uphold the rules," Rose said. "In Dallas, we had access to the president's clothing and to the medical team who had treated him."[24]

It is possible that some of the unending controversy about the JFK autopsy
would have been resolved or would never have occurred had the procedure
been done in Dallas. As it happened, the autopsy performed at Bethesda Naval Medical Center (which began just after eight P.M. and ended shortly before four A.M. on November 23) was inadequate in some ways. The Bethesda
physicians did not confer with the Parkland medical team before they began
the procedure, which put them at a considerable disadvantage. Nor did they
have the opportunity to examine the president's clothing, which was removed at Parkland Hospital; this was unfortunate, since the bullet holes in
JFK's coat and shirt were critical in understanding one bullet's trajectory.
Apparently because of the pressure of time—the Kennedy family was waiting
to go back to the White House with the body—they did not dissect Kennedy's
back-to-neck wound, which could have proven quite useful. While the doctors insisted later that they did not experience direct interference in their
work, the autopsy occurred under highly irregular conditions with many
military, staff, and Secret Service observers buzzing about and asking questions.[25] The close proximity of so many influential individuals and their in-
determinate role in the substance and pace of the autopsy has generated
suspicion and debate for decades.[26*]

The Bethesda doctors did examine Kennedy's shattered head thoroughly,
which led them to determine that the entrance wound was "situated in the
posterior scalp."[27] In other words, they claimed the bullet that destroyed
Kennedy's brain had come from the rear, not from the front, contrary to the
view of Dr. McClelland and many others. There is a good deal of evidence
that on this key point, they were correct. The path of the bullet from back to
front is distinguishable, thanks in part to the pattern of the bullet fragments
that remained in Kennedy's head. Furthermore, additional analyses in the
years following the assassination have shown a "jet propulsion effect" from a
bullet exiting the front of the brain, pushing the body violently backward and
helping to explain the backward and leftward movement of JFK's moribund
body in the Zapruder film, occurring at the instant the bullet exited his skull.
For example, in the 1970s, Dr. Alfred G. Olivier, director of biophysics at the

---

* Kennedy's need for protection expired with his life. The body of Abraham Lincoln had a
state-of-the-art autopsy inside the White House in April 1865, with no prying and meddling
from others. See Dr. Robert King Stone's "Report on Lincoln's Death and Autopsy," Library
of Congress website, http://myloc.gov/Exhibitions/lincoln/hebelongstotheages/ExhibitObjects
/AutopsyReport.aspx [accessed July 26, 2011].

Army's Edgewood Arsenal, told the Rockefeller Commission that "the violent motions of the president's body following the head shot could not possibly have been caused by the impact of the bullet . . . [Olivier] explained that a head wound such as that sustained by President Kennedy produces an 'explosion' of tissue at the area where the bullet exits from the head, causing a 'jet effect' which almost instantly moves the head back in the direction from which the bullet came." Thus, to the untrained eye, the Zapruder images would suggest a bullet striking Kennedy from the front and pushing him back, but as in so many other ways, our eyes can deceive when split-second supersonic effects are involved.[28]

While they may well have gotten the big things right, the Bethesda physicians understood the imperfections in their work within hours. In a report to his commanding officer, Colonel Pierre Finck cited the various limitations he was forced to work under during the autopsy: "no clothing of the deceased at [the] time of [the] autopsy; no photos to view at [the] time of [the] autopsy; no information from Dallas; and his impression that the Kennedy family did not want a 'complete' autopsy."[29] The doctors felt pressure from the attorney general, White House aides, and Mrs. Kennedy to finish as quickly as possible. They were refusing to leave the hospital until the autopsy was finished and the body was prepared to lie in state at the White House. The family had initially resisted the procedure, but Bobby ultimately relented and allowed a complete autopsy on his brother's corpse.[30] The rushed procedure, saving an hour or two, would be regretted for years. Dr. James Humes, one of the three physicians who performed the autopsy, would later admit that he and his colleagues "were influenced by the fact that we knew Jackie Kennedy was waiting upstairs to accompany the body to the White House and that Admiral Burkley wanted us to hurry as much as possible."[31] Nonetheless, Humes (now deceased) always insisted that his team's conclusions, though rushed, were basically accurate, and he was delighted when an independent panel of experts appointed by Attorney General Ramsey Clark in 1968 agreed with his assertion.[32]

The initial autopsy report contained information on only three of the president's wounds—the entrance and exit wounds associated with the skull, and the small wound occupying the lower posterior neck of the president. The physicians were unaware of a possible exit (or entrance) wound on JFK's throat and only noticed the small entrance wound on his back. Therefore, they assumed that the president still had a bullet lodged in his back. Humes testified that "[a]t Colonel Finck's suggestion, we then completed the X-ray examination by X-raying the president's body in toto."[33] When the X-rays did not reveal any projectiles, the autopsy team manually probed the president's back wound. The result was the same: no bullet. When Humes learned about the bullet that had been discovered on the gurney at Parkland Hospital, he simply assumed that it was the same one that had penetrated President Kennedy's back.[34] However, the next day, Humes spoke to Dr. Perry at Parkland and learned about the apparent bullet hole in the president's throat. Humes went home and drafted a new autopsy report for the Warren Commission in which he described this wound as the probable exit point for the bullet that had pierced Kennedy's back.[35]

HUMES'S TEAM TOOK fourteen X-rays and fifty-two photographs of the president's corpse. The X-rays showed that the bullet that struck Kennedy's head "had shattered into about forty dustlike particles, appearing on the X-ray film like 'stars at night.'" In addition, Humes said the doctors found a small 6-millimeter-diameter entrance wound in the rear of Kennedy's head. Humes believed that a high-velocity rifle bullet had entered through the rear of the skull, then fragmented and exited through the top of the skull.[36] Below is a diagram that roughly explains Humes's conclusion (produced in the 1970s by the House Select Committee on Assassinations). The medical evidence, autopsy photos, and analyses in the decades that followed mainly

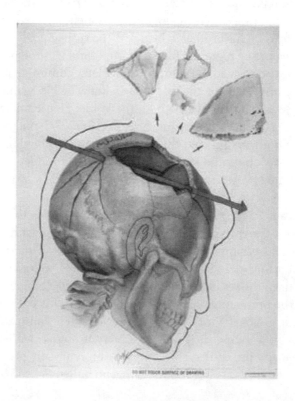

support this theory of the fatal bullet's path. Initial controversy was caused by the Warren Commission's placement of the head wound entry point a full four inches below the one shown in the diagram we have reproduced.[37]

Why did the commission get the placement so wrong? It relied on the inaccurate written notes of Dr. Humes, who told the House Select Committee on Assassinations a decade later that he had been up all night on November 23–24 and had drafted the final autopsy report based on rough notes he jotted down during the procedure. He testified that he did not take greater care with the wounds' placement since he assumed the autopsy photographs would be used to precisely establish their location.[38] Understandable exhaustion and less excusable haste created a long-term controversy that could easily have been avoided.[39]

The National Archives and Records Administration (NARA) has never released the autopsy photos to the press or public; they are, after all, fundamentally private medical records. They have been made available on a limited basis to congressional investigators, forensic experts, and government agents with the approval of the Kennedy family. It was completely appropriate to withhold the photos in the years immediately following JFK's death. But after a half century, this is pure American history, and a vital piece of the assassination puzzle. It is time to release all of the medical evidence so that everyone with an interest in the case can sort out the truth from varying perspectives.[40]

THE LOCATIONS OF Kennedy's wounds, and the subsequent autopsy, have proven controversial, but the ballistic evidence from the assassination is even more disputed. The Warren Commission concluded that the shots that killed the president and wounded Governor Connally came from the southeast corner window of the sixth floor of the Book Depository, an assertion based on (1) eyewitness accounts of a gun present in the window, seen either during the firing or immediately after the shots; (2) the forensic matches among bullet fragments found in the front seat of the presidential limousine, the whole bullet discovered on the hospital stretcher that purportedly transported Connally, and the grooves made on the bullet by the rifle found on the sixth floor; (3) the presence of three spent cartridge cases located below the key sixth floor window, which were forensically matched to the rifle and bullets "to the exclusion of all other weapons"; (4) the damage on the inside front windshield of Kennedy's limousine, presumably caused by a bullet fragment striking, but not penetrating or shattering, the glass surface;[41] and (5) the nature of the wounds inflicted upon Kennedy and Connally, which seemed to indicate that the bullets had come from an elevated position behind the limousine on Elm

Street rather than from any other location along the parade route, such as the triple overpass or the grassy knoll.

The commission also found that three bullets were fired from the Depository. The first bullet missed the car entirely. The second bullet entered the back of the president's neck and exited through the flesh at the lower front of the neck, near his tie knot. (Most of the Parkland physicians, including Dr. Robert McClelland, believed that this wound was dangerous but survivable by the president.) The same second bullet continued on, entering the right side of Connally's back and exiting from the right side of his chest immediately below the nipple before again entering his body, apparently passing through the top of his right wrist near his hand and then causing a minor wound on his left thigh, possibly remaining just under the skin, where it later exited while Connally was on the Parkland stretcher. The third and final bullet ended Kennedy's life as it entered the right rear quadrant of the president's head, shattering the cranial area.[42]

Though the commission's report indicated there had been some internal dissent over attributing Connally's wounds to the same bullet that had passed through Kennedy's throat, the document concluded that expert-derived "persuasive evidence" had demonstrated beyond any doubt that Oswald alone had fired the shots from his Mannlicher-Carcano rifle. Oswald could not have fired more than three bullets in the elapsed time, and one bullet unmistakably missed the limo and struck a curb near the triple underpass. Therefore, for the Warren Commission, the remaining two bullets had to account for all the wounds in JFK and Connally. The first of these has often been derisively termed the "magic bullet" or the "pristine bullet" because of its relatively good condition after allegedly doing so much damage to two men. The dispute about this bullet aside, the commission and subsequent investigations concluded that Oswald had sufficiently expert marksmanship to aim and fire the gun with deadly effect from the Depository to the street (a distance of no more than 88 yards). Finally, ballistics also matched several cartridge cases found at the scene of the shooting of police officer J. D. Tippit to a revolver found in Oswald's possession at the time of his arrest, another gun that had been purchased by Oswald.[43]

A number of other vital details were analyzed by the commission. The panel said the shots rang out at 12:30 P.M. CST. Roy Kellerman and William Greer, two of the president's bodyguards, agreed on the time, which was reinforced by a photograph of the limousine speeding to Parkland just past the grassy knoll and the triple overpass, with the large Hertz clock on the Depository clearly showing exactly half past twelve. The president's vehicle was moving forward very slowly on Elm Street in the critical seconds before and during the shooting. Frame-by-frame analysis of the Zapruder film produced a speed estimate averaging 11.2 miles per hour.[44]

However, agreement on the other particulars is elusive. The accounts of those in the presidential limo differ significantly on the most important point. From the rear left seat of the vehicle, Mrs. Kennedy heard a noise and subsequent cry of pain from Governor Connally, who was seated directly in front of her husband. Upon turning right, she observed the president raising his hands to his throat with a puzzled expression on his face. JFK realized what had happened. "My God, I am hit" were his last words. Mrs. Kennedy was attempting to help her husband when she heard the fatal shot and saw what the fatal bullet did. Mrs. Kennedy's testimony would tend to support the theory that one bullet struck both JFK and Connally.[45]

But the recollections of Governor Connally and his wife, Nellie, sharply contrasted with those of Mrs. Kennedy, and both insisted throughout their lives that separate bullets struck Kennedy's back and Connally's back.[46] The governor reported that he heard the first shot originating from a direction over his right shoulder and contorted his body in that direction to trace the origin of the noise. While turning his head in the other direction to check on an already wounded Kennedy, he was struck in the back by a bullet. Connally testified that he did not hear the shot that penetrated his body. It is possible that Connally heard the first shot that missed the limousine entirely and caught a glimpse of the wounded president at the very instant he (Connally) was struck by the bullet that had just exited JFK's throat; perhaps Connally's brain had not had time to process the noise from the second shot. It is also possible that Connally was struck by a separate bullet.[47]

Mrs. Connally, who was not hurt, confirmed her husband's recollections. Moments after she had turned to JFK and chirped, "Mr. President, you can't say that Dallas doesn't love you," she heard a shot fired from the right. Glancing over her right shoulder, she saw the president noiselessly clutching his throat before slumping toward Mrs. Kennedy. She insisted that a second separate shot then struck her husband, who exclaimed, "My God, they're going to kill us all." Mrs. Connally pulled her badly wounded husband downward onto her lap. From this position, with his head in her lap, both Governor and Mrs. Connally said they heard another shot, whereupon they were hit with blood and tissue from JFK's head wound.[48]

The remaining occupants of the presidential limousine, two Secret Service agents who were in the front seats facing forward and did not directly observe all the key moments, were unable to sort out whether Mrs. Kennedy's or the Connallys' version was correct. Roy Kellerman, the occupant of the front right passenger seat of the vehicle, reported hearing a firecracker-like pop;

upon turning his head to the right he saw the president clutching his throat. By all accounts it was Kellerman who ordered Agent Greer to accelerate while radioing the president's condition. The Connallys said that they heard Kellerman's call only after the tissue-splattering shot. Greer's version of events is similar to Kellerman's. He heard a loud noise, which he attributed to a nearby police motorcycle. Upon hearing a second such noise, he turned to look over his shoulder and spotted Connally slumped over in his wife's lap. He stepped on the vehicle's accelerator at the precise moment Kellerman issued a similar order. Kellerman claimed to have heard "a flurry of shells" for five seconds after the first shot rang out.[49]

Gerald Blaine, one of the other agents assigned to Kennedy's Texas detail, believes the bullet that struck Kennedy's head (and left behind fragments in the president's skull) caused a large flap of skin to move in the same direction as the projectile, which is visible in the Zapruder film. Could the remnants of this slug still be buried inside Dealey Plaza? Blaine thinks so: "That [bullet] is probably laying up in the rail yard [or] embedded in the [grassy] knoll somewhere."[50]

Secret Service agents in the follow car, trailing the president's car by five feet or so, reported much the same sequence of events: a firecracker-like noise, the sight of Kennedy grabbing his throat and "lurching" left, followed by a second shot and the shattering of the president's skull. Agent Clint Hill, who demonstrated great courage in the face of gunfire, remembered leaping from his position in the follow car, struggling to gain his footing on the presidential limousine as Greer pushed the gas pedal, and helping a frantic Mrs. Kennedy, who had climbed up on the car's trunk, back into the rear seat.

As the motorcade accelerated through the underpass to Parkland Hospital on Kellerman's orders, most agents drew their weapons, including George Hickey, who was armed with an AR-15 rifle.[51] Agent Rufus Youngblood in the front passenger seat of the vice presidential vehicle—about a hundred feet behind Kennedy's limousine—reported hearing an explosive noise before seeing the crowd lined up along the parade route suddenly disperse.[52] Vice President Johnson confirmed hearing several sharp "explosions" in a row; he heard one or two of the shots from a position on the vehicle floor, where he had been pushed down for protection by Youngblood.[53] Agent Clifton Carter, in the vehicle behind the vice presidential limousine, reported hearing two shots after Youngblood had secured LBJ.[54] All Secret Service agents in the motorcade remained with their vehicles—per agency policy—until they reached Parkland Hospital.[55] Despite the eyewitness testimony about Secret Service agents on and near the grassy knoll after the shooting, the Secret Service and the Warren Commission say that the first agent to return to Dealey Plaza, Forrest Sorrels, did not do so until approximately 12:50 P.M.[56]

There are contradictions aplenty here. Few of those likely to be most alert to the facts—the limousine occupants and the Secret Service agents following every instant intently—explicitly acknowledge a first shot that missed the limo. Some participants, including the Connallys, are sure Governor Connally was hit by a separate bullet from the one that struck JFK's throat. Others have memories that differ on various specific points, including the exact number of shots they heard. Police homicide detectives often report that well-meaning eyewitness accounts can diverge wildly. But these aren't average eyewitnesses.

Of course, critics see multiple problems with various elements of the scenario we have just described. For example, Ray and Mary La Fontaine, the husband and wife team behind the book *Oswald Talked: The New Evidence in the JFK Assassination*, and Mark Lane, who authored the highly influential 1966 volume *Rush to Judgment* as well as *Plausible Denial* in 1991, have argued that another gun, a 7.65 Mauser, was initially identified by Officers Seymour Weitzman and Eugene Boone as the weapon found on the sixth floor of the Depository. A Weitzman-signed affidavit described it as a "7.65 Mauser bolt action equipped with a 4/18 scope."[57] Boone was the first person to view the weapon and believes that Lane and the La Fontaines are assigning sinister motives to an honest mistake. "That probably was my fault," he told me during a phone interview. "I referred to it as a Mauser. There were a lot of World War II weapons [on] the market at that time, and 'Mauser' really refers to a bolt action weapon." Boone means that he was using the brand name in a generic sense in the same way that one might ask for a Kleenex instead of a tissue. But journalists ran with his description until authorities later identified the murder weapon as an Italian-made Mannlicher-Carcano.[58]

Bertrand Russell, the noted Cambridge philosopher and mathematician, wanted to know how the authorities could have missed a man walking into a "building while allegedly carrying a rifle over three feet long?" Russell observed that along a motorcade route swarming with police and Secret Service agents on heightened alert, it was strange that no one noticed Oswald lugging such a weapon.[59] Was the rifle taken to, or planted in, the Depository much earlier? This is possible; multiple reports suggest that the Depository's back loading dock was frequently open and unguarded, and the freight elevators to the sixth floor could be accessed from that location. Of course, say lone-gunman advocates, there is a logical explanation that would show how Oswald could bring in a rifle on the morning of the motorcade. The neighbor with whom he hitched a ride early on the morning of November 22, Wesley Buell Frazier, said Oswald was carrying a brown-paper-wrapped package that contained "curtain rods"—Oswald's cover for his disassembled rifle. As in so many respects that day, Oswald was devilishly lucky. The slight, physically unremarkable Oswald was dropped off nearby the Depository, wasn't stopped by any policeman or guard on his way into the building (there may not have been any law enforcement personnel stationed in the plaza five hours before the motorcade was to pass), and could have proceeded unmolested once inside up to the sixth floor to drop off his deadly parcel for later use.

Yet Frazier, who had the opportunity to handle and measure an Italian Carcano rifle in later years, insists that Oswald's package was too small to be the weapon discovered on the sixth floor of the Depository. "You know, they asked me, 'How long was the package?'" he recalls. "I said, 'Oh, around two feet, give or take an inch or two.' [So] even if it were disassembled, it wouldn't fit in there." Frazier stuck to his estimate of the size of Oswald's package from the day of the assassination through to his interview with the Warren Commission staff in Washington the next year. The commission put him through a comical routine in which he had to cut up wrapping paper to demonstrate the dimensions of Oswald's object—and staffers made him do it over and over, hoping that he would produce one version large enough to accommodate the rifle.[60] Lending further credence to Frazier's story is the testimony of an FBI firearms expert who told the Warren Commission that the length of the rifle's longest component when disassembled was 34.8 inches—considerably longer than the brown paper package Frazier had observed.[61]

The commission determined, however, that the homemade bag discovered near the sniper's nest measured 88 inches in length (roughly seven feet), which would have been more than enough to conceal Oswald's rifle.[62] In addition, photos taken on the afternoon of the assassination clearly show curtains hanging from the windows inside Oswald's boarding house room, which suggests that Oswald had been lying to Frazier about the need for curtain rods.[63] Frazier recalls the conversation they had the day before the assassination: "He came up to me during the day on Thursday. And he asked me, 'Can I ride home with you this afternoon?' I said, 'Well, sure.' A few minutes later, I realized it wasn't Friday. So when I ran back into him on the first floor, I said, 'Why do you want to go home with me today?' I said, 'Today is Thursday, not Friday.' He says, 'I know. I need to go home because Marina's got some curtain rods for me and I'm gonna put some curtains up in my room.' So I said, 'Okay.'"[64]

This suggests that Oswald had decided on his plan of action, either by himself or with the help of conspirators, by Thursday during the day; and that he either came across or was shown the motorcade route on Wednesday or Thursday. Oswald's assassination plan was not a last-minute snap decision, as some have suggested. Rather, he thought about it for at least a day or two, maybe longer. Moreover, Oswald told Frazier he would not be going back with him on Friday, again suggesting he knew what he was going to do—and that he would either be dead after shooting at the motorcade or he had an escape plan in place, on his own or with the help of co-conspirators.[65]

NO SINGLE PIECE of evidence has sown more doubt than the "magic bullet" fired from the Carcano rifle. Part of the bullet's allure for conspiracy theorists arises from the inexplicable gap in the "chain of custody" surrounding the projectile, which police say was matched with forensic evidence to Oswald's gun.

Upon arrival at Parkland Hospital, Governor Connally—who had fainted from shock and loss of blood—regained consciousness and was immediately helped onto a stretcher.[66] About 1:20 P.M. the bullet was found on the stretcher by Parkland's chief engineer, Darrell Tomlinson. Even though, in retrospect, Tomlinson was uncertain that this stretcher was the one used for Connally, the Warren Commission so designated it. Others wondered whether the bullet had been planted in order to implicate Oswald during the approximately forty minutes the stretcher had been empty.[67] Further questions have been raised about the condition of this 1.2-inch-long bullet, which was only slightly compacted at its base despite having allegedly passed through two bodies and broken bones in Governor Connally. The skeptics insist a bullet that had such a destructive path would have shed more shards along the way.

This is not the only bullet that has proven controversial. One other person besides President Kennedy and Governor Connally was injured in Dealey Plaza at 12:30 P.M. James Tague, a bystander at the base of the triple underpass, on the opposite side of the street from the grassy knoll, was struck in the face by flying debris presumably caused by a stray bullet. The Warren Commission says it was the first bullet that missed the limo entirely and hit a curb near Tague. However, Tague insists that he was struck by the debris—whether curb concrete or bullet fragments—when he heard the second or third shot, not the first one. In addition, the FBI investigated a scar on a curb near where Tague was standing and found that the indentation did not contain any copper residue. This finding suggests to some observers that the ricocheting bullet was not one of the copper-encased projectiles fired from Oswald's gun.[68]

Recently, a team of Texas A&M University scientists, using modern chemical and forensic techniques, concluded that the bullet fragments recovered on November 22 could have come from more than one gun.[69] The scientists discovered "that many bullets within a box of Mannlicher-Carcano bullets have similar composition, leading them to conclude that two-element chance matches to assassination fragments are not extraordinarily rare." In other words, a second undiscovered assassin could have fired a weapon using Mannlicher-Carcano ammunition from another location around Dealey Plaza, and the bullet fragments would have resembled the composition of those that came from Oswald's gun.[70]

Bullet fragments recovered during JFK's autopsy at Bethesda add to the puzzle. The attending physicians identified two wounds in the president's head: a 6-by-15-millimeter wound to the right and above the center back portion of the skull, and a more irregular, nearly 13-centimeter-diameter fracture of the skull that matched chunks of bone recovered by law enforcement personnel from along the parade route.[71] Two small metal fragments were recovered from the larger wound. X-rays revealed particulate fragments of metal in a line from the rear wound to the front portions of the skull, and an embedded metal fragment above the president's right eye.[72]

Yet for many, the Zapruder film contradicts the ballistic path analysis. Kennedy's head and upper torso are clearly thrown backward in a manner seemingly inconsistent with a shot coming from the rear. For example, author Paul Chambers has studied the Zapruder frames using mathematical equations derived from Newtonian physics and concluded that the recoil of the president's head proves that the fatal shot was not fired from the Depository but rather from a location in front of Kennedy's limousine. By no means is Chambers's analysis unanimously supported; others use photographic and scientific perspectives to insist that the Zapruder film shows that the president initially fell forward, having been hit from behind.[73] The ambiguous nature of the visual evidence can lead to diametrically opposite conclusions. More generally, this survey of X-rays and ballistics has demonstrated that so-called hard evidence can prove to be softer than expected.

THE SUGGESTION SHOCKS, but more than a few assassination researchers put forward the theory that Lyndon Johnson was a willing co-conspirator in the killing of his predecessor, or at the very least, had prior knowledge that something was afoot. The linchpin of this conjecture is the belief that Johnson was far more amenable than JFK to the plans of the military, defense industry, and CIA to escalate in Vietnam.[74]

That Johnson lusted after the White House is obvious. He had run for the Democratic nomination himself in 1960, and he regarded John Kennedy as a lightweight in the Senate. RFK was his enemy; their personal dislike was intense and barely containable on both sides. Johnson believed that he had been ill-treated as vice president, his talents underutilized and his influence marginalized by the Kennedy inner circle that called him "Uncle Cornpone." And anyone who has studied Johnson's career has to acknowledge that, for all his dazzling legislative and strategic skills, he was exceptionally devious and capable of great cruelty even to those personally and professionally close to him.[75]

It may be that every vice president who has succeeded his president in midterm has been secretly delighted. All seconds-in-command realize, as did John Adams in describing his position as the first vice president, that "In this I am nothing, but I may be everything."[76] Nevertheless, Johnson was probably more delighted than most. Power, every bit as much as blood, coursed through his veins and kept his weak heart beating.[77] Astoundingly, despite needing to assimilate and recover from the enormous shock of Dallas and with the heavy immediate burden of burying Kennedy and uniting the country, a pajama-clad LBJ was already planning out the legislative initiatives of his administration with close aides in his bedroom in the wee hours of November 23. In this same meeting, the new president even startled the exhausted Lady Bird Johnson—after she declared their new burdens would last only a few months until a new presidential nominee was selected in the summer of 1964—by announcing that he would be running for *at least* one full term in the White House.[78]

It also escaped the notice of few that President Kennedy had been murdered in LBJ's Texas. JFK had gone there mainly to assist in brokering a truce in Democratic factional fighting in which Johnson was a key player. Some friends and advisers, aware of the harsh treatment of United Nations ambassador Adlai Stevenson, who had been spat upon in Dallas one month earlier, wanted Kennedy to cancel. Much like Jack Ruby's rubout of Oswald, Johnson's ascension to ultimate power, thanks to Kennedy's death in LBJ's state, seemed suspicious and convenient.[79]

Kennedy loyalists quickly made the connection, as revealed by a note penned by Evelyn Lincoln, JFK's personal White House secretary, only a couple of hours after the assassination. Mrs. Lincoln was with Kennedy in Dallas and flew back to Washington aboard Air Force One with LBJ and Mrs. Kennedy. During the flight, she compiled a list of people and groups that she thought might have been responsible for the president's death. At the top of her list was the name "Lyndon." Lincoln was completely devoted to JFK and evaluated everyone with one simple standard: Would they help or hurt her president? She may have been reflecting the inner circle's views of LBJ's loyalty, since she had access like few others to the Oval Office, the president, and his closest advisers.[80] Yet one of Johnson's comments made during the flight, reflecting his fear of a possible conspiracy involving enemies of the United States, casts doubt on Lincoln's assertion. "I wonder if the missiles are flying," he told his aide, Bill Moyers, who had asked what was on his mind.[81] Moreover, according to a key eyewitness, General Godfrey McHugh, the new president was not as calm on Air Force One as one might have hoped, at least for a time. McHugh reported, "I walked in the toilet, in the powder room, and there he was hiding, with the curtain closed, saying, 'They're going to get us all. It's a plot. It's a plot. It's going to get us all.' He was hysterical, sitting down on the john there alone in this thing."[82]

Author Craig Zirbel is convinced that Johnson played a role in Kennedy's murder. In his bestselling book *The Texas Connection*, Zirbel writes, "From the outset Lyndon B. Johnson was involved with the planning of the president's trip. A specific motorcade route was demanded which led to Kennedy's death. The connections to Johnson, while regularly ignored, are so clear that undisputable evidence publicly ties Johnson through his friends to not only the Dallas murder, its criminal investigation, but even to Oswald and Jack Ruby." Zirbel is certain that H. L. Hunt, a wealthy conservative oil baron with close ties to LBJ, was involved in the assassination. The author claims that Hunt, who apparently despised JFK, was among several people who helped recruit Oswald and Ruby on Johnson's behalf.[83] As with other theories of the Kennedy assassination, there are wisps of smoke here and there about H. L. Hunt, but no smoking gun that convinces an objective observer it is true.[84]

Conspiracy theorists believe they know why Johnson would have risked his career and even his life: By the autumn of 1963, rumors were circulating that LBJ would be dropped from the 1964 ticket. On the very day Kennedy died, the *Dallas Morning News* announced: NIXON PREDICTS JFK MAY DROP JOHNSON. Evelyn Lincoln also claimed years later that she had discussed with President Kennedy his 1964 vice presidential plans shortly before JFK left for Dallas, and Kennedy told her that he had decided to drop LBJ and substitute North Carolina governor Terry Sanford.[85] Johnson had superb political antennae, so if JFK's intention was to replace him, he likely knew his days as the man a heartbeat away from the Oval Office were numbered.

The problem with this scenario is that not a shred of real evidence—the kind that would survive under competent cross-examination—has emerged in the past half century to back up the suspicions about LBJ's involvement. Top Kennedy aides have insisted that the Kennedy-Johnson ticket would have been kept intact for the 1964 campaign; Jackie Kennedy also confirmed her husband's intention to keep LBJ as his running mate.[86] Texas was still a critical state for JFK, and it was in the throes of party factionalism and realignment that would have been made worse if Johnson were dumped from the ticket. And many ask why President Kennedy would go to Texas on a fence-mending mission if he secretly knew he would be changing his reelection paradigm in a few months.

Another conclusion about the Sanford-for-Johnson swap is possible. JFK was thick as flies with top reporters and loved to hear their gossip. It is quite likely he had been informed about press investigations of LBJ's corrupt business practices in Texas that were being undertaken even as the Dallas trip was being scheduled.[87] JFK may have hatched a contingency plan: If he needed to drop Johnson from the ticket in 1964, Terry Sanford, a moderate Southerner, was a reasonable substitute. Kennedy might well have shared this with Lincoln. He often told her what was on his mind at the moment—a kind of thinking out loud to a confidential secretary, just to hear the idea verbalized. The contingency plan might or might not have ever been put into effect. If Johnson's financial shenanigans had been exposed before the spring of 1964, Kennedy probably would have dropped him. In living memory at the time, FDR had dropped two separate vice presidents (John Nance Garner in 1940 and Henry Wallace in 1944), so it wouldn't have been seen as terribly unusual. On the other hand, if LBJ was able to suppress or squelch the press inquiries—quite possible in those days—then he likely would have survived on the ticket.

Johnson arguably had the means, motive, and opportunity to kill Kennedy. But so did dozens, if not hundreds, of other individuals and groups. And during the five decades since, his involvement is nothing more than conjecture, with no proof even of real smoke, much less fire. It is more like misty fog, generated by the need to find a larger-than-life villain to explain the great evil that ended a promising leader's life.

ANOTHER AREA OF controversy concerns the protection accorded JFK. This much is obvious: The federal agencies that were supposed to protect him failed at one of their most fundamental responsibilities, and then tried to paper over their mistakes. The FBI destroyed evidence and assembled a self-serving report. The CIA withheld crucial information from the public, the press, and the Warren Commission for decades—and may still be doing so. The Secret Service fell short in two ways. The agents designated to protect Kennedy's life were unable to accomplish the paramount mission of the Secret Service. And the administrative leadership of the Secret Service and its parent Treasury Department had not made an aggressive case for more agents and stricter standards to guard the president when he was outside the safe confines of the White House "bubble." The individual agents are the least culpable even though no group has blamed itself more. These men were shockingly overworked and overextended, almost beyond human endurance at times.[88] Also, the agents were too few in number to do the job fully, and they were kept too far away from the president to help in the kind of split-second attack that occurred in 1963. Their supervisors knew the dangers for years, yet nothing was done to stop a tragedy waiting to happen.

In combination, the Secret Service's errors were fatal to John Kennedy. The Service did not have Lee Harvey Oswald on any of its watch lists. When agent Win Lawson found out about the trip to Dallas, he instructed the Protective Research Section (PRS) of the Secret Service to investigate people in the area that might potentially pose a threat to JFK—individuals who had demonstrated hostility toward the president as well as groups that might back a political assassination. A great deal of this information came directly from threatening letters or telephone calls to the White House. Other names were sent along by the FBI, CIA, and state and local police departments, mainly because individuals or organizations had been forthright about their possible intentions. In the early 1960s a person such as Oswald—despite being a defector and having demonstrated hostility toward the United States and its leadership—could easily escape notice, since he had not telegraphed his intentions about the president in palpable ways. In practice, the Secret Service depended heavily on regional law enforcement to provide them with the names of dangerous local residents. This was barely a safety net at all, and the Secret Service knew it, which is one of the reasons agents were always nervous during presidential trips.[89] As is too often the case, a monumental tragedy was needed to produce commonsense reforms in presidential safety. After November 22, the Secret Service tightened protection in ways that should have been evident well before President Kennedy's murder.[90]

MUCH LIKE THE FBI and CIA, the Secret Service tried hard to exonerate itself. A month after the assassination, Gerald Behn, who had been the special agent in charge during JFK's Dallas visit, issued several statements designed to deflect criticism away from his agency. "The United States Secret Service never releases the exact route of any presidential motorcade," read one such statement. "The route, after it has been decided upon by the Secret Service advance agent, the local police and the local committee, is released either by the White House Press Secretary or by the local committee, usually after they have checked with the White House Press Secretary." This misses the point entirely. When the route is released and publicized by any individual or group, it is then the responsibility of the Secret Service to make safe the path. Kennedy's motorcade track had been published in the Dallas newspapers and aired on television for three days, as was inevitable.[91] The purpose of a motorcade is to enable a president to be seen. Why hadn't the agency provided in Dallas what in modern times would be considered a minimal level of security? Behn said that it was "almost impossible" to inspect buildings during presidential visits "because of the shortage of time and manpower"—which argued for more time and manpower, not a suspension of precautions. This is

1963. Some three hours after the assassination, photographer Jerry Cabluck of the *Fort Worth Star Telegram* took this shot of Dealey Plaza from a rented helicopter. Police cars and officers are on and near the grassy knoll, just below and to the right of the Depository.

1963. At Parkland Hospital, with the president having been taken to Trauma Room One, police and federal agents surround the presidential limousine. Almost unbelievably, two agents appear to be wiping down the blood in the car, which is a crime scene. (Note the bucket on the ground near the motorcycle policeman's left foot.) Blood splatter patterns were used even in the 1960s to help determine bullet trajectories.

2012. Dr. Robert McClelland, one of the physicians who tended to President Kennedy at Parkland Hospital on November 22, 1963, holding his shirt from that day, still stained with President Kennedy's blood.

1963. Back at Love Field in Dallas, President Kennedy's staff struggles to load his coffin onto Air Force One. Some seats were removed in the back of the plane to accommodate the fallen leader and his grieving widow and close aides. Mrs. Kennedy is accompanied by Larry O'Brien, a future Democratic National Committee chairman (whose office bugging triggered the Watergate scandal that eventually resulted in President Nixon's resignation). In a simple tribute, a policeman places his cap over his heart in the background.

1963. The famous photo of President Johnson's swearing in aboard Air Force One at 2:40 P.M. LBJ personally arranged his wife Lady Bird on one side and Jackie Kennedy on the other as he was sworn in by Federal Judge Sarah T. Hughes, personally requested by LBJ for the task. Hughes was the first woman to swear in a president.

1963. President Kennedy's casket is placed inside a hearse after Air Force One's landing at Andrews Air Force Base just before 6 P.M. EST on November 22, 1963. Mrs. Kennedy, still dressed in the same pink outfit and accompanied by Attorney General Robert Kennedy, prepares to accompany the body to the autopsy at Bethesda Naval Hospital.

2012. The Dallas jail cell that housed Lee Harvey Oswald for the final two days of his life. This facility is now abandoned.

1963. Bob Jackson received a Pulitzer Prize for this historic photo of Jack Ruby firing a single, deadly shot into Lee Harvey Oswald on November 24, 1963. This was the first live televised murder in American history. Ruby was later sentenced to death, though he died of cancer before the execution could be carried out. The Dallas police officer attempting to pull Oswald away from Ruby's gun is Jim Leavelle, who was also stationed at Pearl Harbor on December 7, 1941.

1963. In perhaps the most memorable moment of the weekend, John F. Kennedy, Jr. salutes his father's coffin. The small boy's moving gesture brought millions to tears and reminded Americans of the very personal tragedy for a young family.

1963. Catholic nuns gather to pray at the grassy knoll in Dallas's Dealey Plaza during President Kennedy's funeral on Monday, November 25, 1963.

1964. President Johnson solemnly bows before JFK's final resting place in Arlington National Cemetery on the day before Kennedy would have turned forty-seven years old, May 29, 1964.

1965. Senator Robert F. Kennedy and his family kneel before JFK's Eternal Flame, June 1965.

1967. This photograph, taken May 27, 1967, captures the moment of christening the USS *John F. Kennedy* at Newport News, Virginia, as nine-year-old Caroline Kennedy smashes a bottle on the ship's bow while her younger brother observes under Jackie's watchful gaze and that of President Johnson.

1968. JFK's bust was present for most Cabinet meetings during Lyndon Johnson's presidency. The White House was presented with Kennedy's likeness on November 19, 1964. In early 1963, sculptor Felix de Weldon was chosen by Jacqueline Kennedy to produce the bust that was to be a featured item in JFK's eventual presidential library. President Kennedy posed for the work in the White House, but it was unfinished at the time of his death.

1968. Pallbearers carry Senator Robert F. Kennedy's body to its final resting place near President Kennedy's grave in Arlington National Cemetery, June 1968. RFK's murder rekindled painful memories of his brother's assassination and caused many people to wonder if the gunman, Sirhan B. Sirhan, had been part of a conspiracy.

1969. President Nixon hands Senator Edward Kennedy a pen while approving amendments to the Older Americans Act, September 1969. Despite Kennedy's Chappaquiddick scandal in July that year, Nixon and his aides were still worried that JFK's potent legacy might help his youngest brother win the White House in 1972.

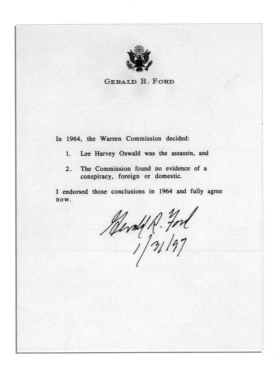

GERALD R. FORD

In 1964, the Warren Commission decided:

1. Lee Harvey Oswald was the assassin, and

2. The Commission found no evidence of a conspiracy, foreign or domestic.

I endorsed those conclusions in 1964 and fully agree now.

Gerald R. Ford
1/31/97

1997. President Gerald R. Ford had served on the Warren Commission while a member of the U.S. House, and he was the longest surviving member of the commission. He emphatically supported the Warren Report's conclusions for the rest of his life, as this signed letter from 1997 indicates.

2001. In 2001 President Ford received the John F. Kennedy Foundation's "Profiles in Courage" ward for his controversial pardon of Richard Nixon, which may have cost Ford a full White House erm of his own. Senator Edward Kennedy, one of Ford's harshest critics at the time of the pardon, nd JFK's daughter Caroline were on hand to present the award.

1979. President Carter shakes hands with Senator Edward Kennedy as Kennedy's wife Joan looks on during the dedication of the John F. Kennedy Library, October 20, 1979. Kennedy's attempt to oust Carter the following year helped Ronald Reagan win the White House and created lasting animosity between Carter and the Kennedys.

1981. Despite deep differences in philosophy, the Kennedys and the Reagans shared a mutual respect for one another and maintained a cordial relationship during Reagan's eight years in office. Here Rose Kennedy and son Ted pay a friendly visit to the Oval Office on November 12, 1981.

1985. President Reagan delivers a glowing tribute to JFK during a June 24, 1985, fundraiser for the John F. Kennedy Library at Ted Kennedy's home in McLean, Virginia. Reagan's genuine admiration for President Kennedy helped bridge the political divide between the two families.

1985. Mrs. Kennedy and Mrs. Reagan were both traumatized by the shootings of their husbands, but according to Mrs. Reagan, they never shared their experiences with one another. The two First Ladies are shown here at the June 1985 reception for the JFK Library.

1958. As two of the most famous and enduring families in American politics, the Kennedys and the Bushes have often interacted. In this photograph from June 26, 1958, Senator Kennedy (right), who founded the New England Conference of Senators, meets with the group's members in the office of Senator Prescott Bush (center, seated), the father of future president George H.W. Bush and the grandfather of future president George W. Bush.

1963. "The Torch Is Passed." Bill Clinton, a seventeen year-old Boys Nation delegate from Arkansa and the future forty-second president, shakes hands with the thirty-fifth president in the Whit House's Rose Garden on July 24, 1963. This was a much-seen photograph during Clinton's 199. campaign. Clinton's mother, Virginia, would later describe the moment this way: "When he cam home from Boys Nation with this picture of John Kennedy and himself shaking hands, I've neve seen such an expression on a man's face in my life. He just had such pride. And I knew then tha government in some form would be his goal."

1993. President-elect Clinton receives a tour of JFK's gravesite in Arlington National Cemetery from JFK, Jr. and Senator Ted Kennedy on inauguration eve, January 19, 1993.

1993. President Clinton speaks at the John F. Kennedy Library in October 1993 during the dedication of the new Kennedy museum.

2004. President George W. Bush and Senator Edward Kennedy talk during the December 3, 2004, signing of a bill increasing educational opportunities for those with disabilities. Despite many political differences, Bush and Kennedy made common cause in educational policy.

2008. Caroline Kennedy joined her uncle Ted on January 28, 2008, at American University in giving the Kennedy blessing to Senator Barack Obama. They compared Obama with their father and brother, saying both JFK and Obama had inspired a younger generation to get involved. Given the closeness of the Obama-Clinton contest, the Kennedy imprimatur may well have made the difference.

not a modern discovery. Fifty years ago, the Secret Service had precise proce-dures for inspecting buildings in Washington during inaugural parades and events for visiting dignitaries. Under these circumstances, the Secret Service required building managers to:

1. [K]now the occupants of each room in their building.
2. Keep people off the ledges of their buildings.
3. Know who is on the roof or lock the door(s) to the roof.
4. [C]ontact the highest official in each office which has windows facing on the parade route and request them not to allow any strangers or any persons they cannot vouch for into the room.
5. [C]ontact the top official in each office with windows facing on the parade route and request them to make certain that nothing is thrown out of the windows.
6. [C]heck each unoccupied room or office and then lock it.[92]

Why were these requirements in effect only for special D.C. events? Weren't they even more essential for road trips where the locales and threats might be less well defined and known in advance—especially when a president is sitting in an open car with nothing to stop bullets fired from any direction? If the Secret Service's standards used in the nation's capital (and sometimes elsewhere) for important presidential appearances had been followed in Dal-las, John Kennedy might have survived the trip. Just four days earlier, during JFK's visit to Tampa, Florida, where serious threats against Kennedy's life had been made, the sheriff's office had secured the rooftops of major buildings along the president's motorcade route.[93] Surely the Dallas of 1963 was anti-Kennedy enough to have justified similar measures. It is obvious in hindsight that the Secret Service should have asked the Dallas police department and sheriff's office to post guards on top of the government buildings overlooking Dealey Plaza, such as the Criminal Courts Building and the Post Office. There was a decent chance that police sharpshooters on the roof with binocu-lars could have spotted the barrel of a rifle extended from the sixth floor window of the Depository.

In 2010 some Secret Service agents who were assigned to protect JFK pub-lished a book, *The Kennedy Detail*, that contains what some say is a blame-the-victim charge. The agents claim that during a trip to Tampa just days before the assassination, Kennedy called the agents "Ivy League charlatans" and ordered them off the back of his limousine. "Tell them to stay on the fol-low-up car," the president allegedly remarked. "We've got an election coming up. The whole point is for me to be accessible to the people." JFK supposedly issued similar orders during the Dallas trip.[94] After so much time it is not possible to know for sure whether these words were uttered, and no contemporaneous paperwork records such instructions. At the same time, the agents are a reliable lot who have been loyal to the Secret Service and mainly kind in their reminiscences about the Kennedys.[95] (Still, some assassination researchers adamantly refute the ex-agents' claim.)[96] Even if the report about Kennedy's instructions is true, the director of the Secret Service could have approached Bobby Kennedy or JFK's close aides to insist that tight security was essential. Such intervention might well have worked, and if it did not, resignation in protest is an honorable way to bring attention to a potential calamity. (Sadly, this is a rare practice in American government.)

Gerald Blaine, a member of JFK's security team and author of *The Kennedy Detail*, told me that he and fellow agents "had to diplomatically beg for resources to handle the motorcade routes and the venues." "In Dallas, they . . . did not have enough resources to man all of the roof tops," Blaine notes. "In 1963 there was little air conditioning and [therefore an] office building window could be raised and lowered." The former agent also says that the modern-day Secret Service does a much better job of protecting the president in part because of lessons learned in Dealey Plaza: "If we would have had the 4,000 agents they have today—some of which are trained in counter sniping—and we had the armored vehicle used by President Obama, Dallas might not have happened. Instead, JFK's assassination is the reason they have those resources [and] new technologies."[97]

Blaine's comments suggest that the Dallas trip provided a perfect opportunity for the Secret Service to press its case. As mentioned, JFK and many of his supporters were apprehensive about the visit due to Dallas's reputation as a right-wing mecca.[98] There had been warnings of possible trouble. Lyndon and Lady Bird Johnson had been accosted in Dallas during the 1960 campaign. While traveling to an event at the Adolphus Hotel, the Johnsons were swarmed by a group of demonstrators who shouted insults and waved signs with slogans such as LET'S BEAT JUDAS and TEXAS TURNCOAT. "It makes me sad to know that people could be so bitter and so frustrated and so discourteous and desperate," LBJ said after one protestor screamed in his wife's face. As mentioned earlier, a Dallas mob had also attacked United Nations ambassador Adlai Stevenson when he was visiting Dallas just weeks before Kennedy was scheduled to come.[99] The protestors spat on Stevenson and hit him in the head with a placard.[100]

The pre-Dallas Secret Service had inadequately studied the sad history of assassinations, and not just in the United States. Around the globe, a chastened Secret Service noted in 1964, "There has been an assassination or a serious attempt at one in every nation during every generation." In France, assassins tried to kill Napoleon III eight times. In England, Queen Victoria survived an equal number of attempts on her life. In China, T. V. Soong and Chiang Kai-shek cheated death a total of nine times. The rulers of Spain, Italy, Germany, and Russia have been targeted dozens of times.[101] In 1962, in a disturbing incident that President Kennedy himself had noted, French president Charles de Gaulle only narrowly escaped death when a would-be assassin using a submachine gun sprayed de Gaulle's car with bullets as it drove through a Paris suburb. One bullet shattered the car's rear window, while another came within two inches of de Gaulle's head. Police found hand grenades and plastic explosives at the scene and connected the attack to a group protesting France's withdrawal from Algeria. Afterward, Kennedy sent a message to de Gaulle "expressing gratitude that the French president escaped unhurt."[102]

To be a head of state is to invite attacks from mentally disturbed or politically motivated persons. The threat cannot be eliminated; the only antidote is unrelenting security. The modern Secret Service is much more adept at doing so, thanks to greatly increased manpower and a heightened sense of the dangers after so many actual and attempted presidential assassinations. In 1996, for example, President Bill Clinton was visiting the Philippines for an Asia-Pacific Economic summit when his Secret Service agents "picked up radio chatter mentioning the words wedding and bridge." Aware that the word "wedding" has often been used by terrorists as a code word for "assassination," agents decided to change the motorcade route, which had previously included traversing a bridge. It was a smart decision. Authorities later found explosives on the bridge, which could have killed Clinton and many in his entourage.

Secret Service agents have occasionally gone to extreme measures to protect the president. For example, President George H. W. Bush's security team once changed a motorcade route in Oklahoma after a psychic told them that a sniper would be waiting at a certain location along the route. But even the most gifted soothsayer or Secret Service agent cannot foresee every threat. During a 2005 event at Tbilisi's Freedom Square in Georgia, a would-be assassin threw a grenade at President George W. Bush. Fortunately, the grenade landed more than thirty yards away from the president and did not explode. Presidential aides have privately admitted that a more competent assassin would have found his mark, unimpeded by the security arrangements on stage.[103]

What few realize is that, in every presidency, there are many potential dangers that are never uncovered by security personnel, despite procedures that are many times better than those existing in 1963. Most who have worked on presidential events or in presidential protection can cite examples, though they do so only on an off-the-record basis (preventing authors like me from recounting them). At my college, the University of Virginia, we still recall the lengthy visit of President George H. W. Bush for his "education summit" in 1989. One major event, a breakfast for the nation's governors and spouses, was held out in the open air, on the terraces of Thomas Jefferson's Rotunda, at the head of his architectural masterpiece, an "academical village" consisting of ten large faculty pavilions and dozens of student rooms on "the Lawn." Towering right above the terrace on one side is Pavilion II, which the Secret Service tried to secure because of the obvious danger of a sharpshooter's perch just a few feet away from the president and his summit cohost, at the time a little-known governor by the name of Bill Clinton. But the Secret Service never checked the pavilion's attic, where there is a window with a direct view of the terrace. A couple of days after the summit, hunting rifles and ammunition were discovered there. As one university official put it, "So much for bomb-sniffing dogs and Secret Service thoroughness."[104]

Circumstances only became tenser with the election of the nation's first African American chief executive. The journalist and author Ronald Kessler reported that "threats against [Barack] Obama [have risen] by as much as 400 percent compared with when President [George W.] Bush was in office." In November 2011, a disturbed twenty-one-year-old man from Idaho opened fire on the White House, striking a pane of protective glass on the south side of the mansion. Fortunately, no one was injured during the incident. In 2012, police arrested another twenty-one-year-old who posted threats against the president on his Twitter page and compared himself to Lee Harvey Oswald.[105]

Looking back, it is mind-boggling how naïve—some would say lax—the Secret Service was about presidential security in 1963. Contrary to some published accounts, the limousine was not armored, and even the bubbletop was just a glassy plastic called Plexiglas.[106] Even more surprising is the fact that FBI director J. Edgar Hoover enjoyed greater protection than the president of the United States. In 1964, Hoover lent his government-owned bulletproof car to President Johnson while the presidential limousine received long-overdue security upgrades.[107] There was also little crowd control in many instances. Presidents were permitted to ride in long motorcades past tall buildings with hundreds of open windows, any one of which could have hidden an assassin. This was a disaster waiting to happen, and just about everyone in authority at the time knew it.

INEVITABILITY:
THE ASSASSINATION THAT
HAD TO HAPPEN

IT HAS TAKEN FIFTY YEARS TO SEE part of the truth clearly. John F. Kennedy's assassination might have been almost inevitable. It didn't have to happen on November 22, 1963, but given a host of factors, one could reasonably argue that JFK was unlikely to make it out of his presidency alive. This assertion is jarring but completely supported by the facts that have emerged.

Almost no one disputes that the security surrounding President Kennedy was thin on November 22, as it often was. The leader of the free world, the most powerful person on the globe, was guarded by twenty-eight Secret Service agents in Dallas, only twelve of whom were actually in the motorcade. Hundreds of local law enforcement personnel assisted with the Dallas visit, but they were neither assigned specifically to, nor trained for, presidential protection.[1] Only a few of JFK's agents were close enough to do him any good in case of attack, yet he was passing an estimated two hundred thousand people from Love Field to Dealey Plaza—most just a few feet away, others gathered with a view of him from open windows in buildings along the way. It had been no different in Fort Worth that morning, when he spoke to hundreds of unscreened people outside his hotel, or in other stops on the Texas trip.

No one had even considered that the president's back brace, needed to stabilize his war-injured torso, would make it difficult for him to duck or be pushed down in the limo in the event of an attack. Nellie Connally was able to pull her wounded husband into her lap. Jackie Kennedy could probably not have quickly done something similar even if she had tried. Some believe the back brace kept JFK upright after the first traumatic back-to-neck wound, giving the assassin a clear follow-up shot to Kennedy's still-erect head.

Much has legitimately been made of the fact that Secret Service agents were not on the runners of JFK's car, which was specifically designed to permit agents to stand guard just a few feet away near the back bumper. While not certain, it is probable that an agent would have blocked Oswald's line of sight to Kennedy most of the time, though perhaps not enough to keep the president completely out of harm's way. Had the agents been on the runners, however, they would have saved precious seconds if the president had been hit with the first bullet, probably jumping on top of him to shield him from the head shot, as Lyndon Johnson's Secret Service agent did in a follow car. (However, Oswald might have chosen to shoot Kennedy from the front or side, just as the limo was turning from Houston Street onto Elm Street; even with agents on the runners, the president was terribly vulnerable.)

Kennedy certainly understood his frightening degree of exposure, and thought a good bit about the possibility of assassination—though he was fatalistic about it. He had a false sense of invulnerability, perhaps relying on history's odds. His White House predecessors had taken their chances and (since McKinley) all had survived. In addition, for the Texas trip, JFK undoubtedly preferred to avoid criticism that he was anxious about his reception in a place perceived as opposed to him.

Then there was the Kennedy clan's penchant for risk—very apparent in JFK for sure, but also a trait on display in his father and most of JFK's siblings. It was quite a gamble for a forty-three-year-old Catholic to think he could be elected president of the United States; far safer to have stayed in the Senate, as Harry Truman had advised, and run for the White House at a more mature, traditional age. Some friends and biographers have noted Kennedy's past brushes with death, from disease as a child, the Japanese during World War II, and back injuries in the 1950s as experiences that inured him to danger. A long-standing Kennedy family joke was that when a mosquito bit JFK, the mosquito died. Moreover, JFK's almost unfathomable level of recklessness in pursuing women of all types, even prostitutes, clearly suggests someone who enjoyed the adrenaline high of getting away with edgy behavior. In any event, Kennedy's role in waving off the Secret Service agents from the runners on November 22 may have been a fatal miscalculation, assuming this allegation is accurate.

Kennedy's staff bears some indirect responsibility for creating the security conditions that made the assassination possible. There is no indication anywhere that his closest advisers made the case to him for tighter security.[2] If they had insisted on greater protection, especially the aides in his longtime inner circle, Kennedy likely would have acceded to the request.

No president had been assassinated since the current Secret Service had begun to provide protection in late 1901.[3] That bred overconfidence; as one agent was heard to say in the aftermath of the assassination, "We've never lost a president before," as though that record had been created by airtight security instead of a large dose of luck. There were many avenues open to the then-director of the Secret Service, James Rowley, to appeal the overall lack of funding, point out the giant holes in presidential protection, and object to a thoughtless decision by the staff or even the president himself about the degree of security around the motorcade. Back channels to RFK or Mrs. Kennedy might have yielded results. According to former Reagan aide Mike Deaver, Nancy Reagan gathered key staffers and Secret Service officials together after the attempt on her husband's life and insisted on greater presidential protection.[4] By the time Reagan left office, procedures had been tightened in dozens of ways and the president's protective cordon had been considerably strengthened.

Kennedy, his staff, and the Secret Service had plenty of company in self-delusion. In 1963 it was alarmingly easy for a disturbed man such as Oswald to obtain a deadly scoped rifle by mail order under a false name. As J. Edgar Hoover said to Lyndon Johnson less than a day after JFK's killing, "It seems almost impossible to think that for $21.00 [the amount of Oswald's money order for the gun] you could kill the president of the United States."[5]

The real conundrum is why this observation had not inspired the man who had headed the FBI and its predecessor for nearly forty years to take action much earlier. In addition to the actual slayings of Presidents Lincoln (1865), Garfield (1881), and McKinley (1901), many presidents before Kennedy had survived attempts on their lives—some of them close calls.[6] Andrew Jackson lived when a man pointed two pistols at him at point-blank range in 1835; both guns misfired, but when police tried them later, they discharged perfectly. Before John Wilkes Booth's bullet found its mark, Lincoln had survived at least two other assassination plots and received scores of death threats. At one point, Lincoln showed a newspaper reporter the eighty-plus threatening letters he kept in his desk and said, "I know I am in danger; but I am not going to worry over threats like these."[7] There were probably disturbed individuals like Oswald represented in the sixteenth president's letter packet, but Lincoln's actual assassin was perhaps the most famous actor in America, a national celebrity. In that sense, Booth's accomplishments and notoriety created a macabre equilibrium in the Lincoln case: A luminary killed a superstar. Lee Harvey Oswald, on the other hand, was a complete nobody—even less than a nobody. The psychological dissonance created by this vast imbalance encourages conspiracy talk in the JFK case.

During the final weeks of the administration of Lincoln's successor, Andrew Johnson, a crazed woman accosted him in the halls of the White House before she was easily subdued.[8] Theodore Roosevelt, running for president again in 1912 after a term out, was shot in the chest on the campaign trail in October. A thick speech manuscript in his pocket helped slow the bullet, which was never removed from his body—a wise choice, since operations often did as much damage as projectiles in that era. Argentinean police foiled a serious attempt on President-elect Herbert Hoover's life during a December 1928 goodwill tour of Latin America. Police found guns, grenades, and a railway map inside the house of four anarchists who were determined to "vindicate those who have been exploited by capitalism." This plot had the potential for success, since someone had leaked Hoover's detailed itinerary to the would-be assassins.[9] An assassin, Guiseppe Zangara, also nearly claimed the life of Franklin Roosevelt before he took the oath of office four years later. In mid-February 1933 while in Miami, bullets fired at President-elect Roosevelt from close range proved fatal to Chicago Mayor Anton Cermak instead and wounded four others sitting with Roosevelt and Cermak in FDR's automobile.[10] In an example of the serendipity sometimes accompanying a failed assassination attempt, the gunman's aim was deflected at the last instant by bystanders Lillian Cross and Thomas Armour. Their efforts, combined with a rickety seat on which Zangara was standing, spared the life of a man who was shortly to become one of America's most consequential presidents. Incidentally, FDR personally cradled Cermak, who survived for three weeks, on the way to the hospital; the president-elect's car served as the ambulance that transported the wounded. He visited the victims the next day, bearing gifts. Mrs. Cross received a warm thank-you note from FDR, plus an invitation to the inauguration and a White House tea. Mr. Armour, who apparently was more reticent about his role, was ignored.[11]

Harry Truman was attacked by pro-independence Puerto Rican nationalists in November 1950. The assailants killed a policeman and wounded a Secret Service agent, but Truman escaped injury. Richard Nixon was targeted by a man who very nearly hijacked a commercial airliner, with plans to crash it into the White House. Nixon was also trailed by Arthur Bremer, the man who instead turned his gun on presidential candidate George C. Wallace in 1972. Gerald Ford had two serious assassination attempts in the month of September 1975, both in California by troubled women, Lynette "Squeaky" Fromme of the murderous Charles Manson cult and Sara Jane Moore. Jimmy Carter was stalked by John Hinckley on the campaign trail in 1980, and his nonpartisan assassination plans to impress actress Jodie Foster continued through the Reagan transition, when he managed to get into a press conference that announced cabinet appointments. Reagan failed to show for the event. Hinckley finally achieved infamy in March 1981 when he shot Reagan and three others. George H. W. Bush was the target of a foiled plot by Saddam Hussein while Bush visited Kuwait shortly after leaving the White House in 1993. In addition to the bridge-bombing incident on foreign soil that has been mentioned already, Bill Clinton was targeted twice domestically in 1994, once by a man who opened fire outside the White House gate and by another who crashed his Cessna into the White House. (Clinton was indoors the first time, and away entirely during the second incident.)[12] Another man fired a gun directly at the White House just three weeks after George W. Bush took office. Beyond the 2005 grenade incident in Tbilisi, Georgia, that we have already recounted, Bush was possibly a target on September 11, 2001—not just by a plane headed for the White House but early that morning near Sarasota, Florida, where Bush was to speak at an elementary school that became the backdrop for his first statement about the 9/11 attacks. The terrorist Mohammed Atta had been in this area earlier in September, and a van showed up at Bush's hotel full of men described as "of Middle Eastern descent" claiming they had a nonexistent "poolside interview" with him. They were turned away and have never been identified.[13]

Keep in mind that these enumerated actual and attempted assassinations probably represent only the tip of a large iceberg; undoubtedly, as mentioned before, some plots and threats throughout history have not been discovered or disclosed. Looking back at the number of incidents we see on the public record, mainly luck has kept the number of assassinated presidents to a total of four. If the presidency was judged by the usual standards employed by the life insurance industry, the job would be almost uninsurable. This much was evident well before 1963. The refusal to learn from our bullet-ridden past—guaranteeing that we would repeat it—is a massive failure all around. Government leaders virtually denied history in the years leading up to November 22 with a conceit that suggested somehow it could not happen again.

Even prior to 1963, President Kennedy had experienced some close calls that should have given all the warnings needed to dramatically tighten security.[14] Twin scares occurred five days before the 1960 election, on November 4 in Chicago. Police arrested two men with guns who were on their way to see JFK speak at Chicago Stadium. The first man, twenty-three-year-old Jaime Cruz Alejandro, "closed in" on Kennedy's car as it moved toward its destination. Alejandro was tackled by a policeman, who needed the help of five other officers to subdue him. At the time of his arrest, Alejandro was carrying a .25-caliber automatic pistol. A sixty-one-year-old minister, Israel Dabney, was also arrested after he tried to push past an officer while carrying a .38 revolver in a brown paper bag. Both men claimed to be carrying their guns for self-defense and said they had no intention of harming Senator Kennedy; both were charged with a misdemeanor for carrying a concealed weapon.[15] Police concluded that Alejandro and Dabney did not intend to harm Kennedy, but the fact that people could get within twenty feet of JFK with concealed weapons was a warning.

A genuine plot unfolded in Palm Beach, Florida, in December 1960, when a disturbed seventy-three-year-old man, Richard Pavlick, carefully planned to kill President-elect Kennedy.[16] Pavlick was well known to the Secret Service because he had written threatening letters to a series of presidents, and he was in the database of possible assassins used by law enforcement. But Pavlick lived in New Hampshire; no one had calculated that he might simply drive to Palm Beach and take up residence waiting for the right moment to strike. Angered by a belief that the president-elect's father had bought the election, Pavlick wired his car with a considerable amount of dynamite, ready to crash it into the president's.[17] The Secret Service later admitted the plan might have worked, since Kennedy was usually driven in a single car during this interregnum. As it happened, Mrs. Kennedy saved her husband from a prepresidential death. As Pavlick waited in his car just outside the Kennedy compound one Sunday, preparing to turn his car bomb into JFK's path, Jackie came out with her husband. Pavlick's twisted conscience was still sensitive enough to deter him, since he had no desire to kill Mrs. Kennedy.

The would-be assassin waited a week until Kennedy turned up at Mass at a nearby Catholic Church. A disheveled Pavlick wandered into the church to make sure JFK was there, spotted him, and made a beeline for that pew. An alert agent grabbed him and whisked him around—but let him go without a clear identification and without knowing whether the man was armed. Before Pavlick drove away, the agent did record the license number and description of Pavlick's decrepit Buick sedan. An all-points bulletin was later issued, and four days later, Pavlick was found in his car, still dynamite-laden—close to the Kennedy compound yet again. As with FDR in 1933, the nation had come close to losing a president before he had ever served a day.[18]

Even after JFK's slaying, the nation was slow to recognize the full importance of security. There was little public or institutional pressure to protect presidential candidates until Robert F. Kennedy was killed in 1968. Shortly after RFK died, one fretful FBI agent sent a telegram to Hoover which read, PLEASE MAKE CERTAIN THAT TED KENNEDY GETS ALL THE PROTECTION HE NEEDS WE ARE DOWN TO ONE KENNEDY THANKS.[19] Robert Kennedy's assassination brought Secret Service protection for future presidential candidates, though not early in the campaign.[20] Protection or not, shortcuts have been taken on the campaign trail when aides to a candidate want a full auditorium but the lines behind the magnetometers is long.[21] The imperfect security arrangements have continued under Presidents Bush and Obama, according to some in and out of the Secret Service. Ari Fleischer, George W. Bush's former press secretary, recounted an odd and potentially threatening incident that occurred during his boss's first inauguration. Shortly before the inaugural parade began, a nondescript man managed to slip through the Secret Service cordon and press a religious message and medallion or "coin" (as Fleischer describes it) into the president's hand. The interloper turned out to be a harmless preacher from California named Richard Weaver, but Bush's bodyguards eventually caught up with Weaver and banned him from attending future presidential events. The Secret Service, according to Fleischer, had some explaining to do to the new administration, especially when it was learned this same individual had slipped through security and confronted the first President Bush and President Clinton at various times.[22]

Unauthorized guests have also found their way face-to-face with President Obama at state dinners.[23] As it happened, the intruders were just publicity-seeking party crashers, but who is to say the next ones could not be well-trained assassins? The Kennedy legacy ought to produce constant vigilance in the realm of presidential security, but failing memory and human weakness inevitably take their toll.[24]

President Kennedy's preventable assassination on November 22 proved that we did not take the steps necessary to protect our leader, and we suffered in a thousand ways on account of it. One of the greatest, saddest lessons of JFK's short White House tenure is that there are terrible costs when we fail to imagine and believe the worst could occur at any moment. Everyone is guilty, not least the partisans who would have pointed fingers at an "overprotected" chief executive had the Secret Service requested a major appropriations hike in order to better safeguard JFK. There was a precedent for such criticism. In 1861, Abraham Lincoln had taken reasonable precautions before his inauguration. Rumors of an assassination plot forced him to board a train to Washington disguised as an invalid, guarded by a heavily armed companion. Once in the District he slipped into his hotel by the ladies' entrance. Lincoln was denounced as a coward and mocked for his prudence.[25]

Kennedy came to power just as inexorable forces in American life were colliding in a way certain to produce social upheaval during his term. Foremost was the civil rights movement. The dream of equality for black Americans could no longer be deferred, yet the clash with deeply rooted traditions of segregation, especially in the South, ensured considerable violence. Just as in the 1860s, the shedding of blood was a precondition for racial justice. An army of racists such as James Earl Ray, convicted assassin of Dr. Martin Luther King, Jr., would have been gunning for JFK after civil rights legislation passed.

The Cold War had generated deep fears of Communism, especially on the right. Any attempt at compromise, any effort to decrease tensions between East and West was viewed by millions as betrayal. The leaflets distributed in Dallas for Kennedy's visit that bore his photo and the caption WANTED FOR TREASON were just a hint of what might have come. Kennedy had made lasting enemies among an intransigent community of anti-Castro exiles who would never have forgiven him for the Bay of Pigs. Names from this group constantly appear on researchers' lists of possible Kennedy assassins, as do organized crime individuals.

In addition, many in the defense and intelligence establishment, active and retired, eyed Kennedy with great suspicion, dismayed by what they regarded as Kennedy's "weak" response to Cuba and Russia during the Cuban Missile Crisis, as well as by the Nuclear Test Ban Treaty with the Soviet Union. The vast majority of these individuals would never have considered taking violent action against their commander in chief. The elaborate coup d'état theory of the Kennedy assassination, prominent in Oliver Stone's film *JFK*, appears especially overwrought. However, rabble-rousers, such as retired General Edwin Walker (Oswald's first assassination target), had thousands of extremist followers whose animus toward Kennedy was visceral; they could have grown to menacing proportions had JFK de-escalated the Vietnam conflict in his second term.

Lyndon Johnson avoided Kennedy's fate for two obvious reasons. First, LBJ benefited from the lessons of the Kennedy assassination. The Secret Service was determined not to lose two presidents in a row, and the agency took security precautions for Johnson that had never been employed for Kennedy. Johnson's first trip out of D.C. after the assassination was to attend the funeral of former New York governor Herbert Lehman. When Air Force One landed at New York's Idlewild Airport on December 8, it was met by police helicopters and uniformed officers standing guard on the roof of the airport hangar and oil storage tanks overlooking the tarmac. Johnson rode to the funeral in a closed limousine escorted by thirty-five police motorcycles and dozens of Secret Service agents. James Rowley, the head of the Secret Service, rode in the motorcade. Two thousand police officers guarded the bridges and highway overpasses along the route. Mrs. Johnson was flown in on a separate plane—possibly at the request of the president—to ensure her safety.[26]

Just as important, Lyndon Johnson—as controversial as he came to be because of Vietnam and civil rights—was not John Kennedy. There was something about JFK that engendered in many Americans a loathing that was the full equal of the loyalty and love that others had for him. Indeed, this was true of the entire Kennedy family. JFK and his clan had everything—power, wealth, youth, looks, celebrity, style, and a soaring trajectory for the future that might have included a presidential dynasty. In the early 1960s, it was assumed in many quarters that Bobby Kennedy would try to succeed JFK in 1968, with Ted waiting in line to follow Bobby.[27] It may even have been true. In the warped minds of some potential assassins, the gun might have been the only way to short-circuit old Joe Kennedy's money and connections before they produced a long line of Kennedys in the White House.

Add it all together: JFK's surfeit of enemies, racial turmoil greater than we had seen since the Civil War era, social upheaval that unsettled millions, the clash between the anticommunist right wing and those willing to negotiate with the Reds, and most of all, a shockingly casual approach to presidential security based on utterly false assumptions. This toxic combination of trends and events made Kennedy appallingly vulnerable, an easy target for murder.

JFK was a marked man. If Lee Harvey Oswald had never been born, if the Texas trip had never been scheduled, John F. Kennedy would still have been in jeopardy every day of his presidency. Given all the factors threatening JFK's safety, even without Dallas, Kennedy would have been very lucky to have been found next to a successor on the inaugural stand come January 20, 1969.

The Assassination and the Kennedy Legacy

Revenge his foul and most unnatural murder!
—Shakespeare, *Hamlet*

HUNDREDS OF BOOKS AND STUDIES have been written about the Kennedy assassination. Alert readers have noticed that their authors often use the words "alleged," "claimed," and "supposedly"—just as I have done in this book. The debate over the Kennedy assassination is one of the longest-running sagas in American history, involving hundreds of subplots. Facts and quasifacts have dribbled out over five decades. Quite a few of these "facts" are unverifiable or only partially verifiable—which does not necessarily mean they are incorrect. Stories are told by respectable and dubious witnesses alike that are based on murky memories of long-ago events. Some legitimate evidence is contradictory. The cast of characters in this historical enterprise, many of them colorful and quirky, could fill a bookshelf of Shakespearean plays. The search for the truth of JFK's assassination is like the quest for El Dorado, the mythical city of gold that tantalized European explorers in the sixteenth century. Inspired by vague clues and Amerindian legends, these explorers spent years in the wilderness hoping to strike it rich, but often died of disease and starvation instead.

This book is a synthesis of what we know after fifty years, not a misguided attempt to solve the insoluble. Too many cases are called "the murder of the century," but other than the killing of Archduke Franz Ferdinand, which sparked the death of millions in the Great War, the slaying of John Kennedy may well qualify for the twentieth century's slot. Few would question that it is one of the most tangled, tortuous, and intimidating political executions of all time.

In these pages I have tried to do justice to the accumulated evidence, and I have attempted to weigh it fairly in evaluating the major theories about November 22 that have been proposed. This has been a difficult undertaking for two reasons. First, Americans did not get all the facts at the time when the assassination might have been solved to most people's satisfaction. Many powerful forces were determined to keep the public from learning the full story, and they handicapped the initial investigation lest it uncover the entire embarrassing truth. Everyone can now see that obscuring the government's efforts to kill Fidel Castro (and perhaps other foreign dictators) was part of the motivation, but there was more. Whether these powerful figures simply wanted to avoid blame for having missed obvious signals about Oswald's potential as an assassin, or were trying to obscure their outright culpability in a more direct sense, will be argued for years to come. Second, a comprehensive appraisal of November 22 is impossible because many government documents are *still* classified. The public has not been trusted with the entire record about the murder of the thirty-fifth president, when the forty-fourth is sitting in the White House. Many of these documents are finally scheduled to be released in 2017.[1] Americans may or may not learn anything new at that time. One doubts that intentionally incriminating paperwork will be found intact at this late date. The true outrage is that it will have taken more than a half century for the people's government to reveal these taxpayer-produced documents about a long-ago seminal event.[2]

Advances in technology may eventually permit researchers to do more with the physical evidence that remains, such as the Zapruder film and the existing still photographs of the crucial moments.

One vital piece of evidence, the police Dictabelt recording that was thought to have preserved the sounds of the shots in Dealey Plaza, was my choice for advanced analysis. I briefly mentioned the Dictabelt earlier in the book. For a long time, the evidence appeared to suggest that, by accident (via a stuck microphone on a policeman's motorcycle in the motorcade), the sounds of the assassination were recorded back at Dallas police headquarters on a Dictabelt—a recording device of the era that was primitive but fairly reliable.[3] The Dictabelt was preserved by the Dallas police because it recorded various instructions given by its officials during the motorcade. In 1976 a radio program director, Gary Mack, who was interested in the Kennedy assassination and had recently moved to Dallas, learned of the Dictabelt's existence.[4] An audio specialist, Mack asked a question no one had thought to pose earlier: In addition to routine police commands, could this Dictabelt have also recorded the shots fired at JFK? If so, could the Dictabelt be the long-sought Rosetta stone that could at least reveal how many bullets had been fired and from what direction(s)?

During its investigation, the House Select Committee on Assassinations was informed of the Dictabelt's existence and potential. James Barger, a well-known acoustics expert with a Harvard doctorate in applied physics, was hired to analyze the Dictabelt.[5] Barger organized and executed an elaborate plan to have police sharpshooters target sandbags every few yards on Elm Street in Dealey Plaza.[6] The street was closed on a Sunday in August 1978 and

sensitive microphones were placed around the plaza to record the echo patterns from a shot into each sandbag from various locations, such as the Depository's sixth floor window as well as the grassy knoll/picket fence area.
Barger knew the motorcade's speed and thought he had some idea of the
placement of the motorcycle in the motorcade. The sound patterns on the Dictabelt seemed to match up well with some of the simulated shots. Barger concluded there was a 99.5 percent probability of gunfire on the Dictabelt. Further,
Barger saw four gunshots in the echo patterns that matched the Dictabelt's
sounds, three of them coming from the Book Depository and one from the
grassy knoll. When Barger first interpreted what the Dictabelt showed, "It
horrified me," he said. He instantly realized its implications.[7]

Barger was cautious in his statistical interpretation of the sound patterns,
and he would only say that there was a 50 percent probability that all four
shots were real and not an artifact of a fifteen-year-old Dictabelt. The House
Committee then engaged two academics, Mark Weiss and Ernest Aschke-
nasy of the City University of New York, who further refined Barger's research, concluding that the probability of four shots, with one from the grassy
knoll, was 95 percent or better. The House Committee was stunned. It had
been preparing to endorse the basic finding of the Warren Commission Report, that Lee Harvey Oswald was the lone assassin, but reversed course and
declared JFK's murder the result of an undefined conspiracy.[8]

Naturally, no conclusion this spectacularly revisionist was going to stand
unchallenged for long. Even during the House hearings, police motorcyclist
H. B. McLain—the cop who was identified as having the stuck microphone—
insisted he was not where Barger's analysis said he should be. As Robert
Blakey admitted, "If it could be proved that no motorcycle was in the predicted location at the time of the shots, then serious doubt would be raised
about the reliability of the acoustics project."[9] While one analyst later concluded that McLain was correct—he was not in position to record the gunfire
in the prescribed location—others have disagreed, and this has been an unresolved matter.[10] In addition, various researchers have claimed that the Dictabelt had odd voice-overs out of sync with the timing needed for the
assassination sequence; that the Dictabelt had deteriorated to the point where
it was not reliable; and even that the Dictabelt used for Barger's analysis was
not the original but a duplicate that had been tampered with.[11]

In 1982 the National Academy of Sciences commissioned a panel of experts
to review the work of the House Committee's consultants. Headed by Professor Norman Ramsey of Harvard, the panel concluded that the committee's
work was "seriously flawed," and wrote there "was no acoustic basis" for the
claim of a grassy-knoll shooter.[12] Yet, in direct contradiction to the NAS report, the House Committee's work has been endorsed by a recent peer-

reviewed study in *Science & Justice*.[13] The House Committee's Robert Blakey summarized the newest study this way: "This is an honest, careful scientific examination of everything we did, with all the appropriate statistical checks. It shows that we made mistakes, too, but minor mistakes . . . The degree of confidence that the shot from the grassy knoll was real [was increased from] 95% . . . to 96.3%. Either way, that's beyond a reasonable doubt."[14]

This is no airy academic dispute. Either the House Select Committee on Assassinations was correct when they asserted that there were too many shots (four) to have been fired just by Oswald with his bolt-action rifle in the shooting sequence on the Zapruder film. Or the HSCA was wrong when it claimed the Dictabelt was the long-sought proof of a conspiracy, with the evidentiary key to more than one marksman and the shooters' positions in Dealey Plaza.[15]

The mystery that has surrounded the Dictabelt for decades can now be solved, and its real value to the puzzle of November 22, 1963 will be revealed here for the first time.

New technologically advanced audio research conducted for this book on all the Dallas police recordings of the Kennedy assassination conclusively proves that the Dallas police motorcycle with the stuck microphone was *not* traveling as part of the presidential motorcade at the time the shots were fired at President Kennedy. Thus, the 1979 conclusion by the House Select Committee on Assassinations is wrong. Not only does the Dictabelt not prove the Committee's assertion about a shot from the grassy knoll, we can find no evidence of gunfire at all, and thus it cannot be used to prove either that Oswald was the lone gunman or that there was more than one shooter in Dealey Plaza.* Previous scientific studies of the Dictabelt have either been fundamentally flawed because of a belief that the motorcycle was an integral part of the presidential motorcade, traveling close to President Kennedy's limousine, or because of their incorrect or nonexistent identification of the officer with the stuck microphone.[16]

Our research demonstrates that the police officer with the open microphone was traveling at a high rate of speed at the time the slow-moving presidential motorcade progressed through the streets of downtown Dallas. The officer was well past the Dealey Plaza site and in the vicinity of the Trade Mart, over two miles from Dealey Plaza, at the time of the assassination. Furthermore, following the shooting, the presidential limousine carrying the dying president approached and then rushed by this officer and motorcycle on its way to Parkland Hospital. At this moment, the motorcycle was parked

---

*The highly technical study commissioned for this book, and conducted by the internationally recognized firm of Sonalysts, is voluminous. It will be published separately in a Kindle version and will be presented on this book's website, TheKennedyHalfCentury.com. The Dictabelt sounds, and a complete transcript that we have compiled, will accompany the Sonalysts report.

and idling. The sounds of the presidential entourage gunning toward Park-land are unmistakable, and they passed the stationary motorcycle within sight of the officer. There were no other siren-equipped emergency vehicles of any type operating in Dallas at this critical time.*

In addition, we believe we have been able to identify the officer with the stuck microphone. He is Willie Price, who had joined the Dallas police de-partment seventeen years earlier and was much liked and respected within the force. Earlier on November 22, Price had been assigned to monitor the corner of McKinney and Harwood Streets, about three-quarters of a mile from downtown Dallas. After Kennedy passed there without incident, his instructions were to go to the Trade Mart, which he did. Our analysis strongly suggests it is his motorcycle engine that is heard on the Dictabelt running at high speed. Once at the Trade Mart, Price was located in the parking lot, awaiting the president's arrival.†

Why is the officer with the stuck microphone very likely to be Price? Every piece of available evidence points in his direction. Our audio analysis demon-strates that the officer with the stuck mic is well ahead of the motorcade at the time of the assassination, where Price is indisputably positioned. The sounds of the limousine carrying JFK screaming by Price's stationary post at the Trade Mart are heard precisely where they should be, a few minutes past 12:30 P.M., and the mic becomes "unstuck" just in time for Price to talk to police headquar-ters once at Parkland. More important, on that very morning, Price had been given a substitute motorcycle to use on November 22 that had demonstrated prior problems with a stuck microphone. Finally, Price himself was convinced that his cycle was the source of the difficulty, as was the police dispatcher on duty, Jim Bowles. This was not a long-delayed revelation. Price drew this conclu-sion within hours of the assassination, and he indicated as much to other Dallas officers at Parkland and also to Bowles, who agreed with his assessment.

As just indicated, instead of turning into the Trade Mart, the president's limousine and accompanying police vehicles whizzed by Price's vantage point on its way to Parkland, just over a half mile further down the highway. Price and the other officers were ordered to leave the Trade Mart and go to Parkland; as it happened, Price intercepted and accompanied the car carry-

---

*Telephone interview with police dispatcher James C. Bowles, May 23, 2013. Bowles had direct knowledge of all emergency vehicles operating in Dallas on November 22, 1963. He stressed to me that: "All emergency vehicles operated through the Dallas Police dispatcher's office. I've checked our transcript on emergency runs. We logged no fire calls, no analyst calls, no Dallas Power and Light Company power line calls, no Lone Star Gas leak calls, and we had nothing else that was running."

†His exact location was about halfway down Industrial Boulevard (today called Market Center Boulevard) between Stemmons Freeway and Harry Hines Boulevard.

ing Lyndon Johnson on its journey to the hospital. LBJ's car lagged behind the presidential limo. Price was also among the officers at Parkland who assisted in moving Kennedy's body into Trauma Room One, and then guarded the room from the outside to prevent unauthorized entry.[17]

Now that we know the location of the stuck microphone, something else is obvious. Given the distance of Price's open microphone from Dealey Plaza—nearly two and a quarter miles at the time of the assassination—it is unlikely in the extreme that gunshots will ever be detected on the Dictabelt recording, no matter how sophisticated sound analysis becomes in the future. Keep in mind that the motorcycle's microphone quality was primitive, on par with a telephone receiver, and that a blunt stylus was simply recording sound impressions on a waxed plastic belt back at police headquarters.

While gunshots in the immediate vicinity of the microphone would have been loud enough to be recorded on the Dictabelt, shots more than two miles away were unheard and unrecorded. Had H. B. McLain in Dealey Plaza been the motorcycle officer with the stuck mic, as the HSCA insisted, the Dictabelt could have answered the basic question of the number and location of shooter(s). Willie Price's motorcycle at this substantial distance from the assassination could not.

Therefore, the long-hoped-for Rosetta Stone of the Kennedy assassination is nothing of the sort. And the much-publicized conclusion of proven conspiracy by the 1979 House Select Committee on Assassinations was deeply flawed and demonstrably wrong. What many believed was the best remaining opportunity to solve the Kennedy murder definitively by means of hard evidence has turned into yet another dry well in a half-century quest to illuminate fully what happened on November 22, 1963.

Despite incontrovertible evidence that the open microphone was not in a location where it could have recorded the sound of gunfire, a puzzling question remains: What is one to make of the "impulses" identified as gunshots by the HSCA?

Our acoustics experts found that some of the impulses attributed to gunfire are very similar to other clusters of impulses found in neighboring regions of the Dictabelt's audio file and even within the span of the alleged gunshot impulse sequences on the Dictabelt.

These observations suggest that at least some of the impulses attributed to gunfire are not unique, nor are they discernible from other impulses contained on the recording. In fact, there are no less than twelve similar impulses in a period spanning just over a three-minute segment of the open microphone audio. Three of these impulses were said to represent gunfire by the HSCA, but the other nine were not. The sounds are so similar that there are no characteristics that reliably distinguish any of the impulses from the rest.

Sonalysts found it likely that all these impulses have the same or similar origin, and they are probably of a mechanical origin associated with the motorcycle (for example, a vibrating metal part or perhaps the result of the policeman handling some equipment attached to the motorcycle). Regardless of the source, what is clear is that the HSCA's analysis mistook individual features of unrelated sounds generated by vibrating, resonant objects for gunfire impulses.

We found the third of four "shots" identified by the HSCA, the one which the committee concluded came from the grassy knoll, to be no different than other "ordinary and common features of the audio recording." It is "nearly identical" to no less than three other impulses occurring around the same time. The HSCA appears to have selected this particular impulse simply because it matched their timing of the Dealey Plaza gunshots.

With the assistance of cutting-edge audio technology, we discovered that when the motorcycle engine noise is filtered out, many of the peaks selected by the HSCA as gunshot impulses disappeared almost entirely. A closer examination of the test methodology used by the HSCA's experts revealed an over-reliance on timing estimates and an under-reliance on amplitude information; this flaw produced "gunfire" matches that under more rigorous testing would have been seen as very unlikely.

While the Dictabelt is not the time tunnel to ultimate truth about the source of the Dealey Plaza shots that it was once heralded as being, the recording is invaluable nonetheless. What we call the Dictabelt is actually a collection of belts that recorded all police communications on two channels from 9:44 am until 3:57 pm on November 22.* Our transcript of the day's chatter (akin to listening to a modern police scanner) is more complete than any ever compiled due to the sound techniques we employed. It totals more than thirty thousand words and includes comments by dozens of police personnel and officers stationed at key locations around Dallas.

These Dictabelt recordings are dramatic living history, a kind of "black box" for the crash that occurred on November 22, 1963. They not only give us new insights into a day that changed America but collectively they serve as a police sound track that can supplement, though not precisely match, the silent films taken on the motorcade route.

In the morning, there are standard police communications about a presidential visit, from the arrival of Air Force One at Love Field to the difficulties of holding back enthusiastic crowds pressing to get a better view of the Kennedys. Occasionally, due to transmitting over the same lines, non-police con-

---

*Technically, the Dictabelt was used only to record channel one. Channel two was recorded using a separate machine called a Gray Audograph. This device recorded onto a plastic disk resembling a phonograph record.

versations from telephone calls bleed over into the police channels: a man profanely curses his favorite but losing football teams, a man and woman alternate between romance and argument, and someone asks a friend for money—and the friend begs off.

Suddenly, routine conversation ends, and police work turns chaotic. Sheriff Decker issues an order to investigate the area behind the grassy knoll: "Have my office move all men available . . . into the railroad yard in an effort to determine what happened in there and hold everything secure until Homicide and other investigators should get there." There is discussion about "victims" remaining in Dealey Plaza, the possible shooting of a Secret Service agent (which did not happen), and an early description of "a suspect." Officers report the contradictory claims of witnesses about the sources of the gunshots: Some said the shots originated at the grassy knoll, others at the Dallas courts building, and still others at the book depository.

The Dictabelt captures the chilling moments of absolute panic as President Kennedy was taken to Parkland for a futile attempt at resuscitation. Officer Price, after he arrives at Parkland and views the extent of President Kennedy's wounds, calls in a report to the dispatcher: "I believe the president's head was practically blown off." Price immediately regretted his comment and declined to repeat it when asked, noting, "It's not for me to say, I can't say." Jim Bowles, the Dallas dispatcher who provided an original, partial transcript of the Dictabelt in 1964, assisted his fellow officer by labeling Price's remark "inaudible"—something Bowles admitted to me that he did purposely to protect Price from embarrassment.[18]

Officers at the Trade Mart ask what they can tell the hundreds of people assembled for a speech President Kennedy would never deliver. The dispatcher asks Officer One [Dallas chief Jesse Curry], who is at Parkland with the presidential entourage and is well aware of the fatal nature of the wounds, "[Is] the president going to appear at the Trade Mart?" The sad, sparse answer from Chief Curry: "It's very doubtful . . . I feel reasonably sure that he will not." There are also Dictabelt references to a series of post-assassination events, from the shooting of Officer Tippit to the arrest of Oswald to the police transporting of LBJ, Jackie Kennedy, and JFK's body back to Air Force One. At the end of a horrible day, there is also the bizarre, jarring reintroduction of everyday life as the police dispatcher tells an officer to "go over to Wholesome Bakery and pick up eight packs of hamburger buns" and deliver them to the Deluxe Diner. "Tell 'em down there at the bakery to charge 'em to the Deluxe Diner."

Yet no out-of-place note of normality can expunge the earth-shattering words heard in Dallas on November 22. From tiny sound impressions made on crude recording devices on that long-ago day, the shock and horror comes to life again, and a listener cannot help but to be mesmerized.

While we now have a firm resolution of the truths both contained in and absent from the Dictabelt, by no means do we have all the available facts needed for an airtight finding about the assassination—certainly not one that will satisfy the warring theorists. Perhaps as-yet unreleased documents will help, though it is doubtful that any eureka revelations will emerge from fifty-year-old bureaucratic paperwork. The missed opportunities for full resolution of John Kennedy's death occurred early. The assassination tragedy continued unabated thanks to a sloppy initial investigation whose purpose was to nail Oswald rather than inquire about the murder more comprehensively. The death of most principals and the mists of time have permanently obscured the full truth. Therefore, we have to accept a somewhat unsatisfying ending, the inability of a balanced analyst—much like the Dictabelt—to reveal with absolute certainty what really happened.

Recognizing these limitations, the following two conclusions seem reasonable. First, the chance of a conspiracy of some sort—either a second gunman in the grassy knoll–picket fence area or a plot involving more than a single shooter who fired the bullets in Dealey Plaza—cannot be dismissed out of hand. The conspiratorial scenario includes the possibility that a lone gunman was supported or encouraged by others. At the same time, the known and incontrovertible hard proof simply does not permit a definitive declaration of conspiracy. The advocates of this point of view have offered several plausible theories but have never been able to produce powerful evidence that would stand up in a court of law—evidence sufficient to warrant a clear confirmation of a conspiracy.

The second conclusion is based on the undisputed evidence we have today. There is no reasonable doubt that at least one of John F. Kennedy's assassins was Lee Harvey Oswald. It may well be that Oswald was the only killer in Dealey Plaza on November 22, and that he alone concocted the plan to murder the president, but that is less certain than Oswald's manifest individual guilt.

Those who insist Oswald was "a patsy"—an innocent front man, set up to take the blame for a murder he did not commit—ignore far too much. As I have reviewed, and as others have devoted lengthy books to confirming, there is a mountain of evidence establishing his culpability. For example, despite all of the Warren Commission's inadequacies, I believe the facts support the commission's assertions about the origin point of the bullets that struck President Kennedy (that is, the sixth floor of the Book Depository) and the paths that they took (back-to-front, with the first successful shot—the so-called magic bullet—striking both President Kennedy and Governor Connally). There are multiple, believable eyewitness reports of a man with a rifle in the sixth floor window of the Depository. Unfortunately, since no photographs or positive identifications of Lee Oswald (or anyone else) in the window were made, there will always be room to suggest that someone else fired the gun in the Depository and that Oswald was framed in an elaborate plot. Yet the weight of evidence is overwhelming that Oswald was there in the window and fired the bullets. He is the only logical suspect from the Depository, the place where he worked and from which he fled. The murder weapon was Oswald's rifle, his palm print was on the gun, and (despite the dispute over the size of Oswald's "curtain rods" package) he likely brought it to work with him the morning of the assassination.

Moreover, anyone attempting to exonerate Oswald must ignore the ballistic evidence found at the scene of Officer J. D. Tippit's murder.[19] Three bystanders—Domingo Benavides, Barbara Jeanette Davis, and Virginia Davis—found four spent cartridge casings in the bushes that were traced to Oswald's .38-caliber Smith & Wesson. Four bullets were retrieved from Tippit's body, one of which matched Oswald's revolver "to the exclusion of all others." The analysis on the other three bullets suggested they very likely came from Oswald's gun, too.[20] Slaying a policeman who has stopped you for questioning is not the act of an innocent man.*

Oswald's life was a virtual template for a potential assassin. He was an acutely unhappy, troubled young man who had long been an angry loner, perpetually dissatisfied with his personal circumstances but hopelessly incapable of changing them. He had led a life marked by wild fluctuations, alienation, deceit, lack of sustainable love, and violent tendencies. At the time of the assassination, Oswald was at the end of his rope; he had exhausted his options for escape from a dead-end existence. Oswald may have disagreed with Kennedy politically on certain subjects such as Cuba, but in a disturbed and agitated mind, was politics really the paramount motivator? This most political of murders may not have been terribly ideological from Oswald's perspective. If ideology entered into it, it may have been more of a secondary justification for an intense emotional impulse. Kennedy was the ultimate symbol of a society Oswald hated because it

---

* One of Tippit's fellow officers, Paul McCaghren, told me about a September 1956 incident that he thinks may have caused Tippit to hesitate when Oswald drew his pistol. "It was about three o'clock in the morning," McCaghren recalled. "I was [at police headquarters] with my partner, working on an accident report, and Tippit and his partner were down at the other end of the hall . . . Tippit was sitting there not saying anything, and I got his partner over to one side and I said, 'What's going on?' And he said, 'Tippit just had to shoot a guy.' The guy [had] tried to draw on him at a bar. [After Parkland Hospital called to say the suspect had expired], "I told Tippit, 'your suspect died.' Well, Tippit almost collapsed. He put his head in his hands—it really shook him up. [During the November 22, 1963, altercation with Oswald], "I think it crossed Tippit's mind that here's the same situation [that happened] years ago. And I just think that Tippit was thinking about that, and not protecting himself." Telephone interview with Paul McCaghren, February 26, 2013. See also Dale K. Myers, "J. D. Tippit, Biography: 1952–1963," J. D. Tippit Official Home Page, http://jdtippit.com/ [accessed February 27, 2013].

had left him, with his considerable help, at the very bottom, with little money or food, a deeply unsatisfying marriage, and no real prospects for a brighter future. Kennedy was the pinnacle of success in a world where Oswald had failed utterly at everything. By chance and fate, Lee Oswald ended up close enough to the motorcade and he had a serviceable weapon that he had almost certainly used before in the assassination attempt on General Walker. Oswald saw an opportunity to fulfill the delusions of grandeur he had always nursed. An explosion of suppressed rage and a sick determination to destroy his human opposite helped Oswald get even with the world for his miserable existence, and in spectacular fashion. The instant the bullets hit Kennedy, Oswald, a nobody, became a historic somebody. This momentous "accomplishment" delivered unto Oswald a triumph for the ages. It is no wonder that in his few public moments after the assassination, luxuriating in worldwide attention, he looked so self-satisfied, the famished cat who had gobbled up the prize canary.

Does this mean all the other theories about November 22 hold no water? Much of the conjecture is groundless, no matter how enticing it may be for those inclined to believe. As distasteful a man as Lyndon Johnson could often be, LBJ did not kill JFK. The Secret Service agents didn't pull guns and accidentally shoot the president, as some absurdly charge, nor did the agents conspire with others to leave the president undefended.[21] The military establishment and the leadership of the FBI and CIA did not join in a massive conspiracy to kill Kennedy in a banana-republic-style coup d'état. Castro and the Russians had no rational motive to do the deed, and the risks would have been enormous for them. There wasn't a UFO involved, either.

But the chance of some sort of conspiracy involving Oswald is not insubstantial. For all the attempts to close the case as "just Oswald," fair-minded observers continue to be troubled by many aspects of eyewitness testimony and paper trails. There remains the live possibility of a second gunman in the grassy knoll area. It is not just the number of Dealey Plaza spectators who believe one or more shots came from that locale. Who were the individuals representing themselves as Secret Service agents, with credentials good enough to fool Dallas policemen familiar with official identification? Who were the armed men and suspicious individuals seen in the vicinity of Dealey Plaza before, during, and after the assassination? What exactly has the CIA been trying to hide about Oswald all these years? Maybe these questions, and others that we have posed, have innocent explanations, but they have eluded honest investigators to this point.

The odds of conspiracy include a second possibility: There was no second gunman, but private assistance or encouragement was given to Oswald in achieving his murderous hit. The most likely suspects, based on the available evidence, would be the Mafia, the anti-Castro Cubans (who had an undisclosed cell operating in Dallas at the time of the assassination), or a small unsupervised cabal within the CIA.[22] All three potential suspects had the means, motive, and opportunity to reach out to Oswald either as a lone assassin or in partnership with someone behind the picket fence. I have already laid out what rationale exists in all three categories. If Oswald was a lone gunman but people from one of these groups encouraged him, the silencing of Oswald by Jack Ruby, even if uninitiated by the co-conspirators, makes it improbable we will ever find out. A smoking gun for conspiracy has never emerged—though, again, technological advances applied to surviving physical evidence such as film and photos might one day prove that *somebody* participated in the shooting with Oswald in Dealey Plaza. If that person existed on November 22, he would have been a person with substantial backing, not because the murder required elaborate planning (it was all too easy) or special equipment (tens of millions of weapons qualified for the job), but because the clean getaway was complicated to arrange and sustain. To disappear without a trace for fifty years, to have no credible deathbed confessions, to have no accomplices disclose the plot in exchange for a great deal of media money— well, all this is possible but adds to one's doubts about conspiracy.

We should also not forget about another intriguing twist that may prove true with time. As I stressed earlier, no one has offered a convincing explanation for the CIA's special treatment of Oswald's paperwork in the weeks leading up to the assassination. It is beyond question that the CIA lied to the Warren Commission in 1964 and then again to the House Select Committee on Assassinations in the late 1970s. What were they hiding? What was so important that the CIA risked intense public condemnation had their dissembling been discovered at those sensitive times? This was especially true in the atmosphere of the 1970s, when the CIA had become widely unpopular. Some politicians and activists were calling for the CIA's dismantling after exposure of its foreign assassination plots, the CIA's role in the bugging of the Democratic National Committee headquarters at the Watergate hotel, and the agency's extensive spying on U.S. citizens domestically.[23] Given its long history of double-talk and dishonesty regarding the Kennedy assassination, and the agency's undeniable misleading of two separate government inquests, the CIA has little credibility left on the subject. Journalist Jefferson Morley believes that, at the very least, CIA agents and directors who withheld information on Oswald "should be stripped of any medals or commendations they received for their job performance in 1963."[24] That is reasonable, but punishing long-departed CIA officials will not end the debate over who killed JFK.

And why does this debate matter so much? It is because the assassination is critical both to understanding America's past and future paths and to the lasting legacy of John Kennedy that is the subject of this book. Concerning the first, a quiet civil war has been raging for a half century. This war has not been fought with bullets, and it has not been a battle of economic ideologies like the chilly one that marked the standoff between the United States and the Soviet Union. Instead, American culture has been engulfed in a war of words between those who have embraced the fundamental conclusion of the Warren Commission that Lee Harvey Oswald was the lone gunman, and those who insist that a broader conspiracy lies behind the assassination.

This is no minor dispute. The commission's backers accuse the conspiracy supporters of stirring feelings of deep cynicism in the American people and encouraging a lack of faith in those who run government with their wild accusations of complicity in Kennedy's murder by senior political figures and civil servants. Further, say the lone gunman theory's advocates, the widespread accusations that senior political, governmental, and military figures participated in the planning, execution, or cover-up of the assassination of President Kennedy have damaged the image of the United States around the globe, fueling anti-American sentiments by undermining the very basis of our democratic system.

The most adamant supporters of the lone gunman theory say that it is irresponsible to question the "carefully considered" conclusions of the Warren Commission report. That is certainly the establishment view, even today, in the halls of government and many media organizations, perhaps reinforced by the reaction to Oliver Stone's everybody-did-it movie. Yet if the Warren Commission's conclusion was so compelling and convincing, why did the man who created the commission and all but mandated the lone-gunman finding, Lyndon Johnson, himself believe until his dying day that Kennedy had been killed by a conspiracy? And why did the two people closest to Kennedy in his presidency, Robert F. Kennedy and Jackie Kennedy, privately judge their brother and husband's death to have been the result of a larger plot?[25] During a January 2013 interview in Dallas with the television commentator Charlie Rose, RFK Jr. said that his father "believed the Warren Report was a shoddy piece of craftsmanship" and gave orders for officials at the Justice Department to conduct a secret investigation of possible ties between Oswald and the CIA and Mafia. "He publicly supported the Warren Commission report," the younger Kennedy confessed, "but privately he was dismissive of it. He was a very meticulous attorney. He had gone over reports himself. He was an expert at examining issues and searching for the truth." Of course, the late attorney general's private doubts about the Warren Commission report have been long documented and discussed in assassination circles for years.[26]

Not to be outdone, those who suspect a broader plot in the assassination see the Warren Commission itself as the cynicism maker. Among other sins, they cite a rushed inquiry pushed along by naked political motives, the failure to pursue legitimate lines of inquiry or even to interview many key witnesses, and the desire of some members with CIA ties to hide the whole truth from the commission on subjects such as U.S. attempts to assassinate Fidel Castro. Many of these critics, at great personal cost and sacrifice, have devoted large chunks of their lives to uncovering the commission's inadequacies. They see themselves as David facing Goliath rather than Don Quixote tilting at windmills, and they have been determined to uncover the truth that has been buried by the alleged hidden perpetrators of this monstrous crime. From their perspective, the pro-commission establishment is more interested in protecting its charter members than in seeking justice for the murder of a president.

The echoes of this war are with us daily. Americans far too young to have any memory of November 22 instantly react to terms that entered the lexicon because of disputes about the assassination: grassy knoll, magic bullet, single bullet theory, conspiracy buff, and many more. More important, younger and older Americans have made their choice between the warring camps. Overwhelmingly—and consistently since the time of the assassination—people believe that Oswald did not act alone. (New polling, discussed later in the book, underlines and expands upon the public's choice of conspiracy.)

Perhaps, as I suggested earlier, it is mainly this: The enormity of the act of negating the decision of 69 million voters does not square with the insignificance of Lee Harvey Oswald. In addition, the silencing of Oswald so soon after the president's murder would cause suspicion even among the most naïve. Maybe most of all, though, it was the sixth sense of many Americans that they were being sold a bill of goods they did not want to buy from the usual group of elite suspects. The United States government has so often covered up the truth and politicians have so frequently lied to the citizenry that there is every reason to imagine the Kennedy story is much bigger than the official line suggests. The moral mendacity in prosecuting the Vietnam War, the sordid tale of Watergate crimes, and the thousand other scandals and schemes since 1963 have only confirmed the widespread public belief in a conspiracy to kill JFK.

Public support does not mean the conspiracy theorists are correct. Nor does the supposed superior knowledge of establishment leaders give them a monopoly on truth about the assassination. Both sides are blinded by contempt for one another and sure that the other group's motives are impure. In fact, impartial observers can find some legitimacy in the viewpoints of both camps, as we have tried to show in this chapter. Whether one embraces a conspiracy theory or prefers the lone gunman explanation, there is simply no question that—at the very least—negligence and deception among some officials contributed to the death of a president and the incomplete public explanation of his demise that followed. This is no minor matter, but some have treated it like a typographical error, to be overlooked without full accountability.

The never-ending controversy about who shot JFK, and why, is central to the thesis of this book. November 22 has kept John F. Kennedy on the front pages and on television and movie screens for fifty years. Every anniversary has been marked by TV specials, magazine spreads, and remembrances of various kinds. The assassination has become iconic, from the Zapruder film and Jackie's pink suit to the sixth floor window and Dealey Plaza. The continuing mystery surrounding the event, and the otherworldly cast of characters connected to it, has transfixed generations not alive at the time. It is a puzzle palace, and no James Bond novel ever had so many twists, turns, and subplots. There is also no epilogue that neatly ties all the strands together. The experts, the investigators, and the witnesses disagree with one another about critical details and fundamental conclusions. The enduring mystery of the assassination is irresistible for historians, journalists, Hollywood producers, and average citizens alike.[27] Just as we are reading books and watching television specials questioning vital aspects of the Lincoln assassination almost 150 years after the event, so, too, are Americans likely to relive the Kennedy assassination centuries from now.[28]

But this is no mere murder mystery for the millions still alive who personally and vividly recall four dreadful days in November 1963 as though they occurred last week. The essential connection between the long-ago tragedy and the fifty years of Kennedy dominance of American culture is simple: profound human emotion. The World War II generation came of age with television and a made-for-TV family named the Kennedys. It makes perfect sense that most Americans told pollsters in the wake of November 22 that they were grieving as though they had lost a member of their own family. In practical effect, they were. We grew up with make-believe television families such as the Cleavers, the Reeds, the Nelsons, the Ricardos, and the Taylors, and the Kennedys appeared to be the real-world match.[29] We felt that we knew this atypical young family of four, and we spoke easily of them as though they were cousins—Jack, Jackie, Caroline, and John-John. No other White House occupants had ever before been in the living rooms of most households on a daily basis, and not since Teddy Roosevelt had any First Family been so photogenic.

Then, horribly, abruptly, with no warnings and no good-byes, the Kennedy presidency and its TV show were canceled, never to return except in permanent, hard-to-watch reruns. The camera-friendly youth and vigor—the picture of what a vibrant postwar United States wished to project to the world—vanished in an instant, replaced by a politically able but dowdy old-style couple who were a throwback to an era that seemed obsolete. Few were able to quickly dispel the deep sadness that shook them to their foundations as they witnessed the youngest elected president become the youngest to die; the elegant First Lady—the Princess Diana or Kate of her day—have her husband gruesomely killed while sitting inches away; the White House children they found delightful but who would now grow up without a father; the little boy who, with one salute of his daddy's casket, caused the whole of America to dissolve into tears. Even now, the scenes conjure up great pain for some and recur in nightmares for others. I was struck by the number of interviewees for this book who openly cried or had to pause to collect themselves as they recalled these long-ago dark days.[30]

Not long after the assassination, Dan Fenn, who later became the first director of the John F. Kennedy Presidential Library, heard one of Jackie's assistants say, "We'll never laugh again." Fenn corrected her, "We'll laugh again, but we'll never be young again." (This quotation was mistakenly attributed to Daniel Patrick Moynihan, later a U.S. senator from New York.)[31] Most Americans felt much older, and more morose, after November 22, 1963. A half century ago, the nation barely recognized depression as a serious mental disorder, and had few effective treatments for it. If we had been more advanced, though, there would have been an unprecedented number of Prozac and Xanax prescriptions written. For the first time ever, because television news was finally able to offer continuous coverage, virtually the whole nation, and much of the world, did little but watch TV, in dazed shock, day after day—the kind of communal mourning that set a precedent for the reaction to the trauma of September 11, thirty-eight years later.

Yet another emotion, that of guilt, played a part in the public's postassassination reaction. In an election divided by religion as much as by party, millions of voters had cast their ballots against Kennedy on account of his Catholicism. Three years later, it was obvious even to the most extreme Kennedy critics that the United States had not been governed from the Vatican, as they had forebodingly projected. Others who had resented the Kennedy clan for its celebrity saw their grievances melt away as they said good-bye to a fallen leader. Almost everyone believed that a terrible injustice had been done to the presidential family, and their own families. Many citizens, even some of Kennedy's political enemies, resolved to right the scales by remembering the man and his legacy, and forgetting about, or outright denying, their past opposition to JFK. The resulting mental gymnastics were a wonder to behold. By 1964 an academic survey found that 64 percent of Americans claimed to have voted for John Kennedy in 1960, when he actually received 49.7 percent of the vote.[32]

Whatever the cynics may think, in a democracy, when the people clearly want something, they usually get it. Politicians and policymakers from the White House to the local school board rushed to respond. Hundreds of schools and sites would be named for Kennedy around the world in the wake of the assassination—not to mention an aircraft carrier. There seem to be few places abroad without a Kennedy plaza or street, and almost no states or major cities have failed to dedicate some monument, avenue, or educational facility to JFK. These daily reminders of a brief presidency, a direct result of November 22, have kept the Kennedy image alive. Most other modern presidents have far fewer concrete testimonials; only Ronald Reagan comes close.[33]

The assassination created a wistful tale of what might have been, at least as we imagine it, and we refuse to let go. Many Americans look back to the Kennedy moment as the country's high-water mark of world influence and domestic tranquillity. In part, this is reconstructed fantasy. The United States was more powerful right at the end of World War II than it had ever been before, or is likely to be again, and given the cauldron of racism that was steaming to a boil during the Kennedy years, it is difficult to call the domestic reality of 1961 to 1963 tranquil. Nonetheless, America was unquestionably the dominant Western nation in November 1963. After the scare of the Cuban Missile Crisis and the hopeful step represented by the Nuclear Test Ban Treaty, the two great powers appeared to be moving toward more tolerant coexistence. Whether it would have happened or not, John Kennedy and Nikita Khrushchev seemed to be approaching a kind of détente a decade before it finally arrived under Richard Nixon and Leonid Brezhnev.

Moreover, nostalgia for Kennedy's one thousand days in office was created by the savage developments that unfolded later in the 1960s and 1970s—widespread race riots, the draining Vietnam defeat, Nixon's megascandals, disturbing revelations about the hidden activities of the FBI and CIA, gasoline lines, high inflation, stubborn unemployment, skyrocketing interest rates, multiple recessions, and international humiliations such as the Iran hostage crisis. We will never know how JFK would have dealt with the tests that came America's way from 1964 to 1969, but retrospectively, to most of his countrymen, his record looked sterling by comparison to the performances of Presidents Johnson, Nixon, Ford, and Carter. Perhaps simplistically, Americans tend to classify public officials as "good guys" and "bad guys." Kennedy received one of the permanent good-guy berths, a designation impervious to revelations about JFK's private life shenanigans, while the four subsequent chief executives went out of office far less popular than they entered it.[34]

Maybe all this is unfair to Kennedy's successors. Andrew Johnson also struggled in the White House in part because he was not Abraham Lincoln. It is impossible to compete with a political martyr, and both Johnsons learned this to their dismay.[35] But as JFK famously said in one of his press conferences, "Life isn't fair." Presidents always discover that politics is one of the least fair parts of life.

As we move on from the shock and sorrow of the Kennedy assassination, and the long-term effects of its flawed investigation, we will explore how LBJ and eight other White House occupants interpreted, capitalized upon, and lived with the semi-saintly ghost of John F. Kennedy.

"LET US CONTINUE": LYNDON JOHNSON— PRETENDER TO THE THRONE

LYNDON JOHNSON HAD WANTED TO be president for a long time. As majority leader of the Senate in the 1950s, he saw the job up close and felt certain he could handle it. At his first real opportunity to chase the presidency, Johnson ran, albeit at the last moment, against Kennedy in 1960, and very probably would have run again in 1968 to succeed JFK, possibly against brother Bobby in the Democratic primaries. In November 1963 Johnson got his White House wish, but in the worst way. For over five years he would be haunted by the memory of the man whose death had delivered unto him the Oval Office.

Kennedy's murder did more for Johnson than put him in the White House. On the very day Kennedy was gunned down, a Maryland insurance broker, Don Reynolds, told a Senate investigative committee that he had bribed LBJ in return for business favors and knew about illegal contributions made to Johnson's campaign fund. Reynolds was able to produce invoices and canceled checks that partially backed up his claims. At the same time, the editors of *Life* magazine were deciding what to do with a muckraking story by one of their staff writers on Johnson's business operations in Texas, which had the odor of corruption about them. Either bad headline could have taken Johnson off the 1964 ticket, ending his hopes of being president. Both the Reynolds scandal and the *Life* magazine story disappeared on account of November 22. The new president was given a clean slate, his old sins wiped away by the tears from an assassination. In practical terms, the Senate committee dropped the investigation and *Life*'s editors spiked the story.[1]

Partly because of all Johnson had gained—and avoided—as a result of the events in Dallas, unfair suspicions about his involvement in his predecessor's murder dogged him from the start, but they were mainly whispered privately in the immediate wake of the assassination. By all firsthand accounts, Johnson was personally shocked as the events of November 22 unfolded, and genuinely concerned about Mrs. Kennedy and her children. Johnson understood the powerful symbolism of having Jackie Kennedy at his side for the swearing-in on Air Force One, and he could not help but be moved by the sight of the former First Lady in her bloodstained outfit.[2] One of his first calls on the flight back to Washington was to JFK's mother, Rose; Lady Bird also participated in the call. At 7:20 P.M., shortly after arriving back in his vice presidential office, he penned affectionate notes to Caroline and John Jr., as well as to their mother.[3]

The new president put every foot right in the tear-drenched hours and days after the assassination. His statement upon landing at Andrews Air Force Base was affecting and appropriately brief. Johnson met with congressional leaders, reached out to the living former presidents and key heads of state around the world, and reassured the country that he was in charge without overstepping delicate boundaries during a period of intense mourning. Disregarding (perhaps unwisely) the urgent advice of the Secret Service, he walked openly in Kennedy's funeral procession. Jackie wrote Johnson the day after the funeral, "Thank you for walking yesterday—behind Jack. You did not have to do that—I am sure many people [forbade] you to take such a risk but you did it anyway."[4] The new president was also solicitous of the feelings of President Kennedy's appointees and understood that he was viewed by many of them as an interloper and usurper. Whatever his personal attitude toward some JFK associates, Johnson did not push them out of office, as was his right. He asked them to stay and help, for he needed them "more than John Kennedy ever did."[5]

Of course, Johnson also understood that the Kennedy staffers and cabinet officers were part of his link to JFK's legacy and a key to his legitimacy as Kennedy's successor. Better to keep them in the tent than have them undermine him from outside. And instinctively, Johnson knew some of them would transfer their allegiance to him quickly. Sure enough, Secretary of State Dean Rusk and Labor Secretary Willard Wirtz, in particular, became close to LBJ over time. It did not hurt that Rusk and Bobby Kennedy were not close.[6] At least at first, the wishes of all the Kennedy family members, not just Jackie, were granted almost without question. When JFK press secretary Pierre Salinger advised Johnson to let Ethel Kennedy and other Kennedy associates fly on Air Force One with him to a deceased congressman's funeral, LBJ answered, "Damn sure is better to ride with me than a separate plane . . . Wherever I go, [they] go and anybody else named Kennedy—or anybody that's ever smelled the Kennedys."[7]

But the other side of Lyndon Johnson was in motion from the start, out of public sight. The striving politician was delighted to be president and determined from his first hours in office to make his mark. No vice president is without ambition for the top job, whatever he may pretend in public. Johnson was no average vice president. He was big, Texas big, and he realized some-time in the afternoon or evening of November 22: Potentially and constitu-tionally, he could serve longer as president than anyone except his hero, Franklin D. Roosevelt.[8] Late that night, in the bedroom of his home, The Elms, on Fifty-second Street NW in D.C.,[9] an exhausted Lady Bird Johnson attempted to go to sleep while her husband was already discussing with aides his plans for what would become the Great Society. "At least this is only for nine months," until the Democratic National Convention would presumably select someone else to carry on, Lady Bird commented. An LBJ aide quickly corrected her: "It is more likely to be nine years." "I'm afraid [he's] right," added LBJ. "At least it's for five years," he said.[10] Mrs. Johnson groaned, pushed earplugs into her ears, put on black shades to block out the light, and pulled the bedcovers up.

Just two days after John Kennedy's burial, on the eve of the nation's shell-shocked Thanksgiving, President Johnson went before a joint session of Con-gress that was televised to the nation. He knew precisely what he wanted to do, and he expected the Democratic Congress to act quickly. Reminding his audience of JFK's inaugural address mandate, "Let us begin," Johnson de-clared, "Let us continue . . . Let us here highly resolve that John Fitzgerald Kennedy did not live—or die—in vain." LBJ outlined the breathtaking scope he intended for his new administration, calling for the urgent passage of bills concerning civil rights, education, tax cuts, youth employment, medical care for the elderly, foreign aid, and more. Having served in the House and Senate, Johnson knew that legislative emotions could dissipate quickly. Despite the danger of overloading Congress, he was determined to press hard for ev-erything, labeling it all a memorial to JFK. This was the same Congress, dominated by a conservative coalition of Southern Democrats and some right-leaning Republicans, that had thwarted most of Kennedy's agenda. Johnson knew he could combine his legislative skills with overwhelming public grief to break the logjam and produce a cornucopia's plenty from Capitol Hill. LBJ revealingly couched Kennedy's unfulfilled goals as "dreams." Johnson knew he could never match the late president's eloquence, so his legacy would be achievement, the translation of JFK's lofty objectives into concrete action. "And now the ideas and the ideals which [Kennedy] so nobly represented must and will be translated into effective action," Johnson told Congress.[11] All this Johnson had shrewdly processed and gamed out barely a hundred hours after taking the oath of office.

Quietly, Johnson and his staff went to work almost immediately to orches-trate what would become one of the most productive congressional legislative sessions in history. This was all the more remarkable because the session was the 88th Congress's second, held in the presidential and congressional election year of 1964. Throughout American history, election year sessions have often been little more than empty shells, marking time until November, with legislators avoiding controversial topics lest they alienate voters just before ballots are cast. Prodded by LBJ and public opinion, this unusual Congress would throw caution to the wind in the rush to memorialize JFK and to please the insistent White House occupant.

The press and public did not directly see much of this work in the remaining days of 1963, a period of mourning that was devoted to finding ways to etch John Kennedy's name everywhere. President Johnson kicked off the efforts on Thanksgiving Day. In a special proclamation, Johnson renamed the NASA Launch Operation Center in Florida the John F. Kennedy Space Center, which had been requested by Mrs. Kennedy.[12] In a companion move not sought by Mrs. Kennedy, LBJ struck the centuries-old geographic name Cape Canaveral from the surrounding area, substituting Cape Kennedy.[13] Locals were furious and protested loudly; Cape Canaveral was finally restored to the map in 1973 after a decade of dissent in the Sunshine State. The Kennedy family released a letter saying they "understood" why JFK's name was removed. It is a small but telling example of LBJ's "Texas big" philosophy from the earliest days of his presidency; he would do even Jackie Kennedy one better. Johnson also offered the ambassadorship to Mexico to the Spanish-fluent Jackie. She declined. "Hell, I'd make her pope if I could," Johnson said, as reported by JFK aide Kenneth O'Donnell.[14]

President Johnson also wasted no time in adopting another, more private part of the Kennedy legacy. During a trip to Austin on the final day of 1963, Johnson announced to top members of the White House press corps, "One more thing, boys. You may see me coming in and out of a few women's bedrooms while I am in the White House, but just remember, that is none of your business." Given the rules of the day about coverage of a politician's personal life, and the precedent set by JFK and others, Johnson had little to worry about. LBJ did his best to continue the sexually predatory practices of his predecessor, and he had a number of affairs while living in the White House.[15]

Meanwhile, suggestions for Kennedy memorials flooded in from across America and the world. JFK was proposed for the Nobel Peace Prize by Peru's Chamber of Deputies, though the Nobel Institute demurred.[16] Domestically, there was little or no resistance to most such efforts. Some required federal action, while others were taken by state and local authorities. The Benjamin Franklin half dollar was replaced by the Kennedy fifty-cent piece, and a five-cent stamp with JFK's likeness was authorized.[17] LBJ named President Kennedy a recipient of the Presidential Medal of Freedom, and also ensured that the forthcoming 1964 World's Fair in New York City would have a suitable memorial to him.[18] The planned Washington, D.C., cultural institute was rechristened the John F. Kennedy Center for the Performing Arts, with a federal appropriation of $30 million in matching funds for private gifts.[19] New York City's Idlewild Airport became John F. Kennedy International a month after the assassination.[20] Schools and hospitals and highways from every corner of the country were renamed for the late president. Bay City, Alaska, near Anchorage, became John Fitzgerald Kennedy City. The "city" had thirty-five residents, and the mayor believed the new name would make it a mecca; today it is still on the map but a ghost town with a population of zero.[21]

Popular tunes, solemn marches, and cantatas were composed as musical tributes by well-known artists and anonymous amateurs.[22] Thousands of letters were written to the White House and the Kennedys offering condolences.[23] Tens of thousands of people requested photographs of the late president and his family.[24] They were not available from the government, but private companies quickly offered lithographs as well as long-playing albums of JFK's speeches and even toy replicas of his famous Oval Office rocking chair, which Kennedy used to ease the soreness in his back.[25] Dozens of memorial magazines and newspapers appeared on the stands and were snapped up as keepsakes as soon as they arrived. A blizzard of instant books rained down in the next year, and JFK's own *Profiles in Courage* returned to the best-seller list.[26]

On December 10, nineteen days after the assassination, Walter Cronkite decided that a depressed country needed a break from the constant barrage of assassination-related reports, and on his evening news program he ran a feel-good story about a new musical group from England called the Beatles. Fellow CBS journalist Mike Wallace had run a five-minute morning segment on the Beatles' rising popularity on the day their new album was released (November 22), and it had been scheduled to rerun that evening, before Kennedy's murder canceled all scheduled items. But Cronkite had seen Wallace's piece and liked it. Cronkite's judgment was proven correct, and Americans welcomed the opportunity to focus on a foreign diversion. This was the televised start of the phenomenon called Beatlemania that swept the United States in early 1964. The death of one cultural icon thus gave way to a new one.[27]

The Beatles sensation was a mere respite from, not a substitute for, the spotlight on John Kennedy. Citizens of all stripes were determined that their fallen leader would be remembered by future generations. The memorial with the most impact on JFK's legacy was not made of paper, or of brick and mortar. It was an idea hatched by Jackie Kennedy a week after the assassination. Over the years, the image most associated with the short Kennedy term has been Camelot, inspired by the Broadway play and song about King Arthur's reign. Never during JFK's life was Camelot linked to him. Mrs. Kennedy invented it with a simple anecdote she shared with presidential election chronicler Theodore White, whom she had summoned to Hyannis Port on the day after Thanksgiving. White was writing for *Life* magazine, and Jackie trusted him to convey her message intact. She also verified the trust by dictating and editing the article herself—and resisting attempts by *Life*'s editors to tone down the repeated allusions to Camelot. The widely read and discussed article, published December 6, 1963, contained this paragraph:

> "When Jack quoted something, it was usually classical," she said, "but I'm so ashamed of myself—all I keep thinking of is this line from a musical comedy. At night, before we'd go to sleep, Jack liked to play some records; and the song he loved most came at the very end of this record. The lines he loved to hear were: *Don't let it be forgot, that once there was a spot, for one brief shining moment that was known as Camelot.*"[28]

The mythic dimensions of the Kennedy presidency were now set. His widow had decreed that JFK had been King Arthur, his aides and cabinet the Round Table, and the time of John Kennedy would never be forgot. At that moment, after the strength she had shown and the sadness she had borne, Jackie Kennedy had more power to influence America than President Johnson, Congress, and the Supreme Court put together. Her word was cultural law, and the code of Camelot remains dominant fifty years later in the minds of those who lived then.[29]

The month of national mourning for John F. Kennedy had been a rare respite from partisan politics. Johnson himself had ordered all administration officials to cease "partisan political speeches of any sort," a ban that occurs only during extraordinary moments of national shock and grief.[30] The bombing of Pearl Harbor and the terrorist attacks of September 11 have been the only other modern examples of a complete, lengthy cease-fire in party warfare.

Replacing the partisan angst was a gnawing sense that the nation had lost its way, that it was becoming a "sick society"—a widespread feeling that would only grow throughout the troubled sixties and beyond. Religious and secular leaders suggested that materialism, the decline of national unity that had defined the years of World War II, and a degradation of timeless American values in the postwar years had culminated in the Kennedy assassination. The conservative *Reader's Digest*, one of the most widely read publications at the time, expressed this sentiment in a statement from the editors:

> What is happening to this beloved country of ours? Have we carried the violent spirit of war over into our peacetime lives? Have we become so complacent in our enjoyment of our material blessings that we have forsaken those nobler things of the spirit? Have we forgotten the ancient truths spoken by the prophets? Does the compassion of Christ no longer mean anything to large numbers of our people? Have Abraham Lincoln's immortal words " . . . this nation, under God" ceased to lift the heart and fortify the conscience?[31]

In retrospect, the tendency to blame all of American society for the actions of one or a few assassins appears ridiculously overblown, but it was a reaction to the enormity of the crime. There had to be greater meaning to such a horrific act with untold consequences. The blaming of established institutions and values accelerated with each new assassination in the 1960s, just as it does in contemporary society in the wake of repeated mass shootings. While he obviously disagreed with the assertions, President Johnson had to account for this as he sought to reassure a nation suffering from profound shock and jangled nerves.

The official national mourning period expired on December 22, 1963, but no single month could begin to contain the long-term impact of the events in Dallas. Not long after the assassination, a despondent Robert Kennedy commented privately that public memory was short and Americans would quickly move on. In this prediction, he could not have been more wrong, as he himself would discover in time.

NATURALLY, THE AMBITIOUS new president hoped to move out from under John Kennedy's shadow in the new year. This aspiration was encouraged by his staff. Aide Jack Valenti, who had been with LBJ on Air Force One in Dallas, wrote Johnson in early January 1964, "Up to this point, you have been carrying on Kennedy's programs—now, it's your show."[32] But even Johnson understood he had no real chance to become his own man until he won a term in his own right. The affection for his predecessor had grown exponentially since his death, and LBJ the consummate politician knew that JFK's murder had created enormous banked capital in an account marked Kennedy. Better to acknowledge this golden reserve and use it to build a joint record than to pretend it was not still the Kennedy-Johnson administration.

President Johnson sensed and heard the deep suspicions about him and his intentions in Democratic circles. There had been not a day's respite from the doubts since November 22. In fact, on the front page of the November 23

New York Times, just below the dark headline KENNEDY IS KILLED BY SNIPER, was a news analysis entitled "Republican Prospects Rise—Johnson Faces Possible Fight Against Liberals":

> President Kennedy's assassination . . . elevated into the Presidency . . . an older, more conservative man still emerging from his Southern heritage. It increased immeasurably, for the leaders of the Republican party, prospects of electing a President next November.[33]

As preposterous as this projection seems now, the dispatch captured the immediate conventional wisdom about Johnson's allegedly precarious position. The truth was quite different. American voters were never likely to give the country three presidents in one year, much less a Republican one.[34] Yet Johnson had learned from his disputed 1948 Senate squeaker not to take anything for granted in politics.[35] He had to hold the Kennedys close personally; be more Kennedy than Kennedy on policy; and accomplish as much as possible in the short window he had before the onset of the 1964 campaign. It was a tall task, but Johnson wasted not an hour.

By the time President Johnson delivered his State of the Union address on January 8, 1964, the plan was set. LBJ would secure passage of key parts of the unfulfilled Kennedy agenda while laying the groundwork for his own legacy. "Let us carry forward the plans and programs of John Fitzgerald Kennedy— not because of our sorrow and sympathy, but because they are right," Johnson intoned before Congress and the nation. But the new man would get to refine, redefine, and extend JFK's "plans and programs."[36]

The first major Kennedy bill to become law was the Revenue Act of 1964, passed on February 26. In a move that today sounds more Republican than Democratic, JFK had called for an $11.5 billion tax cut for individuals and corporations in order to "remove the brakes" of high federal tax rates and stimulate the economy—the largest tax reduction to that point in American history.[37] The proposal was a year old, although it had already made some legislative progress. Johnson wanted it immediately so that it would have the maximum time to work its wonders before November. Two thirds of what amounted to a substantial 19 percent slashing of taxes went into effect retroactive to January 1, 1964.[38] Many economists now believe this fiscal move had its intended effect, and just as important, it enabled Johnson to set forth a credible claim that his actions had produced the prosperity that was evident in the fall.[39] While the Revenue Act received considerable attention at the time, no one then understood how influential it would be in characterizing Kennedy's legacy for future generations. The tax cut enabled Republican candidates and officeholders to seize part of JFK's image and legacy for themselves, making Kennedy much more bipartisan in memory than he was in life.

The tax cut bill paled by comparison with Johnson's premier goal in 1964, the passage of the Civil Rights Act.[40] Even Lyndon Johnson's fiercest critics would admit that he was masterful in his maneuvering to secure this landmark legislation, long sought by African Americans and their allies. Johnson understood that such a massive change in the nation's culture would have to be backed by bipartisan majorities in both houses of Congress, not just to ensure enactment but to achieve compliance, however grudging, especially in the South. This was an era when both Democrats and Republicans had large liberal and conservative wings. It was possible for a skilled president to assemble a coalition that bridged partisanship and calmed party fervor. Knowing all members of the Senate and many members of the House—their strengths as well as their flaws—Johnson went to work to stitch together what is arguably his greatest achievement.

At every stage, LBJ made the bill a memorial to John Kennedy. In public and in private he cajoled and pleaded for his bill, insisting that JFK had been a victim of hatred and violence, much as civil rights workers had been. Ironically, if LBJ's FBI and Warren Commission were to be believed, Kennedy had been killed by a leftist who was sympathetic to civil rights for African Americans.[41] But no one was going to argue this point with Johnson, not for the great cause of equal rights, not when JFK's family and supporters were calling the Civil Rights Act a fitting monument to the late president. Even some conservative Southern Democrats realized the gathering momentum was probably irresistible.

On the other side of the aisle, Republicans of moderate and liberal stripes saw the Civil Rights Act as an opportunity to inoculate themselves in advance of a building Democratic tide in the November election. Politically astute GOP legislators realized early that public sentiment about JFK combined with LBJ's formidable personage would likely deliver victory to the Democrats. Voting for the Civil Rights Act would be one way to avoid being at the top of the Democrats' list of targets. The impending presidential nomination of conservative U.S. senator Barry Goldwater (R-AZ), who opposed the Civil Rights Act, underlined the electoral concerns of northern GOP members of Congress. Voting for civil rights was one way to separate themselves in the public's mind from Goldwater.

In the end, Johnson's legislative victory was as complete as it was historic. In Congress as a whole, 63 percent of Democrats and 81 percent of Republicans voted for the Civil Rights Act.[42] (It is surprising but true: Republican legislators were more liberal on civil rights than the Democrats in Congress.) This time, conservatives in the Senate found the filibuster was not sufficient to thwart the popular bill. Impressively, Johnson had also been able to keep the act strong and intact. At every step LBJ refused easy compromises to water down the bill in exchange for the backing of this or that senior legislator, as he had seen done with earlier civil rights legislation in 1957 and 1960.[43] While public opinion had begun to turn in favor of civil rights before LBJ took office, and JFK had proposed a bill in June 1963 that had been approved by the House Judiciary Committee the month before the assassination, there was no question that President Johnson secured a law with far broader reach than one that might have passed had Kennedy lived.

Signing the bill just before Independence Day, a proud LBJ saluted its original author, "our late and beloved President John F. Kennedy," but he knew history would record the moment as among his own finest. "Let us close the springs of racial poison," Johnson said. "Let us lay aside irrelevant differences and make our nation whole."[44] A few days after the signing, Johnson noted in a letter, "No doubt President Kennedy's death provided a dramatic and important catalyst for consideration of the legislation, but I believe he would have been able to pass the legislation had he lived."[45] That was for the public record. No political observer then or historian now would assert that JFK could have wrangled as strong a civil rights bill from a Congress that frustrated so many of his objectives.[46] Had Kennedy been reelected handily, though, he might have secured passage of a muscular bill in his second term.

With the revenue act and the civil rights bill, President Johnson had gone a long way toward discharging his obligations to the man who chose him for the vice presidency. But Johnson saw an opening to reach farther, to use the Kennedy imprimatur to create the beginnings of his own program. LBJ was the first in a long line of presidents to realize John Kennedy's name and image, properly applied, could speed along acceptance of a new proposal. In Johnson's case, it was his "war on poverty."

On November 19, 1963, just before President Kennedy left for Texas, he met with Walter Heller, chairman of the Council of Economic Advisers. Almost a year earlier, Kennedy had asked Heller to look into the poverty problem in America, which JFK had seen up close during his campaigning for the West Virginia primary in May 1960.[47] Heller hoped for a major assault on poverty, but Kennedy seemed inclined toward a pilot program, applying to perhaps a handful of cities, to be included in his 1964 legislative package sent to Congress. It was an election year and Kennedy feared that the large, heavy-voting middle class would interpret a larger program as redistribution of income, another welfare subsidy.[48] (The echoes of this debate are still with us every time new ideas from health care to immigration reform are proposed.)

The day after the assassination, Heller went to see the new president to tell him about the program and his conversation with JFK the week before.[49]

Johnson stunned Heller by seizing the idea. Johnson reportedly replied, "That's my kind of program. It's a people's program . . . Go ahead. Give it the highest priority. Push ahead full tilt."[50] Unlike Kennedy, Johnson was not born to wealth, and he had personally seen extreme poverty as he grew up in Texas. Johnson emotionally identified with the have-nots because he saw himself as one of them, a hardscrabble graduate of Southwest Texas State Teachers College rather than Harvard.

Soon President Johnson was fashioning an "unconditional war on poverty" as though it had been John F. Kennedy's final wish, a key proviso in the late president's last will and testament, with LBJ as the official executor.[51] Those familiar with Kennedy's cautious approach to most domestic matters were supportive but amused; they knew Kennedy had intended no such thing. Yet this extension of the Kennedy legacy could be quite useful, both to JFK's historical image and LBJ's own presidency. A marriage of conviction and convenience ensued.

Thus was conceived the Economic Opportunity Act. The idea was carefully nurtured by Johnson until its legislative birth in near-record time for a major, novel bill, with a signing on August 20, 1964, and a billion-dollar budget. The alphabet soup of agencies spawned by its administrative Office of Economic Opportunity rivals the New Deal's productivity in some ways: the Job Corps, training disadvantaged youth in employment skills; Volunteers in Service to America (VISTA), a domestic form of the Peace Corps; the Model Cities Program to encourage urban redevelopment; Upward Bound, providing educational tutoring to impoverished high school students so that they could compete and gain admission to college; Head Start, organizing preschool training for the disadvantaged; and more besides. Additional billions added throughout the Johnson years generated the traditional left-right split on government expenditures. Democrats hailed LBJ's initiatives to make society fairer, and cited a significant drop in poverty during the Johnson years as proof they had worked.[52] Republicans argued that government was spending too much, overstepping its bounds, and continuing down the road to socialism.[53] (Little has changed in partisan terms over fifty years.) Unsurprisingly, later Republican administrations sharply reduced the scope and then the funding of the antipoverty programs, though many of them survive in some form today.

The antipoverty efforts comprised much of the heart of Johnson's "Great Society," which he had announced with fanfare, though without much specificity, in a May 22 graduation speech at the University of Michigan.[54] Kennedy's New Frontier had inspired with style more than substance. In Johnson's view, the New Frontier was a mere appetizer to the Great Society's ample menu of entrees that would comprise the most transformative era for government since Franklin Roosevelt. In a way, the behind-the-scenes theme song of Johnson's nascent administration was, "Anything You Can Do I Can Do Better,"[55] though in the fourteen presidential months he had inherited from JFK, Johnson never forgot his mandate of continuity. His choice to head the new Office of Economic Opportunity underlined this. John Kennedy's brother-in-law, R. Sargent Shriver, was plucked from the directorship of JFK's Peace Corps to take command of the OEO. Kennedy's "final wish" was reality, and headed by a member of his family.

The real Lyndon Johnson was emerging from the embers of his predecessor's consumed presidency. The reminders of John Kennedy were constant— extensive memorial services for what would have been his forty-seventh birthday on May 29, 1964,[56] endless books and magazines and dedication ceremonies, photos from time to time of Kennedy family members or dignitaries visiting the Arlington gravesite, Senator Ted Kennedy's near-fatal plane crash in June 1964 that revived the chatter about a "Kennedy curse."[57] But the work of government and the theater of politics had set schedules, and prompted people to look to the future.

The Democratic National Convention, held in Atlantic City, New Jersey, from August 24 through 27, was a critical turning point for the new president. From the first hours after JFK's assassination, the sizable political lobe of Lyndon Johnson's brain had been focused like a laser on securing his own nomination and election. Johnson had reassured liberals with his successful efforts to achieve civil rights and an antipoverty program. Almost as important, conservatives were pleased with his reaction to the Gulf of Tonkin incidents that may (or may not) have taken place in early August off the coast of Vietnam. On August 2, the crew of the USS *Maddox*, engaged in an intelligence mission, reported that North Vietnamese gunboats had fired on them, and two days later the *Maddox* and the USS *Turner Joy* claimed further military provocations had taken place. It is likely that no second attack occurred, and even the first one, though probably real, is disputed. Some senior U.S. officials at the time were skeptical.[58] But perhaps recalling the weakness John Kennedy had projected at the Bay of Pigs, Vienna, and Berlin, LBJ saw an opportunity to stake out an early, hawkish position to the Communist world in this, his first major international test.

With little debate and a nearly unanimous vote in Congress, the Gulf of Tonkin Resolution was passed on August 7. It gave carte blanche to Johnson to use conventional military force in Southeast Asia and, as interpreted by Johnson, became essentially a declaration of war that produced the massive troop buildup in Vietnam during LBJ's tenure. This saber rattling assisted Johnson's short-term political needs as he faced a virulently anticommunist Republican challenger, but it led to long-term political disaster.

The other preconvention business was even more directly related to John F. Kennedy. It was Lyndon Johnson's turn to pick a running mate. In these pre–Twenty-fifth Amendment days, Johnson had no vice president. This selection would define him and his judgment as much or more than anything else he had done since succeeding JFK. There was no question which candidate Democrats preferred.[59] They wanted a return to a ticket of Kennedy and Johnson, except in reverse order and with a Kennedy named Robert. As attorney general and his brother's closest adviser, RFK had supported Jackie Kennedy throughout those four solemn days in November. His grief was palpable and, much as Mrs. Kennedy did, he had the nation's sympathy and support.

Letters poured into the Johnson White House urging the selection of RFK for VP, starting within weeks of Kennedy's death. Catherine Emrick of Oakland, California, wrote to President Johnson in January: "Isn't it possible to have Robert Kennedy as your Vice President? His loyalty and dignity during his late brother's tragedy won the hearts of all who saw him . . ."[60] In March, Mary Emily's letter not only pushed RFK but warned LBJ off another choice: "I certainly feel Robert Kennedy—with his three years experience with his wonderful brother at the White House—is qualified to be Vice President . . . Senator Hubert Humphrey does not seem to have the world-wide appeal of Robert Kennedy."[61] By July the correspondence was even more insistent. A Jesuit priest, Father Joseph F. X. Erhart, fairly begged the president to choose Kennedy:

> Mr. President, if you announced Bobby as your choice, a surge of joy would go around the world. I have been back in the United States for six weeks after spending a year in Europe. I talked with hundreds of Europeans, with Africans, Arabs, Indians, Poles, Russians, South Americans; from this sample I judge that President Kennedy had transformed the image of the U.S. around the world. People identified with him personally. Their hope for peace and a better world was placed in him personally. I don't want to make John Kennedy greater than he was; but the attitude of these people is a fact—a fact to be reckoned with. People need heroes; John Kennedy was an authentic world hero. But they don't know you well, Mr. President; they are uncertain about you; your image is incomplete. By selecting Bobby as your running mate, you would identify yourself emphatically with the Kennedy tradition. I suggest that paradoxically, only thus can you establish your own international political identity.[62]

President Johnson was well aware of the groundswell, but he made it clear privately to his team that he would never put Robert Kennedy on his ticket.

The animosity between the two had been intense from the start. Bobby did not want his brother to put LBJ on the ticket in 1960. He and his friends had been especially dismissive of Johnson during his term as vice president, and his combined fury and grief on November 22 led him to rush right past Johnson on Air Force One without so much as a nod to the new president—a slight that Johnson never forgot.[63] In an extraordinary postpresidency confession to the historian Doris Kearns Goodwin, LBJ unloaded on Robert Kennedy:

> Somehow it just didn't seem fair. I'd given three years of loyal service to Jack Kennedy. During all that time I'd willingly stayed in the background; I knew that it was *his* Presidency, not mine. If I disagreed with him, I did it in private, not in public. And then Kennedy was killed and I became the custodian of his will. I became the President. But none of this seemed to register with Bobby Kennedy, who acted like *he* was the custodian of the Kennedy dream, some kind of rightful heir to the throne . . . I'd waited for my turn. Bobby should've waited for his. But he and the Kennedy people wanted it now. A tidal wave of letters and memos about how great a Vice President Bobby would be swept over me. But no matter what, I simply couldn't let it happen. With Bobby on the ticket, I'd never know if I could be elected on my own . . . If they tr[ied] to push Bobby Kennedy down my throat for Vice President, I'[d] tell them to nominate him for the Presidency and leave me out of it.[64]

Johnson was not about to let such a thing happen. As frank as he was with his loyalists, he had teased Bobby Kennedy (and many others) with the prospect of being chosen for the ticket's second spot. But when he met with Kennedy at the White House on July 29, 1964, it was obvious even to RFK that he was not going to get the prize. Johnson issued a statement saying he had ruled out all members of his cabinet, so valuable were they in their current posts.[65] No one was fooled; no cabinet member but Robert Kennedy was considered a serious possibility for vice president.

This was the moment that marked the informal end of the Kennedy administration. Johnson had fully declared his independence. Bobby Kennedy would go his own way, running for and winning a U.S. Senate seat in New York, though assisted greatly by LBJ's long presidential coattails in November 1964.[66]

By no means did all Democrats acquiesce easily in Kennedy's being shown the door. The White House mailbox was stuffed with angry missives as soon as the news spread. Mrs. Walter Curry of Nashville sent a fiery telegram to

Lady Bird Johnson, asking for her intercession: "In striking at Robert Kennedy your husband has struck at the hearts of millions of American citizens. He has struck at the memory of John Kennedy. Please try to make him understand what he has done."[67] Rose and Harold Kogan wrote President Johnson, "We were shocked at your dropping [of RFK] . . . We feel this move is an insult to our adored and beloved President Kennedy. Because we are ardent Democrats, we feel we must convey to you our deep feeling of personal hurt."[68] And Mrs. Mary Perry of Upper Darby, Pennsylvania, had a prediction for LBJ: "Just heard the news over the radio . . . that you eliminated [RFK]. I am sure you also eliminated the state of Pennsylvania . . . Mark my words, you will lose Pennsylvania."[69]*

As for his real choice, Johnson kept the country, and the contenders, guessing. Three U.S. senators had reason to believe they were destined for the ticket, based on hints dropped by LBJ: Thomas J. Dodd of Connecticut, Eugene McCarthy of Minnesota, and Hubert H. Humphrey, also of Minnesota.[70] Johnson let the speculation build an audience for his unopposed convention renomination, announcing the news of Humphrey's elevation during the Democratic conclave itself.[71] LBJ had almost certainly leaned to Humphrey all along. He was the link to liberals and the North that Johnson required, and his legislative talents were unquestioned. Like Johnson, Humphrey had felt the Kennedy family sting. During the 1960 Democratic primaries, Humphrey was not just defeated but humiliated.[72] The Kennedys left no stone unturned nor insult undelivered in the key primary of West Virginia, where Humphrey was all but accused of cowardice for not serving in World War II. (He had repeatedly tried to enlist but was turned down for various reasons.)[73] Like Johnson and unlike John Kennedy, Humphrey was a serious, well-respected senator—but the amateur had won in 1960. Four years later, it was time for the professionals' revenge. Humphrey understood this potential alliance as early as the previous November 22. After Johnson returned from Dallas, he held a late-night meeting with congressional leaders in his Old Executive Office Building suite. All the assembled Senate and House luminaries pledged their fealty to Johnson, but Humphrey lingered after the meeting, stressing how much he wanted to help LBJ in his new duties.[74]

The formal business of the Democratic National Convention was nominating Lyndon Johnson and Hubert Humphrey. The highlight, though, was memorializing John F. Kennedy, and this was not an entirely welcome prospect for LBJ. For weeks memos had streamed back and forth about how to handle the Kennedys in Atlantic City. In LBJ's view, this was *his* convention, *his* opportunity to emerge fully from John Kennedy's shadow. But to the

---

* Johnson won the Keystone State with 65 percent of the vote in November.

Kennedys, and a large portion of Democrats and the public, it was impossible to forget that this would have been JFK's moment of triumph, where he would have been launched toward a second term.

A twenty-minute film was commissioned to salute JFK. It was, in the words of presidential assistant Douglass Cater, a "tearjerker," utilizing Mrs. Kennedy's allusion to Camelot as its theme. "Camelot was a highly schmaltzy musical about a semi-mythical kingdom," wrote Cater to LBJ press secretary Bill Moyers. "I have quite mixed feelings about its propriety at a convention," he huffed.[75] Cater's real concern became quickly apparent:

> Certainly, the delegates will be left weeping. It would be less dramatic but probably less risky to show that film sequence without the music. I have vague unrest about engaging in such an emotional bender just before the Johnson acceptance speech.

At first the film had been scheduled for showing on the convention's first night. But Johnson and some of his aides worried that it could stampede the delegates into nominating Bobby Kennedy for vice president, regardless of Johnson's preference. This was never a very likely prospect, but such was the wariness about RFK and the Kennedy family's intentions. LBJ's solution was shrewd: the film would be delayed until the final evening when the ticket was already set.[76]

The Johnson entourage was right about one thing. The emotional impact of this film, and its introduction by Robert Kennedy, was overwhelming. When RFK appeared, the delegates launched a spontaneous, twenty-two-minute standing ovation, and they simply refused to let him start speaking. They wanted the moment to last; they wanted him to know how they felt. RFK's short oration finished with a passage from *Romeo and Juliet* that some read, perhaps overread, as a contrast between JFK (the heavenly night stars) and LBJ (the garish sun):

> . . . *when he shall die*
> *Take him and cut him out in little stars*
> *And he will make the face of heav'n so fine*
> *That all the world will be in love with the Night*
> *And pay no worship to the garish Sun*[77]

Virtually the entire convention hall was crying, and millions at home as well. The film recounted JFK's achievements, but the personal glimpses—such as Kennedy teaching John Jr. to tickle his chin with a buttercup—were most affecting, and hard to watch. Meanwhile, RFK had left the stage, gone out to sit on a staircase, and inconsolable, he broke down in tears. No one knew better what that evening could have been.[78]

The general election was fiercely fought. Barry Goldwater detested Lyndon Johnson, thinking him corrupt and unfit for the Oval Office. Senator Goldwater told friends he had looked forward to a race with JFK, who apparently at one point had suggested to the Arizonan that the two might fly around the country on Air Force One, debating the issues at each stop.[79] Kennedy may or may not have been serious, and if he were, it was because he knew Goldwater was simply too far right to pose a serious challenge to his second term. In any event, Johnson refused to debate Goldwater, while most campaign observers believed that Kennedy would have done so, given his success against Nixon in 1960. Unlike Kennedy, Johnson was no television president, and he was not about to give Goldwater a free audience of millions in debates similar to those of 1960.

An embittered Goldwater lashed out at LBJ at every turn, while Johnson commissioned some of the nastiest television spots ever aired. The "bombs away" commercials, including the infamous "Daisy Spot,"[80] all but called Goldwater crazy, likely to use nuclear weapons and, in effect, end all life on earth. Surprisingly few positive advertisements were aired by Johnson, who missed an opportunity to build support for the sweeping programs he had planned for a full term. But Johnson was swept back into the White House with a popular vote majority that even exceeded that of his hero, FDR.* He lost only five Deep South states[81] and, narrowly, Goldwater's Arizona. Best of all, Johnson's margin helped to produce an overwhelmingly Democratic Congress that would bend to his will.[82]

The other aspect of the campaign worth noting was Johnson's reluctance to cite JFK more than he had to. He could not avoid it when Goldwater charged the Cuban Missile Crisis of October 1962 had been timed for maximum political effect in the following month's midterm elections,[83] and occasionally LBJ would mention how he got to the Oval Office.[84] But Johnson wanted to create his own mandate, not slip back into office on Kennedy's ghostly one—though public grief and guilt about the assassination were a big part of the Democratic landslide, whether LBJ acknowledged it or not. At last, Johnson was looking forward to his own term with his own team. However, he underestimated the Kennedy faction in this sense: They viewed his new term as John Kennedy's second, the triumphant term snatched away on the streets of Dallas. In their eyes, Lyndon Johnson would never really be his own man. He would forever be a president who owed everything to John Kennedy—and a well-placed bullet.

---

* In 1936, FDR's best election, Roosevelt received 60.8 percent; LBJ in 1964 garnered 61.1 percent.

No sooner was LBJ elected than he had to face the haunting first anniversary of the assassination.[85] It would be a highly public reminder of how his presidency began, and he had to proceed cautiously. Johnson and his staff agreed on several steps. A presidential proclamation was issued, calling for a day of prayer on November 22 (which conveniently fell on a Sunday in 1964). Johnson visited the Kennedy grave site "quiet[ly], without fanfare" five days before the anniversary to pay respects. A sculpture of JFK was received by LBJ on November 19 and placed in the cabinet room of the White House. And Johnson, after returning to the LBJ Ranch in Texas for Thanksgiving week, attended an interdenominational service at Austin's University Methodist Church on the anniversary itself.[86] Aide Jack Valenti also counseled the president, "It would be ill-advised to be out hunting on Sunday the 22. I know you have visitors that day—but I submit the backlash from this could be severe."[87]

Much as Americans' eyes had been riveted on Arlington in November 1963, and then again on John Kennedy's May 1964 birthday, the eternal flame at JFK's grave site drew television cameras and forty thousand mourners on November 22, 1964. Bobby Kennedy led other family members to kneel in prayer "on the first anniversary of that day of national horror, shame and grief." Among the earliest visitors had been the two daughters of President and Mrs. Johnson, who left yellow roses.[88] Three million people had made the pilgrimage to Arlington just between JFK's funeral and the end of May; tens of millions would follow over the decades.[89]

On December 15, 1964, President Johnson wrote to Jackie Kennedy about matters pertaining to the Kennedy Center for the Performing Arts. He added a poignant thought: "Time goes by swiftly, my dear Jackie. But the day never goes by without some tremor of a memory or some edge of a feeling that reminds me of all that you and I went through together."[90]

14

CROSSED SWORDS:
CAMELOT VS.
THE GREAT SOCIETY

ON JANUARY 20, 1965, POLITICAL observers were almost united in their belief that LBJ was the new FDR, a big-picture, big-government, big-action president who would be in office until the Constitution said he had to go in January 1973. Johnson was at the peak of his powers on the highest mountaintop, and his vista included a robust economy, compliant congressional supermajorities, and unambiguous dominance of the Western world. John F. Kennedy's time was past. Lyndon Johnson's independence day had dawned.

Perhaps because LBJ had already been in office for fourteen months, inauguration day lacked the drama that had accompanied many other swearing-ins in American history. Whatever the level of excitement, Johnson was determined that the day would be free of Kennedy dominance. He had always seen himself as far more experienced and better qualified to be chief executive than his young predecessor. In his short time in office he had already compiled a legislative record more impressive than JFK's. He had won the 1964 election in grand style, a massive landslide compared with Kennedy's squeaker. Therefore, in the reality that Johnson saw, this was entirely his own term. John F. Kennedy was not mentioned in Johnson's inaugural address, and that was part of a larger plan.[1] LBJ's close aide Horace Busby had sent him a memo in December, reminding the president that he had already designated the year as the 175th anniversary of the presidency. Busby recommended this also be the inauguration's premise: "Adoption of the 175-year theme would, as no small benefit, eliminate adverse comments or unwelcome pressures for associating the late President Kennedy with your Inauguration . . . All former presidents would be, in this context, subject to equal treatment, rather than any [that is, JFK] being singled out for special treatment."[2]

Of course, the Johnson White House could not control the media coverage, which naturally mentioned the events of four years prior, nor could it stanch the flow of emotions among the citizenry, which inevitably understood that

John Kennedy would probably have been beginning his second term save for November 22. The reminders were everywhere. While Mrs. Kennedy understandably did not attend the inaugural ceremonies, two Senators Kennedy were now on the inaugural platform, Ted representing Massachusetts and Bobby newly elected from New York.[3] Moreover, nine of JFK's cabinet officers (out of eleven slots) continued serving Johnson as he began his elective term.[4] The principals included Secretary of State Dean Rusk, Secretary of Defense Robert McNamara, Secretary of the Treasury C. Douglas Dillon, Secretary of the Interior Stewart Udall, and United Nations Ambassador Adlai Stevenson.[5]

The Kennedys were not the only interesting omission in LBJ's inaugural speech. The growing American involvement in Vietnam was also ignored. For all of Johnson's achievements in the four years to come, no other matters would so dominate his presidency as the Kennedy name and the Vietnam War. The combination would prove lethal to LBJ's hopes for a lengthier White House stay.

These were faraway drums in January of 1965. Johnson set to work pushing the massively Democratic Congress for a laundry list of new programs and policies. He still had his magic touch on Capitol Hill, with an intimate understanding of the legislative process, and the strengths and weaknesses of virtually every legislator. CBS's Bob Schieffer, who watched his fellow Texan closely, tells a story that illustrates the effectiveness of the fabled "Johnson treatment." When Schieffer's friend Bill Stuckey (heir to the Stuckey's restaurant empire) won election to the House in Georgia's eighth district, LBJ called Stuckey at home and insisted that he come to the White House right away. "They sent a government airplane down there," Schieffer recalls. "Bill got on the airplane. He flew to Andrews Air Force Base. The White House helicopter was waiting, which took him directly to the South Lawn of the White House. He landed on the South Lawn. An aide met him at the helicopter door and took him directly into the Oval Office and there stood the President of the United States who put his arm around him and said, 'Son, I'm really going to need your help.' Bill told me he never once voted against Lyndon Johnson."[6]

The Kennedy legacy also helped LBJ muscle his grand schemes through the House and Senate. The new Congress was responding less to the wave of public sympathy for the party's goals that followed the assassination and had driven the prior year's legislation. Rather, the 1965 legislature was akin to FDR's first, swollen with party adherents who wanted to rubber-stamp just about anything the president sent down from the White House. Both the 1964 and 1965 sessions were part of JFK's bequest—the first a visceral reaction and a direct consequence of November 22, the second an aftershock. Never in American history has grief over a presidential death so shaped the statute books. There was no such precedent after Lincoln's murder, nor following the deaths of Harrison, Garfield, McKinley, Harding, and even Franklin Roosevelt. (There was considerable congressional action post-Lincoln, but Congress wrested control of the agenda from a weak presidential successor and enacted stringent Reconstruction laws that Lincoln likely would have avoided.)[7]

Lyndon Johnson probably thought little about the tunnel of history or John Kennedy's role in his success as he signed a torrent of legislation in 1965, including the Elementary and Secondary Education Act, providing the first substantial federal assistance to schools across the nation, and the Higher Education Act;[8] the groundbreaking Medicare bill, sought first by President Truman and brought to life in his presence in Independence, Missouri;[9] the Voting Rights Act, which empowered the federal government to oversee voter registration in states and localities with a history of racial discrimination as well as outlawing literacy tests used to limit the franchise;[10] the founding of the Department of Housing and Urban Development (HUD) and the appointment of its secretary, the first African American in any cabinet, Robert Weaver;[11] and major pieces of environmental legislation, the Water Quality Act and the Highway Beautification Act (the latter, Lady Bird Johnson's pet project).[12] In later years, LBJ added to his breathtaking record of legislative triumphs with the Public Broadcasting Act that led to the creation of the Public Broadcasting Service and National Public Radio;[13] the establishment of the Product Safety Commission;[14] the Air Quality Act;[15] the Land and Water Conservation Fund Act;[16] and the Wild and Scenic Rivers Act, and the National Trails Systems Act.[17] Many of these advances in education, senior citizen health care, and protection of the environment are taken for granted today as part of the national fabric, but they were revolutionary in their time.

Perhaps the Johnson presidency should be more closely associated in the public mind with these achievements than it is, but for those who lived through LBJ's five years in the White House, one subject dominates all others: Vietnam. And it is not to Johnson's benefit.

JOHNSON WAS NOT the first president to make bad decisions about Vietnam—Eisenhower and Kennedy deserve some blame—nor was he the last, as Nixon would show.[18] But Johnson was unquestionably the chief executive who took Vietnam from back-burner involvement and made it the whole stove. When LBJ succeeded Kennedy, there were 16,300 troops and advisers in Vietnam; when he left, there were more than 535,000.[19]

Early in Johnson's administration there was close to a consensus that America needed to continue the fight against Communism by helping South

Vietnam, although people differed about the precise means. Some members of the press corps were among the most enthusiastic cheerleaders of decisive action in Southeast Asia. Before Lyndon Johnson even took the oath for a full presidential term, he found the influential columnist Joseph Alsop all but questioning his manhood. Alsop compared LBJ unfavorably to JFK during the Cuban Missile Crisis: "If Mr. Johnson ducks the challenge [in Vietnam] we shall learn by experience about what it would have been like if Kennedy had ducked the challenge in October 1962."[20] White House staffers reported that Johnson was furious. Within weeks he had decided to pursue a tough policy against the Communist North Vietnamese, and he gradually committed Marines to the protection of an air base in Danang. First, they were allowed only defensive operations, then offensive, then more divisions were sent, then two Army brigades. In July 1965 came the next major escalation, with the number of GIs in Vietnam increased from 75,000 to 125,000. The die was cast. So, too, was the reaction, which escalated along with the troops. Twenty college campuses and a hundred other communities across America witnessed their first major anti-Vietnam protests in October 1965.[21]

By 1967 President Johnson had sent an astounding number of American troops to Vietnam—close to a half million—and the bombing in Indochina had already been so massive that the United States had dropped more tonnage of explosives there than on all of Europe and Asia during World War II.[22] By the spring of 1967, antiwar demonstrations were widespread—not just at colleges but in cities large and small throughout the nation. In October more than fifty thousand marched on the Pentagon to insist on an end to the Vietnam conflict. Everywhere LBJ went, he was met by increasingly vociferous protestors, who often chanted, "Hey, hey, LBJ, how many kids did you kill today?" At the end of 1967, American casualties numbered 19,560 dead and many thousands more wounded.[23] Television evening news reported the fighting daily, and at week's end contained the grim and growing body count (as well as fantastical U.S.-government-supplied estimates of North Vietnamese and Viet Cong troops supposedly killed, which viewers increasingly disbelieved).[24]

In May 1967, aide Harry McPherson sent a somber memo to Johnson, quoting his wife as saying, "The President never goes anywhere anymore—in America. I feel as if he's a prisoner in the White House."[25] Indeed, LBJ was serving a kind of incarceration, no doubt preferred by the Secret Service given Johnson's low ratings and the intense animus directed at him from the antiwar left. The right wing had also never forgiven Johnson for his civil rights legislation. LBJ achieved the rare status of being hated about equally by both sides of the ideological spectrum.

Partly because of the emergence of Bobby Kennedy as Johnson's premier rival, LBJ and his staff began an unsubtle effort to blame President Kennedy for their Vietnam travails. Johnson was urged to remind the press and public that he was following Kennedy's Vietnam policy, and that JFK had supported the "domino theory"—the belief that if South Vietnam fell, the Communists would succeed in conquering (or at least be emboldened to attempt revolution in) other Southeast Asia countries, not to mention Central and South America. Columnist Joseph Alsop recalled that Johnson "was not very gracefully telling everyone at that time that his was, so to say, a world he'd never made; that he'd inherited this mess from President Kennedy; that it was all President Kennedy's fault, not his fault; and that if we encountered disaster there it would be President Kennedy's disaster, not his disaster."[26] As former president Johnson explained it to the historian Doris Kearns Goodwin, it was his determination to carry out JFK's pledge to save Vietnam—and fear of what Bobby Kennedy and other Kennedy backers might say if he didn't—that produced the whole morass:

> [I]f we lost Vietnam . . . there would be Robert Kennedy out in front leading the fight against me, telling everyone that I had betrayed John Kennedy's commitment to South Vietnam. That I had let a democracy fall into the hands of the Communists. That I was a coward. An unmanly man. A man without a spine. Oh, I could see it coming all right.[27]

Johnson's very personal interpretation that his "manhood" was at stake requires a psychologist rather than a political scientist to interpret. But LBJ's other deep insecurities and resentments toward the Kennedy clan and their Ivy League supporters are easy to fathom:

> [T]here were all those liberals on the Hill squawking at me about Vietnam. Why? Because I never went to Harvard. That's why. Because I wasn't John F. Kennedy. Because I wasn't friends with all their friends. Because I was keeping the throne from Bobby Kennedy. Because the Great Society was accomplishing more than the New Frontier. You see, they had to find some issue on which to turn against me and they found it in Vietnam. Even though they were the very people who developed the concept of limited war in the first place.[28]

No one will ever know how John F. Kennedy would have handled the Vietnam challenge had he lived, though that has not stopped a battalion of historians, JFK aides, and others from trying to divine it.[29] President Johnson was correct to say that his predecessor had set the course in Southeast Asia, and those who claim that all would have been sweetness and light on Vietnam in a second Kennedy administration are blind to reality. Yet JFK and LBJ could not have been more different as people or presidents. Kennedy's strength was foreign affairs, given his family upbringing, life in Great Britain, intellectual interests, and World War II service; Johnson's expertise was mainly domestic. In the crucible of the Oval Office, Kennedy had learned from the Bay of Pigs and the Cuban Missile Crisis not to rely overly on the advice of the military; Johnson was far more deferential. And perhaps most of all, the Ivy League Kennedy's premier base was among the academics at universities; Johnson, always a bit suspicious and perhaps envious of intellectuals, was more at home among hardscrabble Democrats and Capitol Hill politicians.

Given the existence of the military draft and the left-leaning views of most faculty, the first and most vociferous opposition to the Vietnam War naturally emerged from the campuses, locus of JFK's ardent supporters. It is difficult to believe that John Kennedy would have risked his political foundation by pursuing a years-long, highly unpopular war in Vietnam, or ever escalated it to the top of his agenda as LBJ did, and without the Vietnam War, the country would have gone down a very different path in the 1960s and beyond. At the very least, it is difficult to imagine Richard Nixon as Kennedy's successor in 1969—another profound reason why November 22, 1963, had such a wide-ranging effect on modern American history.

JFK's counselor Theodore Sorensen could be expected to defend his president, yet it is difficult to deny the essence of his argument:

> Some historians make too much of the fact that [Johnson's] advisers on that war had been Kennedy's. JFK had more judgment and international experience than LBJ, better positioning him to evaluate and reject some of that advice. [Kennedy] had in fact rejected the repeated advice that he send combat troop divisions to South Vietnam and bomb North Vietnam, the very actions that LBJ took, stimulated by a fake crisis in the Gulf of Tonkin . . . I refuse to agree with LBJ's whine . . . that it was all Kennedy's fault. Johnson's major failure to win the confidence of black and student rioters cannot be traced back to JFK; he had their confidence. [And] JFK was already beginning the withdrawal of the military advisers he had increased in order to reinforce Eisenhower's original commitment.[30]

Vietnam, more than any other single factor, reignited the smoldering hatred between Lyndon Johnson and Robert Kennedy. There had never been reconciliation between the two, although in the months immediately after Johnson's ascension to the presidency—when grief was at its peak and RFK entertained some hope of being picked for the 1964 Democratic ticket—the feud had been submerged. Kennedy's nomination to the Senate created a temporary marriage of convenience between the two political heavyweights. But by 1965 the old angers and grievances were surfacing anew. Harry McPherson sent a scathing memo to the president in mid-1965 that called RFK "a man of narrow sensibilities and totalitarian instincts." McPherson saw that the "intellectuals" who were "as easy a lay as can be found" were gravitating to RFK because of his "'pure' voting and adventurous speeches." The problem, he said, was one of divided loyalties within the administration itself. Would they "go to the wall" for LBJ or be mainly faithful to the Kennedys?[31] Realizing a "polygraph-loyalty test" would be controversial, McPherson stoked Johnson's long-simmering resentment against the Kennedys, reminding LBJ that, "While you were *of* the Senate [in the 1950s], and took responsibility for getting the hard bills through . . . [John] Kennedy was merely *in* the Senate [and] had to lean on you to get his labor bills through . . ."[32] By the way, none of the resentment toward the Kennedys has waned in almost a half century. McPherson told me in 2011 that LBJ is a far more significant historical figure than RFK, whatever popular tastes may suggest: "One of them [LBJ] is a whale and the other one is a minnow. [RFK] was a tuna at best."[33]

Another aide, press secretary Bill Moyers, took pleasure in sending the president an "anti-Kennedy piece done by one of the most distinguished writers in Britain." The right-wing British commentator, Peregrine Worsthorne, scalded RFK: "The crucial decision [on American involvement in Vietnam] was President Kennedy's. For [Bobby] to exploit its consequences to destroy his brother's successor might have struck Machiavelli as the epitome of princely conduct . . ."[34]

For Lyndon Johnson, the true test of loyalty became Vietnam, and Bobby Kennedy was to receive a failing grade. This infuriated LBJ because he truly believed he was carrying out John Kennedy's policy; indeed, he saw Vietnam as a continuation of all post–World War II presidential actions. As he asserted in his State of the Union address in January 1966, "We have defended against Communist aggression—in Korea under President Truman—in the Formosa Straits under President Eisenhower—in Cuba under President Kennedy—and again in Vietnam." In a fatal error that jumps out at anyone reading Johnson's words, the president insisted, "This nation is mighty enough, its society is healthy enough, its people are strong enough, to pursue our goals in the rest of the world while still building a Great Society here at home."[35] This combination of "guns and butter" would sink Johnson and his party over the next three years, and it would have far-reaching consequences in the age-old battle about the proper size of the federal government.

Bobby Kennedy came slowly to full-throated opposition to the Vietnam

War. In 1966 he could still be found writing an encouraging note to President Johnson:

> Reading the newspapers and their columnists and listening to my colleagues in Congress (including myself) on what to do and what not to do in Viet Nam must become somewhat discouraging at times.
>
> I was thinking of you and your responsibilities while I was reading Bruce Catton's book "Never Call Retreat."
>
> I thought it might give you some comfort to look again at another President, Abraham Lincoln, and some of the identical problems and situations that he faced that you are now meeting . . .
>
> In closing let me say how impressed I have been [with] the most recent efforts to find a peaceful solution to Viet Nam . . . [36]

Johnson replied genially to "Dear Bob":

> Your warm letter arrived at an appropriate time. It was one of those hours when I felt alone, prayerfully alone.
>
> I remembered so well how President Kennedy had to face, by himself, the agony of the Cuban missile crisis. I read the paragraph in Catton's book that you had marked, and then I went to a meeting in the Cabinet Room with the Congressional leaders of both parties . . .
>
> You know better than most the gloom that crowds in on a President, for you lived close to your brother. Thus, your letter meant a great deal to me and I tell you how grateful I am for your thoughtfulness . . . [37]

The friendly chain of LBJ-RFK correspondence didn't last. Much of Johnson's last two calendar years as president was marked by mounting tensions and recriminations between the two, which both sides tried to keep private at first. But Johnson's staff monitored RFK and comments about him closely, sending gossipy, negative notes to LBJ or one another. When TV talk show host David Susskind all but endorsed RFK for president in a March 1967 chat with a British parliamentarian, presidential aide Mike Manatos made sure that LBJ knew "no one in the audience clapped, creating an embarrassing moment for Susskind."[38] Presidential press secretary George Christian received a note from a former Johnson White House staffer about a conversation with a reporter, who allegedly said, "I used to be a very close friend of Bobby's, but I don't like him worth a damn now. He is standing on Jack Kennedy's casket and running for the presidency on that coffin."[39]

Long-held suspicions that Bobby might challenge Johnson for renomination deepened throughout 1967, culminating with RFK's appearance on CBS's *Face the Nation* on November 26. During that show, Kennedy went well beyond the public intimations he had made about Johnson's prosecution of the Vietnam War. For the first time, RFK openly insisted that Johnson had "turned [and] switched" the policy of his brother: "We're killing South Vietnamese, we're killing women, we're killing innocent people . . ." LBJ was incensed, demanding to see all of John Kennedy's remarks about Vietnam while being assured by Secretary of State Dean Rusk that President Kennedy had been headed in the same direction in Southeast Asia.[40] When Johnson was reminded of some rare pro-Johnson statements Bobby had made in an earlier speech, he ordered it surreptitiously distributed to the Democratic National Committee and every state party chairman.[41]

Other Kennedy strands wove themselves in and out of Johnson's White House tenure, among them race riots in major cities, the relationship with Jackie Kennedy, and the growing dissatisfaction with the Warren Commission report.

Even LBJ's worst critics would concede that he did more for the civil rights of African Americans than any president since Lincoln and, indisputably, far more than John Kennedy had achieved. JFK's tentative steps were replaced by historic legislation and many African American firsts (not least Supreme Court justice Thurgood Marshall). Yet legal equality had not yielded de facto or economic parity with whites for the black community, and these frustrations exploded in four successive "long hot summers" across America. Beginning with the Watts neighborhood in Los Angeles on August 11, 1965, racial riots caused immense destruction, deaths, injuries, and looting in hundreds of urban areas from 1965 to 1968.[42] The insurrection in Detroit in July 1967 was so massive that LBJ had to send forty-seven hundred federal troops to restore order. Johnson's role as the "civil rights president" did not prevent him from being reviled in many black communities as the enforcer of law and order, and the defender of economic inequality. At the same time, John Kennedy, with his meager record in civil rights, was regarded as a hero and a martyr—something that Johnson found hard to take. His abandonment by many blacks, Johnson told Doris Kearns Goodwin, was an act of rank ingratitude:

> How is it possible that all these people could be so ungrateful to me after I had given them so much? Take the Negroes. I fought for them from the first day I came into office. I spilled my guts out in getting the Civil Rights Act of 1964 through Congress. I put everything I had into that speech before the joint session in 1965. I tried to make it possible for every child of every color to grow up in a nice house, to eat a solid breakfast, to attend a decent school . . . But look at what I

got instead. Riots in 175 cities. Looting. Burning. Shooting. It ruined everything.[43]

Of far lesser importance but still often on the radar screen was Jacqueline Kennedy. "Managing Jackie" was a subtext for both Lyndon and Lady Bird Johnson. The new First Lady named a White House garden[44] after her predecessor in April 1965, but Mrs. Kennedy begged off attending the ceremony, writing, "It is my hope that you can understand my feelings at this time—that it would be quite painful to return to Washington and so many associations with the past. Perhaps some day I shall return but right now it would be too difficult to relive so many memories."[45] When LBJ offered to let Jackie and JFK's two brothers use a presidential jet to attend the dedication of the Runnymede battlefield[46] in May 1965, Jackie thanked him but pleaded, "Do not let it be Air Force One, and please let it be the 707 that looks the least like Air Force One inside."[47] Mrs. Kennedy understandably wanted no reminders of her last flight aboard Air Force One, and she was instead given a regular jet for the trip.

Then there was the strange incident involving the "Resolute desk," a gift from Queen Victoria to President Rutherford B. Hayes in 1880.[48] White House social secretary Bess Abell wrote a distressed note to Lady Bird Johnson in July 1965:

> In the spring of 1964 the Kennedy family requested the [Resolute desk] which President Kennedy had used during his years in office as a loan to the Kennedy family exhibit in New York.
>
> Since this time the exhibit has toured the world and apparently the Kennedy family has no intention of returning the desk.
>
> Because it has been used by 16 Presidents it is probably the single most valuable piece in the White House collection.
>
> I bother you with this because there is a possibility you or the President—or both—may receive a call from Mrs. Kennedy or some member of the family asking for the desk.
>
> Legally, it would take an act of Congress to give it to them.[49]

There is no record of any request by Mrs. Kennedy or any other Kennedy to keep the desk permanently. Theoretically, it was a possibility to be guarded against, yet even today, Bess Abell's alarm puzzles Stephen Plotkin of the John F. Kennedy Library:

> Ms. Abell's letter seems to me sensationalistic at best. I have a difficult time believing that Mrs. Kennedy, who had spent so much time on the White House renovation, and therefore would have had a

working knowledge of the legalities involved, could have contemplated something so egregious as removing the Resolute desk into private ownership.

The exhibit in question was not a "Kennedy family" exhibit, but rather a publicity exhibit for the building of the proposed Kennedy Library, and therefore at least as much a government project as it was a private project. At the conclusion of the tour, the desk was turned over to the Smithsonian. To the best of my knowledge it was never requested by President Johnson; that does not surprise me, given the degree to which the public identified the desk with John F. Kennedy. The desk stayed in the Smithsonian until the election of President Carter, who requested it back.[50]

Secret Service protection for Mrs. Kennedy and her children led to another subterranean controversy. At the time of JFK's assassination it was unprecedented for a former First Lady and family to have government-paid security. But the wrenching, instantaneous nature of Mrs. Kennedy's White House departure and, apparently, some menacing communications had caused President Johnson and Congress to extend Secret Service protection for two years.[51] In the summer of 1965 Senator Robert Kennedy requested a further two-year extension. LBJ aide Marvin Watson, in a memo to the president, argued that since "it has been six months since Mrs. Kennedy has received a threatening letter or phone call," just a one-year extension should be approved.[52] Johnson signaled his agreement. However, at about the same time, Congress passed a bill providing for extensive security coverage for the spouses and children of former presidents.

Thanks to recollections Mrs. Kennedy shared with the historian and JFK aide Arthur Schlesinger, Jr., in April 1964 that were published in 2011, we now know the depth of the tension that existed between Jackie and the Johnsons.[53] Mrs. Kennedy was merely petty concerning Lady Bird.[54] But on President Johnson himself, she was scathing, claiming that on several occasions, JFK had said to her or Bobby, "Oh God, can you ever imagine what would happen to the country if Lyndon was president?"[55] According to Jackie's recollections, Johnson had been drunk when asked to be on the ticket in 1960 and JFK regarded him as a nonentity as vice president, of little help when needed and vague in his opinions when asked.[56] Some of this is probably bitterness that the Johnsons, not Kennedys, were at the center of the nation's attentions. Nonetheless, the words sting even after a half century, and hint at a relationship that was less than ideal.[57]

Yet former Johnson aides vehemently dispute the portrait painted by Mrs. Kennedy. Harry McPherson, LBJ's chief speechwriter, rejects Jackie's version of events. "When you listen to the tapes that the Johnson Library has put out, it's clear that Johnson is doing everything he can to ingratiate Mrs. Kennedy and she is responding with, 'I can't tell you how much I appreciate what you've done,' 'you've been so wonderful,' and so on. Anyway, that's the Jackie Kennedy you hear on the [tapes], and then to think that that same Lyndon Johnson would be referred to [in the manner] she apparently did with Arthur is just appalling and to me, it's not the case. It's not what happened." McPherson insists that JFK and LBJ had a cordial working relationship. "[It] was by no means a warm, untroubled, loving, admiring relationship on both sides, but [it] did reflect an accepting, good spirited understanding . . . They understood who they were and Jack Kennedy understood that Lyndon Johnson was an enormously significant person for him."[58] Still, comparing "the kind of president Jack was and the kind Lyndon is," Mrs. Kennedy made an observation some would find prescient: "When something really crisis [sic] happens, that's when they're going to miss Jack. And I just want them to know it's because they don't have that kind of president [JFK was] and not because it was inevitable."[59]

The Kennedy-Johnson dispute broke out into the open during the "Manchester affair" in 1966 and 1967. William Manchester had penned a book entitled *The Death of a President*,[60] and prepublication press accounts were filled with sensational details, including an introductory passage that portrayed Johnson as vulgarly goading a reluctant JFK into killing a deer on the LBJ ranch—a contrast between New England refinement and Texan boorishness.[61] President Johnson was convinced that the purpose of the book, which had Mrs. Kennedy's initial cooperation, was to defame him and position Robert Kennedy for a 1968 run for president.[62]

However, Mrs. Kennedy was no happier about the book than LBJ was.[63] Jackie had instructed JFK press secretary Pierre Salinger to contact Manchester in February 1964 to write what she intended to be a dignified, comprehensive account of the assassination.[64] Apparently, she expected Manchester to be as discreet with her intimate recollections as Arthur Schlesinger would prove to be, but Manchester did not have the same close ties to the Kennedy family. He was also determined to make a great deal of money on the project. The world serialization rights with *Look* magazine alone amounted to $665,000, a fantastic sum in the 1960s. Much of the sensational material came from ten hours of interviews Manchester conducted with Mrs. Kennedy, and she believed the money should go to the Kennedy Library. So Jackie sued in December 1966, filing for a court injunction to stop publication of the book. It was a disaster all around.[65] Most leading journalists sided with Manchester, as did much of the public, which wanted to learn the truth about JFK's assassination. Mrs. Kennedy settled out of court, the book was published, and Jackie had given it such publicity that it likely sold tens of thousands more copies than it would have otherwise.[66] A Lou Harris poll found that a third of the public thought less of Mrs. Kennedy because of her attempt at what some saw as censorship.[67]

LBJ wrote Jackie when her suit was filed, trying to soothe her:

> Lady Bird and I have been distressed to read the accounts of your unhappiness about the Manchester book. Some of these accounts attribute your concern to passages in the book which are critical or defamatory of us. If this is so, I want you to know while we deeply appreciate your characteristic kindness and sensitivity, we hope you will not subject yourself to any discomfort or distress on our account. One never becomes inured to slander but we have learned to live with it. In any event, your own tranquility is important to both of us, and we would not want you to endure any unpleasantness on our account.[68]

Jackie responded in kind:

> I was so deeply touched by your letter—I am sick at the unhappiness this whole terrible thing has caused everyone—
>
> Whatever I did could only bring pain. Not to sue would have been to let them print everything and take such cruel and unfair advantage. Every day since I returned from Hawaii I have been pleading by letter, phone or in person with one or more of their side.
>
> The author and publishers always broke their word, and I finally understood that was what they intended to keep on doing—play cat and mouse [with] me until I was exhausted and they had gone to press.
>
> Now I suppose I am "winning"—but it seems a hollow victory—with everything I objected to printed all over the newspapers anyway. At least I made it known that I object . . .
>
> I am so dazed now I feel I will never be able to feel anything again.[69]

PERHAPS PARTLY BECAUSE of the Manchester book, interest in JFK's assassination was renewed and skeptics of the Warren Commission's official version of the events of November 22 were becoming outspoken and publishing widely—years after the report was issued.[70]

The first congressional resolution to establish a joint committee of the House and Senate to reinvestigate the Kennedy assassination was filed on

September 28, 1966, by the New York Republican representative Theodore Kupferman.[71] Newspaper and television reports carried a drumbeat of disbelieving voices, especially around the time of the large, widespread, continuing commemorations held twice a year for President Kennedy's May 29 birthday and the November anniversary of his death.[72] Among observers who were astounded at the unceasing questioning of the Warren Commission was Chief Justice Earl Warren himself, who wrote to one correspondent, "It is really amazing how many people choose to doubt [the commission] without reference to facts."[73] As for a Washington, D.C., television station's invitation to Warren to attend a November 1966 program on a "Reexamination of the Warren Commission Findings," the chief justice sent word he would not be in attendance.[74]

The dam of skepticism and doubt about the Warren Commission burst on February 18, 1967, when Jim Garrison, the district attorney of Orleans Parish in Louisiana, told the press that he had proof President Kennedy was assassinated as the result of a conspiracy hatched in New Orleans. On March 2, Garrison arrested a prominent city businessman, Clay Shaw, and charged him with plotting to kill JFK. Younger Americans are mainly familiar with this seminal event because of Oliver Stone's movie *JFK*, which was based in large part on Garrison's investigation.[75] It took two full years for the case to reach trial, and in that time Garrison became famous, appearing on many domestic and foreign television broadcasts, including *The Tonight Show with Johnny Carson*, and granting interviews not just to the traditional press but to *Playboy* magazine. Unfortunately for Garrison, his evidence against Shaw was so weak that the jury took less than one hour to acquit the defendant in March 1969.[76]

Garrison did not get a conviction, but he had an unmistakable effect on public opinion. Between February and May 1967, the proportion of Americans believing in a JFK assassination conspiracy jumped from 44 to 66 percent, according to a Louis Harris survey.[77] President Johnson was given several days' advance notice of the poll results, which were released on what would have been JFK's fiftieth birthday. Johnson made no public comment and consistently refused entreaties to reopen the investigation into his predecessor's murder.[78] LBJ may have later felt justified in this decision by the results of a widely seen series by CBS and the Associated Press in the summer of 1967. Over four days the network and the AP reported on their own reinvestigation of the Warren Commission's findings, concluding that "Despite critical flaws, the [report] stands up as the most intelligent, most reliable view of what happened in Dallas on November 22, 1963."[79] The CBS anchor of the series, Walter Cronkite, told me in 1991 that he had been suspicious of the Warren findings, and set out to prove them wrong. He secured the support of the top CBS brass, which approved a million-dollar budget. To Cronkite's surprise, the pieces of the reinvestigation kept coming in affirming the Warren Commission. "I accepted it. I reported it the way it was," reprising a version of his longtime sign-off for the *CBS Evening News*—his trademark phrase, "And that's the way it is." Critics have since found errors in CBS's reenactment of the Dallas gunshots—so it may not have been quite "the way it was."[80]

ASSISTED BY MOUNTING controversy over Vietnam and increasing unpopularity of the Johnson administration at home and abroad, the myth of Camelot flourished as LBJ's time in office wore on. A 1966 film on JFK by the United States Information Agency had a considerable impact. Designed mainly for international viewers, the hagiographic movie, entitled *John F. Kennedy: Years of Lightning / Day of Drums* and narrated by the actor Gregory Peck, was in such demand that it was distributed to regular theaters throughout the United States. The distributor fees were waived and the profits sent to the Kennedy Center by special congressional legislation.[81] The emotive script shifts back and forth between November 1963 and the key events of the Kennedy presidency, and Peck concludes: "The day of drums is over, but the years of lightning glow in everyone he touched and in everyone he continues to touch . . . John F. Kennedy is now silent and invisible, but so is peace and freedom and so is love and faith and so are memories and dreams."

Other tributes to John F. Kennedy continued at a pace somewhat astonishing, considering the assassination was years removed. A permanent JFK gravesite was consecrated in Arlington on March 15, 1967, with President Johnson and the Kennedys present.[82] Kennedy's birthplace in Brookline, Massachusetts, was designated a national historic site. A new 13-cent stamp was issued with Kennedy's visage.[83] And in one of the largest ceremonies of the year, the aircraft carrier *John F. Kennedy* was launched at Newport News, Virginia, on May 27, 1967. Mrs. Kennedy and her two children headed a large delegation of Kennedys that witnessed Caroline christening the ship with the traditional bottle of champagne before a forest of TV cameras and a crowd of ten thousand people.[84]

The main speaker was the incumbent president—and his staff saw the dilemma. As aide Ben Wattenberg advised LBJ, the event "may well be the most dramatic single appearance you will make all year . . . an occasion that is, at once, a great opportunity and a great hazard."[85] With Senator Robert Kennedy looking on, the elephant in the room was once again Vietnam. Even calling JFK "a man of peace" or someone who "brought a new style of politics to America" were considered dangerous phrases, since an increasingly skeptical press corps might flip the terms to suggest that Johnson was, by contrast, a warmonger and an old-style politician. The speech LBJ actually delivered was gracious to his predecessor, but it also contained some veiled messages about Vietnam for RFK as well as the nation and world. "John Kennedy understood that strength is essential to sustain freedom . . . In times past, it has often been our strength and our resolve which have tipped the scales of conflict against aggressors, or would-be aggressors. That role has never been an easy one. It has always required not only strength, but patience—the incredible courage to wait where waiting is appropriate, to avoid disastrous results to shortcut history. And sacrifice—the tragic price we pay for our commitment to our ideals."[86]

The launch of an aircraft carrier is hard to miss—an obvious legacy—but the heritage of the Kennedy years is also found in America's basic document of state. A few months before Johnson spoke in Newport News, Americans ratified the Twenty-fifth Amendment to the U.S. Constitution, a direct result of the Kennedy assassination and worry over possible scenarios affecting future presidential successions. For the first time, clear procedures for the temporary or permanent replacement of a living but incapacitated president were delineated. And presidents were given a notable new power—the selection of a replacement vice president, subject to the approval of both houses of Congress, whenever the vice presidency became vacant through death, resignation, or succession to the Oval Office. A mere six years after its ratification, the amendment produced a vice president, Gerald R. Ford, following the 1973 resignation in disgrace of Vice President Spiro Agnew. Also, without the Twenty-fifth Amendment, American history would have recorded the name of the thirty-eighth president of the United States, succeeding upon the resignation of Richard Nixon in 1974, as Carl Albert, not Gerald Ford. Albert was the Democratic Speaker of the U.S. House of Representatives, next in line to be president under the old pre–Twenty-fifth Amendment order.[87]

EXCEPT FOR THE Civil War period, it is difficult to identify a sadder year in U.S. history than 1968—twelve long-suffering months clouded by tragedies, disasters, disappointments, and broken dreams. Nothing underlined the transformation that the nation had undergone from JFK to LBJ better, or worse, than that year. The prelude to the presidential campaign was the Tet Offensive in January, a broad-based attack by North Vietnamese and Viet Cong troops on U.S. installations and thirty-eight provincial capitals throughout South Vietnam, including assaults on the U.S. embassy and the presidential palace in the capital city of Saigon. While some military historians have insisted that Tet was actually a major setback for Communist forces,[88] the American public saw it quite differently. Instead of winning the war, the United States appeared to be sinking ever deeper into the jungle quicksand of an endless conflict. One of the most trusted newsmen of his time, Walter Cronkite, reported, "To say that we are mired in stalemate seems the only realistic, yet unsatisfactory, conclusion." Lyndon Johnson supposedly remarked, "If I've lost Cronkite, I've lost Middle America."[89]

The Tet Offensive's aftermath effectively ended any real chance of reelection for President Johnson. On March 12, LBJ narrowly won the New Hampshire primary over antiwar candidate Senator Eugene McCarthy of Minnesota, then shocked the nation on March 31 by announcing that he would "not seek, nor will I accept, the nomination of my party for another term as your president."[90] A presidency that had begun in blood and tragedy unraveled in much the same way. Johnson bowed out by quoting John Kennedy's inaugural address in almost a plaintive way, reminding Americans that they would have to continue to "pay any price . . . to insure the survival and the success of liberty." To the last, LBJ seemed to want his fellow citizens to understand that, at least in his mind, he was fulfilling JFK's pledge to support freedom, at an admittedly high cost, in Southeast Asia.

Only two weeks before, the long-simmering feud between LBJ and RFK had broken out into total warfare, as Bobby Kennedy announced his candidacy for president on March 16. Wearing a gold PT 109 tie clasp and speaking in the same room JFK had used in 1960 for his White House announcement, Kennedy declared, "I do not run for the presidency merely to oppose any man . . . but to propose new policies." This move enraged not only Johnson but also Gene McCarthy, who had decided to challenge Johnson after Kennedy had hesitated. The McCarthy backers viewed Kennedy as an interloper, a Bobby-come-lately who ran only because McCarthy had just demonstrated Johnson's electoral weakness in New Hampshire. Vietnam, said Kennedy, and not the Granite State results, was the proximate cause of his fateful choice.[91] Two days before his announcement, on March 14, an uncertain Kennedy and Ted Sorensen met with LBJ's defense secretary, Clark Clifford, at the Pentagon. According to a revealing memo by Clifford:

> [Kennedy] said that he had talked to [Mayor] Dick Daley in Chicago and had also talked to [JFK counselor] Ted Sorensen and his brother [Edward], and they thought that consideration should be given to a plan that he had evolved. He suggested that Sorensen present the plan. Sorensen said that if President Johnson would agree to make a public statement that his policy in Vietnam had proved to be in error, and that he was appointing a group of persons to conduct a study in depth of the issues and come up with a recommended course of action, then Senator Robert Kennedy would agree not to get into the race.

> I said I thought there were three major points he should con-
> sider. 1. It was my opinion that the possibility of his being able to
> defeat President Johnson for the nomination was zero . . . 2. That
> I thought Senator Kennedy would be making a grave mistake if he
> assumed that the situation in Vietnam would be the same in Au-
> gust of this year as it is now . . . 3. That if by chance he were able to
> gain the Democratic nomination, I thought it would be valueless
> because his efforts in displacing President Johnson would so split
> the Democratic Party that the Republican nominee would win
> easily.[92]

Clifford, who had been advising Democratic presidents since Truman, was probably correct about Kennedy's slim chances of defeating President Johnson for the nomination and winning the general election if he somehow dethroned Johnson. Of course, as it happened, RFK would instead be running against Johnson's heir, Vice President Hubert Humphrey, who was less politically sure to win than LBJ but, at a time when bosses ruled the party, was still the favorite for the Democratic nomination. Clifford was dead wrong about his second point. Vietnam was still a jungle quagmire come August, and if anything, domestic discontent had escalated to a fever pitch. Alas, Bobby Kennedy would not live to know that, or to joust with Humphrey and McCarthy in Chicago at the convention.

Lyndon Johnson had many sides to his complex persona, and one can see the good and bad within the prism of his relationship with RFK. Initially, as he told Doris Goodwin, the imperial Johnson was apoplectic, and feeling rather sorry for himself:

> And then the final straw. The thing I feared from the first day of my
> Presidency was actually coming true. Robert Kennedy had openly an-
> nounced his intention to reclaim the throne in memory of his brother.
> And the American people, swayed by the magic of the name, were
> dancing in the streets. The whole situation was unbearable for me.
> After thirty-seven years of public service, I deserved something more
> than being left alone in the middle of the plain, chased by stampedes
> on every side.[93]

Once Johnson had withdrawn from the race, Bobby Kennedy quickly sought out LBJ, and a conciliatory president was on view. When LBJ hosted RFK in the White House on April 3, Johnson's loyal aide Walt Rostow took notes, mainly from LBJ's perspective, and they are worth citing at length:

The President went on to say that in fact he had not wanted to be Vice President and had not wanted to be President. Two men had persuaded him to run in 1960: [House Speaker] Sam Rayburn and [*Washington Post* publisher] Phil Graham. They had said that unless Johnson were on the ticket, John Kennedy could not carry the South. Without the South, Nixon would win. He would have greatly preferred to have continued to be the leader of the Senate.

The Vice Presidency . . . is inherently demeaning: although no one ever treated a Vice President better than President Kennedy had treated him.

The President said, "I found myself in this place and did the best I could." He had the feeling that perhaps Senator Kennedy did not understand his feeling about President Kennedy. When he accepted the Vice Presidency, he felt he went into a partnership with President Kennedy. They disagreed seldom, but . . . a few times President Kennedy was a little irritated with him and showed it; but no one ever knew . . .

As President he had continued to look on his task as a partnership with President Kennedy. He felt he had a duty to look after the family and the members of the firm which they had formed together. He had never asked a Kennedy appointee to resign. He had never accepted the resignation of a Kennedy appointee without asking him to stay. As President, he had felt President Kennedy was looking down on what he had done and would approve.

The President said he felt the press had greatly exaggerated the difficulties between Senator Kennedy and himself.

The President said that if there were any way in which he could have avoided being a Presidential candidate in 1964, he would have not run then. He wants Senator Kennedy to know that he doesn't hate him, he doesn't dislike him, and that he still regards himself as carrying out the Kennedy/Johnson partnership.[94]

LBJ's remarks are not entirely credible. Johnson wanted the vice presidency in order to position himself to run for the White House eventually. No one who knew Johnson would ever have believed that, once president, he would not have run to continue in office in 1964. Most of all, Johnson disliked, even hated, Bobby Kennedy, and the mutual loathing and distrust were self-evident. When LBJ tried to secretly tape their April 3 meeting, Kennedy (or one of his aides) apparently smuggled in a scrambling device that prevented the magnetic tape from recording. This may or may not be true, but LBJ apparently believed it to be so, and was furious that he had been outsmarted.[95] But at that late date, Johnson's goal was rapprochement with Kennedy, to the degree possible, since he had less than ten months left to mend his tattered presidential reputation. He planned to focus on achieving peace both in Vietnam and in America's racially torn cities.

The following day, Dr. Martin Luther King, Jr., was shot and killed in Memphis, and Johnson's hopes for a statesmanlike exit became impossible. Riots raged across the country, and Johnson did not possess the stature in the African American community to calm the waters. His attempts to wind down the Vietnam War went nowhere, too, despite the beginning of peace talks in Paris in 1968. The country and the world, including the Communists, were waiting for a new president.

Bobby Kennedy would not be that president. On June 5, 1968, just after he declared victory over Gene McCarthy in the crucial California primary, Kennedy was gunned down in the Ambassador Hotel in Los Angeles, purportedly by a lone assassin, Sirhan B. Sirhan. Despite a gunshot wound in the head, he lingered for a little more than twenty-four hours before dying.[96] The nation was in complete disbelief; the nightmare of Dallas had returned. People relived the horror and grief of November 1963, as the awful yet familiar rituals of political assassination and Kennedy family mourning played out.

Within hours, the Johnson White House was preparing talking points for a televised presidential address to the nation. Press Secretary George Reedy advised LBJ that he should stress two points above all. "The greatest immediate danger arising out of the attempted assassination of Senator Kennedy is the rapidly developing sense of national guilt and the feeling that there is a 'sickness in our society.' . . . The danger of the 'sickness in our society' thesis is that it can breed further violence and acts of desperation. It can lead to widespread acts of violence committed from a sense of outrage and a warped determination to 'avenge' Senator Kennedy . . . It has nothing to do with 'sickness in our society' but with sickness in individuals . . ." Second, in an echo of the Johnson White House's immediate impulse following JFK's assassination, Reedy was already arguing—before all the facts could possibly be known—that Kennedy's shooting was "a formless act committed by a psychopath [Sirhan] who found as his victim the most prominent man in sight . . . The truth is that no man in this, or in any country, can be prominent without risking his life."[97] (In fact, Sirhan expressed a clear motive in his own private writing. The assassin shot RFK on the first anniversary of Israel's Six-Day War, and he fulminated over Kennedy's positions that favored the Jewish state over the Palestinians.)

Johnson's address on the evening of June 5 followed Reedy's prescription for the most part. Kennedy was still clinging to life as LBJ intoned, "We pray to God that He will spare Robert Kennedy and will restore him to full health and vigor. We pray this for the nation's sake, for the sake of his wife and his children, his father and his mother, and in memory of his brother, our beloved late President. The Kennedy family has endured sorrow enough, and we pray that this family may be spared more anguish."[98] Johnson continued:

> It would be wrong, it would be self-deceptive, to ignore the connection between . . . lawlessness and hatred and this act of violence. It would be just as wrong, and just as self-deceptive, to conclude from this act that our country itself is sick, that it has lost its balance, that it has lost its sense of direction, even its common decency.
>
> Two hundred million Americans did not strike down Robert Kennedy last night any more than they struck down President John F. Kennedy in 1963 or Dr. Martin Luther King in April of this year.[99]

Throughout the one day that RFK lived after the shooting, people gathered before their televisions and in churches, hoping for a miracle. At my Catholic high school in Norfolk, Virginia, we said the rosary for RFK in between final exams, much as we had grasped our rosaries for a briefer time on a Friday afternoon in November 1963. Kennedy never regained consciousness and died at 1:44 A.M. on June 6, the twenty-fourth anniversary of D-Day. His body was flown to New York for a funeral Mass at St. Patrick's Cathedral on June 8, where a stirring eulogy was delivered by the lone surviving Kennedy brother. Paraphrasing the Irish playwright George Bernard Shaw, Senator Ted Kennedy said of Bobby, as his voice broke from the strain, "My brother need not be idealized, or enlarged in death beyond what he was in life, to be remembered simply as a good and decent man, who saw wrong and tried to right it, saw suffering and tried to heal it, saw war and tried to stop it . . . As he said many times, in many parts of this nation, to those he touched and who sought to touch him, 'Some men see things as they are and say why. I dream things that never were and say why not.'"[100] Many Americans, like my father, watched and remarked, "Ted's going to be president one day." The family torch, and the burden of expectations, had been passed to the youngest member of his Kennedy generation, the sole surviving son.

An extraordinary funeral train ride from New York to Washington then took place. RFK's coffin, accompanied by his pregnant widow, Ethel, his ten children, and dozens of family, friends, and working press, made its way as average Americans, many holding flags, wearing military and Scout uniforms, and saluting, gathered in train depots and simply alongside the tracks for hundreds of miles. An uncomprehending sadness was etched onto all their faces. Upon arrival in D.C., the casket was borne by thirteen pallbearers, mostly family but also former astronaut John Glenn and former secretary of defense Robert McNamara, among others. The procession stopped at the Lincoln Memorial where the Marine Corps Band played "The Battle Hymn of the Republic." The motorcade arrived at Arlington National Cemetery at 10:30 P.M. and made its way to the hallowed ground occupied by John F. Kennedy. Bobby was interred nearby. Sunday, June 9, was an official national day of mourning, as a depressed nation tried to recover from a tragic spring.[101]

President Johnson appointed yet another commission, this one headed by Dr. Milton S. Eisenhower, brother of President Dwight D. Eisenhower, to investigate the causes and prevention of violence.[102] In 1969 and 1970, the commission released a series of reports that called for tough new gun control laws, additional curbs on television violence, and other reforms aimed at controlling what appeared to be a national epidemic of bloodshed.[103] Many similar ideas are still circulating in twenty-first-century America, where mass shootings are far more common than in the 1960s.

The parallels between the Kennedy assassinations are many, not least the persistent belief in conspiracy.[104] The convicted assassin Sirhan was sentenced to death in the gas chamber, though his life was spared by a California Supreme Court ban on capital punishment.[105] As with Oswald, though, many people do not believe that Sirhan acted alone.

Just as a Dictabelt was long thought to have recorded the gunshots in Dealey Plaza (though we have now disproven it), a reporter's tape machine is believed to have caught the volley of gunfire in the Ambassador Hotel pantry. An audio analysis of free-lance newsman Stanislaw Puszynski's recording may indicate as many as thirteen gunshots, while Sirhan's gun contained only eight bullets. Given what we learned about the JFK Dictabelt by means of sophisticated testing, however, it might be best to consider the RFK recording's finding as an initial possibility rather than a hard conclusion. Sirhan has regularly applied for parole in California, claiming he was in a trancelike state and does not recall shooting Kennedy. His most recent attorney insisted at a 2011 parole hearing that another gunman shot RFK.[106] Conspiracy theories have also abounded about the assassination of Dr. Martin Luther King, Jr.[107]

Only recently, a Western Union telegram surfaced on the antiques market. Dated 1968, it reads simply, "Please accept my sincerest and deepest sympathy." The recipient was Sirhan's mother, Mary. The sender was Lee Harvey Oswald's mother, Marguerite.[108]

WHEN THE DEMOCRATIC National Convention met in Chicago in late August to nominate Vice President Hubert Humphrey, fury about Vietnam turned downtown Chicago into a domestic war zone, as youthful demonstrators clashed with Mayor Daley's police. Inside the hall, where tear gas occasionally could be smelled and reporters were fair game for pummeling by Daley's angry allies, there was little peace. But calm prevailed for the showing of yet another film about yet another lost Kennedy, *An Impossible Dream*, narrated by Richard Burton—the same actor who had narrated John Kennedy's celluloid memorial at the 1964 Democratic Convention.[109] Politics continued for the living, and the last Kennedy brother was the focus of intrigue. Mayor Daley tried, unsuccessfully, to convince Ted Kennedy to permit a draft from the floor so that he could carry the party's banner instead of Humphrey.[110] By contrast, no one tried to draft Lyndon Johnson for another term. Johnson had hoped to give a valedictory speech as the retiring chief executive. The conclave had been timed originally to coincide with his birthday. But he chose to stay away lest his presence result in embarrassing anti-LBJ displays by many delegates on the convention floor. Also, Johnson probably would have turned the anger on Chicago's streets into complete anarchy.

No comparable good comes from great evil, but the assassinations of Robert Kennedy and Martin Luther King enabled President Johnson to notch his last major legislative achievement. On October 22, Johnson signed the Gun Control Act, which outlawed mail order gun sales and made it illegal to sell guns to anyone indicted or convicted of serious crimes, the mentally ill, drug addicts, and illegal immigrants.[111] In the main, these restrictions are still in effect today—and gun control has not been greatly expanded since.[112] In addition, Secret Service protection was extended to major party candidates for president and vice president.[113]

The tragic decade of the Kennedys was coming to a close. The queen of Camelot stunned the world on October 20, 1968 by marrying the Greek shipping magnate Aristotle Onassis. "Ari" Onassis was the antithesis of John Kennedy in youth, looks, and charm, but in his vast fortune and isolated foreign retreats, the divorced, often unscrupulous wheeler-dealer offered Jackie Kennedy security and escape for herself and her children.[114] Public reaction was not kind; as one *New York Times* report put it, Americans showed "a combination of anger, shock, and dismay."[115] And in Europe, the feedback was summed up in a much-cited headline, JACKIE—HOW CAN YOU?[116]

Camelot was in retreat, if not receivership. The presidential heir was leaving office deeply unpopular and reviled. The family's crown prince had been assassinated. The living symbol of that one brief shining moment had fled to the Mediterranean. John F. Kennedy's vanquished opponent, Richard Nixon, was elected the new president in November, which seemed to many a repudiation of the Kennedy-Johnson years and the tumult they had brought. Pundits prematurely wrote an end to John Kennedy's era, as the second term he might have had came to a close.

But there were enduring signs that Americans were not willing to let go of their fallen leader. On the fifth anniversary of JFK's assassination, thousands again showed up spontaneously at the Arlington gravesite to pay tribute. Memorial services were held in many places, not least Dallas, where the mayor placed flowers in Dealey Plaza and the nurses at Parkland Hospital left a wreath on the door of Trauma Room One.[117] And when *Apollo 8* circled the moon on Christmas Eve, at last providing a soaring achievement to conclude America's *annus horribilis*, John Kennedy's pledge of manned space exploration was prominently cited by the news media. Despite all that had happened since November 1963, the nation's memory of the Kennedy years was fresh and mainly favorable, its admiration for a martyred president undimmed.

As he prepared to leave office, Lyndon Johnson must have reflected upon his own star-crossed presidency. In 1964 he had won an electoral mandate as large as any president had ever enjoyed. Yet despite that, or perhaps because of it, Johnson had overreached and now his departure was mourned by few. His fall from power was tied to his own shortcomings, but in the background, and occasionally the foreground, was the unresolved conflict with the Kennedys. Whose presidency was it anyway? The tug-of-war continued until the day Johnson left office. During his entire White House tenure, Johnson was haunted by the question: What would John Kennedy have done? History still asks it, unanswerable though it is.

15

"Tin Soldiers and Nixon Coming": JFK's Repudiation and Revival

THE RESURRECTION OF RICHARD Nixon has no clear parallel in American politics. Defeated for the presidency by a whisker in 1960 and then beaten decisively for governor of California in 1962, Nixon was so washed up that ABC television ran a program in mid-November 1962 entitled "The Political Obituary of Richard Nixon."[1] Astonishingly, he became president in 1968, put in office by a "silent majority" (actually, a 43 percent plurality) fed up with the Democrats' handling of the Vietnam War and urban riots. The 1960s had zigged left, and far wrong in the eyes of many, so the electorate responded by zagging right to secure Nixon's promised "law and order" and "peace with honor."

Having been elected to the U.S. House of Representatives in the same postwar year of 1946, John Kennedy and Richard Nixon became friends.[2] The two young, ambitious politicians were both World War II veterans, of different parties but a similar frame of mind. While they could not have imagined their lives would be so intertwined, and that both would reach the White House, Kennedy and Nixon recognized each other's talents. As with any political pair in Washington, affable acquaintanceship was mixed with competition and, inevitably, jealousy.

Probably to Kennedy's surprise, given his advantages of education and family finances, Nixon was the one who got fast-tracked. As a freshman congressman, the Republican became a central figure in the 1948 investigation of the former State Department official Alger Hiss, who was accused of being a Communist and later convicted of perjury.[3] As chairman of a special subcommittee of the House Un-American Activities Committee (HUAC), Nixon thrust the hearings into the spotlight with allegations of espionage and skulduggery. This propelled Nixon from the House to the U.S. Senate from California in 1950, and then—at the remarkably young age of thirty-nine—to the vice presidency under President Eisenhower.[4] While never especially close to

Ike, Nixon served dutifully and could possibly have become president during Eisenhower's serious illnesses, such as a heart attack and a stroke, suffered during his White House years. Much more vigorous than Eisenhower, Nixon was sent abroad on a number of high-visibility missions, including the Soviet Union in 1959, where he famously argued with Soviet premier Nikita Khrushchev about the relative merits of capitalism and Communism in the so-called kitchen debate. (It occurred in a mock American kitchen at the American National Exhibition in Moscow.) Nixon was still deeply controversial because of the Hiss case and a "secret fund" scandal during the 1952 presidential campaign,[5] but he was a universally recognized national and international force by 1960. Meanwhile, John Kennedy waited until 1952 to win election to the Senate from Massachusetts, and he lost his bid to be the Democratic vice presidential nominee in 1956. Worse, JFK spent much of the 1950s in pain and on occasion, near death from war-related back injuries. He was never a major force in the Senate.

Nixon was the inevitable 1960 Republican presidential nominee, but Kennedy's path to the Democratic nod was not carefree. Nonetheless, through a combination of pluck, luck, and just enough "time for a change" sentiment—and the help of Chicago's Mayor Daley and LBJ's Texas allies—JFK defeated the more experienced Nixon.[6] It was a bitter pill for the vice president, who believed that he was much better prepared to assume the highest office—and on that score, he was certainly correct. However, Nixon was realistic enough to know after a very close election and at the still-young age of forty-seven, he could stage a comeback. Even after his crushing and somewhat unexpected defeat for the Golden State governorship in 1962, Nixon saw a path to eventual victory, though not in 1964.

It is a supreme, coincidental irony that Richard Nixon was in Dallas on November 20–22, flying out on the morning of the assassination. Nixon had never stopped crisscrossing the country, campaigning for GOP candidates and causes, though he was in Dallas to attend the board meeting of the Pepsi Cola Bottlers Association. (The soft drink company had a financial association with the former vice president.) One can only imagine Nixon's inner thoughts as he heard about President Kennedy's assassination, but the next day, he wrote a note to Jackie that suggests he had been genuinely saddened:

> In this tragic hour, Pat and I want you to know that our thoughts and prayers are with you. While the hand of fate made Jack and me political opponents I always cherished the fact that we were personal friends from the time we came to the Congress together in 1947. That friendship evidenced itself in many ways including the invitation we

received to attend your wedding. Nothing I could say now could add to the splendid tributes which have come from throughout the world. But I want you to know that the nation will also be forever grateful for your service as First Lady. You brought to the White House charm, beauty and elegance as the official hostess of America, and the mystique of the young in art which was uniquely yours made an indelible impression on the American consciousness. If in the days ahead we could be helpful in any way we shall be honored to be at your command.[7]

At the same time, Nixon's keen political mind no doubt analyzed the aftermath quickly: President Johnson would be a heavy favorite for election in 1964, but the natural cycles of politics might make 1968 a very different situation. Few establishment Republicans, and certainly not Nixon, thought Barry Goldwater would have a chance to win; his decisive defeat would strengthen Nixon's opportunity for 1968. After all, Nixon had nearly won the presidency and he was already the party's senior statesman.

History played out precisely that way. Nixon became the GOP's workhorse in 1966, as he campaigned for 105 candidates in thirty-five states and picked up invaluable chits everywhere.[8] The strong Republican showing in 1966—the GOP won an additional forty-seven U.S. House seats as voters expressed disaffection with LBJ's war policy—gave Nixon a real boost. By 1967 he was the Republican presidential frontrunner, and despite challenges from three governors—New York's Nelson Rockefeller, California's Ronald Reagan, and Michigan's George Romney—Nixon won his second White House nomination on the first ballot in August 1968.*

Despite all of Nixon's advantages, not least the deep unpopularity of Johnson and his Vietnam policy, the general election turned out to be exceptionally close. The Republican had held a sizable edge in the Gallup poll in early September over Vice President Hubert Humphrey, but the anti-Democratic vote was split because of former Alabama governor George Wallace, who ran a racist, populist campaign that took 13.5 percent of the vote and 46 electoral votes.[9] Nixon would have won a solid majority except for Wallace; instead, he squeaked to victory over Humphrey by a margin of 43.4 to 42.7 percent.[10]

---

* According to LBJ White House aide James Jones, President Johnson was privately rooting for Rockefeller to become the next president. Nixon was an old adversary, so he would never have been Johnson's preference, but the surprise was that Johnson preferred "Rocky" to his own Democratic vice president. "I think he felt that Hubert [Humphrey] was maybe too nice to be president," Jones told me. "He thought [Rockefeller] was the most talented." Personal interview with James Robert Jones, November 22, 2011.

Almost 57 percent of Americans had voted for someone other than Nixon, making his task ahead much more difficult.

THE AMERICA RICHARD Nixon inherited from Lyndon Johnson—deeply divided over Vietnam and polarized about race—was a far cry from the generally tranquil one John Kennedy received from Dwight Eisenhower. Nixon had little margin for error and less of a honeymoon than any modern president. The conditions were ripe for a contentious administration, not least because Democrats retained large majorities of both houses of Congress and some of Nixon's most fervent detractors, such as Senator Edward Kennedy, resided there.

Nixon had long nursed grievances, many of them justified, about his treatment by the news media and Democratic elites in 1960 and 1962. JFK had been a press favorite throughout his presidential campaign and White House years, and it was an article of faith for Nixon that he had not gotten a fair break in 1960 from many, maybe most, reporters. This carried over to Nixon's presidency. References abound in Nixon's notes and his staff's memos to JFK's media coverage and public relations successes. Just weeks into his presidency, Nixon prodded his chief domestic adviser John Ehrlichman to set up a Kennedy-like network as pushback on press coverage of his actions:

> I still have not had any progress report on what procedure has been set up to continue . . . the letters to the editor project and the calls to TV stations. Two primary purposes would be served by establishing such a procedure. First, it gives a lot of people who were very active in the campaign a continuing responsibility which they would enjoy having. Second, it gives us what Kennedy had in abundance—a constant representation in letters to the editor columns and a very proper influence on the television commentators . . . I do not want a blunderbuss memorandum to go out to hundreds of people on this project, but a discrete and nevertheless effective Nixon Network set up. Give me a report.[11]

Displeased by a mild joke on the television comedy show *The Smothers Brothers*, Nixon again urged Ehrlichman, "I think it is not too late . . . to have a few letters go to the producers of the program objecting to this kind of comment particularly in view of the great public approval of RN's handling of foreign policy, etc. etc. As I have pointed out ad infinitum this was [the] automatic reaction on the part of the Kennedy adherents and it should be an automatic reaction wherever we are concerned, both when we find something we want to approve and when we find something we want to disapprove."[12]

President Nixon also repeatedly stressed to his chief of staff, H. R. "Bob" Haldeman, that he should brief the press about Nixon's extemporaneous responses at press conferences. "I never memorize an answer," wrote Nixon, also noting that his press confabs had "no planted questions." "This was the Kennedy way. It is not our way."[13]

When Democratic National Committee chairman Lawrence O'Brien, a Kennedy man, accused Nixon of generating "the worst recession since the 1950s," Nixon wrote that Senator Bob Dole, the Republican National Committee chairman, should "hit fast that Kennedy had high unemployment for [19]61-62-63 . . ."[14] An editorial in the *Richmond News Leader* as Nixon's first year as president came to a close, entitled "Nixon v. JFK," delighted Nixon. It read in part, "Mr. Kennedy comes off as the acolyte, Mr. Nixon as the more effective minister . . . Mr. Kennedy had solid Democratic majorities in Congress . . . Yet in his first year as President, Mr. Kennedy was rebuffed by Congress on practically all his major programs . . . In the Republican Nixon's first year, he wrenched far more out of a Democratic Congress . . ." Nixon wrote to Haldeman, "I hope you are following through with unprecedented letters to columnists and commentators . . ."[15]

Similarly, Nixon ordered aide Charles Colson to "circulate broadly" a third-year retrospective on Nixon's presidency by liberal pundit Mike Royko that was even tougher in its assessment of JFK and more generous in its evaluation of Nixon.[16] Royko's no-holds-barred opinion piece blasted Kennedy as a "lazy, girl-watching senator" who "used his old man's dough to blitz one state primary after another." In contrast, he portrayed Nixon as a skilled statesman who knew what was best for the country.[17] When the liberal reporter Mary McGrory praised Kennedy to Nixon's detriment, Nixon told Haldeman, "Here is where our people should be talking about our bold foreign policy initiatives *never* undertaken by JFK et al."[18] When a newspaper reporter wrote of a Gallup poll that showed Kennedy leading Nixon in all categories of leadership except for foreign affairs, Nixon fumed. The president wrote to Haldeman, "This shows the effectiveness of the J.F.K. P.R."[19] When Nixon saw a quotation from a young business executive that Nixon had "provided courage and leadership—not Kennedy-style brinksmanship," the president brought it to the attention of his team, calling it "an excellent line for our speakers to quote."[20] The competition even extended to First Ladies. Aide Harry Dent made sure President Nixon saw a Gallup poll that showed the public approved of Pat Nixon's job as First Lady by a 9-to-1 margin. The ratio for Jackie Kennedy, noted Dent, was only 6 to 1. Nixon forwarded this information to Haldeman and Ehrlichman with an unusual notation about his own wife: "An asset we should use more."[21]

Any fair analysis of the substantive accomplishments of the two White House administrations would give Nixon bragging rights over Kennedy in several key areas, including international affairs. But Nixon and his aides understood that in the public's affections, Nixon could not compete. Speechwriter Patrick J. Buchanan told Nixon bluntly, "I have never been convinced that Richard Nixon, Good Guy, is our long suit; to me we are simply not going to charm the American people; we are not going to win it on 'style' and we ought to forget playing ball in the Kennedys' Court."[22] A campaign strategy memo from Colson to Haldeman claimed JFK's appeal was pure "charisma":

> Despite a mediocre Administration, an undistinguished record in foreign affairs and a poor legislative tally, [Kennedy] might well have been re-elected in 1964; if so it would probably have been largely due to the successful mystique he created (with the help of a friendly press). The fact that he was able to maintain a substantial base of political support a year before the election would suggest that even a relatively ineffectual President can support himself on personality alone.[23]

The observations about Nixon in this strategy memo were telling. "It would be foolish . . . to try to build a Kennedy-type mystique—there isn't time [and] the press would never let us get away with it . . ." The remarkable conclusion, perhaps borne out in the results of Nixon's landslide 1972 reelection, read, "A President doesn't have to be likeable, have a sense of humor, or even love children . . ."[24]

WHILE THERE ARE many JFK references in the documents comprising the Nixon administration, to suggest that John Kennedy was an obsession would be misleading. The late president was no longer a threat. But another Kennedy was. Almost from the first, President Nixon and his circle viewed JFK's brother Ted as their foremost adversary and obstacle to reelection. They plotted and planned about how to deter him, and kept close watch on the heir to Camelot. John Ehrlichman told Nixon that he was "covering" Kennedy "personally," getting reports about what the senator did each night during a 1971 trip to Hawaii, for instance. Perhaps surprisingly, given Kennedy's womanizing proclivities, he was well behaved on this tropical vacation, prompting Nixon to comment, "He's being careful now . . . The thing to do is, just watch him, because what happens to fellows like that, who have that kind of problem, is that they go quite a while, and then . . ." But Nixon wondered if they would find anything since Ted might be restrained while "trying for the big thing [the presidency] . . . although [JFK] was damn careless."[25]

For a while after the Chappaquiddick Island incident on July 19, 1969, the White House breathed easier about Ted Kennedy, wondering how he could survive the enormous scandal following the drowning death of the young campaign worker Mary Jo Kopechne.[26] Kennedy had been the driver of the car when it careened off a bridge late at night. Despite knowing that his passenger had not escaped and was certainly injured, drowning, or dead, Kennedy did not even report the accident to police for ten hours, appearing far more concerned about contacting family friends and protecting his political career than assessing Kopechne's fate.*

Many had assumed that the 1972 election would feature the next Kennedy versus Nixon in the presidential matchup. Seeing a golden opportunity, and fearing that the Kennedy family would cover up the scandal, the president ordered Ehrlichman to do what he could to keep the Chappaquiddick tragedy a high-profile subject of discussion. Ehrlichman hired Jack Caulfield, a former New York detective, to follow up. "For two weeks, [Caulfield] dug through the available evidence, asked damaging questions at press conferences, anything to keep the dirt flying," noted Chris Matthews.[27] Nixon operatives also placed a wiretap in the Georgetown house where Mary Jo Kopechne had lived with several other women.

Nixon had many sources about Chappaquiddick and was interested in the gossip. Just a couple of weeks after the accident, he sent a memo to Ehrlichman: "I would like for you to talk to Kissinger on a very confidential basis with regard to a talk he had with Galbraith as to what really happened in the Kennedy matter. It is a fascinating story. I'm sure Kissinger will tell you the story and then you of course will know how to check it out and get it properly exploited."[28] Nixon also watched as Kennedy went through the court proceedings—the senator was given a very lenient two-month suspended jail sentence—and then began to rehabilitate his image.[29] When Kennedy's friend Senator Birch Bayh noted that he had "a tremendous hold on young people—it amounts almost to worship—and young people are prone to forgive and forget," Nixon underlined Bayh's remarks and wrote in the margins to Ehrlichman, "The fix must be in."[30] Kennedy's first post-Chappaquiddick trip out of Massachusetts and Washington was to a Democratic Party fund-raiser in Miami in February 1970. A White House observer

---

* The Chappaquiddick tragedy would dog Kennedy throughout the rest of his life, and it did in fact help to sink the one presidential bid he would launch in 1980.

sent to the event reported to Ehrlichman that Kennedy "did pretty well."[31] At the same time, Nixon saw that some in the press were beginning to push Kennedy forward again, and he brought it to the attention of Haldeman and others: "The wish is probably father to the thought. But a major rebuilding job is going on—our people should do what they can to blunt it."[32] When a British newspaper reported in November 1970 that Kennedy "danced until dawn with an Italian divorcee in a Paris night club the day of the funeral of [President Charles] deGaulle" and declared that "the French consider that he insulted the memory of deGaulle," Nixon wanted to know if the photo of Kennedy and the woman that accompanied the U.K. article was going to be published in the United States. White House counsel John W. Dean wrote in reply, "[Chuck] Colson has discussed with H[aldeman] and is following through."[33]

The Nixon White House had every reason to keep close tabs on Edward Kennedy. By mid-1971, in spite of Chappaquiddick, Kennedy led Nixon in Gallup's presidential trial heats by as much as ten percentage points.[34] Until Nixon's brilliant opening to China and détente with the Soviet Union in the first half of 1972, the president appeared vulnerable in his reelection bid. Assuming that Kennedy would not launch a campaign due to Chappaquiddick, senior Democrats hoped that Senator Edmund Muskie of Maine, who had polled strongly since his bid as the Democratic nominee for vice president in 1968, would be the party's nominee against Nixon. But Muskie's campaign flopped badly, and the strongly antiwar senator George McGovern gained traction over Muskie and former vice president Hubert Humphrey, who had rejoined the Senate from Minnesota in 1971. McGovern was a deeply flawed, left-wing candidate, and the Nixon guard could not help but think the Democrats would toss McGovern aside and draft Ted Kennedy for a presidential rescue mission late in the process.

President Nixon carefully followed Kennedy's press, underlining sections of newspaper and magazine articles about him and scribbling comments such as "a plug for Teddy."[35] When Kennedy attacked the administration on Vietnam in April 1972, Nixon became enraged—and completely engaged. Kennedy declared himself "appalled" by the "moral and military bankruptcy" of Nixon's war policy. To Nixon's delight, Senator Bob Dole was dispatched to say that Kennedy's remarks deserved "the condemnation and contempt of every decent American." Referring directly to Kennedy's ties to JFK and LBJ's Vietnam involvement and perhaps indirectly to Chappaquiddick, Dole asserted that Kennedy "should never accuse anyone of having blood on his hands."[36]

Nixon's aides, including William Safire and Pat Buchanan, produced detailed analyses of Kennedy's strengths and weaknesses as a candidate. Safire's memo from November 1971 was especially perceptive:

SUBJECT: Kennedy Victory Scenario

I notice some people around here actually looking forward to Kennedy as the Democratic nominee as "easiest to beat." To dispel that notion, here is a quick rundown of ways he can be expected to turn Chappaquiddick to his advantage.

Pre-Convention

1. Carrying the torch. "The torch has been passed" was a memorable quotation from JFK. Teddy will constantly harp on the brother's fallen torch theme. Not subtly, either—"we Kennedys can't make plans" is a sledgehammer, strictly emotional, playing on the guilt feelings of many Americans, and because it is bad taste does not make it bad politics.

2. The Sudden-Maturity rationale. How do they come to grips with the failure of courage at the [Chappaquiddick] bridge? Answer: Each of the brothers underwent a deep sea-change at some stage of their lives. The Bay of Pigs changed JFK, enabling him to rise to greatness at the Cuban Missile Crisis; Bobby, too, underwent an enormous change from the [Joseph] McCarthy counsel, ruthless and coldblooded, to the warm and compassionate friend of the underprivileged he came to appear to be in 1968 . . . Kennedys traditionally overcome their pasts; the "record" has never been held against them, and to more people than we like to think, will not be this time either.

The Campaign: Making Chappaquiddick work for Kennedy.

3. The pressure to open up the sealed verdict will be allowed to grow; then, probably in Houston, scene of the Ministers Conference where JFK "faced up" to the Catholic issue, Teddy will break his silence on Chappaquiddick. The same people who deride a "Checkers speech" as cornball will see this as a human appeal for fairness and a brave exposition of a man's soul. The tape will then be played wherever it is most useful to Teddy.

4. The President can avoid television debates with any other candidate; but a public yearning for a Nixon-Kennedy rematch on television would be well-nigh irresistible. Ducking or delaying would only play up their "courage" pitch, which would directly answer that loss of courage at the bridge.

5. The polls will be far more volatile than usual, reflecting the emotional responses sure to be triggered in a campaign that plays on national guilt, past assassinations, pleas to rise above vicious innuendo, and the like . . .

6. Great stress will be laid on the number of threats he receives, the impassioned pleas of the Secret Service to limit his campaigning to safe television appearances, and his courageous refusal to be kept away from

crowds. He will motorcade Dallas. The "old" Teddy ran away from trouble; the "new" Kennedy will not run away. He will prove his courage once and for all in Dallas, on the final weekend of the campaign.

Why do I write this memo? I think we can beat Kennedy. But it is important that we recognize the wild and wooly nature of the campaign he could put on and stop thinking he would be the easiest candidate to beat.[37]

A bit earlier, Pat Buchanan—ever the hardball combatant—had also urged an aggressive posture to distinguish the liberal Ted from his much more centrist brother, JFK:

No matter that EMK [Ted] is adored by the Party's Left, we have a serious problem only if he gets well with the Party's Center. The more he acts like Brother Bobby the better off we are; the less he acts like brother John, the better off we are.

Socially, Kennedy is out of touch with the political mood. The Jet Set, Swinger, See-Through Blouse cum Hot Pants crowd, the Chappaquiddick-Hoe down and Paris hijinks—the more publicity they all get, the better.

Since EMK will be trafficking on the JFK myth, it would be well to document JFK's tough line on defense, foreign policy, Vietnam, Europe, etc. over against EMK's positions—to provide conservative Democrats with some rationale for abandoning the little brother of their hero.[38]

Nixon and everyone else with political sense in the White House understood that a campaign against Kennedy would be fraught with peril, and best avoided. The goal was clear: Avoid goading Ted into the race while building up McGovern to the extent possible. As Buchanan put it in an April 1972 memo, "Though [Kennedy] would be unacceptable to the South, in a national election, he would bring to his candidacy all the McGovern support, plus the Kennedy charisma, plus the support of the Meanys [George Meany, head of the AFL-CIO] and Daleys. A Democratic Party deeply divided, thirsting for unity and victory, would welcome a Kennedy. For this reason, we do *not* believe our strategy should be to flush Kennedy out. As Kennedy is elevated, McGovern recedes—and We Want McGovern."[39]

And McGovern they got, on their way to a forty-nine-state landslide victory in November. McGovern had hoped that Kennedy would run as his vice presidential candidate, but Kennedy would have no part of it. If this third

Senator Kennedy was going to endure unrelenting scrutiny because of Chappaquiddick and risk possible assassination on the campaign trail, he would run not for the second slot but for the top job, and in a year more promising for Democrats than 1972 was turning out to be. After the withdrawal of McGovern's eventual pick for vice president, Missouri senator Thomas Eagleton (who was discovered to have had electric shock treatments for depression), McGovern tried to recover with a dose of Kennedy glamor, choosing JFK's brother-in-law Sargent Shriver as Eagleton's replacement. But the former head of the Peace Corps was no antidote for the Democratic ticket's long list of electoral handicaps.

The demise of the Ted Kennedy specter for Nixon's reelection did not make the president any less wary of the Massachusetts senator. By this time, Nixon's psychology was purely Kennedy-averse, and he was always wary. As John Dean suggested, "It always was apparent to me that Nixon had not forgotten how close the 1960 election with John Kennedy had been. After Watergate Ted Kennedy was one of the first to start investigating in the Senate . . . Nixon didn't think Ted was going to run against him. At that point it was too late and McGovern was the nominee. But Nixon just sees this hand again, the fine hand that denied him [in 1960], and he wonders whether the Kennedy people might have the wherewithal to deny him a second term."

Kennedy campaigned extensively for McGovern in the fall of 1972, and after a direct appeal to Nixon by family matriarch Rose Kennedy, who worried about her last son's safety, Ted was provided with Secret Service protection until after election day. Nixon and Haldeman seized upon this opportunity to collect political intelligence, planting a Nixon loyalist, retired agent Robert Newbrand, in Kennedy's Secret Service detail, though all indications are that Newbrand turned up little actionable intelligence.[40]

Already looking to 1976 and the possibility that Kennedy could emerge as the consensus choice to reclaim the White House for the Democrats, the Irish American Nixon shared a few thoughts about the Irish American Kennedy during an Oval Office discussion. White House aide Ken Clawson recorded for posterity Nixon's unusual views about his own ethnic group in a September 1972 memo:

> The President . . . discussed at length the disciplines required of the Nation's Chief Executive . . . Referring to Senator Kennedy, the president wondered aloud whether the potential presidential candidate might not lack the stringent disciplines of a President. He said that the Irish, in particular, deteriorate rapidly without strong personal discipline. Such a deterioration might remove many of the appealing

qualities that Senator Kennedy now appears to possess, the President said.[41]

WHILE THE NIXONS and Kennedys kept their distance during the Nixon White House years, given the partisan history between them, one exception occurred the evening of February 3, 1971, when Jacqueline Kennedy responded to an invitation from the Nixons for a private visit and dinner at the White House.[42] This event marked her and the children's first visit since they had moved out in early December 1963. By all accounts it was a pleasant, sentimental occasion, enjoyed by all the participants.[43] But there are political considerations in everything for a White House occupant. Two aides had reports on Haldeman's desk the next morning. Mort Allin called it "truly an outstanding move here in having Jackie in and just the initial reports look very good. One thing we might avoid—too much description . . . of what a warm evening it was . . . Any more pushing of that theme could become overkill."[44] Another assistant, Robert C. Odle, Jr., agreed but offered, "It might be pointed out quietly to friendly columnists that this is Mrs. Onassis's first visit since 1963 and that she refused LBJ's invitations."[45]*

During his presidency, Richard Nixon avoided other Kennedy gatherings, including all commemorations of November 22, 1963—sending only emissaries with wreaths to JFK's grave and mentioning the anniversary in an official proclamation just once, on the tenth anniversary in 1973, which coincided with Thanksgiving.[46] When Haldeman suggested to Nixon very early in his first term that he might want to reopen the Warren Commission's investigation of the Kennedy assassination, Nixon wasn't at all interested; such a move, favored by Haldeman because he recognized the growing controversy about the commission, would have been astonishing and might have overshadowed the new administration's initiatives.[47] Privately though, Nixon admitted that the Warren Commission's investigation had been deeply flawed. When presidential hopeful George Wallace was shot and seriously wounded during a campaign stop in Laurel, Maryland, the president called FBI senior official Mark Felt (later made famous for his role in bringing Nixon down as "Deep Throat" during the Watergate investigation) and said, "Be sure we don't go through the thing we went through—the Kennedy assassination, where we didn't really follow up adequately. You know?"[48] Nixon also declined to attend the opening of the Kennedy Center on September 8,

---

* Jackie had in fact refused repeated offers from President Johnson and Lady Bird to come back, though we will never know whether it was because of her opinion of LBJ or because the timing simply wasn't right.

1971, giving as the excuse his desire not to steal the spotlight from the famous family. The president was harshly criticized by some for skipping the event.[49] In fact, Nixon may have been trying to avoid the left-wing politics of the featured entertainer, Leonard Bernstein.[50]

On the whole, Nixon seemed to prefer to avoid mentioning JFK at all—with the exception of two big subjects where Kennedy's actions helped Nixon's public case, Vietnam and Watergate. On one occasion Nixon's omission of JFK caused a controversy. Despite having a dozen or more opportunities in official and unofficial forums, Nixon never mentioned President Kennedy in connection with the July 1969 moon landing, which had been achieved because of Kennedy's bold commitment in 1961.[51] Such a salute would not have detracted from Nixon's ceremonial role and might well have enhanced its public relations value with a sprinkling of bipartisan graciousness. Imagine if Nixon had included JFK's 1961 call for a moon landing on the plaque that now rests on the moon's surface—an act that would have forever linked his name and Kennedy's in a powerful symbol of national unity to denote a supreme human triumph. Yet Nixon could not bring himself to do it, and the obvious exclusion generated censure.[52] Nixon finally acknowledged Kennedy's role in the moon program only when it ended, with the return of *Apollo 17* in December 1972.[53]

It was also never consciously or explicitly acknowledged that Nixon's innovative, dramatic moves in foreign policy followed the post–Cuban Missile Crisis plans of a chastened President Kennedy. Having come so perilously close to war in 1962, JFK had begun to explore the pathways to peace, encouraged by the similar desires of Premier Khrushchev. JFK's American University speech in June 1963 and the Nuclear Test Ban Treaty later that year were the antecedents of détente. Yet Nixon went far beyond Kennedy's tentative steps with the Soviet Union and reconstructed the nature of U.S.-USSR relations. And there is no indication Kennedy ever conceived of constructive engagement with China, nor would it have been politically possible for a Democrat in the 1960s to have reached out to "Red China" in the way Nixon did in 1972. Nixon's fierce anticommunism protected him from soft-on-Communism attacks, while Democrats were already perceived in some quarters as too eager for accommodation with the Reds—plus, China had fallen behind the Iron Curtain under the Democratic Truman administration. In any event, Nixon's stellar foreign policy realignments were a source of justifiable pride for him and his party, far outstripping what even a reelected President Kennedy could have hoped to do.

Nixon's fundamental relationship with JFK was competitive, but not always. Few realize that Nixon saved one of JFK's best-known programs, the Peace Corps. Early in his presidency, Nixon had been inclined to phase out the Corps, as well as other activist divisions of the New Frontier and Great Society, but he thought better of it in time. When Southern conservatives in Congress linked the Peace Corps to the widely despised spending category of foreign aid and slashed the Peace Corps budget, Nixon found funds in other areas to transfer to the Corps, enabling it to continue operating at full strength.[54] Had Nixon wanted to damage JFK's legacy in a prized area, and do so without fingerprints, this would have been the perfect opportunity.

PRESIDENCIES ARE PERSONAL in the moment, but in history, they are judged by substantive achievements and epic failures. In many ways, Nixon had the better of Kennedy in both historic categories. Nixon's painfully slow but successful winding down of Vietnam, his shrewd playing off of China and Russia to produce spectacular diplomatic breakthroughs, and some creative domestic policies (such as the establishment of the Environmental Protection Agency and a reorganization of the federal government) may eventually restore some luster to a presidential reputation destroyed by extensive Watergate abuses.[55] That was Nixon's hope in retirement.

That Richard Nixon resented John Kennedy is obvious, and his antipathy was not irrational. For reasons ranging from personal charm to Democratic tilt within the news media, JFK was loved and touted by the press throughout his national career in a way that Nixon could never match or even approach. Press adulation probably made at least 119,000 votes' worth of difference in 1960, and Nixon lived with this bitter reality for years. Where JFK triumphed, as in the Cuban Missile Crisis, he was assured of glowing, long-lasting coverage; when he fell short (the Bay of Pigs), the press moved on. His private vices, such as reckless womanizing, were ignored. In cases where Kennedy policy led to disaster (Vietnam), there was an automatic might-have-been excuse to the discussion. Because of his assassination, John Kennedy was untouchable, and this must have galled the flesh-and-blood, here-and-now Nixon from time to time. Nixon's feats seemed to fade more quickly, his fiascoes were sometimes exaggerated, and like Lyndon Johnson, Nixon could never compete with a saintly ghost.

It is hard to fault Nixon for insisting that the Vietnam record prominently display its Kennedy-Johnson lineage. Johnson's role was far greater, but JFK initiated the era of major involvement. Nixon was determined to remind the public of this fact, and he quoted JFK at length in his much ballyhooed November 1969 televised address on Vietnam: "In 1963, President Kennedy, with his characteristic eloquence and clarity, said: 'We want to see a stable government there, carrying on a struggle to maintain its national independence. We believe strongly in that. We are not going to withdraw from that effort. In my opinion, for us to withdraw from that effort would mean a collapse not only of South Vietnam, but Southeast Asia. So we are going to stay there.'"[56] Even more important in Nixon's assessment, Kennedy played a central role in the overthrow and murder of Vietnamese president Ngo Dinh Diem. Nixon had long believed the Diem assassination was a crucial turning point in forcing more U.S. involvement, and he frequently referred to it in public and private.[57]

Nixon tried to resolve the Indochina catastrophe he had been handed as best he could, given his determination not to let the Communists win and to achieve "peace with honor." Along the way, Nixon and his staff never hesitated to let the two prior administrations take the political hit. Of the two, Nixon preferred to target Kennedy's. Johnson had been bedeviled by the same band of Kennedy loyalists and "Eastern establishment, Ivy League elites" that targeted Nixon, even though many of them had supported Kennedy's original Vietnam involvement.[58] When the Pentagon Papers were published in 1971, giving the public access to the secret history of U.S. involvement in Vietnam, Nixon aide Charles Colson wrote to chief of staff Haldeman, "The [Democrats] are very well aware that the major thrust of this controversy will eventually become the Kennedy-Johnson mishandling of the war . . . We should encourage [Capitol] Hill to carry on well publicized hearings [on] the Kennedy-Johnson papers and over how we got into Vietnam [and] the skill with which the President is managing to get us out." The dirty-tricks side of Colson also surfaced here: "We could of course plant and try to prove the thesis that Bobby Kennedy was behind the preparation of these papers because he planned to use them to overthrow Lyndon Johnson. (I suspect that there may be more truth than fantasy to this.)"[59]

A legitimate Nixon inquiry into the Diem assassination morphed into another dirty trick. During the Pentagon Papers controversy, Nixon ordered his senior staff, including Haldeman, Ehrlichman, and national security adviser Henry Kissinger, to comb through everything they could find on Diem's murder and the Kennedy role in it.[60] At the same time, Nixon asked Richard Helms, the director of the CIA, to share his agency's classified internal documents with White House staffers. Nixon promised to keep the documents secret. "Listen, I've done more than my share of lying to protect [the CIA and] it was totally right to do it," he said. Nixon wanted unrestricted access to Langley's JFK files. "Who shot John?" he asked Helms. "Is Eisenhower to blame? Is Johnson to blame? Is Kennedy to blame? Is Nixon to blame?"[61] Helms never turned over the JFK files, but he cooperated with the Diem investigation.

The Diem assignment worked its way down the chain of command into the hands of White House aide E. Howard Hunt.[62] As he investigated, he found that certain critical, timely diplomatic cable traffic was conveniently missing or possibly tampered with. Years later, it was learned that JFK had indeed engineered a cover-up and ordered incriminating cables at the State Department, the CIA, and the Defense Department destroyed.[63] Instead of pursuing this legitimate angle, Hunt—claiming orders from Colson—forged documents incriminating Kennedy and his administration in the Diem debacle.[64] As ex-Nixon counsel John Dean told me, "Hunt had a rather simple solution as a former CIA operative. He got his scissors and craft knives out and started phonying up cables by using other cables and patching them together and then Xeroxing them . . . [Colson] convinced a journalist to publish this story which would've indeed hung the murder of Diem on John Kennedy. The story fell apart, however, when the editors asked to see the original copy and the cut-and-pasted version didn't look as good as the Xeroxed version." When the forgery was eventually revealed in the spring of 1973, it became a larger scandal than the killing of Diem.[65]

In this and so many other episodes, one is drawn to a lesson learned too late by President Nixon. In the conclusion to his final speech in the White House on August 9, 1974, Nixon told his assembled staff, "never be petty; always remember, others may hate you, but those who hate you don't win unless you hate them, and then you destroy yourself."[66] That became the central lesson of the multilayered scandal that demolished any chance Nixon had of being as well remembered as John Kennedy.

As he began to sink under the weight of Watergate, Nixon and his associates often insisted that dirty tricks and eavesdropping had been the techniques of a series of presidents, certainly including JFK, and again they were correct. For example, Kennedy had left 125 tapes and 68 Dictabelt recordings of conversations, and Lyndon Johnson had made extensive tapings, too, without the knowledge or permission of the other participants.[67] In March 1973, Nixon urged John Ehrlichman to "make the subtle point that the highest number of [FBI wire]taps was when Bobby Kennedy was Attorney General and, incidentally, that was before the war in Vietnam had heated up . . . [G]et across the fact that it was during the Kennedy Administration and the Johnson Administration that the FBI was used for surveillance on newsmen and everybody else . . . Bobby Kennedy had FBI agents rout newspapermen out of bed in the middle of the night and put them under grilling as to what they knew about a possible price rise by steel companies. This kind of thing, of course, goes far beyond anything we have attempted in the national security area."[68] Later, in July, Nixon urged his new chief of staff, General Alexander Haig, to pursue similar themes: "This Administration has never used the FBI for purely political purposes—both Kennedy and Johnson did . . . In other words, rather than being the most repressive Administration in these areas it is perhaps the least repressive Administration despite the fact that we had a massive problem to deal with in terms of domestic violence and, therefore, had much more justification than either Johnson or Kennedy had for enlisting all agencies of the government to deal with that violence."[69] After his resignation, in his memoirs, Nixon stressed the excuse that "everybody did it":

> My reaction to the Watergate break-in was completely pragmatic. If it was also cynical, it was a cynicism born of experience . . . [DNC chairman] Larry O'Brien might affect astonishment and horror, but he knew as well as I did that political bugging had been around nearly since the invention of the wiretap. As recently as 1970 a former member of Adlai Stevenson's campaign staff had publicly stated that he had tapped the Kennedy organization's phone lines at the 1960 Democratic convention. Lyndon Johnson felt that the Kennedys had had him tapped; Barry Goldwater said that his 1964 campaign had been bugged; and Edgar Hoover told me that in 1968 Johnson had ordered my campaign plane bugged . . . [70]
>
> . . . I decided that I wanted all the wiretaps of previous administrations revealed. It was Bobby Kennedy who had authorized the first wiretaps on Martin Luther King. Ultimately King was subjected to five different phone taps and fifteen microphone bugs in his hotel rooms. The Kennedys had tapped newsmen. They had tapped a number of people instrumental in the passage of a sugar import bill they considered important.[71]

Nixon's memory was selective, though. His administration extensively used the FBI, the Internal Revenue Service, and the CIA to serve its political needs just as his predecessors had. The age of the imperial presidency had enabled Kennedy and Johnson to get away with their deeds. Nixon was caught, and his web of lies, deceits, and unconstitutional pretensions during Watergate brought down his presidency in an unprecedented way, through resignation in the face of near-certain House impeachment and Senate conviction. Had John Kennedy lived and if his extramarital entanglements had been exposed, he would probably have been forced to resign. Had Lyndon Johnson won a second full term and continued the Vietnam War as Nixon did, he might have triggered abuse-of-power revelations, too, and been forced to leave office early. But JFK by assassination and LBJ through early retirement avoided that fate.

Nixon believed that his political enemies were behind the Watergate revelations. He pointed to Ben Bradlee, the executive editor of the *Washington Post* who had been a close JFK confidant, and to Watergate special prosecutor

Archibald Cox, who had worked for JFK in 1960 and been recommended for the prosecutor's role by Ted Kennedy.[72] Nixon might have added that his many foes in a heavily Democratic Congress were eager to do their part in his collapse. (JFK and LBJ were fortunate to have had their party firmly in charge of Capitol Hill throughout the 1960s.) Yet for all the assistance and cheerleading that President Nixon's adversaries gave to his demise, Nixon caused his own downfall, and he was also the man occupying the White House when the hefty bill came due for long-term presidential abuse of power. That bill would have arrived eventually in any event, but Nixon hastened it with his attitudes as well as deeds. "The more successful Nixon became, the more vengeful he became," noted John W. Dean. "It's really quite remarkable. Nixon didn't mellow with his success, he became embittered by it."

For a short period, mainly in 1972, JFK's legacy had dimmed because of Nixon's spectacular foreign policy successes, just as Kennedy's domestic record was almost completely eclipsed during the 1965 heyday of the Great Society. But Richard Nixon discovered what Lyndon Johnson already knew: In the broad sweep of history, their presidencies were judged inadequate. Nixon and Johnson had much longer lists of achievements, but fundamental personal faults led to policy disasters and, ultimately, their undoing. More than a decade after Kennedy's death, compared to both his successors, JFK retained the lion's share of the American people's affections.

Ironically, as Nixon fought to keep the White House in his final days, he argued that the nation could not endure another failed presidency, specifically citing Kennedy's assassination and Johnson's early exit.[73] When he resigned, he elevated his handpicked vice president, Gerald R. Ford, to the nation's highest office.* Americans immediately recognized that he was a pleasant, uncomplicated man who had none of the neuroses that had troubled LBJ and Nixon. After more than a decade of trauma, citizens welcomed a chance to heal.[74]

Nonetheless, Ford started with a self-inflicted wound only a month after taking the presidential oath, a complete pardon for his disgraced predecessor for any and all crimes he may have committed in office. Having lost his honeymoon glow, Ford plummeted almost overnight from 71 percent to 49 percent in the Gallup poll.[75] He then rode a roller-coaster of recession, oil shocks, foreign crises, and intraparty rebellion as he filled out Nixon's term.

---

* In the previous century only two presidents have had a shorter tenure of office than JFK's two years and ten months. Warren Harding served about two years and five months before dying on August 2, 1923, while Gerald Ford occupied the Oval Office for about two years and six months, beginning August 9, 1974.

As did his predecessors, the new thirty-eighth president had a direct connection to the thirty-fifth. Ford had served on the Warren Commission and was an unwavering advocate of its conclusions during his presidency and throughout his long life.[76] Nonetheless, Watergate had jimmied open the Pandora's box of CIA and FBI horrors, raising suspicions about their possible role in the Kennedy assassination, and both the electorate and lawmakers demanded to know more. In part to try to head off more intrusive investigations, President Ford appointed a commission in 1975, headed by his newly confirmed vice president, Nelson Rockefeller, to "determine the extent to which the [CIA] had exceeded its authority."[77] The resulting, rather limited, report disclosed the CIA's illegal mail opening and surveillance of dissident groups domestically. It also dealt with some lingering questions about John Kennedy's assassination, though its findings were clearly designed to reinforce those of the Warren Commission. In addition to insisting that "there was no credible evidence of any CIA involvement" in JFK's murder, the Rockefeller Commission denied any CIA connection to Lee Harvey Oswald or Jack Ruby.[78]

Further, the Rockefeller Commission took an extraordinary action in the wake of the March 1975 public screening of Abraham Zapruder's home movie. Keep in mind that the Zapruder film had been kept out of the public domain for more than eleven years—something that would almost certainly prove impossible today in the Internet age, with its much higher public expectations for prompt disclosure. Conditions had been very different in the 1960s. Immediately after the assassination, Zapruder made several copies of his soon-to-be-famous 8-millimeter amateur film. He turned over one copy to the Secret Service and sold the original to Time-Life for $150,000 plus a percentage of future proceeds. New Orleans district attorney Jim Garrison subpoenaed the original from Time-Life during the trial of Clay Shaw, which led to the widespread distribution of bootleg copies among assassination researchers. In 1969, an optical technician named Robert Groden obtained a copy of the film and spent four years improving and enhancing its images. Groden's extremely graphic version shocked the public when it debuted on ABC television in March 1975. In addition, the "back and to the left" movement of President Kennedy's head when it was struck by the fatal bullet appeared to contradict the Warren Commission's insistence that JFK had been shot from behind.[79] So the Rockefeller Commission convened a panel of military and medical experts to refute the impressions left by the Zapruder film. They cited experiments "conducted at Edgewood Arsenal [Maryland] [that] disclosed goats shot through the brain evidenced just such a violent neuromuscular reaction ... [A] head wound such as that sustained by President Kennedy produces an 'explosion' of tissue at the area where the bullet exits from the head, causing a 'jet effect' which almost instantly moves the head back in the direction from which the bullet came."[80]

At a time when the manifest sins of the federal government had been exposed in both domestic and international affairs, Americans were disinclined to accept such findings at face value. Moreover, the heavily Democratic Congress, just elected in the wake of Watergate, was unwilling to leave the investigation to the Republican executive branch. Shortly after the appointment of the Rockefeller Commission, the Senate voted overwhelmingly to create a special eleven-member committee to examine the CIA, headed by Idaho's Democratic senator Frank Church.[81] The Ford administration was not pleased, and pointed to Church's presidential ambitions.*

Whatever political dimensions existed, the well-staffed Church Committee produced plenty of damaging revelations about the CIA—and more than a few about the Kennedy administration.[82] The first indications of the Kennedy-authorized assassination attempts on Fidel Castro came from the Church Committee, encouraging the belief that JFK was killed by Cuban agents intent on retaliation.[83] Moreover, a staff leak from the committee generated the first sordid story of Kennedy's extensive, irresponsible White House philandering. JFK's long affair with Judith Campbell, including her ties to mob boss Sam Giancana, was laid bare in December 1975 press reports.[84] Kennedy's secrets, carefully protected by his friends in the media for many years, started oozing out, shocking many Americans who had accepted the post-Dallas image of sainthood conferred upon the dead president.[85] Other tales of Kennedy's adultery reached the front pages, such as his two-year affair with socialite Mary Pinchot Meyer, and the Kennedy family's exertions to cover up JFK's sexual shenanigans became controversial, too.[86] By 1976, the political cartoonist Charles Brooks could publish a drawing, unthinkable in the 1960s, of a very full garbage pail labeled "John F. Kennedy's Secret Sex Life While President" behind a phony castle marked "Camelot."[87] In the sixties, a barrelful of worshipful books about JFK were written by former Kennedy aides and friends and eagerly published to good reviews and sizable sales.[88] Now revisionist history was taking hold, and new volumes told a fuller, seamier truth about John F. Kennedy. The cynical 1970s were a decade when illusions of all sorts would be shattered, and JFK was no longer immune from severe criticism and personal exposure.

This skeptical era as well as prevailing political conditions combined to produce a full review of the Warren Commission's conclusions. President Ford was not in favor of it, but if anything, his opposition made Democratic congressional efforts to reopen the investigation more determined. The pub-

---

* Church ran unsuccessfully for president in 1976.

lic's intense response to the Zapruder film—both to the gruesomeness of its 486 frames and the questions raised in viewing JFK's and Connally's physical reactions to the bullets—added to the demand for a new inquiry. So, too, did revelations that the CIA had gone to considerable lengths to counter and discredit some authors of books proposing conspiracy theories about November 22, 1963.[89] In 1976 the House of Representatives established its Select Committee on Assassinations (HSCA), discussed in an earlier chapter. Because this was an internal House action, President Ford had no voice in the matter, and he was already distracted by a difficult and ultimately losing election campaign. It would take the committee three years to complete its work, concluding that a conspiracy of some sort had existed in JFK's murder. The committee issued its report and twelve volumes of appendices in 1979.[90]

Eerily, given his Warren Commission membership, Gerald Ford became the target for the first fully executed assassination attempts on a sitting president since JFK. Both would-be assassins were women and both struck in California during September 1975. Lynette "Squeaky" Fromme, a member of the notorious Charles Manson gang that had brutally murdered pregnant actress Sharon Tate and others in 1969, tried to kill Ford in Sacramento on September 5. Fromme pointed a .45-caliber automatic pistol at Ford as he was shaking hands near the state capitol, but an alert Secret Service agent grabbed her just in time. She was a mere two to three feet from the president and might easily have fatally wounded Ford.[91] Some two weeks later, on September 22, Ford was visiting San Francisco when Sara Jane Moore fired a .38-caliber pistol at the president from across a crowded street. She missed Ford by a few feet, mainly because a former Marine, Oliver Sipple, deflected her arm at the last moment.[92] The bullet was a highly destructive one similar to a dum-dum, and after striking a planter box and ricocheting off the pavement, it wounded a taxi driver in the groin. Adding to the Secret Service's frustration, Moore had been arrested only two days earlier for illegal possession of another gun, and she was questioned by agents to see if she was a threat to Ford. The gun was confiscated, and in a serious error, Moore was released the day before Ford arrived. Fromme and Moore were not known to the Secret Service prior to September 1975—though at the time, almost thirty-nine thousand Americans were in the Service's active file of potential assassins, including three hundred considered so dangerous that they were under surveillance in an operation code-named Watchbird.[93]

In a fascinating twist, Ford's fall 1976 presidential campaign against Jimmy Carter planned to use the memories of these assassination scares—as well as a reference to the city where JFK was killed—to suggest that Ford was a survivor who had helped America turn the corner from a difficult decade. In a nearly five-minute commercial set to upbeat patriotic music entitled "I'm

Feeling Good about America," Ford continued giving a speech despite a loud firecracker blast. The narrator said, "Neither the cherry bombs of a misguided prankster, nor all the memories of recent years can keep the people and their president apart." The scene then shifted to Dallas; Ford stood and waved through the open top of his automobile, as the narrator continued: "When a limousine can parade openly through the streets of Dallas, there's a change that's come over America."[94] At the last minute, Ford's campaign leaders, fearing adverse public reaction, got cold feet and substituted generic footage of Ford for the "cherry bomb" and Dallas segments of the advertisement before it aired.

Ford proved more durable than his presidency, living longer than any other American president and dying in 2006 at age ninety-three. But the nation looked back at his tenure with some fondness. Republicans saw that Ford helped the country, and their party, recover from the Nixon scandals, while Democrats focused on the social liberalism (pro-choice on abortion, in favor of the Equal Rights Amendment) embraced by Ford and his wife, Betty.

In 2001, the John F. Kennedy Foundation gave Ford, then eighty-eight, its "Profiles in Courage" award for putting the nation's interests above his own career when he pardoned Nixon on September 8, 1974—the highly controversial decision that almost certainly cost Ford an elective term of his own. Presenting the award to Ford was Senator Ted Kennedy, who in 1974 had said that the president's pardon showed that he was "clearly out of touch with the vast majority" of Americans.[95] Accepting the honor, Ford offered a telling observation that applied to JFK as well as himself:

> To know Jack Kennedy, as I did, was to understand the true meaning of the word [courage]. Physical pain was an inseparable part of his life, but he never surrendered to it—any more than he yielded to freedom's enemies during the most dangerous moments of the nuclear age. President Kennedy understood that courage is not something to be gauged in a poll or located in a focus group. No adviser can spin it. No historian can backdate it. For, in the age-old contest between popularity and principle, only those willing to lose for their convictions are deserving of posterity's approval.[96]

Ford also left behind a somewhat surprising call for the complete release of all classified documents relating to the Kennedy assassination—an entreaty yet to be heeded, since fifty-thousand-plus pages of information, including key CIA records, are still kept from the public.[97] In a conversation with a trusted journalist, Thomas DeFrank, Ford gave permission to publish the following comment after his death, which DeFrank did in 2007: "The time has come to do it, but you have to be forewarned: there are some stories that'll come out that were never verified that could be harmful to some people . . . I'll just say some people that are known. You know how that happens— somebody investigates, somebody asks questions, and they make a statement. They're never verified, it's rumor, et cetera. That's gonna happen, and that's too bad."[98] Unfortunate or not, the revelations are a part of history, and after fifty years of delay, few will disagree with Ford's suggestion.

16

THE CARTERS AND THE KENNEDYS: DEMOCRATIC HATFIELDS AND McCOYS

NOT LONG AFTER JOHN KENNEDY'S ASSASSINATION, Democrats almost everywhere began to assume that at some point there would be a "Kennedy restoration"—another Kennedy in the White House. Bobby was the natural successor, but after his murder, all eyes turned to Edward. However, in 1968, while in mourning, and in 1972, following Chappaquiddick, Ted declined to run, much to the delight of Richard Nixon. To the surprise of many, burdened by family responsibilities, scandal's hangover, and probably concern for his own safety, Teddy refused to run in 1976, too. This was Kennedy's great missed opportunity to be president. While Chappaquiddick would still have been a considerable impediment for him, Richard Nixon's fall, a bad economy, and a weak, appointed GOP president might have given him enough openings to win.

Instead, a little-known former one-term governor of Georgia burst onto the scene with narrow wins in Iowa and New Hampshire, and before anyone knew all that much about him, Jimmy Carter was the Democratic candidate for president and the favorite to win in November. Carter's amazing rise was a product of the public's intense desire to find someone who was untainted by scandal and unfamiliar with the sordid ways of Washington. In that sense, Carter represented a clean break with the past.

Carter could not be called the inheritor of the JFK mantle in any tangible sense. If anything, the election of a man from the South recalled Lyndon Johnson, and the outcome contradicted the widespread expectation since Kennedy's assassination that somehow, some way, the next Democratic president would reinstate and continue what had been lost on November 22, 1963. Perhaps Carter's inability to fill the bill made his conflict with the Kennedys inevitable. Unavoidable or not, it came, and helped to destroy the Carter White House in time.

Carter's one true—if slight—connection to John Kennedy was through his mother, Lillian. She had been an alternate delegate to the 1964 Democratic National Convention, and brought home the very emotional story of RFK's tribute to his assassinated brother. "My mother was very deeply committed to the Kennedys, much more than I was, I have to say," Carter told me during a recent interview. "My favorite president in my lifetime was Truman." At age sixty-eight, "Miss Lillian," as she was known, joined JFK's Peace Corps and spent two years in a small village in India between 1966 and 1968. And as preposterous as it sounds today, the younger Jimmy Carter had often been compared to John Kennedy.[1] From certain angles there was a slight resemblance in hair, face, and smile, and a practiced gesture or two, which Carter and his supporters were more than happy to emphasize. Nothing has changed since; most Democrats who have run for president in the past half century have tried to evoke Kennedy comparisons.

Astonishingly, Carter had never even met a Democratic president when he was elected, and he felt no real obligation to defend their administrations. Carter put distance between himself and the immediate past president from his party, the still-unpopular Johnson—which necessitated a call of apology to his widow, Lady Bird Johnson (Carter was quoted in *Playboy* as saying, "I don't think I would ever take on the same frame of mind that Nixon or Johnson did—lying, cheating and distorting the truth . . .").[2] By contrast, Carter was more willing to embrace John Kennedy. Despite recent revelations about his private life, Kennedy retained the affections of much of the public. More important, JFK's story met Carter's political needs in 1976. Many of the attacks on Carter were reminiscent of those on Kennedy, such as those centered on religion. Carter's fundamentalist, evangelical Christianity was as alien to many Americans in 1976 as Catholicism had been for most Protestants in 1960. Given the JFK precedent, and the arguments Catholics made during the Kennedy-Nixon contest, it was a special irony that Catholics appeared especially suspicious of the Baptist Carter. In attempting to assuage Catholics, Carter cited Kennedy's campaign address to the Protestant ministers in Houston. Speaking to a meeting of the National Conference of Catholic Charities in early October 1976, Carter said Kennedy's prediction that one day a Jew or a Baptist would also be questioned because of his faith "has come to pass. I welcome the scrutiny, and I have not the slightest doubt that this year, once again, our national tradition of tolerance and fairness will prevail . . ."[3]

Carter also invoked President Kennedy to rebut the "inexperience" charge, reminding voters that JFK was viewed as not ready for the presidency and insufficiently trained in senior office. Like Kennedy in 1960, Carter was relatively young (fifty-two), and eleven years younger than President Ford. From his acceptance address at the Democratic National Convention to stump speeches around the nation, Carter echoed Kennedy's call to "get the nation moving again."[4]

In addition, Carter used Kennedy to ease the concerns of Northern liberals about electing a Southerner from a state with a troubling history on race. Carter's predecessor as governor had been the segregationist clown Lester Maddox, who won election in 1966 mainly on the strength of barring African Americans from his chicken restaurant.[5] So Carter reminded audiences around the country that Georgia had provided an even larger percentage of the vote for Kennedy than Massachusetts (62.5 percent, more than two points higher than the Bay State). Of course, this was due to Georgia's diehard, post–Civil War devotion to the Democratic Party, not a love for JFK. The Democratic streak in the Peach State ended in 1964, when Georgia became one of only six states to choose Barry Goldwater over Lyndon Johnson.

Even as he was praising John Kennedy and using him for his own purposes, Jimmy Carter was clashing with other Kennedys. One of Carter's opponents for the Democratic nomination was JFK's brother-in-law R. Sargent Shriver, the first director of the Peace Corps. Shriver naturally claimed the Kennedy mantle when announcing on September 20, 1975.[6] Surrounded by Kennedy relatives, Shriver invoked JFK's legacy and made clear that, with Ted Kennedy out of the race, he was the closest thing to a Kennedy in the ring. There were no memorable confrontations with Carter, though, since Shriver's bid was as uninspiring as it was brief. Shriver garnered only 8 percent of the vote in the New Hampshire primary, and he was quickly out of the contest.[7]

There were other "Kennedy moments" during the 1976 campaign. Jackie Kennedy, who had avoided most overtly political events since Robert Kennedy's assassination, made an appearance at the Democratic National Convention, not to give a speech but simply to sit in the VIP section. Bedlam ensued, and practically the entire convention assemblage, on the floor and the bleachers, moved as one thunderstruck herd in her direction.[8] An early indication of the friction that would define Carter's relationship with Senator Edward Kennedy emerged. Perhaps feeling a bit of replacement envy, Kennedy charged Carter with being "intentionally . . . indefinite and imprecise" on a host of issues.[9] Carter responded by asserting that he "didn't have to kowtow to anyone" to get the Democratic presidential nomination. Carter also all but admitted that he had used some salty language privately in rebutting Ted Kennedy: "I don't have to kiss his ass."[10] Senator Kennedy no doubt remembered that exchange. He may also have taken note of the occasional odd statement by Carter about President Kennedy. For instance, in a widely publicized July 1976 interview in the *Atlantic Monthly,* Carter made this comment: "I can see in retrospect what President Kennedy meant to the deprived people in this country and abroad . . . He never really did that much for them, but he made them think he cared."[11] The Kennedy clan was not the sort to let an insult pass without eventual retribution.

Meanwhile, Carter found John Kennedy helpful in yet another critical way. He studied the 1960 debate tapes for tips to use in his four encounters with President Ford.[12] Ford carefully reviewed the JFK-Nixon face-offs, too. After all, these were the only presidential debates in American history up to that time, and the precedent had led Ford and Carter to their own debate pact. The relatively green Carter needed to show he could endure high-pressured scrutiny and stand toe to toe with the incumbent, and Ford was desperate to regain some ground after every poll showed him well behind Carter after Labor Day.[13] Contemporaneous notes and reports indicate that both men studied the gestures, facial expressions, and other visual cues of the 1960 candidates closely.[14] The lesson of Kennedy's debate triumph—achieved as much by style as substance—had not been lost in the ensuing sixteen years. Meanwhile, Nixon still served as an example of what not to do.

Just as JFK would not have been elected without his face-offs with Nixon, Jimmy Carter might well have lost his close battle with Ford had it not been for the incumbent president's "free Poland" gaffe in a mid-October debate. Thanks to an improved economy and fading memories of the Nixon pardon, Ford had been gaining steadily on Carter, but his mistake in appearing to suggest the Soviet Union did not control Eastern Europe derailed the Republican's momentum. Ford's own polling showed how badly the mistake, and his refusal to clarify it quickly, cost him.[15] Some observers believed that if the campaign had been a week or so longer, Ford would have had time to recover fully and surpass Carter, at least in the Electoral College.

Like John F. Kennedy, Jimmy Carter gained the White House on a thin mandate. On November 2, 1976, Carter was elected with just 50.2 percent of the national vote and a close Electoral College margin of 297–240 over President Ford. His majority was built on a sweep of the South (save Virginia) plus all the Dixie Border States except Oklahoma. Twenty states were decided by five percentage points or less—the hallmark of a highly competitive, truly national contest.* What had seemed an easy prospective victory in the summer became a nail-biter in the fall, and Carter recognized he had not done as well as he had hoped or expected. When Mississippi finally fell into his column and put him over the top in the wee hours of election night, Carter pledged to be a better president than he had been a candidate.[16]

Almost all Democrats in the House and most in the Senate had won easily,

---

* Compare this to the mere four states decided by 5 percent or less in the 2012 presidential contest between President Obama and Republican nominee Mitt Romney.

far outpacing Carter's vote totals, and so they felt no special obligation to the new president they barely knew.[17] Despite a long campaign, Carter was nearly unknown to Washington when he arrived to take the oath of office in January 1977. He would need the help of longtime Capitol Hill power brokers, including Ted Kennedy, to succeed, but more often than not, Carter did not receive the assistance—or failed to ask in time-honored Washington ways. The thirty-ninth president didn't enjoy after-hours schmoozing with legislative barons, and even worse, he thought of the U.S. Congress as a national version of the part-time Georgia legislature. As Carter would learn to his dismay, he could not dictate even to a heavily Democratic Congress, especially when he was a stranger in their midst. Many members of Congress, including Ted Kennedy, were much more liberal than Carter and, now that Democrats again ruled the roost in Washington, they were determined to extend the New Deal and Great Society in ways that a budget-balancing Carter disliked. The seeds of conflict were sown even before Carter had unpacked his bags.

LITTLE OF THIS was apparent on January 20, 1977, as Carter began his presidency in a moment of hope and good feelings, but also amid stark national limitations that did not seem evident at John Kennedy's inauguration sixteen years earlier. JFK's boldness and high-flying rhetoric at a time when the United States was utterly preeminent in the world were replaced by Carter's subdued delivery, his modest goals of governmental competence and simple ethics, and the admonition that "we cannot afford to do everything."[18] Vietnam, Watergate, oil shocks, and inflation had humbled America and the presidency itself. The most memorable part of the day was not Carter's address but his open walk with the entire Carter family from the Capitol all the way to the White House—a decision that worried, indeed horrified, the Secret Service.[19]

Once he reached the Oval Office for the first time as president, Carter was surprised to find that the desk was not the one he had seen in pictures from John Kennedy's time. In his memoirs, Carter recalled that his first decision as chief executive was to restore the Kennedy era's "Resolute desk," the nineteenth-century gift from Queen Victoria to America; it was stored at the Smithsonian but was quickly brought to the White House.[20]

President Carter's White House staff was dominated by his "Georgia Mafia," including campaign aides Hamilton Jordan (appointed chief of staff) and Jody Powell (press secretary). Yet the new Democratic president also needed experienced hands, and he relied on at least a few recycled appointees from the Kennedy years. JFK's secretary of the Army, Cyrus Vance, became Carter's secretary of state, for example, and Harold Brown, who held a middle-rank post in Kennedy's Defense Department, became Carter's secretary of defense. Probably the best known of the Kennedy aides tapped by Carter was the JFK counselor and speechwriter Theodore Sorensen, designated now to be director of the CIA. Alas, this appointment was not to be.

Sorensen had backed Carter and helped to smooth tensions with liberals, and Carter was clearly grateful. But prior to confirmation, it was revealed that Sorensen had registered for the military draft as a conscientious objector who would serve only in a noncombat role. Another charge was that he had removed classified papers from the White House at the end of the Kennedy administration. Carter quickly withdrew the nomination,[21] a decision that still rankled Sorensen more than three decades later: "Do not exaggerate [Carter's] admiration of me, inasmuch as he pulled the rug out from under me soon after appointing me . . ."[22]

With these few exceptions, though, Jimmy Carter's time in the White House marked a considerable change from the struggles that had gripped JFK and his three immediate successors. America seemed ready for a blank slate, and the nation appeared determined to move on. Events, however, tugged the nation backward. A persistent energy crisis that began in the Nixon-Ford years deepened and dragged the economy lower. The Watergate-inspired end to the imperial presidency kept Carter on a shorter leash than his predecessors, and he was stripped of some of the majesty of the executive office. After the multitude of Nixon scandals, Carter had to be very sensitive to any appointee's behavior that could be construed as unethical. In addition, the Vietnam hangover made Americans wary of any attempt by Carter to take military action and commit the country to prolonged involvement abroad. If not real isolationism, the public's sentiment was akin to fear of flying after a rough crash landing. Most citizens had had their fill both of the world and of politicians, and were far less inclined to "ask what they could do for their country."

At first Carter believed that a large Democratic Senate majority would help speed his programs to passage. But he hadn't counted on the determined opposition of Ted Kennedy as his term wore on. "The first year that I was in office Kennedy had the best voting record of any member of the House or Senate in supporting my proposals," Carter recalled. In time, however, Kennedy began derailing bills that had originated in the Oval Office—even some he mostly agreed with in principle. President Carter cited Medicare as a major example. "The last two years I was in office he was always opposing anything I did, even including comprehensive health care. He blocked my effort to apply Medicare to all ages step-by-step, which would have been, and still is, the best approach to comprehensive medical care. I had the money to move Medicare to cover not only old people, but also the first number of years of life, like [ages] one to five, and then I had a step-by-step proposal to cover every age group in the nation. It was a very good program and we had the money to do it then. But he blocked it and he was powerful enough that his opposition prevailed." President Carter didn't sugarcoat his view of his erstwhile foe from Massachusetts: "Ted Kennedy was a pain in my ass the last two years I was in office—the worst problem I had [during] the last two years."[23]

Kennedy's obstructionism notwithstanding, Carter's personal failures, such as an uninspiring oratorical style, the inability to deal successfully with Congress on many big agenda items, and his devotion to minutiae in the Oval Office (including assigning use of the White House tennis courts), did not help his presidency. But mainly Carter was overcome by events that spun far out of his control, from high inflation, interest rates, and unemployment to the Iran hostage crisis and the Soviet invasion of Afghanistan. Carter appeared incapable of dealing with these problems, and the United States took on the image once more of the pitiful, helpless giant. Jimmy Carter was vulnerable in 1980, and politicians in both parties sensed it.

INTO THE BREACH stepped Ted Kennedy. After having refused to run for president in the three previous elections, he startled the political world by announcing his candidacy on November 7, 1979. It was easy to see why Kennedy made the race: Most liberals and labor unions were clamoring for him to oust Carter, and virtually every national poll for a year or so had shown Kennedy defeating Carter handily, often by as much as two to one.[24] President Carter's popularity had fallen into the twenties, and he was widely seen as an ineffective leader. By August 1979 Kennedy had made the decision to challenge Carter, and some Democrats made the incorrect assumption that it was all over but the shouting. Instead, a feisty Carter focused again on Ted Kennedy's posterior. Having asserted in 1976 that he did not have to kiss Kennedy's ass to become president, Carter now said privately (at a White House breakfast with some Democratic members of Congress) that he would "whip his ass." "When I went to Alaska, the governor gave me a whip," Carter remembered with a chuckle.[25]

The president proceeded to do just that in a difficult primary campaign. The personal antagonism between Carter and Kennedy would grow to the point where it directly contributed to Carter's landslide defeat in the fall of 1980. As Carter harshly sized it up, he was running against someone who "felt entitled to be president because of the tragic legacy of his brothers" but had done little to earn the office on his own.[26] After a lunch with Vice President Walter Mondale, Carter wrote down his view of Ted Kennedy in a diary: "As a student he was kicked out of college; he's my age but unsuccessful; as majority whip in the Senate, he was defeated after his first term; his preoccupation [is] with national health insurance while never able to get the bill out of his own subcommittee in twelve years . . ."[27]

A special moment intervened before the battle commenced, an opportunity for President Carter to use his shared office with John Kennedy to draw distinctions with Ted—and perhaps to assert why the incumbent was a more fitting White House occupant than JFK's brother. On October 20, 1979, the John F. Kennedy Library was dedicated in Boston, and as tradition dictates at these occasions, the sitting president was the main orator. In rare form, Jimmy Carter rose to the rhetorical challenge in front of a strongly pro–Edward Kennedy assemblage. Every inch the president, he gave a moving address. Carter first tweaked Ted with the words of Jack, to the loud laughter of the gathered dignitaries, including Ted:

> In a press conference in March 1962, when the ravages of being president were beginning to show on his face, he was asked this two-part question: "Mr. President, your brother Ted said recently on television that after seeing the cares of office on you, he wasn't sure he would ever be interested in being president." And the questioner continued, "I wonder if you could tell us whether, first, if you had it to do over again, you would work for the presidency and, second, whether you can recommend this job to others?" The president replied, "Well, the answer to the first question is yes, and the second is no. I do not recommend it to others—at least for a while." As you can well see, President Kennedy's wit and also his wisdom is certainly as relevant today as it was then.[28]

Carter skillfully wove together Kennedy's great goals of civil rights at home and peace abroad with his own emphasis on human rights and arms control. He also pointed out the main difference created by the energy crisis, economic scarcity, and the public reaction to Vietnam: America could no longer do whatever it wanted, and the nation's president had far less maneuverability than in John Kennedy's time. The abundant resources and optimistic national character that defined JFK's years were absent in the 1970s. Perhaps again with Ted in mind, Carter insisted, "The world of 1980 is as different from what it was in 1960 as the world of 1960 was from that of 1940." Carter continued,

> But . . . the essence of President Kennedy's message—the appeal for unselfish dedication to the common good—is more urgent than it ever was. The spirit that he evoked—the spirit of sacrifice, of

patriotism, of unstinting dedication—is the same spirit that will bring us safely through the adversities that we face today. The over-arching purpose of this nation remains the same: to build a just so-ciety in a secure America living at peace with the other nations of the world.[29]

The crowd was hushed as the usually unemotional Carter told an intimate story about November 22, 1963:

On that November day, almost sixteen years ago, a terrible moment was frozen in the lives of many of us here. I remember that I climbed down from the seat of a tractor, unhooked a farm trailer, and walked into my warehouse to weigh a load of grain. I was told by a group of farmers that the president had been shot. I went outside, knelt on the steps, and began to pray. In a few minutes, I learned that he had not lived. It was a grievous personal loss—my president. I wept openly for the first time in more than ten years—for the first time since the day my own father died. People wept in Boston and in Paris, in Atlanta and in Warsaw, in San Francisco and in New Delhi. More than anyone had realized before that day, the spirit of this young American president had taken hold of the hearts and the imaginations of countless millions of people all over the world.

At the time, the tragedy in Dallas seemed an isolated convulsion of madness. But in retrospect, it appears near the beginning of a time of darkness. From Vietnam to Cambodia, from Los Angeles to Memphis, from Kent State to Watergate, the American spirit suffered under one shock after another, and the confidence of our people was deeply shaken.[30]

Had Carter been this eloquent regularly, had he more often explained the forces shaping the United States and the globe persuasively, his presidency might have thrived to a much greater degree, with or without the opposition of Ted Kennedy.

Even at this intentionally unifying event, there were overt signs of the Carter-Kennedy feud. "I remember when I went to the Kennedy library, it was my Southern custom that when I met a woman, I went to kiss her on the cheek," President Carter observed. But when he reached out to Jackie in that way, "She flinched away from me. And that may have been because of the women's liberation movement or something like that. I didn't pay much attention to it, but one of the *Washington Post* reporters wrote an article about it. And one of Robert Kennedy's sons, before I spoke, had some fairly negative things to say about me. But I was president, I just grinned and ignored it. I felt that maybe I didn't need to respond to that."[31]

Edward Moore Kennedy formally announced for president in Boston's Faneuil Hall on November 7, but he had damaged himself a few days earlier in an interview on CBS with the journalist and Kennedy family friend Roger Mudd, when the senator could not seem to answer in a coherent fashion a simple question: "Why do you want to be president?"[32] Nonetheless, Kennedy came galloping out of the gate when he attacked Carter's leadership in his announcement: "For many months we have been sinking into crisis. Yet, we hear no clear summons from the center of power. Aims are not set; the means of realizing them are neglected. Conflicts in directions confuse our purpose. Government falters. Fears spread that our leaders have resigned themselves to retreat. This country is not prepared to sound retreat. It is ready to advance. It is willing to make a stand. And so am I." Kennedy's candidacy launch was given massive coverage, as would be expected, but—perhaps anticipating an eventual showdown with Carter—reporters had swarmed Kennedy's public events for much of the president's term. "He became an almost constant problem for me," Carter noted. "Every time Kennedy spoke he got more coverage than I did as president. You know, the Kennedy family had [broad] access to the news media, and still does, as a matter of fact."[33]

Yet despite a lifetime of political experience, Kennedy had forgotten that a candidate looks best before he becomes a formal contender; the above-the-fray statesman being pursued by partisan admirers who hope he will run is always superior to the grubby politician lusting after high office while soliciting votes in the trenches. Ted Kennedy was also well to the left of an American electorate growing more conservative in the late 1970s. This gave Carter the opportunity to claim that he, not Ted, was the true inheritor of John Kennedy's moderate-conservative political philosophy, which included fiscal responsibility and a strong defense. While Carter acknowledged Ted was "blood kin" to Jack, he asserted that, based on critical issues facing America, "I feel a very close kinship with President Kennedy also." As Carter put it, in retrospect, "There's no doubt that John Kennedy was more [of a] pragmatist than Ted Kennedy. I think Ted was more of a pure liberal. I was very conservative on improving the military and on balancing the budget. But I was deeply committed to human rights, so I had kind of a mixture. So I was much more compatible with John Kennedy's basic philosophy than Ted's."[34]

Carter supporters and many news organizations were soon reviewing the unflattering story of Chappaquiddick and the death of Mary Jo Kopechne. The character issue generated by Chappaquiddick and many whispered reports of Kennedy's extramarital activities would follow the candidate every day of the campaign, just as he had always feared. And passions ran so high that the Secret Service took extraordinary precautions to try to preserve Kennedy's life. A pair of bulletproof vests—one built into a raincoat and the other constructed as an undergarment—became a frequent part of Kennedy's wardrobe, especially in parades.[35]

While Kennedy remained safe, his candidacy was mortally wounded by an event no one could have foreseen. Just three days before Kennedy announced, American hostages were taken in Tehran. Few understood at the time how this would work against Kennedy, in combination with the late-December Soviet invasion of Afghanistan. The twin foreign crises gave Carter the excuse to run a presidential "Rose Garden" campaign, as he ignored Kennedy's attacks and created nonpartisan headlines with regular White House briefings about vital international concerns. In the first months, as is usually the case, the public rallied around the commander in chief while he focused on battling foreign enemies, not Ted Kennedy. The weekly "death to Carter" rallies in Iran had the unintended effect of elevating a previously unpopular president.

Sure enough, Carter rode the Rose Garden wave through Iowa in January, where the caucuses gave Carter a landslide 59 percent victory, and New Hampshire in February, where Carter defeated Kennedy 47 to 37 percent in a state next door to Massachusetts. Carter proceeded to sweep the South in March and even won critical Illinois, where Kennedy once seemed to have had a large edge, by 65 to 30 percent on March 18. Early on, it appeared that Kennedy had failed and Carter would be renominated—a realization that conversely freed up Democrats to express their underlying unhappiness with the president. On March 25, aided by Jewish support generated by a Carter administration vote in the United Nations against Israeli settlements in the West Bank, Kennedy shocked Carter by capturing New York, 59 to 41 percent, and he won neighboring Connecticut as well. A small but significant Kennedy win in Pennsylvania followed in April. Even though Carter won almost all of the May primaries in friendlier territory, the season ended on a disastrous note for the president. On June 3 Ted Kennedy won California by 8 percentage points and New Jersey by 18, as well as New Mexico, Rhode Island, and South Dakota. Overall, Carter had garnered 9.6 million votes in the primary contests (51 percent of the total) to Kennedy's almost 7 million (37 percent), and Carter had far more than the minimum number of delegates needed to secure the nomination, but the senator's strong finish gave him the incentive to refuse to withdraw. Instead of quitting, Kennedy launched a new campaign to have the Democratic National Convention pass a rule to "unpledge" the delegates—that is, free them up to "vote their conscience" in an open convention.[36] It was yet another nightmare for President Carter, an extension of the divisive internecine battle all the way to the edge of the general election, with little time for the wounds to heal before he faced the Reagan challenge. The Republican had cleanly wrapped up his nomination in May, when his most serious challenger, former CIA director George H. W. Bush, gave way. Reagan had not completely reunited the GOP, but the party's delight at President Carter's continuing troubles—and its sense that victory was possible—kept dissension to a minimum.

This was hardly the only worry on Carter's plate. The U.S. economy continued to exhibit severe weakness, and his efforts to free the hostages in Iran took a tragic turn.[37] Convinced that the leaders of Iran were not seriously pursuing negotiations, Carter gave his approval to a secret April 1980 rescue mission. The well-trained troops never reached Tehran, though, because of a terrible helicopter accident in the Iranian desert, which killed eight men, aborted the mission, and gave a huge propaganda victory to the hostage takers.[38] Secretary of State Cyrus Vance, who had become disenchanted with Carter and opposed the mission as reckless, resigned in protest.[39]

Discouraged by the disaster in the desert and understanding he needed to take responsibility, Carter asked press secretary Jody Powell to get him the speech President Kennedy had made after the Bay of Pigs invasion.[40] In a press conference at the end of April, Carter delivered a statement not unlike that of JFK: "It was my responsibility as president to launch this mission. It was my responsibility to terminate the mission when it ended . . . There is a deeper failure than that of incomplete success, and that is the failure to attempt a worthy effort, a failure to try. This is a sentiment shared by the men who went on the mission."[41] Long afterward, Carter would say, when asked to name his regrets about his presidency, he most wished he had sent along an extra helicopter on the rescue mission. Whether that would have resulted in a successful hostage rescue will forever be unknown, but this incident, as much as any in Carter's last year, solidified his image as that of a struggling leader whose bad luck or incompetence made solving the country's deep-seated problems all but impossible.

Carter's summer of misery culminated at the mid-August Democratic Convention in New York. What should have been a celebration of a hard-earned nomination instead became a soap opera about Ted Kennedy. The entire first day was devoted to the Kennedy effort to open up the convention, which was ultimately defeated. The convention's second day was consumed by speculation about how Kennedy would handle the end of his campaign. That night, Kennedy gave his answer in a fiery speech; along with his 1968 eulogy of his brother Bobby, it may have been his best. Recounting his views of what the Democratic Party stood for, Kennedy mounted a rhetorical tour de force that concluded with these lines: "For me, a few hours ago, this campaign came to an end. For all those whose cares have been our concern, the work goes on, the cause endures, the hope still lives, and the dream shall never die."[42] The Kennedy delegates went wild, and the convention was at a standstill for a lengthy period. While Kennedy had run an ineffective campaign and had often been an inarticulate candidate, his final effort exceeded anything Carter could deliver in his acceptance address.

As expected, Carter's speech at the convention's conclusion was mainly forgettable. Worse, Kennedy decided to sulk about his defeat, and he put his pique on display that evening in an exceptionally damaging way. Having missed Carter's address, Kennedy drove over from his hotel for the traditional end-of-convention love feast on stage, when all the party's grandees, whatever their real feelings, are expected to join hands in victory salutes and give unity smiles to network cameras and voters at home. With balloons and confetti falling, Carter spied Kennedy on the platform and sought him out for the traditional raising of the arms. Embarrassingly, the incumbent president chased the vanquished challenger all over the stage but never got what he sought. TV anchormen detailed every humiliating second for the millions watching, as Carter's convention finale flopped. Here is how Carter himself later described it: "Ostentatiously, Kennedy refused to shake my extended hand, and this became one of the main news stories from the convention . . . [A]fter much reflection, I have concluded that there is little I could have done to prevent Kennedy's attempt to remove me from the political office that he considered his justifiable family heritage." Carter confirmed this opinion during our 2013 conversation: "Ted Kennedy just felt that he should have been president, that he was the descendant of John Kennedy and Robert Kennedy, and therefore he deserved to be president."[43] President Carter was never able to put the pieces of the Democratic coalition back together. Senator Kennedy campaigned for Carter and the Democratic ticket as the autumn wore on, and a "Carter-Kennedy Unity Celebration" was held in mid-October at which nice things were said and pleasant gestures were made. Just as at the JFK Library dedication a year earlier, Carter made John Kennedy one of the prime subjects of his address, in an attempt to woo Edward Kennedy and his followers. Carter even presented a watercolor of JFK, given to Carter by artist Jamie Wyeth during the 1976 campaign, as a gift for the JFK Library. But nothing could soften Kennedy's negative view of the president. "After I got the nomination, I met with Ted Kennedy twice privately, to see what he wanted, what I could do to assuage him, how I could get him to support me," Carter remembered. "And he was very cool toward me personally. He was determined, after he lost the nomination, that I would not be elected. I think Kennedy was very happy when Reagan was elected. Kennedy was very bitter toward me for the rest of his life."[44]

The electoral damage done by Kennedy's split with Carter was lasting.

Many Kennedy Democrats defected to Republican Reagan or the moderate independent candidate, Congressman John Anderson of Illinois, which partially explains Reagan's carrying of Massachusetts and a host of normally liberal Northeastern and Midwestern states. Just 61 percent of Kennedy's voters from the Democratic primaries stayed with the party and backed Carter in November. A remarkably high 28 percent cast a ballot for Reagan, and 11 percent voted for Anderson. Voting studies indicated that Anderson took votes from both Carter and Reagan, uniting some Democrats and Independents disappointed with the president's performance as well as some Republicans who believed Reagan was too conservative. Overall, however, Anderson's presence was probably more damaging to Carter; the independent often joined Reagan to double-team the incumbent, who seemed increasingly enfeebled.[45]

One question that can never be definitively answered is whether Ted Kennedy, America's foremost liberal, was secretly pleased that his nemesis Carter, a moderate, lost to Reagan, the most conservative president in generations. In a 1980 diary entry, Carter puzzled about the truth of Kennedy's intentions, asking, "We were uncertain about Kennedy's ultimate goal. Was it to be elected himself, or did he just want to prevent my reelection?"[46] While Kennedy fought Reagan's programs and nominees with relish throughout the Californian's White House years, aides of both men noted their warm personal relationship for most of that time.[47] If the personal is the political, then we have our answer.

Whatever the truth about Ted Kennedy's outlook, it is difficult to dispute that the Kennedys had played a role in the destruction of the two Democratic presidencies succeeding JFK. For Jimmy Carter, one nagging question remained: How did Ted Kennedy manage to block key Carter initiatives in the Senate? The president offered an intriguing theory, that Senator Kennedy had a private alliance with Democratic Majority Leader Robert Byrd of West Virginia. "My impression is that Kennedy promised Bob Byrd that if he was elected president that he would appoint Byrd to the Supreme Court."[48]

Both Lyndon Johnson and Jimmy Carter came to be seen by the Kennedy clan as usurpers. Policy was ostensibly at the heart of the opposition provided by both Robert and Edward Kennedy to LBJ and Carter, yet some measure of jealousy and resentment may also have been motivations. The elite band of national players, certainly including the Kennedys, is not known for small egos and tiny vanities. That a Kennedy could help to end a Democratic presidency in 1980 was a measure of the continuing power of the name; that a Kennedy would once again fail to attain the highest office suggests the limitations of the family name. Perhaps an unintended consequence of John F. Kennedy's large legacy in the popular imagination was that no other, lesser Kennedy seemed worthy of the White House.

In a comparative way, the manifest failures and deep unpopularity of the Carter presidency enhanced the memory of the Kennedy White House. Whereas Kennedy presided over a soaring, preeminent American economy, Carter represented a nation whose financial system could no longer produce the bounty of the 1960s. JFK scored a foreign policy triumph for the ages in the Cuban Missile Crisis, while Carter's longest-lasting international episode was the humiliating Iran hostage saga. (The Panama Canal treaty and the Camp David peace between Israel and Egypt were Carter coups, but most Americans have to search their memories for them, while the wounds from Iran remain fresh thirty years later.)

John Kennedy's rhetoric and policies inspired the people of his time and generations to come; despite many notable achievements, little of what Jimmy Carter did or said as president is remembered. Doom and gloom, and a weary, exhausted persona, came to define Carter in his time. Fortunately for Carter, his lengthy post-presidency, filled with humanitarian acts and global efforts to conquer disease and strengthen human rights, have added considerable luster to his record. In 2002 the former president received the Nobel Peace Prize. Partly, the award came to Carter because of his many peace-keeping and election-supervising missions abroad, which are often potentially perilous, putting him at greater risk than he felt he was as president. "I have had two or three threats to my life after I came home [to Georgia] from the White House. When I go on an overseas trip almost invariably, I get a report from the Secret Service that where I'm going is very dangerous," Carter revealed. "And sometimes they ask me not to go, and I go anyway. They and I both just laugh about it. So I have been more concerned about my safety in doing the Carter Center's business overseas than I ever was in the White House."[49]

President Carter was the fourth arguably unsuccessful chief executive to follow JFK, and the combined calamities of LBJ, Nixon, Ford, and Carter elevated Kennedy's mainly successful tenure further. Could no one else get it right? Ronald Reagan would finally provide an answer that pleased most Americans. Few would have thought at the outset that a sixty-nine-year-old conservative Republican would eventually offer the closest approximation to Kennedy's White House, but the conventional wisdom would be transformed during the 1980s.

REAGAN AND KENNEDY: OPPOSITES ATTRACT

AT FIRST GLANCE, JOHN F. KENNEDY and Ronald Reagan might appear to have had little in common other than the presidency. Democrat Kennedy was the youngest elected president and Republican Reagan the oldest. Kennedy came from inherited wealth, while Reagan grew up poor. Kennedy's whole adult lifetime was devoted to politics, while Reagan had a long first career in Hollywood. Kennedy was a pragmatic, generic Democrat, while Reagan was the leader of an ideological crusade among conservatives to take control of the Republican Party.

All these differences hold true, yet among Kennedy's successors in the White House, none came closer to embodying the "Kennedy mystique" than Ronald Reagan. Perhaps a bit of it was the shared Irish blood; a genealogical tracing linked the Kennedy and Reagan clans, which were both related to the famed tenth-century Irish king Brian Boru.[1] Confident and self-assured, comfortable in his own skin, Reagan governed with qualities reminiscent of JFK. No characteristic linked the two presidents more than a playful, self-deprecating sense of humor—a trait lacking in almost all other modern occupants of the Oval Office.[2] Reagan was a Democrat for much of his life, and he was bound to a place and a culture that Kennedy loved well—Hollywood. Perhaps as a consequence, no two modern presidents have ever been so comfortable in front of the camera; both were naturals, with their communication skills key to their success as chief executive.

Ideologically, they were not as far apart on many issues as observers would first have guessed. The Kennedy tax cut became the model for Reagan's. To the extent that social issues were addressed in the early 1960s, Kennedy was as much a traditionalist as Reagan. Both Kennedy and Reagan were Cold Warriors, with a hard-line stance against the Communists from Russia to Cuba. Still, both negotiated major arms control treaties during their time.

Perhaps the parallels make sense because Kennedy and Reagan were generational contemporaries. JFK is frozen in time in his forties, but he would have been sixty-three years old when Reagan took office at age sixty-nine.

They were shaped by the same domestic upheavals, world wars, and social norms. And they were both blessed by fate and family with winning personalities and great good luck in the political arena.

THE TRANSFORMATION OF Ronald Reagan from loyal FDR Democrat to Goldwater Republican may have been a natural evolution promoted by second wife Nancy Reagan's conservative stepfather, the neurosurgeon Dr. Loyal Davis.[3] But it was also a by-product of Reagan's transition from Hollywood B-movie star to the national spokesperson for General Electric, beginning in 1954. Reagan's eight years of hosting *General Electric Theater* on TV and touring the nation as a GE representative, giving speeches to conservative, business-oriented audiences, encouraged the development of Reagan's Republican political perspectives.

By 1956 Reagan was campaigning as a Democrat for President Eisenhower's reelection campaign, and he continued to play the role for Vice President Nixon in 1960 despite having worked hard for Nixon's 1950 Democratic opponent for U.S. Senate, Helen Gahagan Douglas. In a revealing letter to Nixon dated July 15, 1960, Reagan made clear that he had already fully embraced the philosophy that would become his presidential trademark:

> Unfortunately, [Kennedy] is a powerful speaker with an appeal to the emotions. He leaves little doubt that his idea of the "challenging new world" is one in which the Federal Government will grow bigger and do more and of course spend more. I know there must be some short-sighted people in the Republican Party who will advise that the Republicans should try to "out liberal" him. In my opinion this would be fatal.
>
> One last thought—shouldn't someone tag Mr. Kennedy's bold new imaginative program with its proper age? Under the tousled boyish haircut is still old Karl Marx—first launched a century ago. There is nothing new in the idea of a Government being Big Brother to us all. Hitler called his "State Socialism" and way before him it was "benevolent monarchy."[4]

Reagan's comparison of JFK's views to those of Marx, Hitler, and long-ago kings is outlandish, given Kennedy's moderate to conservative presidency, and it would be contradicted by President Reagan's own firm embrace of some of JFK's foreign and domestic policies. Yet Reagan's 1960 anti-Kennedy broadside has become a standard rhetorical theme in GOP evaluation of Democrats over the decades—evocative of the party's modern-day critique of

Barack Obama (though Obama is unquestionably well to the left of JFK). Democratic presidential nominee Walter Mondale tried to use this letter to Nixon to discredit Reagan in 1984, an effort that failed badly, further reinforcing Reagan's fabled "Teflon" coating.[5] The usual rule in politics is that invoking Hitler in order to smear opponents results in backfire and backlash. The letter was not made public in 1960, and for that, Nixon could be grateful.[6]

During the 1960 campaign, Reagan was apparently shown photographs of JFK "going in and out of hotel rooms with different women." Perhaps reflecting lessons learned in Hollywood, Reagan opposed their use in the campaign, reportedly saying, "We have to base elections on issues and a candidate's ability to lead. There are bad husbands who are good leaders, and there are good husbands who are bad leaders. Those photos are about a personal matter between Mr. Kennedy and his wife."[7]

Even more to Reagan's credit, once he shifted to the GOP, he made no attempt to curry favor with JFK's popular Democratic administration. The GE platform kept Reagan in demand, and he held little back, attacking Washington on everything from JFK's alleged kowtowing to the "roughnecks of the Kremlin" to "welfare statism" at home. Reagan also claimed that some told him, "I was the most popular speaker in the country after President Kennedy. And after a while I noticed something very interesting. I would go into a city and find out at the other end of town, there'd be a member of the Kennedy cabinet. After a while I realized it was deliberate. I guess I was getting too much attention to suit them."[8] It may be that the Kennedy White House saw what millions of Republicans were starting to recognize: Ronald Reagan offered Kennedyesque glitz and glamor with a conservative flavor.

There may have been something to Reagan's allegation about a Kennedy vendetta against him. Michael Reagan has asserted that General Electric "was in the midst of negotiating some government contracts" when "Bobby Kennedy, the attorney general of the United States, bluntly informed GE that if the company wished to do business with the U.S. government, it would get rid of *General Electric Theater* and fire the host . . . Within forty-eight hours of Bobby Kennedy's call, the show was cancelled and Ronald Reagan was out of a job."[9] The irony here is that had Reagan continued to host *General Electric Theater*, he probably wouldn't have run for governor of California, or become president. Could the Kennedy administration have started Reagan on his elective path to the White House?

To no one's surprise, Reagan changed his party registration from Democrat to Republican in 1962. He went all out for Barry Goldwater in 1964, giving the most memorable televised defense of the GOP presidential nominee in the entire campaign on October 27, 1964, near the campaign's conclusion.[10] This effort endeared Reagan to conservatives everywhere, and the response encouraged him to seek the governorship of California in 1966. This midterm election year was a perfect environment for Reagan's tough rhetoric about welfare, crime, student protests, and government waste. The anti-LBJ undercurrent helped Reagan soundly defeat two-term Democratic governor Edmund G. "Pat" Brown, the father of future governor Jerry Brown. Reagan's long climb to the presidency had begun in earnest.

As a new governor, Reagan's trajectory intersected once more with the Kennedys. In May 1967, CBS decided to pair him up with Senator Robert F. Kennedy in a transcontinental debate about Vietnam and U.S. foreign policy. Reagan was a staunch supporter of the Vietnam War—though not the manner in which Lyndon Johnson was waging the conflict—while RFK was beginning his turn to become a fierce critic of Johnson and Vietnam. An estimated 15 million Americans watched the face-off between Reagan in Sacramento and Kennedy in New York City, with students in London asking tough questions of them both. Reagan took the confrontation seriously, commissioning a lengthy memo from his staff and rehearsing with aides a day before the event, but Kennedy did no preparation. As a consequence, Reagan scored big, robustly defending the U.S. role abroad while Kennedy appeared hesitant and meek. It was no surprise that Kennedy remarked afterward, "Who the fuck got me into this?"[11] Had Reagan been the cunning sort, he might have seen his debate victory as revenge for RFK's earlier role in his firing from General Electric.

Already impressed with Reagan, Republicans took further note of him after the Reagan-RFK face-off. Finally, they had a champion who could best a Kennedy on television. The contrast with the 1960 JFK-Nixon debates was stark. Even though Reagan had served only a few months in his first office, whispers began that Reagan should run for president in 1968. He hesitated at first, and two other governors—Michigan's George Romney and New York's Nelson Rockefeller—became the main rivals for former vice president Nixon. By the spring, however, with Romney out of the race and Rockefeller faltering, Reagan warmed to the idea and assumed "testing the waters" status. But Nixon was too far ahead. Reagan secured over 20 percent of the vote in just two primaries, Nebraska on May 14 and Oregon on May 28. He was accorded "favorite son" status in California and garnered 1,525,000 votes on June 4, 100 percent of the total on the GOP side, though this received little attention in the aftermath of the shooting of Robert Kennedy late that night. Because of California, though, Reagan actually outpolled Nixon, 1,696,000 (37.9 percent) to 1,679,000 (37.5 percent) in all the 1968 primaries combined. By the time of the convention, Reagan had considered joining forces with Rockefeller in a "stop Nixon" coalition, but it was far too late. Nixon already had a majority (692) of the delegate votes, to Rockefeller's 277 and Reagan's 182.

The presidential bug had burrowed deep into Reagan's core, however. He ran for and won reelection as governor in 1970, and looked to 1976. Wisely, Reagan decided not to run for a third term as governor in the heavily Democratic year of 1974, when he might well have lost, and planned instead to target the politically weak incumbent president, Gerald Ford. In a titanic battle that went right to the 1976 convention, the more moderate Ford defeated Reagan by a close delegate tally of 1,187 to 1,070. When Jimmy Carter defeated Ford in November, Reagan, at age sixty-five, figured his time had passed. If Carter served eight years, Reagan would be seventy-three in 1984, probably too old to win nomination or election.

During the Carter years, Reagan stayed in the public eye and delivered a series of radio broadcasts focused on contemporary political issues. When the House Select Committee on Assassinations released its final report on JFK's murder in 1979, Reagan may have surprised some of his listening audience by laying out the case for a Communist conspiracy:

> I'd like to comment on a conspiracy theory in the Kennedy case that seems to have been overlooked . . . [H]ave we hesitated to investigate the possibility that Oswald might have been carrying out a plot engineered by an international agency? Even the original investigation by the Warren Commission seems to have ignored some obvious clues and been rather in haste to settle for Oswald as a lone killer.
>
> Former Marine Lee Harvey Oswald gave up his American citizenship and moved to Russia. He learned the Russian language before he defected. Someone must have helped him do this. Once in Russia, he married the niece of a colonel in the Soviet spy organization, the KGB. Thanks to that marriage, he lived at a level of luxury above that of the average citizen in Russia. While he is supposed to have recanted his favorable views on the USSR, it does seem strangely unlike the Soviets that he was allowed to return to the United States with his Russian wife . . . The Warren Commission was evidently unimpressed with the fact that he was an enthusiastic member of the pro-Castro Fair Play for Cuba Committee.
>
> Nor did the commission find it significant that two months before the assassination, he went to the Soviet embassy in Mexico City and was seen in the company of two known Cuban agents. After his arrest, his wallet was found to contain the addresses of the *Communist Daily Worker* and the Soviet embassy in Washington. It has been reported by more than one source that President Johnson and the commission were fearful that evidence of a Communist conspiracy involving, as it would the Soviet Union and/or Cuba, would anger

the American people and lead to a confrontation, possibly even to war. It is also reported that the FBI files indicate there might have been a Communist conspiracy involving Oswald, but that the commission was unwilling to pursue this. The files further show that the Justice Department and the Warren Commission wanted to establish Oswald as alone in the case, and to get this conclusion to the American people as quickly as possible. Maybe someday, a new investigation will start down that trail.[12]

SHORTLY AFTER THIS, history began to turn in Reagan's favor. First, Reagan had underestimated his staying power within the Republican Party. The increasingly conservative GOP base, fed up with leaders they considered too ideologically unreliable (such as Nixon and Ford), championed the California conservative who had won their hearts two decades earlier. President Ford's loss took the steam out of the moderate wing, whose central political argument had always been that the party got victory in exchange for tempering its right wing. As President Carter sank lower and lower in the popularity polls, Republicans believed they could take the chance of nominating Reagan despite his age and sharp rhetoric. The script for the old actor was set, and with just a few rewrites, the year 1980 unfolded as the fulfillment of Reagan's long-held dreams. JFK had been elected president at his first chronological and political opportunity, and Reagan was elected at his last. After a scare from George H. W. Bush with a loss in the Iowa caucuses, Reagan swept to the nomination and (after seriously considering Gerald Ford for the ticket) chose Bush as his running mate. Burdened by a bad economy, the Iran hostage crisis, and the Ted Kennedy challenge, President Carter was doomed and lost badly to Reagan in November. A new Irish American presidency was born.

Personally and politically, in the oddest kind of yin and yang, the Reagan White House and the Kennedy White House would complement each other. LBJ, Nixon, Ford, and Carter labored in JFK's long shadow. Reagan enthusiastically sought to forge a legacy partnership, using selective policies and a warm bond with President Kennedy's surviving family.

The release of the fifty-two remaining American hostages by Iran on inauguration day helped President Reagan get off to a hopeful start. In a final insult to the departing chief executive they had helped to destroy, the Iranians had made sure the hostages did not leave their control until a few minutes after Carter had left office. In a conciliatory gesture, Reagan asked Carter to greet the ex-hostages in Germany. A celebratory inaugural evening on January 20, 1981, featured Frank Sinatra, once one of JFK's closest Hollywood pals, as chairman of the inaugural committee. The many other stars in attendance or performing for the Reagans reminded some of Camelot—though not the seamier side that saw Sinatra facilitate the extramarital affair between Kennedy and Sam Giancana's mistress, Judith Campbell.

Like Carter, Reagan chose JFK's Resolute desk for the Oval Office. As the president settled in, observers noticed that similarities in style linked Kennedy and Reagan. Both had a wicked sense of humor and enjoyed joke telling, some of it off-color, using it to break the ice in groups large and small. By nature, both enjoyed the social side of the presidency, welcoming legislative leaders and Washington's grandees to parties and after-hours drinks. The contrast with Jimmy Carter, who did not enjoy schmoozing and preferred quiet work and family time, was unambiguous. Reagan and Kennedy focused on the big picture, the top priorities, and left the details to staff. And both had a firm, realistic grasp of what they wanted to accomplish. Unlike JFK, though, Reagan had a faithful marriage to, and a full partner in, Nancy Davis Reagan, and he would soon need her strength in overcoming a personal and national nightmare with echoes of Dallas.

Ronald Reagan's presidency nearly ended before it had really begun. On Monday, March 30, 1981, Reagan left the White House and arrived around 1:50 P.M. at the Washington Hilton hotel to address a large group of AFL-CIO representatives. An uneventful speech followed, and Reagan made his way out at 2:27 P.M. through a side passage. The presidential limousine was just ten yards from the door, and a small press contingent waited on the exit's side to film Reagan and shout a few questions. Reagan turned toward them, smiled, and waved, but didn't stop (fortunately, since that would have made him an easier target). In that instant, shots rang out from the press line. John Hinckley, Jr., had managed to insinuate himself in the knot of reporters and photographers, armed with a Röhm .22-caliber revolver loaded with "Devastator" exploding cartridges.[13] Uncannily, the gun had been purchased in a Dallas pawnshop, a mere mile from Dealey Plaza.[14] Hinckley managed to get off six shots in 1.7 seconds before being subdued by bystanders and Secret Service personnel. In addition to wounding a Secret Service agent, a D.C. policeman, and Reagan's press secretary, James Brady, Hinckley shot the president by means of a bullet that ricocheted off the limousine and hit Reagan in his left underarm, as he was still in midwave while being pushed into the bulletproof car. This one-in-a-hundred shot was nearly enough to kill Reagan, as the bullet hit a rib, tore into a lung, and lodged a mere inch from his heart. Brady, shot through the head, was disabled for life. The agent and policeman, though seriously wounded, recovered.[15]

Just as in Dallas, the assassination's events occurred in the blink of an eye. Only those closest to Kennedy's car immediately knew the awful truth on November 22, 1963, and on March 30, 1981, even Reagan and his Secret

Service agents in the limo did not at first realize that the president had been hit. While speeding back to the White House, Reagan started coughing up red blood, thought at first to have been a result of a rib broken in pushing him hard into the backseat. The right call—to go to George Washington University Hospital—was made by Jerry Parr, head of Reagan's Secret Service detail, the man who had shoved the president into the limo just in time to avoid a possible shot to Reagan's head. As in the case of JFK, the car reached the hospital in about five minutes.[16]

Had they gone back to the White House, Reagan probably would have died. Walking into the hospital, the president nearly collapsed from internal bleeding and was rushed to treatment for critically low blood pressure. Once stabilized, the surgery began to remove the bullet—which was not then known to be a Devastator and could have exploded during the operation. Before the surgery, a distraught Nancy Reagan had arrived. Mrs. Reagan's recollections of her trip to GW Hospital included a flashback to Dallas: "As my mind raced, I flashed to scenes of Parkland Memorial Hospital in Texas, and the day President Kennedy was shot. I had been driving down San Vicente Boulevard in Los Angeles when a bulletin came over the car radio. Now, more than seventeen years later, I prayed that history would not be repeated, that Washington would not become another Dallas. That my husband would live." She could have added, "That I would not become the next Jackie Kennedy." Mrs. Reagan never spoke about the assassination attempt with Mrs. Kennedy, who did not call or write Mrs. Reagan during the period of the president's shooting and recovery. Possibly it was too painful a memory for Mrs. Kennedy to invoke.[17]

Upon seeing his wife in the hospital, Reagan quipped in his usual self-deprecating way, "Honey, I forgot to duck." Shortly before being anesthetized, Reagan looked up at his doctors and said, "Please tell me you're Republicans!" The head surgeon replied, "Mr. President, today we are all Republicans."[18] Given Reagan's age and the seriousness of the wounds, it was touch-and-go for a while, with a difficult recovery behind the scenes. The president was unable to return to the White House for thirteen days, and once there, was still mending for weeks more.[19] The nation was not told at the time how badly off Reagan had been, and he put on the actor's face whenever out in public. Although he was back making speeches by the end of April, Reagan was on a reduced schedule of activity for months, and some felt his full vigor did not return until the autumn.

Meanwhile, the nation was in shock. At first, the public was told that Reagan was unharmed. Shortly thereafter came the dreadful truth, and real fear that Reagan would die from a gunshot wound. The confusion and contradictory announcements—including a widely broadcast claim that Jim Brady had died—led many to suspect that we were purposely not being given all the facts. In yet another echo of 1963, Vice President Bush was in Texas, and some speculated that he was being rushed back to Washington to take control. Bush's absence from D.C. led to the famous not-quite-right declaration by Secretary of State Alexander Haig that he, Haig, was next in line and "in control" at the White House.[20]

Reagan's midday assassination attempt generated immediate comparisons to JFK's murder in Dallas. Regardless of partisan affiliation, Americans were in total disbelief that this could have happened again.[21] Just as with Kennedy, many wondered about the motive of the assassin. Like all presidents, Reagan had many domestic and international opponents who may have nursed grievances about the 1980 election results. International intrigue was never far from our minds in the era of superpower confrontation. Could foreign agents be involved? The Cold War was still icy and Reagan had been fiercely anti-Soviet and anti-Cuban. And then there was Iran, whose hatred of the Great Satan was undiminished by the transfer of power from Carter to Reagan.

But it quickly became apparent that there were no complicated plots, second shooters, or grassy knolls attached to this sordid event. John Hinckley was more akin to Garfield's loony killer Charles Guiteau than to Lincoln's cause-motivated John Wilkes Booth. Mentally ill, Hinckley had stalked both Carter and Reagan in an attempt to impress the actress Jodie Foster, his imagined girlfriend. That Hollywood's president would be felled by an assassin trying to win over a Tinseltown star was among the more bizarre aspects of the case. Foster had played an underage prostitute in the 1976 movie *Taxi Driver*, and the film had become a Hinckley obsession. The attempted assassination of a senator running for president was part of the plot, and in Hinckley's warped mind, a similar effort in real life against a sitting president would make him a national figure worthy of Foster's affections.

Hinckley was eventually found not guilty by reason of insanity—a highly controversial decision—and he has mainly remained in mental institutions for most of the last thirty years.[22] When Hinckley appeared in court about a month after the shootings, he was forced to wear a bulletproof vest, and spectators underwent a triple security check, two metal detectors, and a frisking. Authorities were clear on their motive: to prevent "another Jack Ruby" from killing the accused.[23] Hinckley was not the only one to receive extra protection. Almost immediately after the attempted assassination, temporary Secret Service protection was extended once more to Senator Ted Kennedy.[24] There were no specific threats, but the Capitol Hill police and Secret Service anticipated the possibility of a deranged copycat being "inspired" to take action.

Not unexpectedly, the Secret Service insisted that its procedures had not been at fault on March 30. The Service's spokesman, Jack Warner, noted that

the agents "were competing with a bullet" and "the fact that we live in a democracy has to be taken into account." A few days after Reagan was shot,
Warner told a reporter, "We do not at this time anticipate any changes in
procedure."[25] Reagan's close friend and White House counselor Edwin
Meese (later U.S. attorney general) noted he had known the president for
many years and he would not lower his public profile on account of his near-
fatal experience. Neither Warner nor Meese properly calculated the determination of Nancy Reagan, who, according to former White House aide Mike
Deaver, gathered key staffers and Secret Service officials together and demanded improvements in presidential security.[26]*

Whether that discussion happened or not, the Secret Service eventually
accepted that changes were in order, just as they had done after Dallas. The
failure to have an agent check press credentials and watch spectators at the
Washington Hilton rope line, or to have the president's exit more carefully
shielded, was nearly fatal. In a July 1981 report on the assassination attempt, the
Treasury Department, which supervises the Secret Service, admitted that the
Warren Commission's recommendations for improving the Service were never
fully implemented. Greater protection would require "significantly increased
manpower and financial resources" as well.[27] At the Washington Hilton—
known to this day inside the Secret Service as "the Hinckley Hilton"—the
president is now driven into a special interior entrance before disembarking. In
fact, whenever possible, especially at unsecured sites, presidents since Reagan
avoid walking in full view of unscreened people; most present-day presidential
arrivals and departures are "covered" and unseen, with presidents shielded from
unanticipated attacks.

As with Lee Harvey Oswald, the FBI had not connected the dots—and
quickly the Secret Service tried to shift blame to the Bureau. Hinckley had
been arrested in October 1980 at the Nashville airport by alert screeners
for the illegal possession of firearms, specifically three revolvers, a box of
.22-caliber ammunition, and a pair of handcuffs in his luggage. A judge
fined Hinckley $62.50 and let him go on his way. Even though President
Carter was in town for a campaign stop, the FBI never questioned Hinckley
closely or reported the incident to the Secret Service. Sometimes, a coincidence is more than a happenstance, and that was the case with Hinckley and
Carter together in Nashville.[28]

Mrs. Reagan was so distraught over nearly losing her husband that she
consulted an astrologer, Joan Quigley, about the president's schedule; events
would be postponed or canceled to accommodate the astrologer's advice.

---

* Mrs. Reagan, now in her nineties, relayed to us through her son Ron Jr. that she does not remember any such conversation taking place. E-mail from Ron Reagan, Jr., May 10, 2012.

Quigley's assistance was not known until 1988, when embittered ex-Reagan chief of staff Don Regan, who had been fired by the Reagans, released a book.[29] But as questionable a "science" as astrology is, few Americans faulted the traumatized First Lady when her habit became public. Understandably, Mrs. Reagan did not think she could fully trust the Secret Service alone to keep her husband safe.

The Secret Service's resistance to change and defensive justification of its "procedures" in the face of obvious evidence that they did not work is typical of bureaucracies everywhere. It is true, as President Kennedy once said, "If anyone wants to do it [kill me], no amount of protection is enough. All a man needs is a willingness to trade his life for mine."[30] But as the country learned in both 1963 and 1981, the Secret Service is obligated to work ever harder to make its most valuable protected official as safe as humanly possible. Every security slipup is potentially fatal. Presidents know this, and while they do not usually express concern for their safety publicly, they are aware of the dangers. It is the First Family that suffers the most, though. Both Mrs. Reagan and son Ron Jr. separately urged President Reagan not to seek a second term, fearing further attempts on his life.[31]

Reagan's remarkable presence of mind and humor in a life-threatening moment won over the country and gave his presidency a big boost in poll ratings and congressional support. He chose to use this painfully won political capital to get his economic program passed. But perhaps the greatest postassassination impact was on Reagan himself. He believed that his life had been spared by God for larger purposes—a belief apparently encouraged by another assassination survivor, Pope John Paul II, who was nearly killed in May 1981 while riding in the open "popemobile" in Vatican Square.[32]

The harsh world of politics has little time for might-have-beens. Ronald Reagan was lucky—the first incumbent president to be hit by a bullet and survive—while John Kennedy was not. Yet the Reagan experience reminds us that President Kennedy's personal and political path would have been altered had he been wounded but survived on November 22. Assuming full recovery, Kennedy would certainly have used the inevitable popularity spurt to unfreeze some of his legislation in Congress, quite possibly the civil rights bill. His reelection would virtually have been assured, and by a large enough margin to have carried in much friendlier Democratic majorities in the legislature. Whether he would have pursued a war on poverty and the other components of what became LBJ's Great Society is a mystery. Kennedy was more cautious than Johnson in some ways. Still, the assassination attempt would have rearranged his plans and perhaps his thinking in ways that are not predictable. The varying trajectories of the bullets marked for Kennedy, and the one that struck Reagan, remind us that an inch one way or the other can make an enormous difference in history.

Other than a successful congressional effort to tighten up the insanity plea by shifting the burden from the prosecution to the defense, the only significant piece of federal legislation that can be directly tied to the March 30, 1981, shootings came not from Reagan but from another victim, James Brady. While he remained the titular press secretary throughout Reagan's eight years in office, Brady was too severely impaired to return to the job. Nonetheless he and his wife, Sarah, went to work on designing gun control legislation that eventually passed a dozen years after the shooting. As president, Reagan had always opposed gun control measures, but on the tenth anniversary of his near-assassination, Reagan endorsed the Brady bill.[33] The Brady Handgun Violence Prevention Act was signed into law by President Clinton in November 1993. For the first time, it required background checks for most firearms purchases.[34]

RONALD REAGAN BEGAN his presidency with no honeymoon bump; Gallup measured his job approval at just 51 percent after ten days on the job—the precise proportion of the vote he had received in November. While he gained steadily, the events of March 30 sent his job approval soaring to 67 percent in Gallup and above 70 percent in some other polls.[35] Reagan and his staff knew just what to do. On April 28, the recovering president appeared before a joint session of Congress to a hero's welcome and marshaled his and the nation's emotion: "The warmth of your words, the expression of friendship and, yes, love, meant more to us than you can ever know. You have given us a memory that we'll treasure forever. And you've provided an answer to those few voices that were raised saying that what happened was evidence that ours is a sick society . . ."[36] And from there, Reagan made clear that he wanted to cash in his new political chips for his domestic agenda of across-the-board tax cuts as well as defense spending increases to contain the Communists. By summer's end, the president had most of what he desired. The legislation was delivered to his California ranch and he signed it with a flourish.[37]

Ronald Reagan had an unusual rhetorical ally in achieving his fiscal and international goals—John F. Kennedy. It is extraordinary how often Reagan employed JFK's words to his own ends. As one scholar wrote: ". . . while [Reagan] quoted [Franklin] Roosevelt 76 times between his 1980 inauguration and his 1984 reelection, he cited John Kennedy on 133 occasions. (By contrast, he referred to Hoover once, to Nixon sixteen times, and to Coolidge [one of Reagan's favorites] in only twenty-four instances.) Even Abraham Lincoln appeared only sixty-seven times—nine fewer than Roosevelt, sixty-six fewer than Kennedy. All but a handful of these references to Kennedy were highly complimentary."[38]*

Reagan's recurrent use of JFK was a carefully planned political strategy, on a par with Lyndon Johnson's regular invocation of President Kennedy. It was difficult for Democratic politicians to contradict their patron saint, and John Kennedy's imprimatur made Reagan's policies more palatable to the public. Late in Reagan's first term, the Republican National Committee undertook a study of Kennedy's positions and assembled a "quote file" that could be used by the White House to undergird its proposals. The report opened:

> Liberal Democrats have sought, for twenty years now, to embellish their policies and proposals with the theme of carrying forward the "vision" of President John F. Kennedy. They would have the American people believe that their big-government, tax and spend, anti-defense, anti-business policies are what JFK would have pursued had he lived.
>
> A review of the actual words of President Kennedy has yielded an astoundingly different story. In reality, from national defense to tax policy, from foreign policy to the federal budget, from the economy to education—the views of JFK ring far closer to those of President Reagan than to those of the self-appointed "torch carriers." The fact is that many Democrats and their media sympathizers have grossly distorted the views of President Kennedy, building a false image, possibly, to play upon the reverence accorded an assassinated President to suit their own ends.
>
> The following quotes reveal a man who was strong on defense, ever-mindful of the Soviet threat, sought tax cuts to stimulate the economy, supported the free market, sought to limit domestic spending and the growth of the federal government and was opposed to racial quotas. Indeed, few of the words of JFK contained here would be alien to President Reagan and, in fact, are amazingly consistent with his views of foreign, domestic and economic policy. They provide fascinating reading.[39]

In no area did President Reagan use JFK to greater effect than for his tax cuts. It was incontrovertible that Kennedy pushed for slashing the top individual rates from a sky-high 91 percent to 65 percent, a reform that was on

---

* This was not just a first-term phenomenon; my own study of presidential citations, detailed later in the book, shows that Reagan continued to cite President Kennedy with frequency in his second term.

track to occur when he went to Dallas and was passed in February 1964.[40] From his first month in office, Reagan linked his tax program to Kennedy's, and when Reagan's critics accused him of helping the rich, he quoted JFK's argument, "A rising tide lifts all boats."[41] Deficit hawks feared the tax cuts would increase the national debt (as they did), but Reagan used the Kennedy economy to rebut them, employing JFK's words: "'Our true choice is not between tax reduction on the one hand and avoidance of large federal deficits on the other. An economy stifled by restrictive tax rates will never produce enough revenue to balance the budget, just as it will never produce enough jobs or enough profits.' John F. Kennedy said that back in 1962, when he was asking for a tax decrease, a cut in tax rates across the board. And he was proven right, because that—the last tax cut, literally, that we've had—actually produced more revenue for government, because the economy was stimulated and more people were working and there was more industry and productivity in America."[42]

Over and over again, all the way through his reelection and beyond, President Reagan cited the same passages from John Kennedy and the matching statistics about the post-tax-cut growth of government revenue in the 1960s to deflect concerns about federal deficits in the 1980s. Democrats used Ted Kennedy to attempt to seize back JFK's mantle, with limited success. "President Kennedy's tax cut concentrated relief on middle income families. [Reagan's] tax cut would give the most to the wealthiest segment of our society," claimed Senator Kennedy in April 1981. In fact, JFK's tax cut had also done far more for the rich than the middle class.[43]

Ironically, President Reagan took President Kennedy's side of the tax cut argument and ignored one of the JFK tax cut's chief opponents—none other than Barry Goldwater, Reagan's conservative hero, who believed Kennedy's tax policies would fuel runaway deficits.[44] However, what didn't happen in the 1960s, when the United States maintained a stronger position in the world economy and much smaller federal expenditures, unfolded with a vengeance in the 1980s. Reagan's "supply-side economics," built around his tax cuts, greatly expanded federal debt; promised spending cuts never occurred, mainly because of staunch Democratic opposition.[45] The Kennedy tax cut legacy was truly double-edged, an economic boost in the go-go sixties and a fiscal fount of red ink in the more complicated eighties.[46]

Ronald Reagan also employed JFK, with much less success, in his repeated attempts to reduce federal social spending. The president took to quoting the most famous lines from Kennedy's inaugural speech ("Ask not what your country can do for you . . ."), but insisting "it's time . . . to remember the second part of what JFK said, 'Ask what you can do for your country.'"[47] His point was unmistakable—Americans should accept less largesse and fewer federal entitlements. Not even John F. Kennedy could help Reagan with that goal, still unrealized three decades later.

EQUAL TO TAX cuts on the list of President Reagan's passions was his fervent anticommunism. Again, President Kennedy was Reagan's faithful rhetorical ally. Except for a relative handful of liberals and radicals in the 1950s and 1960s, there was little sympathy for Communism, and on this, John F. Kennedy was no liberal. In the 1950s he had defended his personal friend, Richard Nixon, on his rigid anticommunism, and had even told associates that if he (Kennedy) could not get the Democratic nomination for president, he would vote for Nixon.[48] Opposition to the Reds was a basis for bipartisan unity, and opposing candidates such as Kennedy and Nixon tried to out-do one another in bashing Communism.

Once in the Oval Office, JFK faced crisis after crisis—the Bay of Pigs, Berlin, the Khrushchev summit, Soviet missiles in Cuba—generated by the great ideological conflict between East and West. The consensus at the time was that Communism and capitalism were engaged in a life-or-death struggle that would leave one side's philosophy and civilization on the scrap heap of history. Every American adult was familiar with Premier Khrushchev's declaration to the West, "We will bury you!" Even schoolchildren at the time remember that frightening sentence emblazoned on placards fixed to the walls of school buses.[49] Civil defense shelters dotted the map in every urban locality and bomb shelters in individual homes were common. Kennedy's rhetoric about Communism was tough and harsh, beginning with his inaugural address: "Let every nation know, whether it wishes us well or ill, that we shall pay any price, bear any burden, meet any hardship, support any friend, oppose any foe, in order to assure the survival and the success of liberty." President Reagan had many such JFK passages from which to choose.

Reagan's first use of Kennedy was to adopt his own version of JFK's "missile gap" charge. President Reagan's favorite data on defense spending became a staple of his speeches: Under JFK, defense spending accounted for 46 percent of the federal budget, compared to 29 percent for social programs. Twenty years later, just 29 percent of federal money was devoted to defense and more than 50 percent to social spending "that mushroomed during the Great Society."[50] Reagan even included an animated graph of this trend, with credit to Kennedy for keeping America strong, in a televised address to the nation on November 22, 1982, the nineteenth anniversary of the assassination.[51] Interestingly, Reagan blamed the shift away from defense not just on the Great Society but "neglect in the 1970s," when two of his foes, Gerald Ford and Jimmy Carter, were president: "[T]he 1970's were marked by neglect of our defenses ... Too many forgot John Kennedy's warning that only when our arms are certain beyond doubt can we be certain beyond doubt they will never be used. By the beginning of this decade, we face three growing problems: the Soviet SS-20 monopoly in Europe and Asia; the vulnerability of our land-based ICBM [intercontinental ballistic missiles]; and the failure of arms control agreements to slow the overall growth in strategic weapons."[52]

Just as Kennedy's allegation that the United States was falling behind the Soviet Union in the production and deployment of nuclear missiles proved to be false, so, too, was part of Reagan's accusation that post-Kennedy leaders in the 1960s and 1970s had let America fall behind. In absolute terms, defense expenditures had skyrocketed from $53 billion in 1963 to $134 billion in 1980, the year before Reagan took office—Reagan's case depended on the high inflation of the 1970s.[53] Whatever the truth of the candidates' assertions, the fear of Communism was such that most voters seemed to side with Kennedy and Reagan, preferring to be prepared rather than sorry.

Like Kennedy, Reagan was a member of the World War II generation, though unlike JFK, he had only served domestically, mainly in a special Hollywood filmmaking military unit.[54] Yet Reagan's global views were shaped in part by the events of the 1930s and '40s, just as Kennedy's were. Reagan again found reason to make common cause with JFK by touting Kennedy's 1940 book, *Why England Slept*:

> Even after war broke out in Asia and in Europe, our own country was slow to take the steps necessary to defend itself. Warning us of the impending crisis, a young Harvard student, John Fitzgerald Kennedy, wrote a book titled *Why England Slept*. His thoughtful study holds as true now, forty-two years later, as when it was first published. After describing how a dictatorship with a controlled press and the power to silence political opposition can carry on a vigorous arms program, he noted, "In contrast, in a democracy, the cry of warmonger would discourage any politician who advocates a vigorous arms policy. This leaves armaments with few supporters. Among the reasons for England's failure to rearm in time," Kennedy wrote, "probably the most important was a firm and widely held conviction that armaments were one of the primary causes of war." Well, the Western democracies didn't wake up till it was too late. It took Pearl Harbor to shake Americans from their complacency.
>
> Today, in this era of much more dangerous weapons, it is even more important to remember that vigilance, not complacency, is the key to peace.[55]

In using Kennedy to compare 1980s Communism with 1930s Fascism, Reagan cleverly linked bipartisan lessons learned by the World War II generation to the modern struggle with "the Evil Empire," Reagan's term for the Soviet Union and its allies.

In Reagan's view, the Communist threat still resembled the one from Cuba and Vietnam, an international conspiracy to extend its influence and take over nation-states that would fall, one by one, like dominoes. In our own hemisphere, Reagan fought the Communists in Nicaragua, El Salvador, and Grenada with arms and rhetorical ferocity that often included references to JFK. For example, in a televised address to the nation on May 9, 1984, about his policies in Central America, Reagan made Kennedy the star attraction:

> We're in the midst of what President John F. Kennedy called "a long twilight struggle" to defend freedom in the world. He understood the problem of Central America. He understood Castro. And he understood the long-term goals of the Soviet Union in this region.
>
> Twenty-three years ago, President Kennedy warned against the threat of Communist penetration in our hemisphere. He said, "I want it clearly understood that this government will not hesitate in meeting its primary obligations which are to the security of our nation." And the House and Senate supported him overwhelmingly by passing a law calling on the United States to prevent Cuba from extending its aggressive or subversive activities to any part of this hemisphere. Were John Kennedy alive today, I think he would be appalled by the gullibility of some who invoke his name.[56]

President Reagan's second term placed a special emphasis on defeating the Communist-friendly Sandinistas in Nicaragua, an effort that led his administration into the infamous Iran-Contra scandal.[57] In the midst of his efforts to secure congressional funding and marshal public opinion for the anticommunist Nicaraguan "Contras," Reagan addressed the nation and told an anecdote about President Kennedy that defined Reagan's own fundamental mission in international affairs, the containment and eventual elimination of Communism:

> You know, recently one of our most distinguished Americans, Clare Boothe Luce,[58] had this to say about the coming vote: "In considering this crisis," Mrs. Luce said, "my mind goes back to a similar moment in our history—back to the first years after Cuba had fallen to Fidel. One day during those years, I had lunch at the White House

with a man I had known since he was a boy, John F. Kennedy. 'Mr. President,' I said, 'no matter how exalted or great a man may be, history will have time to give him no more than one sentence. George Washington, he founded our country. Abraham Lincoln, he freed the slaves and preserved the Union. Winston Churchill, he saved Europe.' 'And what, Clare,' John Kennedy said, 'do you believe my sentence will be?' 'Mr. President,' she answered, 'your sentence will be that you stopped the Communists—or that you did not.'"

Well, tragically, John Kennedy never had the chance to decide which that would be. Now leaders of our own time must do so. My fellow Americans, you know where I stand. The Soviets and the Sandinistas must not be permitted to crush freedom in Central America and threaten our own security on our own doorstep. Now the Congress must decide where it stands. Mrs. Luce ended by saying: "Only this is certain. Through all time to come, this, the 99th Congress of the United States, will be remembered as that body of men and women that either stopped the Communists before it was too late— or did not."[59]

Reagan's recurrent summoning of JFK's spirit to back ideas not favored by contemporary Democrats provoked a reaction, and from time to time, Senator Edward Kennedy would take umbrage. Perhaps he remembered that Reagan had been a severe critic of JFK in the early 1960s and had backed Nixon enthusiastically. However, the Kennedys were remarkably chummy with the Reagans during the 1980s, and at some level, the family must have been pleased that JFK was mentioned so frequently and prominently by an Oval Office successor, even a conservative Republican.

The keepers of a legacy often try to sand down the rough edges of history, and even rewrite a few chapters to keep a departed statesman relevant to current events he could scarcely have imagined. The truth in this instance is that John Kennedy was conservative (in today's terms) on both economic policy and foreign affairs. The same holds for social policies. Feminism, gun control, gay rights, abortion rights, and environmentalism were fringe advocacy concerns in JFK's day. That is not his modern image, as cultivated and refined by the Kennedy family and Democratic Party leaders, but President Reagan actually hit closer to the mark in reviving the John F. Kennedy who ran for and served as president. It is another inconvenient truth of history.

On the other hand, President Reagan's selective invocation of Kennedy's words and programs was sometimes misleading. Reagan and Kennedy were diametrically opposed on a wide range of matters, not least civil rights for African Americans—which Kennedy finally supported and Reagan mainly opposed.[60] Yet the presidency set both men on somewhat the same course to achieve peace and prosperity in their time. That tax cuts were the centerpiece of both men's economic strategy is revealing. So too is the fact that both gradually moved from confrontation to negotiation with the Soviets. Kennedy secured the 1963 test ban treaty and clearly wanted to go much further with Khrushchev in a second term. After complaining that Soviet leaders kept "dying on me"—two of them, Premiers Yuri Andropov and Konstantin Chernenko, served brief tenures during Reagan's first term—Reagan found a willing partner in Mikhail Gorbachev, and substantial arms reduction progress was made in his second term.[61] Ted Kennedy privately urged Reagan in 1985 to seek accommodation with the Soviets by reminding him of his brother's "proudest achievement": "As you know I am off to Geneva this weekend as part of the Senate observer group for the negotiations on arms control [and] want to add my hopes for your success in the forthcoming arms negotiations. Jack always felt that the Partial Test Ban Treaty of 1963, coming as it did on the heels of the Cuban Missile Crisis, was the proudest achievement of his presidency. You above all are in a unique position to be blessed as the peacemaker of the century and the prayers of all of us in Congress and the country are with you in this historic undertaking."[62]

Arms control was in the interests of both East and West in the 1960s and 1980s. But on the central issue of the Soviet system itself, Presidents Kennedy and Reagan were actually close together, and on the right side of history. That was demonstrated dramatically on several days separated by five U.S. administrations, in events happening at the tense crossroads of East and West, the city of Berlin. Divided since the end of World War II with its German families separated by a military-enforced wall built in 1961, Berlin became the flashpoint for Cold War intrigue, and the site of two great presidential speeches. President Kennedy's "Ich bin ein Berliner" declaration of June 1963 underlined the harsh reality of Communist tactics. Ronald Reagan, as a private citizen, had fumed that President Kennedy did nothing to stop the wall's construction. Not long before he began his 1980 campaign, Reagan was still unhappy, complaining about "the lost opportunity in Berlin, when we could have knocked down and prevented the completion of the wall with no hostilities following."[63] But by the time Reagan first came to Berlin as president, in June 1982, he was citing Kennedy's "stirring words" to which he added, "We in America and the West are still Berliners . . . and always will be."[64] On his final presidential trip to Berlin, in June 1987, Reagan delivered an address that was the equal of Kennedy's. Reminding his audience of JFK's speech and others by American presidents, Reagan explained that, "We come to Berlin . . . because it's our duty to speak in the place of freedom." Then Reagan made perhaps the most famous challenge of his time in office: "General Secretary

Gorbachev, if you seek peace . . . come here to this gate! Mr. Gorbachev, open this gate! Mr. Gorbachev, tear down this wall!"[65] In two years' time, as a result of solidarity among nine presidential administrations and constant pressure by the United States and its allies, not to mention enormous sacrifice in lives and dollars, the Berlin wall came tumbling down at last.

In the case of Berlin and hundreds of others, presidents depend on the precedents set by earlier chief executives. Some precedents are followed easily, especially when administrations are of the same party and twinned by the accidents of history, such as FDR and Truman, or JFK and LBJ. Never in modern times, though, has a president of one party utilized the words and policies of a president of the other party as much as Reagan did with Kennedy. It is a circumstance that demonstrates the long-term power and bipartisan appeal of John Kennedy, both his image and his reality.

OF THE EIGHT years Ronald Reagan served as president, none produced more Kennedy references than 1984, not coincidentally, Reagan's reelection year.[66] By then the Republican had well learned the power JFK's words had to catch the attention of Democrats and Independents.

Democrats had a spirited contest for their party's presidential nomination that featured, among others, two candidates with Kennedy credentials—one who was a national hero and personal favorite of JFK, former astronaut and Ohio senator John Glenn, and another who consciously fashioned himself after John Kennedy, Colorado senator Gary Hart.

Before these contenders could come to the fore, Ted Kennedy had made an early decision not to run, announced on December 1, 1982. He had been thought likely to try again after his defeat in 1980, but he probably realized that the odds were not favorable for victory. Moreover, Kennedy was in the midst of a divorce from his wife, Joan, guaranteeing lots of journalistic inquiries about his often-wild personal life.[67] A third factor may have been crucial: His family actively dissuaded him from a second campaign out of fear for his safety.[68] Ted had been lucky throughout his 1980 effort, but the nearly successful Reagan assassination attempt surely reminded the Kennedys that two brothers lost to bullets were enough. Some family loyalists talked hopefully of a future quest, once Chappaquiddick had supposedly faded completely from the public's mind, but others began to realize that Ted Kennedy's home would always be the Senate. It was left to a retired president, whose obsession with Edward Kennedy had helped to bring about his own downfall, to offer a postmortem. "The train has left the station" and Kennedy's presidential moment was gone, said Richard Nixon.[69] As a five-time national candidate, the canny Nixon knew that other ambitious Democratic politicians had already deferred for years to Ted and would now insist on their turn.

John Glenn moved quickly to seize the Kennedy mantle. He appeared in the Senate press gallery on the day Kennedy withdrew as a possible candidate to suggest that he was the natural heir. Glenn's haste was not appreciated by Ted Kennedy, who had never been as close to Glenn as his brothers had.[70] In any event, Glenn was never able to achieve much of a liftoff for his campaign; the quietly spoken moderate could fire his space rockets but not political crowds. After finishing a poor third in New Hampshire, he never won a single primary and dropped out on March 16, 1984.

Though Gary Hart had no strong Kennedy connections like Glenn, he fit the JFK mold better, at least superficially. Hart said he became interested in politics after hearing JFK at a 1960 rally, and by 1972 he had managed George McGovern's presidential campaign. This was Hart's springboard to a Senate seat from Colorado in 1974. Ruggedly handsome, polished, and articulate, the forty-seven-year-old Hart proclaimed himself the man of "new ideas" who could rescue the Democratic Party from its post-Carter doldrums. His main opponent, considered the heavy front-runner at the start, was Carter's vice president, Walter Mondale of Minnesota. Burdened with defending the Carter record, Mondale was also a Great Society liberal closely associated with Hubert Humphrey, whose Senate seat he had taken when Humphrey was elevated to the vice presidency in 1965. Hart was something of a loner in D.C., while Mondale was well liked in political circles. Yet there was no comparison on the stump between the unexciting, bland Mondale and the energetic, charismatic Hart.

As the campaign began, Mondale had checked all the boxes and taken the stands expected by the various Democratic Party constituencies, such as labor unions and women's groups. His nomination was considered almost inevitable. But as Democrats began to grasp that a rebounding economy was lifting President Reagan toward a second term, they looked for an alternative to shake up the race. Gary Hart loomed large, with his "Kennedy hair," hands thrust in his pockets à la JFK, and a practiced rhetorical cadence that was reminiscent of John Kennedy's. The public's innate yearning for a JFK revival had been pretested by Hart's campaign in focus groups. Political impressionists had a field day mimicking Hart mimicking Kennedy.[71] Hart stunned Mondale by roaring to a ten-percentage-point victory in New Hampshire, followed by wins in Florida and Massachusetts. Mondale fought back, capturing states where the party organization was strongest, such as Illinois and New York. The party was still deeply split as the primary season drew to a close in June; Hart snagged California, New Mexico, and South Dakota, while Mondale triumphed in New Jersey and West Virginia. Overall, Mondale edged

Hart in all primaries combined, 6.8 million votes to Hart's 6.5 million, with the civil rights activist Jesse Jackson pulling in another 3.3 million.

If there was a turning point in such a close battle, it may have been the stripping away of Hart's pseudo-Kennedy persona. Many observers criticized Hart for too much conscious imitation of JFK, and it was found that Hart had remade himself in other small but telling ways, such as shaving a year off his real age, changing his name from Hartpence to Hart, and dramatically altering his signature.[72] Never much of a sound-bite politician, Mondale nevertheless borrowed a fast-food slogan when he asked Hart, the man of new ideas, "Where's the beef?"—the punch line of a popular Wendy's hamburger commercial that permitted Mondale to claim Hart's proposals were vague and gauzy and that the candidate was more style than substance.

In the end, Mondale managed to thwart Hart by the slim margin of 224 delegates out of 3,933 at the party's July 1984 convention in San Francisco. Recognizing his own lack of pizzazz, Mondale tried to generate enthusiasm with the historic nomination of a woman, New York representative Geraldine Ferraro, for vice president. But the temporary boost she provided soon evaporated as questions about her family's finances were raised.[73] An uphill campaign became even more so.

Reagan's team needed little encouragement to play the Kennedy card, but Hart's defeat enabled them to appeal to Democratic voters attracted to a defeated JFK look-alike. In speech after speech, Reagan quoted Kennedy, and he often added Franklin Roosevelt, Harry Truman, and other prominent Democrats for good measure. At his renomination convention in Dallas on August 23, 1984, Reagan enlisted the pumped delegates for audience participation with this theme:

> THE PRESIDENT. Ten months ago, we displayed ... resolve in a mission to rescue American students on the imprisoned island of Grenada. Democratic candidates have suggested that this could be likened to the Soviet invasion of Afghanistan—
>
> AUDIENCE. Boo-o-o!
>
> THE PRESIDENT. —the crushing of human rights in Poland or the genocide in Cambodia.
>
> AUDIENCE. Boo-o-o!
>
> THE PRESIDENT. Could you imagine Harry Truman, John Kennedy, Hubert Humphrey, or Scoop Jackson [a hawkish Democratic U.S. senator from Washington state who died in 1983] making such a shocking comparison?
>
> AUDIENCE. No![74]

As Reagan traveled from Iowa to Michigan to Connecticut in the fall, he carried the same message: that he was closer to the policies of JFK and other Democratic presidents than the liberal Mondale and his band of "San Francisco Democrats." Reagan especially sought crossover votes from Democrats who believed in an interventionist, anticommunist foreign policy: "Harry Truman believed—with FDR before him and John Kennedy after him—in strength abroad and self-reliance at home. To all those Democrats—and I hope there are many here—who feel that under its present leadership the Democratic Party no longer stands behind America's responsibilities in the world, that it no longer represents working men and women, we say to you: 'Join us.'"[75] The technique even worked in Boston. On his way to carrying JFK's Massachusetts for the second time, Reagan would stifle hecklers by quoting JFK, and daring them to interrupt Kennedy's words.[76]

The only high point of the general election campaign for Mondale came at the first presidential debate, when Reagan lost his place and showed his age— and possibly demonstrated the earliest effects of his then-undiagnosed Alzheimer's disease. (Reagan famously recovered in the second and final debate, joking that he would not exploit his opponent's age and inexperience for political purposes.) Mondale used his brief opening remarks to associate himself with his own version of John Kennedy:

> The president says that when the Democratic Party made its turn, he left it. The year that he decided we had lost our way was the year that John F. Kennedy was running against Richard Nixon. I was chairman of "Minnesotans for Kennedy"; President Reagan was chairman of a thing called "Democrats for Nixon." Now, maybe we made a wrong turn with Kennedy, but I'll be proud of supporting him all of my life. And I'm very happy that John Kennedy was elected, because John Kennedy looked at the future with courage, saw what needed to be done, and understood his own government . . .
>
> The question is our future. President Kennedy once said in response to similar arguments, "We are great, but we can be greater." We can be better if we face our future, rejoice in our strengths, face our problems, and by solving them, build a better society for our children.[77]

Judging by the postdebate polls, swing Democrats were unmoved by Mondale's tactic, though some JFK loyalists were again furious that Reagan was appropriating Kennedy for his own purposes. Ted Kennedy fumed about it with friends, and a hundred academics purchased a full-page advertisement in the *New York Times* to protest Reagan's use of Roosevelt, Truman, and Kennedy as "a flagrant distortion of reality."[78]

Distortion or not, the technique, combined with a rebounding economy, clearly worked. On November 6, 1984, President Reagan not only won 58 percent of the popular vote and forty-nine states—all but Mondale's Minnesota—he attracted the backing of 26 percent of Democrats. Mondale received a miniscule 7 percent of the Republican vote by comparison.[79] There would be no Kennedy revival in 1984, unless one considered Reagan himself the Kennedy substitute.

PRESIDENT REAGAN'S PUBLIC relationship with Senator Edward Kennedy ran hot and cold, depending on the issue of the day, and Kennedy rarely aligned himself with any major administration initiative. In particular, Kennedy fiercely opposed Reagan's tax cut, Central American policy, and many key appointments. Even today, conservatives have not forgotten Kennedy's key role in sinking Supreme Court nominee Robert Bork; Kennedy's 1987 Senate speech about "Robert Bork's America" contained a litany of horrors that would descend upon America if Bork took a high court seat.[80]

But privately, a very different relationship unfolded between Kennedy and Reagan, one that was usually initiated by Ted and included the whole Kennedy family. The record of the Reagan White House is replete with examples. On the thirteenth anniversary of Bobby's assassination, the congressionally approved Robert F. Kennedy Medal was awarded in honor of the late senator's service and presented to Ethel Kennedy in the White House Rose Garden. The ceremony was preceded by an informal Oval Office meeting with Mrs. Kennedy and her children as well as Senator Kennedy. In what would become standard for these events, Reagan was exceptionally eloquent and generous in his remarks, saying in part, "[Robert Kennedy] wrote to his son, Joseph, on the day of President Kennedy's death, 'Remember all the things that Jack started. Be kind to others that are less fortunate than we and love our country.' And it is the final triumph of Robert Kennedy that he used his personal gifts to bring this message of hope and love to the country, to millions of Americans who supported and believed in him." Ted Kennedy responded, "Let me thank you, Mr. President, for this great honor that you have given to Robert Kennedy. And it is appropriate that he should receive it from you, for he understood so well that the common love of our country transcends all party identification and all partisan difference. And you should know that after he debated you on international television in 1967, my brother Bob said that Ronald Reagan was the toughest debater he ever faced and, obviously, he was right. [Laughter]"[81]

Rose Kennedy visited Reagan in the Oval Office, accompanied by Ted, and Reagan wrote her a letter on her ninety-second birthday.[82] He taped a television commercial for Eunice Shriver, JFK's sister, for her "Special Olympics"—and attended a White House ceremony for the Special Olympics winners, followed by warm correspondence between Reagan and Shriver about this annual event.[83] At Ted Kennedy's request, Reagan permitted Ted Reardon, a devoted friend of President Kennedy's, to be buried close to JFK at Arlington.[84] On November 22, 1983, the twentieth anniversary of the assassination, at Ted Kennedy's invitation, President and Mrs. Reagan attended a memorial mass for President Kennedy at Georgetown's Holy Trinity Church. The church was packed with the surviving principals of the New Frontier as well as JFK's extended family, and the solemn sense of loss was again palpable. Caroline read from her father's speeches and Ted Kennedy took the opportunity to thank the Reagans, who "have been very kind to our family on this and other occasions."[85] Perhaps remembering his own close call, Reagan issued a stirring statement about the Dallas tragedy and the long-lasting "trauma and grief" of that day.[86]

Senator Kennedy later asked the president for his backing in raising an endowment for the JFK Library. Reagan agreed to meet with Caroline and John Jr., who noted in a letter to Reagan that their father was unable to do what other former presidents do as a matter of course—make the calls and visits necessary to secure the financial future of his library and museum.[87] President Reagan took a personal interest and agreed to speak at an event on June 24, 1985, at Ted Kennedy's McLean, Virginia, home. It became the site of Reagan's most moving tribute to JFK:

> It is a matter of pride to me that so many men and women who were inspired by his bracing vision and moved by his call to "ask not," serve now in the White House doing the business of government. Which is not to say I supported John Kennedy when he ran for president; I didn't. I was for the other fellow. But you know, it's true, when the battle's over and the ground is cooled, well, it's then that you see the opposing general's valor.
>
> He would have understood. He was fiercely, happily partisan. And his political fights were tough—no quarter asked, none given. But he gave as good as he got. And you could see that he loved the battle.
>
> Everything we saw him do seemed to betray a huge enjoyment of life. He seemed to grasp from the beginning that life is one fast-moving train, and you have to jump aboard and hold on to your hat and relish the sweep of the wind as it rushes by. You have to enjoy the journey; it's unthankful not to . . .
>
> And when he died, when that comet disappeared over the continent, a whole nation grieved and would not forget. A tailor in New

York put up a sign on the door: "Closed because of a death in the family." The sadness was not confined to us. "They cried the rain down that night," said a journalist in Europe. They put his picture up in huts in Brazil and tents in the Congo, in offices in Dublin and Warsaw. That was some of what he did for his country, for when they honored him they were honoring someone essentially, quintessentially, completely American. When they honored John Kennedy, they honored the nation whose virtues, genius, and contradictions he so fully reflected.

Many men are great, but few capture the imagination and the spirit of the times. The ones who do are unforgettable. Four administrations have passed since John Kennedy's death; five presidents have occupied the Oval Office, and I feel sure that each of them thought of John Kennedy now and then and his thousand days in the White House.

And sometimes I want to say to those who are still in school and who sometimes think that history is a dry thing that lives in a book: Nothing is ever lost in that great house; some music plays on.

I've even been told that late at night when the clouds are still and the moon is high, you can just about hear the sound of certain memories brushing by. You can almost hear, if you listen close, the whir of a wheelchair rolling by and the sound of a voice calling out, "And another thing, Eleanor!" Turn down a hall and you hear the brisk strut of a fellow saying, "Bully! Absolutely ripping!" Walk softly, now, and you're drawn to the soft notes of a piano and a brilliant gathering in the East Room where a crowd surrounds a bright young president who is full of hope and laughter.

I don't know if this is true, but it's a story I've been told. And it's not a bad one because it reminds us that history is a living thing that never dies. A life given in service to one's country is a living thing that never dies—a life given in service, yes.

History is not only made by people; it is people. And so, history is, as young John Kennedy demonstrated, as heroic as you want it to be, as heroic as you are.[88]

Ted, Caroline, and John Jr. all wrote Reagan to thank him for his extraordinary tribute. But the most memorable lines had been written just after the Oval Office meeting with Reagan by John Jr., in a postscript that cemented the warm mutual feelings that had developed between families of different partisan stripes: "I was not one of the 'irritated Democrats' when you quoted my father. I thought it was great! Please quote him all you want!"[89]

Much of this tale of two clans is simply smart political relationship building in the snake pit of Washington, where the era of good feelings ended with President James Monroe. As Jimmy Carter learned too late, genuine friendships in your own party and across the aisle can make a difference when a president gets into a tight spot. Ronald Reagan and Edward Kennedy were naturally congenial and enjoyed bipartisan repartee. Unlike many prominent politicians of our own era, they could usually separate their public statements—the ones predetermined by ideology and partisanship—from after-hours personal relationships. They also shared a love of the game and an intimate knowledge of the Oval Office's hothouse. Families that have made it to 1600 Pennsylvania Avenue have much in common, since they are members of the most select club in the country. It may also be true that Reagan understood that a cordial relationship with the Kennedys would give him more leeway to cite JFK in his speeches without fear of rebuke from Ted or others.

Reflecting on the ties that developed between his parents and the Kennedys, Ron Reagan, Jr., detected shared admiration for those who performed well under the hot lights of the public stage. "My parents were show folk, basically, and while the Kennedys didn't come from Hollywood, they understood that leadership required good performance. There was a respect and appreciation for the way the Kennedys handled the public spectacle. Ted Kennedy became a very good friend of my mother's and would call to check up on her, particularly when my father was out of office and ill. They became rather close and my mother was very fond of him."[90]

Whatever the basis of their reciprocated esteem and friendliness, it worked politically for both families, especially the political patriarchs, Ronald Reagan and Edward Kennedy. It was the kind of bipartisan arrangement that is difficult to achieve today, when the personal and the political are one and the same.

DESPITE THE LOSS of Republican control of the U.S. Senate in 1986 and the subsequent Iran-Contra scandal that cost him much of his effectiveness throughout 1987, President Reagan enjoyed an economy robust enough to support a rebound in popularity, just in time for the 1988 presidential election. Reagan had a favorite, his onetime foe, George H. W. Bush, who had been his loyal vice president for eight years. On paper, Bush was an odd combination of the Boston-Austin, Kennedy-Johnson ticket. Born in Massachusetts, Bush had developed his political career in Texas, though he was unlike the Bay State's JFK or the Lone Star State's LBJ. Bush had no well-defined style or base, but he was fortunate to have Reagan, and as the election unfolded, that was all that mattered.

Bush's political career was long, varied, and intertwined with that of every modern president. The son of a senator, Prescott Bush of Connecticut, Bush won his first elected post in February 1963 as chairman of the Harris County (Houston, Texas) Republican Committee. But he had his eye on something much bigger: the U.S. Senate seat of liberal Democrat Ralph Yarborough. Conservatives who dominated Texas politics were unhappy with some of Yarborough's views, and it was mainly this dispute between John Connally's conservative faction and Ralph Yarborough's liberal faction that would, at Lyndon Johnson's urging, draw President Kennedy to the state in November 1963. Had the assassination never happened, Republican Senate nominee Bush might well have defeated Yarborough in 1964. Texas was turning increasingly Republican—the GOP's John Tower had captured LBJ's vacated Senate seat in a 1961 special election—and the Kennedy-Johnson ticket, which squeaked to victory in the Lone Star State in 1960, probably would not have won the same massive majority (63 percent) that Johnson on his own secured in Texas in 1964. But Johnson's presidential coattails sank Bush's first Senate bid, and he lost 56 to 44 percent.

Bush was persistent. He won election to the U.S. House from a conservative Houston district in 1966, and with his strong familial Capitol Hill ties, became the first freshman in sixty years to gain a seat on the powerful Ways and Means Committee. The GOP House caucus was a sharp spur in Lyndon Johnson's side, but Bush was careful to maintain his family's good relations with the president.[91] In January 1969, when Johnson yielded the presidency to Nixon, Bush broke away from the inaugural ceremonies and went to the airport to help see off LBJ and Lady Bird.[92] The Johnsons never forgot this kindness, extended at a time when Johnson's popularity was at low ebb.

Of course Bush knew Johnson's influence in Texas would still be considerable in 1970, when Bush intended to try again to defeat Yarborough. It was to be a reasonably good Republican year in the South, and Bush would probably have succeeded in his quest—except conservative Democrat Lloyd Bentsen took out Yarborough first, in a Democratic primary. Bush went down to his second Senate defeat against Bentsen by 54 to 46 percent.

The resilient Bush became the Nixon-appointed U.S. ambassador to the United Nations in 1971, and then the chairman of the Republican National Committee as Nixon began his second term in 1973. Defending Nixon during Watergate was not a choice assignment, but Bush managed to avoid being tarred. President Ford considered Bush for vice president, before choosing Nelson Rockefeller, and sent Bush instead to head the U.S. liaison office in the People's Republic of China. His last assignment for Ford, extending a year until Jimmy Carter assumed the presidency, was to head the CIA. In 1976, Ford again thought about Bush to replace Rockefeller as vice president, but Bob Dole was selected.

Bush had hoped Carter might keep him on as CIA director, and if that had happened, Bush might never have become president. Instead, Carter gave him a pink slip. Out of office for the first time in a decade, Bush set his sights on the White House in 1980, announcing his candidacy in May 1979. After winning Iowa and a few other contests, he yielded to Reagan and was eventually asked to join the GOP ticket as a safe backup to a failed effort to make Gerald Ford Reagan's running mate.

In 1988, Bush's moment had finally arrived, though politically he was not in a commanding position at first. There was a natural desire for change after eight turbulent years under Reagan, and Bush was the personification of the status quo. Democrats sensed impending victory, and other Republicans saw an opportunity to dislodge Bush by presenting themselves as standing for both change and continuity. Bob Dole was foremost among them, and he bested Bush in Iowa, where the sitting vice president did so poorly he placed third, behind the evangelical preacher Pat Robertson. With the critical help of Governor John Sununu in New Hampshire, Bush turned it around in the Granite State and became the Republican nominee presumptive.

Yet Bush's general election poll ratings were still dismal, and a bevy of Democrats was attracted to compete for their party's nomination. Once again, several of them decided that modeling their candidacy after John F. Kennedy—and presenting themselves to the voters as the next JFK—was the ticket to victory. Gary Hart came back for a second bite at the apple, and was the presumed frontrunner, until his extramarital affair with Donna Rice was revealed in May 1987.[93] Delaware senator Joseph R. Biden, in the first of two unsuccessful campaigns for president, seized the Kennedy mantle by consciously applying JFK's inaugural dictum about defense policy to domestic concerns: "In the spirit of another time, let us pledge that our generation of Americans will pay any price, bear any burden, accept any challenge, meet any hardship to secure the blessings of prosperity and the promise of America for our children."[94] Biden invoked John Kennedy so often that the other candidates kidded him about it, suggesting that in Oklahoma, for example, he might want to announce, "Ich bin ein Sooner."[95] Congressman Richard Gephardt of Missouri was another "neo-Frontiersman," as the *New York Times* dubbed the Kennedy imitators. Gephardt frequently compared his ambitious agenda to JFK's moon landing challenge. The eventual Democratic nominee, Michael Dukakis, was governor of Kennedy's Massachusetts, so the comparisons were inescapable. Dukakis declared that he would follow JFK's example of negotiating with the Soviet Union—though Kennedy's record was full of Cold War clashes and superpower competition. Like Hart and many other Democrats, Dukakis attributed his involvement in politics to JFK's inspiration. Clearly, there was an emotional tie for the famously unemotional

Dukakis, who was seen wiping away tears at the dedication of a Bay State park to President Kennedy.[96]

Kennedy fever mainly touched the Democrats, but it was occasionally apparent on the Republican side, too. One of Bush's early opponents for the GOP presidential nomination, Congressman Jack Kemp of New York, possessed a persona and appearance that had often reminded people of Kennedy. As he campaigned, Kemp claimed Kennedy had set the precedent for a full follow-through on Ronald Reagan's much discussed but never implemented "Star Wars" missile defense system:[97] "John F. Kennedy didn't just talk about researching and testing [for] putting a man on the moon. John F. Kennedy said we would put a man on the moon by the end of the decade. Ladies and gentlemen, we should not just research and test [the Strategic Defense Initiative]. We should research, test and deploy SDI."[98] And the Reverend Pat Robertson, also in the race, used Kennedy's Catholicism to deflect criticism of his evangelical Protestant faith. His final newspaper advertisement in Iowa featured JFK's photo, and reminded readers that Kennedy had been criticized for his religion.[99] Of course, Kennedy was not a priest, and he had been elected to the House and Senate; Robertson, a preacher, had never held any elected office, though his father had been a United States senator.[100]

The best-known intersection of John F. Kennedy and the 1988 campaign occurred on October 5 during the vice presidential candidates' debate. In fact, it was the single most celebrated moment of that entire political year. George Bush's choice for the second office, Indiana senator Dan Quayle, had had a difficult couple of months and was seen by some as insufficiently qualified to be a heartbeat away from the presidency. In an effort to dispel that impression, Quayle had been noting in speeches that he had had almost as many years in Congress (twelve) as JFK had served when he ran for president (fourteen). In 1960, of course, Kennedy had been widely criticized for moving too soon with too little preparation for the White House, but almost three decades and an assassination later, JFK was untouchable and, figuratively at least, he had an honored place on Mount Rushmore. Fair or not, Quayle was not perceived by anyone to be in Kennedy's league. The Republican aspirant had been warned by his staff against utilizing the comparison to JFK, but he had either discounted the advice or forgotten it.[101] Quayle's opponent for vice president, Democratic senator Lloyd Bentsen of Texas—the man who had defeated Bush for Senate in 1970—had noticed Quayle's invocation of JFK. During the debate, panelist Tom Brokaw of NBC asked Quayle if he had a plan in mind for what he would do if he became president.

> QUAYLE: Let me try to answer the question one more time . . . because the question you are asking is what kind of qualifications does

Dan Quayle have to be president . . . ? I would make sure that the people in the Cabinet and the people that are advisors to the president are called in, and I would talk to them, and I will work with them . . . I will be prepared not only because of my service in the Congress, but because of my ability to communicate and to lead. It is not just age, it's accomplishment; it's experience. I have far more experience than many others that sought the office of vice president of this country. I have as much experience in the Congress as Jack Kennedy did when he sought the presidency . . .

BENTSEN: Senator, I served with Jack Kennedy, I knew Jack Kennedy, Jack Kennedy was a friend of mine. Senator, you are no Jack Kennedy . . . [Prolonged shouts and applause]

QUAYLE: That was really uncalled for, Senator. [Shouts and applause]

BENTSEN: You are the one that was making the comparison, Senator—and I'm one who knew him well. And frankly I think you are so far apart in the objectives you choose for your country that I did not think the comparison was well taken.[102]

Quayle never really recovered from this exchange. He became vice president because Bush soundly defeated Dukakis by 53.4 to 45.6 percent, though it is possible Quayle cost Bush a percentage point or two.[103] More damaging for Quayle, the image of a not-ready-for-prime-time player stuck, reinforced by other verbal gaffes he committed while in office.[104] When Quayle sought the presidency himself in 1999, he fared so poorly—finishing eighth in the well-known Ames, Iowa, straw poll—that he withdrew and backed George W. Bush. Ironically, Quayle had more governmental experience than any other 2000 Republican presidential contender, including Bush, but it was too late for experience to do Quayle much good. It is only a slight exaggeration to say that Quayle became the second Republican, after Richard Nixon, whom John Kennedy defeated in a nationally televised debate.

Unlike President Reagan, President Bush rarely mentioned John F. Kennedy in his public speeches and comments. Perhaps the 1988 Quayle incident was part of the explanation; any JFK reference by Bush could be turned by comics or political opponents into a dig at the vice president. Perhaps the Kennedy strategy was also too closely associated with Reagan. Once in office, Bush put some distance between his approach—a "kinder, gentler" one—and Reagan's more hard-edged ideology. It is also true that the policies Reagan tied to Kennedy were no longer on the front burner. Instead of tax cuts, Bush agreed to a tax increase as part of a 1990 budget deal, a decision that violated his "no new taxes" campaign pledge and would harm his reelection bid.

Moreover, the JFK-Reagan Cold War rhetoric became passé when Communism collapsed in 1989 throughout the Soviet empire.

It is also true that Bush's father, Senator Prescott Bush of Connecticut, had not been keen on the Kennedy clan, and he had surely made his views known to his son, the future president. In April 1969, the elder Bush, then a former senator, sent a letter to Clover Dulles, the wife of JFK's former CIA director, expressing disgust with the Kennedy brothers' handling of the Bay of Pigs episode:

> I recall in the summer of 1961, after the ill-fated Bay of Pigs affair, you were away and we called Allen to come for supper, and he accepted. That afternoon he called and asked if he could bring a friend, and we said "surely." So he brought John McCone, whom we had known well, but had not thought of as a particular friend of Allen's. But Allen broke the ice promptly, and said, in good spirit, that he wanted us to meet his successor. The announcement came [the] next day. We tried to make a pleasant evening of it, but I was rather sick at heart, and angry too, for it was the Kennedys that brought about the fiasco. And here they were making Allen seem to be the goat, which he wasn't and did not deserve. I have never forgiven them. [*Misspellings corrected here.*][105]

Occasionally, though, Bush gave a nod to Camelot. His inaugural pledge to honor the old virtues of patriotism and community service, and his call to Americans to give of their time and energy to do what government cannot, struck some as reminiscent of John Kennedy's "ask not" entreaty.[106] Bush's robust foreign policy, from Panama to Kuwait to the former Soviet and Eastern European republics, was in the Kennedy tradition. And though not as frequent as in the Reagan administration, Bush extended courtesies to the Kennedys, such as a proclamation in honor of Rose Kennedy's hundredth birthday in 1990.[107]

As with his predecessors, Bush could not avoid leftover controversies from November 22, 1963. Bush lived in Houston in 1963, and he actually called the Dallas office of the FBI soon after the assassination to report an individual who had made a threat against the life of President Kennedy.[108] From time to time, conspiracy theorists have sought to tie Bush to the assassination itself, based on references to Bush here and there in the voluminous records of the assassination. Not a shred of convincing proof of Bush's involvement has ever been produced, and this claim appears even more specious than the insinuation than LBJ was behind John Kennedy's murder.[109]

Actually, President Bush made a positive, if limited, contribution to the effort to reveal all the facts about the assassination when he signed the Assassination Records and Collection Act (ARCA).[110] This law, passed by Congress in 1992, was a direct result of the public's demand for full disclosure by the government after the release of Oliver Stone's controversial 1991 movie *JFK*. Near the twentieth anniversary of the release of *JFK*, I asked Oliver Stone how his film had approached the body of evidence accumulated about the Kennedy assassination. He admitted that he had employed artistic license to go beyond the known facts. "I view the JFK assassination as the Moby Dick of American stories," Stone said. "It is the great mystery and is the white whale . . . I felt like Ahab going after the white whale . . . There were just too many weird things that happened . . . All you can say is [my movie is] a countermyth. We can't prove it." A filmmaker has no obligation to produce a historically faithful documentary, and in that, Stone is on solid ground. Still, Americans—especially those too young to remember November 22, 1963—often interpret Stone's film as a cross between documentary and exposé. Stone's own term "countermyth" ought to be part of the advertising for all showings.[111]

President Bush may or may not have seen Stone's film during its original release, but his ARCA signing statement shows that he had some reservations about the structure of the board that would review JFK-related documents, and more broadly, a former CIA director was probably not enthusiastic about shining sunlight into some of the dark corners of the agency he loved. Nonetheless, he was presented with the bill as his reelection campaign drew to a close, and given the substantial popular support for it, Bush affixed his signature on October 26, 1992.[112] Ten days later, Bush would be ousted as president by a man who idolized President Kennedy. Enforcement of the Assassination Records and Collection Act—and preservation of the Kennedy legacy—would pass to Bill Clinton.

CLINTON GRABS
KENNEDY'S TORCH

RARELY IF EVER IN AMERICAN HISTORY has one president hero-worshipped another president the way Bill Clinton idolized John F. Kennedy.

On July 24, 1963, seventeen-year-old Bill Clinton was an Arkansas delegate to Boys Nation in Washington. He had met with his state's U.S. senators on the trip but was most looking forward to a brief audience with President Kennedy in the Rose Garden. The youthful Clinton had long identified with the Democratic Party and its new star. He recalled sitting in front of the TV set, "transfixed," as JFK fought a losing battle to be Adlai Stevenson's 1956 running mate at the Democratic National Convention. In 1960, encouraged by a couple of Democratic teachers in a heavily Republican county, Clinton had sided with Kennedy in a ninth-grade civics class debate.[1] And he had been delighted that November when Arkansas, and the country, voted for JFK.

Now in close proximity to his president, Clinton planned to make the most of the moment. The future president positioned himself at the front of the line so that, even if Kennedy "shook only two or three" hands, his would be one of them. After receiving a Boys Nation T-shirt, JFK strode down the steps and outstretched his hand. Sure enough, Bill Clinton's hand met his.[2] And fortuitously for Clinton, a black-and-white movie camera recorded the second that the thirty-fifth president met the forty-second. That brief segment of film would show up again in TV ads and a Democratic National Convention video presentation in 1992. The torch had been passed yet again.

The Rose Garden handshake was much on Clinton's mind after he was told of President Kennedy's assassination. His calculus teacher broke the news to the class, and Clinton recalled a man "so full of life and strength" four months earlier. He also remembered a classmate from that afternoon who remarked that "maybe it was a good thing for the country" that JFK was shot—her feelings no doubt stemming from civil rights controversies that had rocked Arkansas since the 1950s.[3]

After Clinton moved to Washington to attend Georgetown University in 1964, he became friends with a dormitory floor mate, Tommy Caplan, who had interviewed JFK in 1960 and later convinced members of his administration to establish a pilot project for a "junior Peace Corps" so that youngsters could correspond with their peers in developing countries. Inevitably Clinton and Caplan pursued their common interest as friends, from visiting President Kennedy's grave to exploring the National Archives, where JFK secretary Evelyn Lincoln was cataloging the late president's personal items for history. Mrs. Lincoln showed the young men President Kennedy's famous rocking chair and many other mementos.[4] "[The JFK assassination] was the first real tragedy that any of us had ever confronted," Caplan recalls. "It wasn't that Bill Clinton and I uniquely talked about it, we were probably two of the only people who had any direct connection to the [Kennedy] White House."[5] Caplan's comments reinforce the notion that Clinton's brief encounter with Kennedy in the White House Rose Garden helped guide his destiny.

Like John Kennedy had been, Bill Clinton was a young man in a hurry. His years at Georgetown were followed by a Rhodes scholarship to Oxford University (though he failed to get a degree in the end), law school at Yale, and a quick return to Arkansas to begin his political career with a close but losing run for the U.S. House of Representatives in 1974. His marriage to Yale classmate Hillary Rodham in 1975 was quickly followed by his election as state attorney general in 1976 and successful campaign for governor in 1978. At age thirty-two, Clinton was one of the youngest governors in American history, marking Clinton as a comer.

From time to time, Clinton quoted JFK in his speeches,[6] but the governor of this socially conservative Southern state gave a wide berth to Ted Kennedy's presidential candidacy in 1980. Clinton stuck with Jimmy Carter, much to the dismay of his friends from the 1972 McGovern campaign.[7] But politically, Clinton could hardly have done otherwise.

The irony is that Carter's growing unpopularity, combined with the White House's decision to send thousands of Cuban refugees to be housed in Arkansas, created a Republican tidal wave in 1980 that swept Clinton out of office after a single two-year term.[8] Reagan's coattails elected the GOP's Frank White to replace Clinton as governor, and his once-bright future seemed shattered. Clinton had contributed to the debacle himself, trying to do too much all at once, instituting a hated increase in the car tax and assembling a staff that looked and acted too liberal for Arkansas.[9] As Clinton himself later wrote, "I organized the governor's office without a chief of staff . . . President Kennedy had organized his White House in a similar way, but his guys all had short hair, boring suits, white shirts, and dark, narrow ties. [Clinton's top staffers] all had beards and were less constrained in their dress code."[10]

But Clinton quickly demonstrated the resilience that would mark his political exploits. In a campaign noted for its emphasis on humility, listening instead of talking, and redemption, Clinton worked his way back into Arkansans' favor. Assisted by a deep recession that hurt Republicans in the 1982 midterms, the youthful ex-governor ousted Frank White to secure a nonconsecutive second term. Clinton never let down his guard again, and he never faced another serious challenge in Arkansas, winning gubernatorial reelection in 1984, 1986 (when the term was lengthened to four years), and 1990.

In the midst of his fourth term, Clinton seriously considered a presidential run. Preparations were well under way, and the national press corps was called to Little Rock in July 1987 to hear Clinton's long-awaited announcement. But Clinton had long before chosen to emulate the seedier side of John F. Kennedy, and his many sins of the flesh caught up with him. Not long after his gubernatorial defeat in 1980, journalists in Arkansas had received tips about Clinton's extramarital activities. Sure enough, Clinton eventually hinted that he had first "brought pain" into his marriage at about that time.[11] (Close observers of Clinton say it started long before then.)

Over the years, the evidence had mounted—inescapable proof both to Clinton's fellow politicians and those closest to Clinton in his political circle. At National Governors Association meetings in Washington and around the nation, Clinton's fellow state chief executives would sometimes make bets on which young woman in the room would be approached by their Arkansas colleague, who usually was not accompanied by his wife. The governor's Arkansas staff was loyal, but it was impossible for them to overlook the accumulating evidence that was close at hand. The night before Clinton's scheduled presidential announcement, his gubernatorial chief of staff, Betsey Wright, reviewed a lengthy list of women who had been linked to the handsome governor. After a number of replies from the governor along the lines of "She'll never say anything," it was obvious that Clinton had a big problem. Looking back, decades later, Wright said, "I felt betrayed. He lied to me. He lied to a lot of people about [adultery], not least of whom was himself."[12]

Two months before Clinton's announcement, in May 1987, Democratic presidential front-runner Gary Hart had been forced out of the race in the midst of an extramarital scandal, and Hart had been asked, "Have you ever committed adultery?"[13] Given the widespread, substantive rumors about Clinton's womanizing, the question was inevitable, and the answer was unavoidable. To the considerable surprise of the gathered media, a subdued Clinton accepted reality and declared that he would not run, citing the classic excuse that he wanted to spend more time with family.[14] Even at that time, the scuttlebutt throughout the national political community was about Clinton's extramarital affairs. This experience was just a hint of what was to come, and amazingly, the highly intelligent Clinton learned little or nothing from his brush with private life revelations.

The year actually got worse for Clinton. He was invited to give the main nominating speech for Michael Dukakis at the 1988 Democratic National Convention in Atlanta, potentially a great opportunity to shine and position himself for the future. Instead, Clinton showed he lacked John F. Kennedy's flair when it came to rhetorical ability. Clinton's address quoted JFK in its final paragraph:

> In closing, I want you to remember that in November, when Michael Dukakis is elected president, we will observe the twenty-fifth anniversary of President Kennedy's death. But Mike's victory will be a tribute to the life and legacy of John Kennedy, to the boundless optimism, the grace, the courage, and the sheer joy with which he urged us forward. The great Israeli statesman Abba Eban began his memorial tribute to President Kennedy with this simple, stirring statement: "Tragedy is the difference between what is and what might have been." Michael Dukakis has spent his entire public life closing the gap between what is and what might have been.[15]

It was Clinton's best paragraph, not because of the Kennedy passage but because it began, "In closing..." Clinton talked much too long, with little apparent emotion, and the crowd turned restless with delegates and guests loudly talking over the Arkansas governor in a thousand private conversations. The magic words "in closing" generated Clinton's only real ovation. A few days later, arranged by a couple of backers with Hollywood ties, Clinton appeared on *The Tonight Show with Johnny Carson*. In a prearranged gag, when Clinton sat next to him, Carson pulled out an hourglass to set a time limit on the governor's gab. A good laugh washed away much of the convention embarrassment.[16]

AS IT HAPPENED, Clinton was fortunate his White House dreams were deferred. Peace, prosperity, and a popular GOP incumbent probably would have defeated any 1988 Democratic nominee, though a more appealing candidate than Michael Dukakis might have made the contest closer. With his long governorship very likely in its final term, and no U.S. Senate vacancy in sight, Bill Clinton realized that 1992 might well be his best shot at the presidency.

George H. W. Bush's sizable winning margin in 1988 and subsequent victory in the 1991 Persian Gulf War led most Democrats to think he would be unbeatable for reelection. Yet a mild recession in 1991 gave Clinton reason to think otherwise. Moreover, as a small-state governor with some obvious personal baggage, he benefited from the decisions of party heavyweights such as New York governor Mario Cuomo and New Jersey senator Bill Bradley to skip the 1992 race. Against the odds, Clinton took the plunge in October 1991 and launched his campaign.

One of his themes from the start was to emulate, as he put it, "John Kennedy's ethic of mutual responsibility, asking citizens to give something back to their country . . ."[17] Clinton soon announced that one of his presidential goals would be the creation of a "Democracy Corps" of American legal, financial, and political specialists sent abroad to augment the Peace Corps.[18] Clinton's campaign speeches contained many references to JFK and his policies, from investment tax credits to spur business expansion to the need for religious tolerance.[19] Much like Jimmy Carter had done in 1976, Clinton even reversed roles with JFK—going to Notre Dame as a Southern Baptist to appeal for Catholic votes.[20] "Clinton always thought of Kennedy as a performer [and] Clinton viewed Kennedy as a kind of 'third way' [moderate] Democrat," says James Carville, Clinton's chief campaign strategist.[21] Thus, Clinton's gestures, speech patterns, and less liberal, more pragmatic politics show a clear Kennedy influence.

As the early front-runner, Clinton was expected to win the New Hampshire primary, even though another candidate given to Kennedy allusions, former Massachusetts senator Paul Tsongas, was also running. The first hurdle was Clinton's Vietnam-era draft record, which was decidedly un-Kennedy-like. In order to avoid the unpopular war, Clinton had used his connections to evade the military draft and was less than forthcoming about the details.[22] PT 109 it was not. Of course, prominent Republicans such as Defense Secretary Dick Cheney had used multiple deferments to skip Vietnam service, and future president George W. Bush and the incumbent vice president, Dan Quayle, had joined the National Guard. All had connections of some sort within the system, and they used them, like many thousands of potential draftees in that era. But while legal, and given the nature of the war, somewhat understandable, these actions were not admirable in a political context.

Clinton's draft controversy was chicken feed compared to the full feast on the table laid by Gennifer Flowers. The onetime Arkansas lounge singer stunned the political world in January 1992 with an allegation that she had had a longtime affair with Clinton. Her charges were published in the *Star*, a supermarket tabloid that paid Flowers for the story, but they were given credence thanks to her tapes of private phone conversations with Governor

Clinton about how she should handle questions concerning their relationship. Flowers held a full-blown press conference carried live on CNN to present her evidence, and many analysts at the time thought Clinton was finished politically. As *Newsweek* put it, "Old CW [conventional wisdom]: Hooray, the new JFK. New CW: Uh-oh, the new JFK."[23]

Clinton fought back, with unconvincing, misleading blanket denials and with a more effective, not-so-secret weapon, Hillary Rodham Clinton. In a joint appearance on *60 Minutes,* the Clintons presented the image of a modern couple that had worked through problems in their marriage, with Hillary insisting she was not "some little woman standing by my man like Tammy Wynette."[24] Once the front-runner, Bill Clinton finished second behind Paul Tsongas in the New Hampshire primary. But he had survived the crises that threatened to eject him from presidential politics, and he declared himself to be "the Comeback Kid" as he declared "victory" with his second-place showing. Clinton won the Democratic nomination mainly because there was no convincing, credible alternative to him in the race. What did not kill Clinton made him stronger—at least until the Monica Lewinsky scandal during his presidency. Though there would be many other lower-level rumors and allegations about Clinton's past and present womanizing in 1992, some of them likely true, he never again faced scrutiny so intense that his candidacy was endangered.[25]

Volumes have been written about the Clintons' marriage, but it may not be all that different from the one that existed between President and Mrs. Kennedy. John Kennedy and Bill Clinton loved their wives, had children with them, and understood they were great assets politically. At the same time, both men were driven by their own apparently uncontrollable desires and demons to commit adultery on a regular basis, oblivious to, or uncaring about, the pain this caused their spouses. For their part, the wives placed a high priority on protecting the children, as well as preserving their marriages and their status. Jackie and Hillary were often angry at their husbands, and privately lashed out at them in various ways, Jackie with her free-spending habits and frequent absences from White House duties, and Hillary by her berating of Bill in private settings. Still, the wives stood by their husbands stoically in public, maybe hoping in vain for maturation in their behavior as they grew older. Politics is careerist for couples, and political marriages are partnerships that benefit husbands *and* wives. The professional bargain that is struck can often outlast the intimate bonds of a spousal relationship.

The personal aspects receded as the strange politics of 1992 continued to unfold. A sputtering economy erased the polling heights once enjoyed by

President Bush. Triumph in the 1991 Persian Gulf War seemed a long time past, and the Clinton campaign adopted the perfect slogan to reflect the public's anxieties: "It's the economy, stupid!" Bush and his campaign team, expecting Clinton to collapse under the weight of various scandals, did not take the Democrat seriously until it was too late. "Can you imagine Bill Clinton sitting there?" Bush quipped a few months before the election, pointing toward his chair in the Oval Office as his closest advisers laughed.[26] The overconfidence was supplemented by a lack of energy and focus on Bush's part that may well have been a consequence of Graves' disease, an immune disorder caused by an overactive thyroid gland that was diagnosed in the president in 1991. His friend and campaign manager Fred Malek recalled, "[During the '88 campaign] I would get calls from [Bush] two or three times a week around seven A.M., with kind of a rat-tat-tat of different recommendations that he wanted me to think about and follow up. I'd get calls a couple of times a week to come up to the vice president's residence after work and chat with him and Barbara . . . He was just full of ideas and thoughts and initiatives. Contrast that with 1992 when I came back and had frequent contact once again. It was altogether different. He wasn't reaching out. He wasn't doing those things. Of course, he was president then and had a full-time job. But it was quite clear there was a profound change in his energy and demeanor."[27]

Just as consequential as the economy and Graves' disease was the independent candidacy of the billionaire businessman Ross Perot. Bush's fellow Texan aimed most of his fire at Bush, double-teaming the president with Clinton. Polls, studies, and opinions differ about whether Perot's sizable 19 percent of the November vote* enabled Clinton to win with 43 percent (to Bush's 37)—or whether by then, Clinton would have won an outright majority against Bush had it been a two-man contest. Certainly, polls at the time showed Clinton thumping Bush in a head-to-head matchup.[28]

Clinton's own superbly focused campaign played a role in his remarkable yearlong resurrection. The Gallup poll had Clinton in third place, behind both Perot and Bush, as late as June 1992.[29] Yet Clinton never let Bush up off the mat on the economy, and Perot eliminated himself from serious consideration by withdrawing in July after some bizarre charges about Republican plans to disrupt his daughter's wedding. (Perot reentered the contest in early October, but by then he had forfeited any real chance of winning.)[30] This process of elimination left Clinton, even with his credibility problems and the

---

* Perot was the second most successful independent presidential candidate in U.S. history, after former president Theodore Roosevelt, who garnered 27.4 percent of the vote in 1912 as the candidate of the Progressive or "Bull Moose" Party.

strong scent of scandal, as the only possible route to change in the country's direction.

Clinton seized the opportunity and converted himself from the second coming of JFK the womanizer to the reincarnation of JFK the inspirational leader. Like Kennedy, Clinton fared well in debates, mastering the art of "feeling the pain" of people in distress. "You ought to read my mail," Clinton told *Rolling Stone*. "People my age writing me, saying they haven't felt this way since Kennedy was president . . ."[31] In Clinton's campaign proposals and speeches, President Kennedy, as the journalist Joe Klein suggested, "made Clinton seem larger—large enough, ultimately, to unseat the incumbent President of the United States."[32] His nominating convention in New York City in mid-July was consciously designed to evoke Kennedy parallels, not least because a Hollywood producer on his team had studied the films of the 1960 Democratic National Convention.[33] An elaborate tribute to Robert Kennedy featured his son, Congressman Joseph P. Kennedy II, and Senator Ted Kennedy.[34] When Clinton broke with tradition and appeared in the convention hall on the night he officially won the nomination—usually, candidates appear only to give an acceptance address on the closing night—Clinton explained his reasoning to the cheering delegates: "Thirty-two years ago another young candidate who wanted to get this country moving again came to the convention to say a simple thank you."[35]

The next night, a film was shown on national television and in the hall to introduce Clinton just before his big speech; the emotional highlight for excited delegates, and probably for the audience at home, was the brief clip of Boys Nation delegate Bill Clinton shaking hands with President Kennedy. In the film, Clinton's mother drove home the point: "When he came home from Boys Nation with this picture of John Kennedy and himself shaking hands, I've never seen such an expression on a man's face in my life. He just had such pride. And I knew then that government in some form would be his goal."[36] (On Clinton's first day in office, he took pride in showing his mother precisely where he had stood in the Rose Garden when he shook JFK's hand.)[37] The selection of Senator Albert Gore as vice president reinforced the theme of generational change. Even the convention's musical theme, Fleetwood Mac's "Don't Stop Thinking About Tomorrow," was designed to contrast Clinton's youthfulness and energy with President Bush's age (sixty-eight) and his alleged personal and policy exhaustion.

Whatever the precise combination of factors that elevated him, Clinton's almost lifelong ambition to be president became a reality on November 3, 1992. At forty-six, just three years older than John F. Kennedy was when he entered the White House, Clinton was the seventh president to succeed JFK. The twenty-two years in age that separated Clinton from his predecessor

Bush was the second largest in American history, only exceeded by the twenty-seven-year age gap between JFK and Eisenhower.

CLINTON'S EMBRACE OF John F. Kennedy was no campaign gimmick or passing fancy. The news media sensed it and emphasized the theme. Within forty-eight hours of the election, the incoming Clinton White House was being compared to Camelot in TV news programs.[38] *Time* stressed the Kennedy-Clinton parallels in naming Clinton its 1992 Man of the Year.[39] The public caught the wave, with a sizable plurality in a *Wall Street Journal* / NBC News poll saying the past president most reminiscent of Clinton was, of course, JFK.[40] And the nation's premier satirical program, *Saturday Night Live*, produced a skit with Madonna singing "Happy Inauguration Day" to an actor portraying Bill Clinton, in a takeoff of Marilyn Monroe's sexy rendition of "Happy Birthday to You" for JFK.[41]

The Clinton administration began with a symbolic nod to the new president's idol. On inauguration eve, January 19, 1993, President-elect and Mrs. Clinton joined Ted Kennedy, Ethel Kennedy, and John F. Kennedy, Jr., to visit the graves of JFK and RFK in Arlington Cemetery.[42] Clinton placed a long-stemmed white rose on each grave.[43] To no one's surprise, President Clinton's inaugural address the next day contained echoes of President Kennedy's. "Let us begin anew," said both men. JFK asserted, "Now the trumpet summons us again," as the torch was passed to a new generation, with Kennedy asking what "you can do for your country," with God's work on earth being our own. Clinton intoned: "We have heard the trumpets. We have changed the guard. And now, each in our own way and with God's help, we must answer the call."[44] Clinton also became the first president since JFK to invite a poet to participate in the inaugural ceremony; Maya Angelou succeeded Robert Frost in this special role.[45]

Though Bill Clinton's devotion to JFK was real, he also certainly understood the political advantages of the juxtaposition. However, at least at first, Clinton might not have fully realized the risks inherent in competing with a heroic myth. Immediately, Clinton's workmanlike but uninspiring inaugural address was held up to JFK's gold standard and found wanting. The historian Garry Wills called Clinton's language "flimsy" next to Kennedy's: "Great writing is something you can lean your weight against; it will resist . . . Flimsy language 'gives,' as if you were putting your hand through stage scenery."[46]

Throughout his presidency, Clinton was often called articulate but not eloquent. John Kennedy possessed an unusual gravitas—perhaps a combination of handsome visage, vocal distinctiveness, natural wit, and the ability to turn a memorable phrase (with wordsmith Ted Sorensen's considerable aid). JFK also instinctively knew that in politics, at the presidential level, less is more. By contrast, Bill Clinton personified his generation's rhetorical (and other) excesses. More is better; extra words can create escape hatches; phrases must be inserted to cover all constituency bases. With the possible exception of one powerful speech after the Oklahoma City bombing in 1995, the only universally memorable public utterance from the Clinton years is the pitiful and untruthful, "I did not have sexual relations with that woman, Miss Lewinsky."[47]

Given Clinton's embrace of all things Kennedy, it is not unreasonable to think about the Clinton presidency in Kennedy-like terms, both in similarities and differences. Both men were resilient: Kennedy bounced back from serious illnesses, and Clinton came back from defeats for Congress and governor, as well as surviving enough scandals to sink a battleship. Of course, Kennedy never lost an elective contest, primary or general, unless one counts the vice presidential nomination at the 1956 Democratic National Convention. Nor did Kennedy have to struggle to rise to the top; he was to the manor born. Clinton didn't have a father like Joseph Kennedy. His real father, William Jefferson Blythe, Jr., died in a traffic accident even before Clinton was born, and Clinton—originally named Blythe III—took his surname from his sometimes angry, wife-beating stepdad, Roger Clinton. JFK floated into prep school and Harvard, but Clinton had to work very hard to travel from Arkansas to Georgetown, Oxford, and Yale Law.

After choosing two different pathways to the presidency—Kennedy the Senate, Clinton a state governorship—they entered office with many opponents questioning their legitimacy. To this day many Republicans insist that JFK and LBJ stole the 1960 election with vote fraud in Illinois and Texas, while Clinton had difficulty overcoming his low 43 percent plurality of the vote in 1992.

The most telling similarity between the two administrations may be the trouble both Democrats had getting their programs through a heavily Democratic Congress. In both cases, an alliance between Republicans and conservative Democrats frustrated many of their legislative initiatives, including health care. Kennedy's Medicare proposals had to wait for LBJ's term, while Clinton's "Hillary-care" effort collapsed entirely. Clinton ended up in a far worse situation, since his failures early in his administration produced GOP control of both houses of Congress in the 1994 midterm election and for the rest of Clinton's tenure. Two government shutdowns in 1995 and 1996 were the result of executive-legislative deadlock, although eventually Clinton and Republican leaders were able to reach compromises on some topics, such as free trade, welfare reform, and crime control. Even had he completed two terms, JFK would never have had to face a Republican majority in either house, given his era's Democratic dominance on Capitol Hill.

Every White House has its share of crises, and there were elements of Kennedy's in the early 1960s that still resonated for Clinton in the 1990s. Bill Clinton had to deal with an early domestic disaster that paralleled JFK's Bay of Pigs fiasco: the Waco tragedy. Just three months after Clinton assumed the presidency, seventy-six people (including more than twenty children and two pregnant women) were killed after a fifty-one-day siege at the Branch Davidian compound near Waco, Texas. This Protestant sect's flock was under the control of an unstable cult leader, David Koresh. The Bureau of Alcohol, Tobacco, and Firearms and the FBI, supervised by Attorney General Janet Reno, were the government agencies directly in charge of the situation. Clinton himself delegated final decision-making authority on Waco to Reno. Even though he had actually wanted to hold out longer to try more peaceful means of conflict resolution, he gave in to the insistence of Reno, among others, for a more aggressive approach. In retrospect, Clinton would regret this, though he continued to back Reno publicly.[48]

Both sides at Waco were exceptionally well armed, and soon after the final assault began, the entire complex was consumed by fire. The government asserted the conflagration was a result of arson by the Davidians themselves, while the surviving sect members insisted that the FBI's equipment and tactics led to the calamity. In any event, much of the public was horrified by the results—and some Americans were radicalized by it. The Waco siege figured prominently in the motives cited by Timothy McVeigh, the convicted (and later executed) Oklahoma City bomber. McVeigh chose April 19, 1995—the second anniversary of Waco—to explode his car bomb at the city's federal building, killing 168 people including many children, with roughly seven hundred injured.[49]

Waco occurred for Clinton at almost precisely the same moment in his young presidency that the Bay of Pigs invasion did for Kennedy (April 16–19). New presidents can make mistakes, trusting too much in their advisers' judgments, and these tragedies are classic examples. Just as the Bay of Pigs led in some ways to the Cuban Missile Crisis—the Russians became convinced Kennedy was weak and they could take advantage—so, too, did Waco lead to a greater catastrophe at Oklahoma City. Nonetheless, for both JFK and Clinton, a by-product of their early missteps was a strengthening of their two presidencies, and the subsequent crises enhanced their position. JFK had no greater triumph than the Cuban Missile Crisis, and Clinton's skillful comforting of the shell-shocked residents of Oklahoma City is the moment some mark as the beginning of his political recovery after the 1994 Republican midterm landslide, on his way to a successful reelection.[50]

The connections between and among presidents, even those serving decades apart, are inevitable. For example, President Clinton replaced the last remaining JFK appointee on the Supreme Court in 1993. Kennedy friend Byron "Whizzer" White, having served three decades, retired and was replaced by Clinton's choice, Ruth Bader Ginsburg. Foreign policy ties among presidencies are especially strong. Containing the Soviet Union was an overriding focus for every White House occupant from Truman through Bush. Clinton was the first to benefit from the absence of the Cold War—though it was soon replaced by the threat of terrorism. As much as Cuba bedeviled JFK, the island nation ninety miles to the south of Florida proved to be a major irritant for Clinton. Thirty-eight years after the Cuban Missile Crisis, he had to deal with the fallout from the repatriation of a six-year-old Cuban refugee, Elian Gonzalez. The boy's mother had drowned while trying to escape to the United States from Cuba, but Elian made it and was placed with relatives. The boy's father, still in Cuba, then demanded his return, and the American courts eventually agreed. In a raid on the Miami home of Elian's relatives in April 2000, the youngster was seized and sent back to Cuba by U.S. government agents, again supervised by controversial attorney general Reno. A famous photo shows Elian hiding in a closet, terrified by the appearance of an armed-to-the-teeth law enforcer.[51] This angered many Cuban Americans, a key voting bloc, and the searing incident may well have cost Al Gore far more than the 537 votes by which he lost Florida and the White House in the fall 2000 election.

A poignant JFK-Clinton link was forged on Vietnam, as Clinton brought to a final conclusion the greatest foreign policy mistake of the 1960s. As the first opponent of the Vietnam War to be elected president, and having evaded military service, Clinton was handicapped in his role as commander in chief in the eyes of some. His 1993 initiation of the "don't ask, don't tell" policy for gays and lesbians in the military was deeply controversial at the time, in part because of Clinton's draft record. But Clinton saw an opportunity to bring the era of divisiveness over American involvement in Vietnam, begun in earnest during the Kennedy administration, to an end. Clinton was encouraged by a letter he had received as president-elect from JFK and LBJ's defense secretary Robert S. McNamara, a primary architect of the bloody conflict in Southeast Asia. McNamara referred to Clinton's Oxford roommate, Frank Aller, who resisted the Vietnam draft and committed suicide in 1971: "For me—and I believe for the nation as well—the Vietnam War finally ended the day you were elected president. By their votes, the American people, at long last, recognized that the Allers and the Clintons, when they questioned the wisdom and morality of their government's decisions relating to Vietnam, were no less patriotic than those who served in uniform."[52] With the help of Vietnam veterans in Congress from both parties, Clinton pursued normalization of relations with Vietnam. In 1995, diplomatic relations were established between the former foes, and shortly after the 2000 election, Clinton journeyed to Vietnam for the first official state visit by a president of the United States.

Dramatic events aside, the underlying foundation for the popularity of both Kennedy and Clinton as president was a strong economy. JFK's tax cut in public memory is attributable to Republican praise of it, not Democratic support. Clinton was associated with the opposite, an income tax increase, which he engineered in 1993.[53] (Clinton also signed GOP-sponsored tax reductions in estate and capital gains levies in 1997.)[54] Both Kennedy and Clinton were considered fiscal moderates; they were tight-fisted in some ways and ran up relatively small deficits, or in Clinton's case, eventually achieved a balanced budget.[55] What mattered most, however, was that the gross domestic product expanded at a fast clip under JFK (5.5 percent) and Clinton (5.8 percent), while joblessness averaged just under 6 percent for Kennedy and 5.2 percent for Clinton.[56] Whether their policies were wise or they were just lucky, both presidents are linked in history with prosperity. Nothing leaves a better impression on the American public than a robust economy.

Another direct JFK-Clinton bond could be seen in the establishment of AmeriCorps.[57] President Clinton fulfilled a campaign promise by further applying the idea of the Peace Corps to opportunities for domestic service, from after-school tutoring to environmental protection.[58] Young people who work 1,700 hours over the typical eleven-month term of service earn a living allowance and up to $5,550 that can be applied to college or graduate school. When he signed the AmeriCorps legislation in September 1993, the Peace Corps' first director, JFK brother-in-law Sargent Shriver, was on hand and lent Clinton one of the pens Kennedy had used to sign the Peace Corps bill in 1961.

BILL CLINTON HAD a luxury denied to President Kennedy—eight full years in office. After the 1994 Republican landslide, Clinton looked very vulnerable to defeat for reelection. But by the time 1996 arrived, the economy was rebounding vigorously, and there was little question that Clinton would beat Republican nominee Bob Dole, the former Senate majority leader and 1976 GOP vice presidential nominee. A triumph JFK had hoped for was earned by Clinton, as he swept 379 electoral votes and won the popular vote by 8 percentage points (49 to 41 percent), with Ross Perot again on the ballot and securing about 8 percent.

Clinton's second term turned out to be anything but a victory lap, though. Instead of building "the bridge to the twenty-first century" that he had talked about on the campaign trail, Clinton mainly answered for scandals in his past and present. The problems, many stemming from Clinton's gubernatorial tenure, had been mounting throughout his White House years. Less than a year into his presidency, some Arkansas troopers and other state employees began talking to various news media outlets, claiming they had facilitated Governor Clinton's extramarital affairs in Little Rock and elsewhere.[59] Precisely a year after the inauguration, Attorney General Reno acceded to Republican demands and named an independent counsel, Robert Fiske, to investigate Bill and Hillary Clinton's investment in an Arkansas real estate development called Whitewater, which had been discussed during the 1992 campaign and became a press obsession in 1993 and 1994.[60] A few months later, a former Arkansas state employee, Paula Jones, filed a civil lawsuit claiming Governor Clinton had made explicit sexual advances toward her, including exposing himself, in 1991.[61] The water was rising behind a dam that, fortunately for Clinton, would not burst until after he was safely reelected.

Just short of a year into Clinton's second term, the die was cast when former solicitor general Kenneth Starr, who had replaced Robert Fiske as the independent counsel in 1994, received permission from Janet Reno to expand his investigation beyond Whitewater. His focus was on some explosive information he had received—that President Clinton had carried on an affair with a young White House intern named Monica Lewinsky from November 1995 until March 1997. On January 17, 1998, Clinton gave sworn testimony for the Paula Jones lawsuit. In the deposition, he denied having a sexual relationship with Lewinsky. Within a few days, the story was fully public, virtually wiping out all other news and dominating the headlines until 1999.[62] In front of reporters and TV cameras in the White House, an angry President Clinton wagged his finger and repeated his denial in the most-replayed video clip of his tenure ("I did not have sexual relations . . .").[63]

The country avidly followed a presidency that became a high-stakes soap opera. By August Clinton was forced to admit to a grand jury (the first ever in which a president appeared in his own defense) and then to the nation in a televised address that he had had "a relationship with Miss Lewinsky that was not appropriate."[64] By this time, Clinton knew that Ken Starr had accumulated evidence of the affair; as it happened, the proof included a blue dress worn by Lewinsky during one of her encounters with Clinton that was stained with his semen.[65] Clinton continued to insist that he had not lied in the Jones deposition because of his use of the present tense—that is, denying only that the affair was a current one. By that time, he was no longer seeing Lewinsky. Clinton also claimed that because only fellatio was involved, no real sexual relations took place—an assertion that produced widespread scorn and gave late-night comedians a ratings boost.

On September 9, 1998 Starr delivered to Congress a scathing, explicit report about his four-year investigation. Having lied under oath, Clinton was an impeachment target in the Republican-controlled U.S. House of Representatives. On December 16 President Clinton became the second chief executive, after Andrew Johnson, to be impeached by the House, which justified its action on the basis of Clinton's perjury and obstruction of justice. There was never any chance Clinton would be convicted by the Senate, since a two-thirds vote (67 senators) was required for conviction and there were only 55 GOP senators. Clinton's long ordeal officially ended on February 12, 1999, when the Senate failed to convict on any charge. Two months later Clinton was held in civil contempt of court by a federal judge, and he was eventually compelled to pay Paula Jones's lawyers $90,000 in compensation for the extra work they performed because of Clinton's false testimony.[66] Separately, Paula Jones had also been awarded $850,000, though all but $200,000 of that was for her legal expenses.[67] Clinton paid from a legal fund he had established, but admitted no wrongdoing in her case. In a final indignity, handed down just a day before he left the White House in 2001, Clinton's law license was suspended for five years by the Arkansas Supreme Court's Committee on Professional Responsibility, and Clinton had to pay an additional fine of $25,000.[68]

While Clinton was a diminished president after the airing of his very dirty laundry, the Republicans did themselves no favor either. The public wanted Clinton censured, not ousted from office, and the electorate punished the GOP for overplaying its hand, depriving the party of expected gains in Congress during the 1998 midterm election. The Republicans lost five seats in the House, and added no seats in the Senate, despite early expectations that they would gain substantially in both houses. Instead of Clinton leaving office, it was Republican Speaker Newt Gingrich who resigned his post, forced out by an unhappy GOP caucus that learned he had been conducting an extramarital affair at the same time he had been capitalizing on Clinton's woes.[69] The nation learned anew that hypocrisy is often the lifeblood of politics.

The contrast between the standards for presidents applied in the 1960s and the 1990s is stark. John Kennedy's sexual shenanigans in the White House were likely more frequent and every bit as outrageous as Bill Clinton's. JFK carried on an affair with a young intern, too, and did so more or less openly in front of trusted staffers.[70] The moral reprehensibility is clear in both cases, but the accepted norms under which the men operated were akin to night and day. In JFK's time, public men, even presidents, were given a free pass by the press on their dalliances, while Clinton had had lesson after lesson on the dangers of adultery during his governorship, his 1992 campaign, and his pre-Lewinsky White House days. Clinton paid dearly for pretending that he was above the rules that applied to his contemporaries. And of course JFK, for all his talents, could never have survived the press and legal scrutiny of the 1990s.

BILL CLINTON MAY have duplicated some of JFK's bad behavior, but he was determined not to make Jimmy Carter's political mistake. Clinton stayed close to Ted Kennedy and the Kennedy family throughout his presidency.[71] Substantively, the Clinton-Kennedy intersection was health care. While in the end, the Clinton plan to provide health insurance for every American would not be passed, Clinton took care to consult with Senator Kennedy and gain his imprimatur for the approach he and Mrs. Clinton were taking.[72] And Kennedy, who had dreamed of universal health care coverage for decades, did his best to advocate for the Clinton plan, especially within the balky Democratic Senate caucus.[73]

On a personal level, the ties between the first families were strong and well tended. No doubt the Kennedys were delighted that a JFK acolyte who cited President Kennedy at every turn was in the White House. They had already accepted that Ted would never run again, and the younger Kennedys were years away from any potential presidential bid. Thus, there was little direct competition or jealousy, unlike the case of Carter, who had been seen as supplanting or even usurping the Kennedys' place of honor. For good measure, Clinton appointed Jack and Ted's sister Jean Kennedy Smith as U.S. ambassador to Ireland.[74] He spoke at the memorial service for Robert Kennedy on the twenty-fifth anniversary of his assassination and offered a moving tribute to JFK at the formal dedication of the John F. Kennedy Library Museum.[75] He celebrated the quarter-century mark of the Kennedy Center for the Performing Arts and the thirty-fifth anniversary of the Peace Corps.[76] He was everywhere the Kennedys asked him to be.

Few were surprised when the Clintons vacationed at Martha's Vineyard with the Kennedys in August 1993. Jackie Kennedy was the official hostess for a five-hour sailing luncheon, and she was joined by daughter, Caroline, and brother-in-law Ted, among others.[77] Just a few months later, in January 1994, Jacqueline Kennedy was diagnosed with non-Hodgkins lymphoma. A heavy smoker for most of her life, she died on May 19 at home in New York, just sixty-four years old, surrounded by her family. President Clinton said upon her death, "Even in the face of impossible tragedy, she carried the grief of her family and our entire nation with a calm power that somehow reassured all the rest of us."[78] Most Americans paused to remember an elegant First Lady who had endured the unspeakable. Homes were again filled with the images of Camelot's sparkling years, and the four black November days that ended it. She was buried next to President Kennedy and her two children who did not survive infancy, with the eternal flame she had lit thirty-one years earlier providing light and warmth.

If there can be fortune in early death, it was in Mrs. Kennedy's passing away before her son, John Jr., aged thirty-eight, was killed on July 16, 1999, in the crash of a small plane he was piloting to a family wedding. John's wife and her sister also died. The crown prince of Camelot, as he was often called, was expected to enter politics eventually, perhaps even aspire to the presidency. News channels provided round-the-clock coverage of the search for his plane at sea as Americans came to terms with yet another awful Kennedy heartbreak. Born late in the month his father was elected president, John Jr. had never lived a day without being a public person. If his father's had been, in the words of historian Robert Dallek, "an unfinished life," John F. Kennedy, Jr.'s was a life of enormous potential, now never to be realized on the public stage. As his uncle Ted said at his funeral, "Like his father, he had every gift but length of years."[79] For Americans of the second half of the twentieth century, John Jr.'s enduring image would always be the innocent courage and unknowing loss of a little boy saluting his daddy's coffin.

With the deaths of Mrs. Kennedy and her son, President Kennedy's legacy was, more and more, slipping into the past. But it was still a past often invoked. For his entire term, President Clinton never failed to revel in his moment with President Kennedy in the Rose Garden. For six of his eight years, he hosted the Boys Nation group, joined by the Girls Nation delegation, at the White House. Clinton would bring out special guests, such as Vice President Gore or Senator Kennedy or the Joint Chiefs of Staff, and regale the youngsters with stories of his special day in 1963. Once, he recalled that his Boys Nation group had passed a resolution against racial discrimination just before the trip to the White House. President Kennedy thanked them, noting "that we had shown more initiative than the nation's Governors," who had recently refused to do something similar at their national conference. "We [of Boys Nation] loved it, but the Governors didn't like it very much, and it got [President Kennedy] in a lot of hot water with them."[80] Most of all, President Clinton would take the time to shake hands and pose for a photograph with each delegate. As Clinton wrote in his autobiography, "I hope some of those photos turn up in campaign ads someday."[81]

When evaluating the unusual historical relationship between John Kennedy and Bill Clinton, it is vital to remember that the bond was created by Clinton's memory of a moment. A brief handshake may be enough for a powerful political commercial, but it hardly suffices to explain anything. The two were of dissimilar generations and mindsets, and the challenges they faced as president were dramatically different. The old Lloyd Bentsen line, "I knew John F. Kennedy, and you're no John F. Kennedy," applied almost as well to

Bill Clinton as it had to Dan Quayle. The two Vietnam War–avoiding Baby Boomers had little in common with a man shaped by World War II.

In Clinton's case, it was more about hero worship than anything else. He adopted JFK as a role model in his youth, and while he may have striven to be like Kennedy, Clinton was his own person, and certainly no photocopy of Kennedy. Clinton was as smart and politically shrewd as the thirty-fifth president, but less polished and suave. Instinctively and generationally, Clinton was more liberal than Kennedy on a host of issues, his positioning as a "New Democrat" notwithstanding. How could Clinton not be more to the left? JFK had not lived to see the counterculture sixties, the cynicism-producing disasters of Vietnam and Watergate, the economic failures of the seventies, and the defining movements for women's rights, gay rights, and the environment—all of which molded the nineties version of Bill Clinton. Just to cite one direct result of cultural changes: The Clinton administration was packing to leave the White House as First Lady Hillary Clinton, who was her husband's RFK during his presidency, was elected to the U.S. Senate from New York. In the 1960s, no one—least of all Jackie—could ever have imagined that Jacqueline Kennedy would run for office.

Aside from the pure adulation that Clinton felt for Kennedy, there was a clever political calculation. Clinton understood well that Democrats—and most of the country—had longed for a Kennedy restoration since the 1963 assassination. But they wanted a credible, nonthreatening restoration. Ted Kennedy seemed too liberal and scarred by Chappaquiddick. So Clinton became the next best thing: the same age as JFK when he died, quoting Kennedy frequently and ardently, full of vigor and New Frontier–like proposals, a moderate presence compared to the leftist candidates that had dominated the Democratic Party in many recent presidential cycles. This image can be sustained for the duration of a campaign, but it fades into the reality of the presidency, when Americans live with a man day in, day out for eight years and get a better sense of the individual behind the political pose.

Bill Clinton truly was no John F. Kennedy, and Kennedy was not Clinton's doppelgänger. Clinton was Clinton, with all the good and bad his own persona dictated. Judging by his postpresidential popularity and the positive retrospective view most people have adopted about his policies (as opposed to his regrettable personal failings), Clinton carved a distinctive path. It was a legacy quite different than John Kennedy's, but still agreeable to the electorate for the most part.

PRESIDENTS AND PRESIDENTIAL candidates often express admiration for certain White House predecessors. Washington, Jefferson, and Lincoln are relatively uncontroversial choices (slave ownership aside for the first two). A couple of sons of former presidents, John Quincy Adams and George W. Bush, had the fondest affections for their fathers. Men who succeeded to office through the death of a president will invoke their patron's name habitually. Occasionally, a chief executive will make a past president a role model for a combination of political and policy reasons, as Gerald Ford did with Give-'Em-Hell Harry Truman or as Ronald Reagan chose to do with small-government proponent Calvin Coolidge. Youthful idolization led Bill Clinton back to John Kennedy.

Citing President Kennedy has been a staple for all modern Oval Office occupants, of course. A couple of graphs can illustrate the number of times every post-JFK president invoked Kennedy in public. The top chart shows the total number of times each president publicly mentioned JFK in speeches, press conferences, and the like, while he served in the White House. The second chart plots the same thing, but from year to year: As one would expect, Lyndon Johnson mentioned the man who made him vice president and originated many of his programmatic objectives with great frequency. JFK's rival, Richard Nixon, barely cited JFK, and neither did Gerald Ford. The first Democratic president since LBJ, Jimmy Carter, brought Kennedy into play more than Nixon and Ford, but less than a third as often as Johnson. John Kennedy was linked frequently to Reagan's central proposals so there was a JFK revival in the 1980s. George Bush the senior rarely referred to Kennedy. And then along came Bill Clinton, who managed to summon the Kennedy name and legacy so often he exceeded Johnson's mountainous total.

This was a genuine impulse in Clinton, but it was also a conscious strategy by a young Democratic candidate and president to link himself to the Kennedy era's hopes and dreams—and older voters' memories of them. Clinton's mainly popular two-term presidency is a measure of his success in capitalizing on JFK's style and rhetoric.

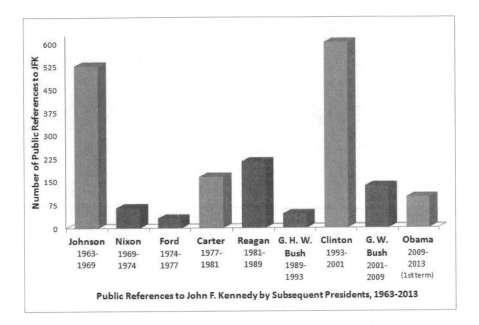

Public References to John F. Kennedy by Subsequent Presidents, 1963-2013

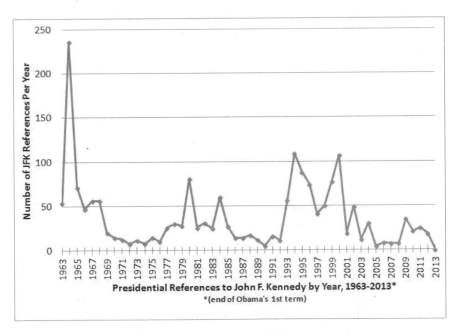

Presidential References to John F. Kennedy by Year, 1963-2013*
*(end of Obama's 1st term)

G. W. Bush: Back to the Republican Kennedys

A FREAKISHLY CLOSE VOTE IN FLORIDA set the stage for one of the most contested elections ever. Once the November vote was counted, Vice President Al Gore, the Democratic nominee, led Republican nominee George W. Bush, the Texas governor and son of President George H. W. Bush, by 540,000 votes in the national tally (out of 105 million cast). But in the all-important electoral vote, Gore had 267, three short of victory, Bush had 246, and the decisive 25 electoral votes were the Sunshine State's—where Bush and Gore were virtually tied. It took a hotly disputed recount and ultimately a divisive Supreme Court decision in *Bush v. Gore*[1] to resolve the matter. Democrats viewed the Court ruling as partisan, with the five most conservative justices siding with Bush against the four more liberal justices' preference for Gore, but in the end, Bush was declared the winner by an astonishingly tiny 537 votes in Florida—2,912,790 for Bush to 2,912,253 for Gore. This gave Bush a final electoral count of 271 votes, one more than the minimal majority needed for election.[2]

Thus, the offspring of president number 41 became president number 43, a Bush restoration after just eight years. Compare this to the twenty-four years that separated the two chief executives from the Adams family, John Adams who left office in 1801 and John Quincy Adams who entered the White House (after losing the popular vote) in 1825. Both of the Adamses served only one term, but George W. Bush would get two. The dozen years of Bush White House occupancy compares to less than three for the Kennedy family. The Bush family also accumulated eight years in the vice presidency (the senior Bush), fourteen years in the governorships of Texas and Florida (George W. and Jeb), ten years in the Senate (grandfather Prescott of Connecticut), and four years in the House (Bush senior). The Kennedys have had no governorships, but three senators (John, Robert, and Edward) plus scattered House service by several family members and a lieutenant governorship (Kathleen Kennedy Townsend, Bobby's daughter, in Maryland).

There is no real comparison: The more successful family dynasty by far, at least to this point, has the surname of Bush. No one would have guessed this in the 1960s, and it is one of history's sleight of hand tricks. Demography has played as much a part as destiny. In population, wealth, and influence, the Sunbelt has come to dominate the Frostbelt, and thus has the Texas house of Bush outstripped the Massachusetts line of Kennedys. Patriarch Joseph Kennedy's dreams of a long period of Kennedy dominance were dashed by war (Joe Jr.), bullet (Jack and Bobby), scandal (Teddy), and accident (John Jr.). Younger generations of Kennedys, including new congressman Joseph Kennedy III of Massachusetts, may try to even the score, though the Bushes have potential competitors, too, such as Jeb's politically active son George P. Bush—and Jeb Bush himself.

Yet, fifty years on, the short Kennedy presidency is far more admired by the public than either of the Bush tenures, and the iconic legacy of JFK's short White House stay greatly overshadows three full terms of the Bush family. George W. Bush was superficially a good deal like John F. Kennedy. Both had famous and powerful fathers, came from well-heeled, privileged backgrounds, had Ivy League educations, were elected president in squeakers, and saw foreign policy dominate their terms. Yet even Bush jokes frequently about his lack of eloquence and frequent malapropisms. Jack and Jackie Kennedy were the life of the party and led the nation culturally from the White House. Though gracious hosts, George and Laura Bush were famous for going to bed by 9:30 P.M. whenever possible. It may well be that Bush's serious, sober personal style was preferable to JFK's wild living for governance. Still, the public's imagination is rarely captured by bland temperance.

Concerning his presidential agenda and the Kennedys, George W. Bush was more like Ronald Reagan than his father. The second Bush was a determined tax-cutter, unlike his dad, who had famously violated his campaign pledge, "Read my lips, no new taxes," by raising taxes during his term. In seeking across-the-board cuts as part of his early legislative program, Bush copied Reagan in citing JFK before Congress and on the stump. The tax cuts were needed, said Bush, "to, in President Kennedy's words, 'get this country moving again.'"[3] In his most significant early achievement—but one with damaging consequences for the burgeoning national debt—Bush won $1.35 trillion in tax cuts, which he supplemented with still more tax breaks in both 2002 and 2003.[4]

Other than tax cuts, the closest parallel in the Bush presidency to JFK's was a militarily assertive foreign policy. Just as with Kennedy at the Bay of Pigs, the Bush administration was not prepared for its first-year crisis, the terrorist attacks on September 11.[5] But in the aftermath of failure, both administrations were transformed; they reevaluated and recalibrated to prepare for the crises to come. In Bush's case, the decision to strike back in Afghanistan (and later, much more controversially, in Iraq) as well as the actions taken to protect air travel and the homeland defined his White House years. Kennedy and all Cold War presidents were able to use the clear and present danger of a well-defined threat (the Soviet menace) to marshal public opinion and congressional support for their goals. While it came at a high price, terrorism in the twenty-first century returned purpose and clarity to American politics—and restored a natural enemy—that had been lacking since the fall of the Soviet empire. The "axis of evil" (Iran, Iraq, and North Korea, along with terrorism generally) enabled Bush to focus his energies on enemies that unified Americans, at least temporarily. Osama bin Laden and Saddam Hussein became Bush's Fidel Castro and Nikita Khrushchev.

In the view of many, though, this led to the kinds of excesses in the name of national security that had emerged during the Cold War era. The powers of the National Security Agency were broadened to permit eavesdropping on U.S. citizens and foreign nationals domestically, and the FBI's powers were expanded in a wide-ranging new antiterrorism law, the PATRIOT Act.[6] The "imperial presidency" of JFK's era was back, and civil liberties were restrained to meet the threat posed by another "ism"—terrorism this time rather than Communism. President Bush insisted that his national security reforms did not trample civil liberties in a manner reminiscent of the Cold War, and in his memoir, *Decision Points*, he specifically cited the excesses under the Kennedy administration: "Before I approved the Terrorist Surveillance Program, I wanted to ensure there were safeguards to prevent abuses. I had no desire to turn the NSA into an Orwellian Big Brother. I knew that the Kennedy brothers had teamed up with J. Edgar Hoover to listen illegally to the conversations of innocent people, including Martin Luther King Jr. Lyndon Johnson had continued the practice. I thought that was a sad chapter in our history, and I wasn't going to repeat it."[7]

Bush was not so publicly critical of the Kennedys while in office, and certainly not in the opening stages of his administration. To the contrary, he believed his success in securing one of his major goals, an education law called No Child Left Behind, depended heavily on Senator Ted Kennedy. As governor of Texas, Bush had also skillfully wooed powerful Democrats such as Texas House Speaker Pete Laney and Lieutenant Governor Bob Bullock, so he had confidence his technique of bipartisan camaraderie might work in Washington.

For the first film screening in the new Bush White House, the president and Mrs. Bush chose *Thirteen Days*, a movie about JFK's handling of the Cuban Missile Crisis. The guest of honor was Ted Kennedy, and he brought much of the family with him. The occasion was to prove the power of what President Bush's press secretary, Ari Fleischer, called "the amazing soft power of a kindly invite." As Fleischer pointed out, Bush recognized "there were two Ted Kennedys. There was the Ted Kennedy that . . . could take to the floor of the Senate and give the most impassioned, powerful speech anyone has ever heard and he will fight you tooth and nail. The other Ted Kennedy was the one who will reach a compromise with you and reach across the aisle. Both Kennedys existed on any given day . . . Bush knew if he could get the compromising Kennedy to be with him, chances were very good that his legislation was going to make it through the Senate. Kennedy was that type of old bull."

At the time, Bush insisted his gestures of friendship for Senator Kennedy had no connection to legislative deal making, but the ex-president's memoirs noted, "The movie hadn't been my only purpose for inviting Ted. He was the ranking Democrat on the Senate committee that drafted education legislation. He had sent signals that he was interested in my school reform proposal . . ." That night Bush told Kennedy he wanted to be known as "the education president" and emphasized, "I don't know about you, but I like to surprise people. Let's show them Washington can still get things done." The next morning, a note from Kennedy to Bush arrived, reading in part, "Like you, I have every intention of getting things done . . . We will have a difference or two along the way, but I look forward to some important Rose Garden signings."[8]

That same year, while No Child Left Behind was still being negotiated in Congress, President Bush marked the seventy-sixth anniversary of the birth of Robert Kennedy by dedicating the main Justice Department building on Constitution Avenue in Washington to RFK. Before an assemblage of Kennedys and surviving New Frontiersmen, Bush hailed the special relationship between JFK and RFK: "No man ever had a more faithful brother."[9] Asked by a reporter whether the renaming was an attempt to curry favor with Ted Kennedy, Bush laughed and replied, "I'm not quite that devious."[10] But he was. By year's end, Bush signed into law No Child Left Behind, accompanied by praise from the Massachusetts senator: "President Bush was there every step of the way."[11]

The Bush-Kennedy infatuation did not last, and could not. The ideological demands of their very different political parties tore apart the relationship, with Kennedy campaigning for Democrats in 2002, opposing Bush's conservative Supreme Court picks, and clashing repeatedly with the administration over the Iraq War. Still, George W. Bush had learned a lesson his predecessors had also absorbed. When trying to influence public opinion or make congressional deals stick, the Kennedys, past and present, were good allies to have.

Even Bush's vice president, Dick Cheney, who was not a man much given to open sentiment, realized the emotional effect a Kennedy appearance could generate. In September 1963 President Kennedy appeared at the University of Wyoming in Laramie, and Cheney was there to see JFK ride in an open motorcade a couple of months before Dallas. "He had inspired us all," Cheney later wrote, "and at a time when I was trying to put my life back together, I was particularly grateful for the sense of elevated possibilities he described."[12]

Kennedy footprints have been found here and there in the Bush White House years even as the Bushes gave Republicans the opportunity to tout their own dynastic family to rival the Democratic royals. For much of the Bush presidency, JFK had been in eclipse, rarely mentioned and seemingly becoming a distant memory for most Americans. And then something—or someone—unexpected happened in 2008, reviving the Kennedy image and promise. His name, of course, was Barack Obama.

20

FULL CIRCLE: THE TWINNING OF BARACK OBAMA AND JOHN KENNEDY

BOBBY KENNEDY WAS ONE OF THE first to imagine an African American president in the nation's near future. On May 26, 1961, in an interview with Voice of America about the ongoing attacks on integrationist Freedom Riders in the South, Attorney General Kennedy made a startling prediction: "There's no question that in the next thirty or forty years a Negro can also achieve the same position that my brother has as President of the United States, certainly within that period of time."[1] While RFK was eight years too optimistic, the Kennedy family's close association with civil rights causes made the Obama campaign irresistible for many of JFK and RFK's closest relatives.

The Kennedys chose to back a politician whose background could not have been more different from that of the privileged JFK. Barack Obama was a mixed-race child with an absent Kenyan father and a mother whose peripatetic personal journey meant his upbringing in Hawaii and the Philippines was often less than stable.[2] But young Obama got on the right track at age ten when he returned to Honolulu to live with his maternal grandparents. His natural abilities took him to Occidental College and, by transfer, to Columbia University, where he received his B.A. in 1983. From this point Obama's future more precisely resembled Kennedy's in key respects. At Harvard Law School, Obama began to travel in elite circles and served as the first African American editor of the law review, later returning to Chicago to practice civil rights law. JFK's family was full of politics, so he was schooled in the art from birth, while Obama's political training was provided by a stint in the Illinois State Senate from 1996 to 2004 as well as a failed bid for Congress in 2000.

John Kennedy's and Barack Obama's path to the White House converged in five ways. They successfully sought a Senate seat at an early age (thirty-five for JFK and forty-three for Obama) but had no intention of becoming a Senate fixture; both were planning a glide path to the presidency, with the Senate as brief a stop as they could make it. They each drew a following of journalists, elites, and policy wonks who were impressed with their intellect and rhetorical ability. The publication of bestselling books (*Why England Slept* and *Profiles in Courage* for Kennedy, and *Dreams from My Father* and *The Audacity of Hope* for Obama) underlined the candidates' appeal. They both made a splash at the national party convention preceding their presidential nomination; JFK ran for vice president in 1956 and in 2004 Obama delivered a gripping keynote address prior to John Kerry's nomination, saying in part, "There's not a liberal America and a conservative America; there's the United States of America."[3] While they lacked executive experience for the presidency, they tried to compensate by projecting hope, promise, vigor, and sharp change from the status quo. Finally, they each had a political handicap, religion for Kennedy and race for Obama, that caused some to say they could not win but many others to flock to their banner. Their potential "firsts" became causes célèbres, making their candidacies larger than themselves and fueling the massive grassroots activism that got them elected. Volunteers and voters want to believe they are participating in a movement or a grand idea that transcends one moment and personality.

These parallels proved alluring to Caroline Kennedy Schlossberg and Ted Kennedy in 2008. Of course, the ground had been carefully prepared. Obama had made favorable references to JFK in *The Audacity of Hope*, and as a new senator, he had sought out his colleague from Massachusetts for frequent counsel.[4] The celebrated wordsmith Ted Sorensen was one of the first JFK associates on the Obama bandwagon, actively campaigning for him and making New Frontier allusions whenever possible. To the charge that Obama was lacking in foreign policy training, Sorensen attacked presidential candidate Hillary Clinton for siding with George W. Bush on the Iraq War. Critics had called JFK out of his depth, too, until the Cuban Missile Crisis, asserted Sorensen, who added: "Judgment is the single most important quality in a president of the United States. Kennedy had judgment. Obama has judgment."[5] Caroline Kennedy also reported that her children were taken with Obama and pushed her in his direction.[6]

In order to endorse Obama, though, the Kennedys had to move away from the Clintons, a presidential family they had once wholeheartedly embraced. This abandonment was made easier by some Clinton missteps. In Ted's view, Hillary Clinton had slighted his brother during the primaries by praising LBJ for the 1964 Civil Rights Act without mentioning that it had been proposed by John Kennedy and passed in part as a tribute to the late president. Clinton also did not correct a supporter who introduced her and suggested that Obama was another JFK, who merely talked about civil rights, while Clinton was an LBJ, who would actually get things done.[7] Ted and Bill Clinton also had a heated argument by telephone about some of the former president's tactics in trying to get his wife nominated—ploys that in Kennedy's view included the unfortunate injection of race into the campaign.[8] The fraternal keeper of the Kennedy flame had long been sensitive about insults to the memory of his brothers, and this miscalculation by the Clintons proved costly.

Barack Obama had won the Iowa caucus in early January, but Hillary Clinton had roared back to win the New Hampshire primary. The giant "Super Tuesday" contest in twenty-two states was to be held in early February. Just before this critical juncture, on January 28, Ted Kennedy and Caroline Kennedy Schlossberg stepped onto the national stage to crown Obama as JFK's natural successor. Carried live by the cable networks and covered extensively by all media outlets, the endorsement rally was a dramatic turning point that would enable Obama to build a small delegate lead he never relinquished in a nip-and-tuck battle with Clinton that lasted all the way until June. Caroline's blessing was heartfelt and an explicit straight-line linking of her father and Obama. The Obama campaign ran an ad throughout the primaries featuring images of JFK and the moon landing, and using these words from Caroline:

> Once we had a president who made people feel hopeful about America and brought us together to do great things. Today Barack Obama gives us that same chance. He makes us believe in ourselves again, that when we act as one nation we can overcome any challenge. People always tell me how my father inspired them. I feel that same excitement now.[9]

At the endorsement rally, Obama gave an uplifting address that reached across generations and divisions, perhaps especially affecting those who lived in the early 1960s and remembered President Kennedy. On a very political day, Obama insisted, "Today isn't just about politics for me. It's personal. I was too young to remember John Kennedy and I was just a child when Robert Kennedy ran for president. But in the stories I heard growing up [from] my grandparents and mother . . . I think my own sense of what's possible in this country comes in part from what they said America was like in the days of John and Robert Kennedy."[10]

Obama also asserted that his father, Barack Obama, Sr., had been able to travel from Kenya to the United States for study because of an effort by Senator John F. Kennedy and the Kennedy Foundation to pay for his travel expenses.[11] Thus, Obama claimed, JFK enabled his parents to meet and, quite literally, the thirty-fifth president had been partially responsible for young Obama's very existence. This story was almost too good to check, and the candidate clearly did not. But when the *Washington Post* did, they found that the Kennedy Foundation donation had been made too late to help Obama Sr. The Obama campaign admitted the error.[12]

The Clintons were aghast at this turn of the Kennedy wheel of fortune. According to close associates, the former president suffered a kind of betrayal, given his lifetime devotion to JFK and good working relationship with Ted during his White House years. Yet there was little the Clintons could do. Any attack on the Kennedys would backfire in the Democratic race. Hillary's campaign trotted out the backing of a couple of RFK's children, but even this was negated by the support for Obama expressed by RFK's widow, Ethel.[13] Obama was the big winner in the 2008 primary for Kennedy family blessings.

Kennedy clan appearances on behalf of Obama continued for the rest of the campaign, though Ted Kennedy's stumping was essentially eliminated after the May 2008 diagnosis of the brain tumor that would take his life thirteen months later. A very ill Teddy did manage to appear at the late summer Democratic National Convention in Denver, where he delivered a farewell that echoed his 1980 convention address after his loss to Jimmy Carter: "This November the torch will be passed again to a new generation of Americans . . . The work begins anew. The hope rises again. And the dream lives on."[14]*

Unlike the Kennedy-Nixon squeaker of 1960, there was relatively little doubt that Obama would win the election after the economic collapse of September 2008. Obama's Republican opponent, Senator John McCain of Arizona, was hugely burdened by his GOP ties to a deeply unpopular President Bush, whose support had fallen into the twenties because of economic collapse and the lingering Iraq War. Perhaps hoping to establish a link to a better-regarded presidency, McCain referred to JFK from time to time, invoking Kennedy's willingness to engage opponents in urging more debates with Obama, for example.[15] But his most effective use of Kennedy was in tying JFK's wartime preparation for the Oval Office to his own. Like Kennedy in World War II, McCain had been pushed to his limits during the Vietnam War, but unlike JFK, McCain had been captured and interned in a brutal POW camp nicknamed the Hanoi Hilton. Beyond heroics, McCain found another connection to Kennedy that prepared him for the White House's life-or-death decision making: "I was on board the USS *Enterprise* [during the

---

* I searched through the records of every Democratic National Convention from 1964 to 2012 and found 96 substantial segments about, or references to, JFK and his family. There was not one Democratic convention without at least several Kennedy invocations and representations. Other historic Democratic figures, from Jefferson and Jackson to Wilson and FDR, were given short shrift by comparison.

Cuban Missile Crisis], and I sat in a cockpit on the flight deck waiting to take off. We had a target. I know how close we came to a nuclear war and I will not be a president who needs to be tested."[16]

It wasn't nearly enough for McCain. Obama ended up with 53 percent of the popular vote and 365 electoral votes. Remarkably, the first African American ever elected to the nation's highest office had won a larger percentage of the popular vote than all the other Democratic nominees since the Civil War, save only for FDR and LBJ. Race had proved to be less of a determining factor in 2008 than religion had in 1960.[17]

After the election, occasional Kennedy references were sprinkled into President Obama's speeches, and Kennedy symbolism extended even into his choice of White House decor. Once again, JFK's Resolute desk was chosen for the new president's use and, as mentioned earlier, among the five quotations woven into the Oval Office carpet that each new president gets is one from John Kennedy: "No problem of human destiny is beyond human beings."[18]

Yet as Americans got to know Obama better, it became obvious that the new president was not a clone of the one lost in 1963. Strong backers such as Ted Sorensen certainly noticed key differences: "Kennedy, unlike Obama, continued his oratorical skills into his inauguration and presidency [and] was a wittier speaker who enjoyed laughing and making other people laugh."[19] Obama's first inaugural speech was surprisingly flat and unmemorable,[20] though his second, focused squarely on liberal themes such as minority and gay rights, had more historic luster to it.

With some exceptions, Obama's presidential addresses have often been wonky and uninspiring.[21] As Sorensen suggested, one missing element for Obama is off-the-cuff humor, which JFK frequently employed in press conferences and one-on-one media interviews. The professorial Obama sometimes appears more akin to Woodrow Wilson than John Kennedy in style.

Nor has President Obama cited JFK all that much during his time in office. During his first term, Obama referred to Kennedy 99 times—a fraction of the 327 citations by President Clinton in his first term and even less than President Carter's low total (for a Democrat) of 165. Perhaps Obama, having been an infant during the Kennedy administration, simply does not relate much to the events of the early 1960s.[22] This is true even when the parallels are obvious to older generations. For example, one of Obama's signal achievements has been the elimination of 9/11 mastermind Osama bin Laden on May 2, 2011. The president's instrument to achieve his goal was an exceptional group of service personnel, the Navy SEALs, established by President Kennedy in January 1962. JFK's objective then—to develop unconventional capabilities, including clandestine operations to counter guerilla warfare—describes precisely the SEALs' mission to Pakistan to deal with bin Laden.

Obama has certainly not ignored JFK or the Kennedys. In May 2011, while Caroline Kennedy was visiting, the president renamed the famous White House Situation Room, established in May 1961 shortly after the Bay of Pigs, for President Kennedy. (Fifty years ago, it was called the "Cold War Control Room.")[23] Two years later, Obama tapped Caroline to serve as U.S. ambassador to Japan.[24] Famous JFK phrases and sentences certainly show up from time to time in Obama speeches. As he advocated for action on climate change, Obama mentioned Kennedy's well-known formulation that "our problems are man-made; therefore they may be solved by man."[25] References to JFK's efforts to establish the Peace Corps, the Alliance for Progress, and Medicare are sprinkled in appropriate Obama pronouncements about foreign policy and health care.[26] Obama has invoked the Kennedy wit on some occasions, such as at a fund-raiser for his 2012 campaign: "You know, President Kennedy used to say after he took office what surprised him most about Washington was that things were just as bad as he had been saying they were."[27] Still, the encomia for Kennedy from the "new JFK" seem sparse.

Obama critics have employed John Kennedy's record in a few policy areas to poke at the president. For example, Obama's severe cutbacks at NASA provoked the ire of three pioneering astronauts, including the reclusive first man to set foot on the moon, Neil Armstrong.[28] In a widely discussed column coauthored by astronauts Jim Lovell and Gene Cernan, Armstrong (who died in 2012) blasted what he saw as Obama's timidity, contrasting it with Kennedy's boldness. JFK had called the space race "the new ocean, and I believe that the United States must sail on it and be in a position second to none." The retired astronauts concluded, "For fifty years we explored the waters to become the leader in space exploration. Today . . . the voyage is over. John F. Kennedy would have been sorely disappointed."[29] The reproach must have stung a president who recalled "sitting on my grandfather's shoulders in Hawaii, watching the Apollo astronauts return from a journey President Kennedy set in motion. Looking back, I think my own sense that America is a place of boundless possibility comes, in part, from moments like these."[30] Adding to the astronauts' insult, a conservative group aired a tough TV spot against Obama in 2012, contrasting his NASA cutbacks to film clips of JFK asserting, "We choose to go to the moon in this decade and do the other things, not because they are easy, but because they are hard . . . And the moon and the planets are there, and new hopes for knowledge and peace are there." Alluding to JFK's 1960 campaign pledge to "get this country moving," a man on the street comments in the advertisement, "We need a leader that is not scared to get this country moving in the right direction again."[31]

While President Obama had the lion's share of JFK associations to himself in 2008, he got a bit more competition in 2012. The first Mormon candidate for the presidency, Republican Mitt Romney, alluded to JFK's barrier-breaking religious affiliation occasionally, and the press stressed this particular Kennedy-Romney connection. As Romney put it when he first ran for the White House in 2007, "Almost fifty years ago, another candidate from Massachusetts explained that he was an American running for president, not a Catholic running for president. Like him, I am an American running for president. I do not define my candidacy by my religion."[32] By 2012, religious prejudice certainly wasn't as widespread as it had been in 1960. Nonetheless, Romney's task was tougher than Kennedy's in a crucial respect. While both JFK and Romney could rely on overwhelming backing from their coreligionists, Roman Catholics comprised 26 percent of the U.S. population in Kennedy's time, while Mormons were just 2 percent of the population during the 2012 election.[33]

Romney chose one of JFK's coreligionists for his ticket, Wisconsin Republican Paul Ryan, who was an Irish Catholic and the same age (forty-two) as John Kennedy had been when he declared for the presidency in January 1960. Ryan was the second Roman Catholic to be nominated by the GOP for either spot on its national ticket (in 1964, Barry Goldwater picked a Catholic, Congressman Bill Miller of New York, for vice president). The 2012 major party nominees were a measure of how much America had changed since JFK's presidential contest. A Mormon-Catholic duo faced off against the nation's first African American president and his Catholic running mate, Vice President Joe Biden.

JFK's name came up in the foreign policy presidential debate (Cuba and how a White House should handle the inevitable unexpected crisis) and in the vice presidential debate (Kennedy's tax cut, raised by Ryan and dismissed by Biden: "Now you're Jack Kennedy?"). But the 2012 script was different from 1960's. Romney, the most recent nominee from Massachusetts, like Kennedy, won the first debate by a wide margin, but unlike JFK, he lost the election decisively. As with Michael Dukakis and John Kerry, Romney found that the era of Massachusetts miracles ended with JFK.

The Latino vote was a major reason why. Obama in 2012, like Kennedy in 1960, was able to win over this increasingly important voting bloc with a message of inclusivity. Mitt Romney, on the other hand, alienated many Latino voters by opposing immigration reform and endorsing a "self-deportation" policy for undocumented workers. Obama crushed Romney with Hispanics, winning 71 percent of this tenth of the electorate (a gain even over Obama's sizable 67 percent in 2008). The seeds of Democratic victory were sown more than a half century earlier. President Kennedy's last night on earth was spent with a Latino group in Texas in what has been described as a watershed event. The president and First Lady electrified a crowd attending a

Hispanic political gathering in Houston when they showed up unannounced and gave impromptu remarks. Mrs. Kennedy spoke to the crowd in fluent Spanish. The Kennedy campaign realized that Hispanics had helped make the difference in 1960 and might be needed again if Texas turned out to be close in 1964.[34]

THE OBAMA PRESIDENCY coincided with the half-century mark since the Kennedy presidential campaign and term of office. Commemorations abounded from 2010 to 2013.[35] One of the most remarkable occurred at the University of Michigan, fifty years to the night when John Kennedy, after a long day of campaigning, showed up at the campus well behind schedule—in the wee hours of the morning, in fact. He gave a speech proposing the Peace Corps to thousands of excited students and faculty at 2:00 A.M., and on October 14, 2010, despite a cold rain, roughly fifteen hundred people showed up yet again from one to three in the morning to see a new documentary on the Peace Corps and a ceremony marking JFK's visit.[36]

The fiftieth anniversary of Kennedy's inauguration became a major Washington event. A three-week series of performances at the Kennedy Center began on the evening of January 20, 2011, with over a hundred members of the Kennedy clan assembling to hear Morgan Freeman recite excerpts from JFK's speeches and President Obama pay tribute to his predecessor.[37] But more poignant was a gathering earlier that day in the grand rotunda of the Capitol. The powerful listened in silence as Kennedy's fourteen-minute inaugural address was replayed near where it was delivered exactly five decades before. A few months later, on what would have been JFK's ninety-fourth birthday, the U.S. Navy announced that a second aircraft carrier would be named for the late president, the first having been decommissioned in 2007.[38]

Since JFK would have been in his nineties during the Obama administration, the same clock had affected other members of the Kennedy clan, and slowly the older generation of the family America remembered for its vitality departed this earthly realm. Though there had been plenty of advance notice, Edward Kennedy's death from a brain tumor was still a shock to most. Kennedy was seventy-seven years old, but most Americans born before 1960 had a fixed view of him as the youngest of President Kennedy's siblings. His Senate career of about forty-seven years was highly influential by anyone's yardstick, and he had fully earned the title of the Senate's "liberal lion." Most Americans, whatever their politics, probably could agree with the perspective offered by President Obama upon Kennedy's death: "His fight has given us the opportunity we were denied when his brothers John and Robert were taken from us: the blessing of time to say thank you and good-bye . . . For his family he was a guardian. For America he was the defender of a dream."[39] Just weeks before Ted Kennedy's death, his and JFK's sister Eunice Kennedy Shriver, the founder of the Special Olympics, passed away. JFK brother-in-law Sargent Shriver followed in early 2011. Later that year, Kara Kennedy, the only daughter of Ted Kennedy, would die of a heart attack at age fifty-one. RFK Jr.'s estranged wife, Mary, committed suicide in May 2012, reviving for the umpteenth time the age-old discussion about the family curse.[40] Of course, the Kennedys are a sprawling, burgeoning tribe; most families of that size have loads of tragedies over time, but they are out of the public eye.

If there was a sign of waning Kennedy influence in politics, even in Massachusetts, it was the failure of the Kennedy family to put forth one of their own in the special election to succeed Ted Kennedy.[41] After all, this was a Senate seat that had been filled by a Kennedy almost continuously since early 1953.[42] Moreover, a Republican state senator, Scott Brown, was elected to the Kennedy seat in early 2010 as a "Tea Party" favorite, having aired a TV spot featuring President Kennedy and his advocacy of the income tax cut; this invocation of Massachusetts's political patron saint may have eased the blow to the Kennedys a bit.[43] Not surprisingly, Brown's career was a short one in the heavily Democratic Bay State, and he was defeated for reelection in 2012 by Elizabeth Warren, who benefited from an Obama landslide in Massachusetts.

Accentuating the lack of Kennedys in public office, for the second half of President Obama's first term, there was no Kennedy presence in Congress. The last family representative, Congressman Patrick Kennedy of Rhode Island, left in early 2011. Briefly, Caroline Kennedy Schlossberg had been the New York governor's choice to fill Hillary Clinton's U.S. Senate seat once Clinton became secretary of state, but Caroline's selection fell flat as her lack of preparation and knowledge about the intricacies of Empire State politics became apparent.[44] However, the Kennedy interregnum was brief. In November 2012, RFK's grandson, Joseph P. Kennedy III, was elected to represent the liberal Massachusetts district of retiring Democratic congressman Barney Frank. Given the number of adult Kennedy children and grandchildren—numbering in the dozens—it is remarkable that young Joseph Kennedy is currently the only one in any significant elective office at the state or national level.[45] Either the newest generations of Kennedys have moved in nonelective directions or the voters have. It is always possible that, in time, either half of this equation could change; more Kennedys could take up politics, and the electorate may look favorably upon them. Many Massachusetts observers believe that Joe Kennedy III may have the right stuff to move up.

Whatever the family's political prospects, public interest in John Kennedy appears unquenchable. The books, articles, TV documentaries, mini-series, and even music videos and video games continue to multiply.[46] Caroline published a memoir about her mother, containing hours of unreleased tapes of Jackie discussing her late husband.[47] Secret Service agents from the Dallas trip made their case about the assassination in *The Kennedy Detail*.[48] Former CIA operative Brian Latell leveled a *j'accuse* at Fidel Castro concerning Dallas.[49] Stephen King wrote a novel entitled *11/22/63*.[50] Yet another JFK mistress, Mimi Alford, came forward in *Once Upon a Secret*.[51] FOX News commentator Bill O'Reilly published a runaway bestseller, *Killing Kennedy*.[52] Stephen Hunter, author of the Bob Lee Swagger series, released *The Third Bullet*, another fictional assassination whodunit, to critical acclaim.[53] One of the least circulated books with a Kennedy flavor contained one of the most fascinating tidbits. Archbishop Philip Hannan, in his memoir *The Archbishop Wore Combat Boots*, included a previously undisclosed December 20, 1963, letter he had received from Jackie Kennedy. Devout Catholic though she was, Mrs. Kennedy expressed a sentiment that most people who have lost loved ones have probably felt:

> If only I could believe that [Jack] could look down and see how he is missed and how nobody will ever be the same without him. But I haven't believed in the child's vision of heaven for a long time. There is no way to commune with him. It will be so long before I am dead and even then I don't know if I will be reunited with him . . . Please forgive all this—and please don't try to convince me just yet—I shouldn't be writing this way.[54]

One's faith is understandably tested in circumstances similar to Mrs. Kennedy's. And the heartfelt passion she expressed appears to contradict the view that JFK's flagrant adulteries had created an empty, loveless union.[55]

Because of its deep wound to the national psyche, November 22, 1963, was the focus of more books and TV shows than any other aspect of John Kennedy's story. Just in the past several years, the History Channel, the Discovery Channel, and the National Geographic Channel have aired at least six specials on what they claim are new aspects of the assassination.[56] The fascination with the assassination has led to some unfortunate by-products. A British video game called "JFK Reloaded" re-created the assassination scene and permitted players to carry out the assault from different vantage points.[57] Souvenirs of the tragedy are also now selling for incredible prices. The fedora worn by Jack Ruby when he shot Lee Oswald fetched $45,000 at auction, and Ruby's shoes went for $15,000. The toe tag attached to Oswald's corpse generated an obscene $83,000.[58] Even more morbidly, the funeral director who embalmed Oswald sold Oswald's first, discarded coffin, his death certificate, and the instruments and table he used to prepare Oswald's body for $160,000.[59] The old ambulance that carried JFK's body after Air Force One landed in Washington was purchased for $120,000.[60] The owner of the boarding house where Oswald lived in November 1963 decided to put her property on the market to capitalize on the fiftieth anniversary of the assassination.[61]

The reason these items are trading for substantial monies is not simply because people want to own a piece of history, however perverse, but also because the Kennedy assassination is a wound that never healed for many Americans; they are still trying to come to terms with it. Souvenirs of the Lincoln assassination were highly sought after for generations, too, for much the same reasons. In fact, the opera glasses Lincoln was using in Ford Theater were recently put on the auction block with a minimum asking price of half a million dollars.[62] The combination of a senseless act of violence plus historic change of a high order of magnitude—present in both the Lincoln and Kennedy assassinations—traumatized society for years.

21

THE PEOPLE'S PRESIDENT

IT SEEMS MORE THAN A LITTLE STRANGE to apply any populist label to John F. Kennedy. He was a child of privilege, a young man sent to the best schools, a politician with a charmed life fueled by his father's vast wealth and influence, and a refined individual blessed with looks, talents, and worldly goods beyond the hope of most mortals. What real connection did he ever have to the struggles and challenges faced by average citizens? Nonetheless, Kennedy's life, presidency, and death combined to cast a powerful spell that has worked its magic on generations of Americans, and continues to this day.

What elements make up the Kennedy enchantment? As described in this book's introduction, we undertook a detailed public opinion study to determine how and why JFK has maintained his position at the top of the presidential pile over the past half century.

The 2,009 American adults participating in the opinion poll supervised by Peter Hart and Geoff Garin were asked to rate all the presidents from Dwight Eisenhower to Bill Clinton on a scale from 0 to 10, with 10 being the best possible grade. (The two most recent presidents, George W. Bush and Barack Obama, were not included since not enough time has passed for fair, less partisan evaluations.)

John F. Kennedy was the most highly rated by a considerable margin: Finishing immediately behind Kennedy were Ronald Reagan, Dwight Eisenhower, and Bill Clinton. The latter trio served eight full years each, compared to JFK's less than three years. Few historians would claim that Kennedy's actual achievements during his short term compared to those who were given the maximum tenure. Other than JFK, the less-than-two-term presidents all ranked lower: Gerald Ford, George H. W. Bush, Lyndon Johnson, Jimmy Carter, and, in the cellar, Richard Nixon.[1]

In most cases, the evaluations of those age fifty-five and over and those under fifty-five were not much different, although Carter was better liked by younger adults who perhaps knew him more from his popular postpresidential activities than from his generally unsuccessful White House term.

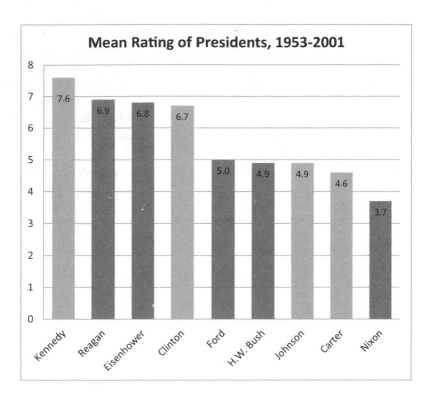

Naturally, partisanship was a significant factor in people's evaluations of presidents, though much less so in the case of JFK than most others. Democrats gave Kennedy his highest grades, with 79 percent calling him one of the country's best presidents[2] while 52 percent of Republicans offered the same superlative. While a considerable difference, the Kennedy results are much more balanced than the partisan findings for Ronald Reagan and Bill Clinton. Fully 87 percent of Republicans hail Reagan as one of the best, but only 31 percent of Democrats do so; 85 percent of Democrats figuratively see Clinton on Mount Rushmore, but a mere 28 percent of Republicans do.

Kennedy received especially high rankings from older voters; 72 percent gave Kennedy a rating of 7 to 10, far more than any other modern president. What is equally remarkable is that all but 16 percent of younger voters knew enough about Kennedy to rate him. Compare this to Kennedy's predecessor and successor in the White House. Fully 42 percent of those under age fifty-five couldn't rate Eisenhower, and 45 percent knew too little about Johnson to judge him. Of course, Kennedy has received far more media attention than less photogenic presidents—but JFK is also intrinsically more interesting and memorable in many ways.

In a separate question, participants were asked how much they knew about different presidents in terms of their personal history and background before becoming and while serving as president. George Washington, Abraham Lincoln, and Franklin Roosevelt were included along with JFK and other modern presidents. Somewhat surprisingly, 62 percent knew a great deal or a fair amount about Kennedy, compared to 56 percent for Lincoln, 49 for Washington, and a mere 36 for Roosevelt. All age groups were equally uninformed concerning long-ago great presidents.

However, Kennedy did not sweep every measure of presidential stature. In an open-ended question, respondents were asked which president, living or dead, they would want to be the next president. Reagan was picked by 24 percent, Clinton by 21, and Kennedy by 13, with Lincoln in fourth place at 9 percent.[3]

IN A REVEALING section of the survey, respondents were asked to specify President Kennedy's most significant attributes and what they most closely associated with him. While some events such as the civil rights struggle were mentioned prominently, most people focused on personal characteristics: decisiveness, strength, youth, family, optimism, idealism, and energy. Participants were then queried about the most profound change JFK made on the country as president. Racial integration, standing up to the Soviet Union, and the space program were the top three choices. Once again, older voters offered more specifics. When asked how much they admired JFK, two thirds of those fifty-five and over replied "a great deal" or "a fair amount" compared to 55 percent of those under age fifty-five. The response was even more robust when people were asked to rate the impact JFK and his policies had on the United States. Two thirds of younger adults said a great deal or a fair amount; among older adults, 78 percent rated JFK's impact highly.

Even more interesting, many of the standard divisions in American society—based on gender, race, religion, and the like—were much less pronounced for President Kennedy than for most political figures, past or present. There was almost no gender gap regarding the degree to which people admire JFK. Roughly three out of five men (57 percent) and women (60 percent) registered a great deal or fair amount of admiration. Not surprisingly, African Americans were high up on the admiration scale (71 percent), but so were Hispanics (63) and whites (58). The affection for Kennedy was naturally substantial among Catholics (62 percent), but Protestants were not far behind (55). Liberals were JFK's biggest admirers (69 percent), yet moderates were close (62), and almost half of conservatives (49 percent) thought positively of him.

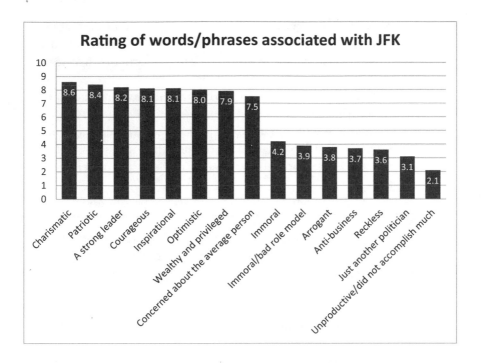

Rating of words/phrases associated with JFK

In the focus groups, participants repeatedly used certain words and phrases to describe JFK, which were then included in the broader poll: Kennedy was most strongly associated with the terms "charismatic," "patriotic," "a strong leader," "courageous," "inspirational," and "optimistic." The poll's respondents also saw Kennedy as "wealthy and privileged"—though it was more descriptive than undesirable—and "concerned about the average person." Negative words and phrases, such as "immoral," "bad role model," "arrogant," "reckless," and "did not accomplish much," were rarely used, even among Republicans. Realistically, anyone could fairly attribute each of these criticisms to aspects of the life and presidency of John Kennedy. Clearly then, JFK is not seen as just another politician, whatever the truth of the matter.

Respondents were also asked to select which two among seven of Kennedy's best-known statements (four of them from his inaugural address) best represent what America would most benefit from today in focusing our approach to government and citizenship:

63%—"Let us not seek the Republican answer or the Democratic answer but the right answer. Let us not seek to fix the blame for the past—let us accept our own responsibility for the future."[4]

49%—"Ask not what your country can do for you—ask what you can do for your country."[5]

28%—"Let every nation know, whether it wishes us well or ill, that we shall pay any price, bear any burden, meet any hardship, support any friend, oppose any foe to assure the survival and the success of liberty."[6]

26%—"If a free society cannot help the many who are poor, it cannot save the few who are rich."[7]

14%—"We choose to go to the moon in this decade and do the other things, not because they are easy, but because they are hard, because that goal will serve to organize and measure the best of our energies and skills . . ."[8]

12%—"It is an unfortunate fact that we can secure peace only by preparing for war."[9]

9%—"Let the word go forth from this time and place, to friend and foe alike, that the torch has been passed to a new generation of Americans—born in this century, tempered by war, disciplined by a hard and bitter peace . . ."[10]

In our era of intense partisan strife and polarization, Americans seek relief from the blame game, perhaps the reason that the highest rated statement was Kennedy's statesmanlike assertion that the "right answer" should be preferred to the Democratic or Republican answer. Older and younger adults liked this sentiment equally well, as did Democrats, Republicans, and Independents. JFK's most famous declaration, "Ask not what your country can do for you—ask what you can do for your country," was chosen by 49 percent—although Republicans were especially enamored of this combination of patriotism and self-reliance.[11] Those over age fifty-five were somewhat more likely to pick this statement, compared to younger adults, perhaps because it was the single most quoted line of JFK's inaugural address, and those alive and aware in 1961 recalled the attention it received. The only Cold War proclamation to draw much backing was Kennedy's "pay any price, bear any burden" litany from the inaugural. Younger respondents were more inclined to pick Kennedy's rationale for helping the poor; 30 percent of those fifty-four and under selected that line from the inaugural, compared with just 20 percent of those fifty-five and older.

Later in the survey, respondents watched short film clips of President Kennedy giving parts of five speeches: the inaugural address on January 20, 1961 (the "ask not" excerpt), a September 12, 1962, address that included a recapitulation of the moon landing goal, the Cuban Missile Crisis address to the nation on October 22, 1962, Kennedy's "peace speech" to American University's graduating class on June 10, 1963, and the following day's television address on civil rights.[12] "Ask not" was the most remembered excerpt: a startling 83 percent of those age fifty-five and over "definitely" recalled having seen or heard it, with 60 percent of those under age fifty-five having also come across it. Of older Americans, 55 percent remembered the Cuban Missile Crisis speech, compared to only 26 percent of younger Americans. The least recognized excerpt was the peace speech, with a mere 5 percent of adults recalling it.

Respondents were then asked to "write a few words or phrases describing how you felt as you watched this video." The inaugural excerpt encouraged people to get involved and make a difference. The Cuban Missile Crisis address evoked many comments about JFK's "firm, strong leadership." Civil rights elicited remarks about Kennedy's boldness and courage in calling for equality (though civil rights leaders in the first couple of Kennedy years would have had a less positive view about JFK's "boldness"). The moon speech produced observations about Kennedy's "good ideas and great, worthy goals." Many saw the peace speech as both a call for national unity and an attempt to avoid war.

The responses to this question were not dramatically different by age, save for the Missile Crisis address. Americans alive and aware in 1962 were almost three times as likely to say they were "scared" or "frightened" while watching the speech as those too young to recall the event. Emotions generated by the very real prospect of nuclear annihilation easily survived a half century.*

Ten concrete goals and achievements of the Kennedy administration were featured in order to test respondents' knowledge of them. These "things that John F. Kennedy did as president" ranged from setting a course for the moon landing to pushing for a major tax cut. Seventy-seven percent of respondents aged fifty-five and older were familiar with JFK's goal of landing a man on the moon, while only 59 percent of younger respondents remembered it. Older participants also demonstrated a greater awareness of the Cold War; 82 percent said that they knew JFK had resisted the Soviet Union's attempt to place missiles in Cuba even as 44 percent of younger respondents admitted to knowing nothing, or next to nothing, about this pivotal event. Few of the younger respondents can recall the crisis in Germany either, while 55 percent of the older group remembered that Kennedy had supported West Berliners in their fight against Communism. JFK's lesser-known accomplishments

---

* I vividly recall the anxiety at age ten when my father packed up the car so that my mother and I could escape death from the nuclear bomb that would certainly be dropped within a couple miles of our home. We lived near the giant naval base in Norfolk, Virginia, where my father worked and would have to stay; some of our relatives resided in a relatively safe, sparsely populated area in the Appalachian Mountains, which would have been our destination had the crisis moved in the direction of imminent danger.

appear to be fading fast from public memory. Only 32 percent of the people in both groups knew that Kennedy signed a Nuclear Test Ban Treaty with the USSR, and only 21 percent were aware that he endorsed a major tax cut.[13]

Even so, in every case, those who lived through the Kennedy years were more familiar with these achievements than younger Americans. More interesting is the consistency of the Kennedy legacy for generations born since his time. Younger people focused on the accomplishments still relevant to modern life, such as space exploration and civil rights. The most remembered event for Americans alive and aware in the early 1960s was the life-or-death Missile Crisis. For the young, though, the Soviet Union is merely a failed piece of discarded history, and the Berlin confrontation with the Soviets an even more obscure episode in the Cold War against Communism. Unexpectedly perhaps, young people appear unaware that JFK established the Peace Corps. Compared with older Americans, the young are also less conscious that JFK's election was a watershed event in the separation of church and state—possibly because the once-palpable prejudice against Roman Catholics in the political arena is almost nonexistent today.

When asked to pick the top three accomplishments of Kennedy's presidency, the poll's entire group of respondents chose (1) standing up to the Soviet Union in Cuba, (2) proposing the legislation that became the Civil Rights Act, and (3) desegregating schools in Alabama and Mississippi, with the moon landing goal a close fourth.[14] Democrats rated JFK's civil rights record highly, while Republicans were more inclined to credit Kennedy's staunch anticommunism and desire to explore space.

In part because of John Kennedy's assassination, Americans are not inclined to focus on his shortcomings. The natural human reaction is to say "He and his family have suffered enough," or "If he had been given additional time, he might have reversed course, changed destructive behaviors, or accomplished more." While understandable and kind, these reactions do not contribute much to a balanced view of JFK's presidency. In the poll, five specific criticisms of Kennedy in the White House were tested, and respondents were asked whether they were matters of concern: the escalation in Vietnam, wiretapping of civil rights leaders, JFK's extramarital affairs, CIA coups and assassinations abroad, and Kennedy's inability to get civil rights legislation passed in his lifetime.[15]

The Vietnam question hovers over Kennedy. Among all adults in the survey, 53 percent had major concerns, and of only those old enough to have clear memories of the Vietnam War's course during the 1960s, 60 percent had major concerns. Younger adults were more uneasy about the wiretapping of civil rights leaders (48 percent) than older adults (42 percent). Remarkably, neither age group was overly alarmed about JFK's role in CIA coups overthrowing foreign leaders. Few held JFK responsible for failing to power the civil rights bill into law; this may be the clearest example of Americans making allowances for the short time that JFK held the White House.

The public's tolerant view of Kennedy's extramarital affairs while president is noteworthy. Just a third of the respondents had major concerns about Kennedy's behavior, and there was essentially no difference based on age. Forty-five percent had "only minor" or "no concerns" about JFK's womanizing. As a follow-up, respondents were asked to assess how Kennedy's many extramarital affairs affected their view of him, and many drew a clear distinction between JFK the president and JFK the person. Only 17 percent said, "This makes me feel more unfavorable to JFK both as a person and as president" while 44 percent replied, "This makes me feel more unfavorable to JFK as a person, but does not affect my view of him as a president." And another 36 percent indicated that their view of Kennedy as both a president and a person was completely unaffected by the affairs.[16] On this topic, though, a large partisan gap emerged about JFK. Only 19 percent of Democrats had major concerns about the extramarital affairs, but 56 percent of Republicans did. And while only 4 percent of Democrats felt more unfavorable to Kennedy as a person and a president on account of his affairs, 34 percent of Republicans rated Kennedy lower as a result.

There may be another psychological factor in the public's tendency to give Kennedy a pass on his unsavory behavior: the expectations human beings have of a powerful, good-looking politician. With great frequency, participants in both the focus groups and the poll cited JFK's charisma, handsomeness, and physical attractiveness (his hair, voice, bearing, and other attributes). Some men said they simply assumed an "alpha male" like Kennedy would assert his supremacy and use his charms to attract members of the opposite sex, while some women openly commented on Kennedy's sex appeal. As a retired Chicago waitress revealingly put it, "This might be too personal . . . but he's the first president I ever had a sex dream about . . . I was young [and] there was an underlying sexual attraction about him." Other women around the focus group table nodded in agreement. Human nature is full of such subconscious realities and the contradictions they encourage. We condemn immoral actions but presuppose and anticipate them in certain "entitled" individuals—while simultaneously resenting and censuring the entitlement.

A final question explored today's public sentiment about press exploration of politicians' private lives, especially referring to the fact that members of the press knew about JFK's extramarital affairs during his presidency but adhered to an unspoken agreement to ignore his transgressions. By a 59 to 41 percent margin, respondents believed we were better off in the 1960s when many of the private details of elected officials' personal lives were considered off-limits by the media. Older adults were more inclined to "strongly agree" with the former rules of coverage than younger adults,[17] and party differences emerged on private life reporting: Democrats and Independents strongly preferred the old "off-limits" press guidelines, but Republicans were almost evenly divided about which set of journalistic procedures is better.

There has been a sea change in opinion on this subject over the decades. The media may have turned a blind and complicit eye, but public tolerance of extramarital affairs by politicians was quite low in Kennedy's time, and if revelations about JFK's behavior had broken then, he would never have been elected president, or would almost certainly have been forced to resign his office. President Bill Clinton survived such exposure in the 1990s, and judging by Clinton's relatively high ratings in our current survey, there has been little lasting damage from his many brushes with scandal. Similarly, we can find no evidence that Kennedy's often egregious womanizing has had any durable effect on his overall public standing, though for specific subgroups, such as evangelical Christians, JFK's private life revelations have indeed hurt his image. For example, born-again Protestants were far more likely (54 percent) than the general population (33 percent) to say that Kennedy's extramarital affairs were of concern to them.

There is little doubt that Americans evaluate Kennedy's life in the shadow of his tragic death, and the survey underlines that belief. Other than the terrorist attacks on September 11, 2001, the Kennedy assassination is far and away the defining event for those aged fifty-five and over. Almost two thirds of the older participants chose November 22, 1963, as one of the days having the greatest impact on their generation. Asked to choose a second day, 72 percent also named 9/11.[18] Other key events in the lifetimes of those over fifty-five trailed far behind: the attack on Pearl Harbor (30 percent), the assassination of Dr. Martin Luther King, Jr. (21), the explosion of the space shuttle *Challenger* (7), and the Oklahoma City bombing (6).

Naturally, because the shocking events of September 11, 2001, were within the living memory of everyone in the poll, 95 percent reported that they had "a clear and vivid memory" of it. At the same time, 84 percent of those fifty-five and older reported a clear and vivid memory of the assassination, which was defined as remembering exactly where they were, to whom they were talking, or what they were doing when they heard the news. By contrast, among those seventy-six or older, only 41 percent had a clear, vivid memory of Pearl Harbor. Time has dimmed the recall of December 7, 1941, but not of November 22, 1963.[19]

Media historians have often commented that television news "came of age" with the Kennedy assassination. Whether that is true, or too generous, it is undeniable that television brought Americans together by sharing the same sights and sounds with everyone, live and unfiltered. We watched TV almost nonstop for four days, in a way that had never happened before. Even after five decades, solid majorities of people fifty-five and older can remember seeing many critical events of the long assassination weekend. A whopping 81 percent recall seeing JFK's funeral procession on live television, with 73 percent reporting that they saw John F. Kennedy Jr.'s heart-wrenching salute to his father happen in real time. Half of the older respondents said they tuned in to Walter Cronkite's coverage of the assassination, and 43 percent watched live footage of Jack Ruby shooting Lee Harvey Oswald. More than half remember seeing other notable events in real time, including the lighting of the eternal flame, Air Force One's arrival at Andrews Air Force Base, and pictures of JFK's flag-draped casket when it was briefly on display in the East Room of the White House.[20]

All these elements had a pronounced emotional effect on most individuals, but respondents were asked to name "the two events that had the greatest impact on you." The top choice was the moment on November 25, 1963, when young John F. Kennedy, Jr., on his third birthday, stepped forward and saluted his father's flag-draped coffin as it passed on its way to burial. Nearly six in ten poll respondents picked the JFK Jr. salute, with 38 percent each choosing President Kennedy's funeral procession and Walter Cronkite's Friday afternoon CBS reports on the assassination. About a quarter selected the shooting of Lee Harvey Oswald, with 15 percent or less for all other events.

Kennedy's fellow Catholics were especially traumatized by those four days in November, and the loss of the first Catholic president weighed heavily on them. In almost every category in the poll, Catholics reported intense memories and robust reactions. The funeral ceremonies centered on Roman Catholic rites and leaders, of course, so JFK's coreligionists could relate closely to ritualistic aspects that may have been less familiar to others.

Large proportions of younger respondents indicated they had seen many of the signal moments of the assassination and its aftermath in subsequent televised replaying over the years. Fully 85 percent have seen images of JFK in the convertible on the Dallas streets and 69 percent have come across the JFK Jr. salute, for instance. There have been dozens of TV shows and movies about the assassination, so it would be unusual if those under fifty-five had not caught glimpses of these images. "Unusual" does not mean impossible. Of those under age fifty-five in the poll, 8 percent said they had never even heard of "the assassination of President Kennedy in a convertible in Texas."

The participants all watched the Zapruder film of the assassination. Nearly seven in ten remembered having viewed it before—83 percent of those aged fifty-five and up had seen it—and it was recalled as much as or more than all the other JFK film clips. When asked to describe their reactions in writing, respondents recorded these words and phrases most often: "sad, devastated, heartbroken, sickened, I cried; shocked, stunned, horrified, couldn't believe this happened; a terrible low point in U.S. history, a sad dark day for our country; I felt angry, disgusted, outraged; disturbing to watch, brutal footage."

Adults of all ages agreed that the assassination "changed America." Fully 91 percent said JFK's murder changed the nation "a great deal" (61 percent) or "somewhat" (30 percent). More than anything else, November 22, 1963, took away America's innocence, according to 57 percent of the poll's respondents and two-thirds of those aged fifty-five and over. Despite a long history of violent acts against presidents, people living in a prosperous, peaceful country in the early 1960s simply did not believe that the madness of Dallas was possible. Respondents frequently used the word "unthinkable" to describe the assassination. Those alive at the time can attest to the deep depression that set in across the country, as the optimism that had mainly prevailed since the end of World War II seemed to evaporate. In a real sense, the Kennedy assassination presaged and psychologically prepared America for numerous devastating events to follow during the decade.

Older Americans are perhaps the best judges of the assassination's effects on the country. Beyond taking away the nation's innocence, those fifty-five and over said Kennedy's murder "marked the end of an era of peace and prosperity" (34 percent), "made Americans more cynical and divided" (27), "contributed to the escalation of the Vietnam War" (25), and "caused Americans to have less trust in government" (20).[21] On the other hand, 18 percent of older adults—and 31 percent of younger ones—believed that the assassination "delayed progress on the civil rights movement." In fact, it had the opposite result, enabling LBJ to use the tragedy to propel the civil rights bill into law.

The last finding of the survey confirms a staple of public opinion since the assassination. An overwhelming majority of respondents—fully three-fourths—rejected the Warren Commission's conclusion that Lee Harvey Oswald acted alone.[22] While the proportions are almost identical for all ages, Americans who lived through the assassination have especially strong feelings about who was responsible. Among those fifty-five and older, 20 percent strongly agree that Oswald acted alone, but almost two and a half times that number, 49 percent, strongly believe that we cannot yet close the case on JFK's killing.[23] While people of all races were inclined to think that too many questions remain unanswered, 87 percent of all African Americans and an astounding 91 percent of blacks aged fifty-five and above were conspiracy-inclined.[24] Clearly, most Americans remain unconvinced that John Kennedy's murder has been solved.*

OUR WIDE-RANGING STUDY of the public's view of John F. Kennedy leads to several overarching impressions and conclusions. Even after the passage of fifty years and in a fast-paced society that appears to shift its focus by the hour, "Kennedy remains a vivid presence ... particularly for those [who have] a living memory of him. Even many younger [people] talk about Kennedy in personal terms and treat him as a modern and contemporary figure, rather than as someone out of history."[25] Younger participants in the survey who could not even identify President Eisenhower spoke about the Kennedy presidency in rich detail—a result of the unrelenting focus on JFK in the news media but also the fact that their older relatives have discussed Kennedy often.

Considering the contempt in which we hold many modern politicians and even some past presidents, it is eye-popping to see and hear the terms of endearment lavished upon John Kennedy. Perhaps selective memory is at work, but people identify JFK as "the polar opposite of the very unhappy views they have of the country today. Whereas [contemporary] America is polarized and divided, Kennedy represents unity and common purpose in the public's mind, as well as a sense of hope, possibility, and optimism."[26] Unlike many former presidents, and almost all current top politicians, Kennedy is not seen as a particularly partisan or ideological figure; he has transcended the liberal label applied to most Democrats, not least because his policies were defined by the Cold War and conservative economics. Moreover, Kennedy's popularity has a bonus for his public evaluation: his faults are usually minimized and his extramarital affairs excused as "the way things were back then." Criticism was voiced about other members of the Kennedy family, including Ted Kennedy, a much more ideologically divisive figure, and some younger Kennedys

---

* If you doubt the stability of public opinion about the Kennedy assassination, consider the Gallup poll study conducted at the fortieth anniversary of November 22 in 2003. Gallup asked a more pointed question than we did about Dallas: "Turning now to the assassination of John F. Kennedy in 1963, do you think that one man was responsible for the assassination of President Kennedy, or do you think that others were involved in a conspiracy?" The public's answer was nearly identical to the one in our survey: 75% said "conspiracy" and 19% said "one man." And for the three-quarters who believed in a conspiracy, the guesses about the guilty parties were divided five ways: the Mafia (37%), the CIA (34%), LBJ (18%), Cuba/Castro (15%), and the Soviet Union (15%). See Lydia Saad, "Americans: Kennedy Assassination a Conspiracy," *Gallup*, November 21, 2003, http://www.gallup.com/poll/9751/americans-kennedy-assassination-conspiracy.aspx [accessed August 13, 2012].

whose hijinks and troubles have challenged the family legacy. "There is re-sentment of the treatment of the Kennedys as 'America's royal family,' and the sense of entitlement that some Kennedys are perceived to have had."[27] Yet this postdates JFK's life, and he is not held responsible.

Certain aspects of the Kennedy legacy have come to dominate our collec-tive memory. Even though some historians of the civil rights movement would question the conclusion, Americans strongly associate JFK with the struggle for civil rights—a cause to which he came late and not always wholeheartedly—and credit is given to him posthumously for the passage of the Civil Rights Act of 1964. Similarly, Kennedy was not around for the moon landing in 1969, but he is fixed in the people's imagination as the one who set that adventurous aim and provided the inspiration to achieve it. Certainly, the astronaut corps from the 1960s appears to agree: They cite JFK, not Johnson or Nixon, in recounting their feats.

Many specifics will fade as the generations alive during Kennedy's time pass on. While the crisis management lessons are durable, the Cuban Missile Crisis already seems as dated as the Soviet Union to younger Americans. The Peace Corps does not define the New Frontier the way it did in the 1960s, and JFK's tax cuts have long since been eclipsed by those of other presidents. The truly enduring legacy for the public is the stirring idealism and the call to public ser-vice that Kennedy and his New Frontiersmen embodied. As long as JFK's "ask not" invocation is aired and the images of an enterprising young president stream across television and computer screens, powerful optics will endure.

Conclusion: A Flame Eternal?

Hello darkness, my old friend,
I've come to talk with you again.
— Paul Simon, "The Sound of Silence," written
in the months following JFK's assassination [1]

Those who remember November 22, 1963, cannot escape the darkness of a moment that has haunted us for fifty years. Most recall every second of the frequently replayed, silent home movies that recorded John Kennedy's last living ride through Dallas. "In the naked light" of a bright Texas sun at noontime we forever see, as Paul Simon did in his assassination-inspired song, the motorcade passing on Dallas streets, "ten thousand people, maybe more—people talking without speaking." It is a nightmare that will never be erased from our national consciousness. The lingering, gnawing questions about the assassination reinforce our inability to forget. The seeds of modern cynicism were planted that day, and their bitter fruit has left us unwilling to trust much of what we are told by the powerful in and out of government.

But a leader's legacy—a kind of life after death—is shaped by a career's beginning and middle, not just an awful ending. Enough time has passed for Americans to put John F. Kennedy, the whole man and his entire career, in perspective.

No president, before or since, has been savvier in his use of mass media to promote his career or agenda. Early on, Kennedy's books projected a substantive, intellectual image that balanced his playboy reputation. Then the dawning of the age of television created a perfect political marriage between candidate and medium. JFK's visage, energy, picture-postcard family, and soaring rhetoric filled the small screen as perfectly as any Hollywood star has ever been able to do on the big screen. He was the first president to hold nationally televised presidential press conferences in real time, with each broadcast drawing an average of 18 million viewers.[2] From his winning 1960 debates to his witty presidential press conferences to the riveting speeches and famous lines that have become part of the tapestry of American history, John Kennedy was a stellar visual and vocal artist. The talented staff of speechwriters and image makers in his entourage enhanced his natural gifts. As a group, they were a public relations firm that could have put the one depicted in *Mad Men* out of business. The true test of Kennedy's success is passed daily: When a critic of JFK's policies or personal behavior sees the young president again on film, he is drawn in anew, wrapped up in the action and eloquence, separating and subordinating his dim view of the low morals and poor judgment of the lesser, hidden John Kennedy.

Thus, it is easy to comprehend why almost every Democratic candidate for president since JFK has been analyzed through the lens of Kennedy. The more fluent contenders try to be Kennedy, and the press often confers the title of pretender for a few months. Reality eventually sets in, however. No flesh-and-blood politician can compete with the larger-than-life monument that is John Kennedy. For Democrats, he was long ago elevated to Mount Rushmore. For Democratic *and* Republican presidents, Kennedy has presented a different challenge. They cannot vie with an apparition. Yet JFK's more clever White House successors have been able to create opportunities for themselves using Kennedy's record. Lyndon Johnson showed the way, but Ronald Reagan was just as skillful and successful, all the more because he had to wave the Kennedy standard to win Democratic support without alienating his own Republicans. Bill Clinton and Barack Obama each ran for the White House as the semiofficial New Kennedy; it worked well on the campaign trail but less well in office, since the press and public eventually discovered that Clinton and Obama were not Kennedy. Jimmy Carter became the un-Kennedy, a precarious posture for a Democrat, and his fate in 1980 proved it. All of Kennedy's successors learned to selectively employ, or at least tread carefully around, JFK's legacy. As our public poll demonstrated, Kennedy has remained an idol unequaled by any of them, save perhaps Reagan. In many ways, Kennedy's cult of personality is as strong today as in the 1960s, when the memory of his presidency was fresh and universal.

Only the terminally starry-eyed still see John F. Kennedy as an ideological crusader, drawn to politics by idealistic fervor about the great issues of the day. Unlike his brother Bobby in the last years of his life, or youngest brother Ted during many of his decades in the Senate, liberalism had little to do with John Kennedy's motives. The long view of JFK's career reveals that he was eager to define himself as more anticommunist, pro-defense, anticrime, pro-business, and cautious on civil rights than many of his contemporaries in both parties. John Kennedy was no leftist; he placed himself squarely in the mainstream of the Democratic Party and the country during his seventeen-year political sojourn.

Burning ambition, transferred by his father's desires from his deceased older brother Joe, was at JFK's core. The Democratic Party and its constituencies were mere instruments in the march to power. Platform planks were walking sticks used to climb the mountain. The New Frontier was no grand governing philosophy, but a piecemeal accumulation of ideas and opportunities that gradually evolved during Kennedy's campaign and presidency. Interestingly, that pragmatism has permitted John Kennedy to become an icon for modern-day Democrats and Republicans alike. His bifurcated philosophy, partly left and partly right (in today's ideological terms), enables Democrats to make civil rights and peace his monument while Republicans herald his tax cuts, muscular foreign policy, and space program.

Kennedy could not have foreseen this, nor was it his motivation. JFK and his entire family were drawn to the exercise of raw power, the perfect accompaniment to their colossal wealth. They were driven by desire for the ultimate clout of the White House, determined to be in the king's castle at the top of that shining city on a hill. Is this really any different from the incentives that have attracted most other men to seek and win the presidency before and after Kennedy? They surfed the waves of public opinion and did what was necessary to grasp the magnificent prize, but always, at the heart of it, they wanted to possess ultimate command and control over others. What sets the Kennedys apart is that never—at least until the Bushes—has a large family acted as one single-minded, unstoppable organism that methodically sought and won the highest office.

For the Kennedys, if there was a subterranean impulse beyond the overriding wish to be in charge, it might have been to achieve domination over the Anglo-Saxon Protestants who had run things for centuries and turned their noses up at Irish Catholic immigrants. It was delicious turnabout that the WASPs would have to come hat in hand to an Irish Catholic clan and beg for favors WASPs had considered their birthright. Anyone who has ever fought an arrogant in-crowd can appreciate it—but sweet revenge is not normally the stuff of heroic legend.

The legend derives instead from sorrow. In the aftermath of JFK's assassination, all things Kennedy were sanctified. Five decades on, that is no longer true, but a transformed Kennedy legacy lives. It certainly is not the one forged in JFK's exciting but vapid 1960 campaign, which in most ways (the new television debates aside) was quite conventional. Like all campaigns it was characterized by exaggerated attacks about minor matters, revolving more around style than substance. Not a sentence from the Kennedy-Nixon debates has lived on, because nothing weighty was uttered in those hours on the air. We recall what Americans watching then perceived. Kennedy looked terrific: movie-star handsome, tanned, and forceful. This is especially remarkable since throughout the campaign his image makers projected youthful vigor in a chronically ill man, not to mention the phony idealization of a secretly dysfunctional marriage. The election of 1960 was not a realigning watershed that set the nation's path going forward, but a narrow tactical victory about little. Regrettably, the Kennedy-Nixon campaign was one of many "Seinfeld elections" in U.S. history—a contest about nothing beyond partisan and tribal loyalties in which the real challenges facing the winner are never much discussed. The 1960 match-up is remembered mainly because it was astonishingly close and JFK managed to break the religious barrier.

Nor is President Kennedy's legacy one of historic achievement in the Oval Office. The seventh-shortest presidency, JFK's time in the White House was too brief for a lengthy list of accomplishments.[3] This recalls Kennedy's litany of reasons about why "life isn't fair" at one of his presidential press conferences.[4] The general principle JFK cited could well apply to the reality that an assassin's bullet deprived him of five more years at the helm to make his full mark in history. The inequity of this does not reduce its harsh effect on an evaluation of Kennedy's presidency: There is simply much less in Kennedy's White House record than there might have been for us to judge.

In the sweep of history, nothing JFK attained will matter more than his daring bet on NASA and a moon landing, which has permanently expanded man's horizons and led to earthbound breakthroughs in science, technology, communications, medicine, and consumer products of all sorts. Humankind's millennia of space exploration to come will always trace its roots to JFK's bold 1961 declaration of intent.

Kennedy also displayed critical growth in the presidency in two areas that changed the course of America. JFK was not especially sensitive to the plight of African Americans at the outset of his term, and he took far too long to make civil rights a central goal. But once he did so in 1963, Kennedy set the stage for the second Reconstruction that delivered the Civil Rights Act of 1964, the Voting Rights Act of 1965, and a far more just society.

Just as important, the bellicose Kennedy of the inauguration gave way to a serious search for peace and common ground with the Communist world. Some say that Kennedy's ineffective failures at the Bay of Pigs, in Berlin, and in early negotiations with the Soviet Union contributed to the near-fatal superpower encounter over Cuba in 1962. However, as Ted Sorensen insisted, "Every generation needs to know that without JFK the world might no longer exist as a result of a nuclear holocaust stemming from the Cuban Missile Crisis."[5] That searing experience turned Kennedy, and probably the Russians,

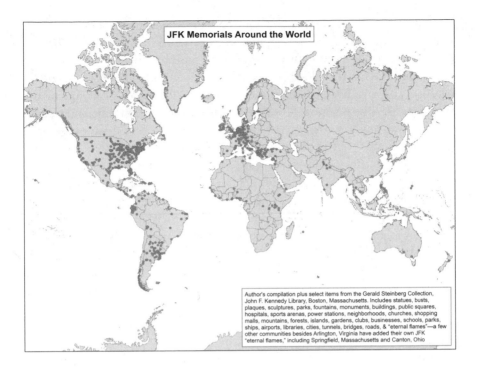

JFK Memorials Around the World

Author's compilation plus select items from the Gerald Steinberg Collection, John F. Kennedy Library, Boston, Massachusetts. Includes statues, busts, plaques, sculptures, parks, fountains, monuments, buildings, public squares, hospitals, sports arenas, power stations, neighborhoods, churches, shopping malls, mountains, forests, islands, gardens, clubs, businesses, schools, parks, ships, airports, libraries, cities, tunnels, bridges, roads, & "eternal flames"—a few other communities besides Arlington, Virginia have added their own JFK "eternal flames," including Springfield, Massachusetts and Canton, Ohio

away from sole reliance on tough rhetoric and military might and toward treaties, détente, and a lessening of international conflict where it was possible. This is a considerable legacy.

Without question, much of the globe has recognized Kennedy's achievements on the world stage in concrete ways. In the United States and around the world, some thirteen hundred JFK memorials have been erected. While this is almost certainly a partial list, this too is the Kennedy legacy accumulated over a half century.

KENNEDY'S PLACE IN the pantheon of presidencies should not be exaggerated. The great conflicts of his time were critically important, but many have faded in relevance and have as little connection to modern existence as the debate about tariffs in the nineteenth century. The Soviet Union no longer exists. The Cold War and its relatively tidy bipolar system have dissolved into a shadowy world of terrorist threats and transnational forces. The United States is no longer the undisputed economic giant of the 1960s that can dictate to other nations; the American century may well be ebbing as China, India, and other countries outstrip the United States in critical ways. The

Democratic Party of Kennedy's time was overwhelmingly male, very sub-stantially white, and dependent upon a segregationist South. That monochromatic status quo is a dinosaur in our century's rainbow reality.

Just as outdated is Kennedy's predatory personal behavior. It was as unrestrained and irresponsible as any ever engaged in by an occupant of the White House. The potential for extortion by Kennedy's domestic and foreign enemies was huge, as was the risk of exposure, which would have destroyed his presidency as well as the dreams of his family and supporters.[6] His jaw-dropping escapades and libertine practices were in complete contradiction to the image he and his handlers projected of the devout Catholic and consummate family man. Had a single one of his dalliances become public, history would have recorded that John Kennedy and not Richard Nixon was the first president to resign in disgrace. In sexual matters, Kennedy's self-control was nonexistent, and virtually on a daily basis, he risked everything. In addition, Kennedy's successful attempt to hide the fragile state of his health and his use of potent, mind-distorting drugs on a regular basis, with the help of accommodating medical personnel, was an equal deception of the public. We ought to remember this because it is a cautionary tale. Americans in any century can be too inclined to accept consultant-crafted images of flesh-and-blood people. Just as important, the courtiers of the powerful, including many in journalism, can conspire to deceive us, or acquiesce in the deception, as they did with JFK.

This is the underbelly of JFK's legacy. Standards for personal behavior and disclosure were far different in the 1960s than today. That fact does not absolve John Kennedy, but it does explain the mental process that enabled him to justify his conduct to himself and others.

Why, then, do so many Americans pine for the Kennedy era? Why is John Kennedy consistently rated one of the nation's best presidents? Why have JFK's successors so often sought to wear his mantle? Style and tragedy are the answers.

There will probably never be a more attractive couple in the White House than Jack and Jackie Kennedy. Their good looks and fashion sense transcended time; they could walk down the street today and not just fit in but command notice. JFK's oratory was often so powerful that it was hypnotic. Compared to most politicians of his time and ours, Kennedy could have read the telephone directory and held our attention. Even to their political opponents, President and Mrs. Kennedy were the precise image America wanted to project to the world: youth, vitality, charm, wit, optimism, confidence, fearlessness about the future. Kennedy benefited from serving at a time when citizens still trusted their government, and his infectious enthusiasm and big-picture worldview made people, especially the young, want to participate in remaking the world. The Peace Corps is only the most obvious example.

JFK's apparent personification of the nation's best qualities made November 22 all the more incomprehensible. At least during the lifetime of Americans who personally remember the assassination, the Kennedy legacy will remain vivid and indestructible. Mrs. Kennedy's postassassination creation of Camelot was a brilliant fiction, but we were ready to believe it. We wanted a larger-than-life myth, and Camelot gave us a happier story to summon up and heroic possibilities to realize. Those who loved John Kennedy—his powerful family and influential supporters such as Arthur Schlesinger and Ted Sorensen—were determined that his life's work would continue so his death would not be in vain, and they nurtured and extended the legend that Jackie built.

These efforts mattered because Kennedy's death gave life to all the promises that might have remained unfulfilled had Kennedy served a second term. Even with a solid 1964 reelection victory, JFK would probably not have swept into power a Congress willing to enact the kind of controversial civil rights, antipoverty, and health care policies that were irresistible only as a tribute to an assassinated president. Had Kennedy been on the ballot in 1964, his margin over Barry Goldwater probably would not have been as great as that achieved by his successor, who capitalized on the nation's remorse and grief over JFK's murder. For Kennedy, Democratic legislative majorities would have been less swollen, and the public's eagerness to erect legal monuments to a fallen leader would not have been a factor.

Kennedy's assassination created the big picture, the full Kennedy legacy, both in the statute books and in the hearts of his countrymen. November 22, 1963—its mysteries and tragedies—will continue to be the focal point that defines John F. Kennedy for the ages. Had this president not been assassinated, it is doubtful that the Kennedy years—however they played out—would have been able to sustain a dominating presence for half a century. The bullets in Dallas have made Kennedy's image bulletproof. His Shakespearean end transformed Kennedy into a Lincolnesque martyr-saint whose casual observations have become profound additions to politicians' speeches and students' term papers. JFK is frozen not just in time, but at a moment of peace, prosperity, and surging American power. Given all that has happened since, that Americans look back to the early 1960s as idyllic and associate the loss of Kennedy with the country's long "decline" is not surprising.

The likelihood that most people will remain unsatisfied with the official explanations of JFK's murder extends the shelf life of an increasingly distant presidency. The continued efforts of the CIA and others to conceal or redact relevant documents about the Kennedy assassination a half century after the event helps neither the agency's credibility nor public trust in government. The Kennedy family, for its part, has often been less than cooperative with researchers and scholars, too. The people of the United States own their country's history, and the public's money has paid for most of the materials that remain under lock and key.[7]

Even without the assassination documentation, though, the perspective of time can resolve a second cold war—not the one waged between the United States and the Soviet Union, but the more enduring battle between the defenders of JFK's legacy and the guardians of Lyndon Johnson's. The two Democratic ticketmates and presidents could not have been more different in personal history, style, and symbolism. The transfer of power from Kennedy to Johnson is a line of demarcation in history, symbolizing the end of Frostbelt dominance in American politics. Since Kennedy, seven of eight elected presidents have been from the South or West—the Sunbelt—where an ever-increasing share of voters is living.[8] Kennedy personified the old Frostbelt culture, while Johnson was the epitome of Sunbelt swagger. Still, their relationship in history is symbiotic, not parasitic. Most of the big achievements of Johnson's first two years, from civil rights to Medicare, and even the war on poverty, became law because they could be sold as tributes to a slain president. Johnson did what Kennedy could not because Kennedy's murder enabled it. JFK and LBJ should rightfully share credit, fairly equally, for the signal legislative accomplishments in 1964 and 1965. At the same time, while Johnson bears the lion's share of responsibility for the massive escalation of the Vietnam War, and for its subsequent shattering failure, Kennedy must shoulder culpability, too. JFK's acolytes have been too eager to absolve him of all blame. The thirty-fifth president may or may not have followed through on plans to scale down or end American involvement in Southeast Asia if he had lived, but his assertive anticommunism in that region set the stage for Johnson's calamitous policy. LBJ could plausibly claim yet another faithful attempt to continue the Kennedy program as it existed on November 22, 1963.

This struggle for credit and stature is cyclically waged by historians, and also by the surrogates and descendants of presidents. Over time it becomes less relevant than other, more impressionistic aspects of a president's image and his bequest to the nation. Ultimately, public opinion resolves any disputes—and public opinion can shift.

Younger Americans do not have rich recollections that give full life to the Kennedy legacy. As the nation adds decades and presidents, and the millions of baby boomers with firsthand memories pass on, Kennedy will not loom as large on the horizon as he has for the first fifty years since his death. The flame at JFK's grave site has a flashing electric spark near the tip of a gas nozzle that reignites the fire whenever rain and wind extinguish it; no passing storm can ever snuff it out. But the symbolic flame that has glowed so brightly since the one at Arlington Cemetery was lit will not prove as lasting. The Kennedy magic, which has entranced people for a half-century, will lose potency as his brief presidency ceases to have an outsized effect on personal memory and a nation's history.

The American people's idealization of John Kennedy, their determination to overlook his obvious flaws, and successive presidents' use of the Kennedy record for their own ends have been the sparks that have repeatedly reignited JFK's influence. Some of this effect will linger. Inspiring rhetoric and a charismatic leader captured forever on film will continue to fire the imagination of Americans yet unborn, and a young president's torch of possibilities and public service will be passed again and again to new generations. Yet time and distance will at last enable a country to put Kennedy's legacy in perspective. What endures will be what matters—not just the stark reminder that even the most charmed life can be defined by brutal tragedy, but genuine inspiration from John Fitzgerald Kennedy's public words and deeds, the things that moved history and people's minds and hearts.

NOTES

INTRODUCTION: THE BIRTH OF A LEGACY

1. "Etymology: Medieval Latin *legatio*, from Latin *legare* to bequeath," Dictionary.com, http://dictionary.reference.com/browse/legacy [accessed July 13, 2011].

2. See Eyal J. Naveh, *Crown of Thorns: Political Martyrdom in America from Abraham Lincoln to Martin Luther King, Jr.* (New York: New York University Press, 1990), 1.

3. John Kennedy and Richard Nixon are both excellent examples. But JFK's martyrdom has minimized the impact of revelations about his private life, while Nixon's resignation in the midst of scandal has given his image no protection.

4. Merrill D. Peterson, *The Jefferson Image in the American Mind* (Charlottesville: Thomas Jefferson Memorial Foundation and University of Virginia, 1998), xiii.

5. Few presidents have ever had as devoted a group of aides determined to shape his image long after his death as has John Kennedy. See John Hellmann, *The Kennedy Obsession: The American Myth of JFK* (New York: Columbia University Press, 1997).

6. Hart Research Associates, "Internet Survey of 2,009 Adults Nationally," June 7–13, 2012, http://survey-na.researchnow.com/wix/p337243575.aspx [accessed September 12, 2012] and "Focus Group Interviews in Richmond, Virginia, Chicago, Illinois, and Los Angeles, California: Men and Women, 55 and Older, 40–54, 30–39, and 20–29," July 11–18, 2012. Commissioned by the University of Virginia Center for Politics, all rights reserved.

1. "PRESIDENT KENNEDY DIED AT 1 P.M. CENTRAL STANDARD TIME"

1. Kenneth P. O'Donnell, David F. Powers, and Joe McCarthy, *"Johnny, We Hardly Knew Ye": Memories of John Fitzgerald Kennedy* (Boston: Little, Brown, 1970), 26.

2. Robert Dallek, *An Unfinished Life: John F. Kennedy, 1917–63* (Boston: Little, Brown, 2003), 693; Arthur Schlesinger, Jr., *A Thousand Days: John F. Kennedy in the White House* (Boston: Houghton Mifflin, 1965), 1023. Jackie's chief secret service agent, Clint Hill, says that the Roosevelts tried to talk her out of making the trip to Dallas. See Clint Hill, *Mrs. Kennedy and Me* (New York: Gallery Books, 2012), 266–67. Hill does not specify which Roosevelts, but he is probably referring to FDR son James Roosevelt and his wife. Gerald Blaine, one of the other agents assigned to the Texas detail, told me that the "trip to Dallas was like any other trip the president took. There were no special concerns and the president loved his reception." E-mail from Gerald Blaine, January 9, 2013. The split was between the liberal

wing of the Texas Democratic Party (led by Senator Ralph Yarborough) and the conservative wing (led by Governor John Connally). According to the PBS journalist Bill Moyers, this infighting weighed heavily on JFK's mind in the weeks leading up to the Dallas trip, and he ordered Moyers to fly to Texas ahead of time to calm the waters. When Moyers resisted, citing his responsibilities at the Peace Corps, Kennedy said, "Well, Bill, I'll tell you what: You go to Texas and think about politics and I'll be here in Washington thinking about the Peace Corps. Okay?" Needless to say, Moyers went to Texas. Bill Moyers, letter to Jeb Byrne, April 13, 2010, forwarded by Harold Pachios via e-mail, December 6, 2011.

3. Connally's use of the word "murdered" presaged what the governor would cry out just after having been shot on 11/22/63: "My God, they're going to kill us all!"

4. "Phone Call Between President Kennedy and John Connally, November 7, 1962," YouTube, http://www.youtube.com/watch?v=bWYZBePl4Lk&feature=channel&list=UL [accessed September 4, 2012].

5. Vincent Bugliosi, *Reclaiming History: The Assassination of President John F. Kennedy* (New York: W. W. Norton, 2007), 24–25. JFK visited Dallas three times during his presidency. The other two trips were on October 9, 1961, when he visited House Speaker Sam Rayburn in the hospital, and a November 18 return trip for Rayburn's funeral. E-mail from Gary Mack, curator of the Sixth Floor Museum at Dealey Plaza, January 17, 2012.

6. You can see the Warren film for yourself at http://www.jfk.org/go/collections/ward-warren-film [accessed January 15, 2013].

7. The fiction writer Stephen King published a bestseller in 2011 with a similar story line. King's protagonist, Jake Epping (a divorced high school teacher who is unhappy with life in the twenty-first century), discovers a time tunnel to 1958, which he uses in an attempt to stop the Kennedy assassination. See Stephen King, *11/22/63: A Novel* (New York: Scribner, 2011).

8. Barbara A. Perry, *Jacqueline Kennedy: First Lady of the New Frontier* (Lawrence: University Press of Kansas, 2004), 176; *The Lost JFK Tapes: The Assassination*, DVD, directed by Tom Jennings (Washington, DC: National Geographic Video, 2010).

9. A local television reporter narrated the event live for Dallas area viewers: "President in obvious good spirits . . . and here they come. Right down toward us. And the people who have waited all morning in suspense are rewarded with a close look and a handshake with the president of the United States and his wife. Boy, this is something. The press is standing up high, getting a lot of shots of this. He's broken away from his clan and gone right up to the fence to shake hands with people. This is great for the people and makes the eggshells even thinner for the Secret Service, whose job it is to guard the man . . . Back they go to the cars."

10. Gerald Blaine with Lisa McCubbin, *The Kennedy Detail: JFK's Secret Service Agents Break Their Silence* (New York: Gallery Books, 2010), 200.

11. Lehrer's wasn't the only journalistic career given an unexpected boost by the assassination. Dan Rather and Bob Schieffer, who both went on to celebrated careers at CBS, were reporters in Dallas at the time, and both managed to get major scoops from the tragic events. See Ciera Lundgren, "Bob Schieffer Explains How JFK's Assassination Shaped His Career," CBS News, October 11, 2011, http://www.cbsnews.com/8301-503544_162-20118863-503544.html [accessed October 13, 2011] and Alan Weisman, *Lone Star: The Extraordinary Life and Times of Dan Rather* (Hoboken, NJ: John Wiley and Sons, 2006), 39–52. Interview with Jim Lehrer, April 20, 2011.

12. Blaine with McCubbin, *Kennedy Detail*, 196–202.

13. "Report of United States Secret Service on the Assassination of President Kennedy," C. Douglas Dillon Papers, Box 43, Folder "The President's Committee on the Warren Report," John F. Kennedy Library, Boston, Massachusetts; *Guide to U.S. Elections*, vol. 1, 6th ed. (Washington, DC: CQ Press, 2010), 789; Telephone interview with Ralph Dungan, May 24, 2011.

14. Bugliosi, *Reclaiming History*, 28–31; Jim Bishop, *The Day Kennedy Was Shot* (New York: Funk and Wagnalls, 1968), 116–17; Blaine with McCubbin, *Kennedy Detail*, 204–5.

15. Bugliosi, *Reclaiming History*, 31; "Report of the President's Commission on the Assassination of President Kennedy, Chapter 3: The Shots from the Texas School Book Depository," 68. JFK Assassination Records, National Archives and Records Administration website, http://www.archives.gov/research/jfk/warren-commission-report/chapter-3.html #witnesses [accessed March 8, 2011].

16. Blaine with McCubbin, *Kennedy Detail*, 206.

17. *The Lost JFK Tapes: The Assassination*. DVD, 2010; Blaine with McCubbin, *Kennedy Detail*, 51, 196, 206; "United States Secret Service Lecture Outline on Protection of the President for Guidance of Special Agents Appearing Before Police Schools," C. Douglas Dillon Papers, Box 42, Folder "The President's Committee on the Warren Report," John F. Kennedy Library, Boston, Massachusetts; Bob Greene, "The Man Who Did Not Kill JFK," *CNN Opinion*, October 24, 2010, http://articles.cnn.com/2010-10-24/opinion/greene.jfk.arrest_1_kennedy-family-mansion-election-lee-harvey-oswald?_s=PM:OPINION [accessed March 18, 2011]; "Crime: The Man from Peyton Place," *Time*, December 26, 1960, http://www.time.com /time/magazine/article/0,9171,895131,00.html [accessed March 18, 2011]; Philip Kerr, "JFK: The Assassin Who Failed," *New Statesman*, November 27, 2000, http://www.newstatesman .com/200011270016 [accessed March 18, 2011].

18. "Report of United States Secret Service on the Assassination of President Kennedy," C. Douglas Dillon Papers, Box 43, Folder "The President's Committee on the Warren Report," John F. Kennedy Library, Boston, Massachusetts.

19. Blaine with McCubbin, *Kennedy Detail*, 207–8.

20. "Report of United States Secret Service," Dillon Papers, Box 43, Kennedy Library.

21. "Report of the President's Commission, Chapter 3," 68–71.

22. "Report of the President's Commission on the Assassination of President Kennedy, Chapter 4: The Assassin," 149–54. JFK Assassination Records, National Archives and Records Administration website, http://www.archives.gov/research/jfk/warren-commission -report/chapter-4.html [accessed March 9, 2011]; Bugliosi, *Reclaiming History*, 47–48.

23. "Report of the President's Commission, chapter 4" 149–54; Bugliosi, *Reclaiming History*, 47–48.

24. Bugliosi, *Reclaiming History*, 55–65.

25. Hugh Aynesworth, a journalist for the *Dallas Morning News*, interviewed Roberts on the day of the assassination; she did not mention the police car during this interview. Nor did she mention it during a second interview with Aynesworth. During two subsequent interviews with the reporter, however, she expanded upon her story, even recalling a number on the police car—though the number was different in two separate tellings. It is impossible to say what actually happened. The Dallas police have no record of a cruiser in her neighborhood at one P.M. on 11/22/63, but in the massive confusion of the day, a police car might have been there, for whatever reason—innocent or nefarious, as discussed in a later chapter.

26. United Press International scooped the story. At 12:34 P.M., four minutes after the shooting, Merriman Smith, UPI's Dallas correspondent, called in the incident from a radio-phone in the White House press pool car; he held the lone phone away from another re-porter, AP's Jack Bell, and didn't give it to Bell until they had arrived at Parkland Hospital. Smith's report quickly spread across the globe. Smith is also the person who first called the strip of green on the right side of Dealey Plaza "the grassy knoll." A myth exists among the public that breaking news reports in the 1960s were more accurate than modern ones. An honest review of the record, however, shows that reporters covering the Kennedy assassina-tion made mistakes and spread misinformation in the same way their counterparts have done during recent crises such as the Boston Marathon bombing. CBS initially told viewers that "a man and a woman" had fired shots at President Kennedy and Governor Connally using a machine gun; that a Secret Service man had been killed in a hail of gunfire; that the Secret Service had arrested a suspect when the chief murder suspect, Lee Harvey Oswald, was still at large; and that "a witness saw a colored man fire three shots" from the fourth floor of the Texas School Book Depository. See "Two Hours of Uncut 11/22/63 CBS-TV Cov-erage, Starting at 1:30 P.M.," YouTube, http://www.youtube.com/watch?v=t_Ry9-bpixM [accessed April 23, 2013].

27. "Top 125 Most Memorable Political Moments. #1 Assassination of JFK (November 22, 1963)," Museum of Broadcast Communications, http://www.museum.tv/exhibitionssection .php?page=440 [accessed March 10, 2011]; Bugliosi, *Reclaiming History*, 57.

28. Mary Ann Watson, *The Expanding Vista: American Television in the Kennedy Years* (Durham, NC: Duke University Press, 1994), 214–15.

29. Steven M. Gillon, *The Kennedy Assassination—24 Hours After: Lyndon B. Johnson's Pivotal First Day as President* (New York: Basic Books, 2009), 55–57; Blaine with McCubbin, *Kennedy Detail*, 223–25; Hill, *Mrs. Kennedy and Me*, 293; interview with H. B. McLain, March 17, 2011.

30. Another strange story involves a phone call that was received at Fort Sam Houston in San Antonio (headquarters of the 4th Army) a few minutes before the assassination. Be-tween 12:15 and 12:30 CST, a base operator contacted the Deputy Chief of Staff Operations and Training office and asked for help in directing a call from an unidentified man who wanted to speak with the "Silver Dollar War Room." The operator was told to put the caller through to extension 2703. At approximately 12:25, the caller said, "This is Silver Dollar call-ing to test communications. I read you loud and clear, loud and clear. How do you read me?" A voice on extension 2703 replied, "I read you loud and clear, loud and clear." The caller then said, "Roger, over and out," before hanging up. "Silver Dollar" turned out to be the code word for the National Emergency Airborne Command Post, a specially equipped Air Force jet that had been designed to carry the president and his national security advisers during a nuclear war. Records show that the NEACP plane was in the air between 10:40 A.M. and 2:30 P.M. CST on 11/22. The question is why. Was it just an eerie coincidence? And who was the un-identified male caller? Larry Haapanen and Alan Rogers, "A Phone Call from Out of the Blue," Mary Ferrell Foundation website, http://www.maryferrell.org/mffweb/archive/viewer /showDoc.do?docId=4275&relPageId=13 [accessed May 31, 2011]. In recent years, other strange radio conversations have surfaced that deserve closer scrutiny. A tape of never-before-heard radio traffic from Air Force One was discovered in General Chester Clifton, Jr.'s belongings after he died. Topics on the Clifton tape include General Curtis LeMay's whereabouts on 11/22; a debate about where to take JFK's body for the autopsy; and tantaliz-

ing references to various unknown individuals with code names like Monument and WTE. See John Loviglio, "Lost JFK Assassination Tapes on Sale," Associated Press, November 15, 2011, http://www.google.com/hostednews/ap/article/ALeqM5hyPT4jpoo6hsWvJ6SJRquXZ _1qyw?docId=2dccd4eca1584b24974c118c4a50311e [accessed November 15, 2011]. Audio excerpts from the Clifton tape can be found at http://www.raabcollection.com/kennedy-air -force-one-tape/ [accessed November 15, 2011].

31. "JFK: Inside the Target Car, Part 1," *Discovery Channel*, YouTube, http://www.you tube.com/watch?v=e246B581jH0 [accessed April 20, 2011]; Blaine with McCubbin, *Kennedy Detail*, 243–45.

32. "Report of the President's Commission on the Assassination of President Kennedy, Appendix 8: Medical Reports from Doctors at Parkland Memorial Hospital, Dallas, Tex.," 529–30. JFK Assassination Records, National Archives and Records Administration website, http://www.archives.gov/research/jfk/warren-commission-report/appendix8.html [accessed March 11, 2011]; Gerald Posner, *Case Closed: Lee Harvey Oswald and the Assassination of JFK* (New York: Anchor Books, 1994), 287–88.

33. Blaine with McCubbin, *Kennedy Detail*, 229; Posner, *Case Closed*, 287.

34. Although based on the Eisenhower-Nixon succession agreement (or "Disability of President Memo"), the JFK-LBJ agreement included a telling addition: "There is no provision of the Constitution or of law prescribing any procedure of consultation, but the president and vice president felt, as a matter of wisdom and sound judgment, that the vice president would wish to have the support of the Cabinet as to the necessity and desirability of discharging the powers and duties of the presidency as acting president as well as legal advice from the attorney general that the circumstances would, under the Constitution, justify his doing so." In other words, JFK and RFK revised the Ike-Nixon agreement in order to rein in LBJ and give RFK more power over the succession. The memo that Eisenhower sent to Nixon is friendlier and less formal: "However, it seems to me that so far as you and I are concerned in the offices we now respectively hold, and particularly in view of our mutual confidence and friendship, we could do much to eliminate all these uncertainties by agreeing, in advance, as to the proper steps to be taken at any time when I might become unable to discharge the powers and duties of the president." Undated memo from JFK to LBJ, Vice Presidential Papers, 1961 Subject File, Box 119, Folder, "Vice President, Office of," Lyndon Baines Johnson Library, Austin, Texas; Louis Galambos, Daun Van Ee, Elizabeth S. Hughes, Janet R. Brugger, Robin D. Coblentz, Jill A. Friedman, and Nancy Kay Berlage, eds., *The Papers of Dwight David Eisenhower: The Presidency: Keeping the Peace*, vol. XIX (Baltimore: Johns Hopkins University Press, 2001), 711–14.

35. Gillon, *Kennedy Assassination*, 60–64; "U.S. Constitution: Article II, Section 1," Avalon Project: Documents in Law, History, and Diplomacy, http://avalon.law.yale.edu/18th _century/art2.asp [accessed March 14, 2011].

36. Personal interview with Robert McClelland, January 14, 2011, Dallas.

37. Posner, *Case Closed*, 291.

38. G. Paul Chambers, *Head Shot: The Science Behind the JFK Assassination* (Amherst, NY: Prometheus Books, 2010), 38; Bugliosi, *Reclaiming History*, 83–84; Posner, *Case Closed*, 292–93.

39. Cronkite was not the first journalist to report Kennedy's death on the air. That sad distinction belonged to Eddie Barker, news director of KRLD television in Dallas. Barker's unconfirmed report was based on a single but reliable source who worked at Parkland

Hospital. Interview with Eddie Barker, November 20, 2003, *The NewsHour with Jim Lehrer*, http://www.pbs.org/newshour/bb/white_house/kennedy/barker.html [accessed March 5, 2012].

40. "Top 125 Most Memorable Political Moments," Museum of Broadcast Communications website, http://www.museum.tv/exhibitionssection.php?page=440 [accessed March 15, 2011]. Some of those closest to the president were unaware of his passing until later that evening. Gerald Blaine, one of the Secret Service agents assigned to protect Kennedy, first heard the news when his plane touched down at around seven P.M. "The flight contained all of the agents in Austin and also John Bailey, the Democratic Committee chairman," Blaine told me. "All Air Force [planes] were put on radio silence. It was only after we landed at Andrews Air Force Base that we found out the president was dead." E-mail from Gerald Blaine, January 9, 2013.

41. Max Holland believes that Lee Harvey Oswald may have had as much as eleven seconds to fire three shots. Other researchers disagree. See Dale K. Meyers and Todd W. Vaughn, "Max Holland's 11 Seconds in Dallas," *Secrets of a Homicide*, June 25, 2007, http://jfkfiles.blogspot.com/2007/06/max-hollands-11-seconds-in-dallas.html [accessed November 21, 2011]. Holland also believes that the first bullet that missed Kennedy may have struck the "mast arm" of a traffic light on Elm Street, but he admits that further tests are necessary to confirm his theory. See "The DeRonja-Holland Report," November 20, 2011, *Washington Decoded*, http://www.washingtondecoded.com/site/2011/11/the-.html [accessed November 28, 2011].

42. Arthur M. Schlesinger, Jr., *Robert Kennedy and His Times* (Boston: Houghton Mifflin, 2002), 609.

43. Robert Caro, the award-winning LBJ biographer, says that it was RFK, not one of Johnson's aides, who called Katzenbach for the oath. See Robert Caro, *The Passage of Power* (New York: Alfred A. Knopf, 2012), 328.

44. As time passed, LBJ and RFK would bicker over the details of their conversation. LBJ gave the impression that taking the oath in Dallas had been Bobby's idea, which is doubtful on its face. RFK certainly rejected this version of events. Kennedy and some other family loyalists portrayed LBJ as a power-hungry politician who needed immediate control and who perhaps feared that if he didn't take the oath in Dallas that the Kennedys would somehow find a way to keep the presidency from him. A more neutral appraisal—while not denying that these motives may have played a role—would certainly admit the importance of reassuring a shaken nation of continuity in the Oval Office. Nothing could do that like the visible swearing-in of the next president. And Johnson was already legally the president, oath or not. The Constitution was clear on that point, even before the ratification of the Twenty-fifth Amendment regarding presidential succession in 1967. Gillon, *Kennedy Assassination*, 114–15.

45. Bishop, *Day Kennedy Was Shot*, 231–44.

46. Ibid., 210.

47. Bugliosi, *Reclaiming History*, 10.

48. Amanda Hopkinson, "Cecil Stoughton: Kennedy's In-House Photographer, Best Known for Capturing the Swearing-in of LBJ," *The Guardian*, November 20, 2008, http://www.guardian.co.uk/world/2008/nov/20/photographer-obituary-cecil-stoughton [accessed March 16, 2011]; "President Lyndon B. Johnson Taking the Oath of Office: November 22, 1963 and Beyond," Lyndon Baines Johnson Library and Museum website, http://www.lbjlib

.utexas.edu/johnson/kennedy/index.htm [accessed March 16, 2011]; Bishop, *Day Kennedy Was Shot*, 243.

49. The announcement was also broadcast over channel two at 12:45 P.M.

50. "Report of the President's Commission, Chapter 4," 165–76. The journalist and assassination researcher Henry Hurt is not convinced that Oswald killed Tippit, and he has raised questions about the timeline of events and the credibility of the eyewitnesses. See Hurt's book *Reasonable Doubt: An Investigation into the Assassination of John F. Kennedy*, especially chapter 7 ("Tippit's Murder: Rosetta Stone or Red Herring?").

51. Ibid., 176–78; Bosley Crowther, "Oozing Conflict: 'Cry of Battle' Opens at the Victoria," *New York Times*, October 12, 1963, http://movies.nytimes.com/movie/review?res=9C01 E0DC133CEF3BBC4A52DFB6678388679EDE [accessed March 17, 2011].

52. "Report of the President's Commission, Chapter 4," pages 178–80; Bugliosi, *Reclaiming History*, 104–6. The Texas Theatre has been preserved and is both a community center and a tourist attraction in Dallas. But the row of seats where Oswald was sitting was removed by a previous owner and is in the hands of a private collector.

53. Jeff Carlton, "Paul Bentley; Detective Helped Arrest Oswald," *Boston Globe*, July 25, 2008, http://www.boston.com/bostonglobe/obituaries/articles/2008/07/25/paul_bentley _detective_helped_arrest_oswald/ [accessed March 17, 2011]. There is also existing film of Oswald being driven away from the theater. Bentley was related to L. C. Graves, one of the officers escorting Oswald when he was shot by Jack Ruby. He later told Graves, "I arrested him and you let him get shot!"

54. William E. Scott, *November 22, 1963: A Reference Guide to the JFK Assassination* (Lanham, MD: University Press of America, 1999), 25; "Report of the President's Commission, Chapter 4," 179–80.

55. "Who was Lee Harvey Oswald? 9: Capture," *Frontline*, PBS website, http://www.pbs .org/wgbh/pages/frontline/shows/oswald/view/ [accessed March 21, 2011].

56. Telephone interview with Jim Lehrer, April 20, 2011. Understandably, Lehrer has chosen not to identify the agent. Actually, it is entirely possible that the bubbletop would have been removed anyway. Roy Kellerman, the Secret Service special agent in charge of the Dallas trip, had been told that unless the weather clearly prevented it, the bubbletop was not to be used. The White House staff apparently wanted Dallasites to get a good look at the Kennedys. We will never know for sure what might have happened. "Report of United States Secret Service," Dillon Papers, Box 43, Kennedy Library. The bubbletop was made of quarter-inch Plexiglas and was designed to fit in the trunk of the presidential limousine when not in use. It was not bulletproof. The Secret Service had approached Swedlow, Inc., a plastics manufacturing company, about designing a bulletproof model, but Swedlow's engineers could not come up with a suitable model. In October 1963, the Secret Service enlisted the help of a retired army colonel who "furnished the Service with names of two commercial concerns" in mid-November—far too late to help John F. Kennedy.

57. The reporter, Bill Mercer of KRLD, had outdated information. Henry Wade, Dallas County's district attorney, did not formally charge Oswald with the murder of JFK until 1:30 A.M. on November 23.

58. "Who Was Lee Harvey Oswald? 10: Jack Ruby and the Murder of Oswald," *Frontline*, PBS website, http://www.pbs.org/wgbh/pages/frontline/shows/oswald/view/ [accessed March 21, 2011]; Bugliosi, *Reclaiming History*, 188.

59. Various advertisements for the Carousel Club, Richard "Chick" Ramirez Collection, Sixth Floor Museum at Dealey Plaza, Dallas, Texas; "Report of the President's Commission on the Assassination of President Kennedy, Appendix 16: A Biography of Jack Ruby," page 801. JFK Assassination Records, National Archives and Records Administration website, http://www.archives.gov/research/jfk/warren-commission-report/appendix-16.html [accessed March 21, 2011]; "Who Was Lee Harvey Oswald? 10," Frontline, PBS website [accessed March 21, 2011]; Hugh Aynesworth with Stephen G. Michaud, *JFK: Breaking the News* (Richardson, TX: International Focus Press, 2003), 166.

60. Lyndon B. Johnson, "Remarks upon Arrival at Andrews Air Force Base, November 22, 1963," John T. Woolley and Gerhard Peters, *American Presidency Project* [online], Santa Barbara, CA, http://www.presidency.ucsb.edu/ws/index.php?pid=25976#axzz1HFMxZC9n [accessed March 21, 2011].

61. These were almost the precise words of my own father.

62. Interview with James I. Robertson, Jr., May 7, 2013.

63. Ibid.

64. Undated interview with James I. Robertson, Jr., "Storytelling with James I. Robertson, Jr.—John F. Kennedy," Virginia Tech website, University Relations, http://www.unirel .vt.edu/audio_video/2011/01/2011-01-14-robertson-JFK.html [accessed March 24, 2011].

65. Perhaps Mrs. Kennedy's decision also spurred the widely seen 1963–64 circular that connected Lincoln to Kennedy. The parallels included elections a hundred years apart, vice presidents named Johnson, and Southern assassins who were known by three names. See "Linkin' Kennedy," http://www.snopes.com/history/american/lincoln-kennedy.asp [accessed August 8, 2011].

66. Theodore H. White, *The Making of the President 1964* (New York: Atheneum, 1965), 9.

67. Texas law requires autopsies in homicide cases. The district attorney for Dallas County, Henry Wade, very reluctantly allowed the autopsy to be performed in Washington, D.C. The Secret Service agents, angry and in no mood for interference, had insisted. This conflict is discussed in a later chapter.

68. Posner, *Case Closed*, 299.

69. Wesley Buell Frazier, who drove Oswald to work on Friday, November 22, said, "I will tell you this, he did not carry lunch with him on Friday. And I noticed that. And I said, 'You don't have your lunch with you today?' because when he rode back with me on Monday he always had lunch. 'No,' he says, 'I'm going to buy my lunch today.'" Telephone interview with Wesley Buell Frazier, April 16, 2013.

70. Bugliosi, *Reclaiming History*, 213–18.

71. Gladwin Hill, "Evidence Against Oswald Described as Conclusive," *New York Times*, November 24, 1963.

72. Robert A. Caro, *The Years of Lyndon Johnson: The Passage of Power* (New York: Alfred A. Knopf, 2012), 409–10.

73. James Reston, "Cabinet Convenes," *New York Times*, November 24, 1963; Gillon, *Kennedy Assassination*, 199–204; E. W. Kenworthy, "Johnson Orders Day of Mourning," *New York Times*, November 24, 1963; "Johnson Proclaims a Day of Mourning," *Washington Post and Times Herald*, November 24, 1963.

74. Dan B. Fleming, Jr., *Ask What You Can Do for Your Country: The Memory and Legacy of John F. Kennedy* (Clearwater, FL: Vandamere Press, 2002), 207–23; Tom R. Taylor,

untitled article in *Quinto Lingo*, November 1971, Box 239, "JFK Tributes 1972," Rose Kennedy Papers, John F. Kennedy Library, Boston, Massachusetts; "Analysis of World Reaction to President Kennedy's Assassination," December 13, 1963, Records of the Central Intelligence Agency, RG 263, Box 51, "Personality File of Lee Harvey Oswald," The National Archives at College Park, Maryland.

75. James Reston, "Why America Weeps," *New York Times*, November 23, 1963; "President's Assassination Brings Statements of Sadness and Shock from Faculty Members," *Temple University News*, November 25, 1963, Rose Fitzgerald Kennedy Papers, Box 237, "JFK Commemorative Publications and Tributes, 1963, sent to JPK," John F. Kennedy Library, Boston, Massachusetts.

76. Interview with Bob Schieffer, March 4, 2013.

77. Telephone interview with Senator Mitch McConnell, December 2, 2011.

78. Interview with Lynda Robb, May 22, 2013.

79. John Glenn to Mr. and Mrs. Joseph Kennedy, Western Union telegram, November 23, 1963, Marlene Dietrich to Mr. and Mrs. Joe Kennedy, RCA Communications Telegram, November 23, 1963, and John Edgar Hoover to the Honorable Joseph P. Kennedy, November 22, 1963, Box 236, "Special Letters, Notes, and Telegrams, etc., 1963," Rose Kennedy Papers, John F. Kennedy Library, Boston, Massachusetts.

80. Tim Weiner, *Enemies: A History of the FBI* (New York: Random House, 2012), 237.

81. Carolyn H. Williamson to Mrs. Joseph P. Kennedy, November 27, 1963, Rose Fitzgerald Kennedy Papers, Box 237, "JFK Commemorative Publications and Tributes, 1963, sent to JPK," John F. Kennedy Library, Boston, Massachusetts.

82. Commander Gerald J. Murray to Mr. and Mrs. Joseph P. Kennedy, November 23, 1963, Mrs. William J. McCluggage to Mrs. Kennedy, November 29, 1963, Theresa A. Twaddle to Ambassador and Mrs. Kennedy, November 23, 1963, Box 236, "Cards & Letters, 1963," Rose Kennedy Papers, John F. Kennedy Library, Boston, Massachusetts.

83. "Statement by Pope Paul VI, November 23, 1963," Box 1, Folder 1, William Fine Papers, Library of Congress Manuscripts Division, Washington, DC.

84. "Mass card from the Seraphic Mass Association for the support of the Capuchin Foreign Missions, November 24, 1963," Box 236, Series 10, "Mass Cards from Ireland," Rose Kennedy Papers, John F. Kennedy Library, Boston, Massachusetts.

85. R. Bresnahan to Mrs. Rose Kennedy, November 30, 1963, and Martin J. Maehr to Mr. Joseph P. Kennedy & Family, November 29, 1963," Box 236, "Cards and Letters, 1963," Rose Kennedy Papers, John F. Kennedy Library, Boston, Massachusetts.

86. "Sermon Preached by Reinhold Niebuhr," Box 1, Folder 1, William Fine Papers, Library of Congress Manuscripts Division, Washington, DC.

87. "Sermon Preached by Monsignor John S. Kennedy from Cathedral of St. Joseph, Hartford, Connecticut," "A Tribute by Dr. Julius Mark, Senior Rabbi of the Congregation, Temple Emanu-el, New York, New York," "Sermon Preached by Norman Vincent Peale from Marble Collegiate Church, New York, New York," Box 1, Folder 1, William Fine Papers, Library of Congress Manuscripts Division, Washington, DC.

88. Partly because of the black eye Oswald suffered at the Texas Theatre when he resisted arrest, some wrongly suspected Oswald was being beaten by police.

89. Wayne Thomis, "60 Officers on Scene; Killer Seized," *Washington Post and Times Herald*, November 25, 1963; "A Photographer's Story: Bob Jackson and the Kennedy Assassination at the Sixth Floor Museum Closing Sunday," *Dallas Art News*, October 13, 2010,

http://www.dallasartnews.com/2010/10/a-photographers-story-bob-jackson-and-the-ken nedy-assassination-at-the-sixth-floor-museum-closing-sunday/ [accessed March 29, 2011]; Bugliosi, *Reclaiming History*, 273–84; Posner, *Case Closed*, 396.

90. "Analysis of World Reaction to President Kennedy's Assassination," December 13, 1963, Records of the Central Intelligence Agency, RG 263, Box 51, "Personality File of Lee Harvey Oswald," National Archives at College Park, Maryland; Aleksandr Fursenko and Timothy Naftali, *"One Hell of a Gamble": Khrushchev, Castro, and Kennedy, 1958–64* (New York: W. W. Norton, 1997), 347–50; Earl Lively, Jr. and Herbert A. Philbrick, "The Strange Death of President Kennedy" [outline], Box 223, Folders 9 & 10, Herbert Philbrick Papers, Library of Congress Manuscripts Division, Washington, DC.

91. "John Fitzgerald Kennedy Grave Research Report," LBJ Papers—EX FG 1 3/26/68, Box 18, FG 1, 3/26/68–4/18/68, Lyndon Baines Johnson Library, Austin, Texas.

92. "A Widow's Courage Catches at the Heart of a Nation as Kennedy Lies in State," *New York Times*, November 25, 1963; White, *Making of the President 1964*, 15–16; Mike Mansfield, Earl Warren, and John W. McCormack, *John Fitzgerald Kennedy. Eulogies to the Late President Delivered in the Rotunda of the United States Capitol* (Washington, DC: U.S. Government Printing Office, 1963), available on John F. Kennedy Presidential Library and Museum website, http://www.jfklibrary.org/Research/Ready-Reference/JFK-Miscellaneous-Informa tion/Eulogies.aspx [accessed March 30, 2011]; William Manchester, *The Death of a President: November 20–November 25, 1963* (New York: Harper and Row, 1967), 541–42; James Piereson, *Camelot and the Cultural Revolution: How the Assassination of John F. Kennedy Shattered American Liberalism* (New York: Encounter Books, 2007), 59.

93. Manchester, *Death of a President*, 542; Robert Drew, *Crisis: Behind a Presidential Commitment* [bonus film: *Faces of November*]. DVD (New York: New Video Group, 2008).

94. "John F. Kennedy: The Last Full Measure," *National Geographic* 125 (March 1964): 307–55; Blaine with McCubbin, *Kennedy Detail*, 291; Philip Hannan with Nancy Collins and Peter Finney, Jr., *The Archbishop Wore Combat Boots: Memoir of an Extraordinary Life* (Huntington, IN: Our Sunday Visitor Publishing Division, 2010), 18–22.

95. Hannan, *Archbishop Wore Combat Boots*, 22; Blaine with McCubbin, *Kennedy Detail*, 295.

96. "The Last Full Measure," 350; Barbara Perry, *Jacqueline Kennedy: First Lady of the New Frontier* (Lawrence: University Press of Kansas, 2004), 185–86; "President John Fitzgerald Kennedy," Arlington National Cemetery website, http://www.arlingtoncemetery .mil/visitor_information/JFK.html [accessed March 31, 2011].

2. "ALL THE MARBLES"

1. Ruth Aull and Daniel M. Ogden, Jr., eds., *Official Report of the Proceedings of the Democratic National Convention, Chicago, Illinois, August 13 through August 17, 1956, resulting in the re-nomination of Adlai E. Stevenson of Illinois for President and in the nomination of Estes Kefauver of Tennessee for Vice President* (Richmond: Beacon Press, 1956), 36; Willard Edwards, "Details Given of 1st Day of Convention," *Chicago Tribune*, August 14, 1956.

2. John F. Kennedy, *The Pursuit of Happiness*, VHS, produced by Dore Schary (Chicago: International Historic Films, 1985); Aull and Ogden, *Proceedings*, 36.

3. The CBS decision angered the convention delegates who began shouting "Throw 'em out!" when Paul Butler raised the issue. Sig Mickelson, vice president in charge of news for

CBS, said, "At no time did we make any commitment to carry the Democratic National Committee film 'Pursuit of Happiness.' We did not know the film was considered an official part of the keynote address."

4. Theodore C. Sorensen, *Kennedy* (New York: Harper and Row, 1965), 86; "40-Vote Bay State Delegation Delays Preference Vote," *North Adams Transcript*, August 14, 1956; Aull and Ogden, *Proceedings*, 47. Kennedy made a wise decision when he agreed to star in the film. It allowed him to link his name with a long list of Democratic heroes (Jefferson, Monroe, Jackson, Bryan, Wilson, Franklin Roosevelt, and Truman).

5. Clement attacked the Republicans, referring to Richard Nixon as the "Vice-Hatchet Man" and accusing Eisenhower of peering "down the green fairways of indifference." At times Clement sounded more like a fire-and-brimstone preacher than a national leader: "You can justify begging God for guidance. You can justify studying the record and after you have done it going out and fighting and singing in unison, you and I together of every race, creed and color, let's go forward singing in unison the immortal victory hymn, 'Precious Lord, Take Our Hands and Lead Us.'" Aull and Ogden, *Proceedings*, 61. The New York journalist Red Smith almost single-handedly made Clement a laughingstock with a memorable quip: "The young governor of Tennessee, Frank G. Clement, slew the Republican Party with the jawbone of an ass here last night . . ." Jack Bass and Walter De Vries, *Southern Politics: Social Change and Political Consequence Since 1945* (Athens: University of Georgia Press, 1995), 289.

6. Jack Gould, "TV: CBS Outsmarted," *New York Times*, August 14, 1956; Herbert S. Parmet, *Jack: The Struggles of John F. Kennedy* (New York: Dial Press, 1980), 356–57 and 366–69; "Party's Film Aids Kennedy's Drive," *New York Times*, August 14, 1956. The revisionist historian Thomas C. Reeves, author of *A Question of Character*, also sees the Kennedy film as a shrewd political maneuver: "Jack had been selected to narrate the film because he had performed well during television appearances and because *Profiles in Courage* was a best-seller. Kennedy appeared at the rostrum soon after the film's showing, prompting a placard-waving demonstration by the Massachusetts delegation. The movie and the convention proceedings were televised nationally, and Jack became known to tens of millions. (When Jack's Georgetown neighbor and friend, television newsman Charles Collingwood, kidded him about the failure of CBS to air the film, Jack shot him a hateful look and said, 'I know, you bastards.')" Thomas C. Reeves, *A Question of Character: A Life of John F. Kennedy* (Rocklin, CA: Prima Publishing, 1992), 134.

7. Doris Kearns Goodwin, *The Fitzgeralds and the Kennedys: An American Saga* (New York: St. Martin's Press, 1987), 395–405; Parmet, *Jack*, 16, 103, 162. See also David Nasaw, *The Patriarch: The Remarkable Life and Turbulent Times of Joseph P. Kennedy* (New York: Penguin Press, 2012.)

8. Sorensen, *Kennedy*, 81. Sorensen says that JFK wanted the vice presidential nomination because he was a competitive guy, not because he really wanted the job. He also says that "circumstances" more than calculated political strategy explain why JFK was so successful at the convention (Sorensen, *Kennedy*, 80–85.) Kenny O'Donnell claims that JFK's father hit the roof when he learned that his son was seeking the vice presidency (Kenneth P. O'Donnell, David F. Powers, and Joe McCarthy, *"Johnny, We Hardly Knew Ye": Memories of John Fitzgerald Kennedy* (Boston: Little, Brown, 1970), 138. The historian Herbert Parmet agrees and says that JFK was asserting his independence from his father (Parmet, *Jack*, 363). But Thomas Reeves dissents: "That Jack would enter a dangerous factional struggle on

his own and against his father's wishes is contrary to what we know about the relationship between the two men, before and after 1956. And given the ambassador's carefully laid plans for his son to this point, and the Kennedys' long-established and widely known (among insiders) designs on the 1956 ticket, it seems highly unlikely that the elder Kennedy suddenly failed to support his son's bid for national prominence." Moreover, Reeves thinks that Joe Sr. was pulling the strings behind the scenes and that his trip to Èze-sur-Mer (on the French Riviera) was a calculated move to convince the public that Jack was his own man (Reeves, *Question of Character*, 131–32). I am skeptical of Sorensen's claims, and there is plenty of evidence that the Kennedy organization had been carefully preparing the way for JFK's VP effort. For example, see Fletcher Knebel's *Look* article, "Can a Catholic Become Vice President?" which ran in June 1956 (34). Knebel later admitted that Sorensen had given him the story. Similarly, Arthur Krock's *New York Times* article, "In the Nation: The Democratic Party and the 'Catholic Vote,'" which was printed on July 5, 1956 (p. 24) has its roots in the Kennedy camp. The August 6, 1956, *Time* article "Democrats: Who for Vice President?" (http://www.time.com/time/magazine/article/0,9171,862293,00 .html [accessed December 18, 2012]) references the "persuasive statistical arguments that Catholicism is no longer a national political liability," and these "statistical arguments" were almost certainly based on the "Bailey Memorandum," a study that had actually been produced by Sorensen.

9. "Adlai Above Minimum Required for Nomination, AP Tally of Votes Shows," *Newport Daily News*, August 16, 1956; Parmet, *Jack*, 370; "Mrs. Roosevelt's V.P. Choice Must Be Anti-McCarthy," *Washington Post and Times Herald*, August 15, 1956.

10. "Gore Is Reported Stevenson Choice," *New York Times*, August 15, 1956; "2 Senators Lead as Running Mate," *New York Times*, August 16, 1956.

11. Sorensen, *Kennedy*, 86–87.

12. "Democrat Delegates Make Scramble to Stevenson," *Independent Record*, August 16, 1956; John F. Kennedy, *"Let the Word Go Forth": The Speeches, Statements, and Writings of John F. Kennedy* (New York: Delacorte Press, 1988), 83.

13. Kennedy, "Let the Word Go Forth," 85; Sorensen, *Kennedy*, 87.

14. Kennedy, *Speeches, Statements, and Writings*, 84; "John F. Kennedy's Voting Record and Stands on Issues," *CQ Fact Sheet on John F. Kennedy* (Washington, DC: Congressional Quarterly, 1960), http://www.jfklibrary.org/Historical+Resources/Archives/Reference+Desk /John+F.+Kennedys+Voting+Record+and+Stands+on+Issues+Page+3.htm [accessed November 16, 2010]; Robert Dallek, *An Unfinished Life: John F. Kennedy, 1917–63* (Boston: Little, Brown, 2003), 214.

15. Kennedy, *Speeches, Statements, and Writings*, 85–86; "Text of Speeches Nominating Two Major Rivals in Democratic Presidential Battle," *New York Times*, August 17, 1956; Parmet, *Jack*, 372. Kennedy's description of Stevenson as the "top vote-getter" was perceived as a jab at former president Truman, who continued to hold out hope that Governor Averell Harriman (NY) would win the nomination.

16. Before 1940, senior party leaders chose the vice presidential nominee. In 1940, FDR established the current practice by personally selecting Henry Wallace as his running mate. Vice presidential votes since have followed the 1940 FDR model and been strictly ceremonial, with the exception of the 1956 Democratic Convention. Lee Sigelman and Paul J. Wahlbeck, "The 'Veep-Stakes': Strategic Choice in Presidential Running Mate Selection," *American Political Science Review* 91 (December 1997): 855–64. Stevenson wasn't sure whom

to choose as his running mate. As he analyzed it, Kefauver might help him in the Midwest farming regions, but the Tennessean had alienated Southerners by refusing to oppose *Brown v. Board of Education*; Humphrey's close ties to liberals made him unpopular among conservatives; Kennedy was unacceptable to Eleanor Roosevelt and other senior party officials. Parmet, *Jack*, 373–74.

17. James Reston, "Race Is Left Open," *New York Times*, August 17, 1956; *Guide to U.S. Elections*, vol. 1, 6th ed. (Washington, DC: CQ Press, 2010), 609; Sorensen, *Kennedy*, 87; Parmet, *Jack*, 376.

18. *Guide to U.S. Elections*, 609; Willard Edwards, "Running Account of V.P. Nomination," *Chicago Daily Tribune*, August 18, 1956.

19. Sorensen, *Kennedy*, 89.

20. LBJ disliked Kefauver, whom he saw as one of his chief rivals for the White House. His opposition to the Tennessean was also a shrewd political move—most Southerners loathed Kefauver. Although LBJ was friendly with JFK, he never took the Massachusetts senator very seriously. Johnson assumed that both Kennedy brothers were errand boys for their powerful father. Ronnie Dugger, *The Politician: The Life and Times of Lyndon Johnson* (New York: W. W. Norton, 1982), 373; Robert A. Caro, *The Years of Lyndon Johnson: Master of the Senate* (New York: Alfred A. Knopf, 2002), 826–27; Bruce J. Schulman, *Lyndon B. Johnson and American Liberalism* (Boston: Bedford Books, 1995), 54.

21. Aull and Ogden, *Proceedings*, 473; Edwards, "Running Account"; Sorensen, *Kennedy*, 90; Drew Pearson, "Kefauver Aided by Gore Switch," *Washington Post and Times Herald*, August 29, 1956; Parmet, *Jack*, 379. The official report of the convention erroneously credits John Connally with making the Texas delegation's announcement.

22. Robert C. Albright, "Tennessean Wins over Kennedy in Seesaw Contest for No. 2 Place," *Washington Post and Times Herald*, August 18, 1956; Edwards, "Running Account"; W. H. Lawrence, "Finish Dramatic," *New York Times*, August 18, 1956.

23. "Kennedy Gets Ovation As He Yields to Winner," *Los Angeles Times*, August 18, 1956; James MacGregor Burns, *John Kennedy: A Political Profile* (New York: Harcourt, Brace and World, 1959), 190.

24. Richard Reeves, *President Kennedy: Profile of Power* (New York: Simon and Schuster, 1993), 15–16; Guy Paul Land, "John F. Kennedy's Southern Strategy, 1956–60," *North Carolina Historical Review* 56 (January 1979): 41–63; "Kennedy Will Play Big Campaign Role," *Washington Post and Times Herald*, September 15, 1956.

25. "Remarks of Senator John F. Kennedy at United Steelworkers Convention, Los Angeles, California, September 19, 1956," http://www.jfklibrary.org/Historical+Resources/Archives/Reference+Desk/Speeches/JFK/JFK+Pre-Pres/1956/002PREPRES12SPEECHES_56SEP19.htm [accessed September 17, 2010]; "Remarks of Senator John F. Kennedy at the Los Angeles World Affairs Council Luncheon at the Biltmore Hotel on September 21, 1956," http://www.jfklibrary.org/Historical+Resources/Archives/Reference+Desk/Speeches/JFK/JFK+Pre-Pres/1956/002PREPRES12SPEECHES_56SEP21A.htm [accessed September 17, 2010]; "Remarks given at the Springfield Rotary Club, Springfield, Massachusetts, October 19, 1956," http://www.jfklibrary.org/Historical+Resources/Archives/Reference+Desk/Speeches/JFK/JFK+Pre-Pres/1956/002PREPRES12SPEECHES_56OCT19B.htm [accessed September 17, 2010]. In fairness, it should be noted that Kennedy knew that he would be running for reelection in Massachusetts in 1958.

26. Reeves, *Profile of Power*, 16.

27. O'Donnell, Powers, and McCarthy, *"Johnny, We Hardly Knew Ye,"* 144. According to Herbert Parmet, Jack came within "38½ votes of an absolute majority." Parmet, *Jack,* 379.

28. "Presidential Hopefuls Blossom Early," *Los Angeles Times,* January 25, 1957; George Gallup, "Kefauver Leads Kennedy in Poll: Wins over Boston Senator by 49% to 38% as Potential Democrat Candidate in 1960," *Los Angeles Times,* February 15, 1957, and "Poll Finds Democrats More Hopeful for 1960," *Los Angeles Times,* March 22, 1957.

29. Stewart Alsop, "The Dead End Street," *Washington Post and Times Herald,* April 5, 1957.

30. Dallek, *Unfinished Life,* 221–29; Kyle Palmer, "All Roads Lead to Washington," *Los Angeles Times,* May 12, 1957; James Giglio, *The Presidency of John F. Kennedy* (Lawrence: University Press of Kansas, 1991), 12. "Transcript, 'Mike Wallace Interview'—ABC TV," Box 30, Folder 20, Clark Clifford Papers, Library of Congress Manuscripts Division, Washington, DC; letter from JFK to Clark Clifford, April 27, 1958, Box 30, Folder 18, Clark Clifford Papers, Library of Congress Manuscripts Division, Washington, DC. For many years, Sorensen denied that he'd ghostwritten *Profiles in Courage.* At the end of his life, he backpedaled slightly and told a *New York Times* reporter that he had indeed "played an important role." The reporter interpreted this to mean that Sorensen had written "most of the chapters." Michael J. Birkner, a history professor at Gettysburg College, believes that "none of Kennedy's wit, political sagacity, or glamour should obscure a basic fact that Theodore Sorensen's death has now confirmed: Kennedy did not write *Profiles in Courage.* He simply took credit for it." See Michael Birkner, "Ghost's Story," *Weekly Standard* 16 (November 22, 2010), http://www.weeklystandard.com/articles/ghost-s-story_516675.html [accessed November 27, 2012]. Birkner does not, however, support his accusation with incontrovertible evidence.

31. Interview with Julian Bond, April 26, 2013.

32. Telephone interview with Senator Mitch McConnell, December 2, 2011.

33. Willard Edwards, "The Kennedys—Winning Team!" *Chicago Daily Tribune,* April 28, 1957; Giglio, *Presidency,* 13.

34. Theresa Romahn, "Colonialism and the Campaign Trail: On Kennedy's Algerian Speech and His Bid for the 1960 Democratic Nomination," *Journal of Colonialism and Colonial History* 10 (Fall 2009), http://muse.jhu.edu/journals/journal_of_colonialism_and_colonial_history/toc/cch.10.2.html [accessed August 17, 2010]. Romahn sees the speech as a wink and a nod from JFK to civil rights advocates, though it was certainly well disguised. Russell Baker, "Kennedy Urges U.S. Back Independence for Algeria," *New York Times,* July 3, 1957; "Kennedy Calls on U.S. to Back Algeria's Fight," *Washington Post and Times Herald,* July 3, 1957; "'Our' Algerian Problem," *Wall Street Journal,* July 8, 1957. JFK's Irish heritage may also explain his anticolonial views, since the Irish were the first people to be colonized by the English. Kennedy might also have been trying to appease the liberal wing of the Democratic Party. Gilbert Harrison, the editor of the influential *New Republic,* wrote a letter to JFK congratulating him on his Algerian speech ("I think you did right to speak your mind on the Algerian question"). Letter from Harrison to JFK, July 9, 1957, Gilbert A. Harrison Papers, Box 2, "John F. Kennedy 1957–60," Library of Congress Manuscripts Division, Washington, DC.

35. "Lacoste Calls Kennedy Arab Propaganda Victim," *Washington Post and Times Herald,* July 8, 1957; "Foreign Relations: Burned Hands Across the Sea," *Time* (July 15, 1957),

http://www.time.com/time/magazine/article/0,9171,809643-1,00.html [accessed September 16, 2010].

36. John F. Kennedy, "A Democrat Looks at Foreign Policy," *Foreign Affairs* 36 (October 1957): 44–59; "Kennedy Criticizes U.S. Foreign Policy," *New York Times*, September 23, 1957. Ironically, Dulles published an article in the same issue about the merits of massive retaliation.

37. Warner Bros. released a big-budget picture in 1963 entitled *PT 109*; the film was produced under the personal supervision of Jack Warner and starred Cliff Robertson as Lieutenant John F. Kennedy. The film was an undeniable boost for Kennedy as he began to seek a second term.

38. Giglio, *Presidency*, 15; "Television: Review," *Time* (October 28, 1957), http://www.time .com/time/printout/0,8816,810051,00.html [accessed September 16, 2010]; "Democrats: Man Out Front," *Time* (December 2, 1957), http://www.time.com/time/printout/0,8816,825326,00 .html [accessed September 16, 2010].

39. Jacqueline Jones, Peter H. Wood, Thomas Borstelmann, Elaine Tyler May, and Vicki L. Ruiz, *Created Equal: A Social and Political History of the United States*, 2nd ed. (New York: Pearson Longman, 2006), 854; Carroll Kilpatrick, "Kennedy, the Moderate," *Washington Post and Times Herald*, October 24, 1957. Sorensen's biography of JFK supports Kilpatrick's interpretation.

40. "Kennedy Raps Union Lawyers as Unethical," *Los Angeles Times*, October 20, 1957; Arthur M. Schlesinger, Jr., *Robert Kennedy and His Times* (Boston: Houghton Mifflin, 1978), 137–75.

41. John M. Murrin, Paul E. Johnson, James M. McPherson, Gary Gerstle, Emily S. Rosenberg, and Norman L. Rosenberg, *Liberty, Equality, Power: A History of the American People*, 3rd ed. (New York: Wadsworth / Thomson Learning, 2002), 990; "Kennedy Assails U.S. Missile Lag," *New York Times*, November 7, 1957; "Hungarians Get Freedom Award," *New York Times*, October 24, 1957. JFK lived during a time when a large majority of Americans of all stripes were anticommunist. On September 20, 1959, Khrushchev met with American labor leaders at the Mark Hopkins Hotel in San Francisco. Walter Reuther peppered the Soviet premier with hostile questions. For example, Reuther asked: "If you don't exploit them [East German workers], why should three million of them cross the border into West Germany?" Khrushchev: "You are hopelessly sick with capitalist fever." Reuther: "Do you have the credentials to speak for the workers of the world?" Khrushchev: "Do you have credentials to poke your nose into East Germany?" Reuther: "Can you give us one single example in which one of your unions ever disagreed with government policy?" Khrushchev: "Why poke your nose in our business?" and so on. Arthur Goldberg Papers, Box I:60, Folder 6, Library of Congress Manuscripts Division, Washington, DC.

42. "Catholic President Upheld by Kennedy," *New York Times*, November 25, 1957; Roger Creene, "Not Too Reluctant Is the Coy Kennedy," *Washington Post and Times Herald*, November 10, 1957.

43. George Gallup, "Poll Shows Kennedy Leading Democrats," *Los Angeles Times*, June 23, 1957.

44. Dallek, *Unfinished Life*, 219–25; Theodore H. White, *The Making of the President, 1960* (New York: Atheneum House, 1961), 50. Kennedy wrestled with the Kennedy-Ives bill for two years, watching in dismay as its strong pro-labor provisions were gradually diluted. He eventually withdrew his sponsorship, and a version of the bill was later passed as the Landrum-Griffin Act.

45. I attempted to secure documents that would have revealed the underlying texture of the Kennedy-Vatican relationship, but the request was politely declined in a letter sent by Sergio Pagano, one of the archivists at the Vatican, on August 20, 2011. Mr. Pagano wrote, ". . . I regret to inform you that the documentation custody in this Vatican Secret Archives, by sovereign papal disposition, is available for consultation by scholars only through February 1939 (the end of the pontificate of Pius XI). No exception has ever been granted for documents contained in the closed periods which you have requested." Governmental bureaucracies are secretive the world over. Americans are still waiting to see thousands of classified pages relating to President Kennedy's assassination, supposedly scheduled for release in 2017.

46. Dallek, *Unfinished Life*, 230–33; William S. White, "John F. Kennedy and His Money," *Washington Star*, May 9, 1958; Kennedy, *Let the Word Go Forth*, 88.

47. Sorensen, *Kennedy*, 64; letter from John Kennedy to Clark Clifford, February 15, 1958, Clark Clifford Papers, Box 30, Folder 15, Library of Congress Manuscripts Division, Washington, DC.

48. White, *Making of the President*, 51; Sorensen, *Kennedy*, 105; Dallek, *Unfinished Life*, 240–41; Remarks of Senator John F. Kennedy (D-MA), National Rural Electric Cooperative Association, Washington, DC, February 11, 1959; Convocation of United Negro College Fund, Indianapolis, IN, April 12, 1959; National Civil Liberties Clearing House Annual Conference, Washington, DC, April 16, 1959; and AFL-CIO Convention, Seaside, OR, August 3, 1959, John Bartlow Martin Papers, Box 74, Folder 7, Library of Congress Manuscripts Division, Washington, DC.

49. Gerald P. Fogarty, *The Vatican and the American Hierarchy from 1870 to 1965* (Stuttgart: Anton Hiersemann, 1982), 383–84.

50. Marquis Childs, "A Banana Peel for Kennedy?" *Washington Post and Times Herald*, December 2, 1959; James Reston, "The Religious Issue That Won't Go Away," *New York Times*, November 29, 1959.

51. Kennedy, *Let the Word Go Forth*, 89–90; "Statement of Senator John F. Kennedy," January 2, 1960, John Bartlow Martin Papers, Box 73, Folder 3, Library of Congress Manuscripts Division, Washington, DC.

52. At the Democratic Party's 1960 presidential campaign kickoff dinner (January 23), Kennedy said, "The Eisenhower 'peace and prosperity' is a myth. We are not enjoying a period of peace—only a period of stagnation and retreat, while America becomes second in missiles—second in space—second in education—and, if we don't act fast and effectively— second in production and industrial might." "For Release to Sunday Newspapers, January 24, 1960," John Bartlow Martin Papers, Box 74, Folder 8, Library of Congress Manuscripts Division, Washington, DC.

53. James Reston, "Primary Issue Explored," *New York Times*, January 15, 1960. In public, Kennedy worked hard to reestablish his credibility with farmers. In November 1959, he had blamed Ezra Taft Benson, Eisenhower's secretary of agriculture, for the drop in agricultural prices. He called for new Democratic programs that would preserve family farms, foster the growth of cooperatives, and cut farmers' costs. In all likelihood, JFK was also trying to soften up Hubert Humphrey's rural backing before the 1960 primaries. Humphrey needed farmers' support in order to win the Democratic nomination. See "Sen. Kennedy Attacks Ike's Crop Program," *Chicago Daily Tribune*, November 13, 1959, and Russell Baker, "Economic Unrest in Farm Belt Spurs Democratic Hopes for '60," *New York Times*, November 23,

1959. Privately, on at least one occasion, JFK expressed contempt for farmers and their demands. After delivering a speech at the 1960 South Dakota Plowing Contest, he told his speechwriter, Richard Goodwin, "Fuck the farmers after November." Michael O'Brien, *John F. Kennedy: A Biography* (New York: Thomas Dunne Books, 2005), 427.

54. "Kennedy Accepts Humphrey's Dare," *Los Angeles Times*, February 4, 1960; Carroll Kilpatrick, "Kennedy Draws Cheers in 'Humphrey Territory,'" *Washington Post and Times Herald*, February 26, 1960; and "Humphrey Questions Kennedy's 'Liberalism,'" *Washington Post and Times Herald*, March 1, 1960.

55. Sorensen, *Kennedy*, 133; Robert C. Albright, "'60 Previewed in Wisconsin," *Washington Post and Times Herald*, September 27, 1959. According to Theodore White, Kennedy won by "a 9 to 1" margin in New Hampshire in "what was, politically, a trumpet flourish for national publicity but of no real meaning." White, *Making of the President, 1960*, 80. Kennedy said he was "fully aware of the risks and difficulties" involved in running in Wisconsin, but added, "No other candidate, real or unannounced, has indicated a willingness to enter any primary adjoining the home state of another contender—including New Hampshire, which is next to my own state of Massachusetts. Nevertheless, the people of Wisconsin should not be denied their right to help select the Democratic presidential nominee merely because their state happens to [ad]join Minnesota." "Statement of Senator John F. Kennedy, Milwaukee Wisconsin, January 21, 1960," John Bartlow Martin Papers, Box 74, Folder 8, Library of Congress Manuscripts Division, Washington, DC.

56. White, *Making of the President, 1960*, 92–93.

57. *Primary*, DVD, directed by Robert Drew (New York: Docurama, 2003). In 1960, fifteen states and the District of Columbia held primary elections.

58. "Kennedy Schedule," Gerald Bruno Papers, Box 3, Folder "1960 Campaign Wisconsin Primary Scheduling," John F. Kennedy Library, Boston, Massachusetts.

59. White, *Making of the President, 1960*, 94–95.

60. Dallek, *Unfinished Life*, 253–57.

61. Telephone interview with Barry Webb Battle, January 20, 2011.

62. Dallek, *Unfinished Life*, 253–57.

63. "A Personal Message From Franklin D. Roosevelt, Jr.," Gerald Bruno Papers, Box 1, "1960 Campaign Trips 4/60-5/60 West Virginia," John F. Kennedy Library, Boston, Massachusetts; O'Donnell, Powers, and McCarthy, *"Johnny, We Hardly Knew Ye,"* 186; Doris Kearns Goodwin, *No Ordinary Time: Franklin and Eleanor Roosevelt: The Home Front in World War II* (New York: Simon and Schuster), 211–12; Dallek, *Unfinished Life*, 257.

64. Sorensen, *Kennedy*, 146; W. H. Lawrence, "Rival Quits Race," *New York Times*, May 11, 1960. Benjamin C. Bradlee, *Conversations with Kennedy* (New York: W. W. Norton, 1975), 27. Kennedy's campaign team worked tirelessly to neutralize the Catholic issue. An extended version of the famous "Kennedy, Kennedy!" made-for-TV campaign jingle included the following lines: "And do you deny to any man the right he's guaranteed to be elected president no matter what his creed? It's promised in the Bill of Rights, to which we must be true. So, it's up to you, it's up to you, it's strictly up to you." See "John Kennedy Campaign Song," YouTube, http://www.youtube.com/watch?v=7DoUiNxh6_0&NR=1&feature=endscreen [accessed September 25, 2012].

65. Jones et al., *Created Equal*, 859; Dallek, *Unfinished Life*, 260.

66. Arthur M. Schlesinger, Jr., *A Thousand Days: John F. Kennedy in the White House* (Boston: Mariner Books, 2002), 97.

67. W. H. Lawrence, "Kennedy Bandwagon Well-Oiled," *New York Times*, June 26, 1960; Roland Evans, Jr., "Confident Kennedy Maps Plans for Headquarters, Hard Campaign," *Los Angeles Times*, July 12, 1960; Max Lerner, "Truman Crystallizes Kennedy Weaknesses," *Los Angeles Times*, July 10, 1960; W. H. Lawrence, "Johnson Backers Urge Health Test," *New York Times*, July 5, 1960; Robert Dallek, "The Medical Ordeals of JFK," *Atlantic Monthly* 290 (December 2002): 49–61.

68. Ronald Kessler, "Whitewashing Joseph P. Kennedy," *Newsmax*, December 4, 2012, http://www.newsmax.com/Newsfront/Joseph-Kennedy-book-Nasaw/2012/12/04/id/466448 [accessed December 5, 2012].

69. Gary A. Donaldson, *The First Modern Campaign: Kennedy, Nixon, and the Election of 1960* (New York: Rowman and Littlefield, 2007), 72.

70. Dallek, *Unfinished Life*, 265; White, *Making of the President, 1960*, 162; Geoffrey Perret, *Jack: A Life Like No Other* (New York: Random House, 2002), 255.

71. In order to prove his point, Alsop relayed a story. Shortly before the convention, Alsop had called Senator Herman Talmadge (D-GA) to find out what his phone number would be at the convention. "I ain't going to Los Angeles, Joe," Talmadge replied, "because I know exactly what's going to happen. Kennedy is going to be nominated on the first ballot by a thousand votes, and then he's going to offer the vice presidency to Lyndon Johnson, and Lyndon Johnson is going to take it. And I just don't want to be there to see that, so I'm going off to the Great Dismal Swamp for a few days hunting." Alsop couldn't believe his ears: "You cannot tell me that Johnson will take the vice presidency," he exclaimed. "It's unimaginable!" "He'll do it," insisted Talmadge. "You wait and see. I know him better than you do." "Joseph Alsop Oral History Interview," May 28, 1969, Joseph and Stewart Alsop Papers, Box 183, Folder 8, Library of Congress Manuscripts Division, Washington, DC.

72. Paul A. Smith and Richard E. May, eds., *Official Report of the Proceedings of the Democratic National Convention and Committee: John F. Kennedy Memorial Edition with History of Democratic Party* (Washington, DC: National Document Publishers, 1964), 143; Dallek, *Unfinished Life*, 266.

73. Community Television Network, "Pachios and Moyers Special," http://ctn5.org/shows /pachios-news/pachios-and-moyers-special-1397 [accessed December 1, 2011].

74. The dislike was fueled by perceived, often petty slights that accumulated over the years. For example, during a hunting trip to Texas, when Bobby's shotgun recoiled in his face and left a nasty cut, LBJ remarked, "Son, you've got to learn to handle a gun like a man." Bobby was furious. Questioning a Kennedy's manhood was simply not done. Sorensen, *The Classic Biography*, 163; Dallek, *Unfinished Life*, 267–69; Schlesinger, *Thousand Days*, 50–56; Schlesinger, *Robert Kennedy*, 210.

75. Rick Hampson, "Obama Outdoor Speech Echoes JFK's 1960 Move," *USA Today*, August 27, 2008; Todd S. Purdum, "From That Day Forth," *Vanity Fair*, February 2011, http:// www.vanityfair.com/society/features/2011/02/kennedy-201102 [accessed January 24, 2011].

76. Smith and May, *Official Report*, 243. Kennedy waited until after the convention to explain the details of the New Frontier. On October 29, he highlighted seven key domestic challenges during a speech in Valley Forge, Pennsylvania: (1) "the new frontier of population" (requiring more economic growth, more housing, etc.); (2) "the new frontier of longevity" (retirees entitled to "dignity and security and recognition"); (3) "the new frontier of education" (more classroom space, more teachers, more funding); (4) "the new frontier of suburbia" (need for additional schools, transportation, "community facilities" to prevent

suburban "slums"); (5) "the new frontiers in science and space" (air travel safety, airports, space exploration, satellites, desalinization plants, new sources of food and energy); (6) "the new frontier of automation" ("machines are replacing men, and men are looking for work"); (7) "the new frontier of leisure time" (preserve national parks and forests; "If more and more cars on more and more superhighways, requiring more and more parking places replace parks and playgrounds and scenic routes, if we permit the great medium of television to occupy more and more of our time with poorer and poorer programs appealing to the lowest common denominator, then we will be failing the public interest on this frontier . . ."). Edmund S. Ions, *The Politics of John F. Kennedy* (London: Routledge, 1967), 44–48.

77. Telephone interview with Nancy Pelosi, May 26, 2011.

3. VICTORY WITHOUT A MANDATE

1. Father Kell, undated letter, Bruce Ferengul, August 19, 1960, Marsha Casper, August 20, 1960, Carol Burke to Marsha Casper, August 23, 1960, Sandra Cara, August 24, 1960, R. Sargent Shriver Papers, Box 3, Series 1.1, "1960 Presidential Campaign Correspondence," John F. Kennedy Library, Boston, Massachusetts.

2. A. V. Gallagher, July 30, 1960, Joanne Hardman, undated letter, Susan Jacobs, Janis Sherwin, Terri Dee, undated letter, R. Sargent Shriver Papers, Box 3, Series 1.1, "1960 Presidential Campaign Correspondence," John F. Kennedy Library, Boston, Massachusetts.

3. C. David Heymann, *RFK: A Candid Biography of Robert F. Kennedy* (New York: Dutton Books, 1998), 158–59.

4. Ted Ruhig to Elmo Hohman, undated letter, Lewis A. Lincoln, undated letter, R. Sargent Shriver Papers, Box 4, Series 1, "Senior Citizens for Kennedy, October 1960," John F. Kennedy Library, Boston, Massachusetts.

5. Theodore H. White, *The Making of the President, 1960* (New York: Atheneum House, 1961), 247; Clayton Knowles, "Citizens for Kennedy," *New York Times*, July 25, 1960; Milton Viorst, "Kennedy's Top Strategists Organize," *Washington Post and Times Herald*, July 27, 1960. Carmine De Sapio controlled New York's Tammany machine; Adam Clayton Powell, Jr., spoke for African Americans; Eleanor Roosevelt and Herbert Lehman led New York's Reform Democrats. Each group distrusted the others.

6. William G. Weart, "Robert Kennedy Cautions Party," *New York Times*, August 3, 1960; White, *Making of the President, 1960*, 247. The 1956 presidential election was never thought to be tight and wasn't especially interesting, but every late public poll in 1960 suggested that the Kennedy-Nixon matchup would be highly competitive. The excitement of that campaign was remarkable, and many marginal voters clearly got caught up in it after the TV debates. Higher turnout was one result.

7. Land, "Kennedy's Southern Strategy," 43–63. Putting LBJ in charge of the Southern campaign was a good move. Kennedy captured all but three southern states (Virginia, Tennessee, and Florida) on election day. This doesn't necessarily mean that Southerners liked JFK, however. Many Dixiecrats considered him to be the "best of a sorry lot." See Claude Sitton, "Kennedy Scores Heavily in South," *New York Times*, November 9, 1960, and Robert T. Hartmann, "Kennedy Faces Many Problems," *Los Angeles Times*, February 29, 1960.

8. "Lag in Poll Fails to Upset Kennedy," *New York Times*, August 18, 1960; Edward L. Bernays to John Martin, September 15, 1960, Martin Papers, Box 73, Folder 13, Library of Congress Manuscript Division, Washington, DC.

9. Bill Adler, ed., *The Kennedy Wit* (New York: Citadel Press, 1964), 7; Don Forsyth, undated press release, R. Sargent Shriver Papers, Box 8, Series 1, "Response to Anti-Catholic Literature," John F. Kennedy Library, Boston, Massachusetts; John Martin, "Pennsylvania Memo," October 11[?], 1960, "Indiana—Briefing Memo," "Michigan—briefing sheet (JBM)," "Memo to TCS. California Campaign," John Bartlow Martin Papers, Box 73, Folders 4, 6, 7, 9, 11, Library of Congress Manuscripts Division, Washington, DC.

10. Personal interview with Herbert Meza, April 6, 2011.

11. Theodore C. Sorensen, *Kennedy* (New York: Harper and Row, 1965), 189–91; Douglas Martin, "Milton Gwirtzman, Adviser to Kennedys, Dies at 78," *New York Times*, July 26, 2011.

12. Donald E. Pelotte, S.S.S., *John Courtney Murray: Theologian in Conflict* (New York: Paulist Press, 1976), 76.

13. Sorensen, *Kennedy*, 190–91; personal interview with Herbert Meza, April 6, 2011. Shortly before his death, the columnist David Broder wrote an essay for the *Washington Post* in which he called the Houston address "one of the best political speeches I ever heard." Broder also remembered the positive response from his fellow journalists: "At the end, Peter Lisagor of the *Chicago Daily News* turned to a knot of other reporters and said, 'If the editors of this country were smart, they'd pull every reporter covering Kennedy tonight off him for the rest of the campaign. You can't have watched this and still say you're neutral.' I thought he was right." See David S. Broder, "When JFK Defused the Catholic Question," *Washington Post*, September 12, 2010. Mark Massa (Catholic Studies, Fordham) says that JFK's Houston speech "secularized" the presidency and helped "privatize" religion. "Precisely because John F. Kennedy was a Roman Catholic—an adherent (however poorly) of a religious tradition that had been successfully excluded from the 'high priesthood' of American politics for almost two centuries—it might be argued that he had to 'secularize' the American presidency in order to win it." See Mark S. Massa, S.J., "A Catholic for President? John F. Kennedy and the 'Secular' Theology of the Houston Speech, 1960," *Journal of Church and State* 39 (1997): 297–317.

14. Robert Dallek, *An Unfinished Life: John F. Kennedy, 1917–63* (Boston: Little, Brown, 2003), 284.

15. "Santorum Takes On JFK," *Metropolis*, September 19, 2010, http://www.phlmetropolis .com/2010/09/god-rick-santorum.php# [accessed January 31, 2011]. In her book *America by Heart: Reflections on Family, Faith, and Flag* (New York: HarperCollins, 2010), Sarah Palin criticized JFK for failing to reconcile his faith with his public life. RFK daughter Kathleen Kennedy Townsend in turn criticized Palin for missing JFK's point: American public officials are not supposed to be subjected to religious tests (183–86). See K. K. Townsend, "Sarah Palin Is Wrong About John F. Kennedy, Religion and Politics," *Washington Post*, December 3, 2010, http://www.washingtonpost.com/wp-dyn/content/article/2010/12/03/AR2010120303209 _pf.html [accessed October 10, 2012].

16. Ted Sorensen, interview by David Gregory, *Meet the Press*, NBC, September 24, 2010; Stephen Ambrose, *Eisenhower*, vol. 2: *The President* (New York: Simon and Schuster, 1984), 601; Kayla Webley, "How the Nixon-Kennedy Debate Changed the World," *Time*, September 23, 2010, http://www.time.com/time/printout/0,8816,2021078,00.html [accessed November 26, 2010].

17. On August 17, during a campaign stop in Greensboro, North Carolina, Nixon injured his knee on the door of his car. He was forced to go to the hospital after the wound became infected. When he was released, he put in long hours to catch up on the huge backlog of

work. He then contracted the flu, but he continued to push himself. Nixon was wan and not yet fully recovered when the first debate was televised.

18. John W. Self, "The First Debate over the Debates: How Kennedy and Nixon Negotiated the 1960 Presidential Debates," *Presidential Studies Quarterly* 35 (June 2005): 361–75.

19. Ibid., 366.

20. Some sources place the number as high as 80 million.

21. White, *Making of the President, 1960*, 279–87; "Transcript of the first Kennedy-Nixon Presidential Debate: September 26, 1960," Museum of Broadcast Communications website, http://www.museum.tv/debateweb/html/greatdebate/92660transcript.htm [accessed February 1, 2011].

22. Rick Perlstein, ed., *Richard Nixon: Speeches, Writings, Documents* (Princeton: Princeton University Press, 2008), 97–98.

23. White, *Making of the President, 1960*, 289.

24. Richard Stout, "Aides Did Makeup on Nixon, but They Blame the TV Camera," *Chicago Daily News*, September 30, 1960; Stephen E. Ambrose, *Nixon*, vol. 1: *The Education of a Politician, 1913–62* (New York: Touchstone, 1987), 575.

25. Barbara A. Perry, *Rose Kennedy: The Life and Times of a Political Matriarch* (New York: W. W. Norton, 2013), 253.

26. James N. Druckman, "The Power of Television Images: The First Kennedy-Nixon Debate Revisited," *Journal of Politics* 65 (May 2003): 559–71; Webley, "Nixon-Kennedy Debate"; Mary Ann Watson, *The Expanding Vista: American Television in the Kennedy Years* (Durham, NC: Duke University Press, 1994), 13. According to Druckman, a political science professor at the University of Minnesota, "There exists no valid empirical evidence that images played any role in the [first] debate. In their exhaustive review, Vancil and Pendell (1987) find that most of the evidence is anecdotal and impressionistic with one exception—the survey by a [nonpartisan] market research firm, Sindlinger & Company. The survey reported that more self-identified radio listeners thought Nixon won the debate, whereas more self-identified television viewers thought Kennedy won: thus, [the TV] image appears to cause a viewer-listener disagreement. However, a number of problems plague the survey, including a failure to report methodological specifics such as sample size (making statistical significance unclear), a reliance on self-reported measures of debate exposure that can be highly unreliable, and a potentially significant time delay between the debate and data collection. Even more important, the survey makes no attempt to control for a variety of variables including pre-debate preference, religion, and party identification."

27. Sorensen, *Kennedy*, 202; Don Shannon, "Kennedy—Debates Were Key," *Los Angeles Times*, November 13, 1960; Kenneth P. O'Donnell, Western Union telegram dated October 8, 1960, Gerald Bruno Papers, Box 1, "1960 Campaign Trips," John F. Kennedy Library, Boston, Massachusetts; "Dixie Governors Give Kennedy Full Support," *Los Angeles Times*, September 28, 1960. According to Chris Matthews, "Kennedy's triumph in the first debate made him the country's number-one box office attraction. Traveling through Ohio the next day, he was confronted by a new phenomenon in the political world—the 'jumper'—the teenager or young woman who literally jumped up in the crowds to get a better look at the most exciting male sex symbol since the debut of Elvis Presley." Christopher Matthews, *Kennedy and Nixon: The Rivalry That Shaped Postwar America* (New York: Simon and Schuster, 1996), 157. However, Ohio went for Nixon. Only two Democrats

since 1900 have won the presidency without Ohio—Franklin Roosevelt in 1944 and John Kennedy in 1960.

28. Nancy Harrison to Joan Braden, Gilbert Harrison Papers, Box 8, "John F. Kennedy 1960–64," Library of Congress Manuscripts Division, Washington, DC.

29. Thomas C. Reeves, *A Question of Character: A Life of John F. Kennedy* (Rocklin, CA: Prima Publishing, 1992), 165, 173, 202.

30. "Coffee Hours—Little Parties with a Big Purpose!" and "How to Use Campaign Volunteers," Gerald Bruno Papers, Box 1, "1960 Campaign Democratic Convention," John F. Kennedy Library, Boston, Massachusetts. "Kennedy Girls" who were stationed at Democratic offices were under orders to "receive calls from Democratic voters who need babysitters." "Girls will immediately be taken to the house of the voter to carry out the wishes of the voter." They were encouraged to be "courteous and friendly, remembering that any other ways may be the loss of a Democratic or Kennedy vote." See "Kennedy Girls," Gerald Bruno Papers, Box 1, "1960 Campaign Trips," John F. Kennedy Library, Boston, Massachusetts.

31. Howard Kurtz, "Jack Anderson's Nixonian Tactics," Media Notes Blog, *Washington Post*, September 13, 2010, http://voices.washingtonpost.com/howard-kurtz/2010/09/jack _andersons_nixonian_tactic.html [accessed November 29, 2010].

32. Mark Feldstein, "A Half-Century of Political Dirty Tricks," *Washington Post*, January 14, 2011.

33. Larry J. Sabato, *Feeding Frenzy: How Attack Journalism Has Transformed American Politics* (New York: Free Press, 1991), 39; David Halberstam, *The Best and the Brightest* (New York: Ballantine Books, 1992), x.

34. Shortly after the break-in, Kennedy asked Travell to collect his medical records from the hospitals where he had undergone treatment and place them under lock and key. See David L. Robb, *The Gumshoe and the Shrink: Guenther Reinhardt, Dr. Arnold Hutschnecker, and the Secret History of the 1960 Kennedy/Nixon Election* (Solana Beach, CA: Santa Monica Press, 2012), 132–35.

35. Robert Dallek, "The Medical Ordeals of JFK," *Atlantic Monthly* 290 (December 2002): 49–61.

36. Paul H. Nitze Papers, Box 141, Folder 8, Library of Congress Manuscripts Division, Washington, DC; Ambrose, *Education of a Politician*, 592. Nixon was fibbing in order to conceal the administration's invasion plans. On March 17, 1960, Eisenhower had approved a four-point plan concerning Cuba, as presented to him by CIA-operative Richard Bissell. The plan "had four parts: (1) creation of a 'responsible and unified' Cuban government-in-exile; (2) 'a powerful propaganda offensive'; (3) 'a covert intelligence and action organization in Cuba' that would be 'responsive' to the government-in-exile; and (4) 'a paramilitary force outside of Cuba for future guerrilla action.' Eisenhower indicated that he liked all four parts, but put his emphasis on Bissell's first step, finding a Cuban leader living in exile who would form a government that the United States could recognize and that could direct the activities of the covert and paramilitary forces." Ike later denied that he had ever bequeathed a Bay of Pigs battle plan to Kennedy, and the former president went to extraordinary lengths to set the record straight, from his perspective, in the wake of the April 1961 fiasco. Stephen E. Ambrose, *Eisenhower: The President*, vol. 2 (New York: Simon and Schuster, 1984), 557, 639. During the campaign, Kennedy put together a Committee on National Security Policy. Members included William C. Foster, Dean Acheson, Dean Rusk, Chester Bowles, Roswell

Gilpatrick, James Perkins (an executive of the Carnegie Corporation), K. E. Bruce (former undersecretary of state), Paul Nitze, and Walt Rostow. Research was provided by Rand, MIT, Stanford, and other institutions. In August 1960, Kennedy told the press that the committee would "function between November 8, when he hopes to be elected, and January 20, when he would take office" (*Washington Evening Star*, August 30, 1960). He also said that it was "to make sure, if I am successful, that the months of January, February, and March would be used most effectively" (*Washington Post*, August 31, 1960). On November 9, 1960, the committee sent its private report to Kennedy: "In addition to Berlin, the new Administration will be faced with a most serious set of legacies in other parts of the world. These include Cuba, the Congo, Quemoy and Matsu, Algeria, Laos, and the smoldering guerrilla war in South Vietnam. On all these issues the Republicans will be prepared to raise cries of appeasement, war-mongering, or both, depending on the course which the new Administration follows. In the Cuban situation it looks as though Castro's internal support should progressively weaken over at least the next three or four months. It is possible, however, that if no firm action is taken against him during the ensuing period of internal weakness, the Communists might be able increasingly to consolidate their position." "Report of the Committee on National Security Policy," November 9, 1960, Paul H. Nitze Papers, Box 141, Folder 8, Library of Congress Manuscripts Division, Washington, DC. Thus, Kennedy's own team encouraged some sort of action against a "weakening" Castro in the near term. The internal advisers had assessed the situation as poorly as the Eisenhower CIA. During the same period, Kennedy raised the possibility of assassinating Castro. Senator George Smathers (D-FL) campaigned with Kennedy in the South and remembered the candidate "throwing out a great barrage of questions—he was certain [the assassination of Castro] could be accomplished—I remember that—it would be no great problem. But the question was whether it would accomplish that which he wanted it to, whether or not the reaction throughout South America would be good or bad and I talked with him about it." See "From the Archive, 18 August 1970: Kennedy Talked of Possibility of Killing Castro," *The Guardian*, August 17, 2012, http://www.guardian.co.uk/theguardian/2012/aug/17/john-f-kennedy-fidel-castro [accessed September 10, 2012].

37. John F. Kennedy, "Excerpts of Remarks at Granby High School Athletic Field, Norfolk, VA, November 4, 1960," John T. Woolley and Gerhard Peters, *The American Presidency Project* [online], Santa Barbara, CA, http://www.presidency.ucsb.edu/ws/index.php?pid=74320 [accessed November 29, 2010]; "Sound Fiscal Policy Pledged by Kennedy," *Richmond Times Dispatch*, November 5, 1960; "Elsie Carper, "Virginians Wildly Hail Kennedy Raising Party's Hopes for State," *Washington Post*, November 5, 1960; David Bowers, conversation with Alvin Hudson, September 24, 2010.This interview was graciously submitted to the author by Bowers, who is the mayor of Roanoke, Virginia. Virginians voted for Nixon anyway. Virginia's Democratic National Committeeman, G. Fred Switzer, told reporters in January of 1960 that JFK would have a tough time in the Old Dominion: "[Virginians] side with the most conservative candidate, and I believe, generally speaking, Nixon is more conservative than Kennedy. Kennedy's too liberal, he's too pro-labor." See "Switzer Sees Nixon Over Kennedy in Va.," *Washington Post*, January 5, 1960.

38. Willard Edwards, "Ike Asks Election of Nixon," *Chicago Daily Tribune*, November 3, 1960; Gary A. Donaldson, *The First Modern Campaign: Kennedy, Nixon, and the Election of 1960* (New York: Rowman and Littlefield, 2007), 139–40; Dallek, *Unfinished Life*, 293.

39. "Sen. Kennedy Stumped in 237 Cities, Vice President Nixon, 168," *Washington Post and Times Herald*, November 5, 1960; "ADA Joins Kennedy, Asks U.S. Accept World Court Rule," *Boston Globe*, March 27, 1960; "Excerpts from Remarks of Senator John F. Kennedy (Dem. Mass.), Liberal Party Dinner, New York—September 14, 1960," John Bartlow Martin Papers, Box 75, Folder 2, Library of Congress Manuscripts Division, Washington, DC.

40. Emmett P. Malloy to Kay Folger, September 1, 1960, R. Sargent Shriver Papers, Box 4, Series 1, "Washington Correspondence August–September 1960," John F. Kennedy Library, Boston, Massachusetts; Lithuanian American Pamphlet, R. Sargent Shriver Papers, Box 3, Series 1, "Lithuanian American Committee for John F. Kennedy, 1960," John F. Kennedy Library, Boston, Massachusetts; "Demo Aspirant Hailed by King," New Orleans *Times-Picayune*, November 11, 1960.

41. "Speech of Senator John F. Kennedy Prepared for a Dinner Held by the Democratic National and State Committees, Waldorf-Astoria Hotel, New York, NY, October 12, 1960," John Bartlow Martin Papers, Box 75, Folder 3, Library of Congress Manuscripts Division, Washington, DC; Donaldson, *Modern Campaign*, 120; "Matsu Complex," Stanley Karnow Papers, Box 59, "Taiwan, 1955–67," John F. Kennedy Library, Boston, Massachusetts. Kennedy lined up the support of a number of prominent liberals before the convention began. In June 1960, "an open letter to American liberals . . . in support of Senator John F. Kennedy" arrived in mailboxes across the country. Signatories included James Burns (political scientist), Henry Steele Commager (historian), J. Kenneth Galbraith (economist), Arthur Goldberg (attorney), Gilbert Harrison (publisher), Allan Nevins (historian), John Saltonstall (attorney), and Arthur Schlesinger, Jr. (historian). Some of these men later joined the Kennedy administration.

42. In all likelihood, the IBM report came out *before* the returns from Philadelphia and Connecticut were known. "At 7:15 . . . the large television set in the corner of the room carried the news that CBS's IBM 7090 computer had projected a victory for Richard Nixon." Herbert S. Parmet, *JFK: The Presidency of John F. Kennedy* (New York: Penguin Books, 1984), 57–58; Aide Kenny O'Donnell remembered that "The senator made his first appearance in Bobby's house, where all of us were gathered around the television screens and the telephones, around seven-thirty in the evening, when the early returns from the East were full of good news" (Kenneth P. O'Donnell, David F. Powers, and Joe McCarthy, *"Johnny, We Hardly Knew Ye": Memories of John Fitzgerald Kennedy* (Boston: Little, Brown, 1970), 251).

43. "Schedule, Senator John F. Kennedy, Monday, Nov. 7, and Tuesday, Nov. 8, 1960," Gerald Bruno Papers, Box 1, "1960 Campaign Election Day Arrangements 11/8/60," John F. Kennedy Library, Boston, Massachusetts; Sorensen, *Kennedy*, 211–12; O'Donnell, Powers, and McCarthy, *"Johnny, We Hardly Knew Ye,"* 250–51; Parmet, *JFK*, 57–58; Dallek, *Unfinished Life*, 294.

44. Sorensen, *Kennedy*, 212.

45. Legitimate, conflicting arguments can be made about whether Kennedy or Nixon won 1960's popular vote. Some analysts point to anomalies in the Deep South, where voters chose so-called free electors who were not obligated to vote for their party's candidates. Many of these electors eventually cast ballots for Virginia U.S. senator Harry F. Byrd, Sr., a committed segregationist, instead of JFK. If we subtract the number of voters represented by

each free elector, then Richard Nixon appears to have won the popular vote. See Brian J. Gaines, "Popular Myths About Popular Vote-Electoral College Splits," *Political Science and Politics* 34 (March 2001): 70–75; Sean Trende, "Did JFK Lose the Popular Vote?" *Real Clear Politics*, October 19, 2012, http://www.realclearpolitics.com/articles/2012/10/19/did_jfk_lose _the_popular_vote_115833.html [accessed October 24, 2012]; and Gordon Tullock, "Nixon, Like Gore, Also Won Popular Vote, But Lost Election," *Political Science and Politics* 37 (January 2004): 1–2.

46. The *Slate* journalist David Greenberg believes that the vice president's refusal to contest the election was nothing more than a clever ruse: "[W]hile Nixon publicly pooh-poohed a challenge, his allies *did* dispute the results—aggressively." See David Greenberg, "Was Nixon Robbed?" *Slate*, October 16, 2000, http://www.slate.com/articles/news_and _politics/history_lesson/2000/10/was_nixon_robbed.single.html [accessed November 9, 2012].

47. Larry J. Sabato and Glenn R. Simpson, *Dirty Little Secrets: The Persistence of Corruption in American Politics* (New York: Random House, 1996), 277; *Guide to U.S. Elections*, 789.

48. Peter Carlson, "Another Race to the Finish," *Washington Post*, November 17, 2000; David Greenberg, "Was Nixon Robbed?" *Slate*, October 16, 2000, http://www.slate.com/id /91350/ [accessed September 7, 2011].

49. Edmund F. Kallina, "Was the 1960 Presidential Election Stolen? The Case of Illinois," *Presidential Studies Quarterly* 15 (Winter 1985): 113–18.

50. *Guide to U.S. Elections*, 789; Larry J. Sabato, *A More Perfect Constitution: 23 Proposals to Revitalize Our Constitution and Make America a Fairer Country* (New York: Walker, 2007), 146; Sabato and Simpson, *Dirty Little Secrets*, 277; Joseph Alsop to Ted Sorensen, November 10, 1960, Joseph and Stewart Alsop Papers, Box 17, "Nov.–Dec. 1960," Library of Congress Manuscripts Division, Washington, DC.

4. THE TORCH IS PASSED

1. "Walkin' Down to Washington," Gerald Bruno Papers, Box 1, "1960 Campaign Democratic Convention," John F. Kennedy Library, Boston, Massachusetts.

2. "Inaugural Gala in Honor of the Inauguration of the Honorable John Fitzgerald Kennedy, the Honorable Lyndon Baines Johnson, Thursday, January 19, 1961," Gerald Bruno Papers, Box 3, "1961 Inauguration Gala," John F. Kennedy Library, Boston, Massachusetts; Theodore C. Sorensen, *Kennedy* (New York: Harper and Row, 1965), 243.

3. According to some scholars, the famous phrase may date back to JFK's days as a high school student at Choate, a posh Connecticut prep school, where the headmaster would periodically remind his students about what mattered most: "Not what Choate does for you, but what you can do for Choate." In 2011 a document surfaced at Choate that supports this notion. A notebook kept by the school's headmaster for his sermons included the following quotation, attributable to a Harvard dean: "The youth who loves his Alma Mater will always ask, not 'What can she do for me?' but 'What can I do for her?'" Ted Sorensen indicated that Kennedy's inaugural statement was repeated from a televised speech JFK delivered on September 20, 1960: "We do not campaign stressing what our country is going to do for us as a people. We stress what we can do for the country, all of us." See Edward Wyatt, "Two Authors Ask About 'Ask Not,'" *New York Times*, May 10, 2005; Michael Melia, "Document May

Shed Light on Origins of JFK Speech," Associated Press, November 3, 2011, http://articles
.boston.com/2011-11-03/news/30356106_1_sermons-choate-officials-thurston-clarke [accessed
November 8, 2011]; Sorensen, *Kennedy*, 241. John Fitzgerald Kennedy, "Inaugural Address
(January 20, 1961)," Miller Center of Public Affairs, University of Virginia, http://miller
center.org/scripps/archive/speeches/detail/3365 [accessed January 9, 2011].

4. Nathan Rott, "'Ask Not . . .': JFK's Words Still Inspire 50 Years Later," January 19, 2011,
National Public Radio website, http://www.npr.org/2011/01/18/133018777/jfks-inaugural
-speech-still-inspires-50-years-later [accessed February 11, 2011].

5. Telephone interview with Nancy Pelosi, May 26, 2011.

6. Matt Viser, "JFK's Words Echo Once More in Washington," *Boston Globe*, January 21,
2011.

7. Adam Frankel, "Author, Author," *New Yorker*, February 28, 2011, http://www.new
yorker.com/talk/2011/02/28/110228ta_talk_frankel [accessed March 9, 2011]; E. J. Dionne,
"Kennedy's Inaugural Address Presents a Challenge Still," *Washington Post*, January 20,
2011.

8. James N. Giglio, *The Presidency of John F. Kennedy* (Lawrence: University Press of
Kansas, 1991), 28; E. H. Foley, "Inaugural Committee, 1961, Final Report of the Chairman," Gerald Bruno Papers, Box 3, "1961 Inauguration Committee Report," John F. Kennedy Library, Boston, Massachusetts; Frances Wilson, review of *Mistresses: A History of
the Other Woman*, by Elizabeth Abbott, *London Daily Telegraph*, December 12, 2010,
http://www.telegraph.co.uk/culture/books/8188789/Mistresses-A-History-of-the-Other
-Woman-by-Elizabeth-Abbott-review.html [accessed December 24, 2010]; "Oral History
Interview with Joseph W. Alsop, June 18, 1964," Joseph and Stewart Alsop Papers, Box
183, Folder 7, Library of Congress Manuscripts Division, Washington, DC; Thomas C.
Reeves, *A Question of Character: A Life of John F. Kennedy* (New York: Free Press, 1991), 236.

9. During his first dinner at the executive mansion, Joseph Alsop learned from Mrs.
Kennedy that there were "twenty 'calligraphers' working away in the White House basement, to produce place cards, menus and everything else in the White House in [a] copper
plate style." In addition, Mrs. Kennedy asked Alsop to find out if the White House could buy
the "noncommercial crus" that California wine growers produced for their own consump-
tion. According to Alsop, these were the "best" California wines—unpasteurized, mature,
and bursting with "the true taste of the soil." Joseph Alsop, "Dear Ann," January 23, 1961,
and Alsop to Betty Flood, January 31, 1961, Joseph and Stewart Alsop Papers, Box 17, Library
of Congress Manuscripts Division, Washington, DC. In later years, Alsop recalled that the
Kennedys "always gave you too much to drink. They had the best wine I'd ever had in any
house in Washington, including the French embassy . . . We'd start off with this perfectly
wonderful white burgundy . . . And then along comes superb claret and then that champagne that he was so fond of that I always thought was overrated." Alsop added that the
Kennedys themselves never drank much. Joseph Alsop Oral History Interview, June 26,
1964, Joseph and Stewart Alsop Papers, Box 183, Library of Congress Manuscripts Division,
Washington, DC.

10. Some organizations still sponsor Confederate commemorations that do not acknowledge the sickness of slavery. In December 2010, the Sons of Confederate Veterans
sponsored a "Secession Ball" in Charleston, South Carolina, that promised participants a
"joyous night of music, dancing, food, and drink." In 2011, the same group celebrated Jef-

ferson Davis's inauguration in Montgomery, Alabama. See Rick Hampson, "Across the South, the Civil War Is an Enduring Conflict," *USA Today*, February 17, 2011.

11. "January–February 1961 Democratic Digest, Special Inaugural Issue, Vol. 8, No. 1," Gilbert A. Harrison Papers, Box 8, "Inauguration 1961 (Nancy Blaine Harrison 1960–62)," Library of Congress Manuscripts Division, Washington, DC.

12. The civil rights movement was more than just a by-product of *Brown v. Board of Education*. Twentieth-century urbanization also played a key role. In 1870, 90 percent of the nation's blacks lived in the South and worked on farms. By 1940, only 77 percent still lived in the South. "By 1960 only half the black population lived in rural areas; less than one in ten still worked on a farm." Thomas C. Holt, *African-American History* in *The New American History Series: A Publication of the American Historical Association* (Philadelphia: Temple University Press, 1997), 15.

13. Jacqueline Jones, Peter H. Wood, Thomas Borstelmann, Elaine Tyler May, and Vicki L. Ruiz, *Created Equal: A Social and Political History of the United States*, 2nd ed. (New York: Pearson Longman, 2006), 855. Milton Viorst, "D.C. Is a Hardship Post for Negro Diplomats," *Washington Post*, August 28, 1960; John F. Kennedy to the Honorable Christian A. Herter, August 25, 1960, Winifred Armstrong Papers, Box 1, Series 1, "Discrimination Against African Diplomats in Washington, DC," John F. Kennedy Library, Boston, Massachusetts.

14. Harris Wofford, *Of Kennedys and Kings: Making Sense of the Sixties* (New York: Farrar, Straus and Giroux, 1980), 63; Larry Sabato, ed., *The Sixth Year Itch: The Rise and Fall of the George W. Bush Presidency* (New York: Pearson Longman, 2008), 9; John Hart, "Kennedy, Congress and Civil Rights," *Journal of American Studies* 13 (August 1979): 165–78. During the campaign, Senator Kennedy expressed support for sit-ins. On June 24, 1960, he told the press that, "Such action inevitably involves some unrest and turmoil and tension, part of the price of change. But the fact that people are peacefully protesting the denial of their rights is not something to be lamented." See Anthony Lewis, "Kennedy Salutes Negroes' Sit-Ins," *New York Times*, June 25, 1960.

15. Brooks Jackson, "Blacks and the Democratic Party," FactCheck.org, April 18, 2008, http://www.factcheck.org/2008/04/blacks-and-the-democratic-party/ [accessed February 26, 2013].

16. "Harlem Leader Talks to Kennedy," *New York Times*, July 7, 1960; "Jack Robinson Raps Kennedy," New Orleans *Times-Picayune*, December 12, 1960; Jackie Robinson to RFK, May 25, 1961, Box 5, Folder 14, Jackie Robinson Papers, Library of Congress Manuscripts Division, Washington, DC; Jackie Robinson to JFK, February 9, 1961, Box 5, Folder 14, Jackie Robinson Papers, Library of Congress Manuscripts Division, Washington, DC.

17. Mark Stern, "John F. Kennedy and Civil Rights: From Congress to the Presidency," *Presidential Studies Quarterly* 19 (Fall 1989): 797–823; Russell Baker, "Kennedy Pledges Civil Rights Fight," *New York Times*, September 2, 1960; "Democratic Party Platform of 1960, July 11, 1960," John T. Woolley and Gerhard Peters, *The American Presidency Project* [online], Santa Barbara, CA, http://www.presidency.ucsb.edu/ws/index.php?pid=29602 [accessed December 9, 2010]; "He Will Support Negro Rights, Kennedy Tells Jackie Robinson," *Los Angeles Times*, July 2, 1960.

18. Wofford, *Kennedys and Kings*, 151; Arthur M. Schlesinger, Jr., *Robert Kennedy and His Times* (Boston: Houghton Mifflin, 1978), 295–97. Seigenthaler later described the scene in

Montgomery as "absolute war." *Freedom Riders*, DVD, produced, written, and directed by Stanley Nelson (Boston: Firelight Media, 2010).

19. Nelson, *Freedom Riders*.

20. Personal interview with Maxwell Taylor Kennedy during the Virginia Film Festival, November 3, 2012, Charlottesville, Virginia.

21. Susan Page, "The Kennedy Mystique," *USA Today Special Edition*, "JFK's America," Fall 2010, 5; Susan Page, "50 Years After Win, a Legacy Endures: JFK's Short Tenure Is Still Shaping USA," *USA Today*, September 27, 2010.

22. Personal interview with Maxwell Taylor Kennedy during the Virginia Film Festival, November 3, 2012, Charlottesville, Virginia.

23. Schlesinger, *Robert Kennedy*, 299.

24. Howard Zinn, *A People's History of the United States, 1492–Present* (New York: Harper Perennial, 2003), 454.

25. Louis Martin, "Memorandum on Black Muslims," April 12, 1961, Louis Martin Papers, Box 6, Folder 12, Library of Congress Manuscripts Division, Washington, DC.

26. At a speech in San Francisco on November 2, 1960, Kennedy said, "I am convinced that our young men and women, dedicated to freedom, are fully capable of overcoming the efforts of Mr. Khrushchev's missionaries who are undermining that freedom." "Making Economic Aid Effective: An American Youth Peace Corps," *Current* 8 (December 1960): 55.

27. At two A.M. on October 14, 2010, Peace Corps director Aaron Williams and former senator Harris Wofford of Pennsylvania gathered on the steps of the student union at the University of Michigan to commemorate the fiftieth anniversary of the JFK campaign speech that led to the formation of the Peace Corps; fifteen hundred students turned out to celebrate the anniversary. "Peace Corps Director Visits Michigan: Commemorates 50th Anniversary of John F. Kennedy's Speech That Inspired the Peace Corps," *US Fed News*, October 16, 2010.

28. Richard Reeves, *President Kennedy: Profile of Power* (New York, Simon and Schuster, 1993), 69; Kevin Lowther and C. Payne Lucas. *Keeping Kennedy's Promise: The Peace Corps: Unmet Hope of the New Frontier* (Boulder, CO: Westview Press, 1978), 3. The Peace Corps was not Kennedy's idea, but he turned it into reality. Some historians trace the Corps' origins to FDR's CCC program. "In 1950 a group of World Federalists advanced the idea of a voluntary 'peace force' to work in the developing countries. In the same year, the Public Affairs Institute published a pamphlet proposing American 'work centers' in the Third World." "Harris Wofford, one of the major architects of the Peace Corps, helped set up the International Development Placement Association, which, in the early 1950s, sent a small number of college graduates to teach or do community development in the Third World." Sargent Shriver made an unsuccessful attempt to sell his idea of three-man political action teams to the Eisenhower administration. Henry Reuss (D-WI) promoted a "Point Four Youth Corps" in the late 1950s and introduced H.R. 9638, which called for a study on the "advisability and practicability of the establishment of a Point Four Youth Corps." Hubert Humphrey's youth service bill, S. 3675 (June 1960), was the first to use the name "Peace Corps." Kennedy picked up on the idea during the campaign. Gerard T. Rice, *The Bold Experiment: JFK's Peace Corps* (Notre Dame, IN: University of Notre Dame Press, 1985), 4–11.

29. Shriver to JFK, March 8, 23, and 27, 1962, R. Sargent Shriver Papers, Box 12, Series 2, "PC: Memorandums to President Kennedy," John F. Kennedy Library, Boston, Massachu-

setts. The Peace Corps produced its share of headaches as well. At least one volunteer sent to the nation of Gabon brought along a firearm "for recreational hunting purposes." Bill Moyers, deputy director of the Peace Corps, thought that taking guns to Africa sent the wrong message. "White men have been coming to Africa for generations with guns," he wrote; "if we are truly different, it seems we ought to be different on the little issues as well as the big ones." He also argued the presence of guns could be misinterpreted "by the leftists and anti-Americans." Bill Moyers to Sargent Shriver, undated, Box 13, Series 2, "Peace Corps Policy," R. Sargent Shriver Papers, John F. Kennedy Library, Boston, Massachusetts. Shriver came under fire for both preserving the secularity of the Peace Corps and attempting to link it with the service arms of churches. The Catholic-affiliated American Council of Voluntary Agencies expressed their "regret" and "resentment" at Shriver's decision not to award contracts to church groups. Later, when Shriver attempted to strengthen ties between the Corps and the churches, Cardinal Richard Cushing resisted: "I don't want any part of federal aid for anything because I don't see how you can get it without control. It is for this reason that I 'keep my mouth shut' with regard to federal aid to education and other projects." Richard Cushing to Shriver, January 31, 1962, and "Recent Peace Corps Rebuff to Churches," *The Tablet*, December 23, 1961, Box 12, Series 2, "Peace Corps Correspondence," R. Sargent Shriver Papers, John F. Kennedy Library, Boston, Massachusetts. Despite these problems, the Peace Corps remains popular today, having convinced generations of people they could make a difference in the world. It has become the creative basis for many other proposals about national service. See, for example, my own plan for Universal National Service (UNS) in Larry J. Sabato, *A More Perfect Constitution: 23 Proposals to Revitalize Our Constitution and Make America a Fairer Country* (New York: Walker, 2007), chapter 5 (entire).

30. Stephen G. Rabe, "Controlling Revolutions: Latin America, the Alliance for Progress, and Cold War Anti-Communism," in *Kennedy's Quest for Victory: American Foreign Policy, 1961–1963*, ed. Thomas G. Paterson (New York: Oxford University Press, 1989), 105–7. Rabe believes that the United States' Cold War policies undermined the effectiveness of the Alliance for Progress program. "Through its recognition policy, internal security initiatives, and military and economic aid programs, the [Kennedy] Administration demonstrably bolstered regimes and groups that were undemocratic, conservative, and frequently repressive. The short-term security that anti-communist elites could provide was purchased at the expense of long-term political and social democracy."

31. The historical context is instructive. In early 1961 the Communists appeared to be winning the Cold War. They could boast of major economic and technological triumphs and were poised to take control in countries such as Laos and the Congo. Many Americans wanted their government to take a tougher stand against Communism, especially in the Western Hemisphere.

32. Thanks to an FOIA lawsuit filed by the National Security Archive, scholars now have access to four volumes of the CIA's "Official History of the Bay of Pigs Operation." As of August 2011, the CIA has refused to release volume 5, which contains "a rebuttal to the stinging CIA Inspector General's Report done in the immediate aftermath of the paramilitary assault, which held CIA officials accountable for a wide variety of mistakes, miscalculations and deceptions that characterized the failed invasion." See Peter Kornbluh, "CIA Forced to Release Long Secret Official History of Bay of Pigs Invasion," *Global Research*, August 2,

2011, http://www.globalresearch.ca/index.php?context=va&aid=25864 [accessed August 2, 2011].

33. "Report of the Committee on National Security Policy," November 9, 1960, Paul H. Nitze Papers, Box 141, Folder 8, Library of Congress Manuscripts Division, Washington, DC.

34. Bowles landed in hot water when he talked to the press about his opposition to the plan. He was eventually sent packing from the State Department and replaced by George W. Ball.

35. Arthur M. Schlesinger, Jr., *A Thousand Days: John F. Kennedy in the White House* (Boston: Houghton Mifflin, 1965), 240–51; Arthur Schlesinger, Jr., "Memorandum for the President," February 11, 1961, National Security Archive, The George Washington University, http://www.gwu.edu/~nsarchiv/bayofpigs/19610211.pdf [accessed on October 13, 2010].

36. Peter Kornbluh, ed., *Bay of Pigs Declassified: The Secret CIA Report on the Invasion of Cuba* (New York: New Press, 1998), 2; R. Hart Phillips, "A 'Fight to Death' Is Feared in Cuba," *New York Times*, April 9, 1960.

37. Kennedy made some changes to the original CIA plan. He moved the landing site from Trinidad to the Bay of Pigs and reduced the number of airstrikes in order to make the operation "less noisy." Like Eisenhower, Kennedy thought that he could somehow conceal the United States' role in the operation.

38. Kornbluh, *Declassified*, 2–3; Robert Dallek, *An Unfinished Life: John F. Kennedy, 1917–63* (Boston: Little, Brown, 2003), 363; Aleksandr Fursenko and Timothy Naftali, *"One Hell of a Gamble": Khrushchev, Castro, and Kennedy, 1958–64* (New York: W. W. Norton, 1997), 95. Stephen Rabe says that an additional airstrike would not have made a difference since Cuban pilots were "prepared to take off at a moment's notice" after April 15. James N. Giglio and Stephen G. Rabe, *Debating the Kennedy Presidency* (New York: Rowman and Littlefield, 2003), 34. The CIA and Cuban exiles were counting on Kennedy to intervene even though the president had made it clear that U.S. forces would stay on the sidelines.

39. Eisenhower was proven correct. The failure at the Bay of Pigs strengthened the resolve of Nikita Khrushchev, who stiff-armed Kennedy at the Vienna summit and then deployed nuclear weapons to Cuba. The worst consequence may have been that Kennedy decided to take a stronger stand in Vietnam to show the Communists that he meant business, accelerating what was to become the greatest American miscalculation of the postwar period.

40. Stephen A. Ambrose, *Eisenhower: The President* (New York: Simon and Schuster, 1984), 638–39.

41. Kennedy was also deceived by the Central Intelligence Agency. "Despite repeated White House instructions to keep U.S. forces from directly participating in order to preserve plausible deniability of American involvement, the CIA ultimately gave permission for U.S. pilots to fly aircraft over the beaches. The aviators were told that, if they were shot down and captured, they should describe themselves as mercenaries and the U.S. would 'deny any knowledge' of them." Four U.S. airmen were killed in the fighting. It is also clear that top CIA officials did not believe that the invasion could succeed without U.S. military involvement. See Robert Dallek, "Untold Story of the Bay of Pigs" and Peter Kornbluh, "Bay of Pigs

History Held Hostage," *Daily Beast*, August 14, 2011, http://www.thedailybeast.com/news week/2011/08/14/bay-of-pigs-newly-revealed-cia-documents-expose-blunders.print.html [accessed August 25, 2011].

42. Dallek, *Unfinished Life*, 365.

43. Ambrose, *Eisenhower: The President*, 639.

44. Sorensen, *Kennedy*, 308; Dallek, *Unfinished Life*, 370.

45. The columnist George Will is among many who has asserted that the Bay of Pigs disaster convinced Khrushchev, "the 67-year-old grandson of a serf and son of a coal miner, that Kennedy, the 43-year-old son of privilege, was too callow to recognize the invasion's risks and too weak to see it through." George F. Will, "JFK's Berlin Blunder," *Washington Post*, August 12, 2011, http://www.washingtonpost.com/opinions/jfks-berlin-blunder/2011 /08/12/gIQAGOcxBJ_story.html [accessed August 15, 2011].

46. Kornbluh, *Declassified*, 4.

47. Schlesinger, *Thousand Days*, 239.

48. Lucien S. Vandenbroucke, "Anatomy of a Failure: The Decision to Land at the Bay of Pigs," *Political Science Quarterly* 99 (Autumn 1984): 471–91.

49. America in the early 1960s might reasonably be compared to Athens in 400 B.C. Nicias, one of the Greek city state's most prominent politicians, made exaggerated estimates about the number of troops and ships that would be required to invade Sicily, attempting to trick the governing assembly into abandoning the expedition. But the Athenians were so consumed with blood lust that they approved Nicias' faux plan and put him in charge of the invasion. In other words, an absurd military plan took on a foolish life of its own.

50. Piero Gleijeses, "Ships in the Night: The CIA, the White House and the Bay of Pigs," *Journal of Latin American Studies* 27 (February 1995): 1–42.

51. In early May 1961, JFK told Schlesinger, "If it hadn't been for Cuba, we might be about to intervene in Laos." Herbert S. Parmet, *JFK: The Presidency of John F. Kennedy* (New York: Penguin Books, 1984), 136. "Robert Kennedy recalled that 'we would have sent . . . a large number of American troops into Laos if it hadn't been for [the Bay of Pigs failure] because everybody was in favor of it.'" Giglio, *Presidency*, 66.

52. Schlesinger, *Thousand Days*, 329, 336; Giglio, *Presidency*, 63–68.

53. Parmet, *JFK*, 182. Robert Dallek attributes Kennedy's back problem to his use of steroids. Prolonged steroid use can cause osteoporosis and a weakened immune system. "Navy medical records indicate that back surgery Kennedy underwent in 1944 had revealed clear evidence of osteoporosis. The surgeons removed 'some abnormally soft disc interspace material' and anticipated additional problems if he continued to suffer bone loss." In the early 1950s, Kennedy's back problems worsened. X-rays from JFK physician Janet Travell's records show that Kennedy's L-4 "had narrowed from 1.5 cm to 1.1 cm, indicating" an imminent spinal collapse, and they also showed "compression fractures in his lower spine." Kennedy's fifth lumbar vertebra did collapse in the spring of 1954. He opted for a risky operation that never fully solved the problem. See Robert Dallek, "The Medical Ordeals of JFK," *Atlantic Monthly* 290 (December 2002): 49–61, http://www.theatlantic.com/past/docs/issues/2002/12 /dallek.htm [accessed September 1, 2010].

54. John Fitzgerald Kennedy, "The Goal of Sending a Man to the Moon (May 25, 1961)," Miller Center of Public Affairs, University of Virginia, http://millercenter.org/scripps/archive /speeches/detail/3368 [accessed December 16, 2010]; Dallek, *Unfinished Life*, 393. Kennedy's

support for the space program stemmed in part from his concerns over Gagarin's flight on April 12, 1961, and the Bay of Pigs fiasco (April 17, 1961). The success of Alan Shepard's flight on May 5, 1961 proved that the U.S. was still competitive with the USSR in outer space.

55. "Robert C. Seamans Jr.," MIT Tech TV, http://techtv.mit.edu/videos/3083 [accessed August 6, 2012].

56. Kennedy also proposed a U.S.-Soviet joint lunar program before the United Nations in September 1963. After the assassination, Ambassador Adlai Stevenson reminded the assembly that "President Kennedy proposed . . . last September to explore with the Soviet Union opportunities for working together in the conquest of space, including the sending of men to the moon as representatives of all our countries. President Johnson has instructed me to reaffirm that offer today . . ." In his first State of the Union address, President Johnson held out some possibility for such a venture: "We must assure our preeminence in the peaceful exploration of outer space, focusing on an expedition to the moon in this decade—in cooperation with other powers if possible, alone if necessary." On January 31, 1964, Webb advised Johnson not to propose a "new high-level U.S. initiative" until the Soviets responded to his and Kennedy's previous proposals. Because the Soviets never did so, the U.S. moved ahead with the Apollo program on its own. See Hirotaka Watanabe, "The Space Policy of the Johnson Administration: Project Apollo and International Cooperation," *Osaka Law Review* 57 (February 2010): 39–64.

57. Telephone interview with Dan Fenn, December 16, 2010; Mike Wall, "JFK's Moon Shot: Q&A With Space Policy Expert John Logsdon," Space.com, May 24, 2011, http://www .space.com/11762-nasa-kennedy-moon-speech-logsdon-interview.html [accessed May 25, 2011]; Carolyn Y. Johnson, "JFK Had Doubts About Moon Landing," *Boston Globe*, May 25, 2011, http://www.boston.com/news/local/massachusetts/articles/2011/05/25/jfk_had_doubts _about_moon_landing/?p1=Local_Links [accessed May 25, 2011].

58. Jacobson's medical license was revoked by the State of New York in 1975 because of his excessive narcotic prescriptions.

59. According to historian Robert Dallek, there "is no evidence that JFK's physical torments played any significant part in shaping the successes or shortcomings of his public actions, either before or during his presidency." Dallek, "The Medical Ordeals of JFK," 49–61. It is also true that no one will ever know for sure. Narcotics can have subtle but significant effects on any human being, especially one dealing with the extraordinary stresses of the presidency.

60. Franklin's fur cap and spectacles caused a sensation in Paris. "The cap, like that worn by Rousseau, served as his badge of homespun purity and New World virtue, just as his ever-present spectacles (also featured in portraits) became an emblem of wisdom. It helped him play the part that Paris imagined for him: that of the noble frontier philosopher and simple backwoods sage—even though he had lived most of his life on Market Street [Philadelphia] and Craven Street [London]." Walter Isaacson, *Benjamin Franklin: An American Life* (New York: Simon and Schuster, 2003), 328.

61. Robert C. Doty, "Kennedy and De Gaulle Agree to Defend Berlin; Discuss Asia and Africa," *New York Times*, June 1, 1961; Rachel Day, "Suit Worn by Jacqueline Kennedy during Presidential Trip to Paris Now on Display at the JFK Presidential Library and Museum," http://www.jfklibrary.org/JFK+Library+and+Museum/News+and+Press/Suit+Worn+by +Jacqueline+Kennedy+During+Presidential+Trip+to+Paris+Now+on+Display+at+the +JFK+Presiden.htm [accessed December 16, 2010]; Dallek, *Unfinished Life*, 400; Barbara A.

Perry, *Jacqueline Kennedy: First Lady of the New Frontier* (Lawrence: University Press of Kansas, 2004), 86. In some ways, President Kennedy treated the trip to Paris as a campaign stop to win French favor, not votes. The night before the visit began, the French people watched "a nationwide television program, prepared especially for them," featuring the president and First Lady. "[T]he president and Mrs. Kennedy expressed their pleasure in the visit." And "Mrs. Kennedy conducted her part of the proceedings entirely in French. Her accent [as noted by some French observers, was] 'accurate,' which is of course several cuts below the 'flawless' they had been led to expect." Kennedy's PR team weren't sure whether to release pictures of the president alone or ones which included the First Lady. As a result, the shops on Rue de Rivoli displayed both types of shots. Press secretary for the trip Andrew Hatcher and JFK aide Ted Sorensen were sent to Paris ahead of time to line up interviews and make sure that the visit went smoothly. The careful work clearly paid off. The journalist Mary McGrory witnessed two French women "giggling" as they "went from shop window to shop window bowing to every photograph of the president. 'How do you do, Mr. Kennedee,' they said in preparation." Mary McGrory, Western Union Telegram, May 31, 1961, Mary McGrory Papers, Box 96, Folder 8, Library of Congress Manuscripts Division, Washington, DC.

62. Mary McGrory, undated Western Union Telegram, Mary McGrory Papers, Box 96, Folder 8, Library of Congress Manuscripts Division, Washington, DC.

63. Dallek, *Unfinished Life*, 402–3.

64. John M. Murrin, Paul E. Johnson, James M. McPherson, Gary Gerstle, Emily S. Rosenberg, and Norman L. Rosenberg, *Liberty, Equality, Power: A History of the American People*, 3rd ed. (New York: Wadsworth/Thomson Learning, 2002), 936–37; Dallek, *Unfinished Life*, 402.

65. Reeves, *President Kennedy*, 158–66.

66. Perry, *Jacqueline Kennedy*, 86; Reeves, *President Kennedy*, 166; Eddy Gilmore, "Jacqueline Charms All Vienna—Especially K.; Nina Cheered for Accepting Plea," *Washington Post and Times Herald*, June 4, 1961; Schlesinger, *Thousand Days*, 367. Khrushchev may have been more impressed by President Kennedy than he showed. According to Schlesinger, Khrushchev told Soviet ambassador Georgi Kornienko after the meeting in Vienna that he (Kornienko) had been right to describe Kennedy as "independent and intelligent." Schlesinger, *Thousand Days*, 378.

67. Schlesinger, *Thousand Days*, 369–70; Reeves, *President Kennedy*, 167–71; John Morton Blum, *Years of Discord: American Politics and Society, 1961–74* (New York: W. W. Norton, 1991), 46.

68. Contrary to some others, O'Donnell thought that Kennedy seemed calm and in control at Vienna. In his version of events, the president came out of the talks with Khrushchev saying that the chairman was bluffing and would never sign a treaty with East Germany. "Anybody who talks the way he did today, and really means it, would be crazy," said Kennedy. "And I'm sure he's not crazy." Kenneth P. O'Donnell, Dave F. Powers, and Joe McCarthy, *"Johnny, We Hardly Knew Ye": Memories of John Fitzgerald Kennedy* (New York: Pocket Books, 1973), 344.

69. Parmet, *JFK*, 190; O'Donnell, *"Johnny, We Hardly Knew Ye,"* 345.

70. Theodore C. Sorensen, ed., *"Let the Word Go Forth": The Speeches, Statements, and Writings of John F. Kennedy* (New York: Delacorte Press, 1988), 248–50; Reeves, *President Kennedy*, 190–95.

71. Kevin W. Dean, "'We Seek Peace, but We Shall Not Surrender': JFK's Use of Juxtaposition for Rhetorical Success in the Berlin Crisis," *Presidential Studies Quarterly* 21 (Summer 1991): 531–44.

72. Fred Kaplan, "JFK's First-Strike Plan," *Atlantic Monthly* 288 (October 2001): 81–86.

73. In fairness, it should be noted that President Bush was speaking to a group of airline employees in Chicago whose livelihoods depended on public confidence in the safety of air travel. But Bush never asked the public to do anything out of the ordinary to cover the massive human and financial costs of post–September 11 actions. Andrew J. Bacevich, "He Told Us to Go Shopping. Now the Bill Is Due," *Washington Post*, October 5, 2008.

74. John Fitzgerald Kennedy, "Report on the Berlin Crisis (July 25, 1961)," Miller Center of Public Affairs, University of Virginia, http://millercenter.org/scripps/archive/speeches /detail/5740 [accessed December 24, 2010].

75. Schlesinger, *Thousand Days*, 392; Dallek, *Unfinished Life*, 424.

76. Something like this would have been much less possible after November 22, 1963, even for a vice president. Security would have been much tighter anywhere, much less in what was effectively a war zone. Neil Spitzer, "Dividing a City," *Wilson Quarterly* 12 (Summer 1988): 100–122; Reeves, *President Kennedy*, 211; Giglio and Rabe, *Debating*, 27 (quotation); Dallek, *Unfinished Life*, 427.

77. Giglio and Rabe, *Debating*, 27; Kaplan, "JFK's First-Strike Plan," 81–86.

78. See Robert Dallek, *Unfinished Life*, 288–90, and Thomas Reeves, *Question of Character*, 249.

79. Eisenhower authorized the Jupiters in 1959, but never actually deployed them.

80. Joseph A. Loftus, "Gilpatric Warns U.S. Can Destroy Atom Aggressor," *New York Times*, October 22, 1961; "Huge U.S. Arsenal of A-Bombs Bared," *Long Beach Independent Press Telegram*, October 22, 1961; "Unprecedented Disclosure: U.S. Nuclear Weapons Counted 'In Thousands,'" *Zanesville* [Ohio] *Times Recorder*, October 22, 1961; Giglio and Rabe, *Debating*, 19; Dallek, *Unfinished Life*, 433–34. Kennedy, Rusk, and McNamara were also bragging publicly about America's nuclear arsenal.

81. Joseph Alsop thought the president "looked like his old self" during this period. "[H]e has forced himself to lose ten pounds, which is good for him." The journalist had recently dined at the White House and thought that the evening had been "a great relief for the president" who needed to "escape and forget his terrible burdens." Letter written by Joseph Alsop, January 16, 1962, Joseph and Stewart Alsop Papers, Box 183, Library of Congress Manuscript Division, Washington, DC.

82. The Kennedys did achieve some progress on civil rights in 1961. Speaking from Dallas on November 15, 1961, Attorney General Robert Kennedy told the press that "the people of Dallas, Atlanta, Memphis, New Orleans, and many other cities" had shown their respect for orderly progress by "desegregating their schools this fall without disorder or disrespect for the law. In each of these cities, and particularly in Dallas and Atlanta, this was accomplished by citizens from all walks of life, accepting their responsibilities and acting with skill, vigor, and dedication." "Address by Robert F. Kennedy, Associated Press Managing Editors Meeting, Dallas, Texas, November 15, 1961," Victor S. Navasky Papers, Box 3, "Background: Communist Party, General," John F. Kennedy Library, Boston, Massachusetts.

83. John Fitzgerald Kennedy, "State of the Union Address (January 11, 1962)," Miller Center of Public Affairs, University of Virginia, http://millercenter.org/scripps/archive/speeches /detail/5742 [accessed December 29, 2010].

5. STEEL AT HOME AND ABROAD

1. Arthur Goldberg to JFK, March 13 and 20 and April 3, 1962, Arthur J. Goldberg Papers, Box 1:27, Folder 2, Library of Congress Manuscripts Division, Washington, DC; Richard Reeves, *President Kennedy: Profile of Power* (New York: Simon and Schuster, 1993), 294–95. Goldberg was a highly effective secretary of labor at a time when unions wielded considerable power. In September 1961, he helped avert a UAW strike: "The primary cause of this automobile strike was failure to reach agreement on the question of relief time. When I learned of this I suggested the formula which the parties accepted last night." On October 24, 1961, he informed the president that "The threatened strike against the Southern Pacific Railroad was postponed at my request. The parties have been meeting here in the Department in an effort to work out an agreement." In November, a "strike of the Air Line Pilots Association against Pan American World Airways was averted . . . by the creation of an Emergency Board." Goldberg to JFK, September 12, October 24, and November 14, 1961, Arthur J. Goldberg Papers, Box 1:27, Folder 2, Library of Congress Manuscripts Division, Washington, DC. In the summer of 1962, the nation's five major aluminum companies were able to negotiate labor contracts without Washington's help. See "Labor: Forgotten Method," *Time*, July 6, 1962, http://www.time.com/time/magazine/article/0,9171,939998,00.html [accessed March 23, 2011].

2. According to some sources, the original quote was, "My father told me businessmen were all pricks . . ." Others say that it was, "My father always told me that steel men were sons-of-bitches . . ."

3. Ted Sorensen, *Kennedy: The Classic Biography* (New York: Harper Perennial Political Classics, 2009), 447–48; Kenneth P. O'Donnell and David F. Powers with Joe McCarthy, *"Johnny, We Hardly Knew Ye": Memories of John Fitzgerald Kennedy* (New York: Pocket Books, 1972), 471; Arthur M. Schlesinger, Jr., *A Thousand Days: John F. Kennedy in the White House* (Boston: Houghton Mifflin, 1965), 635; James N. Giglio, *The Presidency of John F. Kennedy* (Lawrence: University Press of Kansas, 1991), 131.

4. In February of 1902, President Theodore Roosevelt ordered his attorney general, Philander Knox, to file suit against the Northern Securities Company, "a recently created holding company that comprised the leading railroads of the northwestern quarter of the country." Roosevelt's decision prompted a visit from J. P. Morgan, one of Northern Securities' primary investors, who asked the president if he planned on attacking his (Morgan's) "other interests," which included the "steel trust." "Certainly not," said Roosevelt, "unless we find out that in any case they have done something that we regard as wrong." H. W. Brands, *TR: The Last Romantic* (New York: Basic Books, 1997), 437. One could reasonably conclude that JFK went even further than TR in using the power of government to influence one big business.

5. John F. Kennedy, "President's News Conference, April 11, 1962," John T. Woolley and Gerhard Peters, *The American Presidency Project* [online], Santa Barbara, CA, http://www.presidency.ucsb.edu/ws/index.php?pid=8598 [accessed January 11, 2011].

6. Some researchers believe that the Kennedys also ordered the IRS to audit the uncooperative steel executives' books. Although the evidence is not ironclad that JFK ever used the IRS for political purposes, there is certainly some support for this conclusion. See James Bovard, "A Brief History of IRS Political Targeting," *Wall Street Journal*, May 14, 2013, http://online.wsj.com/article/SB10001424127887324715704578482823301630836

.html [accessed May 17, 2013]; John Gizzi, "IRS Political Abuse Started Long Before Tea Party," *Newsmax*, May 13, 2013, http://www.newsmax.com/Newsfront/irs-tea-party-political/2013/05/13/id/504108 [accessed May 17, 2013]; and Joseph J. Thorndike, "An 'Unthinkable' IRS Scandal? More Like Unavoidable," *Washington Post*, May 17, 2013, http://www.washingtonpost.com/opinions/an-unthinkable-irs-scandal-more-like-unavoidable/2013/05/17/3f89a1ce-bd84-11e2-89c9-3be8095fe767_story.html [accessed May 17, 2013]. When I asked Stephen Plotkin, archivist at the JFK Library, if President Kennedy ever used the IRS as a weapon against his political enemies, Plotkin replied: "I'm missing one thing, which is a direct connection between the office of the president and the IRS activity. It's one thing for JFK to create an atmosphere receptive to IRS investigations of right wing organizations, but it is quite another to imply that he ordered such investigations. And let's not forget that a great many of these organizations richly deserved to be audited." E-mail from Stephen Plotkin, May 15, 2013.

7. Reeves, *President Kennedy*, 298–99; Robert Dallek, *An Unfinished Life: John F. Kennedy, 1917–63* (Boston: Back Bay Books, 2003), 486; Giglio, *Presidency*, 132.

8. Burton Crane, "Stock Prices Dive in Sharpest Loss Since 1929 Break," *New York Times*, May 29, 1929; Thomas C. Reeves, *A Question of Character: A Life of John F. Kennedy* (Rocklin, CA: Prima Publishing, 1992), 332; Giglio, *Presidency*, 132; Theodore C. Sorensen, *Kennedy* (New York: Harper and Row, 1965), 462.

9. Giglio, *Presidency*, 133–35; John F. Kennedy, "Radio and Television Report to the American People on the State of the National Economy, August 13, 1962," John T. Woolley and Gerhard Peters, *The American Presidency Project*, Santa Barbara, CA, http://www.presidency.ucsb.edu/ws/index.php?pid=8812&st=&st1= [accessed January 12, 2011]. Similarly, President Obama tried to repair relations between the White House and the business community in 2011 after two years of health care reform, financial industry regulation, and other battles with business. In February 2011 he delivered a pro-business address at the U.S. Chamber of Commerce in Washington. Previously, the chamber had lobbied against Obama's various reforms. It made little difference, of course. Business interests overwhelmingly opposed Obama's successful reelection in 2012. Scott Horsley, "New Approach: Obama Woos Chamber of Commerce," February 14, 2011, National Public Radio website, http://www.npr.org/2011/02/07/133551752/new-approach-obama-woos-chamber-of-commerce [accessed February 14, 2011].

10. Giglio, *Presidency*, 138.

11. C. Douglas Dillon, JFK's treasury secretary, thought that Kennedy had been sold on tax cuts even before he assumed the presidency: "This was something that was originally discussed by me with the president before my appointment. It was part of our original policy that was mentioned in the tax message of 1961. Our idea then was that the first tax bill would be passed in 1961, and that we would come along the next year with the overall tax cut. We didn't, at that time, know the exact size of the tax cut that we would propose, but we did know that we wanted to reduce the top rates to the area of 65 or 70 percent and other rates accordingly." Interview with Douglas Dillon, C. Douglas Dillon Papers, Box 43, "Dillon Tapes," John F. Kennedy Library, Boston, Massachusetts.

12. Tax rates have jumped up and down over the years. As the Great Depression deepened in June 1932, President Hoover and Congress raised the top income tax rate from 25% to 63% and quadrupled the lowest tax rate from 1.1% to 4%. President Roosevelt raised taxes

at times to pay for his New Deal programs and World War II. Under President Truman, income tax rates were cut across the board, with the top marginal rate, 94% on all income over $200,000, cut to 86.45%. The lowest rate was cut to 19% from 23%, and with a change in the amount of income exempt from taxation an estimated 12 million Americans were eliminated from the tax rolls entirely. There were also changes in the separate corporate tax rate structure. See Alan Reynolds, "The Hoover Analogy Flunks," Cato Institute website, reprinted from *Forbes*, September 29, 2008, http://www.cato.org/publications/com mentary/hoover-analogy-flunks [accessed April 9, 2013], and Burton Folsom, Jr., and Anita Folsom, "Did FDR End the Depression?" *Wall Street Journal*, April 12, 2010, http:// online.wsj.com/article/SB10001424052702304024604575173632046893848.html [accessed April 9, 2013].

13. John Fitzgerald Kennedy, "Yale University Commencement (June 11, 1962)," Miller Center of Public Affairs, University of Virginia, http://millercenter.org/scripps/archive/speeches /detail/3370 [accessed January 13, 2011]; Schlesinger, *Thousand Days*, 648; Matt Viser, "JFK's Words Echo Once More in Washington," *Boston Globe*, January 21, 2011; David Greenberg, "Tax Cuts in Camelot?" January 16, 2004, *Slate*, http://www.slate.com/id/2093947/ [accessed January 13, 2011]. Liberals counter by arguing that JFK was trying to put money in the hands of consumers with a kind of demand-side economics, not further enriching the wealthy. They may be right about the intent, but the effect of the Kennedy tax cut disproportionately benefited the well-off.

14. Bundy knew about the missile sites on October 15, but decided to withhold the information from the president until the following day. Bundy later explained the reasons for his decision: (1) it would take 24 hours to put together a presentation, (2) a hastily-assembled meeting of top officials would alert the press to the crisis, (3) Bundy thought that Kennedy, back from a "strenuous campaign weekend," would benefit from a good night's sleep. Sorensen, *Classic Biography*, 673.

15. Sorensen, *Classic Biography*, 673–74; "Kennedy's Cuba Statement," *New York Times*, September 5, 1962; Aleksandr Fursenko and Timothy Naftali, *"One Hell of a Gamble": Khrushchev, Castro, and Kennedy, 1958–64* (New York: W. W. Norton, 1997), 222–23. Sorensen said Ex-Comm actually consisted of as many as "fourteen or fifteen men."

16. Fursenko and Naftali, *Hell of a Gamble*, 224–25; Sorensen, *Classic Biography*, 675–77; Dallek, *Unfinished Life*, 545–47; Audio Clips from the Kennedy White House, Tuesday, October 16, 11:50 A.M., Cabinet Room, White House, National Security Archive, George Washington University, http://www.gwu.edu/~nsarchiv/nsa/cuba_mis_cri/audio.htm [accessed January 19, 2011].

17. Fursenko and Naftali, *Hell of a Gamble*, 226; Reeves, *President Kennedy*, 376–77.

18. In the autumn of 1963, LeMay occasionally served as acting chairman of the Joint Chiefs of Staff and in that capacity recommended sabotage operations against Cuba. Some conspiracy theorists tie LeMay's aggressive posture toward Cuba, and President Kennedy's refusal to sign off on the general's plans, to LeMay's alleged but unsubstantiated involvement in JFK's assassination. See LeMay's memo to the Secretary of the Army, September 23, 1963, Mary Ferrell website, http://www.maryferrell.org/mffweb/archive/ viewer/showDoc.do?docId=10220&relPageId=1 [accessed January 5, 2012]. LeMay's hawkish views were the inspiration behind Fletcher Knebel and Charles W. Bailey's book *Seven Days in May*, which tells the story of a right-wing general who plots a coup against a

president who is trying to make peace with the Soviets. See Adam Bernstein, "Charles W. Bailey II, 'Seven Days in May' Co-author, Dies at 82," *Washington Post*, January 4, 2012.

19. Fursenko and Naftali, *Hell of a Gamble*, 230; Dallek, *Unfinished Life*, 551–52; Audio Clips from the Kennedy White House, Thursday, October 18, 12:00 P.M., Cabinet Room, White House, National Security Archive, George Washington University, http://www.gwu .edu/~nsarchiv/nsa/cuba_mis_cri/audio.htm [accessed January 19, 2011].

20. Schlesinger, *Thousand Days*, 805; Dallek, *Unfinished Life*, 553.

21. LeMay became the running mate of presidential candidate George C. Wallace in 1968. Wallace was the nominee of the American Independent Party, whose anti-civil rights platform helped Wallace and LeMay win 46 electoral votes in the South.

22. John Morton Blum, *Years of Discord: American Politics and Society, 1961–74* (New York: W. W. Norton, 1991), 82–83; Reeves, *Question of Character*, 374; Dallek, *Unfinished Life*, 55.

23. Sorensen, *Classic Biography*, 692–94; Reeves, *Question of Character*, 375–77.

24. John Fitzgerald Kennedy, "Address on the Buildup of Arms in Cuba (October 22, 1962)," Miller Center of Public Affairs, University of Virginia, http://millercenter.org/scripps /archive/speeches/detail/3372 [accessed January 20, 2011].

25. Herbert S. Parmet, *JFK: The Presidency of John F. Kennedy* (New York: Penguin Books, 1986), 292; Sidey, *Reporter's Inside Story*, 344.

26. On October 23, the OAS voted unanimously to support the U.S. response to the missile crisis.

27. Dallek, *Unfinished Life*, 561; Arthur M. Schlesinger, Jr., *Robert Kennedy and His Times* (Boston: Houghton Mifflin, 1978), 514; Reeves, *Question of Character*, 381.

28. Author Michael Dobbs describes the "eyeball to eyeball" moment as an "erroneous myth." The lead Soviet ship, says Dobbs, was actually 750 miles away from the quarantine line when it turned around and Khrushchev had ordered his ships back to the Soviet Union "some 30 hours earlier." See Michael Dobbs, "The Price of a 50-Year Myth," *New York Times*, October 15, 2012, http://www.nytimes.com/2012/10/16/opinion/the-eyeball-to-eyeball-myth -and-the-cuban-missile-crisiss-legacy.html?_r=1& [accessed October 25, 2012].

29. Parmet, *JFK*, 294; Dallek, *Unfinished Life*, 565.

30. James Rosen, "RFK Files Show Missile Crisis Disrupted Anti-Castro Plots," FoxNews.com, July 25, 2013, http://www.foxnews.com/politics/2013/07/25/rfk-files-show -missile-crisis-disrupted-anti-castro-plots/ [accessed July 26, 2103]. Laurence Chang and Peter Kornbluh, eds., *The Cuban Missile Crisis, 1962* (New York: New Press, 1992), 374–79; Dallek, *Unfinished Life*, 565–68; Blum, *Years of Discord*, 88.

31. Khrushchev's account of the meeting, as told to him by Dobrynin, portrays the Kennedy brothers as worried about the possibility of a military putsch in the U.S. According to Dobrynin, "Robert Kennedy looked exhausted. One could see from his eyes that he had not slept for days. He himself said that he had not been home for six days and nights. 'The president is in a grave situation,' Robert Kennedy said, 'and does not know how to get out of it. We are under very severe stress. In fact we are under pressure from our military to use force against Cuba. Probably at this very moment the president is sitting down to write a message to Chairman Khrushchev. We want to ask you, Mr. Dobrynin, to pass President Kennedy's message to Chairman Khrushchev through unofficial channels. President Kennedy implores Chairman Khrushchev to accept his offer and to take into consideration the peculiarities of the American system. Even though the president himself is very much against starting a war over Cuba, an irreversible chain of events could occur against his will . . . If

the situation continues much longer, the president is not sure that the military will not over-throw him and seize power.'" Jim Hershberg, "Anatomy of a Controversy: Anatoly F. Do-brynin's Meeting With Robert F. Kennedy, Saturday, 27 October 1962," *The Cold War International History Project Bulletin* 5 (Spring 1995), National Security Archive, George Washington University, http://www.gwu.edu/~nsarchiv/nsa/cuba_mis_cri/moment.htm [accessed January 21, 2011]. While we do not know for sure what RFK said to Dobrynin and there is no evidence at all that a military coup was contemplated by anyone, this was perhaps a useful argument to make to a Soviet well aware of how regime change happened in his own country.

32. In 1989 Sorensen admitted that he purposefully omitted the Jupiter missile arrange-ment from Robert Kennedy's book *Thirteen Days*.

33. Dallek, *Unfinished Life*, 570–71.

34. McGeorge Bundy, "Memorandum for the Executive Committee, November 16, 1962," Harlan Cleveland Papers, Box 78, "Cuba—Cuban Crisis 1962," John F. Kennedy Li-brary, Boston, Massachusetts; Tad Szulc, "Navy Gets Order," *New York Times*, November 21, 1962. See also David G. Coleman, *The Fourteenth Day: JFK and the Aftermath of the Cuban Missile Crisis* (New York: W. W. Norton, 2012).

35. Meredith had also been inspired by the New Frontier. According to Arthur Schlesinger, he applied for admission to Ole Miss on the day that JFK delivered his inaugural address.

36. Blum, *Years of Discord*, 73–75; Schlesinger, *A Thousand Days*, 940–49; John Fitzger-ald Kennedy, "Address on the Situation at the University of Mississippi (September 30, 1962)," Miller Center of Public Affairs, University of Virginia, http://millercenter.org/scripps /archive/speeches/detail/5743 [accessed January 25, 2011].

37. J. H. Meredith to "The Attorney General," September 5, 1963, Burke Marshall Papers, Box 8, "Meredith, James H.," John F. Kennedy Library, Boston, Massachusetts. In an un-dated letter to President Kennedy [probably sent in early 1963], Robert Kennedy chose to look on the bright side of the integration struggle: "For the headline writer, rioting and vio-lence at the University of Mississippi overshadowed the civil rights field and painted 1962 as one of resistance by the South to law and the orders of our courts. The historian, however, will find, on the contrary, that 1962 was a year of great progress in civil rights, in large mea-sure because of the responsibility and respect for law displayed by the great majority of the citizens of the South. In 1962 the United States took major steps toward equal opportunity and equal rights for all our citizens and in every area of civil rights—whether voting, trans-portation, education, employment, or housing. During this administration, officials in 29 counties in Georgia, Alabama, Mississippi, and Louisiana have voluntarily made voting rec-ords available to the department in our investigations of voting complaints—without the need for court action." RFK to JFK, undated letter, Burke Marshall Papers, Box 8, "Presi-dential April 8, 1963–August 17, 1964 & undated," John F. Kennedy Library, Boston, Massachusetts.

38. The racism of the 1960s pervaded much of the Southern media. On August 28, 1963, WMOG radio, part of the "Johnnie Reb" chain of stations, ran an advertisement sponsored by the Glynn Society for Democratic Action that allegedly included the follow-ing announcement: "The niggers are now marching in Washington; keep the schools for white people." A subsequent FCC investigation concluded that the word "Negro" had been pronounced "nigra." "The Secretary of the anti-integration society that placed the subject advertisements with the station, in a letter to the FCC, [made] the pithy

comment: 'In one section of the country the word 'vigor' is believed to be pronounced as though it was spelled 'viggah.'" Jerome K. Heilbron to Burke Marshall, September 23, 1963, Victor S. Navasky Papers, Box 3, "Background Civil Rights," John F. Kennedy Library, Boston, Massachusetts. One of JFK's signature words, spoken with a Boston accent, was "vigor."

39. Blum, *Years of Discord*, 75; Rhodes Cook, "The Midterm Election of '62: A Real 'October Surprise,'" *Sabato's Crystal Ball* VIII (September 30, 2010), http://www.center forpolitics.org/crystalball/articles/frc2010093001/ [accessed January 25, 2011].

40. Harris Wofford, *Of Kennedys and Kings: Making Sense of the Sixties* (Pittsburgh: University of Pittsburgh Press, 1980), 170; Martin Luther King, Jr., *Why We Can't Wait* (New York: Harper and Row, 1964), 77–100.

41. Parmet, *JFK*, 264–67; Reeves, *President Kennedy*, 488–89; Letter from Marshall Haynes, Jr., to Burke Marshall, September 18, 1963, Burke Marshall Papers, Box 8, "Attorney General, September–October 1963," John F. Kennedy Library, Boston, Massachusetts; Western Union telegram from Jackie Robinson to JFK, May 7, 1963, Jackie Robinson Papers, Box 5, Folder 14, Library of Congress Manuscripts Division, Washington, DC.

42. Reeves, *President Kennedy*, 501.

43. Wallace's stand in the schoolhouse door was pure political theater. He knew that his action would not prevent the integration of the University of Alabama and that Alabama's elected state attorney general, Richmond Flowers, opposed his policies. In addition, the university's Board of Trustees had previously adopted a resolution promising to obey the orders of the courts. Memorandum from Burke Marshall to RFK, May 22, 1963, Burke Marshall Papers, Box 8, "Attorney General, April–June 1963," John F. Kennedy Library, Boston, Massachusetts.

44. John Fitzgerald Kennedy, "Address on Civil Rights (June 11, 1963)," Miller Center of Public Affairs, University of Virginia, http://millercenter.org/scripps/archive/speeches/detail /3375 [accessed January 27, 2011].

45. Louis Martin Diary, June 16, 1963, Louis Martin Papers, Box 12, Folder 5, Library of Congress Manuscripts Division, Washington, DC; Letter from JFK to Mrs. Medgar Evers, June 13, 1963," Burke Marshall Papers, Box 8, "Presidential, April 8, 1963–August 17, 1964 and undated," John F. Kennedy Library, Boston, Massachusetts; Sorensen, *Classic Biography*, 496–97.

46. Lewis's original line was, "We cannot support the administration's civil rights bill." At Kennedy's behest, he changed it: "It is true that we support the administration's civil rights bill in Congress. We support it with great reservations, however." Lewis also deleted "We will march through the South, through the heart of Dixie, the way Sherman did. We shall pursue our own scorched earth policy and burn Jim Crow to the ground nonviolently." John Lewis has been a Democratic member of the U.S. House of Representatives from Georgia since 1987.

47. Transcript of *Meet the Press*, produced by Lawrence E. Spivak. Guest: The Honorable Robert F. Kennedy, attorney general of the United States. June 23, 1963; vol. 7, no. 24. Merkle Press, Washington, DC, in Victor S. Navasky Papers, Box 3, "Background Civil Rights," Library of Congress Manuscripts Division, Washington, DC; Michael Lind, "The Candidate," review of *Robert Kennedy: His Life*, by Evan Thomas. *New York Times on the Web*, http:// www.nytimes.com/books/00/09/10/reviews/000910.10lind.html [accessed January 28, 2011]; *JFK: A Presidency Revealed*, DVD (New York: A&E Home Video, 2003).

48. Malcolm X criticized King for allowing the Kennedys to dilute the strength of the protest: "And as they took it over, it lost its militancy. It ceased to be angry, it ceased to be hot, it ceased to be uncompromising. Why, it even ceased to be a march. It became a picnic, a circus. Nothing but a circus, with clowns and all." Howard Zinn, *A People's History of the United States, 1492–Present* (New York: Harper Perennial, 1980), 458.

49. E. W. Kenworthy," 200,000 March for Civil Rights in Orderly Washington Rally," *New York Times*, August 29, 1963; Dallek, *Unfinished Life*, 645. There were many moderate and liberal Republicans serving in Congress at the time, and most ended up backing the civil rights bills of the 1960s.

50. James Reston, "Birmingham: The Crisis of Lawlessness in Alabama," *New York Times*, September 18, 1963; Sorensen, *Classic Biography*, 506; Comment by Sarah Collins Rudolph at UVA Center for Politics seminar, Charlottesville, Virginia, April 15, 2013.

6. EUROPE, SPACE, AND SOUTHEAST ASIA

1. John F. Kennedy, "The Strategy of Peace," in Theodore C. Sorensen, ed., *"Let the Word Go Forth": The Speeches, Statements, and Writings of John F. Kennedy* (New York: Delacorte Press, 1988), 282–90.

2. Arthur Schlesinger, Jr., *A Thousand Days: John F. Kennedy in the White House* (Boston: Houghton Mifflin, 1965), 904; Kenneth P. O'Donnell, David F. Powers, and Joe McCarthy, *"Johnny, We Hardly Knew Ye": Memories of John Fitzgerald Kennedy* (Boston: Little, Brown, 1970), 414–15; Bono, "What I Learned from Sargent Shriver," *New York Times*, January 19, 2011. Ireland's obsession with JFK has hardly waned in half a century. In 2013 various tributes to Kennedy were posted on the *Irish Times* website: http://www.irishtimes.com /culture/heritage [accessed June 19, 2013].

3. John Morton Blum, *Years of Discord: American Politics and Society, 1961–74* (New York: W. W. Norton, 1991), 114; John F. Kennedy, "'Ich bin ein Berliner' Speech (June 26, 1963)," Miller Center of Public Affairs, University of Virginia, http://millercenter.org/scripps /archive/speeches/detail/3376 [accessed February 1, 2011]; "Berlin Marks Kennedy Rally," BBC News, June 26, 2003, http://news.bbc.co.uk/2/hi/europe/3020202.stm [accessed February 2, 2011].

4. O'Donnell, Powers, and McCarthy, *"Johnny, We Hardly Knew Ye,"* 417–18.

5. Kennedy's advisers later realized that he should have said, "Ich bin Berliner" instead of "Ich bin ein Berliner" (*ein Berliner* can mean "jelly doughnut" in German). JFK learned the phrase from McGeorge Bundy during the flight to Germany. Bundy later wrote, "Fortunately the crowd in Berlin was untroubled by my mistake; no one in the square confused JFK with a doughnut." Michael R. Beschloss, *The Crisis Years: Kennedy and Khrushchev, 1960–63* (New York: Edward Burlingame Books, 1991), 606.

6. James Robert Carroll, *One of Ourselves: John Fitzgerald Kennedy in Ireland* (Bennington, VT: Images from the Past, 2003), 11–23.

7. Herbert S. Parmet, *JFK: The Presidency of John F. Kennedy* (New York: Penguin Books, 1984), 322–23; Carroll, *One of Ourselves*, 69.

8. O'Donnell, Powers, and McCarthy, *"Johnny, We Hardly Knew Ye,"* 421–23.

9. Carroll, *One of Ourselves*, 184.

10. Parmet, *JFK*, 323; Gerald Blaine with Lisa McCubbin, *The Kennedy Detail: JFK's Secret Service Agents Break Their Silence* (New York: Gallery Books, 2010), 84.

11. See "Travels of President John F. Kennedy," U.S. Department of State, Office of the Historian, http://history.state.gov/departmenthistory/travels/president/kennedy-john-f [accessed August 2, 2012].

12. O'Donnell, Powers, and McCarthy, *"Johnny, We Hardly Knew Ye,"* 424–25.

13. Jacqueline Jones, Peter H. Wood, Thomas Borstelmann, Elaine Tyler May, and Vicki L. Ruiz, *Created Equal: A Social and Political History of the United States,* 2nd ed. (New York: Pearson Longman, 2006), 868; John M. Murrin, Paul E. Johnson, James M. McPherson, Gary Gerstle, Emily S. Rosenberg, and Norman L. Rosenberg, *Liberty, Equality, Power: A History of the American People,* 3rd ed. (New York: Wadsworth/Thomson Learning, 2002), 995.

14. Parmet, *JFK,* 326; Richard Reeves, *President Kennedy: Profile of Power* (New York: Simon and Schuster, 1993), 490, 516.

15. Kennedy vacillated for many weeks. He did not want another Bay of Pigs to unfold in Southeast Asia. During meetings in late August, he peppered his aides with questions: Would it be possible to delay the coup until they could gather more information on the political situation in Saigon? Could the coup really succeed, and if so, what came next? How would the U.S. conceal its role in the operation?

16. Roger Hilsman, *To Move a Nation: The Politics of Foreign Policy in the Administration of John F. Kennedy* (New York: Dell Publishing, 1967), 481; Robert Dallek, *An Unfinished Life: John F. Kennedy, 1917–63* (Boston: Little, Brown, 2003), 674; diplomatic cable from Henry Lodge to JFK, August 30, 1963, John M. Newman Papers, Box 14, "30 August 1963," John F. Kennedy Library, Boston, Massachusetts.

17. Memorandum from Roger Hilsman to Dean Rusk, August 30, 1963, John Newman Papers, Box 14, "August 1963," John F. Kennedy Library, Boston, Massachusetts.

18. Howard Zinn, *A People's History of the United States, 1492–Present* (New York: Harper Perennial, 2003), 474–75; Blum, *Years of Discord,* 132; Parmet, *JFK,* 335; Tim Weiner, *Legacy of Ashes: The History of the CIA* (New York: Anchor Books, 2007), 242.

19. "JFK Library Releases Remaining Presidential Recordings," January 24, 2012, John F. Kennedy Presidential Library and Museum website, http://www.jfklibrary.org/About-Us /News-and-Press/Press-Releases/JFK-Library-Releases-Remaining-Presidential-Recordings .aspx [accessed January 24, 2012].

20. President's press conference, April 11, 1962, Neil Sheehan Papers, Box 69, Folder 13, Library of Congress Manuscripts Division, Washington, DC; John F. Kennedy, "Annual Message to the Congress on the State of the Union, January 14, 1963," John T. Woolley and Gerhard Peters, *The American Presidency Project,* Santa Barbara, CA, http://www.presi dency.ucsb.edu/ws/index.php?pid=9138 [accessed February 7, 2011]; "President Kennedy's Undelivered Remarks at the Trade Mart in Dallas 22 November 1963" in James N. Giglio and Stephen G. Rabe, *Debating the Kennedy Presidency* (Lanham, MD: Rowman and Littlefield, 2003), 92.

21. O'Donnell, Powers, and McCarthy, *"Johnny, We Hardly Knew Ye,"* 443.

22. Reeves, *President Kennedy,* 450; Jack Raymond, "G.O.P. Asks Candor on Vietnam War," *New York Times,* February 14, 1962; "An Open Letter to President John F. Kennedy Against U.S. Military Intervention in South Vietnam," April 11, 1962, and "An Open Letter to President John F. Kennedy For Ending the War and Making Peace in South Vietnam," March 18, 1963, Neil Sheehan Papers, Box 69, Folder 12, Library of Congress Manuscripts Division, Washington, DC.

23. Dallek, *Unfinished Life*, 685–86.

24. James W. Douglass believes that Kennedy had already decided to withdraw from Vietnam, "part of the larger strategy for peace that he and Nikita Khrushchev had become mutually committed to, which in Kennedy's case would result in his death." James W. Douglass, *JFK and the Unspeakable: Why He Died and Why It Matters* (New York: Simon and Schuster, 2008), 94.

25. Giglio and Rabe, *Debating the Kennedy Presidency*, 64.

26. Dallek, *An Unfinished Life*, 154.

27. Ted Sorensen, *Kennedy: The Classic Biography* (New York: Harper Perennial Political Classics, 2009), 734–40; John F. Kennedy, "Remarks at Dedication of Aerospace Medical Health Center, San Antonio, Texas, November 21, 1963," in Sorensen, *"Let the Word Go Forth,"* 181; James Giglio, *The Presidency of John F. Kennedy* (Lawrence: University Press of Kansas, 1991), 142–43.

28. Two court cases strengthened the Equal Pay Act: Schultz v. Wheaton Glass Co. (1970) and Corning Glass Works v. Brennan (1974). In 2009 President Obama expanded the amount of time women have to file a pay related grievance with the government by signing the Lily Ledbetter Fair Pay Restoration Act. For more information on both court cases and the Ledbetter Act, see Borgna Brunner, "The Equal Pay Act: A History of Pay Inequity in the U.S.," http://www.infoplease.com/spot/equalpayact1.html [accessed June 10, 2013].

29. JFK wrote: "Dedicated to my Mr. J. P. Kennedy. My recent allowance is [$].40. This I used for [airplanes] and other playthings of childhood but now I am a scout and I put away my childish things. Before I would spend 20 [cents] of my [40 cents] allowance and in five minutes I would have empty pockets and nothing to gain and 20 [cents] to lose. When I, a Scout, I have to buy canteens, haversacks, blankets, [searchlights], poncho things that will last for years and I can always use it while I can't use a chocolate marshmallow sundae with vanilla ice cream and so I put in my plea for a raise of thirty cents for me to buy scout things and pay my own way more around." Undated letter from JFK to Joseph P. Kennedy, "Correspondence, 1929–35," JFKPP-001-010, John F. Kennedy Presidential Library and Museum website, http://www.jfklibrary.org/Asset-Viewer/Archives/JFKPP-001-010.aspx [accessed May 1, 2013].

30. Seymour M. Hersh, *The Dark Side of Camelot* (Boston: Back Bay Books, 1997), 399; Reeves, *President Kennedy*, 626.

31. Hersh, *Dark Side*, 230; Cynthia R. Fagen, "Teen Mistress Addresses Relationship, Pol's Cold War Fears in Memoir," *New York Post*, February 5, 2012, http://www.nypost.com/p/news/national/inside_my_teen_affair_with_jfk_FGF4aS7OdoQozP4tyySsmK/o [accessed February 7, 2012]; Lance Morrow, "Woman, Interrupted," *Smithsonian* (December 2008): 87–95. In 1964 Meyer was murdered under mysterious circumstances during a botched robbery attempt in Washington, DC.

32. See J. Randy Taraborrelli, *The Secret Life of Marilyn Monroe* (New York: Grand Central Publishing, 2009), 409–17.

33. Mimi Alford, *Once Upon a Secret: My Affair with President John F. Kennedy and Its Aftermath* (New York: Random House, 2011). Mention of Alford, without details or a first-person account, first appeared in Robert Dallek's *An Unfinished Life*.

34. For more information on Kennedy's reckless philandering, see Ronald Kessler, "Secret Service Describes JFK as Reckless," Newsmax, February 13, 2012, http://www.newsmax.com

/Newsfront/Secret-Service-JFK-Alford/2012/02/13/id/429282 [accessed February 13, 2012], and Larry J. Sabato, *Feeding Frenzy: How Attack Journalism Has Transformed American Politics* (New York: Free Press, 1991), 33–42.

35. Sabato, *Feeding Frenzy*, 38.

36. Arthur Schlesinger thought that Kennedy's religion "was humane rather than doctrinal. He was a Catholic as Franklin Roosevelt was an Episcopalian—because he was born into the faith, lived in it and expected to die in it." Schlesinger also told the story of an evening at the White House when Kennedy had argued "with considerable particularity that nine of the ten commandments were derived from nature and almost seemed to imply that all religion was so derived." Sorensen never heard his boss "pray aloud" or "disclose his personal views on man's relation to God." Schlesinger, *Thousand Days*, 107; Sorensen, *Kennedy*, 19. On the other hand, Jackie Kennedy told Arthur Schlesinger in a private interview in the spring of 1964, which has now been made public, that President Kennedy would change into his pajamas prior to his afternoon nap, kneel at the bedside, and say his prayers. See Susan Cheever, "Jackie's Enduring Mystique," *Daily Beast*, September 17, 2011, http://www.thedailybeast.com/newsweek/2011/09/17/jackie-kennedy-tapes-show-us-what-we-lost.html [accessed December 27, 2012].

37. Thomas C. Reeves, *A Question of Character: A Life of John F. Kennedy* (Rocklin, CA: Prima Publishing, 1992), 400; Dallek, *Unfinished Life*, 633; "New York Times Chronology (October 1963)," John F. Kennedy Library website, http://www.jfklibrary.org/Research/Ready-Reference/New-York-Times-Chronology/Browse-by-Date/New-York-Times-Chronology-October-1963.aspx [accessed February 8, 2011].

7. ECHOES FROM DEALEY PLAZA

1. The historian was David Herbert Donald, a scholar of Lincoln and the Civil War. Molly Muldoon, "President John F. Kennedy Predicted His Own Assassination," *Irish Central*, June 3, 2001, http://www.irishcentral.com/news/President-John-F-Kennedy-predicted-his-own-assassination-123115643.html [accessed July 19, 2011]. See also Barney Henderson, "John F. Kennedy Made Ominous Legacy Prediction a Year Before Assassination," *The Telegraph*, June 2, 2011, http://www.telegraph.co.uk/news/worldnews/northamerica/usa/8553200/John-F-Kennedy-made-ominous-legacy-prediction-a-year-before-assassination.html [accessed July 13, 2011].

2. William Manchester, *The Death of a President: November 20–November 25, 1963* (New York: Harper and Row, 1967), 630.

3. Lyndon B. Johnson, "Executive Order 11130 Appointing a Commission to Report Upon the Assassination of President John F. Kennedy [Released November 30, 1963. Dated November 29, 1963]," Lyndon B. Johnson Papers, John T. Woolley and Gerhard Peters, *The American Presidency Project*, Santa Barbara, CA, http://www.presidency.ucsb.edu/ws/index.php?pid=26032#axzz1IeuLBveT [accessed April 6, 2011]. The influential journalist Joe Alsop helped convince LBJ of the need for a blue-ribbon panel to investigate the Kennedy assassination. See "LBJ-Alsop 11-25-63," *History Matters*, http://historymatters.com/archive/jfk/lbjlib/phone_calls/Nov_1963/audio/LBJ-Alsop_11-25-63.htm [accessed May 24, 2011]. In the latest installment of his award-winning series on LBJ, the historian Robert Caro says that Robert Kennedy recommended two of the appointees—McCloy and Dulles. This story, provided by Johnson himself, is almost certainly false. The Kennedys banished the Dulles clan from

Washington after the Bay of Pigs. Bobby convinced his brother to replace Allen Dulles with John McCone as head of CIA and forced Eleanor Dulles (Allen's sister) to resign from the State Department. See Robert Caro, *The Passage of Power* (New York: Alfred A. Knopf, 2012), 442–43; Leonard Mosley, *Dulles: A Biography of Eleanor, Allen, and John Foster Dulles and Their Family Network* (New York: Dial Press / James Wade, 1978), 473–74; and Eleanor Lansing Dulles, *Chances of a Lifetime: A Memoir* (Englewood Cliffs, NJ: Prentice Hall, 1980), 304–7; Rex Bradford, "Whispers From the Silent Generation," Mary Ferrell Foundation website, May 2013, http://www.maryferrell.org/wiki/index.php/Essay_-_Whispers_from _the_Silent_Generation [accessed June 15, 2013].

4. Specter served in the U.S. Senate from 1981 to 2011, representing Pennsylvania. He was a Republican until 2009, when he changed parties and became a Democrat. Defeated for reelection in 2010, Specter died in 2012.

5. Kathryn S. Olmsted, *Real Enemies: Conspiracy Theories and American Democracy, World War I to 9/11* (New York: Oxford University Press, 2009), 131.

6. Arthur M. Schlesinger, Jr., *Robert Kennedy and His Times* (Boston: Houghton Mifflin, 1978), 615. Katzenbach "maintained later that his goal had been to gather, not cover up, evidence against Lee Harvey Oswald, who he was convinced was the lone assassin." Douglas Martin, "Nicholas Katzenbach, Trusted Adviser to JFK and LBJ, Dies at 90," *New York Times*, May 9, 2012.

7. Harris Wofford, *Of Kennedys and Kings: Making Sense of the Sixties* (Pittsburgh: University of Pittsburgh Press, 1980), 415. At 4:01 P.M. EST on November 22, two and a half hours after the assassination, Hoover sent a memo to aides naming Oswald as the prime suspect. See "Memorandum for Mr. Tolson [et al.]," JFK Lancer website, http://www.jfklancer.com /backes/newman/documents/hoover/Hoover_RFK.JPG [accessed May 22, 2013]. Hoover apparently quashed an FBI investigation of the National States Rights Party as well. See IC Robert G. Renfro to SAC, Dallas, November 22, 1963, http://jfkmurdersolved.com/hoover .htm [accessed May 22, 2013].

8. Oswald attempted to kill Major General Edwin Walker in April 1963 (discussed in a subsequent chapter). The case was still open at the time of JFK's assassination.

9. Anthony Summers, *The Kennedy Conspiracy* (London: Sphere Books, 1989), 283–85. Dallas FBI Agent James P. Hosty, Jr., twice visited the Paine residence in November 1963. Hosty had inherited the Oswald file from Fort Worth FBI Agent John Fain. On November 1, 1963, Hosty visited Ruth Paine's house in Irving. Marina and her children were living with Paine at the time. Paine told Hosty that Marina and Lee had separated and that Lee worked at the Texas School Book Depository. Paine also said that Lee lived somewhere in the Oak Cliff neighborhood, but she wasn't sure where. Hosty and a second FBI agent returned on November 5. Paine told the agents that she still didn't have Lee's address, but that he had described himself to her as a Trotskyist-Marxist. James P. Hosty, Jr., *Assignment: Oswald* (New York: Arcade Publishing, 1996); "Papers of James Hosty, Jr.," National Archives and Records Administration website, http://www.archives.gov/research/jfk/finding-aids/hosty -papers.html [accessed June 13, 2011].

10. Without clear written evidence, which is not available, it is difficult to impute a motive here, but surely protection of the FBI's reputation weighed on Hoover at the time observers began to assess blame for the murder of the president.

11. Michael L. Kurtz, *The JFK Assassination Debates: Lone Gunman versus Conspiracy* (Lawrence: University Press of Kansas, 2006), 21; Joseph A. Loftus, "Oswald Assassin Beyond

a Doubt, F.B.I. Concludes," *New York Times*, December 10, 1963; Laurence Stern, "FBI Keeps Silent on Contents As Dallas File Goes to Warren," *Washington Post and Times Herald*, December 10, 1963.

12. Later on, I will review the evidence about this topic, including the stray bullet that hit a curb (missing the target entirely) and the timing of the shots as determined by the available film and photographic evidence.

13. Abraham Zapruder was a Dallas dressmaker who happened to be filming the president's motorcade at the exact moment of the assassination, from a well-positioned perch atop a concrete pedestal on what is now known as the grassy knoll. The Warren Commission obtained the film in January 1964. While some still frames from the film were released from 1963 into the 1970s, the public never saw the entire Zapruder film until 1975.

14. The Warren Commission initially concluded that "A bullet had entered his [JFK's] back at a point slightly above the shoulder and to the right of the spine." Ford wanted the sentence to read, "A bullet had entered the back of his neck at a point slightly to the right of the spine." The final report said: "A bullet had entered the base of the back of his neck slightly to the right of the spine." Mike Feinsilber, "Ford Altered Crucial JFK Report: His Revision Raised the Location of the Wound," *Seattle Post-Intelligencer*, July 3, 1997. Here's the *London Independent*'s version of the same story: "The former U.S. president, Gerald Ford, altered a key sentence in the Warren Commission report to strengthen its conclusion that John F. Kennedy was killed by a single bullet, it emerged yesterday. The effect of his editing was to suggest that a single bullet struck the assassinated president in the neck and severely wounded Texas Governor John Connally—a crucial element in its controversial finding that Lee Harvey Oswald was the sole gunman . . . Ford said last night that it was a small change, one intended to clarify the report and not to alter history." Kate Watson-Smyth, "Ford Tampered with Report on JFK Shooting," *The Independent* (London, UK), July 3, 1997.

15. Mark Lane, *Rush to Judgment* (New York: Thunder's Mouth Press, 1992), 7–8; Kurtz, *Assassination Debates*, 21–22; Olmsted, *Real Enemies*, 128; Joe Stephens, "Ford Told FBI of Skeptics on Warren Commission," *Washington Post*, August 8, 2008; Mike Feinsilber, "Ford Altered Crucial JFK Report," *Seattle Post-Intelligencer*, July 3, 1997.

16. On two separate occasions in the 1990s, Ford told me personally that he was convinced of the commission report's accuracy and of the critics' wrongheadedness. His sincerity in this belief is unquestioned. On January 31, 1997, Ford affixed his signature to a statement on his own letterhead which read in full: "In 1964, the Warren Commission decided: 1. Lee Harvey Oswald was the assassin, and 2. There was no conspiracy, foreign or domestic. I endorsed those conclusions in 1964 and fully agree now."

17. Memorandum from David E. Murphy to the Deputy Director for Plans, April 13, 1964, House Select Committee on Assassinations Segregated CIA Collection, Box 5, NARA #104-10051-10288, Mary Ferrell Foundation website, http://www.maryferrell.org/mffweb/archive/viewer/showDoc.do?docId=39161&relPageId=3 [accessed September 28, 2012].

18. From the 1930s to the mid-1960s, journalists engaged in what I have termed "lapdog" journalism—reporting that served and reinforced the political establishment. During this period, mainstream journalists rarely challenged prevailing orthodoxy, accepted at face value much of what those in power told them, and protected politicians by revealing little

about their nonofficial lives, even when private vices affected their public performance. Wartime necessities encouraged the lapdog mentality but it had already become well established in Franklin Roosevelt's earlier administrations. Lapdog journalism perhaps reached its zenith under John F. Kennedy. See chapter 2 of my book *Feeding Frenzy* (New York: Free Press, 1993), 25–51.

19. Charles Mohr, "President Gets Assassination Report," *New York Times*, September 25, 1964; "The Warren Report: Official Summary and Conclusions of Commission," *Chicago Tribune*, September 28, 1964; Marquis Childs, "Warren Report: Remedy for Rumor," *Washington Post and Times Herald*, September 28, 1964.

20. Max Holland, *The Kennedy Assassination Tapes* (New York: Alfred A. Knopf, 2004), 250. Author and "lone gunman" advocate Gerald Posner credits Holland with debunking some of the myths surrounding Johnson's and Russell's conversation, and his interpretation is different from others': "Although some authors have cited this passage as evidence that the two men did not share the commission's lone-assassin conclusion, they were actually referring to Russell's doubts about the single-bullet theory. Holland rightly points out: 'When Johnson proclaims that he doesn't believe in the single-bullet theory either, it is a blatant example of his tendency to speak for effect. He has not studied the issue; indeed he doesn't understand what the issue is. He is just trying to agree with his old mentor Russell and get to the subject he really wants to talk about: Vietnam'" (249). Gerald Posner, review of *The Kennedy Assassination Tapes: The White House Conversations of Lyndon B. Johnson Regarding the Assassination, the Warren Commission, and the Aftermath*, by Max Holland, *Journal of Cold War Studies* 9, no. 2 (Spring 2007): 154–56. Posner may be right, but it is difficult to get inside LBJ's head and assert with certainty that he is "speaking for effect." One also doubts that the highly intuitive Johnson, who had been present at the assassination and had thought a great deal about it, didn't "understand what the issue is."

21. "Television: Why the Aliens Keep On Coming Back," *Sunday Times*, November 14, 2004, http://entertainment.timesonline.co.uk/tol/arts_and_entertainment/article389474 .ece [accessed April 7, 2011].

22. "John F. Kennedy's Assassination Leaves a Legacy of Suspicion," ABC News Poll: Who Killed JFK? November 9, 2003, http://abcnews.go.com/images/pdf/937a1JFKAssassi nation.pdf [accessed April 8, 2011].

23. Americans are now probably conditioned to believe conspiracy theories. A 2004 Zogby poll found that 49% of New Yorkers say that government officials knew about the 9/11 attacks in advance. See Cass R. Sunstein and Adrian Vermeule, "Conspiracy Theories," Harvard University and University of Chicago Public Law and Legal Theory Research Paper Series, http://papers.ssrn.com/sol3/papers.cfm?abstract_id=1084585 [accessed May 26, 2011].

24. Telephone interview with Nancy Pelosi, May 26, 2011.

25. The London Daily Mail Online, April 19, 2011, http://www.dailymail.co.uk/news /article-1378284/Secret-memo-shows-JFK-demanded-UFO-files-10-days-assassination.html [accessed April 19, 2011].

26. Personal interview with Jerry Dealey, January 14, 2011, Dallas, Texas.

27. The basement is mostly abandoned now, along with the old city jail where Oswald spent his last nights. It is obvious that the basement should have been cleared of all but police personnel and a small pool of reporters and cameras. But in 1963, the Dallas police made the fatal mistake of allowing a crowd to gather in the basement, large enough to enable the murder of the most historically significant prisoner they would ever hold.

28. Kurtz, *Assassination Debates*, 23–26; William E. Scott, *November 22, 1963: A Reference Guide to the JFK Assassination* (Lanham, MD: University Press of America, 1999), 29; Warren Commission Hearings, vol. XXIV, CE 2011, p. 411, Mary Ferrell Foundation website, http://www.maryferrell.org/mffweb/archive/viewer/showDoc.do [accessed June 12, 2012].

29. Interview with Bill and Gayle Newman, July 10, 2003, conducted by Stephen Fagin, Sixth Floor Museum at Dealey Plaza, Dallas, Texas.

30. Almost forty-seven years after the assassination, when I interviewed the Newmans in Dallas on September 24, 2010, Bill Newman clarified that he thought the shots had come from behind him, but not necessarily from the grassy knoll. "What I try not to do, if I'm talking to a group of people . . . and I make the statement that I thought the shot came from behind—the 'shot' meaning the head shot—it was a visual impact that it had on me more so than the noise. Seeing the side of the president's head blow off, see the president go across the car seat into Mrs. Kennedy's lap, in her direction, it gave me the sensation that the shots were coming from directly behind me where I was standing. So, I said 'behind,' and I leave it at that, and then a lot of times, the interviewer or whoever it may be will say, 'Behind to your left?' meaning the School Book Depository. 'Behind to your right?' meaning the picket fence. And I just leave it. I won't define it."

31. "Full Gayle & Bill Newman Interview by Jay Watson," YouTube, http://www.youtube.com/watch?v=3fPpLegSn1k [accessed April 14, 2011]. Officer D. V. Harkness, who was interviewed by the Warren Commission, recalled a similar scenario. "The first shot, Kennedy I think grabbed like this (motions). I was looking right at him. And then the next one he jerked (motions), [and] that was the second shot. And then [the] third one went wild, I think, I don't know." Interview with David V. Harkness, June 29, 2006, conducted by Stephen Fagin, Sixth Floor Museum at Dealey Plaza, Dallas, Texas. This is quite different from the assessment of the Newmans. In fact, witnesses reported many combinations of the number of shots, the impacts of the shots, and the directions from which they came.

32. Interview with Bill and Gayle Newman, July 10, 2003, conducted by Stephen Fagin, Sixth Floor Museum at Dealey Plaza, Dallas, Texas. Also, personal interview with the author, September 24, 2010, Dallas. We often forget the impact that a trauma like 11/22 can have on a family. Bill Newman told me that for several nights following the assassination, he huddled his family together in one bedroom, his 20-gauge shotgun nearby. "My concern was that [the shooter] might have thought we were a threat and could have testified against them in court." Their young son, Billy, asked his mother several days later, "Why did they shoot that man? Did you see all that blood?"

33. E-mail from Gary Mack, June 29, 2011.

34. Personal interview with H. B. McLain, March 17, 2011.

35. Interview with Marilyn Sitzman, June 29, 1993, conducted by Wes Wise with Bob Porter, Sixth Floor Museum at Dealey Plaza, Dallas, Texas; "Abraham Zapruder Film," Sixth Floor Museum at Dealey Plaza website, http://www.jfk.org/go/collections/item-detail?fedoraid=sfm:1999.042 [accessed April 25, 2011].

36. "Filming Kennedy: Home Movies From Dallas, Elsie Dorman," http://www.jfk.org/go/exhibits/home-movies/elsie-dorman [accessed April 15, 2011]; Vincent Bugliosi, *Reclaiming History: The Assassination of President John F. Kennedy* (New York: W. W. Norton, 2007), endnotes on enclosed compact disc, 155, 256–57.

37. The Towners did not come forward voluntarily during the commission's investigation. On the other hand, the commission could have been much more aggressive in urging

witnesses to do so and in attempting to identify witnesses from the many photographs taken in and around Dealey Plaza. The Towners' story and pictures were featured in the November 24, 1967, edition of *Life* magazine. See "Nov. 22, 1963, Dallas: Photos By Nine Bystanders," *Life*, November 24, 1967, 87–94. Personal interview, September 24, 2010, Dallas, with Tina Towner Pender, who was thirteen years old in 1963 and standing next to her parents in Dealey Plaza, Dallas. See also Tina Towner Pender, *Tina Towner: My Story as the Youngest Photographer at the Kennedy Assassination* (Charleston, SC: Createspace.com, 2012).

    38. Interview with Jim, Patricia, and Tina Towner, March 30, 1996, conducted by Bob Porter with Gary Mack, Sixth Floor Museum at Dealey Plaza, Dallas, Texas.

    39. Eugene Boone, a Dallas County deputy sheriff, also encountered a porter (probably Desroe) in the freight yard behind the picket fence. "And we both were scared," Boone recalls. "And it wasn't but just a moment until I could discover . . . that he was back there cleaning up the cars and didn't have anything to do with it." The porter did not report anything suspicious to Boone. Like Jim Towner, Boone does not believe that there were additional gunmen either in front of or behind the picket fence. Interview with Eugene Boone, November 25, 2003, conducted by Stephen Fagin, Sixth Floor Museum at Dealey Plaza, Dallas, Texas. For more information on the Desroes' story, see the interview with Bishop Mark Herbener, February 1, 2006, conducted by Stephen Fagin, Sixth Floor Museum at Dealey Plaza, Dallas, Texas.

    40. Summers, *Kennedy Conspiracy*, 25–26; Jim Marrs, *Crossfire: The Plot That Killed Kennedy* (New York: Carroll and Graf, 1989), 29. See also John Chism's statement to the FBI, 12/18/63, available on Prof. John McAdams's website, "The Kennedy Assassination," http://jfkassassination.net/russ/exhibits/ce2091.htm [accessed July 3, 2012].

    41. See Barry Ernest, *The Girl on the Stairs: My Search for a Missing Witness to the Assassination of John F. Kennedy* (Lexington, KY: CreateSpace Publishing, 2011) and Christopher Means, "JFK Historian Studies 'Missing Witness' Who Should Have Seen Oswald," *Pegasus News*, February 15, 2011, http://news.yahoo.com/blogs/pegasus-news/jfk-historian-studies-missing-witness-seen-oswald-20110215-120738-700.html [accessed January 9, 2012].

    42. Arnold also said that a man in a suit who identified himself as either a CIA or Secret Service agent ordered him away from the railroad bridge overlooking Dealey Plaza before the president's motorcade passed by. Interview with Gordon Arnold, June 6, 1989, conducted by Conover Hunt, Sixth Floor Museum at Dealey Plaza, Dallas, Texas; interview with Mary and Les Arnold, January 13, 2006, conducted by Gary Mack with Stephen Fagin, Sixth Floor Museum at Dealey Plaza, Dallas, Texas. Posner, author of *Case Closed*, rejects Arnold's version of events: "Although Arnold claims he is not visible [in the pictures of the knoll] because he is lying flat on the ground, photo enhancements show no such person." Posner also points out that, "Arnold appeared vindicated when Senator Ralph Yarborough [D-TX] later said he remembered seeing a young man 'throw himself on the ground' as soon as the shooting started. However, Yarborough has since clarified that he was referring to Bill Newman, who was at the foot of the grassy knoll with his family and threw himself, his wife, and their two children onto the grass." Gerald Posner, *Case Closed: Lee Harvey Oswald and the Assassination of JFK* (New York: Anchor Books, 1994), 255–56. Sixth Floor Museum curator Gary Mack disagrees with Posner's conclusions: "My understanding is different, and far more accurate since I spoke to Arnold, Earl Golz, and Dave Murph, the source of the later Yarborough interview. Golz' 1978 *Dallas Morning News* story about Arnold repeatedly referred to him as a *soldier*. After reading Golz' story, Yarborough called him the next day to confirm he

had seen that man (or such a man) hit the ground. So to clarify, a few years later, I asked Arnold what he was wearing that day because Golz had not. That's when Arnold said he wore his 'Army tans,' which explained to me how Yarborough knew that the man who hit the ground was the soldier. Newman didn't look anything like a soldier." E-mail from Gary Mack, May 25, 2012. See Earl Golz, "SS 'Imposters' Spotted by JFK Witnesses," *Dallas Morning News*, August 27, 1978.

43. Arnold said the man who accosted him had very noticeable "dirty fingernails." A Dallas police officer, Joe Marshall Smith, had an encounter with an unusual individual on the grassy knoll immediately after the assassination that fit the same description. This case is discussed on p. 152.

44. Marrs, *Crossfire*, 81–83. Posner says that Hoffman was "some 250 to 300 yards west of the picket fence" and told two different versions of the story. In 1967, he "said he saw two men running from the rear of the Texas School Book Depository, but the FBI concluded he could not have seen them from where he was because a fence west of the Depository blocked his view. He then changed his story to say he saw the men on top of the fence." None of the four policemen stationed "near where Hoffman claimed to be" said that they had seen him there. Posner also reports that there were a number of objects obstructing Hoffman's view, including freight cars and a giant Cutty Sark liquor billboard (Posner, *Case Closed*, 256–57). But Gary Mack, curator of the Sixth Floor Museum at Dealey Plaza, while admitting that there are problems with Hoffman's story, again contradicts Posner: "There were no freight cars at the time and the [Cutty Sark] sign was not in the way from where Hoffman claimed to be." E-mail from Gary Mack, May 25, 2012.

45. Interview with Ken Duvall, May 12, 2009, conducted by Stephen Fagin, Sixth Floor Museum at Dealey Plaza, Dallas, Texas.

46. Gary Mack, who describes Rodriguez's tale as "another false story," told us that the "railroad men were on private property and had every legal right to remain there. Dallas police asked the railroad to ID all of the men to confirm they were employees, and a supervisor was sent over and confirmed every one of them." E-mail from Gary Mack, May 25, 2012.

47. Interview with Victoria Wahlstrom Rodriguez, July 7, 2010, conducted by Stephen Fagin, Sixth Floor Museum at Dealey Plaza, Dallas, Texas.

48. Craig told the Warren Commission that he saw a "Nash Rambler" and that "it looked white to me." In later years, he changed his story and insisted that the vehicle he saw had been "light green" in color. See Warren Commission Hearings, vol. VI, p. 267, Mary Ferrell Foundation website, http://www.maryferrell.org/mffweb/archive/viewer/showDoc.do?docId=35 &relPageId=277 [accessed June 13, 2012].

49. Ruth Paine spoke Russian and befriended the Oswalds when they moved to Dallas. When Marina decided to separate from her husband, she moved in with Ruth. The Paines owned a green 1955 Chevrolet station wagon, not a white Rambler station wagon, though one could argue they are not completely dissimilar.

50. James W. Douglass, *JFK and the Unspeakable: Why He Died and Why It Matters* (New York: Touchstone, 2008), 274–75. Craig said that he reported the Rambler incident to police headquarters on the day of the assassination. Marrs, *Crossfire*, 329–30.

51. See the Warren Report (St. Martin's Press edition, 1991), p. 52: "Other Secret Service agents assigned to the motorcade remained at their posts during the race to the hospital. None stayed at the scene of the shooting, and none entered the Texas School Book Deposi-

tory Building at or immediately after the shooting . . . Forrest V. Sorrels, special agent in charge of the Dallas office, was the first Secret Service agent to return to the scene of the assassination, approximately 20 or 25 minutes after the shots were fired." See also http://www .history-matters.com/archive/jfk/wc/wr/html/WCReport_0038b.htm [accessed November 30, 2012].

52. Gary Mack of the Sixth Floor Museum wrote in an e-mail dated August 30, 2011, "The first officer to 'climb the grassy knoll' up the steps toward the fence and triple underpass was Clyde Haygood, one of the motorcade escort officers. There was no one with him. Within another minute or two, other officers ran there too and a few were accompanied by sheriff's deputies. Joe Marshall Smith was stationed in the Elm-Houston intersection and he ran straight west along the Elm Street Extension directly in front of the Depository, NOT on Elm Street where the motorcade had passed. Smith encountered an unidentified man somewhere behind the [picket] fence and the man claimed to be with the Secret Service (the Service had NO men on the ground at the time). Two short pieces of TV news film (Mal Couch/WFAA and Jimmy Darnell/WBAP) caught Smith as he ran, but it is not possible to identify him since the photographers were in the same car at Smith's left, and the scenes show him essentially from the side."

53. In his 2011 book *JFK Assassination Logic*, John McAdams says that the record shows that the Secret Service agent Smith encountered helped him search the parking lot behind the picket fence, thereby diminishing the possibility of a conspiracy. However, it is not clear from the Warren Commission hearings whether Smith, now deceased, was referring to the agent or another law enforcement officer who was standing nearby. See Joe Marshall Smith's testimony before the Warren Commission, Warren Commission Hearings, vol. 7, p. 535, Mary Ferrell Foundation website, http://www.maryferrell.org/mffweb/archive/viewer/showDoc .do?docId=41&relPageId=545 [accessed December 21, 2011] and John McAdams, *JFK Assassination Logic: How to Think About Claims of Conspiracy* (Washington: Potomac Books, 2011), 16.

54. In an earlier personal interview in Dallas (September 25, 2010), in response to a question about Officer Smith's story, Mack agreed that it was chilling, noting that it is "a good example of what I learned in journalism school. When the logical thing doesn't happen, that's where the story is. Well what's the logical thing in this case? The Warren Commission should have said to the Secret Service, we want to know who that guy [the one claiming to be an agent] is. They did nothing of the sort . . . They [the Commission] questioned the head of the Secret Service and he said 'There's nothing there.' That was the end of it." Smith's testimony before the Warren Commission can also be found here: http://mcadams .posc.mu.edu/russ/testimony/smith_j1.htm. One individual, now deceased, has claimed to be the person who manufactured phony Secret Service credentials for use in Dallas on November 22. His name was Chauncey Holt, a military deserter with a criminal record who supposedly forged documents for the Mafia and the CIA in the early 1960s. Other parts of Holt's story do not check out or cannot be corroborated. See "Bottom Line: How Crazy Is It?" *Newsweek*, December 22, 1991, reprinted on the *Daily Beast* website, http://www.thedaily beast.com/newsweek/1991/12/23/bottom-line-how-crazy-is-it.html [accessed November 8, 2011].

55. Summers, *Kennedy Conspiracy*, 36–37; personal interview with Gary Mack, September 25, 2010, Dallas.

56. In his most recent book, *The Last Word*, Mark Lane argues that the man Smith saw

behind the picket fence was a CIA operative. I had thoroughly investigated Smith's story before I knew about Lane's book. It is one of the most disturbing and unexplained pieces of evidence, so it is not a surprise that other researchers would focus on it. See Mark Lane, *The Last Word: My Indictment of the CIA in the Murder of JFK* (New York: Skyhorse Publishing, 2011), 188–92.

57. Telephone interview with Robert Blakey, July 8, 2011. Blakey has also considered the possibility that the hit man, thinking that Oswald's first bullet or bullets had not yet fatally wounded Kennedy, decided to undertake the task himself. He may have fired his gun almost simultaneously with Oswald's, and perhaps believing that his weapon, not Oswald's, had caused the president's fatal head wound, quickly retreated as the motorcade sped on—leaving his assigned duty of eliminating Oswald undone.

58. Personal interview with Pierce Allman, Dallas, September 24, 2010. Allman thinks that Oswald was the lone gunman, but he is nonetheless puzzled about the incident with the Army Intelligence representative. The FBI interviewed Powell on January 3, 1964. Gary Mack of the Sixth Floor Museum at Dealey Plaza told us the man Allman met is probably Powell. E-mail from Gary Mack, July 5, 2011. Powell's photo of the Depository shows the boxes of books stacked up near the window ledge of the alleged Oswald perch on the sixth floor, though no one is visible. The details about Powell appear at http://www.history-mat ters.com/analysis/witness/witnessMap/Powell.htm and http://jfkassassinationfiles.com /arrb_interview [accessed January 3, 2013].

59. According to Summers, the armed individual may have also said, "You all better not come up here. You can get shot or killed." In any case, Summers believed he understood what the man meant.

60. Like every other aspect of 11/22, there is avid speculation about Oswald's real destination after the assassination. Conspiracy believers think Oswald was supposed to meet some undefined contacts in Oak Cliff, who would then spirit him away to safety. Law enforcement and nonconspiracy researchers are of the opinion that Oswald may have concocted a half-baked plan to escape to Mexico and from there to Cuba or points unknown. While he had left most of his money for Marina, Oswald had a bit less than $15 in his pockets when captured. In the early 1960s this was enough (barely) for bus transportation to Mexico. Other observers speculate that Oswald had not even expected to get away from the Depository, and without a plan, he was simply wandering aimlessly, which is how he ended up inside the Texas Theatre.

61. Interview with Malcolm Summers, March 7, 2002, conducted by Gary Mack, Stephen Fagin, and Arlinda Abbott, Sixth Floor Museum at Dealey Plaza, Dallas, Texas.

62. The officer's correct name is Charles Burnley, but the Warren Report misspells the name as Burnely.

63. "Testimony of Mrs. Earlene Roberts," Warren Commission Hearings, vol. VI, pp. 443–44, *History Matters*, http://www.history-matters.com/archive/jfk/wc/wcvols/wh6 /html/WC_Vol6_0227a.htm [accessed May 16, 2011]; Douglass, *JFK and the Unspeakable*, 289.

64. Interview with Marvin Lynn Wise, November 14, 1977, conducted by Harold Rose, *JFK Assassination Files* website, http://jfkassassinationfiles.com/hsca_180-10112-10156 [accessed June 7, 2012].

65. Gary Mack says that he "started [this] theory from observing video of Harrelson in 1979, after his arrest for killing Judge Wood, and noting the strong similarity with the tall

tramp; this of course was 10 years before anyone knew the names of the arrested tramps."
E-mail from Gary Mack, May 30, 2012.

66. Interview with David V. Harkness, June 29, 2006, conducted by Stephen Fagin, Sixth
Floor Museum at Dealey Plaza, Dallas, Texas; Marrs, *Crossfire*, 333–36; Bugliosi, *Reclaiming
History*, 907; Posner, *Case Closed*, 271–72. You can listen to part of Hunt's deathbed "confession" here: http://www.youtube.com/watch?v=bknUDgKdEJQ&feature=youtube and read
about it in Erik Hedegaard's "The Last Confession of E. Howard Hunt," *Rolling Stone,* April
5, 2007, 44–84. In the mid-1970s, a presidential commission headed by Vice President Nelson Rockefeller studied the past activities and misadventures of the CIA. The commission
compared photographs of the tramps to photographs of Hunt taken before and after November 22, 1963, and found that "even to non-experts it appeared that there was, at best, only
a superficial resemblance between the Dallas 'derelicts' and Hunt . . . The 'derelict' allegedly
resembling Hunt appeared to be substantially older and smaller than Hunt." See Nelson A.
Rockefeller, *Report to the President by the Commission on CIA Activities Within the United
States* (New York: Manor Books, 1975), 257.

67. Telephone interview with Mary Moorman, now Mary Moorman Krahmer, March 5,
2013. As always, it can be argued that Moorman's vision was fixed on JFK and Jackie, and she
might not have noticed something happening on or near the grassy knoll. She told me, for
instance, that she had no recollection of having seen Abraham Zapruder directly across
from her, even though he shows up in her photograph.

68. Interview with Jean Hill, February 1989, conducted by Bob Hays, Sixth Floor Museum at Dealey Plaza, Dallas, Texas; Posner, *Case Closed*, 251–52. During a 1993 interview,
Bill Sloan (who coauthored a book with Hill entitled *JFK: The Last Dissenting Witness*) admitted, "I think though that I cannot in all honesty sit here and tell you that I believe everything Jean said, but I truly believe that Jean believed everything she said. Now, I don't know
if this was a classic case of self-brainwashing or whatever you want to call it, but I think she
had made these statements so many times over the years that she had come to believe them
firmly herself." Interview with Bill Sloan, July 31, 2001, conducted by Bob Porter with Stephen Fagin and Anna Besch, Sixth Floor Museum at Dealey Plaza, Dallas, Texas. By contrast, Mary Moorman's contribution to the history of 11/22 is worth ten thousand words. Her
picture of the president's limousine as it cruised down Elm Street has fascinated researchers
for decades. In 1989, author Jim Marrs wrote, "[An] enlargement of the knoll area in her
photo seems to reveal a man [aka "Badge Man"] firing a rifle. The man is dressed in what
appears to be a police uniform." Marrs, *Crossfire*, 88. The "Badge Man" photo has been analyzed and reanalyzed over the decades. Some say there is a man there, while others insist the
image is just leaves and shadows in an indistinct background. Mary Moorman rejects the
Badge-Man interpretation of her famous photo and told me flatly, "There is no such thing as
the Badge Man." Telephone interview with Mary Moorman Krahmer, March 5, 2013. As for
Hill's later assertions, Moorman said that she could account for all of the photographs she
took on 11/22 and that she and Hill went straight to the sheriff's office after the assassination.
Regarding Hill's claim that she was accosted by Secret Service agents, Moorman says bluntly,
"Didn't happen." "Mary Moorman Breaks Her Silence—iAntique.com Interview," iAntique
.com, May 24, 2011, http://vimeo.com/24228714 [accessed May 31, 2011]. Moorman reaffirmed
this evaluation of Hill's somewhat flamboyant pronouncements in her interview with me.

69. Douglass, *JFK and the Unspeakable*, 297–303; personal interview with Gary Mack,
February 22, 2011, Dallas, Texas.

70. Marina Oswald and Kenneth Porter married in 1965, had a son, and then divorced in 1974. The Porters have apparently reconciled and continue to live together in Texas, though they appear not to have remarried. Porter helped Marina raise Lee Harvey Oswald's children.

71. See, for example, Marina's recent TV interview with former Minnesota governor Jesse Ventura: http://12160.info/video/conspiracy-theory-with-jesse-2?xg_source=shorten _twitter (the second clip at the 11-minute, 30-second mark [accessed January 3, 2013]). See also Marina's correspondence with the Assassination Records Review Board, in which she expresses her doubts about her former husband's guilt: http://www.jfk-info.com/mar04.htm and here: http://www.jfk-info.com/mar09.htm [accessed January 3, 2013].

72. Oddly, Leavelle was stationed at Pearl Harbor on December 7, 1941—the date prior to 11/22/63 that is indelibly imprinted on the American consciousness. As Leavelle put it, he had "double duty" in U.S. history.

73. For example, British author Michael Eddowes convinced Marina that her former husband had been replaced, prior to November 22, with a look-alike Soviet agent who actually killed Kennedy. With Marina's support, the Dallas authorities exhumed Oswald's remains in the fall of 1981, but dental records confirmed beyond any doubt that Lee Harvey Oswald and no one else was buried in his grave. This macabre event received wide national press coverage at the time—just as almost anything concerning the Kennedy assassination has done for fifty years. See Michael Eddowes, *The Oswald File* (New York: Ace Books, 1978) and "JFK Video: The Dallas Tapes," KDFW, Fox 4 Special Project, Dallas–Fort Worth, http://www.myfoxdfw.com/subindex/news/fox_4_projects/jfk_video [accessed March 19, 2012].

74. Personal interview with Jim Leavelle, April 8, 2011, Dallas, Texas.

75. Telephone interview with Henry Hurt, June 1, 2011.

76. Interview with Bob Schieffer, March 4, 2013.

77. Bill Alexander, Dallas's assistant district attorney in 1963 who was the first to gather evidence in Oswald's residence hours after the assassination, is another who believes that Oswald carried out the shootings on his own, and that his own paper trail—"Oswald was a paper-saver," says Alexander—helped the police put together their case quickly. Personal interview, January 14, 2011, Dallas, Texas.

78. Interview with Tom Dillard, July 19, 1993, conducted by Wes Wise with Bob Porter, Sixth Floor Museum at Dealey Plaza, Dallas.

79. Telephone interviews with Mal Couch, March 21 and 23, 2011.

80. Gary Mack, the curator of the Sixth Floor Museum at Dealey Plaza, told me that "Seymour Weitzman is almost certainly the man Mal Couch saw." But Weitzman gave the Warren Commission two seemingly contradictory accounts. As noted in the text, Weitzman said "somebody brought me a piece of what he thought to be a firecracker and it [supposedly] turned out to be . . . a portion of the president's skull." But when asked if he was the one who had picked up the skull fragment off the street, Weitzman replied, "Yes." E-mail from Gary Mack, June 10, 2011.

81. From the transcript of Weitzman's testimony, available at http://jfkassassination.net /russ/testimony/weitzman.htm [accessed January 3, 2013]. Also, e-mail from Gary Mack of the Sixth Floor Museum, Dallas, June 10, 2011. Mack notes, "Amateur photographer Jack Daniel, who filmed the motorcade from the other side of the triple underpass, also saw it happen after walking into the Plaza shortly after [the picking up of the skull fragment]."

82. http://jfkassassination.net/russ/testimony/weitzman.htm [accessed August 3, 2011].

83. Thomas Sills, Jr., for example, watched the parade from the corner of Main and Houston. During a 2008 interview, Stephen Fagin of the Sixth Floor Museum asked Sills how many shots he had heard. "I'm gonna say three," he replied. "You know, that's what I remember. I was nine years old and like I said. I mean, it could've maybe even been just two, but I didn't hear more than three." Fagin: "When you described it a few minutes ago, you only mentioned two shots." Sills: "Yeah." Fagin: "Saying 'three,' does that maybe come from the things you've read later?" Sills: "It might've, it might have . . ." Interview with Thomas Sills, Jr., June 30, 2008, conducted by Stephen Fagin, Sixth Floor Museum at Dealey Plaza, Dallas.

84. For example, see the interviews conducted with Ernest Brandt, May 12, 1994, and John Templin, July 28, 1995, both conducted by Bob Porter, Sixth Floor Museum at Dealey Plaza, Dallas. Brandt and Templin did not come forward as witnesses until 1993. They claim they fled the scene before police could interview them on 11/22/63. Brandt says he is visible in the Zapruder film, wearing a hat, and maybe he is—but it is impossible to tell for sure since so many men were wearing hats (the fashion of the time), and the hats obscure many faces. Both men have detailed accounts about what happened, though they differ on key particulars, such as the number of shots and where they came from. Keep in mind they were supposedly standing next to one another—which could again demonstrate just how confusing the scene and acoustics were in Dealey Plaza.

85. Personal interview with Jim Leavelle, March 17, 2011, Dallas, Texas. Americans who came of age in the late 1960s will recognize this phenomenon as the "Woodstock syndrome." Many more people have claimed to have been at this ultimate music extravaganza, held in Woodstock, New York, in August 1969, than could actually have attended it.

8. 11/22/63: QUESTIONS, ANSWERS, MYSTERIES

1. The Dallas district attorney's office actually told one Dallas reporter late on 11/22 that the assassination was carried out "in furtherance of an international Communist conspiracy."

2. Like many who have lived or studied the confusing saga of November 22, Aynesworth appears to have changed his mind, or at least experienced a moment of doubt, since my last interview with him. In March 2013 he told a reporter that Oswald may indeed have received training and aid from Soviet agents. See Michael E. Young, "Gary Mack and the Evolution of a JFK Conspiracy Theorist," *Dallas Morning News*, March 2, 2013, http://www.dallasnews .com/news/jfk50/explore/20130302-gary-mack-and-the-evolution-of-a-jfk-conspiracy-theo rist.ece [accessed March 5, 2013].

3. Interview with Hugh Aynesworth, March 18, 2011, Dallas, Texas..

4. Said Robert Oswald, "I don't know at what age Mother verbalized to Lee to the effect that she felt he was a burden to her. Certainly by age three, he had the sense that, you know, we were a burden." See the transcript of "Who Was Lee Harvey Oswald?" *Frontline*, PBS, November 16, 1993, available online at http://www.pbs.org/wgbh/pages/frontline/programs /transcripts/1205.html [accessed August 5, 2011].

5. "Report of the President's Commission on the Assassination of President Kennedy, Chapter 1: Summary and Conclusions," pages 9–11, National Archives and Records Administration website, http://www.archives.gov/research/jfk/warren-commission-report/chapter -1.html [accessed April 27, 2011].

6. Not everyone agrees that Oswald was a good shot. Ernst Titovets, one of Oswald's closest friends during his time in the Soviet Union, says that the American defector mishandled a small-bore pistol during a firing demonstration at the Minsk radio factory. "[Oswald] took aim and fired five shots. All bullets went wide, randomly scattering." See Ernst Titovets, *Oswald Russian Episode* (Minsk: Mon Litera Publishing House, 2010), 53–54. On the other hand, the Warren Commission took testimony from a father and son who saw Oswald practicing at a firing range with his rifle on the weekend before the assassination: "Sterling [Wood and his father] observed that Oswald fired approximately 8 to 10 rounds and that each time he was careful in ejecting the hulls, that they were caught in his hand and put into his pocket . . . [T]hey also looked at Oswald's target and both concurred that he did some good shooting since all the rounds fired except one hit the bull's eye." See Warren Commission Hearings, vol. XXIV, CE 2003, pp. 202–3, Mary Ferrell Foundation website, http://www.maryferrell.org/mffweb/archive/viewer/showDoc.do?mode=searchResult&absPageId=144502 [accessed October 9, 2012] and Bill O'Reilly with Martin Dugard, *Killing Kennedy: The End of Camelot* (New York: Henry Holt, 2012), 240–42.

7. Gerald Posner, *Case Closed: Lee Harvey Oswald and the Assassination of JFK* (New York: Anchor Books, 1994), 20–29; Michael L. Kurtz, *The JFK Assassination Debates: Lone Gunman versus Conspiracy* (Lawrence: University Press of Kansas, 2006), 143–44; Anthony Summers, *The Kennedy Conspiracy* (London: Sphere Books, 1989), 93–94.

8. Summers, *Kennedy Conspiracy*, 94–95.

9. Posner, *Case Closed*, 31–32; Kurtz, *JFK Assassination Debates*, 144; "One-of-a-Kind Lee Harvey Oswald Signed Application to Albert Schweitzer College—Upon Acceptance to the Swiss College, He Defected to the U.S.S.R.," Nate D. Sanders Auctions website, http://www.natedsanders.com/ItemInfo.asp?ItemID=32849 [accessed May 12, 2011].

10. Posner, *Case Closed*, 32–33; Summers, *Kennedy Conspiracy*, 102–3.

11. John Newman, *Oswald and the CIA: The Documented Truth About the Unknown Relationship Between the U.S. Government and the Alleged Killer of JFK* (New York: Skyhorse Publishing, 2008), 3–6; "Report on Lee Harvey Oswald," Segregated CIA Collection, Record Group 233, Box 98, Folder "Investigation of JFK Assassination Performance of the Intelligence Agencies," Archives II, College Park, MD.

12. "Ex-Marine Asks Soviet Citizenship," *Washington Post and Times Herald*, November 1, 1959.

13. Some assassination researchers/conspiracy theorists, including Anthony Summers and Jim Marrs, think that Nosenko lied about his relationship with Oswald. James Jesus Angleton, the CIA's counterintelligence czar, did not believe that Nosenko was a legitimate defector and more likely was a double agent. Nosenko failed two lie detector tests, although both of these tests were administered while he was being tortured by the CIA. Nosenko passed a third polygraph exam in 1968 which included questions about Oswald. Nosenko's timely—some said convenient—defection right after the assassination allowed the government to rule out a KGB role in the assassination. Angleton suspected that the KGB had planted Nosenko for this very purpose. By contrast, the FBI believed that Nosenko was a legitimate defector. According to Summers, the FBI considered Nosenko a "godsend" because he could "quash allegations that the Federal Bureau of Investigation had failed to expose a dangerous Communist agent." Adding to the intrigue, Richard Helms, the CIA's deputy director for planning, persuaded the Warren Commission to ignore Nosenko. According to author Michael Kurtz, Helms lied to Earl Warren about Nosenko's value "be-

cause he feared that allowing Nosenko to testify before the Warren Commission would tarnish the agency's image." See Summers, *Kennedy Conspiracy*, 132, and Kurtz, *JFK Assassination Debates*, 148. This is a strange, tangled, murky episode—a classic bureaucratic skirmish between the FBI and the CIA that took precedence over the Warren Commission's mandate to tell Americans the truth about the assassination. The only thing clear about it is that the CIA won the dispute, since Nosenko's name appears nowhere in the Warren Commission report or the volumes of information accompanying it. This is yet another example of the commission's failure to tell the full story behind the assassination— and the CIA's determination to deny the commission information vital to its investigation.

14. In January 1961, Soviet passport officials in Minsk met with Oswald and asked whether he still wanted Soviet citizenship. Oswald later wrote: "I say no[,] simply extend my residential passport . . . and my document is extended unitll [*sic*] Jan 4. 1962." Vincent Bugliosi, *Reclaiming History* (New York: W. W. Norton, 2007), 592–604.

15. "Report of the President's Commission on the Assassination of President Kennedy, Chapter 7: Lee Harvey Oswald: Background and Possible Motives," page 392, National Archives and Records Administration website, http://www.archives.gov/research/jfk/warren -commission-report/chapter-7.html#defection [accessed April 29, 2011]; Posner, *Case Closed*, 43–51; Summers, *Kennedy Conspiracy*, 136; telephone interview with Gary Powers, Jr., February 14, 2011.

16. Telephone interview with Gary Powers, Jr., February 14, 2011. Gary Mack, curator of the Sixth Floor Museum, told me that he is skeptical of Powers's account, since "no one has ever found such a news story in any print or broadcast form." E-mail from Gary Mack, June 15, 2012.

17. I was not able to find any national TV news stories aired at that time that included Oswald. However, Oswald was filmed by two television cameramen in New Orleans as part of his advocacy on behalf of Castro's Cuba. There is a possibility, however remote, that this local footage was distributed more widely. A more plausible explanation, however, is that Powers saw Oswald's picture in a newspaper and later misremembered seeing it on TV, since Oswald was the subject of numerous pre-11/22 newspaper stories. See "Young Ex-Marine Asks to Be Russian Citizen," *Oakland Tribune*, October 31, 1959, p. 1; "Ex-Marine Requests Citizenship," *New York Times*, November 1, 1959, p. 3; "Texan in Russia: He Wants to Stay," *Dallas Morning News*, November 1, 1959, sec. 1, p. 9; "Brother Tries to Telephone, Halt Defector," *Oakland Tribune*, November 2, 1959, p. 8; "U.S. Boy Prefers Russia," *Syracuse Herald-Journal*, December 11, 1959, p. 46; "Third Yank Said Quitting Soviet Union," *San Mateo Times*, June 8, 1962, p. 8; "Marine Returning," *Lima News*, June 9, 1962, p. 1.

18. Marina's comment has raised questions about whether Oswald received language training from an intelligence agency. Gary Mack says he interviewed Marina and asked her if Oswald had ever flubbed a Russian sentence. Mack: "Did he ever say anything to you like 'My, that's a lovely chair you're wearing?'" Mack says Marina laughed at his question and insisted that Lee had never made such an obvious gaffe. She did confirm, however, that his dialect resembled those of the northern Baltic states (Latvia, Lithuania, and Estonia). In 1992 Marina told Gerald Posner that people from the Baltic states "speak with accents and do not speak [fluent] Russian." Earlier, she told the House Select Committee on Assassinations that Baltic residents "don't speak Russian very well" and "have different nationalities than Russians." Personal interview with Gary Mack, February 22, 2011; Posner, *Case Closed*, 64.

19. "Report of the President's Commission on the Assassination of President Kennedy, Chapter 7: Lee Harvey Oswald: Background and Possible Motives," page 393–94, National Archives and Records Administration website, http://www.archives.gov/research/jfk/warren -commission- report/chapter-7.html#defection [accessed May 2, 2011]; Posner, *Case Closed*, 55 and 66–74; Jim Marrs, *Crossfire: The Plot That Killed Kennedy* (New York: Carroll and Graf, 1989), 124–25.

20. On June 13, 1962, Lee, Marina, and their four-month-old daughter arrived in Hoboken, New Jersey. They were met by INS inspector Frederick Wiedersheim and Spas Raikin of the Traveler's Aid Society. Oswald was disappointed that the press had not turned out to interview him. Raikin put the couple in touch with the New York City Department of Welfare, which provided them with temporary housing at a Times Square hotel. Lee borrowed money from his brother Robert and flew his family from New York to Dallas. When Lee arrived at Love Field, he was again disappointed that there were no reporters on hand. He and Marina moved in with Robert's family and stayed for several weeks. Bugliosi, *Reclaiming History*, 638–44.

21. John M. Whitten, "First Draft of Initial Report on GPFLOOR Case," Record Group 263, Box 17, Folder "OSW10:V10B," Archives II, College Park, Maryland.

22. "Memorandum for the Record: [CIA] Meeting With HSCA Staffers," June 29, 1978, Mary Ferrell Foundation website, http://www.maryferrell.org/mffweb/archive/viewer/show Doc.do?docId=49667&relPageId=6 [accessed February 29, 2012].

23. Thomas B. Casasin to Walter P. Haltigan, November 25, 1963, Mary Ferrell Foundation website, http://www.maryferrell.org/mffweb/archive/viewer/showDoc.do?absPageId=248348 [accessed February 29, 2012].

24. Newman, *Oswald and the CIA*, 151–52; Summers, *Kennedy Conspiracy*, 149; confidential cable from Edward L. Freers, U.S. embassy in Moscow, to the U.S. State Department, November 2, 1959, http://www.aarclibrary.org/publib/jfk/wc/wcvols/wh18/pdf/WH18_CE _908.pdf [accessed September 23, 2011].

25. The exact Sicilian translation is "this thing of ours."

26. See Don Bohning, *The Castro Obsession: U.S. Covert Operations Against Cuba, 1959–65* (Washington, DC: Potomac Books, 2005); Marifeli Pérez-Stable, *The Cuban Revolution: Origins, Course, and Legacy*, 2nd ed. (New York: Oxford University Press, 1999); and Aviva Chomsky, *A History of the Cuban Revolution* (Chichester, West Sussex, UK: Wiley-Blackwell, 2011).

27. In another odd twist, CIA director George H. W. Bush wrote de Mohrenschildt a letter in September 1976 in response to a complaint from de Mohrenschildt that he was still being targeted by federal agencies because of his friendship with Oswald. Bush reported that he had found no evidence to justify the grievance.

28. Gerald Blaine, one of the Secret Service agents assigned to the Kennedy detail, also thinks that Oswald would have been a poor choice for a group plotting a political assassination: "[He] had an overwhelming need for recognition. This is the story of most assassins. He also had a personality that would prevent him [from] talking to someone over five minutes without totally alienating them. This would make anyone leery of using him as a conspiracy partner." E-mail from Gerald Blaine, January 9, 2013.

29. Summers, *Kennedy Conspiracy*, 151–72; Newman, *Oswald and the CIA*, 276–79. De Mohrenschildt was the recipient of an inscribed copy of one of the famous photos of Lee Oswald holding a rifle in the spring of 1963. The photo only became publicly known after

de Mohrenschildt killed himself in 1977, when his testimony was being sought by the House Select Committee on Assassinations. It is not clear why de Mohrenschildt committed suicide or whether he received the photo from Lee Oswald or from Marina.

30. The Paines separated in 1962 and were divorced on May 4, 1970, in Dallas. Apparently, the couple reconciled for a brief period following the assassination (see Ruth Hyde Paine's testimony before the Warren Commission, March 21, 1964, vol. 9, p. 353), but the marriage ultimately disintegrated.

31. James W. Douglass, *JFK and the Unspeakable: Why He Died and Why It Matters* (New York: Simon and Schuster, 2008), 169–70; Posner, *Case Closed*, 110; "Report of the President's Commission on the Assassination of President Kennedy, Chapter 7: Lee Harvey Oswald: Background and Possible Motives," pp. 416–18, National Archives and Records Administration website, http://www.archives.gov/research/jfk/warren-commission-report /chapter-7.html [accessed May 4, 2011].

32. You can see all three Oswald gun photos at http://jfk-archives.blogspot.com/2010/06 /backyard-photos.html. Marina's comments on the "backyard photos" appear at http:// mcadams.posc.mu.edu/russ/testimony/oswald_m1.htm [accessed January 3, 2013].

33. Similar actions have been taken by other violence-prone individuals. For example, Seung-Hui Cho, the student who killed thirty-two people at Virginia Tech in April 2007, took a photo of himself just before going on a rampage that ended with his own suicide. The print shows Cho wearing a black T-shirt and ammunition vest while holding two automatic pistols. See Mike Nizza, "Seung-Hui Cho: Who Is This Man?" *New York Times*, August 30, 2007, http://thelede.blogs.nytimes.com/2007/08/30/seung-hui-cho-who-is-this-man/ [accessed May 5, 2011].

34. "Report of the President's Commission on the Assassination of President Kennedy, Chapter 4: The Assassin," pp. 183–87, National Archives and Records Administration website, http://www.archives.gov/research/jfk/warren-commission-report/chapter-4.html#walker [accessed May 5, 2011]; Posner, *Case Closed*, 97–106.

35. On page 249 of the 2002 "Robert Welch University" edition of *The Politician*, the John Birch Society's Robert Welch makes the following claim regarding Eisenhower: "The role he has played, as described in all the pages above, would fit just as well into one theory as the other; that he is a mere stooge, or that he is a Communist . . ." The most common defamatory quote regarding Eisenhower attributed to Birchers is the phrase "conscious, dedicated agent of the Communist Conspiracy," which you can view at http://blogs.abc news.com/thenote/2010/02/farright-john-birch-society-2010.html [accessed October 31, 2012].

36. It is unclear whether Oswald hated Kennedy. During a radio debate with an anti-Castro Cuban named Carlos Bringuier (discussed later in this chapter), Oswald was asked if he agreed with Fidel Castro's description of JFK as a "ruffian and a thief." "I would not agree with that . . . particular wording," he replied. "However, I and the . . . Fair Play for Cuba Committee does [*sic*] think that the United States government through certain agencies, mainly the State Department and the CIA, have made monumental mistakes in its relations with Cuba." "Lengthy Teletype of 1963 Lee Harvey Oswald Debate with Comments on President Kennedy—Only Three Months Before Oswald Assassinated Kennedy," Nate D. Sanders Auctions website, http://natedsanders.com/ItemInfo.asp?ItemID=30696 [accessed May 12, 2011]. Vincent Bugliosi, however, theorizes that Oswald may have been jealous of Kennedy since Marina once described him as "very attractive" and thought that

one of her ex-boyfriends bore a resemblance to the president. Bugliosi, *Reclaiming History*, 711. See also Priscilla Johnson McMillan, *Marina and Lee* (New York: Random House, 1980), 410–13.

37. Bugliosi, *Reclaiming History*, 671–73; interview with Volkmar Schmidt, January 1995, conducted by William E. Kelly, http://jfkcountercoup.blogspot.com/2008/01/volkmar -schmidt-interview.html [accessed May 5, 2011].

38. Ken Holmes, a Dallas resident who has been investigating 11/22 for decades, says that the car belonged to one of Walker's bodyguards. Holmes also says that Walker—who was indisputably on a plane traveling from New Orleans to Shreveport when he heard that Kennedy had been shot—stood up and told his fellow passengers, "I'm General Edwin A. Walker, and I want you to see where I'm at." Walker realized instantly that he could use an alibi. Personal interview with Ken Holmes, January 14, 2011, Dallas, Texas.

39. According to Dallas officer Jim Leavelle, Marina Oswald kept the Walker note to hold over her husband's head and deter him from further violence, and he promised "not to do any more of that silliness." Personal interview with Leavelle, April 8, 2011, Dallas, Texas. In recent years, Marina Oswald appears to have become less reliable and more inclined to change her story, but for the months after the assassination, it seems probable that she told the truth to the authorities as she remembered it—and the memories were fresh.

40. "Report of the President's Commission on the Assassination of President Kennedy, Chapter 4: The Assassin," pp. 183–87, National Archives and Records Administration website, http://www.archives.gov/research/jfk/warren-commission-report/chapter-4.html #walker [accessed May 5, 2011]; Mark Lane, *Rush to Judgment* (New York: Thunder's Mouth Press, 1992), 349–50; *JFK*, special edition DVD, directed by Oliver Stone (Burbank, CA: Warner Home Video, 1997). Robert Frazier, the FBI ballistics expert who worked on the Walker case, was "unable to reach a conclusion" as to whether the bullet found in Walker's home had come from the rifle discovered on the sixth floor of the Book Depository. However, Frazier did say that "the general rifling characteristics of the rifle . . . are of the same type as those found on the bullet . . . and, further, on this basis . . . the bullet could have been fired from the rifle on the basis of its land and groove impressions."

41. "Testimony of Mrs. Lee Harvey Oswald Resumed," Warren Commission Hearings, vol. V, pp. 387–91, History Matters website, http://history-matters.com/archive/jfk/wc/wcvols /wh5/html/WC_Vol5_0199a.htm [accessed December 20, 2012].

42. This behavior by Oswald is oddly predictive of two future assassins: Arthur Bremer, who shot George Wallace in 1972 after first stalking President Nixon, and John Hinckley, who shot President Reagan in 1981 after initially targeting President Carter. See "Portrait of an Assassin: Arthur Bremer," PBS American Experience, http://www.pbs.org/wgbh/amex /wallace/sfeature/assasin.html [accessed December 20, 2012], and Del Quentin Wilber, *Rawhide Down: The Near Assassination of Ronald Reagan* (New York: Henry Holt, 2011).

43. Telephone interview with Wesley Buell Frazier, April 16, 2013.

44. The SV T-1 story comes from John Davis's *Mafia Kingfish: Carlos Marcello and the Assassination of John F. Kennedy* (New York: Signet, 1989), 133–37. SV T-1 was a businessman from Darien, Georgia, who supposedly met with two of his business associates (Salvadore Pizza and Benny Capeana) at a restaurant owned by Marcello. During the dinner, SV T-1 saw a man he believed to be the restaurant's owner passing a wad of cash to a man whom SV T-1 later identified as Lee Harvey Oswald. SV T-1 told his story to a police officer named

Johnny Harris. Davis lists his sources as "Interview of Joseph Albert Poretto by Special Agent Reed Jensen. Dictated 11/27/63. Interview of Mrs. Ella Frabbiele by Special Agent Reed Jensen. Dictated 11/27/63. Interview of Anthony Marcello by Special Agent Reed Jensen. Dictated 11/27/63." But when I looked at the original transcripts of these interviews on a respected independent website, they told a completely different story. Anthony Marcello, one of the managers of the restaurant/motel in question and brother of Carlos Marcello, told the FBI's Jensen that he had never seen Oswald or Ruby at his establishment. Poretto and Ella Frabbiele, a cashier at the restaurant, told Jensen the same thing—neither of them had seen Oswald at the restaurant or anyone who even resembled Oswald. See the Mary Ferrell Foundation website, http://www.maryferrell.org/mffweb/archive/viewer/showDoc .do?docId=56999&relPageId=61, http://www.maryferrell.org/mffweb/archive/viewer/show Doc.do?absPageId=673595&imageOnly=true, and http://www.maryferrell.org/mffweb/ar chive/viewer/showDoc.do?absPageId=673594&imageOnly=true [accessed September 27, 2011].

45. The timeline is as follows: Oswald handed out flyers at the Dumaine Street Wharf on June 16. He was fired from the Reily Company on June 19. He walked into a store owned by an anti-Castro Cuban on August 5, pretending to be anti-Castro himself. The store owner and his associates confronted Oswald on August 9, leading to a scuffle. Oswald appeared in court on August 12, pled guilty, and paid a $10 fine. Johann Rush, a cameraman for WDSU-TV, filmed Oswald as he was coming down the steps of the courthouse building. On August 13, the *Times-Picayune* ran a short article entitled "Pamphlet Case Sentence Given." Oswald handed out pamphlets again on August 16 in front of the International Trade Mart. WDSU-TV and WWL-TV aired brief news footage of the event. Bill Stuckey, a young reporter who hosted a radio program called "The Latin Listening Post," interviewed Oswald on August 17. Stuckey was so pleased with the interview that he invited Oswald to return on August 21 for a debate with two prominent anti-Castro Cubans. Oswald was caught off guard when Stuckey asked him about his undesirable discharge from the Marines and Russian defection. Posner, *Case Closed*, 131–61.

46. Davis, *Mafia Kingfish*, 135–37; Posner, *Case Closed*, 121–30; "Report of the President's Commission on the Assassination of President Kennedy, Chapter 7: Lee Harvey Oswald: Background and Possible Motives," pp. 406–7, National Archives and Records Administration website, http://www.archives.gov/research/jfk/warren-commission-report/chapter-7 .html#attack [accessed May 6, 2011]; Mark North, *Act of Treason: The Role of J. Edgar Hoover in the Assassination of President Kennedy* (New York: Carroll and Graf, 1991), 276–77.

47. During this same period, Oswald accepted an invitation from his cousin, Eugene Murret, to give a brief speech on life in the Soviet Union at Spring Hill College in Mobile, Alabama. Murret was at Spring Hill studying to become a Jesuit priest. According to Murret, Oswald addressed twenty students, plus two priests, and said that he had become disillusioned with life in the USSR after realizing that the Soviet people were "dominated by roughnecks." In addition, Murret remembered that Oswald "was very vague about his leaving Russia to return to the United States." See the Warren Commission Report, vol. XXV, exhibit 2649, pp. 920–22.

48. Bringuier insists that the CIA contacted him on only one occasion, *after* the assassination. But in the 1970s, Isidor Borja, a former DRE leader, told the House Select Committee

on Assassinations that his organization briefed the CIA on the scuffle between Oswald and Bringuier. E. Howard Hunt, the former CIA officer arrested for the Watergate burglary, claimed that his agency had a close relationship with DRE. On his deathbed, without providing the necessary proof, Hunt claimed that LBJ and a handful of rogue CIA agents plotted Kennedy's murder and hired a French gunman to pull the trigger. See Ryan Singel, "Who Killed JFK? Famous Spook Outs the Conspiracy," Wired.com, April 3, 2007, http://www.wired.com/threatlevel/2007/04/who_killed_jfk_/ [accessed June 3, 2011].

49. "Report of the President's Commission on the Assassination of President Kennedy, Chapter 7: Lee Harvey Oswald: Background and Possible Motives," p. 407, National Archives and Records Administration website, http://www.archives.gov/research/jfk/warren-commission-report/chapter-7.html#political [accessed May 9, 2011]; Posner, *Case Closed*, 150–55; Summers, *Kennedy Conspiracy*, 213–16.

50. Marrs, *Crossfire*, 147–49; Summers, *Kennedy Conspiracy*, 229; Posner, *Case Closed*, 139; Newman, *Oswald and the CIA*, 308–9.

51. Bugliosi, *Reclaiming History*, 1348–49; Kurtz, *JFK Assassination Debates*, 163; Robert D. Morrow, *First Hand Knowledge: How I Participated in the CIA-Mafia Murder of President Kennedy* (New York: SPI Books, 1993); David Lee Miller interview with Robert Morrow, *A Current Affair*, YouTube, http://www.youtube.com/watch?v=_3KmGN3gikA&feature=results_main&playnext=1&list=PLAEDFA01CC49C6FA5 [accessed May 9, 2011]. Gary Mack does not consider Morrow a credible source and referred us to Ulric Shannon's biting review of Morrow's book, "First Hand Knowledge: A Review," http://mcadams.posc.mu.edu/morrow.htm [accessed September 26, 2011].

52. Ferrie was forced to relinquish his role as a CAP leader after he was accused of giving inappropriate political lectures to cadets.

53. See Dave Reitzes, "Who Speaks for Clay Shaw?" at http://mcadams.posc.mu.edu/shaw1.htm, and Patricia Lambert, *False Witness: The Real Story of Jim Garrison's Investigation and Oliver Stone's Film "JFK"* (New York: M. Evans, 2000).

54. Posner, *Case Closed*, 141–48; Summers, *Kennedy Conspiracy*, 236–38.

55. Douglass, *JFK and the Unspeakable*, 158–62; Posner, *Case Closed*, 176–77; "Report of the Select Committee on Assassinations of the U.S. House of Representatives," National Archives and Records Administration website, pp. 137–39, http://www.archives.gov/research/jfk/select-committee-report/part-1c.html#odio [accessed May 10, 2011]. Complicating the picture further, a man named Loran Eugene Hall told the FBI on September 16, 1964, that he and two of his associates (one of whom, William Seymour, bore a slight resemblance to Oswald) had visited Odio's apartment on the night in question. Yet Hall recanted his story a mere four days later, and Seymour and another man, named Lawrence Howard, later denied ever being at Odio's apartment. "Howard said Hall was a 'scatter-brain, unreliable, emotionally disturbed, and an egotistical liar.'" Also, payroll records from the Beach Welding Supplies Company of Miami Beach, Florida, show that Seymour worked 40-hour weeks between September 5 and October 10, 1963. Posner, *Case Closed*, 177–78; Bugliosi, *Reclaiming History*, 1306.

56. Some assassination researchers have speculated that the man who appeared at the Cuban and Soviet embassies was not the real Oswald, but an Oswald impersonator. For example, see Jim Marrs, *Crossfire: The Plot that Killed Kennedy* (New York: Carroll and Graf, 1989), 193–96. There is more speculation than proof about this, but as with so many other aspects of the Kennedy case, a fair person cannot make a definitive judgment.

57. Robert Blakey of the House Select Committee on Assassinations said that Oswald may have offered to kill Kennedy for Cuba while visiting the Cuban embassy in Mexico City. Blakey also said the source of this information was none other than Fidel Castro. "We had a high-echelon informant in the Communist Party," Blakey explained, "And that person had an interview with Castro, and Castro told him the story." Castro has denied ever saying anything of the sort. Telephone interview with Robert Blakey, August 10, 2011.

58. Douglass, *JFK and the Unspeakable*, 77–79; Posner, *Case Closed*, 180–86.

59. The cable also explains why officials at the U.S. embassy in Moscow decided to return Oswald's passport to him and grant his wife a visa: US EMB MOSCOW STATED TWENTY MONTHS OF REALITIES OF LIFE IN SOVIET UNION HAD CLEARLY HAD MATURING EFFECT ON OSWALD. The use of the adjective "maturing" in relation to Oswald is ironic in light of history. See "Cable Stating That Lee Oswald Who Called SovEmb 1 Oct Probably Identical to Lee Henry Oswald," October 10, 1963, NARA Record Number: 104-10015-10048, Mary Ferrell Foundation website, http://www.maryferrell.org/mffweb/archive/viewer/showDoc.do?docId=1565&relPageId=3 [accessed January 9, 2013].

60. Oswald turned twenty-four on October 18, 1963.

61. Oleg Nechiporenko, a KGB colonel who was stationed in the USSR's Mexico City embassy at the time of Oswald's visit, believes the mystery man in the photograph "was a former American serviceman, discharged for reasons of health." "I cannot remember the date and purpose of his first visit to our embassy," Nechiporenko wrote, "but in my conversations with him, it became clear that he was psychologically disturbed. Subsequently, he came to see us several times, and the intervals between each visit increased. I remember that during each visit something was explained to him in connection with his requests, and he listened calmly and left fully satisfied." Oleg M. Nechiporenko, *Passport to Assassination* (Secaucus, NJ: Birch Lane Press, 1993), 175. Assassination researcher Bill Simpich told me he is "virtually certain" that the man was a KGB scientist named Yuriy Moskalev. Telephone interview with Bill Simpich, May 23, 2013.

62. Jefferson Morley, "John Brennan and the CIA's Last JFK Secrets," *Huffington Post*, January 11, 2013, http://www.huffingtonpost.com/jefferson-morley/brennan-confirmation-hearings_b_2441856.html [accessed January 14, 2013].

63. James Jesus Angleton was one of the CIA's first officers. He joined the agency in 1947 after serving with the Office of Strategic Services (OSS) during World War II and quickly rose to become chief of the counterintelligence division. Angleton became obsessed with finding spies after a Russian defector, Anatoliy Golitsyn, told him that the KGB had managed to infiltrate the CIA. His zealous hunt for moles alienated many of his co-workers. Angleton resigned from the agency in 1975.

64. John M. Whitten, "First Draft of Initial Report on GPFLOOR Case," Record Group 263, Box 17, Folder "OSW10:V10B," Archives II, College Park, Maryland; Jefferson Morley, *Our Man in Mexico: Winston Scott and the Hidden History of the CIA* (Lawrence: University Press of Kansas, 2008), 192; Kurtz, *JFK Assassination Debates*, 191–92; "1996 Release: Oswald, the CIA, and Mexico City ('Lopez Report')," 87–88, History Matters, http://history-matters.com/archive/jfk/hsca/lopezrpt/html/LopezRpt_0101a.htm [accessed May 11, 2011].

65. Morley, *Our Man in Mexico*, 192–99, and "What Jane Roman Said: A Retired CIA Officer Speaks Candidly About Lee Harvey Oswald," History Matters, http://www.history-matters.com/essays/frameup/WhatJaneRomanSaid/WhatJaneRomanSaid_1.htm [accessed May 13, 2011].

66. Jefferson Morley, "Ray Rocca: 'There Was An Earlier Cable,'" JFK Facts, January 10, 2013, http://jfkfacts.org/assassination/quote/ray-rocca-there-was-an-earlier-cable/ [accessed January 11, 2013].

67. Jefferson Morley, "January 7, 1963: Under U.S. Government Eyes, Oswald Goes to Work," JFK Facts, January 7, 2013, http://jfkfacts.org/assassination/on-this-date/jan-7-1963-under-u-s-government-eyes-oswald-goes-to-work/ [accessed January 11, 2013].

68. Antonio Veciana Blanch, the founder of an anti-Castro group with CIA ties, told the HSCA that a Langley operative named "Maurice Bishop" introduced him to Oswald in September 1963. Some conspiracy theorists believe that Bishop was actually David Atlee Phillips, a CIA agent deeply involved in anti-Castro operations. Phillips denied the accusation and even filed libel suits against publications that tried to link him to the Kennedy assassination. See Gaeton Fonzi, *The Last Investigation* (New York: Thunder's Mouth Press, 1993), and the David Atlee Phillips Papers, Manuscript Division, Library of Congress, Washington, DC. However, Larry Hancock, author of *Someone Would Have Talked* (Southlake, TX: JFK Lancer Productions and Publications, 2010) says that prior to his death, Phillips told an HSCA investigator that JFK was probably killed in a conspiracy involving rogue intelligence officers.

69. According to Morley, who has long investigated the CIA's links to 11/22, Joannides gave the go-ahead to DRE on 11/22/63 to link Oswald to Castro, which caused the Cuban dictator to put his forces on alert and go on the air that evening to deny any connection to Oswald. U.S. newspapers accepted the DRE story and headlined Oswald's Castro connection. This might well have triggered a war had anything come out to substantiate a connection between Oswald and Castro agents. Joannides's efforts with DRE resulted in the disbanding of the Fair Play for Cuba Committee, the best-known pro-Castro group in the United States, in December 1963. See Will Lissner, "Pro-Castro Group Disbanding," *New York Times*, December 28, 1963. Morley theorizes that the underlying goal of implicating the Cuban government in the assassination might have been to prompt an invasion of Cuba or another response that would have resulted in the overthrow of Castro. These actions, however, were undercut by both the Kennedy family and the Warren Commission. Neither the family nor the Warren Report fingered Castro. By using psychological warfare, however, Morley argues that the CIA still accomplished one of its primary goals: the destruction of the FPCC.

70. There is no precise record of what President Johnson said to the CIA on this subject, but as journalist Jefferson Morley suggests, one can "infer" that Johnson expressed his fears about a connection between Oswald and the Communists to the CIA: "[LBJ] spoke with [CIA Director] McCone on the morning of 11/24/63 to find out more about [Oswald] in [Mexico City]. The Katzenbach memo [authored by Justice Department official Nicholas Katzenbach] written later that day after [Oswald] was dead reflects White House determination to quash all conspiracy talk. But did LBJ say that to McCone? That can't be proven. As the week went on LBJ got more updates from CIA but I don't think he ever ordered them not to look into certain things. Remember that he could be confident CIA info would not become public unless he chose to. He wanted to know everything they knew." E-mail from Jefferson Morley, October 11, 2011.

71. Telephone interview with Jefferson Morley, April 18, 2011; Jefferson Morley, "The George Joannides Coverup," May 19, 2005, JFK Lancer website, President John Kennedy, Latest News and Research, http://www.jfklancer.com/morley.html [accessed May 12, 2011].

72. Telephone interview with Jefferson Morley, April 18, 2011. Morley was apparently the one who informed Blakey many years later of the CIA's deceit. "They fucked you," Morley says he told Blakey. Telephone interview with Robert Blakey, July 8, 2011. In a follow-up interview, Blakey said the CIA "had a duty" to disclose that Joannides had once worked with DRE since the agency agreed not to withhold anything from the HSCA. Follow-up telephone interview with Robert Blakey, August 10, 2011. See also Jefferson Morley, "Morley v. CIA: JFK at Issue in Federal Court Next Week," JFK Facts, February 18, 2013, http://jfkfacts .org/assassination/morley-v-cia-jfk-at-issue-in-federal-court-next-week/#more-3023 [accessed February 18, 2013].

73. Telephone interview with Jefferson Morley, April 18, 2011; Jefferson Morley, "Revelation 1963," *Miami New Times*, April 12, 2001, http://www.miaminewtimes.com/2001-04-12 /news/revelation-19-63/ [accessed August 4, 2011]. See also David Talbot, *Brothers: The Hidden History of the Kennedy Years* (New York: Free Press, 2007), and Larry Hancock, *Someone Would Have Talked: The Assassination of John F. Kennedy and the Conspiracy to Mislead History* (Southlake, TX: JFK Lancer Productions and Publications, 2003).

74. George Lardner, Jr., "No Closer to Cracking the Kennedy Case: Meeting Yields Few Answers on Assassination," *Washington Post*, November 21, 2005.

75. "Former HSCA Chief Counsel on CIA Obstruction," JFK Facts, March 23, 2013, http://jfkfacts.org/assassination/quote/former-hsca-chief-counsel-on-cia-obstruction /#more-3171 [accessed March 28, 2013].

76. Morley, "Morley v. CIA," http://jfkfacts.org/assassination/morley-v-cia-jfk-at-issue -in-federal-court-next-week/#more-3023 [accessed February 18, 2013].

77. Historian David M. Barrett's excellent study of CIA explores the agency's complicated relationship with Congress during the height of the Cold War. See *The CIA and Congress: The Untold Story from Truman to Kennedy* (Lawrence: University Press of Kansas, 2006).

78. In 1975, Senator Frank Church held widely publicized Senate hearings into possible abuses by the CIA. The reports from these hearings can be found on the Assassination Archives and Research Center website: http://www.aarclibrary.org/publib/contents/church /contents_church_reports.htm [accessed July 28, 2011].

79. Harry Truman, "Limit CIA Role to Intelligence," *Washington Post*, December 22, 1963.

80. The CIA's unwillingness, or perhaps inability, to shed light on another strange story raises additional questions about the agency's links to 11/22. In 1977 an assassination researcher, Mary Ferrell, discovered a CIA document (dated April 1, 1964) that included a request from the French government for help in finding a French terrorist named Jean Souetre. According to the document, Souetre—a member of the Organisation de l'armée secrète (OAS), a right-wing organization responsible for plotting several assassination attempts against French president Charles de Gaulle—had been in Forth Worth, Texas, during JFK's visit and "[w]ithin forty-eight hours of Kennedy's death . . . was picked up by U.S. authorities in Texas" and "expelled from the United States." There is no official record of who apprehended Souetre or which agency handled his deportation proceedings. Souetre denied involvement during a 1983 interview with a reporter, but suggested that a former French intelligence agent named Michel Mertz may have been in Fort Worth using his (Souetre's) name as an alias. Souetre occasionally used Mertz's name as an alias, as well as the name Michel Roux. Oddly enough, the real Michel Roux had been in Forth Worth on 11/22 visiting

friends. For more information on this tangled tale, see Peter Kross, *JFK: The French Connection* (Kempton, IL: Adventures Unlimited Press, 2012), Brad O'Leary and L. E. Seymour, *Triangle of Death: The Shocking Truth About the Role of South Vietnam and the French Mafia in the Assassination of JFK* (Nashville, TN: WND Books, 2003), and Henry Hurt, *Reasonable Doubt: An Investigation Into the Assassination of John F. Kennedy* (New York: Henry Holt, 1985), 414–19.

81. According to Lamar Waldron and Thom Hartmann, the CIA "claim[ed] the tapes of Oswald's calls were erased shortly after his visits, and before JFK's assassination" (*Legacy of Secrecy: The Long Shadow of the JFK Assassination* (Berkeley, CA: Counterpoint, 2009), 214). But President Johnson's postassassination conversation with J. Edgar Hoover disproves this. See "Telephone Conversation between the President and J. Edgar Hoover, 23 November 1963," Mary Ferrell Foundation website, http://www.maryferrell.org/mffweb/archive/viewer /showDoc.do?docId=807&relPageId=2 [accessed October 10, 2011]. No one disputes that the CIA recorded several conversations in Mexico City that the agency believed included Lee Oswald. In addition to Hoover, there are others who insist the tapes were not erased. W. David Slawson and William Coleman, two lawyers for the Warren Commission, said that the CIA played the Oswald tapes for them several months after the assassination. See John Newman, "Oswald, the CIA, and Mexico City," *Frontline*, http://www.pbs.org/wgbh/pages /frontline/shows/oswald/conspiracy/newman.html# [accessed October 10, 2011]. But at some undefined point, possibly in the 1980s, the tapes were apparently either lost or destroyed. Transcripts of the tapes have survived. See CIA transcripts from Mexico City, September 28 (11:51 A.M.) and October 1 (10:30 A.M.), 1963, CIA January 1994 release (5 brown boxes), Oswald box 15b, folder 56, National Archives and Records Administration, College Park, MD, and http://www.maryferrell.org/wiki/index.php/The_Mexico_City_Tapes [accessed October 10, 2011]. A definitive answer on the status of the tapes might be found in documents scheduled for release in 2017. See Associated Press, "Evidence Indicates 'Oswald' Tapes Survived," *Dallas Morning News*, November 22, 1999.

82. Newman, *Oswald and the CIA*, 364.

83. "The Mexico City Tapes," Mary Ferrell Foundation website, http://www.maryferrell .org/wiki/index.php/The_Mexico_City_Tapes [accessed May 13, 2011]; Summers, *Kennedy Conspiracy*, 275–77; "LBJ-Hoover 11-23-63," *History Matters*, http://www.history-matters .com/archive/jfk/lbjlib/phone_calls/Nov_1963/audio/LBJ-Hoover_11-23-63.htm [accessed May 13, 2011].

84. At the height of the Watergate scandal, Senate investigators discovered that President Nixon kept a voice-activated taping system in the Oval Office. The investigators immediately subpoenaed Nixon's tapes and discovered an 18½-minute gap in a critical conversation between President Nixon and his chief of staff, H. R. Haldeman, concerning an illegal break-in at Democratic National Committee headquarters at the Watergate apartment complex in June 1972. Nixon's loyal longtime secretary, Rose Mary Woods, claimed that she accidentally erased at least some of the tape (about five minutes) while transcribing the conversation. "No one on the president's staff offered an explanation to account for the remaining thirteen and a half minutes." Many believe that President Nixon personally listened to the tape, alone, and possibly erased part of the conversation, intentionally or otherwise, before it was turned over to the Senate. Granted, this is not a certainty and cannot be proven. Jonathan Roscoe of the Richard M. Nixon Library wrote us: "[T]here are some pieces of testimony that suggest the president listened to portions of the White House Tapes

conversation containing the 18.5 minute gap. Unfortunately, it is impossible to say for certain which parts and for how long he listened." E-mail from Jonathan Roscoe, October 18, 2011. Also see Keith W. Olson, *Watergate: The Presidential Scandal That Shook America* (Lawrence: University Press of Kansas, 2003), 127.

85. "Formation of the Warren Commission," Mary Ferrell Foundation website, http://www.maryferrell.org/wiki/index.php/Formation_of_the_Warren_Commission [accessed May 13, 2011]; "The Fourteen Minute Gap [based on a film of the same name by Tyler Weaver]," Mary Ferrell Foundation website, http://www.maryferrell.org/wiki/index.php/The_Fourteen_Minute_Gap [accessed May 13, 2011]. The historian Max Holland points out that "the Johnson Library and the National Archives and Records Administration hired a private contractor, the Cutting Corporation of Maryland, to try to recover an audible version of this conversation. After three months' work, the Cutting Corporation reported that the IBM magnetic belt had been erased and an audible recording could not be retrieved." Max Holland, *The Kennedy Assassination Tapes* (New York: Alfred A. Knopf, 2004), 69.

86. Jefferson Morley, "Did the CIA Destroy An Oswald Tape?" JFK Facts, January 9, 2013, http://jfkfacts.org/assassination/experts/what-happened-to-the-tape-of-oswald-in-mexico-city/ [accessed January 11, 2013].

9. ROUNDING UP THE USUAL SUSPECTS: THE ASSASSINATION'S PUZZLE PALACE

1. "John Moss Whitten," Spartacus Educational website, http://www.spartacus.schoolnet.co.uk/JFKwhitten.htm [accessed May 16, 2011]; Jefferson Morley, "The Good Spy," *Washington Monthly*, December 2003, http://www.washingtonmonthly.com/features/2003/0312.morley.html [accessed May 16, 2011]; and "Newseum to Host Warren Commission Critic Who Got Played By a CIA Spymaster," JFK Facts, April 4, 2013, http://jfkfacts.org/assassination/news/newseum-to-host-edward-epstein-a-warren-commission-critic-suckered-by-the-cia/ [accessed April 8, 2013].

2. Luciano, who was jailed during the war for running a prostitution ring, also encouraged his Italian associates to help the American army during the invasion of Sicily. The federal government later rewarded Luciano by paroling and deporting him to Italy where he ultimately established a lucrative narcotics trade. Dan E. Moldea, *The Hoffa Wars: The Rise and Fall of Jimmy Hoffa* (New York: S.P.I. Books, 1993), 41–42.

3. Mark North, *Act of Treason: The Role of J. Edgar Hoover in the Assassination of President Kennedy* (New York: Carroll and Graf, 1991), 13–17, 181–89.

4. A private investigator, Edward Becker, claimed he heard Marcello make this threat. The FBI dismissed his story, and so did Carlos Marcello. Speaking before the House Select Committee on Assassinations, Marcello insisted that he would never have held a meeting at the location named by Becker—an estate Marcello used for duck hunting. Also, the HSCA decided it was "unlikely that an organized crime leader personally involved in an assassination plot would discuss it with anyone other than his closest lieutenants, although he might be willing to discuss it more freely prior to a serious decision to undertake such an act." See George Lardner, Jr., "Investigator Detailed Mafia Leaders' Threat Against Kennedy," *Washington Post*, July 21, 1979.

5. Lamar Waldron and Thom Hartmann, *Legacy of Secrecy: The Long Shadow of the JFK*

Assassination (Berkeley, CA: Counterpoint, 2009), xi–xii; Anthony Summers, *The Kennedy Conspiracy* (London: Sphere Books, 1989), 197–200.

6. Tim Weiner, *Legacy of Ashes: The History of the CIA* (New York: Anchor Books, 2007), 263.

7. The official memorandum on this incident reads: "On 27 November 1963, Sympathizer/73 showed Richard R. Consley a memorandum which the Dutch Foreign Office had written to SYMPATHIZER. This memo was dated 25 November 1963, and it reported a conversation which one Mr. SLOT, a member of the Dutch Foreign Office, had had with Ricardo SANTOS, 3rd Secretary of the Cuban Embassy, at a reception given by the Soviet Ambassador on 7 November 1963. Mr. SLOT reportedly asked SANTOS a question concerning the attacks made against the Cuban mainland by Cuban refugees. SANTOS' reply to this question was, 'Mr. SLOT, just wait and you will see what we can do. It will happen soon.' Asked by Mr. SLOT to be more specific about what would happen soon, SANTOS merely replied, 'Just wait, just wait.' The memorandum goes on to say that SANTOS [had] a brother living in the U.S. His name and address [were] not known, but he and SANTOS [wrote] to each other regularly. This brother [was] reportedly pro-CASTRO, but went to the U.S. at the insistence of his wife, who [was] 'conservative.' The subject matter of the letters between the brothers is reportedly nothing more than 'family affairs.'" Source: "Memo: For the Record 27 Nov 63," Record Group 263, Personality File on Lee Harvey Oswald, Box 14, Folder "OSW1:V7," Archives II, College Park, Maryland. There is another cable from the CIA to presidential aide McGeorge Bundy dated November 28, 1963: "Our station in the Hague has reported that on 23 November 1963, a local Castroite named Maria Snethlage talked to Third Secretary Ricardo Santos of the Cuban Embassy in the Hague and said that she knew the 'Mr. Lee' (*sic*) who murdered President Kennedy. She characterized 'Lee' as a man full of hate and violence, and speculated that he had been 'misused by a group.' She said she had written to Gibson (undoubtedly Richard Gibson, U.S. citizen of Lausanne, Switzerland, born 13 May 1935, a Castro sympathizer, who had visited the Netherlands recently and was in contact both with the Soviet ambassador and the Cuban embassy). Later on 23 November, Maria Snethlage talked again to Third Secretary Santos and said that, 'Mr. Lee of the Fair Play for Cuba Committee' had been slandered. It was another person, 'named Lee Oswald,' who had done it. Snethlage is reported to have been [in] Cuba in January and again in May 1963." Source: "CIA to McGeorge Bundy and U. Alexis Johnson, 28 November 1963," Record Group 263, Box 4, Russ Holmes Work File, Folder "JFK-RH02:F040B," Archives II, College Park, Maryland.

8. Memo from Richard Helms to Lee Rankin [undated], "Personality File on Lee Harvey Oswald," Box 51, Record Group 263, Folder "V54 OSW 14," Archives II, College Park, Maryland; "Memo: For the Record," November 27, 1963, "Personality File on Lee Harvey Oswald," Box 14, Record Group 263, Folder "OSW 1: V7," Archives II, College Park, Maryland; Memo from Stockholm Embassy to McGeorge Bundy, December 9, 1963, "Personality File on Lee Harvey Oswald," Box 3, Record Group 263, Folder "OSW3: V1," Archives II, College Park, Maryland; Memo from CIA to White House and Secret Service, February 22, 1964, "Personality File on Lee Harvey Oswald," Box 15, Record Group 263, Folder "OSW6: V8," Archives II, College Park, Maryland; Memo from CIA Director to McGeorge Bundy, November 29, 1963, "Russ Holmes Work File," Box 4, Record Group 263, Folder "JFK-RH02:040A," Archives II, College Park, Maryland.

9. "Agency Disseminations to the FBI Et Al Regarding Rumors and Allegations Regard-

ing President Kennedy Assassination," Box 81, Record Group 233, Folder 11, Archives II, College Park, Maryland; "Memo to the director of the CIA from [12] at Station C/WH4," November 30, 1963, "Russ Holmes Work File," Box 12, Record Group 263, Folder "JFK-RH04:F108-II," Archives II, College Park, Maryland; Max Holland, "The Demon in Jim Garrison," *Wilson Quarterly* 25, no. 2 (Spring 2001): 10–17.

10. Aleksandr Fursenko and Timothy Naftali, *"One Hell of a Gamble": Khrushchev, Castro, and Kennedy, 1958–64* (New York: W. W. Norton, 1997), 344–45. Fursenko and Naftali also say that "Walton, and presumably Kennedy, wanted Khrushchev to know that only RFK could implement John Kennedy's vision and that the cooling that might occur in U.S.-Soviet relations because of Johnson would not last forever" (345–46).

11. Thomas P. O'Neill, *Man of the House: The Life and Political Memoirs of Speaker Tip O'Neill* (New York: Random House, 1987), 178.

12. Theodore C. Sorensen, *Kennedy* (New York: Harper and Row, 1965), 750; personal interview with Ted Sorensen, October 22, 2010. Others have been less convinced by the Douglass volume. John McAdams, an associate professor of political science at Marquette University, calls Douglass's book "a self-indulgent political fantasy." "As bad as Douglass' account of Kennedy's foreign policy is," wrote McAdams in a scathing review entitled "Unspeakably Awful," "his depiction of a plot to murder JFK is worse—unspeakably bad, in fact. To paraphrase Thomas Merton, Douglass' muse and inspiration, the bunk and nonsense Douglass recycles goes beyond the capacity of words to describe. He is utterly uncritical of any theory, any witness, and any factoid, as long as it implies conspiracy." John McAdams, "Unspeakably Awful," *Washington Decoded*, December 11, 2009, http://www.washingtonde coded.com/site/2009/12/unspeakably-awful.html [accessed May 18, 2011].

13. Jefferson Morley, "JFK: 'It [A Military Coup] Could Happen in this Country,'" JFK Facts, January 21, 2013, http://jfkfacts.org/assassination/quote/jfk-it-a-military-coup-could -happen-in-this-country/#more-2129 [accessed January 22, 2013].

14. In theory, the cabal could also have been the opposite: Communist-inspired. In April 1961, FBI director J. Edgar Hoover sent Attorney General Robert Kennedy a memo admitting that the Office of Strategic Services (the CIA's parent organization) had been infiltrated by a "Communist element" that "created problems and situations which even to this day affect US intelligence operations." See Hoover to RFK, April 21, 1961, NARA Record Number 124-90092-10011, Mary Ferrell Foundation website, https://www.maryferrell .org/mffweb/archive/viewer/showDoc.do?docId=99112&relPageId=3 [accessed April 16, 2013].

15. Lindsay Porter, *Assassination: A History of Political Murder* (New York: Overlook Press, 2010), 15, 93, 160–61.

16. According to Arthur Schlesinger, "Marvin Watson of Lyndon Johnson's White House staff told Cartha DeLoach, [a senior official] of the FBI that Johnson 'was now convinced [1967] there was a plot in connection with the assassination. Watson stated the president felt that CIA had had something to do with this plot' (*Washington Post*, December 13, 1977)." See Arthur Schlesinger, Jr., *Robert Kennedy and His Times* (Boston: Houghton Mifflin, 2002), 616.

17. Personal interview with Bill Alexander, Dallas, January 14, 2011. It is unclear whether any copies of the newspaper, the *Dallas Morning News*, were actually printed containing this charged information—Alexander says two thousand were—but they were either not distributed or do not survive, as far as we can determine. Yet Alexander is correct that the

"Communist conspiracy" charge was considered Friday afternoon and evening. As Gary Mack of the Sixth Floor Museum notes, this internal debate explains an important aspect of the November 22 timeline: "Clearly, something caused a delay [in charging Oswald with JFK's murder] since Oswald was charged with Tippit hours before he was charged with Kennedy. The decision whether or not to amend the charge by removing 'Communist conspiracy' was a pretty darn good reason." E-mail from Gary Mack, August 30, 2011.

18. Did President Johnson have ironclad evidence of his suspicions, or were these his surmises after the passage of years? The written and testimonial record is not clear, though one naturally assumes that a sitting president has access to the people and documents needed to form conclusions of these sorts.

19. Joseph A. Califano, Jr., "Letter to the Editor: A Concoction of Lies and Distortions," *Wall Street Journal*, January 28, 1992: A15.

20. Max Holland, "The Assassination Tapes," *Atlantic Monthly*, June 2004, http://mcadams.posc.mu.edu/holland_atlantic.htm [accessed July 27, 2011].

21. G. Robert Blakey and Richard N. Billings, *The Plot to Kill the President* (New York: Times Books, 1981), 140.

22. Henry Hurt, *Reasonable Doubt: An Investigation Into the Assassination of John F. Kennedy* (New York: Henry Holt, 1985), 309.

23. "Dousing a Popular Theory," *Time*, October 2, 1978, http://www.time.com/time/magazine/article/0,9171,948669,00.html [accessed August 16, 2011].

24. Jefferson Morley, *Our Man in Mexico: Winston Scott and the Hidden History of the CIA* (Lawrence: University Press of Kansas, 2008), 225–26. Morley believes that Washington silenced Mann because a full investigation could have "revealed that the CIA and FBI had been playing close attention to the FPCC and Oswald in the years, months and weeks before JFK was killed." See "At the Newseum: Epstein's Unconvincing Indictment of the Pro-Castro Assassin," JFK Facts, April 8, 2013, http://jfkfacts.org/assassination/news/at-the-newseum-epsteins-unconvincing-indictment-of-the-pro-castro-assassin/#more-4118 [accessed April 11, 2013].

25. Kennedy told the Florida Chamber of Commerce in Tampa on November 18: "I do not think that there is any doubt that Fidel Castro, as a symbol of revolt in this hemisphere, has faded badly. Every survey, every report, I think every newspaperman, every publisher, would agree that because Mr. Castro has embraced the Soviet Union and made Cuba its satellite, that the appeal that he had in the late fifties and early sixties as a national revolutionary has been so badly damaged and scarred that as a symbol, his torch is flickering. We have not been successful in removing Mr. Castro. We should realize that that task is one which involves not only the security of the United States, but other countries. It involves possibilities of war. It involves danger to people as far away as West Berlin, Germany, countries which border upon the Soviet Union in the Middle East, all the countries that are linked to us in alliance, as the Soviet Union is so intimately linked with Cuba . . . In answer to your question, Mr. Castro still is in control in Cuba, and still remains a major danger to the United States." In Miami later that day, Kennedy added: "It is important to restate what now divides Cuba from my country and from the other countries of this hemisphere. It is the fact that a small band of conspirators has stripped the Cuban people of their freedom and handed over the independence and sovereignty of the Cuban nation to forces beyond the hemisphere. They have made Cuba a victim of foreign imperialism, an instrument of the policy of others, a weapon in an effort dictated by external powers to subvert the other American Republics. This,

and this alone, divides us. As long as this is true, nothing is possible. Without it, everything is possible." These tough words were delivered in two cities with large numbers of Cuban-Americans. It is not unreasonable to assume that Castro would have been interested in monitoring Kennedy's Texas speeches to see if he continued this theme in a state with a different population mix. See John F. Kennedy, "Address and Question and Answer Period in Tampa Before the Florida Chamber of Commerce," November 18, 1963, Online by Gerhard Peters and John T. Woolley, *The American Presidency Project*, http://www.presidency.ucsb .edu/ws/?pid=9526 [accessed January 7, 2013]; and "Address in Miami Before the Inter-American Press Association," November 18, 1963, Online by Gerhard Peters and John T. Woolley, *The American Presidency Project*, http://www.presidency.ucsb.edu/ws/?pid=9529 [accessed January 7, 2013].

26. Brian Latell, *Castro's Secrets: The CIA and Cuba's Intelligence Machine* (New York: Palgrave MacMillan, 2012), 213–21.

27. "JFK Assassination Quotes by Government Officials," Mary Ferrell Foundation, http://www.maryferrell.org/wiki/index.php/JFK_Assassination_Quotes_by_Government _Officials [accessed May 19, 2011]; Harris Wofford, *Of Kennedys and Kings: Making Sense of the Sixties* (New York: Farrar, Straus and Giroux, 1980), 416–18; Henry Hurt, *Reasonable Doubt: An Investigation into the Assassination of John F. Kennedy* (New York: Henry Holt, 1985), 309; "Dousing a Popular Theory," *Time*, October 2, 1978, http://www.time.com/time /magazine/article/0,9171,948669,00.html [accessed May 31, 2011]; "Cable to CIA Director," March 3, 1964, "Latin American Division Work Files," Box 1, Record Group 263, Folder "WF02:F3," Archives II, College Park, Maryland.

28. Martin Roberts, "Cuban Ex-Intelligence Chief Recalls JFK Assassination," *Washington Post*, July 12, 2010.

29. Telephone interview with Edward Martino, May 8, 2013. Martino, who has apparently not sought publicity nor profited from his story, permitted my interview with him to be cited but requested that no direct quotations be used. See also Larry Hancock, "If There Was a JFK Conspiracy, Wouldn't Somebody Have Talked?" JFK Facts, January 2, 2013, http://jfkfacts.org/assassination/experts/if-there-was-a-jfk-conspiracy-wouldnt-somebody -have-talked/ [accessed May 10, 2013].

30. The term refers to an intensely propagandized individual who has been programmed subconsciously to act as an assassin, on the orders of a foreign power. Richard Condon wrote a thriller novel by this name, and it first appeared in a film released in 1962, starring, among others, Frank Sinatra. See Hal Hinson, "The Manchurian Candidate," *Washington Post*, February 13, 1988.

31. "Discussion Between Chairman Khrushchev and Mr. Drew Pearson, RE: Lee Harvey Oswald," May 27, 1964, NARA Record Number: 104-10150-10113, Mary Ferrell Foundation website, http://www.maryferrell.org/mffweb/archive/viewer/showDoc.do?docId=51190 &relPageId=2 [accessed January 7, 2013]. The memo containing the details of this conversation, leaked by Pearson and his wife, was signed by Richard Helms, CIA's Deputy Director for Plans.

32. "Nuclear Test Ban Treaty," John F. Kennedy Library website, http://www.jfklibrary .org/JFK/JFK-in-History/Nuclear-Test-Ban-Treaty.aspx [accessed May 19, 2011]; Arthur Schlesinger, Jr., *A Thousand Days: John F. Kennedy in the White House* (Boston: First Mariner Books, 2002), 905. Interview with Sergei Khrushchev, November 2, 2011, Charlottesville, Virginia. Richard Holmes, a seasoned British diplomat who was stationed in Moscow between

1961 and 1962, believes that JFK might have been the victim of KGB vigilantes seeking revenge for the Cuban Missile Crisis. Holmes raises interesting questions that give pause: Why did three Soviet diplomats stationed in Mexico City spend their Saturday morning meeting with Oswald, a person who was supposedly uninteresting to them? And why did these diplomats send a classified telegram to Moscow immediately after the meeting? See Richard Holmes, *A Spy Like No Other: The Cuban Missile Crisis and the KGB Links to the Kennedy Assassination* (London: Biteback Publishing, 2012).

33. "Yeltsin Gives Clinton JFK File," *Washington Post*, June 20, 1999; Max Holland, "A Cold War Odyssey: The Oswald Files," *Cold War International History Project Bulletin*, issue 14/15, Washington Decoded, http://www.washingtondecoded.com/site/files/a_coldwar _odyssey.pdf [accessed May 24, 2011]. On November 25, 1963, Soviet deputy premier Anastas Mikoyan gave the Kremlin a report on conversations he had with Secretary of State Dean Rusk and other American officials about the assassination. Mikoyan wrote, "Judging from everything, the U.S. government does not want to involve us in this matter, but neither does it want to get into a fight with the extreme rightists; it clearly prefers to consign the whole business to oblivion as soon as possible." See "Documents Handed to President Clinton by Russian President Boris Yeltsin," Mary Ferrell Foundation website, http://www.maryferrell .org/mffweb/archive/viewer/showDoc.do?docId=929&relPageId=72 [accessed August 5, 2011]. The Soviet high command also discovered a letter dated November 9, 1963, that Oswald had apparently sent to the Soviet embassy in Washington asking for information on "the arrival of our Soviet entrance visa's [sic] as soon as they come." The Soviets thought that the letter might be a forgery mailed by the true assassins who wanted to link Oswald to the USSR. See http://www.maryferrell.org/mffweb/archive/viewer/showDoc.do?docId=929&relPageId=95 [accessed August 5, 2011].

34. One of the most intriguing books on the Mafia's ties to the Kennedy assassination is David Kaiser's *The Road to Dallas* (Cambridge, MA: Belknap Press of Harvard University Press, 2008). Kaiser believes that Oswald had originally been hired to kill Castro, but targeted Kennedy after the Cuban embassy in Mexico City turned down his request for a travel visa. The Mafia despised both leaders.

35. Coppola, F. F. (director). (2010). *The Godfather, Part II* (Coppola Restoration) [Blu-ray] [motion picture]. United States: Paramount Home Entertainment.

36. *Godfather III* came out in 1990.

37. Evidently, some mobsters had disdain for Senator Edward Kennedy as well. Three weeks after RFK was assassinated, the FBI recorded a drunken threat made by Al Capone's son, who boasted that EMK might "get it too." See Helen Kennedy, "Al Capone's Son Threatened Hit on Sen. Ted Kennedy Weeks After Robert Kennedy's Assassination: FBI," *New York Daily News*, August 1, 2011, http://www.nydailynews.com/news/national/2011/08/01/2011-08 -01_al_capones_son_threatened_hit_on_sen_ted_kennedy_weeks_after_robert_ken nedys_ass.html [accessed August 2, 2011].

38. It is not clear that Joe Kennedy ever actually engaged in bootlegging. As the author Daniel Okrent points out, "Three times during the 1930s, Kennedy was appointed to federal positions requiring Senate confirmation (chairman of the Securities and Exchange Commission, chairman of the U.S. Maritime Commission, U.S. ambassador to Great Britain). At a time when the memory of Prohibition was vivid and the passions it inflamed still smoldered, no one seemed to think Joe Kennedy had been a bootlegger—not the Republicans, not the anti-Roosevelt Democrats, not remnant Klansmen or anti-Irish Boston Brahmins or

cynical newsmen or resentful Dry leaders still seething from the humiliation of Repeal." Daniel Okrent, "The Biggest Kennedy Myth," *Daily Beast*, April 26, 2010, http://www.the dailybeast.com/articles/2010/04/26/the-kennedy-bootlegging-myth.html [accessed July 27, 2010]. See also "Joe Kennedy Was No Angel But Neither Was He a Bootlegger," *Irish Examiner*, March 14, 2011.

39. This quotation comes from Sam and Chuck Giancana, *Double Cross: The Explosive, Inside Story of the Mobster Who Controlled America* (New York: Skyhorse Publishing, 2010), 308. Sam is the nephew of Sam "Momo" Giancana and the son of Sam's brother, Chuck Giancana.

40. Encouraged both by J. Edgar Hoover and RFK, President Kennedy began to put distance between himself and Sinatra on account of Sinatra's mob friendships. Having worked hard for Kennedy's election, Sinatra felt betrayed, and his fury was such that he even personally destroyed a helipad he had commissioned on his California property for the use of the presidential helicopter. Siobhan Synnot, "The Rat Pack, Booze, Broads and the Coolest Turkey in Film History," *Sunday Mail*, February 3, 2002.

41. See "Tina Sinatra: Mob Ties Aided JFK," *60 Minutes*, http://www.cbsnews.com/stories/2000/10/05/60minutes/main238980.shtml [accessed May 24, 2011].

42. Giancana, *Double Cross*, 308–9, 376, 388–92; Michael L. Kurtz, *The JFK Assassination Debates: Lone Gunman versus Conspiracy* (Lawrence: University Press of Kansas, 2006), 203; David Talbot, "The Man Who Solved the Kennedy Assassination," *Salon.com*, November 22, 2003, http://www.salon.com/news/feature/2003/11/22/conspiracy [accessed May 25, 2011].

43. John Davis, *Mafia Kingfish: Carlos Marcello and the Assassination of John F. Kennedy* (New York: Signet, 1989), 139–45; "The Assassination: Did the Mob Kill J.F.K.?" *Time*, June 21, 2007, http://www.time.com/time/magazine/article/0,9171,956397,00.html [accessed May 25, 2011]. Lee's mother, Marguerite Oswald, knew a number of Marcello's associates, including Sam Termine (Marcello's chauffeur), Clem Sehrt (one of Marcello's lawyers), and Louis Rousell (a financier who allegedly was an associate of Carlos Marcello).

44. Telephone interview with Robert Blakey, July 8, 2011; Waldron and Hartmann, *Legacy of Secrecy*, 50, 753; "Santos Trafficante—It Should Have Been Bobby," Mary Ferrell Foundation website, http://www.maryferrell.org/wiki/index.php/Santos_Trafficante_-_It_Should_Have_Been_Bobby [accessed August 2, 2011]; Frank Ragano, *Mob Lawyer* (New York: Random House, 1996); Gerald Posner, *Case Closed: Lee Harvey Oswald and the Assassination of JFK* (New York: Anchor Books, 1994), 460–61.

45. Moldea, *Hoffa Wars*, 148; Kurtz, *JFK Assassination Debates*, 203–5.

46. David Talbot, *Brothers: The Hidden History of the Kennedy Years* (New York: Free Press, 2007), 86–87; Seymour M. Hersh, *The Dark Side of Camelot* (Boston: Little, Brown, 1997), 203.

47. "Organized Crime Expert Says JFK Assassination Wasn't Mob Related," ABC News, http://abcnews.go.com/WNT/story?id=131460&page=1 [accessed May 26, 2011]; "HSCA Final Assassinations Report," p. 147, *History Matters*, http://history-matters.com/archive/jfk/hsca/report/html/HSCA_Report_0089a.htm [accessed May 26, 2011].

48. Posner, *Case Closed*, 461–62.

49. "Report of the President's Commission on the Assassination of President Kennedy: Appendix 16: A Biography of Jack Ruby," National Archives and Records Administration website, page 781, http://www.archives.gov/research/jfk/warren-commission-report/appendix-16.html#family [accessed June 6, 2011].

50. Marrs, *Crossfire*, 383–84. Dorfman would later develop a close working relationship with Jimmy Hoffa, the corrupt Teamsters Union president who despised RFK.

51. Ibid.; "Report of the President's Commission on the Assassination of President Kennedy: Appendix 16: A Biography of Jack Ruby," National Archives and Records Administration website, p. 801, http://www.archives.gov/research/jfk/warren-commission-report/appendix-16 .html#family [accessed June 6, 2011]; Posner, *Case Closed*, 395.

52. Moldea, *Hoffa Wars*, 155.

53. Ibid., 165–66; Marrs, *Crossfire*, 387; Davis, *Mafia Kingfish*, 180–84.

54. "Report of the President's Commission on the Assassination of President Kennedy: Appendix 16: A Biography of Jack Ruby," National Archives and Records Administration website, p. 801, http://www.archives.gov/research/jfk/warren-commission-report/appendix-16 .html#family [accessed June 6, 2011]. The HSCA's Robert Blakey says that the Warren Commission relied on Lenny Patrick—a Chicago hitman who grew up with Ruby—to prove that Ruby had no connection to organized crime. "Give me a break," Blakey said. "[Ruby's] operation was prostitution, a strip joint. And the women are on a circle that go to these clubs. People don't want to watch the same woman every week. And the union that runs this is mob-dominated. And the place where he got them from, in New Orleans over to Dallas, was run by Carlos Marcello's brother." Telephone interview with Robert Blakey, July 8, 2011.

55. Moldea, *Hoffa Wars*, 152.

56. Kurtz, *JFK Assassination Debates*, 198–99.

57. Giancana, *Double Cross*, 193.

58. Summers, *Kennedy Conspiracy*, 335–40.

59. "Report of the President's Commission on the Assassination of President Kennedy: Appendix 16: A Biography of Jack Ruby," National Archives and Records Administration website, p. 802, http://www.archives.gov/research/jfk/warren-commission-report/appendix-16 .html#family [accessed June 6, 2011]; Kurtz, *JFK Assassination Debates*, 196.

60. Marrs, *Crossfire*, 37.

61. Posner, *Case Closed*, 259. Oliver said she used a camera on 11/22 that did not exist in 1963.

62. Posner, *Case Closed*, 368.

63. Personal interview with Jim Leavelle, April 8, 2011, Dallas.

64. Telephone interview with Nancy Pelosi, May 26, 2011.

65. Posner, *Case Closed*, 396; "Testimony of Barnard S. Clardy," Warren Commission Hearings, vol. XII, p. 412, The John F. Kennedy Assassination Homepage, http://www.jfk-as sassination.de/warren/wch/vol12/page412.php [accessed June 8, 2011]; personal interview with Bill Alexander, Dallas, January 14, 2011.

66. Mel Ayton, "Why Jack Ruby Killed Lee Harvey Oswald," *Crime*, November 25, 2005, http://www.crimemagazine.com/why-jack-ruby-killed-lee-harvey-oswald?page=57 [accessed August 2, 2011].

67. Telephone interview with Jim Cunningham, December 17, 2012. Cunningham, now an Episcopal Church deacon in his eighties, was working in his office near Love Field when the presidential motorcade went by on November 22.

68. "The Assassination: A Nonentity for History," *Time*, January 13, 1967, http://www.time .com/time/magazine/article/0,9171,843229,00.html [accessed June 8, 2011]; "Sequels: A Last Wish," *Time*, December 30, 1966, http://www.time.com/time/magazine/article/0,9171,901898 ,00.html [accessed June 8, 2011].

69. It is important to note that Oswald's transfer schedule was not the equivalent of a space launch; many realized it might not be precisely adhered to. The ten A.M. transfer time was tentative, and established to give the news media plenty of time to arrive and set up. Oswald's interrogating officers were not hurried to finish by anyone inside or outside the police department. See "Shooting of Oswald," http://www.jfk.org/go/exhibits/dallas/oswald -shooting [accessed December 5, 2012], and "Testimony of Harry D. Holmes," Warren Commission Hearings, vol. VII, http://history-matters.com/archive/jfk/wc/wcvols/wh7/html/WC _Vol7_0153a.htm [accessed December 5, 2012].

70. Telephone interview with Robert Blakey, July 8, 2011.

71. Summers, *Kennedy Conspiracy*, 349.

72. Personal interview with Bill Alexander, Dallas, January 14, 2011.

10. EXAMINING THE PHYSICAL EVIDENCE: OLD AND NEW CONTROVERSIES

1. Warren Report, chapter 1, History Matters website, pp. 52–56, http://www.history -matters.com/archive/jfk/wc/wr/html/WCReport_0038b.htm [accessed September 29, 2011]. See also "The Kennedy Connection," Parkland Hospital website, http://www.parklandhos pital.com/whoweare/kennedy.html [accessed June 8, 2011].

2. Warren Commission Hearings, History Matters website, Testimony of Dr. Charles Carrico, March 30, 1964 (vol. 3, p. 359), http://www.history-matters.com/archive/jfk/wc /wcvols/wh3/html/WC_Vol3_0184a.htm [accessed September 29, 2011]. Based upon these faint heartbeats, Dr. Carrico concluded that the president was still technically alive and continued efforts to stabilize the patient. This is a somewhat different definition of "living" than we have today, of course. JFK was brain-dead from the moment the bullet(s) struck his head, and his presidency effectively ended at 12:30 pm CST. See the Warren Report, chapter 1, History Matters website, at pp. 53–54, http://www.history-matters.com/archive/jfk/wc/ wr/html/WCReport_0039b.htm [accessed September 29, 2011].

3. Warren Commission Hearings, History Matters website, Testimony of Dr. Charles Carrico, March 25, 1964 (vol. 6, p. 3), http://www.history-matters.com/archive/jfk/wc /wcvols/wh6/html/WC_Vol6_0007a.htm [accessed September 29, 2011].

4. Warren Commission Hearings, History Matters website, Testimony of Dr. Malcolm Perry, March 30, 1964 (vol. 3, pp. 367-368), http://www.history-matters.com/archive/jfk/wc /wcvols/wh3/html/WC_Vol3_0188a.htm [accessed September 29, 2011].

5. Ibid., 368. Dr. Perry told the Warren Commission that he had considerable experience with gunshot wounds, examining 150 to 200 during his tenure at Parkland Memorial Hospital.

6. Warren Commission Hearings, History Matters website, Testimony of Dr. Malcolm Perry, March 30, 1964 (vol. 3, pp. 369-70), http://www.history-matters.com/archive/jfk/wc /wcvols/wh3/html/WC_Vol3_0189a.htm [accessed September 29, 2011].

7. Warren Commission Hearings, History Matters website, Testimony of Dr. Kemp Clark, March 21, 1964 (vol. 6, p. 20, 25), http://www.history-matters.com/archive/jfk/wc /wcvols/wh6/html/WC_Vol6_0015b.htm [accessed September 29, 2011]; Warren Report, chapter 1, History Matters website, at pp. 54–55, http://www.history-matters.com/archive/jfk /wc/wr/html/WCReport_0039b.htm [accessed September 29, 2011].

8. Warren Commission Hearings, History Matters website, Testimony of Dr. Marion T. Jenkins, March 21, 1964 (vol. 6, p. 48), http://www.history-matters.com/archive/jfk/wc

/wcvols/wh6/html/WC_Vol6_0029b.htm [accessed September 29, 2011]. In all likelihood, Jenkins made a mistake by saying "cerebellum" when he meant to say "cerebrum." See Dennis Breo, "JFK's Death, Part II—Dallas MDs Recall Their Memories," *Journal of the American Medical Association* 267:20 (1992): 2804–7. The cerebrum is at the top of the head—the cerebellum is elsewhere.

9. Clint Hill, the agent who jumped on the back of the presidential limousine in an attempt to shield the Kennedys from additional gunfire, believes that Mrs. Kennedy had been trying to retrieve a large piece of JFK's skull when she climbed on the trunk of the vehicle. Billy Harper, a medical student at Texas Christian University, found a 2¾–inch piece of Kennedy's skull lying in Dealey Plaza, which he quickly turned over to the authorities. E-mail from Gerald Blaine, January 9, 2013. See also G. Paul Chambers, *Head Shot: The Science Behind the JFK Assassination* (Amherst, NY: Prometheus Books, 2010), 93–96.

10. Breo, "JFK's Death, Part II," 2804–7.

11. Warren Commission Hearings, History Matters website, Testimony of Dr. Kemp Clark, March 21, 1964 (vol. 6, p. 20), http://www.history-matters.com/archive/jfk/wc/wcvols /wh6/html/WC_Vol6_0015b.htm [accessed September 29, 2010].

12. "Surgeon Who Operated on JFK in Dallas Dies," Associated Press, March 12, 2005. Quoted in Vincent Bugliosi, *Reclaiming History: The Assassination of President John F. Kennedy* (New York: W. W. Norton, 2007), 71.

13. "The Assassination," *Time*, November 29, 1963, http://www.time.com/time/magazine /article/0,9171,875361,00.html [accessed September 29, 2010]. Only WBAP, the NBC television affiliate in Dallas, made a sound recording of Kilduff's historic announcement, and NBC did not even air it until November 1964. It has made only infrequent appearances in films about the assassination since then. E-mail from Gary Mack, June 15, 2012.

14. Dr. Perry described the throat wound as an "entrance" wound three times during the press conference. See Assassination Records Review Board, Master Set of Medical Deposition Exhibits, available at the National Archives (Box 1, MD 41) or online at http://www .maryferrell.org/mffweb/archive/viewer/showDoc.do;jsessionid=B71BDC6C072CE59FC303 A37418E504DE?docId=622 [accessed August 16, 2011].

15. Warren Commission Hearings, History Matters website, Testimony of Dr. Malcolm Perry, March 30, 1964 (vol. 3, pp. 373–74), http://www.history-matters.com/archive/jfk/wc /wcvols/wh3/html/WC_Vol3_0191b.htm [accessed August 15, 2011]. The doctors who attended Kennedy believed, as Dr. Robert McClelland put it to me, that despite his other health problems, the president "would have very likely survived" the neck wound alone. Personal interview, January 14, 2011, Dallas.

16. Charles A. Crenshaw, M.D., *JFK: Conspiracy of Silence* (New York: Penguin Books, 1992), 79.

17. Gary Mack considers Crenshaw's account "nonsense" and told me that "Crenshaw arrived with McClelland, who testified that when he first saw JFK, the tracheotomy was in progress and the wound was obliterated." E-mail from Gary Mack, June 15, 2012.

18. Some have expressed doubts as to whether Dr. Crenshaw was even present at the time of the resuscitation efforts. See Breo, "JFK's Death, Part II," p. 2804. None of the physicians interviewed during Breo's research remembered seeing Dr. Crenshaw in the trauma room. Of course, the room was crowded and most eyes were undoubtedly fixed on the president or Mrs. Kennedy. No photographs were taken in Trauma Room One, so once again, we will never know for sure.

19. "AARB MD 41—White House Transcript of Dallas Press Conference," Mary Ferrell Foundation website, http://www.maryferrell.org/mffweb/archive/viewer/showDoc.do?docId =622&relPageId=5 [accessed September 29, 2011].

20. Personal interview with Robert McClelland, Dallas, January 15, 2011. Dr. McClelland almost certainly meant to say "cerebrum," not "cerebellum." See note 8 above.

21. "MR. SPECTER: Did you observe the condition of the back of the president's head? DR. McCLELLAND: Well, partially; not, of course, as I say, we did not lift his head up since it was so greatly damaged. We attempted to avoid moving him any more than it was absolutely necessary, but I could see, of course, all the extent of the wound. MR. SPECTER: Did you observe a small gunshot wound below the large opening on the back of his head? DR. McCLELLAND: No." Testimony of Dr. Robert Nelson McClelland, March 21, 1964, Warren Commission Hearings, History Matters website (vol. 6, pp. 30–39), http://www.history -matters.com/archive/jfk/wc/wcvols/wh6/html/WC_Vol6_0023a.htm [accessed September 29, 2011].

22. In another strange twist, McClelland almost physically bumped into John Kennedy at the entrance to Baylor Hospital in late 1961, when JFK arrived to visit terminally ill House Speaker Sam Rayburn. Kennedy returned for Rayburn's funeral, which made the November 1963 trip his third and final visit to Texas as president.

23. Personal interview with Robert McClelland, Dallas, January 15, 2011. McClelland's suit was soaked as well, but he had only two of them, so his wife had it dry-cleaned.

24. Breo, "JFK's Death: Part II," at p. 2806. Practically, it is difficult to see how November 22 would have played out had Kennedy's body been delayed for hours in Dallas so that an autopsy could be performed. Probably new president Lyndon Johnson would have had to leave Mrs. Kennedy and the fallen president behind to take a separate flight to D.C. Mrs. Kennedy also would not have participated in the swearing-in of LBJ, and there would have been additional mass confusion as aides and Secret Service decided who would be assigned to which flight.

25. The last surviving FBI agent to witness JFK's autopsy, James Sibert, died in 2012. In the years after the Kennedy assassination, Sibert told numerous interviewers that he "didn't buy the single bullet theory." See Stephanie Borden, "Last Surviving FBI Agent at JFK Autopsy Dies in Fort Meyers," *Naples News*, April 18, 2012, http://www.naplesnews.com/news /2012/apr/18/last-surviving-fbi-agent-at-jfk-autopsy-dies-in/ [accessed April 19, 2012].

26. See Jim Marrs, *Crossfire: The Plot That Killed Kennedy* (New York: Carroll and Graf, 1989), 368–73.

27. Warren Report, History Matters website, appendix IX, page 541, http://www.history -matters.com/archive/jfk/wc/wr/html/WCReport_0283a.htm [accessed September 29, 2011].

28. See Dennis Breo, "JFK's Death—The Plain Truth from the MDs Who Did the Autopsy," *Journal of the American Medical Association* 267:20 (1992): at p. 2798, http://jama .ama-assn.org/content/267/20/2794.short [accessed September 29, 2011]; Rockefeller Commission Report, chapter 19, p. 262, Mary Ferrell Foundation website, http://www.maryferrell .org/mffweb/archive/viewer/showDoc.do;jsessionid=1A16E8264CA1C009F1291DFB02116 02A?docId=930&relPageId=274 [accessed October 11, 2011]. Also in the 1970s, the Kennedy family allowed Dr. John Lattimer, chairman of the urology department at Columbia University, to examine the autopsy photos and X-rays. Lattimer upheld the main conclusions of the Warren Report—namely that President Kennedy had been struck from behind by two bullets. See Fred P. Graham, "Doctor Inspects Kennedy X-rays," *New York Times*,

January 9, 1972. A few years earlier, an independent panel of medical experts appointed by Attorney General Ramsey Clark arrived at a similar conclusion. See "ARRB MD 59—Clark Panel Report (2/26/68)," page 4, Mary Ferrell Foundation website, http://www.maryferrell .org/mffweb/archive/viewer/showDoc.do?docId=323&relPageId=4 [accessed October 11, 2011].

29. Dennis Breo, "JFK's Death, Part III—Dr. Finck Speaks Out: 'Two Bullets, from the Rear,'" *Journal of the American Medical Association* 268:13 (1992): 1748–54, History Matters website, http://www.history-matters.com/archive/jfk/arrb/master_med_set/md23/html /Image09.htm [accessed September 29, 2011].

30. Henry Hurt, *Reasonable Doubt: An Investigation Into the Assassination of John F. Kennedy* (New York: Henry Holt, 1985), 36. Gerald Posner says that the Kennedys still intended to have an open casket at this point and did not want the president to be disfigured. Gerald Posner, *Case Closed: Lee Harvey Oswald and the Assassination of JFK* (New York: Anchor Books, 1994), 302.

31. Breo, "JFK's Death—The Plain Truth," 2794–2803.

32. Dr. Humes helped persuade Clark to assemble the panel. He and J. Thornton Boswell—one of the other two physicians at Bethesda—wrote a letter to the attorney general requesting a new investigation in order to quell rumors of a conspiracy. See Breo, "JFK's Death—The Plain Truth," p. 2800. However, some medical experts, such as Cyril Wecht, do not accept the findings of the autopsy and other matters related to President Kennedy's assassination. See Wecht with Mark Curriden and Benjamin Wecht, *Cause of Death* (New York: Dutton, 1993).

33. Warren Commission Hearings, History Matters website, Testimony of Commander James Humes, March 16, 1964 (vol. 2, p. 364), http://www.history-matters.com/archive/jfk /wc/wcvols/wh2/html/WC_Vol2_0186b.htm [accessed September 29, 2011].

34. Michael L. Kurtz, *The JFK Assassination Debates: Lone Gunman versus Conspiracy* (Lawrence: University Press of Kansas, 2006), 16. Of course, Humes was correct if this was the same bullet that struck JFK and then Connally—though Humes could not have imagined at the time that the bullet had dropped from Connally's wounded body onto the governor's gurney and not Kennedy's.

35. Breo, "JFK's Death—Part III," 1750.

36. Posner, *Case Closed*, 300; Chambers, *Head Shot*, 98.

37. "The Moving Head Wounds," Mary Ferrell Foundation website, http://www.mary ferrell.org/wiki/index.php/The_Moving_Head_Wounds [accessed July 26, 2011].

38. Humes's testimony can be found at http://history-matters.com/archive/jfk/hsca/re portvols/vol1/html/HSCA_Vol1_0167b.htm [accessed October 11, 2011].

39. Some of the autopsy photos are available at http://jfklancer.com/photos/autopsy _slideshow/index.html [accessed October 11, 2011].

40. In February 2013 I wrote to former U.S. senator Paul G. Kirk, Jr., Ted Kennedy's appointed successor in the Senate and a longtime Kennedy family friend, requesting access to JFK's autopsy records. Kirk replied respectfully but wrote: "[T]he terms of the Deed are explicit, and they do not permit access to these autopsy materials to persons, however serious their purpose or the level of esteem in which they may be held in their own particular field of study, who are not recognized experts in the field of pathology or related areas of science and technology. I trust you can understand the logic of limiting access to those whose conclusions and theories about the assassination would be founded on their own recognized

expertise and academic qualifications in those particular fields or disciplines." Letter from Paul Kirk to author, March 1, 2013.

41. Richard Dudman, a reporter covering the president's trip for the *St. Louis Post-Dispatch*, insisted that he saw a "small hole" (not a "crack") in the windshield of the limousine when it arrived at Parkland Hospital. See Jefferson Morley, "Dec. 1, 1963: The Origins of Doubt," JFK Facts, April 25, 2013, http://jfkfacts.org/assassination/on-this-date/dec-1-1963-the-origins-of-doubt/#more-4321 [accessed April 26, 2013].

42. The ordering of this evidence replicates the Commission's own listing in the summary of its findings. Warren Commission Report, chapter 1, pp. 18–20, History Matters website, http://www.history-matters.com/archive/jfk/wc/wr/html/WCReport_0021b.htm [accessed September 30, 2011].

43. Ibid.

44. The calculations behind this are outlined in the report: The vehicle traveled 136 feet in the 152 Zapruder frames preceding the first shot. At a camera rate of 18.3 frames per second, this yields 11.2 mph.

45. Warren Commission Hearings, vol. V, p. 180, History Matters website, http://www.history-matters.com/archive/jfk/wc/wcvols/wh5/html/WC_Vol5_0095b.htm [accessed October 3, 2011].

46. I personally heard this version from Nellie Connally at a private dinner at the LBJ Library on February 7, 1997. Ironically, the dinner speaker was former president Gerald Ford of the Warren Commission.

47. There are slightly differing assessments of Connally's movements, including Connally's own testimony a week after the assassination. According to the author Michael Kurtz, Governor Connally "turned to his right to see what had happened, but he saw nothing, so he decided to turn around to his left, but he only moved back to a straight ahead position. Then Connally, his movements having consumed about a second and a half, felt the searing pain of a shot that tore through his upper back . . ." (Kurtz, *Assassination Debates*, p. 4). Vincent Bugliosi described the same moment this way: "Unable to see the president over his right shoulder, and deeply concerned for his safety, Governor Connally is in the middle of a turn to look back over his left shoulder into the backseat, to see if Kennedy has been hit, when he feels a hard blow to the right side of his own back, like a doubled-up fist." (Bugliosi, *Reclaiming History*, 40.) For Connally's own recollection, see https://www.tsl.state.tx.us/governors/modern/connally-agronsky-1.html [accessed November 1, 2012].

48. Marrs, *Crossfire*, 12–13; Warren Commission Hearings, vol. IV, p. 147, History Matters website, http://www.history-matters.com/archive/jfk/wc/wcvols/wh4/html/WC_Vol4_0078a.htm [accessed October 3, 2011].

49. Blaine, *Kennedy Detail*, 214–15; Warren Commission Hearings, vol. II, pp. 74 and 117–18, History Matters website, http://www.history-matters.com/archive/jfk/wc/wcvols/wh2/html/WC_Vol2_0063a.htm [accessed October 3, 2011].

50. E-mail from Gerald Blaine, January 9, 2013.

51. Gerald Blaine with Lisa McCubbin, *The Kennedy Detail: JFK's Secret Service Agents Break Their Silence* (New York: Gallery Books, 2010), 216–17.

52. "Testimony of Rufus Wayne Youngblood, http://mcadams.posc.mu.edu/russ/testimony/youngblo.htm [accessed October 4, 2011].

53. Warren Commission Hearings, vol. V, p. 562, History Matters website, http://www

.history-matters.com/archive/jfk/wc/wcvols/wh5/html/WC_Vol5_0286b.htm [accessed October 3, 2011].

54. Warren Commission Hearings, vol. VII, pp. 474–75, History Matters website, http://www.history-matters.com/archive/jfk/wc/wcvols/wh7/html/WC_Vol7_0242a.htm [accessed October 3, 2011].

55. "Report of United States Secret Service on the Assassination of President Kennedy," C. Douglas Dillon Papers, Box 43, Folder "The President's Committee on the Warren Report," John F. Kennedy Library, Boston, Massachusetts.

56. Bugliosi, Reclaiming History, 67.

57. Affidavit of Seymour Weitzman, appendix VI in Mark Lane, Rush to Judgment (New York: Thunder's Mouth Press, 1992), 409.

58. Telephone interview with Eugene Boone, September 14, 2012. Boone also added some comments worth considering on the possible presence of a second gunman; I have included them on my website, TheKennedyHalfCentury.com.

59. Bertrand Russell, "16 Questions on the Assassination," The Minority of One (6 September 1964), 6–8.

60. Telephone interview with Wesley Buell Frazier, April 16, 2013.

61. Testimony of Robert A. Frazier, March 31, 1964, Warren Commission Hearings, vol. III, The Assassination Archives and Research Center website, http://www.aarclibrary.org/publib/jfk/wc/wcvols/wh3/html/WC_Vol3_0202a.htm [accessed April 19, 2013].

62. "Chapter 4: The Assassin," p. 133, JFK Assassination Records, National Archives and Records Administration website, http://www.archives.gov/research/jfk/warren-commission-report/chapter-4.html [accessed April 19, 2013].

63. Bugliosi, Reclaiming History (photo insert.)

64. Telephone interview with Wesley Buell Frazier, April 16, 2013.

65. Frazier's friendship with Oswald initially convinced police that he was involved in the assassination, and they tried to force him to sign a confession. "Captain Will Fritz, after quite a few hours of interrogation . . . [came] through the door, and that was the first time I'd ever seen him, and he had this red-ribbon paper, 8.5" by 11", and he had a pen with him. He put this [confession] down in front of me and said, 'I want you to sign this.' And I looked at him and said, 'I'm not signing that. That's ridiculous.' Well, he drew back his hand to hit me and I put my left arm up for a block. And I told him, 'There's policemen on the other side of that door but we're gonna have a hell of a fight before they get in here.' He got real red-faced. He snatched the paper up in front of me and the pen and walked out the door. I don't think I was treated properly because I never had been in any type of [trouble before]." Frazier says that he had difficulty sleeping in the days that followed. "This was a very terrifying thing for me."

66. Warren Commission Report, chapter 1, p. 53, History Matters website, http://www.history-matters.com/archive/jfk/wc/wr/html/WCReport_0039a.htm [accessed October 3, 2011].

67. Anthony Summers, The Kennedy Conspiracy (London: Sphere Books, 1989), 391.

68. Interview with James T. Tague, March 30, 1999, conducted by Bob Porter, Sixth Floor Museum at Dealey Plaza, Dallas, Texas. However, Vincent Bugliosi says that bullets "consist of 98 to 99 percent lead, the rest being trace elements" (Bugliosi, 813). Chris Kincheloe, owner of Nuckols Gun Works in Staunton, Virginia, told me that copper residue would probably not show up in a scar caused by a copper-encased lead bullet.

69. Cliff Spiegelman, one of the researchers involved in the study, credits a high school government teacher named Stuart Wexler with piquing his interest in the assassination's ballistic evidence. "Wexler and a friend of his had bought some bullets of the same type believed to have been used in the Kennedy assassination," Spiegelman explains. "They were Mannlicher-Carcanos, which were only manufactured in 1954 and are now antiques, mainly because most surviving bullets have been bought up by conspiracy buffs. He was looking for someone to analyze them. I thought it was interesting and that it would be a neat project, so I agreed." Spiegelman told me that Dr. Vincent Guinn, a chemistry professor at the University of California, "testified to the House Select Committee on Assassinations, that he knew what kind of ammunition was used . . . We disagree that he would know that from the chemical composition . . . He also said that he could count the bullets in the Kennedy party . . . From the chemical analysis it's just impossible to count." Telephone interview with Cliff Spiegelman, July 27, 2011. Using a technique known as neutron activation analysis, Guinn told the HSCA that all of the bullet fragments recovered on 11/22 came from just two bullets and that those two bullets closely matched ammunition made by the Western Cartridge Company for Mannlicher-Carcano rifles. But Spiegelman told me, "If Dr. Guinn's wrong and bullets aren't chemically unique [which is what Spiegelman's team basically concluded], then those five fragments could be five different bullets." Telephone interview with Cliff Spiegelman, August 3, 2011. See also Gary L. Aguilar, "Is Vincent Bugliosi Right that Neutron Activation Analysis Proves Oswald's Guilt?", Mary Ferrell Foundation website, http://www.maryferrell.org/wiki/index.php/Essay_-_Is_Vincent_Bugliosi_Right_that_Neutron_Activation_Analysis_Proves_Oswalds_Guilt [accessed September 1, 2011].

70. "Texas A&M Statistician Probes Bullet Evidence in JFK Assassination," May 14, 2007, Texas A&M College of Science website, http://www.science.tamu.edu/articles/550/;%20%20http://arxiv.org/abs/0712.2150 [accessed June 8, 2011].

71. The wound at the base and rear of the president's neck also showed a bullet channel that had terminated at the throat, in the area obliterated by the tracheotomy.

72. Warren Report, chapter 1, p. 60, History Matters website, http://www.history-matters.com/archive/jfk/wc/wr/html/WCReport_0042b.htm [accessed October 3, 2011].

73. See G. Paul Chambers, *Head Shot: The Science Behind the JFK Assassination* (New York: Prometheus Books, 2010). See also David R. Wrone, *The Zapruder Film: Reframing JFK's Assassination* (Lawrence: University Press of Kansas, 2003), 1; Richard B. Trask, *Pictures of the Pain: Photography and the Assassination of President Kennedy* (Danvers, MA: Yeoman Press, 1994), 124. Professor Wrone's argument is especially noteworthy. Wrone used advanced forensic techniques to examine the Zapruder film and concluded that more than one person fired on Kennedy. He doubts that Oswald was one of these gunmen.

74. See Barr McClellan, *Blood, Money, and Power: How LBJ Killed JFK* (New York: Skyhorse Publishing, 2011); Joseph P. Farrell, *LBJ and the Conspiracy to Kill Kennedy* (Kempton, IL: Adventures Unlimited Press, 2011); L. Fletcher Prouty, *JFK: The CIA, Vietnam, and the Plot to Assassinate John F. Kennedy* (New York: Skyhorse Publishing, 2011); and Roger Stone, *The Man Who Killed Kennedy: The Case Against LBJ* (New York: Skyhorse Publishing, 2013).

75. See Robert Caro, *Means of Ascent: The Years of Lyndon Johnson* (New York: Alfred A. Knopf, 1990); Fredrik Logevall, *Choosing War: The Lost Chance for Peace and the Escalation of the War in Vietnam* (Berkeley: University of California Press, 1999); and Robert Dallek, *Flawed Giant: Lyndon Johnson and His Times, 1961–73* (New York: Oxford University Press, 1998).

76. David McCullough, *John Adams* (New York: Simon and Schuster, 2001), 389.

77. Johnson had had a near-fatal heart attack in 1955. Once out of office, Johnson had another serious heart attack in 1972 and finally succumbed to heart disease at the age of sixty-four in January 1973.

78. Randall B. Woods, *LBJ: Architect of American Ambition* (New York: Free Press, 2006), 422. Having succeeded Kennedy with only fourteen months remaining in the term, Johnson was constitutionally eligible to run for two full terms. Had he not been essentially forced out by anti-Vietnam war sentiment in 1968, LBJ might have served over nine years as president, more than anyone except his political hero, Franklin D. Roosevelt.

79. Arthur M. Schlesinger, Jr., *A Thousand Days: John F. Kennedy in the White House* (Boston: Houghton Mifflin, 1965), 1020–21.

80. "Sale 43, Lot 240: John F. Kennedy's Personal Secretary Lists Suspects in His Murder," Alexander Autographs, http://auctions.alexautographs.com/asp/fullCatalogue.asp?salelot=43+++++++240+&refno=+++68450 [accessed June 3, 2011]. Lincoln's other suspects were (in order) the "KKK, [Southern] Dixiecrats, [Teamsters boss Jimmy] Hoffa, [the] John Birch Society, [Richard] Nixon [who had been in Dallas on a well-publicized trip the previous day, perhaps raising suspicions in Mrs. Lincoln's mind], [the late South Vietnam Premier] Diem [presumably, Lincoln meant loyalists to Diem upset about his recent assassination], Rightist[s], [the] CIA in Cuban fiasco [presumably, she meant the Bay of Pigs], [unnamed] Dictators, [and] Communists."

81. David Talbot, *Brothers: The Hidden History of the Kennedy Years* (New York: Free Press, 2007), 252.

82. "Godfrey T. McHugh Oral History Interview, May 19, 1978," John F. Kennedy Presidential Library and Museum website, http://www.jfklibrary.org/Asset-Viewer/Archives/JFKOH-GTM-02.aspx [accessed April 23, 2013].

83. Craig I. Zirbel, *The Texas Connection* (New York: Warner Books, 1991), 226.

84. Zirbel says that Hunt assisted LBJ during the 1960 Democratic primaries by printing and circulating "over 200,000 copies of a speech lambasting Kennedy as a Catholic." Zirbel also believes that Oswald wrote a letter to Hunt or Hunt's son on November 8, 1963, that read, "Dear Mr. Hunt, I would like information concerding [sic] my position. I am asking only for information. I am asking that we discuss the matter fully before any steps are taken by me or anyone else. Thank you, Lee Harvey Oswald." Handwriting experts are divided over the authenticity of the letter. In the 1990s, Christopher Andrew and Vasili Mitrokhin published a book claiming that the Hunt letter was a clever KGB forgery. Mitrokhin was a KGB agent who worked in the agency's foreign intelligence archives; he defected to Great Britain in 1992 and turned over a treasure trove of notes and secret documents. See *The Sword and the Shield: The Mitrokhin Archive and the Secret History of the KGB* (New York: Basic Books, 2000). The Hunts were staunch right-wingers. One of Hunt's sons helped pay for the highly critical advertisement headlined "Welcome Mr. Kennedy" that appeared in the *Dallas Morning News* on 11/22. Hunt Sr. hosted a right-wing radio show called *Life Line* and founded a conservative organization called the Facts Forum. Another wealthy Texan sometimes linked to Hunt and the Kennedy assassination is D. H. Byrd. David Harold Byrd was an oil baron who purchased the Texas School Book Depository in the 1930s. He was affiliated with the so-called Suite 8F Group—a coterie of conservative businessmen who took their name from the Houston hotel room where they would often meet. Lyndon Johnson and John Connally were supposedly affiliated with this group. Byrd also founded an aviation

company called Temco that employed Mac Wallace, a man who was charged with killing the owner of a golf course in Austin (John Kinser) who was allegedly sleeping with Johnson's sister. Wallace also knew Lyndon Johnson, and it has been alleged that LBJ interceded to get Wallace off the hook following the murder. Wallace has also been linked to a palm print found on the sixth floor of the Depository. If Wallace worked for Byrd, it is not unreasonable to think that he might have been in the Book Depository at some point for one reason or another—assuming the palm print was actually his, which is hotly disputed. In 2001 author Vincent Bugliosi interviewed Nathan Darby, a Texas print examiner who identified a print found on the sixth floor of the Depository as Wallace's. Darby told Bugliosi that he'd been given "two fingerprints, one from a card, the other a latent [print]" and that it was "all blind." "I didn't know and wasn't told who they belonged to," said Darby. Bugliosi told Darby that the "latent" print found in the Depository was a palm print, not a fingerprint. Darby replied, "Of course, you can't compare a palm print with a fingerprint." Bugliosi, *Reclaiming History*, 922–23. Gary Mack of the Sixth Floor Museum at Dealey Plaza goes further: "There was no 'Wallace print' found anywhere in the Depository. One partial print [on the sixth floor at the time of the assassination] was unidentified and a study decades later using photocopies, not actual prints, concluded the partial belonged to Wallace. But another examiner found far more points of dissimilarity which, to print experts, immediately rules out a match." E-mail from Gary Mack, August 30, 2011.

85. Robert Dallek, *Lyndon B. Johnson: Portrait of a President* (New York: Oxford University Press, 2004), 142. Other Kennedy loyalists doubted Lincoln's story, including close aide Ted Sorensen. For example, in a personal interview with me, Sorensen said he was unaware of any such plan. However, Jackie Kennedy, in tape-recorded conversations with historian and Kennedy aide Arthur Schlesinger in the spring of 1964, insisted that both JFK and RFK were completely opposed to LBJ as Kennedy's potential successor, and they planned to back someone else to stop Johnson in 1968. No doubt Johnson, who had superb political antennae, was aware of their hostility to his ambitions. See Jacqueline Kennedy, *Historic Conversations on Life with John F. Kennedy* (New York: Hyperion, 2011), 277–78.

86. Kennedy, *Historic Conversations*, 278.

87. In the latest installment of his award-winning series on LBJ, historian Robert Caro reveals that the editors of LIFE magazine were meeting to decide the fate of a muckraking piece on Johnson's questionable business dealings in Texas when news of Kennedy's death came over the wires. See Robert Caro, *The Passage of Power* (New York: Alfred A. Knopf, 2012), 308–9.

88. See Blaine, *Kennedy Detail*, 176, 322, and his "U.S. Secret Service Employee's Monthly Activity Report," November 1963, National Archives and Records Administration, College Park, Maryland. The report shows that Blaine worked 109 overtime hours the month Kennedy was killed.

89. "Report of the United States Secret Service on the Assassination of President Kennedy," C. Douglas Dillon Papers, Box 43, Folder "The President's Committee on the Warren Report," John F. Kennedy Library, Boston, Massachusetts.

90. For example, Secret Service agents produced 30,820 "protection hours" in August 1964 compared to 21,446 the previous August. "Comparative Analysis: August—Protection Hours, U.S. Secret Service," C. Douglas Dillon Papers, Box 43, Folder "The President's Committee on the Warren Report," John F. Kennedy Library, Boston, Massachusetts. The Treasury Department spent time reviewing security procedures during overseas presidential

trips and "the advance detection of people who might [pose a threat] to the president or the vice president." At a press conference held on September 29, 1964, Secretary of the Treasury C. Douglas Dillon announced the completion of a "great many" security improvements. "There has been a great deal more advance preparations of visits to different cities," he said, "buildings have been surveyed, routes have been surveyed; we have used in this process the help of other government enforcement agencies, largely Treasury agencies but also the FBI . . ." See "President's Committee on Warren Report Holds First Meeting," September 29, 1964, C. Douglas Dillon Papers, Box 42, Folder "The President's Committee on the Warren Report," John F. Kennedy Library, Boston, Massachusetts.

91. While no one knows for sure how Lee Oswald learned of the motorcade route, one of his fellow boarders at the Roberts house told the press—forty years after the assassination—that Oswald saw the route on an evening news show a few days before the president's visit. Unless Oswald was part of a well-informed, high-level assassination plot, one assumes he first realized via the local news or from co-workers that Kennedy would be passing right next to his place of employment.

92. "SAIC Behn—White House Detail, Statement on Releasing the Exact Route of Presidential Motorcades," and "Statement on General Procedure When Surveying Individual Buildings along Motorcade Route," December 12, 1963, C. Douglas Dillon Papers, Box 42, Folder "The President's Committee on the Warren Report," John F. Kennedy Library, Boston, Massachusetts. Today, it is accepted practice for the Secret Service to insist that all windows in buildings surrounding a presidential appearance be either closed or covered by agents or police.

93. Gerald S. Blaine to James J. Rowley, "Final Survey Report," December 4, 1963, JFK countercoup website, http://jfkcountercoup.blogspot.com/2012/12/the-tampa-survey-report .html [accessed January 8, 2013]. Blaine explained to me why he finally decided after fifty years to donate this document and others to the National Archives: "[It's] because some of the conspiracy theories indicated that we had a problem in Tampa by an alleged three-man hit team [and that] the president knew about it. This was totally false. The report states that there were no unusual incidents. Tampa went very smoothly and both threat subjects were isolated. One, a young man with psychiatric problems [Wayne Gainey], was placed under the custody of his parents and a local agent had the home under surveillance. The second threat case individual [John Warrington] was in the Tampa jail for making a death threat to the mayor." E-mail from Gerald Blaine, January 9, 2013. During a 1978 interview with the HSCA, one of Blaine's colleagues, Agent Robert Jamison, was presented with documents from November 18, 1963, that showed that the Secret Service was worried about "a mobile, unidentified rifleman shooting from a window of a tall building with a high powered rifle fitted with a scope." Jamison did not recall the incident. Blaine thinks that the memos might have been in reference to Joseph Milteer, a right-wing southern segregationist who told a police informant that JFK could be shot "from an office building with a high-powered rifle . . . He knows he's a marked man." See HSCA interview with Robert J. Jamison, February 28, 1978, HSCA# 180-10074-10394, http://www.jfklancer.com/greer/d-114.pdf [accessed January 10, 2013], and Summers, *Kennedy Conspiracy*, 308–9.

94. Blaine, *Kennedy Detail*, 142–49.

95. It is also true that Kennedy took risks from time to time that further complicated his security arrangements. For example, in March 1963 during a visit to Chicago, JFK ordered his limousine to stop at a busy downtown intersection so that he could shake hands with

well-wishers. A mob scene ensued, as motorists on a nearby highway halted their vehicles and ran across the median to get a better look at the president. See Stephan Benzkofer, "Why Kennedy Came to Town," *Chicago Tribune*, March 17, 2013, http://www.chicagotribune.com /news/local/ct-per-flash-kennedy-ohare-0317-20130317,0,670202.story [accessed March 18, 2013].

96. Vince Palamara, author of *Survivor's Guilt: The Secret Service and the Failure to Protect the President*, does not believe that JFK ever ordered his bodyguards to stand down. "Don't believe the 47-year-old lies told by those seeking to profit from the man they failed to protect," Palamara writes on his blog. See "Vince Palamara's JFK Secret Service President Kennedy Blog: The Real Truth About the Kennedy Detail," http://vincepalamara.blogspot .com/ [accessed June 14, 2011].

97. E-mail from Gerald Blaine, January 9, 2013.

98. A few months after the assassination, Warren Leslie published a book called *Dallas Public and Private: Aspects of an American City* that blamed Kennedy's death on Dallas's right-wing political climate. Leslie's critics complained about his unflattering portrayal of Dallas and pointed out that hundreds of thousands of the city's residents had turned out to welcome the Kennedys. See Dennis Hevesi, "Warren Leslie Dies at 84; Wrote Book That Rankled Dallas," *New York Times*, July 23, 2011, http://www.nytimes.com/2011/07/24/us /24leslie.html [accessed July 25, 2011]. A lot of people shared Leslie's unfavorable opinion of Dallas. The Dallas Cowboys, playing in Cleveland on November 24, were roundly booed by the crowd, and the team members were even warned by Coach Tom Landry not to be conspicuous in public or identify themselves as belonging to the team. See Marc Sessler, "Cowboys Fielded Boos, Anger After JFK's Assassination in Dallas," NFL.com, November 23, 2011, http://www.nfl.com/news/story/09000d5d824651e6/article/cowboys-fielded-boos-an ger-after-jfks-assassination-in-dallas?module=HP11_content_stream [accessed November 30, 2011].

99. Stevenson visited Dallas on October 24, 1963.

100. Blaine, *Kennedy Detail*, 148–49, 162; Donald Janson, "Johnson Caught in Booing Crowd as He Heads for Rally in Dallas," *New York Times*, November 5, 1960; Richard Reeves, *President Kennedy: Profile of Power* (New York: Touchstone, 1993), 634.

101. "United States Secret Service Lecture Outline on Protection of the President for Guidance of Special Agents Appearing Before Police Schools," C. Douglas Dillon Papers, Box 42, Folder "The President's Committee on the Warren Report," John F. Kennedy Library, Boston, Massachusetts.

102. Robert C. Doty, "Attempt to Kill De Gaulle Fails," *New York Times*, August 23, 1962.

103. Marc Ambinder, "Inside the Secret Service," *Atlantic Magazine*, March 2011, http:// www.theatlantic.com/magazine/archive/1969/12/inside-the-secret-service/8390/4/ [accessed June 2, 2011]; "Kessler: Secret Service: LBJ Out of Control, Often Drunk," YouTube, https:// www.youtube.com/watch?v=G41XRl40RL0 [accessed December 5, 2012].

104. The rifles and ammunition belonged to the faculty occupant of the Pavilion, who had forgotten about them. It was all innocent enough—but it might not have been under other circumstances. In presidential security, assumptions should never be made.

105. Kessler is author of *In the President's Secret Service: Behind the Scenes with Agents in the Line of Fire and the Presidents They Protect* (New York: Three Rivers Press, 2009). See also Ronald Kessler, "Threats Against Obama Prompt Secret Task Force," *Newsmax*, July 26, 2010, http://www.newsmax.com/RonaldKessler/Obama–threats–Secret-Service–task-force

/2010/07/26/id/365617 [accessed June 2, 2011]; Mark Memmott, "Alleged White House Shooter Charged With Attempted Assassination," National Public Radio, November 17, 2011, http://www.npr.org/blogs/thetwo-way/2011/11/17/142470201/alleged-white-house-shooter -charged-with-attempted-assassination?ft=1&f=1001&sc=tw&utm_source=twitterfeed &utm_medium=twitter [accessed November 18, 2011]. "Man Pleads Guilty After Threatening to Kill President During DNC," WBTV.com, October 26, 2012, http://www.wbtv.com /story/19927214/donte-sims-guilty-threatening-kill-president-obama-twitter-dnc [accessed October 31, 2012].

106. JFK's limousine is now on display at the Henry Ford Museum in Dearborn, Michigan. The museum's archivists told me, "After the assassination, the midnight-blue, unarmored, open convertible was radically changed. A permanent roof, bullet-proof glass, and extensive armor-plating made the car much more secure. Wearing sedate black paint in place of the distinctive blue, the car served Presidents Lyndon B. Johnson and Richard M. Nixon as front line transportation and remained in the White House fleet as a backup through 1977." The White House approved the plan to refurbish Kennedy's car "around December 12, 1963" and a "committee was formed . . . representing the Secret Service, Army Materials Research Center, Hess & Eisenhardt, and Pittsburgh Plate Glass Company." Changes to the limousine included: a "complete re-armoring of [the] rear passenger compartment; the addition of [a] permanent non-removable top ('greenhouse') to accommodate transparent armor; the replacement of [the original] engine with [a] hand-built, high compression unit, providing approximately 17 percent more power; the addition of [a] second air conditioning unit in [the] trunk; the addition of certain electronic communication devices; the reinforcement of some mechanical and structural components, e.g., front wheel spindles and door hinges, to accommodate additional weight; the complete re-trimming of [the] rear compartment, eliminating damage resulting from the assassination; [and] a new paint treatment, 'regal Presidential Blue Metallic with silver metallic flakes that glitter under bright lights and sunshine.'" E-mail from the Benson Ford Research Center at The Henry Ford Museum, July 3, 2012. One wonders whether LBJ and Nixon ever thought about the fact they were riding in the car in which JFK was killed. The events in this limousine made Johnson president and eventually led to Nixon's political resurrection, after all. The November 22 automobile also served as a symbol of presidential vulnerability and mortality.

107. See "Kennedy Limousine Redone for Johnson," *New York Times*, June 14, 1964. It isn't that an FBI director didn't need or deserve a bulletproof car. Rather, it is that no one believed his boss, the president, should have the same protection.

I I . INEVITABILITY: THE ASSASSINATION THAT HAD TO HAPPEN

1. Warren Commission Report, chapter VIII, p. 446, History Matters website, http:// www.history-matters.com/archive/jfk/wc/wr/html/WCReport_0235b.htm [accessed October 4, 2011]; Gerald Blaine with Lisa McCubbin, *The Kennedy Detail: JFK's Secret Service Agents Break Their Silence* (New York: Gallery Books, 2010), 196.

2. According to the Secret Service, "One of the purposes of the Dallas trip was to afford to as many of the people of Dallas as possible an opportunity to see the president in the limited time available. [Agent Win] Lawson was so informed and was also informed by the White House staff that the motorcade from the airport to the luncheon site (the Trade Mart)

should take approximately 45 minutes." In other words, the president was completely vulnerable to attack for fully three-quarters of an hour, as he passed 200,000 unscreened people. "Report of the United States Secret Service on the Assassination of President Kennedy," C. Douglas Dillon Papers, Box 43, Folder, "The President's Committee on the Warren Report," John F. Kennedy Library, Boston, Massachusetts. JFK aide Kenny O'Donnell did not show the president a letter from a Democratic National Committeeman named Byron Skelton advising JFK to steer clear of Dallas. "Showing the letter to the president would have been a waste of his time," O'Donnell later wrote. Kenneth P. O'Donnell, David F. Powers, and Joe McCarthy, *"Johnny, We Hardly Knew Ye": Memories of John Fitzgerald Kennedy* (Boston: Little, Brown, 1970), 19. Arthur Schlesinger, Jr., says that Adlai Stevenson told him there was "something very ugly and frightening" about Dallas and that he (Schlesinger) should pass on his (Stevenson's) concerns to Kennedy. Schlesinger never did; Stevenson was initially grateful for his colleague's discretion. Arthur M. Schlesinger, Jr., *A Thousand Days: John F. Kennedy in the White House* (Boston: Houghton Mifflin, 1965), 1021. Press secretary Pierre Salinger did not show JFK a letter from a Dallas woman who was worried that "something terrible" would happen to the president if he visited her city. Salinger assumed that Kennedy would have "dismissed the warning out of hand." Pierre Salinger, *P. S.: A Memoir* (New York: St. Martin's Press, 1995), 154–55. See also Jules Witcover, "Kennedy's Aides Got Hints of Peril in Texas," *Los Angeles Times*, August 2, 1971.

3. The U.S. Secret Service was established in 1865 to deal with a massive counterfeiting problem that arose once the Civil War had concluded. "After the assassination of President McKinley in 1901, the U.S. Secret Service was specifically designated to protect the president of the United States." "United States Secret Service Lecture Outline on Protection of the President for Guidance of Special Agents Appearing Before Police Schools," C. Douglas Dillon Papers, Box 42, Folder, "The President's Committee on the Warren Report," John F. Kennedy Library, Boston, Massachusetts.

4. See Michael K. Deaver, *Nancy: A Portrait of My Years with Nancy Reagan* (New York: William Morrow, 2004), 140. Del Quentin Webber has explained how difficult it was for Mrs. Reagan to get beyond the assassination attempt: "A natural worrier, Nancy Reagan found herself sobbing uncontrollably at times. She lost weight and became panicky whenever her husband left the White House gates . . ." Del Quentin Webber, *Rawhide Down: The Near Assassination of Ronald Reagan* (New York: Henry Holt, 2011), 223–24. Stuart Spencer, one of Reagan's closest campaign advisers, had this to say about Mrs. Reagan after the assassination attempt on her husband: "She was scared to death after that. She even lobbied [the president] not to run again. She had real qualms. If she asked me once, she asked me fifteen times whether he should run again or not. It wasn't the fear of winning or losing. Every time he went out after that, she had a fear of him getting shot. Why did she talk to Joan Quigley and all these astrologers? She was looking for help . . . [The president] was very fatalistic about it, but she was scared to death. Big change in her." Stuart Spencer, interview, excerpted in "Reagan Officials on the March 30, 1981 Assassination Attempt," http://millercenter.org/academic/oralhistory/news/2007_0330 [accessed July 13, 2011].

5. Transcript of LBJ-Hoover telephone call, 10 A.M, November 23, 1963, reprinted in Max Holland, *The Kennedy Assassination Tapes* (New York: Alfred A. Knopf, 2004), 71.

6. The successful presidential assassins had political motives of various sorts. Lincoln's John Wilkes Booth was a Confederate sympathizer. Charles Guiteau had sought a political appointment from Garfield and was embittered by his rejection—although he was also

mentally disturbed, if not insane. McKinley's Leon Czolgosz was an anarchist who wanted to bring down the established order. And Oswald clearly had some combination of political and personal intentions.

7. David Herbert Donald, *Lincoln* (New York: Touchstone, 1995), 550.

8. Hans L. Trefousse, *Andrew Johnson: A Biography* (New York: W. W. Norton, 1989), 351.

9. See Associated Press, "Arrest Two Girls in Plot: Buenos Aires Police Hold Them, with Two Men, as Anarchists." *New York Times*, December 13, 1928, and Associated Press, "Anti-Hoover Plot Barred by Raid in Buenos Aires; Reds Seized With Bombs." *New York Times*, December 12, 1928. "CNN's Gut Check for December 11, 2012," CNN.com, December 11, 2012, http://politicalticker.blogs.cnn.com/2012/12/11/cnns-gut-check-for-december-11-2012 / [accessed December 12, 2012].

10. Zangara was a mentally disturbed immigrant.

11. Amy Davidson, "The F.D.R. New Yorker Cover That Never Ran," *New Yorker*, May 5, 2012, http://www.newyorker.com/online/blogs/closeread/2012/05/the-fdr-new-yorker-cover -that-never-ran.html#slide_ss_0=1 [accessed January 30, 2013]; Kirk Semple, "This Means Lore!," *Miami New Times*, September 1, 1993, http://www.miaminewtimes.com/1993-09-01 /news/this-means-lore/ [accessed June 13, 2013]; "Woman Who Diverted Bullet From FDR Dies," *Associated Press*, reprinted in *Victoria* [Texas] *Advocate*, November 11, 1962; "Florida Corrections, Centuries of Progress, 1933–1935," Florida Department of Corrections website, http://www.dc.state.fl.us/oth/timeline/1933-1935.html [accessed June 13, 2013].

12. During the Clinton administration, Congress passed a law limiting Secret Service protection of former presidents to a maximum of ten years. The cost-cutting measure was rescinded in 2013 by Congress and signed into law by President Obama. Former chief executives and their spouses now once again receive lifetime protection. See Olivier Knox, "Obama Signs Law Giving Himself, Bush Lifetime Secret Service Guard," Yahoo! News, January 10, 2013, http://news.yahoo.com/blogs/ticket/obama-signs-law-giving-himself-bush -lifetime-secret-184305122–politics.html [accessed January 11, 2013].

13. I have only covered assassination attempts on U.S. leaders. Unfortunately, the practice is worldwide and all too frequent. To offer just a few modern examples: During a live television debate in October 1960, a Japanese Socialist Party Candidate named Inejiro Asanuma was stabbed to death by a seventeen-year-old anticommunist named Otoya Yamaguchi. Yamaguchi told police that his only regret was that he had been unable to kill two other people, the chairman of the Japanese Teachers' Union and a Communist named Sanzo Nosaka. As briefly mentioned in the text, on August 22, 1962, French president Charles de Gaulle's black Citroën DS was spotted speeding through the Paris suburb of Petit-Clamart, en route with Madame de Gaulle to their estate at Colombey. A host of would-be assassins unleashed a hail of bullets upon the presidential motorcade. One hundred and forty bullets, most of them coming from behind, killed two of de Gaulle's motorcycle bodyguards; twelve bullets shattered the Citroën's rear window and punctured its rear tires. The unarmored car went into a front skid, but de Gaulle's skilled chauffeur was able to accelerate out of it and drive the presidential party to safety. On May 13, 1981, Pope John Paul II was shot four times while blessing crowds in St. Peter's Square in Rome. The gunman was a twenty-three-year-old Turk named Mehmet Ali Agca. The pope came close to death but managed to recover. On June 13, 1981, Marcus Serjeant, a seventeen-year-old British national, aimed a pistol at the queen and fired six rounds (blanks) before being overcome by guardsmen. The queen was on horseback, riding in a ceremony at Buckingham Palace, when the shots were fired. On

November 4, 1995, a twenty-seven-year-old Jewish law student fired three shots at Israeli prime minister Yitzhak Rabin, who died from his injuries.

14. On December 19, 1960, President Eisenhower sent a letter to President-elect Kennedy that read, "I regret that it did not occur to me, earlier, to offer you as president-elect one facility that might be of some possible use, namely the use of a governmental plane. Knowing something about the problems of the Secret Service and their work in providing for the safety of the president-elect and his family, I think it possible that the use of such a plane, during this interregnum, might be of real utility to you." Kennedy wrote back on December 21: "Fortunately, I have been able to use the same plane that carried us through the fall and as I do not plan to travel very much between now and the 20th of January I believe it will serve us very satisfactorily." Personal correspondence, Dwight D. Eisenhower Presidential Library and Museum, Abilene, Kansas.

15. See "Nab 2 Gun Toters at Rally for Kennedy; 1 Is Minister," *Chicago Daily Tribune*, November 5, 1960; "2 Armed Men Seized in Kennedy Crowd," *New York Times*, November 5, 1960; and "Pair Meant Kennedy No Harm, Police Say," *Los Angeles Times*, November 7, 1960; see also http://proquest.umi.com/pqdweb?did=450993452&sid=2&Fmt=10&clientId=8772& RQT=309&VName=HNP. The men appeared in Chicago Municipal Court on November 15, 1960, after the election. Unfortunately, those court records, and the accompanying police reports, have been destroyed and no further information is available. Telephone interview with Cook County Clerk of Circuit Court Archivist Phil Costello, July 5, 2011.

16. Blaine, *Kennedy Detail*, 51–52.

17. According to the journalist Eliot Kleinberg, Pavlick was also "violently anti-Catholic." See Kleinberg, "Kennedy Almost Slain in Palm Beach," *Palm Beach Post*, November 24, 2011.

18. For a thought-provoking look at what might have happened had Pavlick succeeded, see Jeff Greenfield, *Then Everything Changed: Stunning Alternate Histories of American Politics: JFK, RFK, Carter, Ford, Reagan* (New York: Putnam, 2011). Although Pavlick spent several years in psychiatric hospitals after the assassination attempt, the charges against him were eventually dropped. See Eliot Kleinberg, "Palm Beach Police Foiled Plot to Kill JFK," *Palm Beach Post*, December 1, 2011, http://www.historicpalmbeach.com/eliot-kleinberg/2011 /12/palm-beach-police-foiled-plot-to-kill-jfk/ [accessed December 6, 2011].

19. Bill Dedman, "Ted Kennedy FBI File Reveals Threats," msnbc.com, June 14, 2010, http://www.msnbc.msn.com/id/34248485/ns/us_news-life/t/ted-kennedy-fbi-file-reveals -threats/ [accessed July 21, 2011]; Jack Pickell, "FBI Message to Hoover Included Glib Remark on Kennedy," *Boston Globe*, boston.com, June 14, 2010, http://www.boston.com/news/poli tics/politicalintelligence/2010/06/fbi_letter_to_h.html [accessed July 21, 2011].

20. The Secret Service began providing protection for presidential and vice presidential candidates shortly after RFK's assassination. Congress issued a joint resolution (H.J.Res. 1292) on June 6, 1968, which authorized the Secret Service to "furnish protection to persons who are determined from time to time . . . as being major presidential or vice presidential candidates who should receive such protection (unless the candidate has declined such protection)." http://www.cq.com/graphics/sal/90/sal90-331.pdf [accessed July 22, 2011].

21. I witnessed just such a breakdown when Democratic presidential candidate Hillary Clinton appeared before my students in February 2008 at the University of Virginia. At a certain point, with the screening going slowly and the candidate's schedule in jeopardy, many people in line were simply waved through with a cursory glance. I agree with author

Ronald Kessler's assessment that the Secret Service "began cutting corners in 2003 after it was merged into the Department of Homeland Security." Under the auspices of DHS, Kessler argues, the Secret Service has been forced to "compete for funds with other national security agencies," which has "led to a lowering of standards." See Ronald Kessler, "Secret Service Cost-Cutting Leaves President Vulnerable," Newsmax, October 17, 2011, http://www .newsmax.com/RonaldKessler/Secret-Service-Obama-Iranian/2011/10/17/id/414749 [accessed October 17, 2011].

22. Telephone interview with Ari Fleischer, February 19, 2013; David Montgomery, "No Handshake Man at Obama Inauguration," *Washington Post*, November 20, 2008, http:// www.washingtonpost.com/wp-dyn/content/article/2008/11/19/AR2008111904366.html [accessed February 20, 2013]; Chidanand Rajghatta, "Bush's Security and the Handshake Man," *The Times of India*, February 9, 2003, http://articles.timesofindia.indiatimes.com/2003-02 -09/us/27268782_1_weaver-secret-service-national-prayer-breakfast [accessed February 20, 2013].

23. In 2009, Michaele and Tareq Salahi crashed a state dinner being held in honor of Indian Prime Minister Manmohan Singh. A third uninvited guest, Carlos Allen, evaded security by arriving with a group of Indian businessmen who were late for the dinner. See Helene Cooper and Rachel L. Swarns, "At Obama's First State Dinner, the First Crashers," *New York Times*, November 25, 2009, and Amy Argetsinger and Roxanne Roberts, "Secret Service Confirms Third Crasher at White House State Dinner," *Washington Post*, January 5, 2010.

24. Of course, it is probably impossible to protect high officials from every threat. In February 2005, Prime Minister Rafik al-Hariri of Lebanon was killed when a massive car bomb exploded beside his motorcade. Al-Hariri was traveling in a fully armored limousine at the time with two security cars ahead of him and two more, plus an ambulance, following closely behind. The prime minister's security agents were also using sophisticated electronic equipment designed to jam remote-controlled improvised explosive devices (IEDs). The attackers were able to bypass these security arrangements by loading a van with a metric ton of explosives and ordering a suicide operative to detonate his deadly cargo when the motorcade passed by. See Scott Stewart, "Lebanon: Lessons from Two Assassinations," *Stratfor Global Intelligence*, November 15, 2012, http://www.stratfor.com/weekly/lebanon-lessons -two-assassinations [accessed December 17, 2012].

25. See Daniel Stashower, *The Hour of Peril: The Secret Plot to Murder Lincoln Before the Civil War* (New York: Minotaur Books, 2013).

26. Robert Young, "Johnson Guarded by 2,000 in N.Y.," *Chicago Tribune*, December 9, 1963; Robert Alden, "Johnson to Attend Lehman's Funeral In City Tomorrow," *New York Times*, December 7, 1963.

27. Kennedy speechwriter Ted Sorensen confirmed this White House view in a personal interview, May 4, 2010, Charlottesville, Virginia.

12. THE ASSASSINATION AND THE KENNEDY LEGACY

1. As explained by Lamar Waldron and Thom Hartmann, authors of *Legacy of Secrecy: The Long Shadow of the JFK Assassination*, the "1992 JFK Act requires all government JFK assassination files to be released by 2017, but OMB Watch has stated that 'well over a million CIA records' related to the assassination remain unreleased. Even worse, the CIA stated in a

lawsuit last year that they might withhold files related to JFK's assassination even beyond 2017." Legacy of Secrecy official website, http://www.legacyofsecrecy.com/tell.html [accessed August 16, 2011].

2. The movement for quick release of all JFK assassination-related documents is supported by a wide range of prominent individuals including HSCA counsel Robert Blakey. In 2012 Blakey signed a letter addressed to the Archivist of the United States requesting the release of all assassination-related documents prior to the fiftieth anniversary of JFK's death, especially the estimated fifty thousand pages that are still being withheld by the CIA. Letter dated January 20, 2012, from Jim Lesar, president of the Assassination Archives and Research Center, to United States Archivist David S. Ferreiro. It is not clear exactly how many pages or documents the agency is still withholding from the public. Gary Stern, General Counsel at the National Archives, told Jim Lesar, "We believe that the total number of pages is considerably less than 50,000, because our records indicate that the CIA has postponed in full as national security classified a total of 1,171 documents." E-mail from Gary Stern to Lesar, May 9, 2012. The federal government is also withholding documents from the Church Committee's mid-1970's investigation of CIA abuses. Researchers believe that these documents may shed new light on Langley's connections to November 22nd and have called for their immediate release. See Rex Bradford, "Missing JFK Files: The Church Committee Assassination Transcripts," JFK Facts, June 1, 2013, http://jfkfacts.org/assassination/from-the-files/missing-jfk-files-the-church-committee-assassination-transcripts/#more-4842 [accessed June 3, 2013].

3. A Dictabelt machine records sounds by pressing grooves into a plastic belt. In the early 1960s, many police departments used these devices to record radio conversations between officers. Dictaphone-brand "Dictabelts" were cheap and easy to replace.

4. Mack is now curator of the Sixth Floor Museum at Dealey Plaza.

5. Barger worked for Bolt, Beranek and Newman, a well-respected government contractor that specializes in acoustical analysis. BBN scientists helped the U.S. Navy design underwater detection devices. Barger's expertise helped the federal government determine which National Guardsmen fired on students at Kent State University. During the Watergate hearings, his firm provided expert testimony on the infamous 18½-minute gap in one of Nixon's tapes. Summers, Kennedy Conspiracy, 16.

6. According to Paul Chambers, "... three Dallas police sharpshooters fired a total of fifty-six live bullets into three piles of sandbags located along the motorcade route on Elm Street." Chambers also points out that, "An array of thirty-six microphones positioned along the route eighteen feet apart were used to record gunshots from the sixth floor of the [B]ook [D]epository and from the fence along the grassy knoll." Chambers, Head Shot, 119-20.

7. Telephone interview with James Barger, April 15, 2011.

8. Chambers, Head Shot, 118-28.

9. Dale K. Myers, "Appendix II: Rebuttal of the HSCA's Photographic Evidence Offered in Support of the Committee's Acoustic Evidence of Conspiracy," Secrets of a Homicide: JFK Assassination, http://www.jfkfiles.com/jfk/html/acoustics_8.htm#131 [accessed July 20, 2011].

10. The Kennedy Assassination: Beyond Conspiracy, ABC-TV Special, 2003. Here's what Gary Mack told me this about the documentary: "Beyond Conspiracy includes Dale Myers, who has done some interesting work regarding the timing of McLain at various locations in the Plaza as seen in a few of the films. But Dale relied upon camera speeds that had not been

measured by investigators and merely interpolated what they must have been by connecting them to each other. For example, he decided the Towner camera ran at 23 frames per second, which is 28% faster than it was geared to run. Yes, her camera could have been operating that fast IF she had pressed the run button too far, but there's no proof that she did so. He figured the Martin camera also ran at 23 frames per second, which would be either 28% too fast or 44% too fast, depending on which model camera he used. Trouble is, that information is unknown and unknowable. When I substitute standard rates of 18 frames per second, I find that McLain could have been in the right place at the right time . . . but that, of course, is not proof, just an indication. And that's just one more reason why I personally think the acoustics evidence needs to be pursued." Don Thomas is one researcher who believes that McLain's police radio did in fact capture the sound of gunfire. See Donald Byron Thomas, *Hear No Evil: Social Constructivism and the Forensic Evidence in the Kennedy Assassination* (Ipswich, MA: Mary Ferrell Foundation Press, 2010).

11. In July 1979 a rock musician named Steve Barber bought a magazine that included a plastic insert recording of the Dictabelt evidence; the recording had been produced by Gary Mack. Barber listened to the recording dozens of times and heard a faint voice over the final shot saying "Hold everything secure . . ." It turned out to be the voice of Dallas County sheriff Bill Decker. Barber does not accept the HSCA's interpretation of the acoustical evidence. James C. Bowles believes that multiple replays of the Dictabelt may have created scratches that the House Committee acoustics team misidentified as gunshots. See James Bowles, "A Rebuttal to the Acoustical Evidence Theory," http://www.jfk-online.com/bowles.html and Stephan N. Barber, "Double Decker," http://www.jfk-online.com/doubled.html [accessed July 20, 2011].

12. The complete NAS report can be found at http://www.jfk-online.com/nas01.html #intro [accessed July 20, 2011].

13. D. B. Thomas, "Echo Correlation Analysis and the Acoustic Evidence in the Kennedy Assassination Revisited," *Science & Justice* 41, no. 1 (2001): 21–32.

14. Michael T. Griffith, "The HSCA's Acoustic Evidence: Proof of a Second Gunman?" Mary Ferrell Foundation website, http://www.maryferrell.org/mffweb/archive/viewer/show Doc.do?mode=searchResult&docId=413 [accessed July 20, 2011] (quotation).

15. Here is a new wrinkle for a novel or movie. There is a tiny but not fantastically infinitesimal chance two gunmen, Oswald and a picket-fence shooter, independently and without knowledge of the other's intentions, chose Dealey Plaza for the assassination on 11/22. Oswald's selection of shooting location was logical for him, facilitated by his place of employment. The picket fence/grassy knoll site was a sound option for someone else because it was at the very end of Kennedy's motorcade route, therefore likely to have sparse crowds and less security, and it was adjacent to a large parking lot that could facilitate a fast getaway in the immediate chaos of the assassination. This theory strains credulity, and I certainly would not advocate it, but stranger things in human history have happened.

16. The chief Dallas police dispatcher on the day of the assassination, Jim Bowles, theorized correctly about what had happened in his report, James C. Bowles, "The Kennedy Assassination Tapes: A Rebuttal to the Acoustic Evidence Theory", 1979, http://www.jfk-online .com/bowles.html [accessed July 25, 2013.] But he did not have the incontrovertible proof of his theory detailed in our study. Similarly, the National Academy of Sciences' study, Committee on Ballistic Acoustics, National Research Council, "Report of the Committee on Ballistic Acoustics," the National Academies Press, Washington D.C., 1982, while doubting that

the Dictabelt proved what the HSCA claimed it did, suggested (as a possibility for future research) study of the location and the true identity of the motorcycle policeman with the stuck microphone, as well as further investigation of the impulses on the Dictabelt that were marked as potential gunfire.

17. Price Obituary, the *Dallas Morning News,* October 12, 1999. "Services Held for Willie Price, 83", 3rd edition, p. 19A. See also Willie Price Oral History Interview, September 24, 1994 by Wes Wise with Bob Porter; The Sixth Floor Museum at Dealey Plaza, Oral History Collection.

18. Interview with James C. Bowles, May 23, 2013. See also: "Radio Traffic Transcript, by an unknown author. Transcript of radio traffic from President's arrival at Love Field to the arrest of Lee Harvey Oswald" at http://jfk.ci.dallas.tx.us/box14.htm [accessed July 25, 2013.]

19. In November 2012, the city of Dallas unveiled a memorial to Tippit that stands on the street where he died. See Ken Kalthoff, "Dallas to Mark 50th Anniversary of JFK's Assassination with Memorial Ceremony," NBCNEWS.com, November 21, 2012, http://usnews.nbc news.com/_news/2012/11/21/15329670-dallas-to-mark-50th-anniversary-of-jfks-assassination -with-memorial-ceremony?lite [accessed November 26, 2012].

20. "Report of the President's Commission on the Assassination of President Kennedy: Chapter 4: The Assassin," pp. 165–75, National Archives and Records Administration website, http://www.archives.gov/research/jfk/warren-commission-report/chapter-4.html#tippit [accessed June 10, 2011]; Gerald Posner, *Case Closed: Lee Harvey Oswald and the Assassination of JFK* (New York: Anchor Books, 1994), 277.

21. See Bonar Menninger, *Mortal Error: The Shot That Killed JFK* (New York: St. Martin's Press, 1992).

22. It is impossible in this space to summarize all the accusations and possible evidence that researchers have submitted to point the finger at anti-Castro Cubans, but a sampling would include the following: Author Anthony Summers described a meeting of anti-Castro Cubans and John Birch Society members that took place in October 1963 at a house in the Dallas suburb of Farmers Branch. According to Summers, a Bay of Pigs veteran named Nestor Castellanos attended this meeting and said, "We are waiting for Kennedy the twenty-second [of November] . . . We're going to give him the works when he gets in Dallas" (Summers, *Kennedy Conspiracy,* 307–8). It is possible that during the first three months of 1963, Oswald may have attended three meetings (at least) arranged by anti-Castro Cubans living in the Dallas–Fort Worth area (Michael L. Kurtz, *The JFK Assassination Debates: Lone Gunman versus Conspiracy* (Lawrence: University Press of Kansas, 2006), 151, 190). Fabian Escalante, the former head of Cuba's Department of State Security, believes that anti-Castro Cuban exiles recruited by the CIA made plans to kill Kennedy. Escalante has pointed the finger at Luis Posada Carriles, a Miami resident accused of masterminding the 1976 bombing of a Cubana Airlines jet that killed 76 people. Carriles has also been linked to a spate of hotel bombings, which occurred in 1997, that were intended to sow chaos in Cuba and scare off tourists. Escalante is equally sure that Orlando Bosch had something to do with the Kennedy murder. Martin Roberts, "Cuban Ex-Intelligence Chief Recalls JFK Assassination," *Washington Post,* July 12, 2010. Orlando Bosch, who died in April 2011, was a friend of Castro's before he became a rabid anticommunist. In 1968, Bosch fired a homemade bazooka at a Polish freighter that he thought was headed to Cuba. According to the Justice Department, "from 1961 to 1968, Dr. Bosch was involved in 30 acts of sabotage in the United States, Puerto Rico, Panama and Cuba." T. Rees Shapiro, "Anti-Castro Radical Was Acquitted in Jet Bombing," *Washington Post,* April 30, 2011.

23. The CIA suffered multiple wounds from negative press coverage and governmental investigations about Watergate crimes and many other controversies. For example, President Ford admitted that the CIA had participated in the 1973 overthrow of the Allende regime in Chile, an incident Senator Ted Kennedy called "not only a flagrant violation of our alleged policy of nonintervention in Chilean affairs, but also an appalling lack of forthrightness with the Congress." In December 1974 Seymour Hersh published an article in the *New York Times* that accused the CIA of using illegal wiretaps, mail intercepts, and other nefarious methods to spy on American citizens. The Senate investigation of American intelligence activities, chaired by Senator Frank Church (D-ID), exposed CIA assassination attempts against multiple foreign leaders, from the Caribbean to Africa to Southeast Asia. See the Church Committee Reports, Assassination Archives and Research Center website, http://www.aarclibrary.org/publib/contents/church/contents_church_reports.htm [accessed October 5, 2011], and Peter N. Carroll, *It Seemed Like Nothing Happened: The Tragedy and Promise of America in the 1970s* (New York: Holt, Rinehart and Winston, 1982), 168–69.

24. Jefferson Morley, "What Can We Do About JFK's Murder?" *The Atlantic*, November 21, 2012, http://www.theatlantic.com/national/archive/2012/11/what-can-we-do-about-jfks-murder/265520/ [accessed December 4, 2012].

25. Aleksandr Fursenko and Timothy Naftali, *"One Hell of a Gamble": Khrushchev, Castro, and Kennedy, 1958–64* (New York: W. W. Norton, 1997), 344–45; Jefferson Morley, "What JFK Conspiracy Bashers Get Wrong," *Huffington Post*, November 21, 2007, http://www.huffingtonpost.com/jefferson-morley/what-jfk-conspiracy-bashe_b_73722.html [accessed July 20, 2011].

26. David Flick, "Robert F. Kennedy Suspected Conspiracy in His Brother's Assassination, Son Says," *Dallas News*, January 11, 2013, http://thescoopblog.dallasnews.com/2013/01/a-first-in-50-years-two-jfk-relatives-speak-in-dallas.html/ [accessed January 14, 2013], and Michael Granberry, "Robert F. Kennedy Jr. Creates a Story With 'Legs' by Offering Pro-Conspiracy Views on His Uncle's 1963 Assassination in Dealey Plaza," *Dallas News*, January 14, 2013, http://popcultureblog.dallasnews.com/2013/01/robert-f-kennedy-jr-creates-a-story-with-legs-by-offering-pro-conspiracy-views-on-his-uncles-1963-assassination-in-dealey-plaza.html/ [accessed January 16, 2013].

27. In addition to Oliver Stone's *JFK*, there have been numerous films and TV shows that incorporate or have allusions to the Kennedy assassination in their plots, including *Executive Action* (1973), *The Parallax View* (1974), Robert Altman's *Nashville* (1975), *In the Line of Fire* (1993), and the remake of *The Manchurian Candidate* (2004). A *Twilight Zone* TV episode in 1985, "Profile in Silver," used time travel to stop the assassination from happening, at least temporarily. The Kennedy assassination has played a central role in American culture in almost every way, and it is featured in hundreds of plays, comic books, novels, television shows, and with the passage of time, comedies, from *Seinfeld* to *Robot Chicken*. Hunter S. Thompson first used the phrase "fear and loathing" to describe the Kennedy assassination in a November 22, 1963, letter to a friend; it would later become the title of Thompson's most famous book, *Fear and Loathing in Las Vegas* (New York: Random House, 1971). One of the best-known comedy entries is the fraternity movie *Animal House* (1978) starring John Belushi. The film's director, John Landis, has indicated that the climactic homecoming parade scene was intentionally dated November 21, 1963, since the film portrayed a happy-go-lucky postwar America that ended with the JFK assassination. One of the homecoming floats was set to the theme of the New Frontier and dominated by a likeness of President Kennedy, with

the women on the float all dressed in the pink suit and pillbox hat Jackie wore in Dallas. Two well-known songs were written as a result of the assassination: Simon and Garfunkel's "The Sound of Silence" and the Beach Boys' "The Warmth of the Sun." An interesting question with an unknowable answer is: Was Oswald's assassination plan influenced by two movies about presidential assassination that he might well have seen? In 1951, when Oswald was twelve, MGM released *The Tall Target*, starring Dick Powell. It was a film about the alleged Baltimore plot to assassinate President-elect Lincoln as he passed through the Confederate-sympathizing city on February 23, 1861, on his way to Washington for his inauguration. Lincoln was scheduled to leave his train and give a speech, and the conspirators placed their assassin in an open window of a building overlooking the site. The conspirators described a "rifle with a telescopic lens." Then in 1962, when Oswald was back living in the United States, United Artists released *The Manchurian Candidate*, starring Frank Sinatra and Angela Lansbury. This film also spotlighted a potential presidential assassination from a window high above the national convention of an unnamed party. The assassin again uses a rifle with a telescopic lens. Marina Oswald also told the Warren Commission that Lee had watched two assassination-related films, *We Were Strangers* (about the assassination of a Cuban dictator) and *Suddenly* (about the attempted assassination of a U.S. president). The precise dates of viewing have never been determined, though Marina thought her husband might have watched them in October 1963. See Warren Commission Hearings, vol. I, p. 71, and John Loken, *Oswald's Trigger Films: The Manchurian Candidate, We Were Strangers, Suddenly?* (Ann Arbor, MI: Falcon Books, 2000). Gary Mack told me: "I spent a lot of time on this and could not confirm it—there were no double features on local TV or any time when *We Were Strangers* was scheduled. The other film did air on two different days, as I recall, but not *Strangers*." E-mail from Gary Mack, June 15, 2012. Marina was not asked about *The Tall Target*, which is actually closer to the November 22 reality, but then, Oswald might have viewed it years before he met Marina.

28. Recent bestsellers on the Lincoln assassination include Bill O'Reilly and Martin Dugard, *Killing Lincoln* (New York: Henry Holt, 2011); Michael Kauffman, *American Brutus* (New York: Random House, 2005); Kate Clifford Larson, *The Assassin's Accomplice* (New York: Basic Books, 2008); and James L. Swanson, *Manhunt: The 12-Day Chase for Lincoln's Killer* (New York: Harper Perennial, 2007). The History Channel has produced a number of documentaries on the Lincoln assassination, including *The Hunt for John Wilkes Booth* (2008), *Conspiracy? Lincoln Assassination* (2007), and *The Lincoln Assassination* (2004).

29. *Leave It to Beaver, The Donna Reed Show, Ozzie and Harriet, I Love Lucy*, and *The Andy Griffith Show*, all of which aired during the Kennedy years.

30. Former House Speaker Nancy Pelosi was one. On several occasions during our conversation, she became very emotional about President Kennedy's death.

31. Fenn says that he was riding to JFK's burial service with the journalist Mary McGrory when he made the comment and that McGrory mistook him for Moynihan and later misreported the incident. Telephone interview with Dan Fenn, December 16, 2010.

32. These figures are based on a poll conducted by the Survey Research Center at the University of Michigan. See my book *The Rise of Political Consultants: New Ways of Winning Elections* (New York: Basic Books, 1981), 102.

33. It is time-consuming and difficult to identify and count all of the monuments, streets, buildings, and other structures around the world that are named for John F. Kennedy, though we have made an attempt. Our findings appear in the concluding chapter. The

only previous researcher to try, Gerald Steinberg, eventually abandoned the attempt. See the Gerald Steinberg Papers, John F. Kennedy Library, Boston, Massachusetts. A partial list of Reagan memorials can be found at http://www.ronaldreaganlegacyproject.org/ and http://www.reagan.utexas.edu/archives/reference/thingsnamed.html [accessed October 5, 2011].

34. See Robert W. Merry, *Where They Stand: The American Presidents in the Eyes of Voters and Historians* (New York: Simon and Schuster, 2012).

35. Not all successor presidents had as much trouble as Andrew and Lyndon Johnson. It was not long before Theodore Roosevelt had all but consigned William McKinley to the back pages of history. By the end of Roosevelt's seven and a half years in office, it was apparent that TR would be the more significant chief executive by far. Similarly, Harry Truman—though wrongly viewed as inadequate during his tenure—has achieved "near great" status with both historians and average Americans after eight tumultuous years in the White House.

13. "LET US CONTINUE": LYNDON JOHNSON— PRETENDER TO THE THRONE

1. Robert A. Caro, "The Transition: Lyndon Johnson and the Events in Dallas," *New Yorker* (April 2, 2012): 32–49.

2. According to William Manchester, LBJ and Lady Bird saw Jackie in her bloodstained clothes just before the swearing-in ceremony. "As always, this one [Jackie's glove] seemed a part of Jackie. And it was caked with her husband's blood. Bird filled up. She suggested, 'Can we get someone to help you put on fresh things?' 'Oh no,' Mrs. Kennedy replied. 'Perhaps later I'll ask Mary Gallagher. But not right now.' The three of them sat on the bed, Mrs. Kennedy in the middle. After a pause [Lyndon] Johnson said uncertainly, 'Well—about the swearing in.'" William Manchester, *The Death of a President: November 20–November 25, 1963* (New York: Harper and Row, 1967), 316. Steven Gillon describes the swearing-in ceremony this way: "Moments later, Mrs. Kennedy walked into the cabin. The room went silent. Smith described the former First Lady as 'white-faced but dry-eyed.' 'Her pink blouse was spattered with blood and white flecks of her husband's brain,' recalled [LBJ aide] Jack Valenti. Johnson took both of her hands in his and positioned her to his left and Mrs. Johnson on his right . . . Johnson then introduced Hughes, telling Mrs. Kennedy that she was a district judge appointed by JFK." Steven M. Gillon, *The Kennedy Assassination—24 Hours After: Lyndon B. Johnson's Pivotal First Day as President* (New York: Basic Books, 2009), 137–38.

3. At 7:20 P.M. on the day Kennedy died, LBJ wrote, "Dear John: It will be many years before you understand fully what a great man your father was. His loss is a deep personal tragedy for all of us, but I wanted you particularly to know that I share your grief. You can always be proud of him." He penned a similar letter to Caroline ten minutes later. White House Famous Names, Box 7, Folder "Kennedy, Mrs. John F., 1963," Lyndon Baines Johnson Library, Austin, Texas.

4. Letter from JBK to LBJ, November 26, 1963, White House Famous Names, Box 7, Folder "Kennedy, Mrs. John F., 1963," Lyndon Baines Johnson Library, Austin, Texas.

5. Doris Kearns Goodwin writes: "Although Johnson approached these men differently, according to their various relationships with John Kennedy . . . all his appeals ended in the same way: 'I know how much he needed you. But it must make sense to you that if he needed you I need you that much more. And so does our country.'" Doris Kearns Goodwin, *Lyndon Johnson and the American Dream* (New York: St. Martin's Griffin, 1991), 175. The historian

Steven Gillon says that LBJ told Dick Maguire, "I know what a great personal tragedy this is to you, but it is to me too. And you have been so wonderful to the president, that I want you to know . . . that I've got to rely on you more than he did." Gillon, *Kennedy Assassination*, 178. LBJ told Bobby Kennedy, "I need you more than the president needed you." Arthur M. Schlesinger, Jr., *Robert Kennedy and His Times* (Boston: Houghton Mifflin, 2002), 627.

6. Bruce J. Schulman, *Lyndon B. Johnson and American Liberalism* (Boston: Bedford Books, 1995), 69.

7. Randall B. Woods, *LBJ: Architect of American Ambition* (New York: Free Press, 2006), 443.

8. FDR served a bit over twelve years as president, before the passage of the Twenty-second Amendment. Because Johnson was filling out less than half of JFK's elective term, he was eligible to run for two full terms of his own and thus could theoretically have held the White House until January 20, 1973.

9. There was no official home for vice presidents until 1974. As incredible as it may seem today, the second highest official lived in his family's own house in a neighborhood in the Washington area—yet another security nightmare for the Secret Service.

10. The full exchange was as follows. LBJ reportedly said, "I guess we won't be going home for a while," to which Lady Bird responded, "Well, at least it's only for nine months." After realizing that her husband would have to serve beyond the 1964 Democratic Convention, Lady Bird corrected herself: "No, I guess it will be for fourteen months." Horace Busby, who was in the room at the time, said, "Mrs. Johnson, it won't be nine months—it is more likely to be nine years." Lady Bird was irked by Busby's comment. "No," she retorted emphatically. "I'm afraid Buzz is right," LBJ said. "At least, it may be for five years." Gillon, *Kennedy Assassination*, 188–89. See also Woods, *Architect*, 422.

11. Lyndon Baines Johnson, "Address to Joint Session of Congress (November 27, 1963)," Miller Center of Public Affairs at the University of Virginia, http://millercenter.org/scripps /archive/speeches/detail/3381 [accessed July 11, 2011].

12. Mrs. Kennedy also requested that LBJ "affirm that JFK's commitment to the renovation of Washington, D.C. . . . not be sidelined . . . [O]n November 30 Johnson [issued] a special statement reiterating President Kennedy's promise to make Washington a world-class capital." Max Holland, *The Kennedy Assassination Tapes* (New York: Alfred A. Knopf, 2004), 113.

13. Lyndon Baines Johnson, "Thanksgiving Message (November 28, 1963)," Miller Center of Public Affairs at the University of Virginia, http://millercenter.org/scripps/archive /speeches/detail/5657 [accessed July 25, 2011].

14. Woods, *Architect*, 443. Evidently, LBJ was serious about appointing Jackie. Woods reports that LBJ called JFK aide Kenny O'Donnell on December 27 and "told him he wanted to appoint Jackie U.S. ambassador to Mexico. O'Donnell said that he did not think she would accept." LBJ also told JFK's press secretary, Pierre Salinger, "She was always nicer to me than anybody in the Kennedy family . . . [S]he just made me feel like I was a human being. So I'd just like to [appoint her] . . . [T]hat's the biggest thing I got, and I think it'll just revolutionize Latin America." Eric Engberg, "LBJ and Jackie Kennedy," CBS News, February 11, 2009, http://www .cbsnews.com/stories/1998/09/18/national/main17861.shtml [accessed August 23, 2011].

15. Hal C. Wingo, letter to the editor, *New Yorker*, April 23, 2012. Wingo was present at the December 31, 1963, session. See also Larry J. Sabato, *Feeding Frenzy: How Attack Journalism Has Transformed American Politics* (New York: Free Press, 1991), 43.

16. E-mail from JFK Library, August 3, 2011; "World-Wide Fund Drive," *Washington Post and Times Herald*, November 27, 1963.

17. The stamp was issued on what would have been JFK's forty-seventh birthday, May 29, 1964. A quarter of a billion of the stamps were prepared for sale, double the usual number for a commemorative. Marjorie Hunter, "Coin Up to Congress," *New York Times*, December 11, 1963; "Half Dollars—Kennedy Half Dollar, Silver, 1964," *CoinWeek*, October 10, 2010, http://www.coinweek.com/coin-guide/type-coins-silver/half-dollars-kennedy-half-dollar-silver-1964/ [accessed July 21, 2011]; Bart Barnes, "Johnson Leads Tribute at Kennedy Gravesite," *Washington Post and Times Herald*, May 29, 1964.

18. EX FG 2/Eisenhower, Dwight, Box 40, FG 2/Kennedy, John F., 1/1/64– 4/30/64, Lyndon Baines Johnson Library, Austin, Texas; EX FG 2/Eisenhower, Dwight, Box 40, FG 2/Kennedy, John F. 11/22/63–12/31/63, Lyndon Baines Johnson Library, Austin, Texas.

19. Eve Edstrom and Elsie Carper, "Proposal by Johnson Will Rename Cultural Center for Late President," unnamed newspaper clipping, November 30, 1963, Jarold Keiffer Papers, Box 5, Folder: "November 1963," JFK Library, Boston, Massachusetts.

20. Philip Benjamin, "Idlewild Is Rededicated as John F. Kennedy Airport," *New York Times*, December 25, 1963.

21. "Across Knik Arm, a City That Never Was," *Anchorage Daily News*, February 3, 2010, adn.com, http://community.adn.com/adn/node/147535 [accessed August 23, 2011].

22. J. Maloy Roach, a songwriter for Commander Publications in Hollywood, composed "Lincoln and JFK"; Sister Rosalina Abejo wrote the "President Kennedy March"; the Nazareth Academy in Torresdale, Pennsylvania, produced "The Triply Incandescent Flame," which was a "Sacred Cantata for Voices and Organ most gratefully dedicated to John F. Kennedy . . ." See the Rose Fitzgerald Kennedy Papers, Box 237, Series 10, "Musical Tributes," and Box 238, "Musical Tributes and Poems," John F. Kennedy Library, Boston, Massachusetts.

23. Carrol E. Schwaderer heaped praise on JFK's father: "Our debt to you is not only for the sacrifice of two sons to our country [Joe Jr. and JFK], but for your personal efforts in shaping their characters and destinies." Schwaderer to Joseph P. Kennedy, Sr., November 29, 1963. Gloria M. Barron of Muttontown, New York, praised JFK's mother: "You shared him [JFK] with the world and the demands and strain of his office denied to you both the close companionship of years gone by. Today we are all richer for your noble sacrifice." Barron to Rose Kennedy, November 25, 1963. Rose Kennedy Papers, "Cards and Letters, 1963," Box 236, JFK Library, Boston, Massachusetts. Mrs. June Bilimovich of Winnipeg, Canada, wrote, "We, in Canada, feel the pain and sorrow in the very depth of our hearts, minds and souls. We mourn your beloved son with you, your husband and your whole family. His name will be remembered for all times because he showed to . . . mankind a path of enlightenment and gave his young life in the supreme sacrifice. God help us all." Rose Fitzgerald Kennedy Papers, Box 236, Series 10, Folder "Cards and Letters from Other Countries," John F. Kennedy Library, Boston, Massachusetts.

24. EX FG 2/Eisenhower, Dwight, Box 40, FG 2/Kennedy, John F. 1/1/64–4/30/64, Lyndon Baines Johnson Library, Austin, Texas.

25. Letter from Sidney Tarrson to Pierre Salinger, November 29, 1963, and Letter from Cullen Rapp to Pierre Salinger, December 9, 1963, GEN FG 2/A—C , Box 43, FG 2/Kennedy, John F. 11/22/63–12/15/63, Lyndon Baines Johnson Library, Austin, Texas.

26. Tom Wicker, "Kennedy Without Tears," *Esquire*, June 1964, Rose Kennedy Papers, Box 237, Folder: "Newspaper & Magazine Tributes to JFK, 1963," John F. Kennedy Library, Boston, Massachusetts.

27. Martin Lewis, "Hello Goodbye: Why the Great Mike Wallace Instantly Forgot His

Beatles TV Exclusive," *The Huffington Post*, April 8, 2012, http://www.huffingtonpost.com /martin-lewis/hello-goodbye-why-the-gre_b_1411495.html?ref=media [accessed April 9, 2012].

28. Theodore H. White, "For President Kennedy: An Epilogue," *Life*, December 6, 1963, 158–59.

29. Joyce Hoffmann, "How 'Camelot' Lived Happily Ever After; The Rainy Evening When Jackie Kennedy Invented Our National Myth," *Washington Post*, May 21, 1995; Jack Coleman, "1963: Theodore White Eulogy for JFK Links Kennedys and Camelot," *Cape Cod Today*, December 6, 2008, http://www.capecodtoday.com/blogs/index.php/2008/12/06/today _in_cape_history_theodore_white_epi?blog=161 [accessed July 13, 2011].

30. Memo from T. J. Reardon to the Heads of Departments and Agencies, November 29, 1963, EX FG 2/Eisenhower, Dwight, Box 40, FG 2/Kennedy, John F. 1/1/64–4/30/64, Lyndon Baines Johnson Library, Austin, Texas.

31. "A Statement by the Editors: 'This Nation, Under God,'" *Reader's Digest*, January 1964, pp. 37–38, Rose Kennedy Papers, Box 237, Folder: "Newspaper & Magazine Tributes to JFK, 1963," John F. Kennedy Library, Boston, Massachusetts.

32. Memo from Jack Valenti to LBJ, January 11, 1964, White House Central Files, EX PR 18-1, Box 367, LBJ Library, Austin, Texas. As much as Johnson wanted to be his own man, though, he knew that would have to wait until his own elected term. For political and personal reasons, LBJ continued to link his presidency to Kennedy's. During the 1964 Democratic National Convention, for example, LBJ specifically referred to "the four years of the Kennedy administration." See "Remarks Before the National Convention Upon Accepting the Nomination, August 27, 1964," LBJ Library website, http://www.lbjlib.utexas.edu/john son/archives.hom/speeches.hom/640827.asp [accessed September 4, 2012].

33. Warren Weaver, Jr., "Political Picture for '64 Confused," *New York Times*, November 23, 1963, A1.

34. The same effect helped President Calvin Coolidge win a full term in 1924. Coolidge is the only man besides Lyndon Johnson to have succeeded to the Oval Office with fifteen months or less remaining before the next presidential election. Having been shaken by presidential death so soon before an election, the public is understandably hesitant to make another change so quickly. The "honeymoon" glow also helps the new president win his own term.

35. In 1948 Johnson beat Coke Stevenson, a popular Texas governor, in a race for the U.S. Senate. Johnson's razor-thin margin of victory, a mere 87 votes, and various documented irregularities convinced many people that he had stolen the election. His critics subsequently referred to him as "Landslide Lyndon." Robert A. Caro, *Means of Ascent* (New York: Alfred A. Knopf, 1990), 317.

36. Lyndon B. Johnson, "Annual Message to the Congress on the State of the Union, January 8, 1964," John T. Woolley and Gerhard Peters, *The American Presidency Project* [online], Santa Barbara, CA, http://www.presidency.ucsb.edu/ws/index.php?pid=26787#axzz1 SrV9lavY [accessed July 22, 2011].

37. Edward S. Cohen, "First Major Cut in Rates Slated Since 1954," *Washington Post and Times Herald*, February 23, 1964.

38. The rest of the tax cut went into effect in 1965. The 1964 cut was considerably larger than the 10% tax reduction President Eisenhower secured in 1954.

39. The unemployment rate dropped from 5.4% to 4.4% between February 1964 and July 1965 and "the 16.9% rise in GDP in the two years after the February 1964 tax cut made possible a 13.5% rise in government expenditures at lower tax rates." John W. Sloan, "Economic

Policymaking in the Johnson and Ford Administrations," *Presidential Studies Quarterly* 20, no. 1, "Leadership and Crisis Management" (Winter 1990): 112. Middle- and lower-income groups benefited the most from LBJ's economic policies. Charles B. Garrison, "The 1964 Tax Cut: Supply-Side Economics or Demand Stimulus?" *Journal of Economic Issues* 17, no. 3 (September 1983): 681–96.

40. See Bernard Grofman, *Legacies of the 1964 Civil Rights Act* (Charlottesville: University Press of Virginia, 2000); Charles and Barbara Whalen, *The Longest Debate: A Legislative History of the 1964 Civil Rights Act* (Cabin John, MD: Seven Locks Press, 1985); and Aldon D. Morris, *The Origins of the Civil Rights Movement: Black Communities Organizing for Change* (New York: Free Press, 1984).

41. Diane Holloway reports, "Oswald's later writings protested segregation and argued for integration." Holloway, *The Mind of Oswald: Accused Assassin of President John F. Kennedy* (Victoria, BC: Trafford Publishing, 2000), 4. Oswald listed "racial segregation" as one of America's faults during a November 1959 interview with a UPI reporter. Holloway, ed., *Autobiography of Lee Harvey Oswald: My Life in My Words* (Bloomington, IN: iUniverse Books, 2008), 38.

42. United States House of Representatives: 290–130 vote for the Civil Rights Act on February 10, 1964. Democrats voting aye: 152; Democrats voting nay: 96. Democrats 61% for, 39% against. Republicans voting aye: 138; Republicans voting nay: 34. Republicans 80% for, 20% against. United States Senate: 61–27 vote for the Act on June 30, 1964. Democrats voting aye: 46; Democrats voting nay: 21. Democrats 69% for, 31% against. Republicans voting aye: 27; Republicans voting nay: 6. Republicans 82% for, 18% against.

43. The Civil Rights Act of 1957 included a voting rights provision and established a civil rights division within the Department of Justice. As Senate majority leader, LBJ played a major role in getting the bill through Congress. But overall, his record on civil rights was less than stellar and he had blocked passage of a similar bill the previous year. By 1957 Johnson had his eyes on the upcoming presidential contest and knew that he would need liberal and black support to win his party's nomination. David. A. Nichols, *A Matter of Justice: Eisenhower and the Beginning of the Civil Rights Revolution* (New York: Simon and Schuster, 2007), 145. The Civil Rights Act of 1960 aimed to strengthen black voting rights, though it was weak. Southerners blasted LBJ for betraying his region while some liberals accused Johnson of supporting a watered-down bill in order to bolster his presidential prospects in the South. Robert Dallek, *Lone Star Rising: Lyndon Johnson and His Times, 1908–60* (New York: Oxford University Press, 1991), 563; Robert A. Caro, *The Years of Lyndon Johnson: Master of The Senate* (New York: Alfred A. Knopf, 2003), 1033.

44. Lyndon Baines Johnson, "Remarks Upon Signing the Civil Rights Bill (July 2, 1964)," Miller Center, University of Virginia, http://millercenter.org/scripps/archive/speeches/detail/3525 [accessed July 25, 2011].

45. Letter from LBJ to Justin Turner, July 23, 1964, EX FG 2/Eisenhower, Dwight, Box 40, FG 2/Kennedy, John F. 5/1/64–11/19/64, LBJ Library, Austin, Texas. According to the LBJ Library, Turner was the president of the National Society of Autograph Collectors and board chairman of the Abraham Lincoln Sesquicentennial Association. E-mail from Eric Cuellar of the LBJ Library, August 31, 2011. Turner wrote to LBJ after meeting with a group of historians who argued that JFK's assassination had helped expedite the passage of the Civil Rights Act of 1964. Turner wanted to know if this was true and also whether Johnson had expected his bill to pass when he first introduced it. See Justin G. Turner to LBJ, July 13, 1964, WHCF Subject File-LE, LE/HU 2 8/1/64–12/31/66, LBJ Library, Austin, Texas.

46. However, Kennedy played the critical role in another civil rights milestone that is rarely given its due: the ratification of the Twenty-fourth Amendment to the U.S. Constitution. This amendment abolished the "poll tax," an insidious device designed to prevent African Americans and many poor whites from voting in the five Southern states that employed it as of the early 1960s (Alabama, Arkansas, Mississippi, Texas, and Virginia). In order to register to vote, and stay registered, citizens were required to pay an annual tax. FDR had tried to abolish the poll tax, but was stymied by conservative Democrats in the Senate, and Kennedy decided to use the constitutional amendment route instead. The amendment was passed by two thirds of both houses of Congress in 1962, and Kennedy continued to urge the states to ratify it. The required thirty-eighth state, South Dakota, did so in January 1964.

47. A bestselling book by Michael Harrington, *The Other America* (New York: Macmillan, 1962), had stirred concern in the public about widespread poverty in the country.

48. Arthur Schlesinger, Jr., *A Thousand Days: John F. Kennedy in the White House* (Boston: Houghton Mifflin, 2002), 1012; Schulman, *Johnson and American Liberalism*, 70–71.

49. See http://www.lbjlib.utexas.edu/johnson/lbjforkids/pov_weapons.shtm [accessed September 11, 2011], and also http://presidentialrecordings.rotunda.upress.virginia.edu/essays ?series=WarOnPoverty [accessed September 12, 2011].

50. This recollection is Heller's.

51. Nicholas Lemann, "The Unfinished War," *Atlantic Monthly* 262, no. 6 (December 1988): 37–56.

52. "When LBJ took office, 22.2 percent of Americans were living in poverty. When he left, only 13% were living below the poverty line. Not much changed afterwards; at century's end (1999), the poverty level still stood at 12.7%, a disgracefully high level in the context of the great economic boom then under way. But if the Great Society had not achieved quite as dramatic a reduction in poverty as many had hoped, the nation had at least maintained LBJ's program. Without it, "26 million more Americans would have been living below the poverty level." Joseph A. Califano, Jr., *The Triumph and Tragedy of Lyndon Johnson: The White House Years* (College Station: Texas A&M University Press, 2000), 354.

53. Allen Matusow offers some criticism of the Great Society from the left in *The Unraveling of America: A History of Liberalism in the 1960s* (Athens: University of Georgia Press, 1984). Charles Murray, in *Losing Ground: American Social Policy, 1950–80* (New York: Basic Books, 1984), gives a conservative critique, arguing that welfare programs worsened the plight of poor people and minorities.

54. See Lyndon B. Johnson, "Remarks at the University of Michigan, May 22, 1964," John T. Woolley and Gerhard Peters, *The American Presidency Project* [online], Santa Barbara, CA, http://www.presidency.ucsb.edu/ws/?pid=26262 [accessed August 26, 2011].

55. This song, composed by Irving Berlin for the 1946 Broadway musical *Annie Get Your Gun*, was still quite popular in the 1960s.

56. See Nan Robertson, "Kennedy's Birthday Marked in Sorrow; Widow at a Mass," *New York Times*, May 30, 1964, Val Adams, "Kennedy Tribute on C.B.S. Friday," *New York Times*, May 26, 1964, and Bart Barnes, "Johnson Leads Tribute at Kennedy Gravesite," *Washington Post and Times Herald*, May 29, 1964.

57. "Senator Kennedy Hurt in Air Crash; Bayh Injured, Too," *New York Times*, June 20, 1964; "Peter Lawford Stunned by News of Air Crash," *New York Times*, June 20, 1964.

58. Highly classified intercepts indicate that the USS *Maddox*—reconnoitering the Gulf of Tonkin on behalf of the South Vietnamese government—took some fire from North Vietnamese

torpedo boats on August 2, 1964. In all likelihood, the second skirmish on August 4 never took place, but LBJ cited it anyway when asking Congress for authority to "protect our armed forces and to assist nations covered by the SEATO Treaty." See John Prados, "Essay: 40th Anniversary of the Gulf of Tonkin Incident," August 4, 2004, National Security Archive, George Washington University, http://www.gwu.edu/~nsarchiv/NSAEBB/NSAEBB132/essay.htm [accessed September 12, 2011]. Senators Wayne Morse (D-OR) and Ernest Gruening (D-AK) were the only two members of Congress to vote against the Gulf of Tonkin Resolution.

59. In the monthly Gallup samplings from January to May 1964, Robert Kennedy always led the vice presidential pack, often by a wide margin. LBJ's eventual choice, Hubert Humphrey, was well behind RFK consistently. See the iPOLL Databank, Roper Center, University of Connecticut, http://www.ropercenter.uconn.edu/data_access/ipoll/ipoll.html [accessed September 6, 2011].

60. Catherine Emrick to LBJ, January 16, 1964, Gen PL/Kennedy, Robert F./ Pro Coo-CQZ, Box 11, Folder "PL/Kennedy, R. F./Pro. EM-EZ," Lyndon Baines Johnson Library, Austin, Texas.

61. Mary Emily to LBJ, March 2, 1964, Gen PL/Kennedy, Robert F./ Pro Coo-CQZ, Box 11, Folder "PL/Kennedy, R. F./Pro. EM-EZ," Lyndon Baines Johnson Library, Austin, Texas.

62. Rev. Joseph F. X. Erhart to LBJ, July 28, 1964, Gen PL/Kennedy, Robert F./ Pro Coo-CQZ, Box 11, Folder "PL/Kennedy, R. F./Pro. EM-EZ," Lyndon Baines Johnson Library, Austin, Texas.

63. Robert Caro portrays LBJ as a man with "a desire to hurt for the sake of hurting." At one point, says Caro, Johnson told Pierre Salinger, "in a remark he obviously intended to get back to [Bobby] Kennedy," that JFK's death may have been "divine retribution" for the president's role in the assassinations of Ngo Diem (South Vietnam) and Rafael Trujillo (Dominican Republic). See Robert Caro, *The Passage of Power* (New York: Alfred A. Knopf, 2012), 585.

64. Goodwin, *Johnson and the American Dream*, 199–201.

65. During an Oval Office meeting with RFK, LBJ read from a memo prepared by Clark Clifford that said that "Goldwater's nomination and the need for a running mate with appeal to Southern and border states" had convinced the president to offer the second spot to someone other than RFK. (Yet that description hardly fit Hubert Humphrey, a Northern liberal.) The next day, during a luncheon with several journalists, LBJ made fun of Kennedy's response to the announcement. When RFK complained, Johnson denied that he had discussed their meeting with anyone. Schlesinger, *Robert Kennedy*, 659–62. On July 30, 1964, Johnson told the press that as far as the vice presidency was concerned, he had "reached the conclusion that it would be inadvisable for me to recommend to the convention any member of the Cabinet or any of those who meet regularly with the Cabinet." Lyndon B. Johnson, "Statement by the President Relating to the Selection of a Vice Presidential Candidate, July 30, 1964," John T. Woolley and Gerhard Peters, *The American Presidency Project* [online], Santa Barbara, CA, http://www.presidency.ucsb.edu/ws/?pid=26408 [accessed August 30, 2011].

66. Johnson won New York with 68.6% of the vote, while Bobby Kennedy received just 53.5%. LBJ was pleased he had done so much better. Without Johnson's coattails, it is entirely possible that incumbent Republican Kenneth Keating, a popular moderate liberal, would have defeated RFK.

67. Telegram from Mrs. Walter Curry in Nashville, Tennessee, to Mrs. Lyndon Johnson, July 31, 1964, Papers of Lyndon Baines Johnson, President, 1963–69, Gen PL/Humphrey, Hubert, 9/11/64, Box 9, Folder "PL/Kennedy, Robert F.," Lyndon Baines Johnson Library, Austin, Texas.

68. Rose and Harold Kogan to LBJ, August 3, 1964, Papers of Lyndon Baines Johnson, President, 1963–69, Gen PL/Humphrey, Hubert, 9/11/64, Box 9, Folder "PL/Kennedy, Robert F.," Lyndon Baines Johnson Library, Austin, Texas.

69. Mrs. Mary Perry [Upper Darby, PA] to LBJ, undated letter, probably August 1964, Papers of Lyndon Baines Johnson, President, 1963–69, Gen PL/Humphrey, Hubert, 9/11/64, Box 9, Folder "PL/Kennedy, Robert F.," Lyndon Baines Johnson Library, Austin, Texas.

70. It may have been a good thing for the country that Humphrey was chosen. Dodd was later censured by the Senate on corruption charges and McCarthy proved better at leading a 1968 antiwar protest movement than he ever did at governing.

71. LBJ made the official announcement on Wednesday night, August 26, at the Democratic Convention in Atlantic City. Johnson let the decision slip to journalists on the tarmac at Andrews Air Force Base while en route to Atlantic City. "Meet the next vice president," he told the assembled newsmen, showing off the accompanying Humphrey. Walter Trohan, "It's Johnson, Humphrey," *Chicago Tribune*, August 27, 1964.

72. Theodore H. White, *The Making of the President, 1960* (New York: Harper Perennial, 2009), 92.

73. Humphrey's draft history is convoluted. According to the Senate Historical Office, he was put on the back burner at least twice, the first time because he was a father and the second time because of "a right scrotal hernia"; http://www.senate.gov/artan dhistory/history/resources/pdf/hubert_humphrey.pdf [accessed September 12, 2011]. Humphrey "flunked the physical exam for a Navy commission. He was colorblind, and had a calcification of the lungs and a double hernia. And although his draft number was coming up, it seemed doubtful that the Army would take him either." Carl Solberg, *Hubert Humphrey: A Biography* (Minneapolis: Borealis Books, 2003), 97. In his autobiography, Humphrey said, "In 1940, when the draft began, I had been classified 3A, the status given men who were married and had children. But the war was heating up, the draft situation seemed to be changing, my younger friends were going into service, and I was torn between responsibility to my family and a desire to be a part of our military effort" (47). "Shortly before the [Minneapolis mayoral] convention, I had taken an examination hoping for a Naval Reserve officer commission . . . I was embarrassed by again flunking the physical. The reasons seemed to me insignificant: I was color-blind, had a double hernia, and had some calcification and scars on my lungs (probably from drinking unpasteurized, tuberculous milk as a child). I had the hernia repaired, and the other factors would not have had any effect on my ability to function. Those disabilities, if they could be called that, seemed so slight that I pestered the Navy recruiting officer, Rollo Mudge, incessantly. In July, I was classified 1-A Limited and started the whole routine over, but the Army decided it was too expensive to draft and support men with dependents. Muriel and I had three children, so I was deferred once more" (56). Humphrey says he tried to enlist again during the Battle of the Bulge, but was again classified 1-A Limited (57). Hubert H. Humphrey, *Education of a Public Man: My Life and Politics* (Minneapolis: University of Minnesota Press, 1991).

74. *The Kennedy Assassination: 24 Hours After,* History Channel, 2009.

75. Memo from Douglass Cater to Bill Moyers, 7/15/64, Files of S. Douglass Cater, Box 13, Memos to the White House Staff, May-Nov. 1964 and [1967], Lyndon Baines Johnson Library, Austin, Texas.

76. Robert Dallek, *Flawed Giant: Lyndon Johnson and His Times, 1961–73* (New York: Oxford University Press, 1998), 139.

77. Theodore H. White, *The Making of the President, 1964* (New York: Atheneum, 1965), 291–92.

78. Ibid.

79. Historian Jeffrey Matthews quotes Goldwater: "'Kennedy and I . . . had talked the whole thing out . . . [O]ur plans were all laid" for cross-country Lincoln-Douglas-style debates. Matthews, "To Defeat a Maverick: The Goldwater Candidacy Revisited, 1963–64," *Presidential Studies Quarterly* 27, no. 4, "Rules of the Game: How to Play the Presidency" (Fall 1997): 664–65. See also John Nichols, "Goldwater and JFK Set Standard For Today's Pols," *Cap Times*, January 19, 2011, http://host.madison.com/ct/news/opinion/column/john _nichols/article_1899dc22-9347-58b7-9d7b-0d9ea48cfodc.html [accessed September 12, 2011].

80. The "Peace, Little Girl" commercial (better known as the "Daisy Spot") shows a young girl in a field counting petals as she picks them from a flower. When she reaches the number nine, an ominous voice interrupts and begins a missile launch countdown that culminates in a blinding flash of light and the image of a mushroom cloud. We then hear Lyndon Johnson's familiar drawl: "These are the stakes—to make a world in which all of God's children can live, or to go into the dark. We either must love each other, or we must die." A narrator closes solemnly: "Vote for President Johnson on November third. The stakes are too high for you to stay home." The controversial ad was shown only once—during CBS's *Monday Night at the Movies*—but it generated considerable publicity for the Democratic Party and, by inference, portrayed Goldwater as an unstable politician who would wage nuclear war if elected president. Goldwater himself "set the stage for the spot's anti-Goldwater implications" by publicly expressing support for the use of tactical nuclear weapons. "Peace, Little Girl (Daisy Spot)," Lyndon Baines Johnson Library and Museum Media Archives On-Demand, http://www.lbjlib.utexas.edu/johnson/media/daisyspot/ [accessed September 14, 2011]; Larry J. Sabato, *The Rise of Political Consultants: New Ways of Winning Elections* (New York: Basic Books, 1981), 169–70. See also Robert Mann, *Daisy Petals and Mushroom Clouds* (Baton Rouge: LSU Press, 2011).

81. Alabama, Georgia, Louisiana, Mississippi, and South Carolina.

82. For the 89th Congress, Democrats massively outnumbered Republicans in the House by 295 to 140 and in the Senate by 68 to 32.

83. Charles Mohr, "Goldwater Says Kennedy Timed the Missile Crisis," *New York Times*, September 10, 1964; Letter from Clark Clifford to LBJ, 9/11/64, Office Files of Horace Busby, Box 52, Memos to Mr. Johnson, September '64, LBJ Library, Austin, Texas.

84. White, *Making of the President, 1964*, 384.

85. Johnson's aides consulted the historical record and discovered that ceremonies on the first anniversary of the death of a president varied widely. In April 1946, President Truman dedicated Hyde Park, FDR's retreat, as a national shrine, and in Congress, FDR eulogies were in order. In Warren Harding's memory, President Calvin Coolidge lowered the White House flag to half-staff in early August 1924. (This minimal remembrance may have reflected the fact that some of Harding's scandals had become well known in the year following his death, and this was Coolidge's own election season.) Special church services were held for William McKinley in September 1902, including one that President Theodore Roosevelt attended. For poor President Garfield, on the first anniversary of his death in September 1882, nothing special occurred. Abraham Lincoln's anniversary generated a closing of public offices on April 14, 1866, and the House of Representatives adjourned in Lincoln's honor, with the motion being made by Republican U.S. representative James A. Garfield of

Ohio, ironically. See Memo from Benjamin Read to McGeorge Bundy, 11/10/64, EX FG 2/Eisenhower, Dwight, Box 40, FG 2/Kennedy, John F. 5/1/64–11/19/64, Lyndon Baines Johnson Library, Austin, Texas.

86. Memo from Jack Valenti to LBJ, 11/13/64, EX FG 2/Eisenhower, Dwight, Box 40, FG 2/Kennedy, John F. 5/1/64–11/19/64, LBJ Library, Austin, Texas.

87. Memo from Jack Valenti to LBJ, 11/16/64, EX FG 2/Eisenhower, Dwight, Box 40, FG 2/Kennedy, John F. 5/1/64–11/19/64, Lyndon Baines Johnson Library, Austin, Texas.

88. Nan Robertson, "Robert Kennedy Leads the Family as 40,000 Pay Tribute at Arlington," *New York Times*, November 23, 1964.

89. Nan Robertson, "Kennedy's Birthday Marked in Sorrow; Widow at a Mass," *New York Times*, May 30, 1964.

90. LBJ to JBK, December 15, 1964, White House Famous Names, Box 7, Folder "Kennedy, Mrs. John F., 1964," LBJ Library, Austin, Texas.

14. CROSSED SWORDS: CAMELOT VS. THE GREAT SOCIETY

1. See Lyndon Baines Johnson, "Inaugural Address (January 20, 1965)," Miller Center at the University of Virginia, http://millercenter.org/president/speeches/detail/4031 [accessed October 17, 2011]. Johnson did bring up, in passing, "that sorrowful day in November of 1963" as he referred to his oath of office and his original pledge to "do the best I can."

2. Horace Busby to LBJ, December 9, 1964, Office Files of Horace Busby, Box 52, Memos to President-December, LBJ Library, Austin, Texas.

3. "Kennedy Brothers Take Different Role This Time," *Washington Post and Times Herald*, January 21, 1965.

4. Those who stayed on were Secretary of State Dean Rusk, Secretary of the Treasury C. Douglas Dillon, Secretary of Defense Robert McNamara, Postmaster General John Gronouski, Secretary of the Interior Stewart Udall, Secretary of Agriculture Orville Freeman, Secretary of Labor W. Willard Wirtz, Secretary of Health, Education and Welfare Anthony J. Celebrezze, and U.S. Representative to the United Nations Adlai E. Stevenson. Attorney General Robert Kennedy was replaced by Nicholas Katzenbach, and John T. Connor replaced Luther Hodges as secretary of commerce.

5. Rusk, Udall, Secretary of Agriculture Orville Freeman, and Secretary of Labor W. Willard Wirtz served all eight years of the Kennedy-Johnson administrations. McNamara served more than seven years, until February 1968.

6. Interview with Bob Schieffer, March 4, 2013.

7. See Eric Foner, *Reconstruction: America's Unfinished Revolution, 1863–77* (New York: Harper and Row, 1988).

8. Doris Kearns Goodwin, *Lyndon Johnson and the American Dream* (New York: St. Martin's Griffin, 1976), 227; Irving Bernstein, *Guns or Butter: The Presidency of Lyndon Johnson* (New York: Oxford University Press, 1996), 203–5.

9. Bernstein, *Guns or Butter*, 156–82.

10. See LBJ's "Remarks in the Capitol Rotunda at the Signing of the Voting Rights Act, August 6, 1965," Lyndon Baines Johnson Library and Museum website, http://www.lbjlibrary.org/collections/selected-speeches/1965/08-06-1965.html [accessed October 17, 2011].

11. Robert Dallek, *Flawed Giant: Lyndon Johnson and His Times, 1961–73* (New York: Oxford University Press, 1998), 228–29.

12. Bernstein, *Guns or Butter*, 284 and 303.

13. Randall B. Woods, *LBJ: Architect of American Ambition* (New York: Free Press, 2006), 709.

14. Joseph A. Califano, Jr., "Seeing is Believing: The Enduring Legacy of Lyndon Johnson," Lyndon Baines Johnson Library and Museum website, http://www.lbjlibrary.org/about-lbj/seeing-is-believing.html [accessed October 18, 2011].

15. Bernstein, *Guns or Butter*, 298.

16. Ibid., 273.

17. Woods, *Architect*, 664; Sandra L. Johnson, "Federal Programs and Legislation: An Overview of the National Trails System Act," American Trails, http://www.americantrails.org/resources/feds/NatTrSysOverview.html [accessed October 18, 2011].

18. In fairness, it should be noted that Eisenhower refused to get involved in a land war in Vietnam after the fall of Dien Bien Phu, even though the French and the Joint Chiefs pressed him to make just such a move. See Fred I. Greenstein, *The Hidden-Hand Presidency: Eisenhower as Leader* (New York: Basic Books, 1982), 136, 231. For more information on the gradual escalation of U.S. involvement in Vietnam, see David Halberstam, *The Best and the Brightest: Twentieth Anniversary Edition* (New York: Ballantine Books, 1992); David L. Anderson, *The Columbia History of the Vietnam War* (New York: Columbia University Press, 2011); George C. Herring, *America's Longest War: the United States and Vietnam, 1950–75* (New York: McGraw-Hill, 2001); Stanley Karnow, *Vietnam: A History* (New York: Viking, 1983); William J. Fulbright, *The Arrogance of Power* (New York: Random House, 1967); Brian VanDeMark, *Into the Quagmire: Lyndon Johnson and the Escalation of the Vietnam War* (New York: Oxford University Press, 1991); and *The Pentagon Papers: The Defense Department History of United States Decision-making On Vietnam* (Boston: Beacon Press, 1971).

19. Jacqueline Jones, Peter H. Wood, Thomas Borstelmann, Elaine Tyler May, and Vicki L. Ruiz, *Created Equal: A Social and Political History of the United States*, 2nd ed. (New York: Pearson Longman, 2006), 886.

20. Dallek, *Flawed Giant*, 244.

21. Ibid., 268; "Campus Groups Protest Viet Policy Across U.S.," *Los Angeles Times*, October 16, 1965.

22. Bruce J. Schulman, *Lyndon B. Johnson and American Liberalism* (Boston: Bedford Books, 1995), 139.

23. "Statistical Information About Casualties of the Vietnam War," National Archives website, http://www.archives.gov/research/military/vietnam-war/casualty-statistics.html#year [accessed November 9, 2011].

24. William Chapman, "GIs Repel Pentagon Charge; 50,000 Rally Against War," *Washington Post and Times Herald*, October 22, 1967; Daniel Hallin, "Vietnam on Television," Museum of Broadcast Communications, http://www.museum.tv/eotvsection.php?entrycode=vietnamonte [accessed October 18, 2011].

25. Harry McPherson to LBJ, May 12, 1967, EX FG 1 2/11/67, Box 14, FG 1: 5/5/67–5/27/67, LBJ Library, Austin, Texas.

26. Joseph Alsop interview, conducted by Paige E. Mulhollan, May 28, 1969, Joseph Alsop Papers, Box 183, Folder 8, Joseph and Stewart Alsop Papers, Library of Congress Manuscripts Division, Washington, DC.

27. Goodwin, *Johnson and the American Dream*, 252–53.

28. Ibid., 313.

29. See Lawrence Freedman, *Kennedy's Wars : Berlin, Cuba, Laos, and Vietnam* (New York: Oxford University Press, 2000); David Halberstam, *The Making of a Quagmire* (New York: Random House, 1965); Robert S. McNamara and Brian VanDeMark, *In Retrospect: The Tragedy and Lessons of Vietnam* (New York: Times Books, 1995); Theodore C. Sorensen, *Counselor: A Life At the Edge of History* (New York: Harper, 2008); Arthur M. Schlesinger, Jr., *Robert Kennedy and His Times* (Boston: Houghton Mifflin, 1978); and Lawrence Freedman, "Vietnam and the Disillusioned Strategist," *International Affairs* 72, no. 1 (January 1996): 133–51.

30. E-mail from Ted Sorensen, October 12, 2010. Jacqueline Kennedy, speaking privately in 1964, added a bit of evidence to Sorensen's claims when she remarked, "Jack always said the political thing [in Vietnam] was more important than the military and nobody's thinking of that [now, during the Johnson administration]." See Jacqueline Kennedy, *Historic Conversations on Life with John F. Kennedy* (New York: Hyperion, 2011), 272.

31. A Freudian slip is found in McPherson's memo, when he asks whether those with divided loyalties would "go to the wall for you against Jack." He clearly meant Bobby, not Jack.

32. Harry McPherson to LBJ, June 24, 1965, WHCF, Harry McPherson, Box 21, Office Files of Harry McPherson: Kennedy, Robert F., LBJ Library, Austin, Texas.

33. Telephone interview with Harry McPherson, October 5, 2011.

34. Bill Moyers to LBJ, September 10, 1966, Files of Marvin Watson, Box 25, Office Files of Marvin Watson: Kennedy, Robert [2 of 4], LBJ Library, Austin, Texas.

35. Lyndon B. Johnson, "State of the Union (January 12, 1966)," Miller Center website, University of Virginia, http://millercenter.org/scripps/archive/speeches/detail/4035 [accessed August 3, 2011].

36. Letter from RFK to LBJ, January 1966, White House Famous Names Collection—RFK, Box 8, LBJA Famous Names: Kennedy, Robert F. and Family (1965–68), LBJ Library, Austin, Texas.

37. Letter from LBJ to RFK, January 27, 1966, White House Famous Names Collection—RFK, Box 8, LBJA Famous Names: Kennedy, Robert F. and Family (1965–68), LBJ Library, Austin, Texas.

38. Mike Manatos to LBJ, March 29, 1967, EX FG 2/ Kennedy, John F. 12/28/67—LBJ Presidential Papers, Box 41, LBJ Library, Austin, Texas.

39. Tom Johnson to George Christian, August 29, 1967, EX PL/Humphrey, Hubert H./ Pro, Box 26, PL/Kennedy, Robert F., LBJ Library, Austin, Texas. Tom Johnson is no relation to LBJ.

40. Jeff Shesol, *Mutual Contempt: Lyndon Johnson, Robert Kennedy, and the Feud That Defined a Decade* (New York: W. W. Norton, 1997), 386–88.

41. Note from LBJ to staff, December 10, 1967, Files of Marvin Watson, Box 25, Office Files of Marvin Watson: Kennedy, Robert [2 of 4], LBJ Library, Austin, Texas. On June 3, 1967, RFK introduced the president at the Democratic State Committee Dinner in New York by saying, "In 1964 he won the greatest popular victory in modern times, and with our help he will do so again in 1968 . . . He is the head of our nation and of our party, our Commander-in-Chief and our chief diplomat, our Chief Executive and our chief spokesman, and the chief repository of our hopes and our fears, our advice and our consent, our complaints, and, yes, our prayers. I am very proud that we have in our midst President Lyndon Johnson,

President of the United States." See Ben Wattenberg to LBJ, December 8, 1967, Files of Marvin Watson, Box 25, "Office Files of Marvin Watson, Kennedy, Robert [2 of 4]," LBJ Library, Austin, Texas.

42. J. Chris Arndt and Raymond M. Hyser, *Voices of the American Past,* vol. 2 (New York: Wadsworth, 2001), 506.

43. Goodwin, *Johnson and the American Dream,* 340.

44. According to an unofficial White House Museum website, "The East Garden was dedicated by Mrs. Johnson as the Jacqueline Kennedy Garden on April 22, 1965, although it has been called the 'First Lady's Garden' by some later administrations," namely Nixon's— Chris Matthews says that Nixon changed the name. See Matthews, *Kennedy and Nixon: The Rivalry That Shaped Postwar America* (New York: Simon and Schuster, 1996), 276. White House Museum, http://www.whitehousemuseum.org/grounds/kennedy-garden.htm [accessed October 19, 2011]. The staff at the John F. Kennedy Library told me, "The Jacqueline Kennedy Garden is the former East Garden, which is in the same location in front of the East Wing as the Rose Garden is in front of the West Wing."

45. Jacqueline Kennedy to Lady Bird Johnson, March 15, 1965, White House Famous Names, Box 7, Folder "Kennedy, Mrs. John F., 1965," LBJ Library, Austin, Texas.

46. Runnymede is the famous meadow near the Thames River in Southern England where King John signed the Magna Carta in 1215. By placing limits on the king's power, the Magna Carta nurtured the development of English liberties, which in turn helped bring about the American Revolution and the drafting of the Bill of Rights.

47. Jacqueline Kennedy to Lyndon Johnson, March 28, 1965, White House Famous Names, Box 7, Folder "Kennedy, Mrs. John F., 1964," LBJ Library, Austin, Texas.

48. In May 1854, British sailors aboard HMS *Resolute* were forced to abandon their ship "in latitude 74 degrees 41 minutes N longitude 101 degrees 22 minutes W" while searching for another vessel. The following year, an American whaleboat captain discovered the *Resolute,* which was subsequently refurbished and presented to Queen Victoria as a gift from the president and people of the United States. Touched by the kind gesture, Victoria ordered a desk made out of the ship's timbers when it was broken up and had it presented to President Hayes. Since then, the "Resolute desk" has become one of the White House's most iconic furnishings. See "The President's Desk," John F. Kennedy Presidential Library and Museum website, http://www.jfklibrary.org/Research/Ready-Reference/JFK-Miscellaneous-Information/Desk.aspx [accessed October 20, 2011].

49. Bess Abell to Lady Bird Johnson, July 27, 1965, EX FG 2/Eisenhower, Dwight, Box 40, FG 2/Kennedy, John F. 11/20/64–8/31/65, LBJ Library, Austin, Texas.

50. E-mail from Stephen Plotkin, August 1, 2011.

51. Rep. James H. Morrison (D-LA), one of those who voted in favor of extending Jackie's protection, "said it was the unanimous view of federal law enforcement experts that there is still an element of danger to Mrs. Kennedy and the children." See "House Votes Office and Protection to Mrs. Kennedy in Unique Action," *Washington Post and Times Herald,* December 3, 1963. The Senate concurred with the House and passed Public Law 83-195, which provided Secret Service protection for Jackie and her children for two years. See "Senate Passes Bill to Aid Mrs. Kennedy, Children," *Washington Post and Times Herald,* December 12, 1963. In 1965 Congress established the basis of the current spouse protocols, granting former presidents and their spouses lifetime protection, and children of former presidents protection until age sixteen. Prompted by Jackie's marriage to Aristotle Onassis, Congress in 1968

modified the clause for presidential widows to provide coverage until the spouse's own death or remarriage. See the United States Secret Service historical timeline, http://www .secretservice.gov/history.shtml [accessed November 10, 2011].

52. Marvin Watson to LBJ, July 13, 1965, EX FG 2/Eisenhower, Dwight, Box 40, FG 2/Kennedy, John F. 11/20/64–8/31/65, LBJ Library, Austin, Texas.

53. Caroline Kennedy has explained why she decided to publish her mother's interviews with Schlesinger in 2011: "[E]nough time has passed so that they can be appreciated for their unique insight, yet the Kennedy presidency is still within living memory for many who will find her observations illuminating." From the foreword by Caroline Kennedy in Kennedy, *Historic Conversations*, XI.

54. Said Jackie: "And anytime Lyndon would talk that night, Lady Bird would get out a little notebook—I've never seen a husband and a wife so—she was sort of like a trained hunting dog. He'd say something as innocent as—I don't know—'Does your sister live in London?'—and Lady Bird would write down Lee's name and 'London.' Just everything. I mean, she had every name, phone number—it was a—ewww—sort of a funny kind of way of operating." Kennedy, *Historic Conversations*, 85.

55. Ibid., 278. Whatever Kennedy's private view of Johnson may have been, he wisely avoided public spats with the vice president. When Kenny O'Donnell and other Kennedy loyalists attempted to embarrass LBJ by leaking an unflattering story about him to the press, JFK chastised O'Donnell for his indiscretion: "I can't afford to have my vice president, who knows every reporter in Washington, going around saying we're all screwed up, so we're going to keep him happy." Dallek, *Flawed Giant*, 9.

56. Kennedy, *Historic Conversations*, 87, 274.

57. Jackie found out that LBJ had had a gaggle of reporters in the Oval Office listening to one of his December 1963 calls to her—apparently, it infuriated Jackie when she discovered that her private conversation was simply a way for LBJ to prove to the press how "close" they were. See Kennedy, *Historic Conversations*, 86.

58. Telephone interview with Harry McPherson, October 5, 2011.

59. Kennedy, *Historic Conversations*, 273.

60. Anxious to set the record straight on her husband's death, Jackie commissioned the Wesleyan University professor William Manchester to write the definitive account of November 22, 1963. But she quickly became disenchanted with Manchester's warts-and-all manuscript and sued to stop its publication.

61. And, possibly, a suggestion that Texas's culture of gun violence underlay November 22.

62. Dallek, *Flawed Giant*, 520.

63. Barbara A. Perry, *Jacqueline Kennedy: First Lady of the New Frontier* (Lawrence: University Press of Kansas, 2004), 195–96.

64. John Corry, *The Manchester Affair* (New York: G. P. Putnam's Sons, 1967), 18.

65. Sam Kashner, "A Clash of Camelots," *Vanity Fair*, October 2009, http://www.vanity fair.com/politics/features/2009/10/death-of-a-president200910 [accessed August 3, 2011].

66. Manchester dropped about sixteen hundred words from the magazine version, including some personal anecdotes. The notes of the meeting between Manchester and Mrs. Kennedy were also sealed for a hundred years, until 2067. By any accounting, Mrs. Kennedy achieved a minor—and very costly—victory. See foreword by Caroline Kennedy in Kennedy, *Historic Conversations*, XIII.

67. Kashner, "Clash of Camelots," 7.

68. LBJ to Jacqueline Kennedy, December 16, 1966, White House Famous Names, Box 7, Folder "Kennedy, Mrs. John F., 1966," LBJ Library, Austin, Texas.

69. Jacqueline Kennedy to LBJ, undated, White House Famous Names, Box 7, Folder "Kennedy, Mrs. John F., 1966," LBJ Library, Austin, Texas.

70. Harold Weisberg self-published *Whitewash: The Report on the Warren Report* in 1965. Two other major November 22 conspiracy books, Mark Lane's *Rush to Judgment* and Edward J. Epstein's *Inquest*, came out the following year.

71. Kupferman press release dated September 28, 1966, Earl Warren Papers, Box 758, Library of Congress Manuscripts Division, Washington, DC.

72. For example, on what would have been Kennedy's forty-ninth birthday (May 29, 1966), twenty-five hundred people attended a memorial service at the National Shrine of the Immaculate Conception in D.C. Thousands more filed past the Eternal Flame at Arlington Cemetery a few months later to commemorate the third anniversary of JFK's death. See "Service Held in Capital on Kennedy's Birthday," *New York Times*, May 30, 1966, and Richard Harwood and John Carmody, "Mourners Mark Anniversary of Kennedy Death," *Washington Post and Times Herald*, November 23, 1966.

73. Earl Warren to Clayton Fritchey, November 2, 1966, Earl Warren Papers, Box 758, Library of Congress Manuscripts Division, Washington, DC.

74. RSVP from Earl Warren to Robert M. Bennett, Vice President and General Manager of WTTG, October 27, 1966, Earl Warren Papers, Box 758, Library of Congress Manuscripts Division, Washington, DC.

75. Garrison wrote two books on the investigation—*A Heritage of Stone* and *On the Trail of the Assassins*. His third book—*The Star Spangled Contract*—is a fictional thriller loosely based on the Kennedy assassination.

76. George Lardner, Jr., "Shaw Tied to Oswald by Garrison," *Washington Post and Times Herald*, March 3, 1967; James Kirkwood, *American Grotesque: An Account of the Clay Shaw–Jim Garrison Affair in the City of New Orleans* (New York: Simon and Schuster, 1970), 13; Michael L. Kurtz, *The JFK Assassination Debates: Lone Gunman Versus Conspiracy* (Lawrence: University Press of Kansas, 2006), 132.

77. Those believing one man had killed JFK declined from 35% to 19% over the same period. 21% were unsure in February 1967 and 15% in May 1967. See memo from Fred Panzer to LBJ, May 26, 1967, EX FG 2/Kennedy, John F. 12/28/65, Box 41, FG 2/Kennedy, John F. 12/28/65—[1 of 2], LBJ Library, Austin, Texas. See also Louis Harris, "66% See Conspiracy in Kennedy Slaying," *Washington Post and Times Herald*, May 29, 1967.

78. However, in January 1968 the pathologists who performed JFK's autopsy asked LBJ's last attorney general, Ramsey Clark, to empanel a group of medical experts to reexamine their actions. Four such experts, who had no ties to the Kennedy controversy or the original autopsy, were so appointed, partly in response to a suit that had been filed to force disclosure of the autopsy photos and other materials that the Kennedy family wished to keep private. In an April 1968 report to Clark, the experts essentially upheld the professional integrity of the original autopsy, though they did suggest that it would have been preferable to have a sectioning of JFK's neck wound to trace the exact path of that nonfatal bullet. See "ARRB MD 59—Clark Panel Report (2/26/68)," Mary Ferrell Foundation website, http://www.maryferrell.org/mffweb/archive/viewer/showDoc.do?docId=323&relPageId=1 [accessed October 25, 2011]; Dennis L. Breo, "JFK's death—the plain truth from the MDs who did the autopsy,"

JAMA 267, no. 20, May 27, 1992: 2794–803; and Fred P. Graham, "Doctor Inspects Kennedy X-Rays," *New York Times*, January 9, 1972.

79. Leon Jaworski to Earl Warren, July 19, 1967, Earl Warren Papers, Box 758, "Kennedy Assassination Commission Correspondence with Warren, 1964–67," Library of Congress Manuscripts Division, Washington, DC. See also "CBS News Inquiry, June 25, 1967, Part 1," YouTube, http://www.youtube.com/watch?v=iolMAtbkOuo&feature=related [accessed October 25, 2011].

80. Robert Hennelly and Jerry Policoff, "JFK: How the Media Assassinated the Real Story," http://www.assassinationresearch.com/v1n2/mediaassassination.html [accessed October 25, 2011].

81. John F. Kennedy Center bulletin *Footlight*, Summer 1966, Series 2, Box 8, Folder "Subject Files 1959–2004. NCC Publicity [General]," John F. Kennedy Library, Boston, Massachusetts. I saw the film myself as a schoolboy in Norfolk, Virginia, in 1966, and you can view it on YouTube at http://www.youtube.com/watch?v=L4SwEUS4080 [accessed October 26, 2011].

82. Robert B. Semple, Jr., "Johnson at Grave with the Kennedys," *New York Times*, March 16, 1967.

83. Lyndon B. Johnson, "Statement by the President Upon Signing Bill Establishing the John Fitzgerald Kennedy National Historic Site, May 27, 1967," John T. Woolley and Gerhard Peters, *The American Presidency Project* [online], Santa Barbara, CA, http://www.presidency.ucsb.edu/ws/?pid=28275 [accessed August 10, 2011]; "O'Brien Asserts Hero Worship May Obscure Kennedy's Deeds," *New York Times*, May 30, 1967.

84. Laurence Stern, "'I Christen Thee John F. Kennedy': Caroline Christens Carrier Kennedy," *Washington Post and Times Herald*, May 28, 1967. The JFK Library supplied me with an estimate of a crowd of ten thousand, a figure also mentioned in a *Boston Globe* headline detailing the event. Other sources place the number closer to fifteen thousand.

85. Ben Wattenberg to LBJ, May 19, 1967, Office Files of Ben Wattenberg, Box 22, LBJ Library, Austin, Texas.

86. Lyndon B. Johnson, "Remarks at the Christening of the Aircraft Carrier U.S.S. John F. Kennedy, May 27, 1967," John T. Woolley and Gerhard Peters, *The American Presidency Project* [online], Santa Barbara, CA, http://www.presidency.ucsb.edu/ws/?pid=28274, [accessed August 10, 2011].

87. Had Albert succeeded Nixon, a difficult situation would arguably have been made much worse. Nixon had won 61% of the votes over Democrat George McGovern in 1972, yet through the impeachment actions of a heavily Democratic House of Representatives, the Democratic Speaker would have taken the White House, overturning a large popular mandate for the Republicans. To some, it would have looked like a partisan power grab, if not a putsch. Ford, a Republican, was better able to fulfill the mandate his party had won less than two years earlier. For more information on the Twenty-fifth Amendment, see John D. Feerick, *The Twenty-fifth Amendment: Its Complete History and Applications*, 2nd ed. (New York: Fordham University Press, 1992); Birch Bayh, *One Heartbeat Away: Presidential Disability and Succession* (Indianapolis: Bobbs-Merrill, 1968); and Adam Gustafson, "Presidential Inability and Subjective Meaning," *Yale Policy and Law Review* 27, no. 2 (1999): 459–97.

88. See Marc J. Gilbert and William P. Head, *The Tet Offensive* (Westport, CT: Praeger,

1996), Don Oberdorfer, *Tet!: The Turning Point in the Vietnam War* (Baltimore: Johns Hopkins University Press, 2001), David Schmitz, *The Tet Offensive: Politics, War, and Public Opinion* (Lanham, MD: Rowman and Littlefield, 2005), and Ronald H. Spector, *After Tet: The Bloodiest Year in Vietnam* (New York: Vintage, 1993).

89. Dallek, *Flawed Giant*, 506. In a review of Douglas Brinkley's *Cronkite* (New York: HarperCollins, 2012), Louis Menand questions whether LBJ ever uttered these words or even saw Cronkite's broadcast. See Louis Menand, "Seeing It Now: Walter Cronkite and the Legend of CBS News," *New Yorker*, July 9 and 16, 2012, 88–94.

90. Lyndon B. Johnson, "The President's Address to the Nation Announcing Steps to Limit the War in Vietnam and Reporting His Decision Not to Seek Reelection," March 31, 1968, Online by Gerhard Peters and John T. Woolley, *The American Presidency Project*, http://www.presidency.ucsb.edu/ws/index.php?pid=28772&st=&st1=#axzz1btxNKybQ [accessed October 26, 2011]. There had been no public hint of this stunning statement, which came at the end of a national TV address about Vietnam. It was so jaw-dropping that I can recall my father and I, watching it live, turn to one another and mutter in disbelief, "Did you hear him say . . . ?"

91. Shesol, *Mutual Contempt*, 422.

92. "Memorandum of conference with Senator Robert Kennedy and Theodore C. Sorensen," March 14, 1968, Clark Clifford Papers, Box 30, Folder 22, Library of Congress, Manuscripts Division, Washington, DC.

93. Goodwin, *Johnson and the American Dream*, 343.

94. "Memorandum of Conversation: The President, Senator Robert F. Kennedy, Theodore Sorensen, Charles Murphy, and W. W. Rostow, 10:00 A.M., April 3, 1968," White House Famous Names Collection—RFK, Box 8, LBJA Famous Names: Kennedy, Robert F. 1968 Campaign, LBJ Library, Austin, Texas.

95. Mark K. Updegrove, *Indomitable Will: LBJ in the Presidency* (New York: Crown Publishers, 2012), 272.

96. RFK was shot at 12:15 A.M. on June 5; he died at 1:44 A.M. on June 6.

97. George Reedy to LBJ, June 5, 1968, White House Famous Names Collection—RFK, Box 8, LBJA Famous Names: Kennedy, Robert F. Assassination of, LBJ Library Austin, Texas.

98. Lyndon B. Johnson, "Address to the Nation Following the Attack on Senator Kennedy, June 5, 1968," John T. Woolley and Gerhard Peters, *The American Presidency Project* [online], Santa Barbara, CA, http://www.presidency.ucsb.edu/ws/?pid=28908 [accessed August 12, 2011].

99. Ibid.

100. Vincent Bzdek, *The Kennedy Legacy: Jack, Bobby and Ted and a Family Dream Fulfilled* (New York: Palgrave Macmillan, 2009), 141, 145–46.

101. "Robert F. Kennedy Memorial," Arlington National Cemetery website, http://www.arlingtoncemetery.mil/visitor_information/Robert_F_Kennedy.html [accessed August 18, 2011]; Cy Egan and Joseph Mancini, "LBJ Declares Day of Mourning," *New York Post*, June 6, 1968.

102. Lyndon B. Johnson, "Remarks and Statement Upon Signing Order Establishing the National Commission on the Causes and Prevention of Violence," June 10, 1968, Online by Gerhard Peters and John T. Woolley, *The American Presidency Project*, http://www.presidency.ucsb.edu/ws/index.php?pid=28913#axzz1btxNKybQ [accessed October 26, 2011].

103. "Excerpts from the Firearms Statement by the National Commission on Violence,"

New York Times, July 29, 1969; "Excerpts from National Panel's Statement on Violence in TV Entertainment," *New York Times*, September 25, 1969; "Excerpts from the Statement on Civil Disobedience by National Panel on Violence," *New York Times*, December 9, 1969.

104. RFK's murder has evoked some of the same questions and conspiracy theories as JFK's. See for instance, Lisa Pease, "The Other Kennedy Conspiracy," *Salon*, November 21, 2011, http://www.salon.com/2011/11/21/the_other_kennedy_conspiracy/ [accessed November 22, 2011].

105. "Sirhan's Sentence Is Reduced to Life By California Court," *New York Times*, June 17, 1972.

106. James Randerson, "New Evidence Challenges Official Picture of Kennedy Shooting," *The Guardian*, February 22, 2008, http://www.guardian.co.uk/science/2008/feb/22 /kennedy.assassination [accessed October 27, 2011]. See also William Klaber and Philip H. Melanson, *Shadow Play* (New York: St. Martin's Press, 1997); and Shane O'Sullivan, *Who Killed Bobby?* (New York: Sterling, 2008). "RFK Assassin Sirhan Sirhan's Parole Rejected," *Los Angeles Times*, March 2, 2011.

107. See William F. Pepper, *Orders to Kill* (New York: Warner Books, 1995), Philip H. Melanson, *The Martin Luther King Assassination: New Revelations on the Conspiracy and Cover-up, 1968–91* (New York: Shapolsky, 1991), and Mark Lane and Dick Gregory, *Murder in Memphis* (New York: Thunder's Mouth Press, 1993).

108. Marguerite Oswald Telegram to Mary Sirhan, icollector.com, http://www.icollector .com/Marguerite-Oswald-Telegram-to-Mary-Sirhan_i10433007 [accessed October 27, 2011].

109. Charles Guggenheim, the filmmaker, says that his RFK movie nearly caused a riot. See Guggenheim's interview with Jim Lehrer: http://www.pbs.org/newshour/media/biofilms /guggenheim.html [accessed December 6, 2011].

110. Matthews, *Kennedy and Nixon*, 267.

111. The Gun Control Act of 1968 is Public Law 90-618 (82 Stat. 1213). Lyndon B. Johnson, "Remarks Upon Signing the Gun Control Act of 1968," October 22, 1968, Online by Gerhard Peters and John T. Woolley, *The American Presidency Project*, http://www.presidency.ucsb .edu/ws/?pid=29197 [accessed October 27, 2011]; Dan Nowicki and Dennis Wagner, "Concern Over Safety, Rights Shape AZ's Gunslinger Attitude," *Arizona Republic*, July 11, 2011, http://www.azcentral.com/news/articles/2011/07/11/20110711arizona-guns-special-report -history.html [accessed August 18, 2011].

112. The 1986 "Firearm Owners Protection Act" (Public Law No. 99-308) modified several elements of the Gun Control Act, relaxing certain restrictions on gun sellers at the request of the gun lobby while imposing stiffer penalties on individuals convicted of using a firearm while committing certain crimes. A related piece of legislation from the same year, the Law Enforcement Officers Protection Act, defined and outlawed so-called cop-killer bullets, or armor-piercing ammunition. The Brady Handgun Violence Prevention Act of 1993 introduced the five-day waiting period for gun purchases and mandated that firearm sellers conduct background checks on unlicensed purchasers. The FBI was directed to establish within a four-year window a "National Instant Criminal Background Check System" for gun purchasers. Police background checks at licensed gun dealers are now standard, but they do not apply to the sizable portion of guns acquired at private sales and gun shows (the so-called gun show loophole). The Violent Crime Control and Law Enforcement Act of 1994 included a section labeled the "Public Safety and Recreational Firearms Use Protection Act," typically referred to by the press as the assault weapons ban, which prohibited manufacture,

importation, and sale to civilian purchasers of semiautomatic weapons and guns with large-capacity ammunition feeds. The law further prohibited juvenile possession of or trade in firearms. The law expired in 2004 under "sunset" provisions.

113. According to the Secret Service's website, Congress responded to RFK's assassination by authorizing "protection of major presidential and vice presidential candidates and nominees. (Public Law 90-331)." See http://www.secretservice.gov/history.shtml. See especially section 7 of the current code (Title 18, Part II, Chapter 203, Section 3056), which reads in full: "Under the direction of the Secretary of Homeland Security, the United States Secret Service is authorized to protect the following persons: (1) The president, the vice president (or other officer next in the order of succession to the office of president), the president-elect, and the vice president-elect (2) The immediate families of those individuals listed in paragraph (1). (3) Former presidents and their spouses for their lifetimes, except that protection of a spouse shall terminate in the event of remarriage unless the former president did not serve as president prior to January 1, 1997, in which case, former presidents and their spouses for a period of not more than ten years from the date a former president leaves office, except that (A) protection of a spouse shall terminate in the event of remarriage or the divorce from, or death of a former president; and (B) should the death of a president occur while in office or within one year after leaving office, the spouse shall receive protection for one year from the time of such death: Provided, That the Secretary of Homeland Security shall have the authority to direct the Secret Service to provide temporary protection for any of these individuals at any time if the Secretary of Homeland Security or designee determines that information or conditions warrant such protection. (4) Children of a former president who are under 16 years of age for a period not to exceed ten years or upon the child becoming 16 years of age, whichever comes first. (5) Visiting heads of foreign states or foreign governments. (6) Other distinguished foreign visitors to the United States and official representatives of the United States performing special missions abroad when the president directs that such protection be provided. (7) Major presidential and vice presidential candidates and, within 120 days of the general presidential election, the spouses of such candidates. As used in this paragraph, the term "major presidential and vice presidential candidates" means those individuals identified as such by the Secretary of Homeland Security after consultation with an advisory committee consisting of the Speaker of the House of Representatives, the minority leader of the House of Representatives, the majority and minority leaders of the Senate, and one additional member selected by the other members of the committee. The Committee shall not be subject to the Federal Advisory Committee Act (5 App. U.S.C. 2). (8) Former vice presidents, their spouses, and their children who are under 16 years of age, for a period of not more than six months after the date the former vice president leaves office. The Secretary of Homeland Security shall have the authority to direct the Secret Service to provide temporary protection for any of these individuals at any time thereafter if the Secretary of Homeland Security or designee determines that information or conditions warrant such protection. The protection authorized in paragraphs (2) through (8) may be declined." "Powers, Authorities, and Duties of United States Secret Service," Legal Information Institute, Cornell University Law School, http://www.law.cornell.edu/uscode/usc_sec_18_00003056—-000-.html [accessed November 9, 2011].

114. Barbara A. Perry, *Jacqueline Kennedy: First Lady of the New Frontier* (Lawrence: University Press of Kansas, 2004), 197.

115. Judy Klemesrud, "The Reaction Here Is Anger, Shock, and Dismay," *New York Times*, October 19, 1968.

116. "Many in Europe Shocked," *New York Times*, October 19, 1968.

117. Marie Smith, "5 Novembers Later: Thousands at Grave," *Los Angeles Times*, November 23, 1968; "Rites Mark Tragic Date," Gerald Bruno Papers, Box 7, Folder "JFK Assassination," JFK Library, Boston, Massachusetts.

15. "TIN SOLDIERS AND NIXON COMING": JFK'S REPUDIATION AND REVIVAL

1. See "Smith, Howard K.: U.S. Journalist," The Museum of Broadcast Communications, http://www.museum.tv/eotvsection.php?entrycode=smithhoward [accessed December 13, 2011].

2. See Christopher Matthews, *Kennedy and Nixon: The Rivalry That Shaped Postwar America* (New York: Simon and Schuster, 1996).

3. See Susan Jacoby, *Alger Hiss and the Battle for History* (New Haven: Yale University Press, 2009); William Allen Jowitt, *The Strange Case of Alger Hiss* (London: Hodder and Stoughton, 1953); and Alistair Cooke, *A Generation on Trial: U.S.A. v. Alger Hiss* (New York: Alfred A. Knopf, 1950).

4. Nixon turned forty eleven days before his inauguration in 1953.

5. Two months before the election, the press accused Nixon of drawing money from a secret fund set up by corporate lobbyists. The "Checkers Speech" was the national television address given by the vice presidential candidate in September 1952, in which he answered charges about the alleged "secret fund" he had maintained to pay expenses. His appeal to the public was maudlin but worked wonders, as thousands of Americans telegraphed the Republican National Committee to demand that Eisenhower keep Nixon on the ticket. Ike did. See Stephen E. Ambrose, *Nixon: The Education of a Politician, 1913–62* (New York: Simon and Schuster, 1987), pp. 276–91.

6. David Greenberg, "Was Nixon Robbed?" *Slate*, October 16, 2000, http://www.slate.com/articles/news_and_politics/history_lesson/2000/10/was_nixon_robbed.single.html [accessed November 9, 2012].

7. Former Nixon aide Stephen Hess, who was the first of the inner circle to see Nixon after the assassination, reported that Nixon was "very shaken." Stephen E. Ambrose, *Nixon: The Triumph of a Politician, 1962–72* (New York: Simon and Schuster, 1989), 32; Matthews, *Kennedy and Nixon*, 239–40.

8. Ambrose, *Triumph of a Politician*, 86.

9. In September, Gallup had Nixon at 41%, Humphrey at 31%, and independent George Wallace at 20%, with 8% undecided. Conducted by the Gallup Organization, September 1–September 6, 1968 and based on 1,507 personal interviews. Sample: National Adult. [USGALLUP.68-767.R05B]. Gallup Poll (AIPO), Sept. 1968. iPOLL Databank, Roper Center for Public Opinion Research, University of Connecticut, http://www.ropercenter.uconn.edu/data_access/ipoll/ipoll.html [accessed January 30, 2012].

10. *Guide to U.S. Elections*, vol. 1, 6th ed. (Washington, DC: CQ Press, 2010), 791, 881.

11. Richard Nixon to John Ehrlichman, February 5, 1969, President's Personal Files, Box 1, Folder, "Memos—February 1969," Richard Nixon Library, Yorba Linda, California.

12. Richard Nixon to John Ehrlichman, March 11, 1969, President's Personal Files, Box 1, Folder, "Memos—March 1969," Richard Nixon Library, Yorba Linda, California.

13. Richard Nixon to H. R. Haldeman, March 2, 1970, President's Personal Files, Box 2, Folder, "Memos—March 1970," Richard Nixon Library, Yorba Linda, California. See also Nixon to Haldeman, October 1, 1969, President's Personal Files, Box 1, Folder, "Memos—October 1969" and Nixon to Haldeman, January 14, 1971, President's Personal Files, Box 3, Folder, "Memos—January 1971," Richard Nixon Library, Yorba Linda, California.

14. "News Summary—January 19, 1971," President's Office Files, Box 32, Folder, "News Summaries—January 1971," Richard Nixon Library, Yorba Linda, California.

15. Clipping of "Nixon v. JFK," *Richmond News Leader*, January 8, 1970, and the president's handwritten notes, President's Office Files, Box 34, Folder, "News Summaries—January 1970," Richard Nixon Library, Yorba Linda, California.

16. "News Summaries—October 13–20, 1971," President's Office Files, Box 34, Richard Nixon Library, Yorba Linda, California.

17. Mike Royko, "Suppose a President Named Kennedy Did This," *Chicago Daily News*, October 18, 1971.

18. "Weekend News Review—June 12, 1972," President's Office Files, Box 40, Folder, "March 27–31, 1972," Richard Nixon Library, Yorba Linda, California.

19. "News Summary—February 14, 1973," President's Office Files, Box 47, Folder, "February 8–17, 1973," Richard Nixon Library, Yorba Linda, California.

20. News Summary—July 26, 1972," President's Office Files, Box 41, Folder, "July 25–31, 1972," Richard Nixon Library, Yorba Linda, California.

21. Harry S. Dent to Richard Nixon, July 8, 1969, President's Office Files, Box 2, Folder, "President's Handwriting, July 1969," Richard Nixon Library, Yorba Linda, California.

22. Patrick Buchanan to Richard Nixon, September 17, 1971, Patrick J. Buchanan Papers, Box 4, Folder, "Presidential memos—1971," Richard Nixon Library, Yorba Linda, California.

23. Charles Colson to H. R. Haldeman, May 21, 1971, Charles W. Colson Papers, Box 4, Folder, "HRH Memos [1 of 3] [5-10-72–12-16-72]," Richard Nixon Library, Yorba Linda, California.

24. Ibid.

25. Conversation between Richard Nixon and John Ehrlichman, Executive Office Building, Wednesday, September 8, 1971, 3:26 P.M.–5:10 P.M., Tape 274-044, Presidential Recording Program, Miller Center, University of Virginia, http://whitehousetapes.net/transcript/nixon/274-044 [accessed January 10, 2012].

26. See Jack Olsen, *The Bridge at Chappaquiddick* (New York: Ace Books, 1970), and Leo Damore, *Senatorial Privilege: The Chappaquiddick Cover-Up* (Washington: Regnery Gateway, 1988).

27. Matthews, *Kennedy and Nixon*, 280.

28. Richard Nixon to John Ehrlichman, August 7, 1969, John D. Ehrlichman Papers, Box 20, Folder, "Edward Kennedy, 308-A, Stanley," Richard Nixon Library, Yorba Linda, California. Jon Roscoe, an archivist at the Nixon Library, told me that "Aside from President Nixon's initial memorandum regarding information from Kissinger, I was unable to find any materials in John Ehrlichman's papers about an investigation of Kissinger's remarks." E-mail from Jonathan Roscoe, December 22, 2011. Of course, the follow-up could have been accomplished by telephone or in person.

29. "Kennedy could have been charged with manslaughter . . . for leaving the scene of an accident. 'No man stands above the law,' Kennedy would tell Richard Nixon in a few years during the Watergate hearings, but during Chappaquiddick, it appeared to many people that

one man did." Vincent Bzdek, *The Kennedy Legacy: Jack, Bobby and Ted and a Family Dream Fulfilled* (New York: Palgrave Macmillan, 2009), 159.

30. "October 3, 1969 News Summary from Mort Allin to H. R. Haldeman 'For the President,'" President's Office Files, Box 47, Folder, "News Summaries—October 1969," Richard Nixon Library, Yorba Linda, California.

31. Jack Caulfield to John Ehrlichman, February 6, 1970, John D. Ehrlichman Papers, Box 16, Folder, "Chappaquiddick," Richard Nixon Library, Yorba Linda, California.

32. "News Summary—February 5, 1970," President's Office Files, Box 31, Folder, "News Summaries—February 1970," Richard Nixon Library, Yorba Linda, California.

33. "November 1970 News Summary," President's Office Files, Box 32, Folder, "News Summaries—November 1970," Richard Nixon Library, Yorba Linda, California.

34. See Gallup poll numbers, July–Aug. 1971, iPOLL Databank, Roper Center for Public Opinion Research, University of Connecticut, http://www.ropercenter.uconn.edu/data _access/ipoll/ipoll.html [accessed January 27, 2012].

35. "Weekend News Review—November 29, 1971," President's Office Files, Box 36, Folder, "News Summaries—November 24–30, 1971," Richard Nixon Library, Yorba Linda, California.

36. "News Summary—April 6, 1972" and "Weekend News Review—April 10, 1972," President's Office Files, Box 40, Folder, "April 1–11, 1972," Richard Nixon Library, Yorba Linda, California.

37. Bill Safire to H. R. Haldeman, November 16, 1971, H. R. Haldeman Papers, Box 87, Folder, "William Safire—November 1971," Richard Nixon Library, Yorba Linda, California.

38. Pat Buchanan to Richard Nixon, June 9, 1971, Patrick J. Buchanan Papers, Box 4, Folder, "Presidential memos—1971," Richard Nixon Library, Yorba Linda, California.

39. Pat Buchanan/Ken Khachigian to John Mitchell and H. R. Haldeman, April 12, 1972, Patrick J. Buchanan Papers, Box 6, Folder, "Haldeman—1972," Richard Nixon Library, Yorba Linda, California.

40. Interview with John Dean, June 2, 2013; Conversation between Richard Nixon, Bob Haldeman and Alexander Butterfield, Oval Office, Thursday, September 7, 1972, 4:47 P.M.–6:15 P.M., Tape 772-015, Presidential Recording Program, Miller Center, University of Virginia, http://whitehousetapes.net/transcript/nixon/772-015-0 [accessed January 30, 2012].

41. "'Memorandum for the President's file,' September 21, 1972, from Ken W. Clawson," President's Office Files, Box 89, Folder, "Beginning September 17, 1972," Richard Nixon Library, Yorba Linda, California. Nixon's discussion was with the author and journalist Frank van der Linden, who wrote a book entitled *Nixon's Quest for Peace* (Washington, DC: Robert B. Luce, 1972).

42. Jackie was invited to the White House to view the unveiling of the Kennedys' official portraits. She was reluctant to take part in a public ceremony, however, so the Nixons invited her to a private evening and unveiling. Nixon sent a small presidential jet to New York to pick up Mrs. Kennedy and her children. Helen Thomas was the only reporter to find out about the event, but she agreed to delay her story in return for additional details from the White House. Matthews, *Kennedy and Nixon*, 292–94.

43. Sarah Booth Conroy and Sally Quinn, "Jackie Returns," *Washington Post and Times Herald*, February 4, 1971. Nixon handwrote notes to Caroline and John Jr. about the visit, noting they would "always be welcome in this House." Jackie responded that she was

"touched" and the children were "thrilled." "One is most vulnerable where one's children are concerned," she noted. Richard Nixon to JFK Jr., February 28, 1971; Nixon to Caroline Kennedy, February 28, 1971; and Jacqueline Kennedy to Richard Nixon, March 16, 1971, President's Personal Files, Box 10, Folder, "Kennedy, Caroline & John & Jackie," Richard Nixon Library, Yorba Linda, California.

44. Mort Allin to H. R. Haldeman, February 4, 1971, Patrick J. Buchanan Papers, Box 4, "Folder, "Magruder—1971," Richard Nixon Library, Yorba Linda, California.

45. Robert C. Odle, Jr., to H. R. Haldeman, February 4, 1971, Patrick J. Buchanan Papers, Box 4, "Folder, "Magruder—1971," Richard Nixon Library, Yorba Linda, California.

46. "Nixon to Work on Energy During 4 Days at Camp David," *Washington Post and Times Herald*, November 22, 1973.

47. H. R. Haldeman with Joseph DiMona, *The Ends of Power* (New York: New York Times Books, 1978), 39.

48. Tim Weiner, *Enemies: A History of the FBI* (New York: Random House, 2012), 308.

49. Clipping of Gary Wills, "Kennedy Center Shenanigans," in H. R. Haldeman Papers, Box 187, Folder, "JFK Center—Miscellaneous File," Richard Nixon Library, Yorba Linda, California.

50. The Kennedy Center's gala opening included the world premiere of Bernstein's requiem mass honoring President Kennedy. Bernstein and his wife had raised money for the Black Panthers and war protesters such as the Reverend Philip Berrigan—groups and causes certainly not favored by the Nixon White House.

51. E-mail from Jonathan M. Roscoe, Archivist, Richard Nixon Library, October 18, 2011.

52. For example, the editors at the *New York Times* opined, "[B]y accident of the calendar, President Nixon is now the nation's chief executive as the moment approaches for realization of the dream for which his two predecessors worked so effectively with support of the Congress. Against this background, Mr. Nixon's attempt to share the stage with the three brave men on Apollo 11 when they attain the moon appears to us rather unseemly." See "Nixoning the Moon," *New York Times*, July 19, 1969.

53. Richard Nixon, "Statement About the Space Program," December 19, 1972, Online by Gerhard Peters and John T. Woolley, *The American Presidency Project*, http://www.presidency.ucsb.edu/ws/?pid=3718 [accessed December 14, 2011].

54. Richard Reeves, *President Nixon: Alone in the White House* (New York: Simon and Schuster, 2001), 176; Jonathan Movroydis, "How RN Saved the Peace Corps," October 6, 2009, The New Nixon, http://thenewnixon.org/2009/10/06/howrnsavedthepeacecorps/ [accessed October 19, 2011].

55. See Joan Hoff, *Nixon Reconsidered* (New York: Basic Books, 1994), 58–60.

56. Richard Nixon, "Address to the Nation on the War in Vietnam, November 3, 1969," Online by Gerhard Peters and John T. Woolley, *The American Presidency Project*, http://www.presidency.ucsb.edu/ws/?pid=2303 [accessed September 16, 2011].

57. Reeves, *Alone in the White House*, 371; Nixon Tapes Transcripts, Watergate Collection, Thursday, July 1, 1971, 8:45 A.M.–9:52 A.M., Miller Center website, University of Virginia, http://whitehousetapes.net/transcript/nixon/conspiracy [accessed October 25, 2011].

58. Melvin Small, *The Presidency of Richard Nixon* (Lawrence: University Press of Kansas, 1999), 236–37.

59. Charles Colson to H. R. Haldeman, June 25, 1971, Charles W. Colson Papers, Box 14,

Folder, "Misc. Staff Memos 1970–71 [11-5-70–4-5-71]," Richard Nixon Library, Yorba Linda, California. Whether it was true or not, LBJ and Secretary of State Dean Rusk suspected that Secretary of Defense Robert McNamara had commissioned the Pentagon Papers in order to arm RFK with a powerful political weapon. See John T. Correll, "The Pentagon Papers," February 2007, airforce-magazine.com, http://www.airforce-magazine.com/Magazine-Archive/Pages/2007/February%202007/0207pentagon.aspx [accessed January 30, 2012]; see also David Rudenstine, "The Day the Presses Stopped: A History of the Pentagon Papers Case," specifically the paragraph that starts, "Neither President Johnson nor Secretary of State Rusk accepted McNamara's claims that he commissioned the study merely to preserve the historical record," http://www.washingtonpost.com/wp-srv/style/longterm/books/chap1/daythepr.htm [accessed January 30, 2012].

60. Jeffrey Kimball, *Nixon's Vietnam War* (Lawrence: University Press of Kansas, 1998), 28–29 and 255–56.

61. "DCI Richard M. Helms and President Richard Nixon," October 8, 1971, OVAL 587-007a, nixontapes.org, http://nixontapes.org/rmh.html [accessed May 7, 2012].

62. Hunt, a retired CIA officer who worked as a "security consultant" for the Nixon White House, organized the botched break-in of the Democratic National Committee headquarters at the Watergate Hotel. Police found an address book on one of the burglars containing Hunt's name and a White House phone number. It was the first of many clues that led to the unraveling of the Nixon presidency.

63. Matthews, *Kennedy and Nixon*, 306–7; Richard Reeves, *President Kennedy: Profile of Power* (New York: Simon and Schuster, 1993), 577.

64. Colson denied it, saying he had been "misunderstood" by Hunt. See Martin Arnold, "Hunt Says Colson Ordered Forged Data in Diem Death" and "Colson Issues Denial," *New York Times*, May 8, 1973. Given Colson's role in many Nixon White House dirty tricks, it might be best not to take this denial at face value.

65. Interview with John Dean, June 2, 2013; Bernard Gwertzman, "Hunt Was Given Access to 240 Vietnam Cables," *New York Times*, May 9, 1973.

66. Richard Nixon, "Farewell Address, August 8, 1974," PBS *American Experience*, http://www.pbs.org/wgbh/americanexperience/features/primary-resources/nixon-farewell/ [accessed December 15, 2011].

67. Stephen Ambrose, *Nixon: Ruin and Recovery, 1973–90* (New York: Touchstone, 1991), 196.

68. Richard Nixon to John Ehrlichman, March 4, 1973, President's Personal Files, Box 4, Folder, "Memos—March 1973," Richard Nixon Library, Yorba Linda, California. Recently released documents show that the Kennedys did in fact authorize the use of unlawful wiretaps from time to time to spy on journalists in order to uncover their sources. For example, in the summer of 1963 Bobby Kennedy pressured CIA director John McCone into bugging the home and office telephones of Paul Scott, a syndicated columnist who had raised uncomfortable questions about Cuba during a press conference with Secretary of Defense Robert McNamara. Scott's son has attempted for years to force the CIA to reveal all that it knows about the operation code-named Mockingbird. The agency has only partially complied with the younger Scott's requests. See Ian Shapira, "Long-ago Wiretap Inspires a Battle with the CIA for More Information," *Washington Post*, March 2, 2013, http://www.washingtonpost.com/local/long-ago-wiretap-inspires-a-battle-with-the-cia-for-more-information/2013/03/02/8ebaa924-77b0-11e2-aa12-e6cf1d31106b_story.html?hpid=z3 [accessed March 4, 2013].

69. Richard Nixon to Alexander Haig, July 7, 1973, President's Personal Files, Box 4, Folder, "Memos—July 1973," Richard Nixon Library, Yorba Linda, California.

70. Nixon had claimed separately that he was bugged while running for California governor in 1962, presumably by the Kennedys. See the Nixon Tapes Transcripts, Watergate Collection, Friday, September 15, 1972, 5:24 P.M.–6:17 P.M., Oval Office, Miller Center website, University of Virginia, http://whitehousetapes.net/transcript/nixon/everybody-bugs-everybody-else [accessed October 25, 2011].

71. Richard Nixon, *RN: The Memoirs of Richard Nixon* (New York: Simon and Schuster, 1978), 628–29 and 872.

72. Bruce Kehrli to Ron Ziegler, February 27, 1973, President's Office Files, Box 20, Folder "President's Handwriting, January 1973," Richard Nixon Library, Yorba Linda, California; Nixon, *RN*, 910.

73. Interview with John Dean, June 2, 2013; Ambrose, *Ruin and Recovery*, 417.

74. Ford actually entitled his memoirs *A Time to Heal* (New York: Harper and Row, 1979).

75. Ford, *Time to Heal*, 180.

76. Ibid., 76.

77. Ibid., 229–30.

78. Rockefeller Commission Report, chapter 19, page 269, "Allegations Concerning the Assassination of President Kennedy," History Matters website, http://history-matters.com/archive/church/rockcomm/html/Rockefeller_0141a.htm [accessed November 4, 2011].

79. David R. Wrone, *The Zapruder Film: Reframing JFK's Assassination* (Lawrence: University Press of Kansas, 2003), 9–69.

80. Rockefeller Commission Report, chapter 19, p. 262, "Allegations Concerning the Assassination of President Kennedy," History Matters website, http://history-matters.com/archive/church/rockcomm/html/Rockefeller_0132a.htm [accessed November 4, 2011].

81. Republican senator John Tower of Texas was the vice chair.

82. "Historical Minute Essays, 1964–Present," United States Senate website, http://www.senate.gov/artandhistory/history/minute/Church_Committee_Created.htm [accessed November 4, 2011]; Ford, *Time to Heal*, 265.

83. The general public first became aware of the plots to kill Castro when the Church Committee released *Book V: The Investigation of the Assassination of President John F. Kennedy: Performance of the Intelligence Agencies* (also known as the Schweiker-Hart Report). "With the public disclosure of these plots, the idea that Castro 'struck back' gained prominence with many at the time." See Book V, *The Investigation of the Assassination of President John F. Kennedy: Performance of the Intelligence Agencies,* Assassination Archives and Research Center website, http://www.aarlibrary.org/publib/contents/church/contents_church_reports_book5.htm [accessed January 11, 2012].

84. See "More Disclosures by Kennedy Friend Promised," *New York Times*, December 20, 1975; William Chapman, "Sinatra Seen Link Between Woman, Kennedy," *Washington Post*, December 19, 1975; and Bill Hazlett, "John Kennedy's Mystery Woman Tells Her Story," *Los Angeles Times*, December 18, 1975. Two years later, Campbell published a tell-all account of her affair with JFK entitled *My Story* (New York: Grove Press, 1977).

85. Ben Bradlee of *Newsweek* magazine, for example, never disclosed what he knew about JFK's extramarital affairs. See my book *Feeding Frenzy: How Attack Journalism Has*

Transformed American Politics (New York: Free Press, 1991), 42. In 1975, Bradlee published *Conversations with Kennedy,* which hinted at a darker side of Camelot without offering any specifics. The *Newsweek* review of Bradlee's book included this memorable line: "[JFK] swore like a bosun, and—at least from a wishful distance—admired a well-turned ankle." Bradlee knew full well that JFK did not just admire women's ankles from a distance. See Peter Goldman, "A Fond Memoir of JFK," *Newsweek,* March 17, 1975, p. 24.

86. In 1976, Joan and Clay Blair, Jr., published *The Search for J.F.K.,* which included, among other things, information on the Kennedys' cover-up of JFK's health problems and the president's vigorous womanizing. Thomas C. Reeves, *A Question of Character: A Life of John F. Kennedy* (New York: Free Press, 1991), 7–8.

87. "John F. Kennedy's Secret Sex Life While President," Library of Congress website, http://www.loc.gov/pictures/item/2010646178/ [accessed November 11, 2011].

88. Pierre Salinger and Sander Vanocur published *A Tribute to John F. Kennedy* in 1964; Evelyn Lincoln published *My Twelve Years with John F. Kennedy* in 1965; that same year, Arthur M. Schlesinger, Jr., published the first edition of *A Thousand Days* and Ted Sorensen came out with *Kennedy*; Paul "Red" Fay, Jr., published *The Pleasure of His Company* in 1966; Kenny O'Donnell, Dave Powers, and Joe McCarthy published *"Johnny, We Hardly Knew Ye"* in 1972; Walt Rostow published *The Diffusion of Power* in 1972; and Rose Kennedy published *Times to Remember* in 1974.

89. Mark H. Lynch and John H. F. Shattuck to Admiral Stansfield Turner, March 17, 1977, Record Group 233, JFK Task Force, Box 85, Folder, "Downing-House Select Committee on Assassinations," Archives II, College Park, Maryland.

90. The committee also reviewed the assassination of Dr. Martin Luther King, Jr., concluding "that there is a likelihood that James Earl Ray assassinated . . . King as a result of a conspiracy." See "HSCA Final Assassinations Report," p. 5, *History Matters* website, http://history-matters.com/archive/jfk/hsca/report/html/HSCA_Report_0006a.htm [accessed December 20, 2011].

91. Rudy Abramson and Robert Kistler, "Follower of Manson Held After Trying to Kill Ford," *Los Angeles Times,* September 6, 1975.

92. Richard West, "President Escapes Assassin's Bullet," *Los Angeles Times,* September 23, 1975.

93. Jess Bravin, *Squeaky: The Life and Times of Lynette Alice Fromme* (New York: St. Martin's Press, 1997), 221.

94. President Ford Committee Campaign Commercial XXPFC756, "Feeling Good"—foreign trips footage 5:00, Courtesy Gerald R. Ford Library.

95. Spencer Rich and Mary Russell, "Congress Reacts Angrily: Very Few Back Granting of More Pardons," *Washington Post,* September 11, 1974.

96. "Gerald Ford Receiving the Profiles in Courage Award, May 21, 2001," in *USA Today,* Special Edition, "JFK's America," Fall 2010, p. 12.

97. See Jefferson Morley, "The Holy Grail of the JFK Story," *Salon,* November 22, 2011, http://www.salon.com/2011/11/22/the_holy_grail_of_the_jfk_story/ [accessed January 11, 2012], and the *Legacy of Secrecy* official website, http://www.legacyofsecrecy.com/tell.html [accessed August 16, 2011].

98. Thomas M. DeFrank, *Write It When I'm Gone: Remarkable Off-the-Record Conversations With Gerald R. Ford* (New York: G. P. Putnam's Sons, 2007), 176.

16. THE CARTERS AND THE KENNEDYS: DEMOCRATIC
HATFIELDS AND MCCOYS

1. Interview with former president Jimmy Carter, June 18, 2013. For more information on the media's Carter-Kennedy comparisons, see "New Day A'Coming in the South," *Time*, May 31, 1971: 15–20; Robert Shogan, "Georgia's Carter Brings Religion, Idealism to New Hampshire Presidential Primary," *Los Angeles Times*, May 25, 1975; Laurence H. Shoup, *The Carter Presidency and Beyond: Power and Politics in the 1980s* (Palo Alto, CA: Ramparts Press, 1980), 88; and Victor Lasky, *Jimmy Carter: The Man and the Myth* (New York: Richard Marek Publishers, 1979), 45–46.

2. "Lady Bird Johnson Gets Jimmy Carter Apology," *Associated Press*, reprinted in *Nashua* [N.H.] *Telegraph*, September 24, 1976.

3. "Catholics/Image," President Ford Committee Records, 1975–76, Research Office: Carter Quotes—Carter Family, Box H23, Folder "Catholics," Gerald R. Ford Library.

4. Jimmy Carter, "'Our Nation's Past and Future': Address Accepting the Presidential Nomination at the Democratic National Convention in New York City," July 15, 1976, Online by Gerhard Peters and John T. Woolley, *The American Presidency Project*, http://www.presidency.ucsb.edu/ws/index.php?pid=25953#axzz1fJ16eBn6 [accessed December 1, 2011]; Jimmy Carter, *A Government as Good as Its People* (New York: Simon and Schuster, 1977), 138–39 and 163.

5. Maddox attracted national attention in 1964 by refusing to serve three African American Georgia Tech students at his Pickrick Restaurant (a violation of the 1964 Civil Rights Act). "When the three black men tried to buy some of his chicken in July 1964, Mr. Maddox waved a pistol at them and said: 'You no good dirty devils! You dirty Communists!' Some of his customers were sympathetic to his cause and interrupted their meal to take pick handles that Mr. Maddox had put by the door (and sold for $2 apiece) to make it clear that the blacks would not be served. The pick handles, which Mr. Maddox also sold in his souvenir shop, were called 'Pickrick drumsticks' and came to symbolize his resistance to the civil rights movement. On occasion, Mr. Maddox would autograph the handles." Richard Severo, "Lester Maddox, Whites-Only Restaurateur and Georgia Governor, Dies at 87," *New York Times*, June 26, 2003.

6. Jules Witcover, *Marathon: The Pursuit of the Presidency, 1972–76* (New York: Signet, 1977), 161.

7. Shriver received a mere 304,399 votes in all the 1976 primary contests, or 1.9% of the total vote cast. By contrast, Carter won 6,235,609 votes, 39.3% of those cast.

8. Richard Reeves, *Convention* (New York: Harcourt Brace Jovanovich, 1977), 127–28. I attended the 1976 convention as a graduate student researcher, and I vividly recall this electric moment. Like most people there, I had never personally glimpsed Jackie Kennedy. It is no exaggeration to say that we could not take our eyes off her; the convention itself appeared to grind to a halt while thousands of prying eyes kept watch.

9. "Kennedy: Carter Is 'Imprecise,'" *United Press International*, reprinted in *St. Petersburg Times*, May 26, 1976.

10. "Kennedy," President Ford Committee Records, 1975–76, Research Office: Carter Quotes—Carter Family, Box H23, Folder "Carter vs. (1)," Gerald R. Ford Library.

11. President Ford Committee Records, 1975–76, Research Office: Carter Quotes—Carter Family, Box H23, Folder "Congress (1)," Gerald R. Ford Library. Earlier, as governor of Geor-

gia, Carter gave a private indication of his equivocal view of JFK, noting that "Kennedy still occupies a position representing youth, idealism, vigor, etc.—which he may or may not actually deserve. Politically, of course, the image is the reality." See Gary M. Fink, *Prelude to the Presidency: The Political Character and Legislative Leadership Style of Governor Jimmy Carter* (Westport, CT: Greenwood Press, 1980), 18–19.

12. Witcover, *Marathon*, 610–11.

13. See Gallup poll numbers, Sept.–Oct. 1976, iPOLL Databank, Roper Center for Public Opinion Research, University of Connecticut, http://www.ropercenter.uconn.edu/data_access/ipoll/ipoll.html [accessed January 27, 2012].

14. Handwritten notes, Michael Raoul-Duval Papers, Box 30, Folder "Meeting with the President," Gerald R. Ford Library; President Ford Committee Records, 1975–76, Research Office: Carter Quotes—Gay Liberation, Box H27, Folder "Image," Gerald R. Ford Library.

15. For more information on Ford's gaffe and how the intense press coverage of it affected Ford's poll numbers, see my book *Feeding Frenzy: How Attack Journalism Has Transformed American Politics* (New York: Free Press, 1991), 127–29.

16. Carter told a cheering crowd in his hometown of Plains, Georgia, "I had the best organization any candidate ever had. Had the best family any candidate ever had. Had the best home community any candidate ever had. Had the best supporters in my home state any candidate ever had. And the only reason we were close last night was because the candidate wasn't quite good enough as a campaigner. But I'll make up for that when I'm president . . ." Martin Schram, *Running for President 1976: The Carter Campaign* (New York: Stein and Day, 1977), 357.

17. 281 of the 293 Democrats who were elected to the House of Representatives in 1976 received a higher vote percentage than Carter. During the same year, twenty winning Democratic Senate nominees surpassed Carter's vote percentage. John L. Moore, Jon P. Preimesberger, and David R. Tarr, *Congressional Quarterly's Guide to U.S. Elections*, vol. II, 6th ed. (Washington, DC: CQ Press, 2010), 1302–6 and 1434–71.

18. Jimmy Carter, "Inaugural Address," January 20, 1977, Online by Gerhard Peters and John T. Woolley, *The American Presidency Project*, http://www.presidency.ucsb.edu/ws/?pid=6575 [accessed January 4, 2012].

19. I was in attendance with a good seat at the inauguration, thanks to the beneficence of a Virginia politician, former lieutenant governor Henry E. Howell, Jr. Carter's address bore no resemblance to John Kennedy's; it sparked little applause and fell flat even among his most ardent admirers. But the unexpected stroll down Pennsylvania Avenue electrified the tens of thousands of spectators. I do not recall seeing Secret Service personnel, but photographs of the Carter walk show wide-eyed agents understandably looking even more serious and concerned than usual.

20. Jimmy Carter, *Keeping Faith: Memoirs of a President* (New York: Bantam Books, 1982), 24.

21. Sensing defeat, Sorensen requested that Carter withdraw the nomination. Facing stiff opposition from the Senate Select Committee on Intelligence, Sorensen said, "It is now clear that a substantial portion of the United States Senate and the intelligence community is not ready to accept as director of Central Intelligence an outsider who believes as I believe," and "It is equally clear that to continue fighting for this post, which would be my natural inclination, would only handicap the new administration if I am rejected, or handicap my effectiveness as director if I am confirmed." See Wendell Rawls, Jr., "Sorensen

Withdraws, Bowing to Resistance to C.I.A. Nomination," *New York Times*, January 18, 1977.

22. E-mail from Ted Sorensen, October 12, 2010.

23. Interview with former president Jimmy Carter, June 18, 2013.

24. See Gallup poll numbers, Feb.–Nov. 1979, iPOLL Databank, Roper Center for Public Opinion Research, University of Connecticut, http://www.ropercenter.uconn.edu/data_access/ipoll/ipoll.html [accessed January 27, 2012].

25. Peter Maer, "Time Has Not Cooled Jimmy Carter / Ted Kennedy Feud," CBS News, September 17, 2010, http://www.cbsnews.com/8301-503544_162-20016854-503544.html [accessed January 4, 2012]; Interview with former president Jimmy Carter, June 18, 2013.

26. Jimmy Carter, *White House Diary* (New York: Farrar, Straus and Giroux, 2010), 365–66.

27. Ibid., 356.

28. Jimmy Carter, "Boston, Massachusetts Remarks at Dedication Ceremonies for the John F. Kennedy Library," October 20, 1979, Online by Gerhard Peters and John T. Woolley, *The American Presidency Project*, http://www.presidency.ucsb.edu/ws/index.php?pid=31566#axzz1fr6tBNRy [accessed December 7, 2011].

29. Ibid.

30. Ibid. Despite Carter's emotional reaction to November 22, 1963, he made no comment when the House Select Committee on Assassinations presented its report on July 17, 1979. In part, that may have been because of his disagreement with its finding of conspiracy in the JFK assassination. Carter told me in an interview on June 18, 2013, that he had consistently accepted the findings of the Warren Commission from the 1960s onward, in part because of his admiration for Senator Richard Russell of Georgia, a member of the commission.

31. Interview with former president Jimmy Carter, June 18, 2013.

32. Kennedy's reply was clumsy and stumbling: "Well, I'm—were I to make the announcement and to run, the reasons I would run is because I have a great belief in this country. That it is—there's more natural resources than any nation in the world; the greatest education population in the world; the greatest technology of any country in the world; the greatest capacity for innovation in the world; and the greatest political system in the world." Sam Allis, "Losing a Quest for the Top, Finding a New Freedom," *Boston Globe*, February 18, 2009, http://www.boston.com/news/nation/articles/2009/02/18/chapter_4_sailing_into_the_wind/ [accessed January 4, 2012]. Kennedy's staff suggested that the senator feared invoking the formal candidacy provisions of federal campaign finance law—although there were ways to give a powerful, conditional answer ("If I were to run, it would be because . . ."). Vincent Bzdek, *The Kennedy Legacy: Jack, Bobby and Ted and a Family Dream Fulfilled* (New York: Palgrave Macmillan, 2009), 176.

33. Ted Kennedy did not specifically invoke JFK or RFK, and he broke with their tradition in choosing a Boston location to launch his candidacy instead of his brothers' locale, the Senate Caucus Room in D.C. Perhaps he wished to avoid the charge that his candidacy was dynastic, built on legacy and not policy. See Jon Margolis, "Kennedy in Race, Hits Carter," *Chicago Tribune*, November 8, 1979. The portion of Kennedy's speech quoted in the text was transcribed from YouTube: "Kennedy Declares Presidential Bid," ABC News, YouTube, http://www.youtube.com/watch?v=9-UYpwtHopg&feature=youtu.be [accessed January 27, 2012]; Interview with former president Jimmy Carter, June 18, 2013.

34. Jimmy Carter, "Boston, Massachusetts Question-and-Answer Session with Newspaper and Television Reporters," October 20, 1979, http://www.presidency.ucsb.edu/ws/index.php?pid=31567#axzz1iQDToBWW and "East Rutherford, New Jersey Interview With Dick Leone of WNET-TV," October 25, 1979, http://www.presidency.ucsb.edu/ws/index.php?pid=31591#axzz1iQDToBWW, Online by Gerhard Peters and John T. Woolley, *The American Presidency Project* [accessed January 4, 2012]; Interview with former president Jimmy Carter, June 18, 2013.

35. After his father's death, Ted Kennedy, Jr., told *60 Minutes*, "Most people keep coats and umbrellas in their coat closet. My father kept bulletproof vests in his coat closet. And believe me, we would walk by that coat closet every day, fearful about some crazy person out there wanting to make a name for themselves. And that, I think, was in the back of our minds, almost every time that my father would appear in public." See "Kennedy's Son Reflects on Dad's Legacy," CBS, *60 Minutes*, September 13, 2009, http://www.cbsnews.com/2100-18560_162-5303789.html?tag=contentMain;contentBody [accessed January 27, 2012]. According to Richard E. Burke, "They [the Secret Service] provided Kennedy with two versions of a bulletproof vest. One was built into a trench coat and reasonably comfortable; this would come in handy on rainy days. But the fair weather version, made to be worn under a shirt and suit jacket, was heavy and cumbersome." See Richard E. Burke with William and Marilyn Hoffer, *The Senator: My Ten Years with Ted Kennedy* (New York: Macmillan, 2003), 227.

36. *Guide to U.S. Elections, vol. 1, 6th ed.* (Washington, DC: CQ Press, 2010), 638.

37. Peter G. Bourne, *Jimmy Carter: A Comprehensive Biography from Plains to Post-Presidency* (New York: Scribner, 1997), 458–60.

38. Ibid., 460.

39. Carter replaced him with Maine senator Edmund Muskie (D).

40. Hamilton Jordan, *Crisis: The Last Year of the Carter Presidency* (New York: G. P. Putnam's Sons, 1982), 274.

41. Jimmy Carter, "The President's News Conference," April 29, 1980, Online by Gerhard Peters and John T. Woolley, *The American Presidency Project*, http://www.presidency.ucsb.edu/ws/?pid=33342 [accessed December 8, 2011].

42. Bzdek, *Kennedy Legacy*, 182. Bzdek also quotes *Washington Post* reporter Rick Atkinson as saying, "It was the most electrifying speech that I'd ever heard personally . . . People were crying because, I think, it was so evocative of the dead prince."

43. Carter, *White House Diary*, 457–58, 528; Interview with former President Jimmy Carter, June 18, 2013.

44. Jimmy Carter, "Carter/Kennedy Unity Celebration Remarks at the Democratic Party Dinner," October 19, 1980, Online by Gerhard Peters and John T. Woolley, *The American Presidency Project*, http://www.presidency.ucsb.edu/ws/?pid=45328 [accessed December 2, 2011]; Interview with former president Jimmy Carter, June 18, 2013.

45. See http://electionstudies.org/studypages/1980_panelmajor/1980_panelmajor.htm. National Election Studies, 1980 Major Panel Study [dataset]. Ann Arbor: University of Michigan Center for Political Studies [producer and distributor], 1999.

46. Carter, *White House Diary*, 417.

47. Peggy Noonan, "The Reagans and the Kennedys: How They Forged a Friendship That Crossed Party Lines," *Wall Street Journal*, August 28, 2009, http://online.wsj.com/article/SB10001424052970203706604574376951136648912.html [accessed January 5, 2012].

48. Interview with former president Jimmy Carter, June 18, 2013. If President Carter's allegation is correct, Senator Kennedy could have been in violation of a federal statute. The direct or indirect promise of public office by a candidate in order to "procure support" is forbidden by law. See Title 18, Part I, Chapter 29, Section 599 of the U.S. Code, which says: "Whoever, being a candidate, directly or indirectly promises or pledges the appointment, or the use of his influence or support for the appointment of any person to any public or private position or employment, for the purpose of procuring support in his candidacy shall be fined under this title or imprisoned not more than one year, or both; and if the violation was willful, shall be fined under this title or imprisoned not more than two years, or both." However, this is a difficult charge to prove, and the discussion between a candidate and a possible officeholder can be filled with conditional terms that make successful prosecution all but impossible.

49. Interview with former president Jimmy Carter, June 18, 2013.

17. REAGAN AND KENNEDY: OPPOSITES ATTRACT

1. Telephone interview with Ron Reagan, Jr., March 8, 2012.

2. Think through JFK's successors. No one has ever accused LBJ, Nixon, Ford, Carter, Bush 41, Clinton, Bush 43, or Obama of excessive wit, and only the unelected Ford and perhaps Bush 43 demonstrated the ability to make fun of their own shortcomings with any regularity.

3. See Thomas W. Evans, *The Education of Ronald Reagan: The General Electric Years and the Untold Story of his Conversion to Conservatism* (New York: Columbia University Press, 2006), 55–97, and Lou Cannon, *Governor Reagan: His Rise to Power* (New York: Public Affairs, 2005), 83–122.

4. Stephen E. Ambrose, *Nixon: The Education of a Politician, 1913–62* (New York: Simon and Schuster, 1987), 546; "Text of 1960 Reagan Letter," *New York Times*, October 27, 1984.

5. Ibid.

6. As *Time* reported it: "The letter was unearthed from a trove of Nixon's papers in a branch of the National Archives in Laguna Niguel, Calif. Last week Walter Mondale read the passage to campaign audiences to back up his charge that Reagan is guilty of 'political grave robbing' when he invokes the names of such Democrats as Franklin D. Roosevelt, Harry Truman—and, yes, John F. Kennedy. Presidential Spokesman Larry Speakes replied that Reagan 'had been pleasantly surprised to find the difference between Kennedy the candidate and Kennedy the president.'"Source: "Dear Mr. Vice Pres.," *Time* 124 (November 4, 1984): 24. In addition, "Dayton Duncan, Mr. Mondale's deputy press secretary, said the campaign learned about the letter last Wednesday from a hand-writing expert who was doing research on Mr. Nixon's pre-presidential papers at a branch of the Los Angeles Federal Archives in Laguna-Niguel, Calif." Bernard Weinraub, "Mondale Says Reagan Note Compared Kennedy to Marx," *New York Times*, October 24, 1984.

7. Michael Reagan with Jim Denney, *The New Reagan Revolution: How Ronald Reagan's Principles Can Restore America's Greatness* (New York: Thomas Dunne Books, 2010), 103; Larry J. Sabato, *Feeding Frenzy: How Attack Journalism Has Transformed American Politics* (New York: Free Press, 1991), 33–42.

8. Ronald Reagan, *Speaking My Mind* (New York: Simon and Schuster, 1989), 23.

9. Reagan, *New Reagan Revolution*, 110. Whether or not the allegation had a basis in truth, Ronald Reagan believed it to be true and told his son about it.

10. Reagan's speech was entitled "A Time for Choosing" and included such memorable lines as "No government ever voluntarily reduces itself in size. Government programs, once launched, never disappear" and "You and I have a rendezvous with destiny. We will preserve for our children this, the last best hope of man on Earth, or we will sentence them to take the last step into a thousand years of darkness." See Ronald Reagan, "Address on Behalf of Senator Barry Goldwater: 'A Time for Choosing,'" October 27, 1964, Online by Gerhard Peters and John T. Woolley, *American Presidency Project*, http://www.presidency.ucsb.edu/ws /?pid=76121 [accessed April 2, 2012].

11. "The Ronnie-Bobby Show," *Newsweek*, May 29, 1967: 26–31; Paul Kengor, "The Great Forgotten Debate," *National Review Online*, May 22, 2007, http://www.nationalreview.com /articles/220949/great-forgotten-debate/paul-kengor?pg=1 [accessed December 28, 2011]; William Kristol, "In 2008 It's Ronald Reagan vs. Bobby Kennedy," *Time*, March 29, 2007, http://www.time.com/time/magazine/article/0,9171,1604937,00.html [accessed December 28, 2011].

12. Kiron K. Skinner, Annelise Anderson, and Martin Anderson, eds. 2001. *Reagan in His Own Voice: Ronald Reagan's Radio Addresses*. New York: Simon and Schuster. Compact disc.

13. Del Quentin Wilber, *Rawhide Down: The Near Assassination of Ronald Reagan* (New York: Henry Holt, 2011), 65–82.

14. Senator Edward M. Kennedy, "The Handgun Crime Control Act of 1981," *Northern Kentucky Law Review* 10, no. 1, 1982: 1; Charles Mohr, "Guns Traced in 16 Minutes to Pawn Shop in Dallas," *New York Times*, April 1, 1981, http://www.nytimes.com/1981/04/01/us/guns -traced-in-16-minutes-to-pawn-shop-in-dallas.html?scp=1&sq=^%20Guns%20Traced %20in%2016%20Minutes%20to%20Pawn%20Shop%20in%20Dallas&st=cse [accessed April 5, 2012].

15. Wilber, *Rawhide Down*, 203–25.

16. Ron Reagan, *My Father at 100* (New York: Viking, 2011), 195–97.

17. Nancy Reagan, *My Turn: The Memoirs of Nancy Reagan* (New York: Random House, 1989), 5. E-mail from Ron Reagan, Jr., May 10, 2012.

18. Reagan, *My Father at 100*, 195–97.

19. Wilber, *Rawhide Down*, 215.

20. "The Day Reagan Was Shot," CBS News, February 11, 2009, http://www.cbsnews.com /2100-500164_162-287292.html [accessed April 3, 2012].

21. President Ford's two assassination attempts provoked little intense emotion, since Ford was not hit and the disturbing news was immediately linked to the good news of Ford's safety.

22. Unfortunately, Hinckley may soon be back on the streets. In 2009 a judge extended the length of his furlough visits to his aging mother in Williamsburg, Virginia, and Hinckley's doctors have told authorities that he no longer presents a danger to himself or the public. James Polk, "Doctors: Reagan Shooter Is Recovering, Not a Danger," CNN.com, March 26, 2011, http://articles.cnn.com/2011-03-26/justice/hinckley.today_1_john-hinckley-furloughs -insanity?_s=PM:CRIME [accessed April 3, 2012].

23. Eliot Brenner, "Bulletproof Vest for Hinckley," United Press International, April 2, 1981.

24. "Kennedy Gets Secret Service Guard," Associated Press, March 31, 1981.

25. Mike Shanahan, "Secret Service: 'We Were Competing With a Bullet,'" Associated Press, April 4, 1981.

26. Michael K. Deaver, *Nancy: A Portrait of My Years with Nancy Reagan* (New York: William Morrow, 2004), 140.

27. Draft report, "Report on the Performance of the United States Department of the Treasury in Connection with the March 30, 1981 Assassination Attempt on President Ronald Reagan," 07/02/1981, CFOA 28, p. 75, Edwin Meese: Files, Ronald Reagan Presidential Library.

28. Wilber, *Rawhide Down*, 70–71, 225.

29. Regan published *For the Record: From Wall Street to Washington* in 1988. Joyce Wadler, Angela Blessing, Dirk Mathison, and Margie Bonnett Sellinger, "The President's Astrologers," *People* 29 (May 23, 1988), http://www.people.com/people/archive/article /0,,20099022,00.html [accessed April 3, 2012].

30. Johanna McGeary, James Kelly, and Jonathan Beaty, "Protecting the President," *Time*, April 13, 1981, http://www.time.com/time/magazine/article/0,9171,954702,00.html [accessed April 5, 2012].

31. Stuart Spencer, interview, excerpted in "Reagan Officials on the March 30, 1981 Assassination Attempt," http://millercenter.org/academic/oralhistory/news/2007_0330 [accessed July 13, 2011]. Ron Reagan, Jr., told me that when he asked his father not to run for a second term, citing safety concerns, the president demurred, insisting that there were "a lot of things he needed to do and do for the country and it was really important, and so he appreciated my concern but he was just going to have to run anyway." Telephone interview with Ron Reagan, Jr., March 8, 2012.

32. Carl Bernstein and Marco Politi, *His Holiness: John Paul II and the Hidden History of Our Time* (New York: Doubleday, 1996), 357.

33. See Ronald Reagan, "Why I'm for the Brady Bill," *New York Times*, March 29, 1991, http://www.nytimes.com/1991/03/29/opinion/why-i-m-for-the-brady-bill.html?src=pm [accessed April 5, 2012].

34. See the Brady Campaign to Prevent Gun Violence website, http://www.bradycampaign .org [accessed April 5, 2012].

35. See Gallup poll (AIPO), April 10–April 13, 1981, iPOLL Databank, Roper Center for Public Opinion Research, University of Connecticut, http://www.ropercenter.uconn.edu /data_access/ipoll/ipoll.html [accessed May 1, 2012], and ABC News / *Washington Post* poll, April 20–April 22, 1981. iPOLL Databank, Roper Center for Public Opinion Research, University of Connecticut, http://www.ropercenter.uconn.edu/data_access/ipoll/ipoll.html [accessed May 1, 2012].

36. Ronald Reagan, "Address Before a Joint Session of the Congress on the Program for Economic Recovery," April 28, 1981, Online by Gerhard Peters and John T. Woolley, *The American Presidency Project*, http://www.presidency.ucsb.edu/ws/?pid=43756 [accessed April 2, 2012].

37. Ronald Reagan, "Remarks on Signing the Economic Recovery Tax Act of 1981 and the Omnibus Budget Reconciliation Act of 1981, and a Question-and-Answer Session with Reporters," August 13, 1981, Online by Gerhard Peters and John T. Woolley, *The American Presidency Project*, http://www.presidency.ucsb.edu/ws/?pid=44161 [accessed April 2, 2012].

38. Paul D. Erickson, "The Once and Future President: John F. Kennedy in the Rhetoric

of Ronald Reagan" in Paul Harper and Joann P. Krieg, eds., *John F. Kennedy: The Promise Revisited* (New York: Greenwood Press, 1988), 313.

39. Richard Hansen, "John F. Kennedy Quote Compendium: The Reality Behind the Image," ID#190458, FG002-34, WHORM: Subject File, Ronald Reagan Presidential Library. The Reagan Library could not tell me when Hansen's report was written, but Frank Fahrenkopf, chairman of the Republican National Committee at the time, believes the report was done in "late '83 or early '84," just as the Reagan team was gearing up for reelection. E-mail from Frank Fahrenkopf, April 2, 2012. Fahrenkopf's recollection is backed by Bill Greener, the RNC's Director of Communications at the time. Reagan White House political director Ed Rollins suggested a date of October 1983 or perhaps a bit before that. In any event, it is clear that Hansen wrote the report in the critical months leading up to the successful 1984 Republican campaign.

40. John F. Kennedy, "Special Message to the Congress on Tax Reduction and Reform," January 24, 1963, Online by Gerhard Peters and John T. Woolley, *The American Presidency Project*, http://www.presidency.ucsb.edu/ws/?pid=9387 [accessed April 5, 2012].

41. See Ronald Reagan, "Remarks and a Question-and-Answer Session on the Program for Economic Recovery at a Breakfast for Newspaper and Television News Editors," February 19, 1981, Online by Gerhard Peters and John T. Woolley, *The American Presidency Project*, http://www.presidency.ucsb.edu/ws/index.php?pid=43428#axzz1hlMJQkyM [accessed December 27, 2011], and "Remarks in Denver, Colorado, at the Annual Convention of the National Association for the Advancement of Colored People," June 29, 1981, Online by Gerhard Peters and John T. Woolley, *The American Presidency Project*, http://www.presidency .ucsb.edu/ws/?pid=44016 [accessed December 28, 2011]. Stacey Chandler, an archivist at the JFK Library, sent the following e-mail message on 4/6/12: "The earliest record we were able to find of JFK using this phrase is in the "Remarks of Senator John F. Kennedy at Picnic, Muskegon, Michigan," September 5, 1960. The Muskegon speech is available here: John F. Kennedy, "Remarks of Senator John F. Kennedy, Picnic, Muskegon, MI," September 5, 1960, Online by Gerhard Peters and John T. Woolley, *The American Presidency Project*, http:// www.presidency.ucsb.edu/ws/?pid=60414 [accessed April 6, 2012].

42. Ronald Reagan, "Remarks at the Illinois Forum Reception in Chicago ," September 2, 1981, Online by Gerhard Peters and John T. Woolley, *The American Presidency Project*, http://www.presidency.ucsb.edu/ws/?pid=44192 [accessed December 28, 2011].

43. Steven F. Hayward, *The Age of Reagan: The Conservative Counterrevolution 1980–89* (New York: Crown Forum, 2009), 79–80.

44. Dinesh D'Souza, *Ronald Reagan: How an Ordinary Man Became an Extraordinary Leader* (New York: Free Press, 1997), 81.

45. See Benjamin Friedman, "Learning from the Reagan Deficits," *American Economic Review* 83, no. 2 (May 1992): 299–304; and Paul Pierson, *Dismantling the Welfare State? Reagan, Thatcher, and the Politics of Retrenchment* (Cambridge: Cambridge University Press, 2003).

46. Syndicated columnist Robert Samuelson has described Kennedy's tax cut as an economic "disaster" which spawned runaway inflation in the 1970s and 1980s and a permanent "loss of budgetary discipline" in Washington. Samuelson is right about one thing: JFK and his economic advisers set a fiscal precedent that later was misused and led to massive deficits. But the columnist overlooks key root causes of inflation and other economic problems, such as LBJ's "guns and butter" spending in the 1960s and the oil shocks of the 1970s. See

Robert Samuelson, "How JFK's Mistake Led to the Sequester Mess," *Washington Post*, March 3, 2013, http://www.washingtonpost.com/opinions/robert-samuelson-how-jfks-mistake-led -to-the-sequester-mess/2013/03/03/ca4ba654-82bf-11e2-a350-49866afab584_story.html [accessed March 5, 2013].

47. Ronald Reagan, "Remarks and a Question-and-Answer Session with Regional Editors and Broadcasters," April 18, 1985, Online by Gerhard Peters and John T. Woolley, *The American Presidency Project*, http://www.presidency.ucsb.edu/ws/?pid=38498 [accessed December 28, 2011], and "Address to the Nation on the Federal Budget and Deficit Reduction," April 24, 1985, Online by Gerhard Peters and John T. Woolley, *The American Presidency Project*, http://www.presidency.ucsb.edu/ws/?pid=38536 [accessed December 28, 2011].

48. "10 Things You Don't Know About," season 1, episode 3, "John F. Kennedy," *History Channel 2*, original airdate March 5, 2012, available on Amazon Instant Video, http://www .amazon.com/Benjamin-Franklin/dp/B007ET2ZDU/ref=sr_1_1?s=movies-tv&ie=UTF8& qid=1335887154&sr=1-1 [accessed May 1, 2012]. See also Chris Matthews, *Jack Kennedy: Elusive Hero* (New York: Simon and Schuster, 2011), 252.

49. Khrushchev made this chilling statement in the presence of Western diplomats during a November 1956 reception at the Polish embassy in Moscow. See "Foreign News: We Will Bury You!" *Time*, November 26, 1956, http://www.time.com/time/magazine/article /0,9171,867329,00.html [accessed April 6, 2012]. Sergei Khrushchev, son of the Soviet chairman, believes that his father's words have been widely misunderstood in the West: "[T]his was a metaphor . . . Father meant the burial of the outmoded capitalist structure and its replacement by a socialism that would benefit the people. He believed faithfully that the day was not far off when everyone, even the Americans, would ask to enter our paradise. He believed, he held the doors open, but wasn't prepared to chase anyone in by force." Sergei N. Khrushchev, *Nikita Khrushchev and the Creation of a Superpower* (University Park: Pennsylvania State University Press, 2000), 133.

50. Ronald Reagan, "Address Before a Joint Session of the Tennessee State Legislature in Nashville," March 15, 1982, Online by Gerhard Peters and John T. Woolley, *American Presidency Project*, http://www.presidency.ucsb.edu/ws/?pid=42270 [accessed December 28, 2011].

51. Ronald Reagan, "Address to the Nation on Strategic Arms Reduction and Nuclear Deterrence," November 22, 1982, Online by Gerhard Peters and John T. Woolley, *The American Presidency Project*, http://www.presidency.ucsb.edu/ws/?pid=42030 [accessed December 28, 2011].

52. Ronald Reagan, "Remarks at the National Leadership Forum of the Center for International and Strategic Studies of Georgetown University," April 6, 1984, Online by Gerhard Peters and John T. Woolley, *The American Presidency Project*, http://www.presidency.ucsb .edu/ws/?pid=39731 [accessed December 28, 2011]. The Kennedy reference is a paraphrase of JFK's inaugural assertion, "For only when our arms are sufficient beyond doubt can we be certain beyond doubt that they will never be employed."

53. Office of Management and Budget, *Fiscal Year 2012 Historical Tables, Budget of the United States*, Table 3.1, "Outlays by Superfunction and Function, 1940–2016," 49–51, http:// www.gpo.gov/fdsys/pkg/BUDGET-2012-TAB/pdf/BUDGET-2012-TAB.pdf [accessed May 1, 2012]. When measured in 2012 dollars, one could argue that defense expenditures declined slightly from $400 billion in 1963 to $373 billion by 1980.

54. Reagan went on active duty with the army shortly after the attack on Pearl Harbor,

but his poor eyesight prevented him from receiving an overseas assignment. "His first as-signment was at the San Francisco Port of Embarkation, Fort Mason, Calif., as Liaison Of-ficer of the Port and Transportation Office." Reagan was later reassigned to "the 1st Motion Picture Unit in Culver City." See "President Ronald Reagan," National Museum of the US Air Force, September 18, 2009, http://www.nationalmuseum.af.mil/factsheets/factsheet.asp ?id=1660 [accessed May 1, 2012].

55. Ronald Reagan, "Remarks on Presenting the Presidential Citizens Medal to Ray-mond Weeks at a Veterans Day Ceremony," November 11, 1982, Online by Gerhard Peters and John T. Woolley, *The American Presidency Project*, http://www.presidency.ucsb.edu/ws /?pid=41978 [accessed December 28, 2011].

56. Ronald Reagan, "Address to the Nation on United States Policy in Central America," May 9, 1984, Online by Gerhard Peters and John T. Woolley, *The American Presidency Proj-ect*, http://www.presidency.ucsb.edu/ws/?pid=39901 [accessed December 28, 2011].

57. Some of Reagan's top officials sold arms to Iran as part of a secret deal to secure the release of American hostages in Lebanon, and they funneled the profits from these sales to anticommunist forces in Nicaragua (known as the "Contras"). This clandestine arrange-ment directly violated a federal ban on U.S. military aid to the Contras that had been enacted by Congress months earlier. Reagan famously claimed that he could not remember the de-tails of the Iran-Contra plan or whether he had discussed it with aides. See "Reagan: The Iran-Contra Affair," *American Experience*, PBS.org, http://www.pbs.org/wgbh/americanex perience/features/general-article/reagan-iran/ [accessed April 5, 2012].

58. Clare Boothe Luce, the wife of media mogul Henry Luce, was a playwright, a social critic, a journalist, a congresswoman from Connecticut, an ambassador to Italy, and a life-long Republican. See Ralph G. Martin, *Henry and Clare: An Intimate Portrait of the Luces* (New York: Perigee, 1992) and Alan Brinkley, *The Publisher: Henry Luce and His American Century* (New York: Vintage Books, 2010).

59. Ronald Reagan, "Address to the Nation on the Situation in Nicaragua," March 16, 1986, Online by Gerhard Peters and John T. Woolley, *The American Presidency Project*, http://www.presidency.ucsb.edu/ws/?pid=36999 [accessed December 29, 2011]. See also Ronald Reagan, "Address to the Permanent Council of the Organization of American States," October 7, 1987, Online by Gerhard Peters and John T. Woolley, *The American Presidency Project*, http://www.presidency.ucsb.edu/ws/?pid=33514 [accessed December 29, 2011].

60. Lou Cannon writes, "Both Goldwater and Reagan opposed the Civil Rights Act of 1964 on what they believed were constitutional grounds. Neither man was a racist, but their alliance with the Southerners on this touchstone issue opened a gulf between conservatives and blacks that has never healed." Lou Cannon, *Governor Reagan: His Rise to Power* (New York: Public Affairs, 2003), 122. Reagan became more supportive of civil rights during his presidency. In 1988 he championed the Fair Housing Amendments Act and invited Con-gressman John Lewis (D-GA), a veteran of the civil rights movement, to attend the signing ceremony. At the end of his speech, Reagan paid tribute to Lewis while offering a subtle re-minder of JFK's failure to enact similar legislation a quarter century earlier: "Twenty-five years ago, as a young leader of the civil rights movement, Congressman Lewis was standing in this very Rose Garden pressing for federal action to eliminate housing discrimination. John's hard work to achieve that has brought us one step closer to realizing Martin Luther King's dream." Reagan's aides had wanted him to deliver a more cutting remark: "[T]he

president could acknowledge Lewis' presence, note that he stood in the very same spot for the very same reason 25 years ago and tell him that he (the president) is living proof that sometimes you have to wait to get what you want." See Gerald McKiernan to Alan M. Kranowitz, August 31, 1988, and Kranowitz to Mari Maseng, September 9, 1988, Folder "H.R 1158 Fair Housing Bill Signing Ceremony," Box OA 16829, Legislative Affairs, White House Office of Records, Ronald Reagan Library. See also Ronald Reagan, "Remarks on Signing the Fair Housing Amendments Act of 1988," September 13, 1988, Online by Gerhard Peters and John T. Woolley, *The American Presidency Project*, http://www.presidency.ucsb.edu/ws /?pid=36361 [accessed August 15, 2012].

61. The major arms agreement of the Reagan era was the Intermediate-Range Nuclear Forces (INF) Treaty, which banned the use of missiles with ranges of between 500 and 5,500 kilometers. See "Treaty Between the United States of America and the Union of Soviet Socialist Republics on the Elimination of Their Intermediate-Range and Shorter-Range Missiles," Department of State website, http://www.state.gov/www/global/arms/treaties/inf1 .html#treaty [accessed May 2, 2012]. Another major arms reduction treaty accredited to Reagan (introduced in 1982)—START (Strategic Arms Reduction Treaty)—was not signed until after he had left office. See "Treaty Between the United States of America and the Union of Soviet Socialist Republics on the Reduction and Limitation of Strategic Offensive Arms," Department of State website, http://www.state.gov/www/global/arms/starthtm/start /start1.html [accessed May 2, 2012].

62. Edward Kennedy to Ronald Reagan, March 7, 1985, ID#297993, FE008, WHORM: Subject File, Ronald Reagan Library.

63. James Mann, *The Rebellion of Ronald Reagan: A History of the End of the Cold War* (New York: Viking, 2009), 131. Many Cold War experts and observers strongly disagreed with Reagan when he asserted there would have been no hostilities had the United States attempted to stop the wall, which was on East German territory, from going up.

64. Ronald Reagan, "Remarks to the People of Berlin," June 11, 1982, Online by Gerhard Peters and John T. Woolley, *The American Presidency Project*, http://www.presidency.ucsb .edu/ws/?pid=42623 [accessed January 11, 2012].

65. Ronald Reagan, "Remarks on East-West Relations at the Brandenburg Gate in West Berlin," June 12, 1987, Online by Gerhard Peters and John T. Woolley, *The American Presidency Project*, http://www.presidency.ucsb.edu/ws/?pid=34390 [accessed December 28, 2011].

66. Reagan referenced JFK 51 times in 1984, which represents 38% of the 133 total Kennedy references he made during his first term. See *Public Papers of the Presidents of the United States: Ronald Reagan 1984*, vols I & II. Washington, DC: Government Printing Office, 1986.

67. Bill Peterson, "Kennedy, Citing Family, Rules Out Campaign for '84," *Washington Post*, December 2, 1982.

68. Peter Goldman and Tony Fuller with Thomas M. DeFrank, Eleanor Clift, Lucille Beachy, Joyce Barnathan, and Vern E. Smith, *The Quest for the Presidency 1984* (New York: Bantam Books, 1985), 65.

69. Richard Nixon to "friends in the Reagan-Bush campaign," October 29, 1984, reprinted in Goldman et al., *Quest for the Presidency 1984*, 450–53.

70. Goldman et al., *Quest for the Presidency 1984*, 70.

71. Hayward, *Age of Reagan*, 368; Robert S. McElvaine, "The Kennedy Complex," *New York Times*, September 27, 1987.

72. Sabato, *Feeding Frenzy*, 76–77.

73. Ibid., 12–13.

74. Ronald Reagan, "Remarks Accepting the Presidential Nomination at the Republican National Convention in Dallas, Texas," August 23, 1984, Online by Gerhard Peters and John T. Woolley, *The American Presidency Project*, http://www.presidency.ucsb.edu/ws/?pid=40290 [accessed December 29, 2011].

75. Ronald Reagan, "Remarks at a Reagan-Bush Rally in Cedar Rapids, Iowa," September 20, 1984, Online by Gerhard Peters and John T. Woolley, *The American Presidency Project*, http://www.presidency.ucsb.edu/ws/?pid=40407 [accessed December 29, 2011].

76. Ronald Reagan, "Remarks at a Reagan-Bush Rally in Boston, Massachusetts," November 1, 1984,Online by Gerhard Peters and John T. Woolley, *The American Presidency Project*, http://www.presidency.ucsb.edu/ws/?pid=39363 [accessed December 29, 2011].

77. "Debate with Walter Mondale (Domestic Issues) (October 7, 1984)," Miller Center, University of Virginia, http://millercenter.org/president/speeches/detail/5459 [accessed December 29, 2011].

78. Erickson, "Once and Future President," 317; United Press International, "101 Academics Buy Ad to Back Mondale," *New York Times*, October 31, 1984.

79. CBS, Inc., and New York Times Company, CBS News / New York Times Poll: National Election Day Survey (USCBSNYT1984-NATELEC), November 6, 1984. National Election Day Exit Polls Database (Storrs, CT: Roper Center, University of Connecticut, 2012).

80. See Jonah Goldberg, "Ted Kennedy's America," *National Review Online*, October 26, 2007, http://www.nationalreview.com/articles/222638/ted-kennedys-america/jonah-goldberg [accessed April 4, 2012].

81. Ronald Reagan, "Remarks on Presenting the Robert F. Kennedy Medal to Mrs. Ethel Kennedy," June 5, 1981, Online by Gerhard Peters and John T. Woolley, *The American Presidency Project*, http://www.presidency.ucsb.edu/ws/?pid=43909 [accessed December 28, 2011].

82. Edward M. Kennedy to Ronald and Nancy Reagan, November 13, 1981, Presidential Handwriting File, Box 1, Folder 14, Ronald Reagan Library; "The Daily Diary of President Ronald Reagan, July 22, 1982," Ronald Reagan Presidential Foundation and Library website, http://www.reaganfoundation.org/white-house-diary.aspx [accessed January 3, 2012].

83. Eunice Shriver to Ronald Reagan, March 19, 1985, Presidential Handwriting File, Series II: Presidential Records, 3/1/85–5/28/85, Box 12, Folder 175, Ronald Reagan Library; Eunice Shriver to Ronald Reagan, April 24, 1985, Presidential Handwriting File, Series II: Presidential Records, 3/1/85–5/28/85, Box 12, Folder 175, Ronald Reagan Library; Ronald Reagan to Eunice Kennedy Shriver, August 5, 1987, Presidential Handwriting File, Series II: Presidential Records, 2/20/87–8/27/87, Box 18, Folder 299, Ronald Reagan Library.

84. Edward M. Kennedy to Ronald Reagan, October 24, 1985, Presidential Handwriting File, Series II: Presidential Records, 5/29/85–10/31/85, Box 3, Folder 207, Ronald Reagan Library.

85. Lois Romano, "Family, Friends Pay Tribute to Kennedy at Mass Here," *Washington Post*, November 23, 1983.

86. Ronald Reagan, "Statement on the 20th Anniversary of the Death of President John

F. Kennedy," November 22, 1983, Online by Gerhard Peters and John T. Woolley, *The American Presidency Project*, http://www.presidency.ucsb.edu/ws/?pid=40800 [accessed February 14, 2012].

87. Letter from Caroline B. Kennedy and John F. Kennedy, Jr., to Ronald Reagan, March 10, 1985, ID#297993, FE008, WHORM: Subject File, Ronald Reagan Library.

88. Ronald Reagan, "Remarks at a Fund-raising Reception for the John F. Kennedy Library Foundation," June 24, 1985, Online by Gerhard Peters and John T. Woolley, *The American Presidency Project*, http://www.presidency.ucsb.edu/ws/?pid=38816 [accessed December 28, 2011].

89. Letter from John F. Kennedy, Jr., to Ronald Reagan, March 12, 1985, ID#297993 (1), FE 008, WHORM: Subject File, Ronald Reagan Library.

90. Telephone interview with Ron Reagan, Jr., March 8, 2012.

91. Two letters written after the airport meeting are indicative of the men's cordial relationship. Johnson wrote: "Please know that I value your friendship, as I did your father's . . ." When asked why he had broken away from GOP celebrations to see off Johnson, Bush told Joe Frantz, director of the LBJ Oral History project at the University of Texas, at the airport on January 20, 1969: "He has been a fine president and invariably courteous and fair to me and my people, and I thought that I belonged here to show in a small way how much I have appreciated him." E-mail from Liza Talbot, LBJ Library, May 16, 2012.

92. Timothy Naftali, *George H. W. Bush* (New York: Times Books, 2007), 20.

93. Sabato, *Feeding Frenzy*, 148–51.

94. Biden would run for president again in 2008, doing poorly and dropping out early—until Barack Obama put him on his winning ticket for vice president.

95. Representative Richard Gephardt (D-MO) made this quip during a roast for Senator Bill Bradley (D-NJ) that was attended by Biden and other Democratic presidential aspirants. See Robin Toner, "Far Trumpet Is Heard Anew As Candidates Invoke J.F.K.," *New York Times*, July 5, 1987.

96. Ibid.

97. The idea behind the Strategic Defense Initiative (SDI), or "Star Wars" program, was for the Pentagon to launch laser-powered satellites into space that could shoot down enemy missiles before they reached U.S shores. See Frances Fitzgerald, *Way Out There in the Blue: Reagan, Star Wars and the End of the Cold War* (New York: Touchstone, 2000).

98. "Echoes of Kennedy," *New York Times*, July 5, 1987.

99. Peter Goldman, Tom Mathews, and the Newsweek Special Election Team, *The Quest for the Presidency 1988* (New York: Touchstone, 1989), 248.

100. However, Robertson's father had been a U.S. senator from Virginia, Democrat A. Willis Robertson, who served from 1946 to 1966, and the younger Robertson had long been involved in politics.

101. Goldman et al., *Quest for the Presidency 1988*, 383.

102. This is an excerpt of a longer exchange. The complete transcript is available here: Presidential Candidates Debates: "Vice-Presidential Debate in Omaha, Nebraska," October 5, 1988, Online by Gerhard Peters and John T. Woolley, *The American Presidency Project*, http://www.presidency.ucsb.edu/ws/?pid=29424 [accessed January 6, 2012].

103. Lee Atwater, who was George H. W. Bush's campaign manager in 1988, said Dan Quayle cost Bush 2 to 3 percentage points. Roger Simon, "McCain Camp Trying to Scape-

goat Palin," *Politico*, October 30, 2008, http://www.politico.com/news/stories/1008/15073
.html [accessed May 2, 2012]. See also Roger Simon, "Would the Dream Ticket Be a Nightmare?" *Politico*, June 4, 2008, http://www.politico.com/news/stories/0608/10856.html [ac-
cessed May 2, 2012]; and Martin P. Wattenberg, "The Role of Vice Presidential Candidate
Ratings in Presidential Voting Behavior," *American Politics Quarterly* 23, no. 4 (October
1995): 504–14.

104. For a list of some of Quayle's other gaffes, see the "Wisdom of Dan Quayle" website,
http://www.ssqq.com/archive/vinlin03.htm [accessed April 3, 2012]. See also Sabato, *Feeding
Frenzy*, 113.

105. Letter from Prescott Bush to Clover Dulles, April 1969, Allen Dulles Papers, Box 10,
Folder 11, "Bush, Prescott, 1952–69," Mudd Manuscript Library, Princeton University.

106. Herbert S. Parmet, *George Bush: The Life of a Lone Star Yankee* (New York: Scribner,
1997), 363.

107. George Bush, "Proclamation 6159—Rose Fitzgerald Kennedy Family Appreciation
Day, 1990," July 18, 1990, Online by Gerhard Peters and John T. Woolley, *The American
Presidency Project*, http://www.presidency.ucsb.edu/ws/?pid=23750 [accessed January 6,
2012].

108. Bush was president of the Zapata Off-shore Drilling Co. at the time and he phoned
FBI Agent Graham Kitchel at 1:45 P.M. CST on 11/22/63 to pass on a rumor Bush had heard
about a college student named James Parrott. Supposedly, Parrott had threatened to kill
JFK. Memorandum from SA Graham W. Kitchel to SAC, Houston, November 22, 1963, "JFK
Murder Solved," http://jfkmurdersolved.com/bush.htm [accessed April 5, 2012]. The FBI put
two agents, William Schmidt and Kenneth Jackson, on Bush's Parrott tip. Nothing came of
it. Parrott was able to confirm his whereabouts on 11/22. Parrott's mother and one of his
friends insisted that he had been at his home in Houston that day. The documents are available at http://www.maryferrell.org/mffweb/archive/viewer/showDoc.do?docId=62280&rel-
PageId=12 [accessed May 22, 2012].

109. The "Bush did it" theory is mainly linked to two documents. The first is a memo
dated 11/29/63 from J. Edgar Hoover to the Director of Intelligence and Research at the State
Department which contains the following curious sentence: "The substance of the foregoing
information [Cuban ex-patriots' reactions to the assassination] was orally furnished by Mr.
George Bush of the Central Intelligence Agency . . ." When a reporter asked about this document during the 1980s, a spokesperson for Vice President Bush said that Bush had worked
for an oil drilling company in 1963, not the CIA. A man named George William Bush did
work for the CIA in 1963, but he denied that he was the person cited in Hoover's memo
(George William Bush's sworn affidavit is available at http://www.aarclibrary.org/notices
/Affidavit_of_George_William_Bush_880921.pdf). Thus, the Bush reference in Hoover's
memo has never been satisfactorily explained. Perhaps Hoover had confused the CIA's Bush
with another CIA agent who had briefed him. There was also an Army Major General
George Bush found in the calendar of former CIA director Allen Dulles by the Assassinations Records Review Board ("Final Report of the AARB," p. 108). The other document
that raises eyebrows—Kitchel's memo on G.H.W. Bush's call to the FBI—is available here:
http://jfkmurdersolved.com/bush.htm. Tom Flocco and other conspiracy investigators believe that G.H.W. Bush worked for the CIA in 1963 and is untruthful about his whereabouts
on 11/22. Flocco has even posted a photo that supposedly shows Bush in front of the Texas
School Book Depository on the day of the assassination. The photo, which shows a man with

some resemblance to Bush but—to my eye, at least—younger than Bush at the time, is available at http://tomflocco.com/fs/FbiMemoPhotoLinkBushJfk.htm [accessed November 7, 2012].

110. George Bush, "Statement on Signing the President John F. Kennedy Assassination Records and Collection Act of 1992," October 26, 1992, Online by Gerhard Peters and John T. Woolley, *The American Presidency Project*, http://www.presidency.ucsb.edu/ws/?pid=21673 [accessed January 6, 2012].

111. Personal interview with Oliver Stone during the Virginia Film Festival, November 4, 2011, Charlottesville, Virginia.

112. The bill had been passed unanimously by the Senate—one indication of its uncontroversial nature. No doubt, members of Congress were well aware of the public's cynicism about the government's handling of the assassination's aftermath. One poll in this general time frame asked respondents, "Do you think that the American people have or have not been told the whole truth about the assassination of President John Kennedy?" Have been told the truth: 16%, Have not been told the truth: 72%, Not sure: 12%. Survey by Time and CNN. Methodology: Conducted by Yankelovich Clancy Shulman, December 17–December 22, 1991, and based on 1,500 telephone interviews with adults. [USYANKCS.91DEC2.R26] Time/CNN/Yankelovich Clancy Shulman Poll, Dec, 1991, iPOLL Databank, Roper Center for Public Opinion Research, University of Connecticut, http://www.ropercenter.uconn.edu/data_access/ipoll/ipoll.html [accessed May 2, 2012].

18. CLINTON GRABS KENNEDY'S TORCH

1. Michael Takiff, *A Complicated Man: The Life of Bill Clinton as Told by Those Who Know Him* (New Haven: Yale University Press, 2010), 31; Bill Clinton, *My Life* (New York: Alfred A. Knopf, 2004), 35, 43–44; Jim Moore with Rick Ihde, *Clinton: Young Man in a Hurry* (Fort Worth: Summit Group, 1992), 23.

2. Clinton, *My Life*, 62.

3. Ibid., 65.

4. David Maraniss, *First in His Class: A Biography of Bill Clinton* (New York: Simon and Schuster, 1995), 53–55.

5. Telephone interview with Tommy Caplan, June 14, 2012.

6. See, for example, Clinton's speech before the Connecticut Democratic Convention, July 18, 1980, in Stephen A. Smith, ed., *Preface to the Presidency: Selected Speeches of Bill Clinton, 1974–92* (Fayetteville: University of Arkansas Press, 1996), 22.

7. Maraniss, *First in His Class*, 381.

8. From Clinton's autobiography: "In the spring of 1980, Fidel Castro deported 120,000 political prisoners and other 'undesirables,' many of them with criminal records or mental problems, to the United States . . . I knew immediately that the White House might want to send some of the Cubans to Fort Chaffee, a large installation near Fort Smith, because it had been used as a relocation center in the mid-seventies for Vietnamese refugees . . . By May 20, there were nearly twenty thousand Cubans at Fort Chaffee." Clinton, *My Life*, 274–75.

9. Besides the car tax (actually, an increase in license tag fees) and the Cuban immigrant issue, several other factors contributed to Clinton's 1980 defeat, including his proposals for greater regulation of the timber industry and Republican campaign ads linking Clinton to Carter.

10. Clinton, *My Life*, 266.

11. Charles F. Allen and Jonathan Portis, *The Comeback Kid: The Life and Career of Bill Clinton* (New York: Birch Lane Press, 1992), 71, 104.

12. Two well-known Democratic governors, who both supported Clinton's presidential bids, separately shared this anecdote with me on background. Stories of this sort about Bill Clinton are legion. Diane A. Wade, "Bill Clinton TV Biography on PBS: How the Former President Broke the News of Lewinsky Affair to His Aide," *Belle News*, February 21, 2012, http://www.bellenews.com/2012/02/13/world/us-news/bill-clinton-tv-biography-on-pbs-how-the-former-president-broke-the-news-of-lewinsky-affair-to-his-aide/ [accessed February 21, 2012]; Audie Cornish interview with Barak Goodman, February 20, 2012, *All Things Considered*, NPR News, http://www.npr.org/2012/02/20/147164890/clinton-documentary-turns-lens-on-former-president [accessed February 21, 2012].

13. Larry J. Sabato, *Feeding Frenzy: How Attack Journalism Has Transformed American Politics* (New York: Free Press, 1991), 117.

14. Maraniss, *First in His Class*, 443.

15. Smith, *Selected Speeches of Bill Clinton*, 68.

16. Clinton's longtime friends Harry and Linda Thomason came up with the idea. Harry was an Arkansas-born TV and film producer who used his contacts to get Clinton on *The Tonight Show*. Here's his version of the story: "We were very upset, you know, that it [the convention speech] didn't go well. And we knew the press was gonna make mincemeat out of him and people would be making fun of him. So we stew[ed] about it all night, this is a Thursday you know. Sometime in the wee hours Linda wakes me up after a troubled sleep and she said look, he's got to go on the Carson show to make this right and I said, okay, in the morning I'd work on it." See "Clinton's Carson Appearance," PBS *American Experience*, http://www.pbs.org/wgbh/americanexperience/features/bonus-video/clinton-carson/ [accessed July 24, 2012].

17. Clinton, *My Life*, 381.

18. Smith, *Selected Speeches of Bill Clinton*, 120–21. Some aspects of this proposal became reality during the Clinton administration, especially with regard to Russia and newly independent republics that had been a part of the old Soviet Union. See, for example, Carl M. Cannon and Mark Matthews, "Clinton, Yeltsin Begin to Talk about Money: Vancouver Summit Focuses on Issues of Russian Economy," *Baltimore Sun*, April 4, 1993, and William J. Clinton, "Statement on Signing the Foreign Operations Appropriations Legislation," September 30, 1993, Online by Gerhard Peters and John T. Woolley, *The American Presidency Project*, http://www.presidency.ucsb.edu/ws/?pid=47145 [accessed July 25, 2012].

19. Smith, *Selected Speeches of Bill Clinton*, 127.

20. Clinton, *My Life*, 428.

21. Telephone interview with James Carville, February 15, 2013.

22. Clinton was classified 1-A (available for military service) when he graduated from Georgetown in the spring of 1968. But the local draft board in Arkansas, proud of Clinton's academic accomplishments, granted him a temporary reprieve so that he could continue his studies as a Rhodes scholar at Oxford. Opal Ellis, the draft board's executive secretary at the time, told the press: "[W]e were proud to have a Hot Springs boy with a Rhodes Scholarship" [and so] "the board was very lenient with him . . . We gave him more than he was entitled to." Clinton says the board told him that he would probably be called up in September or October of 1969. According to Ellis, Clinton returned to Arkansas after

his first year at Oxford and told her that "he was going to fix [her] wagon [and] pull every string he could think of." Clinton disputed Ellis's version of events and said that he met with an Army ROTC recruiter at the University of Arkansas at Fayetteville and "agreed orally to join the Army officer's program at the law school there." As a result, the Hot Springs draft board changed his classification from 1-A to 1-D, "a draft deferment that a spokesman for the Selective Service System says was only for people who had joined a reserve unit, or who were students taking military training, such as the ROTC." Clinton never joined the program or even enrolled at the university, opting for Yale Law School instead. It is not clear if Clinton ever planned on attending UA-F or simply made a phony promise so that he could avoid the draft. The Army ROTC recruiter, Eugene Holmes, says he was surprised and angered by Clinton's decision not to attend the university and had him reclassified as 1-A. A new draft lottery system was enacted in November 1969 and on December 1, the lucky Clinton drew "number 311." "No one with a number higher than 195 was called, according to the Selective Service System." See Jeffrey H. Birnbaum, "Clinton Received a Vietnam Draft Deferment for an ROTC Program That He Never Joined," *Wall Street Journal*, February 6, 1992.

23. Nigel Hamilton, *Bill Clinton: An American Journey: Great Expectations* (New York: Random House, 2003), 575; Michael Kramer, Laurence I. Barrett and Richard Woodbury, "Moment of Truth: Insisting That Flowers' Charges Are 'False,' Bill Clinton Faces the Biggest Test of His Political Career," *Time*, February 3, 1992; Lucy Howard and Ned Zeman, "'92 Campaign Edition," *Newsweek*, January 27, 1992, p. 4.

24. Transcript of the Clintons' January 26, 1992, interview with *60 Minutes*, "In 1992, Clinton Conceded Marital 'Wrongdoing,'" *Washington Post* website, http://www.washingtonpost.com/wp-srv/politics/special/clinton/stories/flowers012792.htm [accessed July 25, 2012].

25. S. Robert Lichter and Larry J. Sabato, *When Should the Watchdogs Bark? Media Coverage of the Clinton Scandals* (Lanham, MD: University Press of America, 1994).

26. John Micklethwait and Adrian Wooldridge, *The Right Nation: Conservative Power in America* (New York: Penguin Press, 2004), 104.

27. Interview with Fred Malek, November 16, 2011. See also Susan Okie, "Bush's Thyroid Condition Diagnosed as Graves' Disease," *Washington Post*, May 10, 1991, and Bob Woodward, "Watergate's Shadow on the Bush Presidency," *Washington Post Magazine*, June 20, 1999, http://www.washingtonpost.com/wp-srv/politics/daily/june99/shadow20.htm [accessed April 13, 2012].

28. See, for example, this poll conducted by Los Angeles Times, October 2–October 5, 1992, and based on 1,833 telephone interviews that showed Clinton defeating Bush 53% to 39%, with 8% other or don't know. Sample: National adults. [USLAT.100792.R13]. Los Angeles Times poll, Oct. 1992, iPOLL Databank, Roper Center for Public Opinion Research, University of Connecticut, http://www.ropercenter.uconn.edu.proxy.its.virginia.edu/data_access/ipoll/ipoll.html [accessed July 24, 2012].

29. Clinton and Perot were neck and neck in the Gallup poll between April and May 1992. Perot pulled ahead in June (39%), followed by Bush (31%) and Clinton (25%.) By August, however, Clinton held a commanding lead over his two rivals (57%) and won the general election with 43% of the vote. See "Gallup Presidential Election Trial-Heat Trends, 1936–2008," Gallup Politics, http://www.gallup.com/poll/110548/gallup-presidential-election-trialheat-trends-19362004.aspx#2 [accessed June 19, 2012].

30. Perot withdrew from the race on July 16, 1992. At that time, he argued that the Democratic Party's surge meant that the election would likely be thrown into the House of Representatives and "since the House of Representatives is made up primarily of Democrats and Republicans, our chances of winning would be pretty slim." "Excerpts from Perot's News Conference on Decision Not to Enter Election," *New York Times*, July 17, 1992. Perot reentered the race on October 1. Twenty-four days later, he told the press that "he had withdrawn [in July] after hearing that President Bush's campaign was scheming to smear his daughter with a computer-altered photograph and to disrupt her wedding." Richard L. Berke, "Perot Says He Quit in July to Thwart G.O.P. 'Dirty Tricks,'" *New York Times*, October 26, 1992.

31. William Greider, P. J. O'Rourke, Hunter Thompson, and Jann S. Wenner, "The Rolling Stone Interview: Bill Clinton," *Rolling Stone*, September 17, 1992, Jann S. Wenner website, http://www.jannswenner.com/Archives/Bill_Clinton.aspx [accessed February 3, 2012].

32. Joe Klein, *The Natural: The Misunderstood Presidency of Bill Clinton* (New York: Broadway Books, 2002), 215.

33. Howard Fineman with Ann McDaniel, "Minus Perot: The New Math," *Newsweek*, July 27, 1992, p. 24.

34. "1992 Tribute to Sen. Robert Kennedy, Jul. 15, 1992," C-SPAN Video Library, http://www.c-spanvideo.org/program/SenRo [accessed February 2, 2012].

35. Clinton, *My Life*, 418. See also Robin Toner, "Choice Is Affirmed," *New York Times*, July 16, 1992.

36. "Clinton 1992 Acceptance Speech, Jul. 16, 1992," C-SPAN Video Library, http://www.c-spanvideo.org/program/Clinton1&showFullAbstract=1 [accessed February 2, 2012].

37. Clinton, *My Life*, 480.

38. Transcript of NBC *Today*, November 5, 1992, pp. 14–15.

39. Lance Morrow with Tom Curry, "The Torch Is Passed: Bill Clinton Parades into Washington as America Gambles on Youth, Luck and Change," *Time*, January 4, 1993: 22–25.

40. Respondents were asked: "In terms of style, which of the following presidents do you think Bill Clinton will be most like?" Kennedy was named by 43%, Carter by 25%, 15% for other presidents, with 17% unsure / don't know. Survey by NBC News, *Wall Street Journal*, conducted by Hart and Breglio Research Companies, December 12–December 15, 1992, and based on 1,004 telephone interviews. Sample: National adults. [USNBCWSJ.4035.R07C]. NBC News / *Wall Street Journal* poll, December 1992, iPOLL Databank, Roper Center for Public Opinion Research, University of Connecticut, http://www.ropercenter.uconn.edu. proxy.its.virginia.edu/data_access/ipoll/ipoll.html [accessed July 24, 2012]. Sample size: 1,004 respondents—national survey, adults. Margin of error: +/− 3.2 percentage points at the 95% confidence level.

41. "Clinton Inaugural Gala," SNL Transcripts, http://snltranscripts.jt.org/92/92kinauguration.phtml [accessed February 23, 2012].

42. U.S. Representative Joseph P. Kennedy II also attended.

43. Gilbert A. Lewthwaite, "Clinton, Set for Oath, Promises 'New Spirit': Iraq Crisis Shadows Inauguration Eve Marked by Visit to Kennedys' Graves," *Baltimore Sun*, January 20, 1993.

44. See John F. Kennedy, "Inaugural Address," January 20, 1961, Online by Gerhard Peters and John T. Woolley, *The American Presidency Project*, http://www.presidency.ucsb.edu

/ws/?pid=8032 [accessed February 23, 2012], and William J. Clinton, "Inaugural Address," January 20, 1993, Online by Gerhard Peters and John T. Woolley, *The American Presidency Project*, http://www.presidency.ucsb.edu/ws/?pid=46366 [accessed February 23, 2012].

45. Clinton, *My Life*, 478.

46. Garry Wills, "The Art of Oration: Short Is Always Good," *Los Angeles Times*, January 24, 1993.

47. Bill Clinton, "Response to the Lewinsky Allegations (January 26, 1998)," Miller Center website, University of Virginia, http://millercenter.org/scripps/archive/speeches/detail /3930 [accessed July 25, 2012]. If there is any other remembered sentence from the Clinton years, it may be this gem: "It depends on what the meaning of the word 'is' is." The statement was originally made by Clinton before a Starr-convened grand jury investigating Whitewater and other off-shooting scandals. See "The Starr Report," *Washington Post* website, http:// www.washingtonpost.com/wp-srv/politics/special/clinton/icreport/icreport.htm [accessed July 30, 2012].

48. William J. Clinton, "The President's News Conference," April 20, 1993, Online by Gerhard Peters and John T. Woolley, *The American Presidency Project*, http://www.presidency.ucsb.edu/ws/?pid=46451 [accessed February 22, 2012]; Clinton, *My Life*, 498.

49. For more information on McVeigh's life and motives, see Dan Herbeck and Lou Michel, *American Terrorist: Timothy McVeigh and the Oklahoma City Bombing* (New York: HarperCollins, 2001), and Brandon M. Stickney, *"All-American Monster": The Unauthorized Biography of Timothy McVeigh* (Amherst, NY: Prometheus Books, 1996). Senator John Danforth (R-MO) led a federal investigation of the government's handling of the Waco standoff. His report is available at http://www.cesnur.org/testi/DanforthRpt.pdf [accessed June 19, 2012].

50. See, for example, Jack Germond and Jules Witcover, "Clinton Must Deliver on Outrage at Bombing," *Baltimore Sun*, April 21, 1995, and Evan Thomas, *Back from the Dead: How Clinton Survived the Republican Revolution* (New York: Atlantic Monthly Press, 1997), 22.

51. "Federal Agents Seize Elian in Predawn Raid," CNN, April 24, 2000, http://articles .cnn.com/2000-04-22/us/cuba.boy.05_1_helmeted-agent-delfin-gonzalez-lazaro-gonzalez -they?_s=PM:US [accessed June 19, 2012].

52. Clinton, *My Life*, 469–70.

53. See "Bill Summary & Status, H.R. 2264," Library of Congress website, http://thomas .loc.gov/cgi-bin/bdquery/z?d103:H.R.2264 [accessed July 24, 2012].

54. See "H.R. 2014, Taxpayer Relief Act of 1997," Library of Congress website, http:// thomas.loc.gov/cgi-bin/bdquery/z?d105:H.R.2014 [accessed June 19, 2012].

55. See Table 1.1, the Historical Budget tables, http://www.gpo.gov/fdsys/pkg/BUDGET -2011-TAB/pdf/BUDGET-2011-TAB.pdf [accessed November 7, 2012].

56. These averages are based on numbers from "Economic Report of the President," U.S. Government Printing Office, http://www.gpo.gov/fdsys/browse/collection.action ?collectionCode=ERP&browsePath=2001&isCollapsed=false&leafLevelBrowse=false& isDocumentResults=true&ycord=0 [accessed July 30, 2012].

57. William J. Clinton, "Remarks on Signing the National and Community Service Trust Act," September 21, 1993, Online by Gerhard Peters and John T. Woolley, *The American Presidency Project*, http://www.presidency.ucsb.edu/ws/?pid=47092 [accessed February 29, 2012].

58. President Johnson first established a "domestic Peace Corps" in 1965. It was called

VISTA—Volunteers in Service to America—but it was scaled down somewhat in subsequent administrations. AmeriCorps included the remnants of VISTA and broadened the service mandate to other fields. For more information, see the AmeriCorps website, http://www .americorps.gov/about/programs/vista.asp [accessed June 19, 2012].

59. Four of Governor Clinton's "executive protection" troopers, who had allegedly aided and abetted his extramarital pursuits, were very forthcoming about the governor's affairs. An Arkansas state employee, Larry Nichols, had even filed suit against Clinton, ostensibly for employment reasons, but the suit named five specific Clinton paramours, one of whom was Gennifer Flowers. Another was a former Miss America, Elizabeth Ward Gracen, who denied the allegation at the time but in 1998 admitted she had had a one-night stand with Clinton in 1983. See Elizabeth Drew, *On the Edge: The Clinton Presidency* (New York: Simon and Schuster, 1994), 380, 383, and Allen and Portis, *Comeback Kid*, 133–34, 238.

60. John F. Harris, *The Survivor: Bill Clinton in the White House* (New York: Random House, 2005), 109.

61. "Where Are They Now: The Clinton Impeachment: Paula Jones," *Time* Specials, http://www.time.com/time/specials/packages/article/0,28804,1870544_1870543_1870458,00 .html [accessed February 8, 2012].

62. See Jill Abramson, "Clinton Contributor Recommended White House Aide," *New York Times*, January 23, 1998; "Starr Continues Criminal Investigation," CNN, *The World Today*, January 30, 1998; "Descriptions of the taped recordings," *USA Today*, January 22, 1998; Brian Blomquist, "Subpoenas All Round As Starr Cuts Loose," *New York Post*, January 23, 1998.

63. Bill Clinton, "Response to the Lewinsky Allegations (January 26, 1998)," Miller Center website, University of Virginia, http://millercenter.org/scripps/archive/speeches/detail /3930 [accessed July 25, 2012].

64. Address by President Bill Clinton, August 17, 1998, CNN, *All Politics*, http://www .cnn.com/ALLPOLITICS/1998/08/17/speech/transcript.html [accessed July 30, 2012].

65. Clinton must have known that Starr had evidence to prove the Lewinsky affair in the summer of 1998, since it was widely reported that Starr had granted Lewinsky prosecutorial immunity on July 28, the day before Clinton agreed to testify.

66. Judge Susan Webber Wright held Clinton in contempt of court on April 13, 1999. See John M. Broder with Neil A. Lewis, "Clinton Is Found to Be in Contempt on Jones Lawsuit," *New York Times*, April 13, 1999. See also Neil A. Lewis, "Judge Orders Clinton to Pay $90,000 to Jones's Lawyers," *New York Times*, July 30, 1999. This decision came eight months after Clinton agreed to settle the Jones lawsuit out of court for $850,000.

67. Peter Baker, "Clinton Settles Paula Jones Lawsuit for $850,000," *Washington Post*, November 14, 1998; "Paula Jones to Get $200,000 of Settlement," *Baltimore Sun* article reprinted in *San Francisco Chronicle*, March 5, 1999: A6.

68. Associated Press, "Clinton's Ark. Law License Suspension Ends Soon," January 18, 2006, FoxNews.com, http://www.foxnews.com/story/0,2933,182077,00.html [accessed June 19, 2012].

69. See Steven M. Gillon, *The Pact: Bill Clinton, Newt Gingrich, and the Rivalry That Defined a Generation* (New York: Oxford University Press, 2008), 256–57. See also "Gingrich Friend Dates Affair to '93," *Chicago Tribune*, November 11, 1999.

70. See Mimi Alford, *Once Upon a Secret: My Affair with President John F. Kennedy and Its Aftermath* (New York: Random House, 2012).

71. See William J. Clinton, "Remarks at a Reception for Senator Edward M. Kennedy," October 21, 1999, Online by Gerhard Peters and John T. Woolley, *The American Presidency Project*, http://www.presidency.ucsb.edu/ws/?pid=56766 [accessed February 23, 2012]; and William J. Clinton, "Remarks at the John F. Kennedy Presidential Library Foundation Dinner," March 2, 1998, Online by Gerhard Peters and John T. Woolley, *The American Presidency Project*, http://www.presidency.ucsb.edu/ws/?pid=55555 [accessed February 22, 2012].

72. Hillary Rodham Clinton, *Living History* (New York: Simon and Schuster, 2003), 232, 247.

73. Clinton, *Living History*, 232, and Burton Hersh, *Edward Kennedy: An Intimate Biography* (Berkeley, CA: Counterpoint, 2010), 530.

74. Mary McGrory, "Bill as Bobby," March 14, 1993, Mary McGrory Papers, Box 96, Folder 14, Manuscript Division, Library of Congress.

75. William J. Clinton, "Remarks at the Memorial Mass for Robert F. Kennedy in Arlington, Virginia," June 6, 1993, Online by Gerhard Peters and John T. Woolley, *The American Presidency Project*, http://www.presidency.ucsb.edu/ws/?pid=46662 [accessed February 8, 2012]; William J. Clinton, "Remarks at the Dedication of the John F. Kennedy Presidential Library Museum in Boston, Massachusetts," October 29, 1993, Online by Gerhard Peters and John T. Woolley, *The American Presidency Project*, http://www.presidency.ucsb.edu/ws/?pid=46039 [accessed February 8, 2012].

76. William J. Clinton, "Remarks at the 25th Anniversary Reception for the John F. Kennedy Center for the Performing Arts," April 27, 1996, Online by Gerhard Peters and John T. Woolley, *The American Presidency Project*, http://www.presidency.ucsb.edu/ws/?pid=52734 [accessed February 23, 2012]; William J. Clinton, "Remarks on the 35th Anniversary of the Peace Corps," June 19, 1996, Online by Gerhard Peters and John T. Woolley, *The American Presidency Project*, http://www.presidency.ucsb.edu/ws/?pid=52963 [accessed February 22, 2012].

77. Gwen Ifill, "Clinton and Kennedys: In 30 Years, a Full Circle," *New York Times*, August 25, 1993.

78. William J. Clinton, "Remarks on the Death of Jacqueline Kennedy Onassis," May 20, 1994, Online by Gerhard Peters and John T. Woolley, *The American Presidency Project*, http://www.presidency.ucsb.edu/ws/?pid=50207 [accessed February 8, 2012].

79. Edward M. Kennedy, "Tribute to John F. Kennedy, Jr.," July 23, 1999, John F. Kennedy Presidential Library and Museum website, http://www.jfklibrary.org/Research/Ready-Reference/EMK-Speeches/Tribute-to-John-F-Kennedy-Jr.aspx [accessed February 12, 2012].

80. William J. Clinton, "Remarks to the American Legion Boys Nation," July 24, 1993, Online by Gerhard Peters and John T. Woolley, *The American Presidency Project*, http://www.presidency.ucsb.edu/ws/?pid=46901 [accessed February 8, 2012].

81. Clinton, *My Life*, 532.

19. G. W. BUSH: BACK TO THE REPUBLICAN KENNEDYS

1. See "GEORGE W. BUSH, et al., PETITIONERS *v.* ALBERT GORE, Jr., et al.," December 12, 2000, Legal Information Institute at Cornell University Law School, http://www.law.cornell.edu/supct/html/00-949.ZPC.html [accessed June 19, 2012].

2. Larry J. Sabato, *Overtime! The Election 2000 Thriller* (New York: Longman, 2002).

3. George W. Bush, "Address Before a Joint Session of the Congress on Administration

Goals," February 27, 2001, Online by Gerhard Peters and John T. Woolley, *The American Presidency Project*, http://www.presidency.ucsb.edu/ws/?pid=29643 [accessed March 21, 2012]. See also George W. Bush, "Remarks at Western Michigan University in Kalamazoo, Michigan," March 27, 2001, Online by Gerhard Peters and John T. Woolley, *The American Presidency Project*, http://www.presidency.ucsb.edu/ws/?pid=45679 [accessed March 21, 2012].

4. Kelly Wallace, "$1.35 Trillion Tax Cut Becomes Law," CNN, June 7, 2001, http://articles.cnn.com/2001-06-07/politics/bush.taxes_1_child-tax-credit-trillion-tax-tax-relief?_s=PM:ALLPOLITICS [accessed June 19, 2012]. In 2002, Bush signed the "Job Creation and Worker Assistance Act," which allowed businesses to "claim extra deductions for depreciation of a long-term physical capital investment" (essentially a tax cut). In 2003, Bush "reduced taxes on dividends and capital gains and accelerated some provisions passed in earlier tax cuts." See "The Bush Tax Cuts: How Did the 2002 Tax Cuts Change the Tax Code?" and "The Bush Tax Cuts: How Did the 2003 Tax Cuts Change the Tax Code?" Tax Policy Center, http://www.taxpolicycenter.org/briefing-book/background/bush-tax-cuts [accessed June 19, 2012].

5. See *The 9/11 Commission Report: Final Report of the National Commission on Terrorist Attacks Upon the United States* (New York: W. W. Norton, 2004).

6. David E. Sanger and John O'Neil, "White House Begins New Effort to Defend Surveillance Program," *New York Times*, January 23, 2006; "The USA PATRIOT Act: Preserving Life and Liberty," Department of Justice website, http://www.justice.gov/archive/ll/high lights.htm [accessed June 19, 2012].

7. George W. Bush, *Decision Points* (New York: Crown Publishers, 2010), 164.

8. Interview with Ari Fleischer, May 28, 2013, New York, New York; Bush, *Decision Points*, 273–75.

9. George W. Bush, "Remarks on the Dedication of the Robert F. Kennedy Department of Justice Building," November 20, 2001, Online by Gerhard Peters and John T. Woolley, *The American Presidency Project*, http://www.presidency.ucsb.edu/ws/?pid=63476 [accessed February 23, 2012].

10. "Bush Names Justice Department Building for Robert F. Kennedy," CNN Politics, November 20, 2001, http://articles.cnn.com/2001-11-20/politics/justice.rfk_1_kerry-kennedy-cuomo-dedication-ceremony-kennedy-family?_s=PM:ALLPOLITICS [accessed March 22, 2012].

11. Fred I. Greenstein, ed., *The George W. Bush Presidency: An Early Assessment* (Baltimore: Johns Hopkins University Press, 2003), 8–9.

12. Dick Cheney with Liz Cheney, *In My Time: A Personal and Political Memoir* (New York: Threshold Editions, 2011), 40. Thanks to Jonathan Martin for bringing this story to my attention. E-mail from Jonathan Martin, August 28, 2011. Cheney is referring to a troubled period in his youth. By September 1963, the future vice president had flunked out of Yale twice and received two DUIs.

20. FULL CIRCLE: THE TWINNING OF BARACK OBAMA AND JOHN KENNEDY

1. Joseph A. Loftus, "U.S. Tells World of Rights Strife: Attorney General Foresees a Negro as President," *New York Times*, May 27, 1961.

2. See David Maraniss, *Barack Obama: The Story* (New York: Simon and Schuster, 2012).

3. "Transcript: Illinois Senate Candidate Barack Obama," *Washington Post*, July 27, 2004, http://www.washingtonpost.com/wp-dyn/articles/A19751-2004Jul27.html [accessed July 19, 2012].

4. See Barack Obama, *The Audacity of Hope* (New York: Three Rivers Press, 2006), 129, 134, 314–15.

5. Alec MacGillis, "Obama Sells Himself as the New JFK," *Washington Post*, October 3, 2007, http://voices.washingtonpost.com/44/2007/10/post-109.html [accessed March 28, 2012].

6. "Why Caroline Backed Obama," *Daily Beast*, January 29, 2008, http://www.thedaily beast.com/newsweek/2008/01/29/why-caroline-backed-obama.html [accessed July 19, 2012].

7. Mary Ann Akers, "Clinton's LBJ Comments Infuriated Ted Kennedy," *Washington Post*, January 30, 2008, http://voices.washingtonpost.com/sleuth/2008/01/post_11.html [accessed April 18, 2012].

8. Jeff Zeleny and Carl Hulse, "Kennedy Chooses Obama, Spurning Plea by Clintons," *New York Times*, January 28, 2008.

9. Jeff Zeleny, "An Appeal That Looks to (and Uses) the Spirit of the 1960s," *New York Times*, January 30, 2008.

10. "Barack Obama's Remarks at the Kennedy Endorsement," *Huffington Post*, January 28, 2008, http://www.huffingtonpost.com/2008/01/28/barack-obamas-remarks-at-_n_83623 .html [accessed March 28, 2012].

11. Ibid. See also Tom Shachtman, *Airlift to America: How Barack Obama, Sr., John F. Kennedy, Tom Mboya, and 800 East African Students Changed Their World and Ours* (New York: St. Martin's Press, 2009).

12. Michael Dobbs, "Obama Overstates Kennedys' Role in Helping His Father," *Washington Post*, March 30, 2008.

13. Kathleen Kennedy Townsend, Robert F. Kennedy, Jr., and Mary Kerry Kennedy endorsed Hillary Clinton's presidential campaign. See Jeff Zeleny and Carl Hulse, "Kennedy Chooses Obama, Spurning Plea by Clintons," *New York Times*, January 28, 2010.

14. "DNC Tribute and Speech by Sen. Edward Kennedy," C-SPAN, YouTube, http://www .youtube.com/watch?v=f4fh80ZkVNk&feature=player_embedded#! [accessed March 28, 2012].

15. John McCain, "Remarks to a Town Hall Meeting in New Mexico," August 20, 2008, Online by Gerhard Peters and John T. Woolley, *The American Presidency Project*, http:// www.presidency.ucsb.edu/ws/?pid=78611 [accessed May 9, 2013].

16. John McCain, "Remarks in Columbus, Ohio," October 31, 2008, Online by Gerhard Peters and John T. Woolley, *The American Presidency Project*, http://www.presidency.ucsb .edu/ws/?pid=84678 [accessed May 9, 2013].

17. Kennedy received about 37% of the Protestant vote in 1960, so low that it nearly outweighed the 82% of Catholics that he won. According to the 2008 election day exit poll, Obama won 43% of whites, a better showing than some white Democrats have posted among this racial group in past presidential elections. For example, John Kerry (D) garnered only 41% of whites in his contest with President Bush in 2004. Incidentally, it is a measure of how much the religious factor has faded that Obama, a Protestant, secured 54% of the Catholic vote in 2008, but just 45% of the Protestant vote. See Larry J. Sabato, ed., *The Year of Obama: How Barack Obama Won the White House* (New York: Longman, 2010), 65–68; and Donald

R. Kinder and Allison Dale-Riddle, *The End of Race? Obama, 2008, and Racial Politics in America* (New Haven: Yale University Press, 2012), 72.

18. There are also quotations from FDR, Martin Luther King, Jr., Abraham Lincoln, and Theodore Roosevelt. Jon Ward, "Obama Replaces Bush Oval Office Rug with New Quote-Emblazoned Carpet," *Daily Caller*, August 8, 2010, http://dailycaller.com/2010/08/31/obama -replaces-bush-oval-office-rug-with-new-quote-emblazoned-carpet/ [accessed March 29, 2012].

19. E-mail from Ted Sorensen, October 22, 2010.

20. See Barack Obama, "Inaugural Address," January 20, 2009, Online by Gerhard Peters and John T. Woolley, *The American Presidency Project*, http://www.presidency.ucsb.edu /ws/?pid=44 [accessed July 19, 2012].

21. See "Joe Scarborough: State Of The Union Speech 'Boring All Around,'" *Huffington Post*, http://www.huffingtonpost.com/2011/01/25/joe-scarborough-state-of-union-boring_n _814064.html [accessed July 19, 2012], and Colby Hall, "Bill O'Reilly Criticizes Obama's Iraq War Speech for Being Boring," *Mediaite*, August 31, 2010, http://www.mediaite.com /online/bill-oreilly-criticizes-obamas-iraq-war-speech-for-being-boring/ [accessed July 19, 2012].

22. The reason for the lack of Kennedy citations cannot be the Obama speechwriters. In 2009 Obama appointed then twenty-seven-year-old Jon Favreau as director of speechwriting. Favreau cited the Kennedys and Martin Luther King, Jr., as providing some of his inspiration, and said he had done a good deal of reading about them. Ashley Parker, "What Would Obama Say?" *New York Times*, January 20, 2008. Another Obama speechwriter, Adam Frankel, assisted JFK aide Ted Sorensen on his memoirs, and Frankel's paternal grandfather, Stanley Frankel, wrote speeches for Adlai Stevenson, Robert Kennedy, and George McGovern. Peter Nicholas, "The Brain Behind Obama's Speeches," *Los Angeles Times*, September 3, 2010.

23. David Jackson, "Obama Celebrates Birthday of White House Situation Room," *USA Today*, May 13, 2011, http://content.usatoday.com/communities/theoval/post/2011/05/obama -celebrates-birthday-of-white-house-situation-room/1 [accessed July 19, 2012]; Jason Djang, "Inside the Situation Room," White House blog, December 18, 2009, http://www.whitehouse .gov/blog/2009/12/18/inside-situation-room [accessed May 9, 2012]; "Inside the Situation Room: A Guided Tour," *Rock Center with Brian Williams*, May 4, 2012, http://rockcenter .msnbc.msn.com/_news/2012/05/04/11539949-inside-the-situation-room-a-guided-tour?lite [accessed May 9, 2012].

24. David Jackson, "Caroline Kennedy Likely Next Ambassador to Japan," *USA Today*, April 1, 2013, http://www.usatoday.com/story/theoval/2013/04/01/obama-kennedy-japan -ambassador/2041675/ [accessed April 1, 2013].

25. Barack Obama, "Remarks at the United Nations Climate Change Summit in New York City," September 22, 2009, Online by Gerhard Peters and John T. Woolley, *The American Presidency Project*, http://www.presidency.ucsb.edu/ws/?pid=86657 [accessed May 31, 2012].

26. See Barack Obama, "Remarks and a Question-and-Answer Session with Young African Leaders," August 3, 2010, Online by Gerhard Peters and John T. Woolley, *The American Presidency Project*, http://www.presidency.ucsb.edu/ws/?pid=88275 [accessed May 31, 2012]; "Remarks in Santiago, Chile," March 21, 2011, Online by Gerhard Peters and John T. Woolley,

The American Presidency Project, http://www.presidency.ucsb.edu/ws/?pid=90189 [accessed May 31, 2012]; and "Remarks at a Town Hall Meeting and a Question-and-Answer Session on Health Care Reform," July 28, 2009, Online by Gerhard Peters and John T. Woolley, *The American Presidency Project*, http://www.presidency.ucsb.edu/ws/?pid=86479 [accessed May 31, 2012].

27. Barack Obama, "Remarks at an Obama Victory Fund 2012 Fundraiser," January 9, 2012, Online by Gerhard Peters and John T. Woolley, *The American Presidency Project*, http://www.presidency.ucsb.edu/ws/?pid=98855 [accessed May 31, 2012].

28. In February 2010, the *Washington Post* reported on Obama's plans to shelve "Constellation," a program launched by President George W. Bush to return U.S. astronauts to the moon. Obama also proposed cuts to the Ares 1 program, NASA's hoped-for successor to the space shuttle. See Joel Achenbach, "NASA Budget for 2011 Eliminates Funds for Manned Lunar Missions," *Washington Post*, February 1, 2010.

29. Neil Armstrong, Jim Lovell and Gene Cernan, "Is Obama Grounding JFK's Space Legacy?" *USA Today*, May 24, 2011, http://www.usatoday.com/news/opinion/forum/2011-05 -24-Obama-grounding-JFK-space-legacy_n.htm?csp=hf [accessed June 14, 2012].

30. Barack Obama, " 'John Kennedy's Life . . . Was a Source of Inspiration,' " *USA Today Special Edition, JFK's America* (Fall 2010): 9.

31. http://mycmag.kantarmediana.com/videos/PRES_REALLEADER_LED_THE _WAY_60.mov [accessed June 4, 2012].

32. "Romney's 'Faith in America' Address," *New York Times*, December 6, 2007, http:// www.nytimes.com/2007/12/06/us/politics/06text-romney.html?pagewanted=all [accessed May 14, 2012].

33. See Richard Reeves, *President Kennedy: Profile of Power* (New York: Touchstone, 1993), 15; and 1960 Census Data, United States Census Bureau website, http://www2.census .gov/prod2/statcomp/documents/1961-02.pdf [accessed August 2, 2012].

34. Jarod Favole, "Third Presidential Debate," *Wall Street Journal*, October 23, 2012, http://online.wsj.com/article/SB10001424052970203406404578074280108831690.html [accessed November 13, 2012], and "Vice Presidential Debate: Transcript," *Wall Street Journal*, October 12, 2012, http://online.wsj.com/article/SB10000872396390443749204578052240221885884.html [accessed November 13, 2012]; Russell Contreras, "JFK's Last Night Recalled as Watershed Event for Latinos," Associated Press, November 25, 2012, reprinted in *Abilene Reporter News*, http://www.reporternews.com/news/2012/nov/25/jfks-last-night-recalled-as -key-event-for/ [accessed December 3, 2012].

35. One small but telling example: in November 2012, the JFK Fifty-Mile race, one of the oldest "ultramarathon" events in the United States, celebrated its fiftieth anniversary. The race grew out of President Kennedy's challenge to U.S. Marines to march fifty miles in twenty hours in order to demonstrate their physical fitness. Some civilians quickly adopted the Kennedy fifty-mile standard, including eleven members of an athletic club located in Boonsboro, Maryland. Boonsboro continues to host the JFK Fifty-Mile event, which today draws runners from all over the world. See Lenny Bernstein, "JFK 50: A 'Soft American' Accepts the Challenge," *Washington Post*, November 6, 2012, http://www.washingtonpost.com /lifestyle/wellness/jfk50-a-soft-american-accepts-the-challenge/2012/11/05/6066df4a-1d86 -11e2-ba31-3083ca97c314_story.html [accessed December 13, 2012].

36. The University of Michigan commissioned Paul Long Productions to produce the hour-long documentary. The UM commemoration of JFK's Peace Corps speech was brought

to my attention by Ted Sorensen. In an October 15, 2010, e-mail just days before his fatal stroke, Sorensen wrote, "Talk about the JFK legacy!" See the Paul Long Productions website, http://www.paul-long.com/ [accessed June 14, 2012], and also Tom Perkins, "Students Commemorate John F. Kennedy's 'Peace Corps' Speech at the Michigan Student Union," Ann Arbor.com, October 14, 2010, http://www.annarbor.com/news/students-commemorate -john-f-kennedys-peace-corps-speech-at-the-michigan-student-union/ [accessed August 2, 2012].

37. Natasha Lennard, "President Obama, Kennedys Salute JFK," *Politico*, January 21, 2011, http://www.politico.com/click/stories/1101/obama_kennedys_salute_jfk.html [accessed April 19, 2012].

38. Matt Viser, "JFK's Words Echo Once More in Washington," *Boston Globe*, January 21, 2011, http://www.boston.com/news/nation/washington/articles/2011/01/21/jfks_words _echo_once_more_in_washington/?page=1 [accessed June 14, 2012]; "Second Time Around: Caroline Kennedy Helps 'Launch' Second USS John F Kennedy 44 Years After Christening Original Carrier," *The Daily Mail*, May 30, 2011, http://www.dailymail.co.uk/news/article -1392234/Second-time-Caroline-Kennedy-helps-launch-second-USS-John-F-Kennedy-44 -years-christening-original-carrier.html?ito=feeds-newsxml [accessed June 14, 2012].

39. Barack Obama, "Remarks on the Death of Senator Edward M. Kennedy in Chilmark, Massachusetts," August 26, 2009, Online by Gerhard Peters and John T. Woolley, *The American Presidency Project*, http://www.presidency.ucsb.edu/ws/?pid=86565 [accessed April 11, 2012].

40. Jen Doll, "Our Obsession with the 'Kennedy Curse,'" *The Atlantic*, May 17, 2012, http://www.theatlanticwire.com/national/2012/05/our-obsession-kennedy-curse/52451/ [accessed May 17, 2012].

41. Michael Cooper, "G.O.P. Senate Victory Stuns Democrats," *New York Times*, January 19, 2010.

42. Briefly after JFK's election as president, the seat was given to John Kennedy's Harvard roommate, Benjamin Smith, because Ted was not yet of the constitutional age of thirty for Senate service. As planned, Smith stepped aside in 1962 so that Ted, now of age, could run for the seat in the scheduled special election. Abby Goodnough, "Patrick Kennedy Packs Up 63 Years of Family History," *New York Times*, December 16, 2010.

43. See "Different People, Same Message," YouTube, http://www.youtube.com/watch ?v=iddquwGpXMo [accessed March 14, 2012]; and Matt Viser, "For Brown, JFK Transcends Party Lines," *Boston Globe*, December 31, 2009, http://www.boston.com/news/local/massa chusetts/articles/2009/12/31/for_brown_jfk_transcends_party_lines/ [accessed March 14, 2012].

44. Caroline Kennedy was never formally chosen by Governor David Paterson (D), and his appointment went instead to U.S. Representative Kirsten Gillibrand.

45. Patterson Clark, "The Kennedy Family Tree," *Washington Post Online,* http://www .washingtonpost.com/wp-dyn/content/graphic/2009/08/12/GR2009081200033.html [accessed August 7, 2012].

46. See Ted Sorensen, *Counselor* (New York: HarperCollins, 2008); James W. Douglass, *JFK and the Unspeakable* (New York: Touchstone, 2008); Lamar Waldron and Thom Hartmann, *Legacy of Secrecy: The Long Shadow of the JFK Assassination* (Berkeley, CA: Counterpoint, 2009); Steven M. Gillon, *The Kennedy Assassination: 24 Hours After* (New York: Basic Books, 2009); Mark Lane, *Last Word: My Indictment of the CIA in the Murder of JFK* (New

York: Skyhorse Publishing, 2011); Chris Matthews, *Jack Kennedy: Elusive Hero* (New York: Simon and Schuster, 2011); Eliza Gray, "Camelot Tales: Why Is 'Vanity Fair' So Obsessed with the Kennedys?" *The New Republic*, April 12, 2011, http://www.tnr.com/article/politics /86560/vanity-fair-kennedy-middleton [accessed June 14, 2012]; and Brad Watson, "Case Thrown Out Against Seller of Conspiracy Magazines at Dealey Plaza," WFAA.com, December 17, 2010, http://www.wfaa.com/news/local/Case-thrown-out-against–seller–Dealey -Plaza-112050554.html [accessed June 14, 2012]. In 2012, pop star Lana Del Rey and rapper A$AP Rocky reenacted JFK's assassination for the video of Ray's hit single "National Anthem." The video game *Call of Duty: Black Ops* features a special mode that allows players to defend JFK against a zombie attack. See Ann Lee, "Lana Del Rey Plays Marilyn Monroe and Jackie O in National Anthem Video," Metro, June 27, 2012, http://www.metro.co.uk/music /903449-lana-del-rey-plays-marilyn-monroe-and-jackie-o-in-national-anthem-video [accessed June 28, 2012] and Matthew Shelley, "Call of Duty Black Ops Secret Stage: JFK, Nixon and Castro Battle Zombies," CBS News, November 10, 2010, http://www.cbsnews.com/8301 -501465_162-20022370-501465.html [accessed June 14, 2012].

47. Jacqueline Kennedy, *Historic Conversations on Life with John F. Kennedy* (New York: Hyperion, 2011).

48. Gerald Blaine with Lisa McCubbin, *The Kennedy Detail* (New York: Gallery Books, 2010).

49. Brian Latell, *Castro's Secrets: The CIA and Cuba's Intelligence Machine* (New York: Palgrave Macmillan, 2012).

50. Stephen King, *11/22/63: A Novel* (New York: Gallery Books, 2012).

51. Mimi Alford, *Once Upon a Secret: My Affair with President John F. Kennedy and Its Aftermath* (New York: Random House, 2012).

52. Bill O'Reilly and Martin Dugard, *Killing Kennedy: The End of Camelot* (New York: Henry Holt, 2012).

53. Stephen Hunter, *The Third Bullet* (New York: Simon and Schuster, 2013). Hunter's fictional story revolves around a second shooter in the Dal-Tex building, which was directly across the street from the Book Depository. Dallas authorities briefly detained a suspect named Jim Braden who was spotted in the Dal-Tex building around the time of the assassination, but he was released after questioning. See Dave Reitzes, "Phone Factoid: Tortured Connection," Kennedy Assassination website, http://mcadams.posc.mu.edu/factoid.htm [accessed February 21, 2013].

54. Archbishop Philip Hannan with Nancy Collins and Peter Finney, Jr., *The Archbishop Wore Combat Boots* (Huntington, IN: Our Sunday Visitor Publishing Division, 2010), 27–28.

55. Indeed, the archbishop said he included the letter to counter the idea that JFK and Jackie had "a loveless marriage of convenience."

56. The National Geographic Channel aired *The Lost JFK Tapes: The Assassination* (2009) and *JFK: The Lost Bullet* (2011); the History Channel aired *JFK: 3 Shots That Changed America* (2009); and the Discovery Channel aired *Did the Mob Kill JFK?* (2009), *JFK: The Ruby Connection* (2009), and *The Kennedy Detail* (2010).

57. Players' scores are based on how closely their version of the assassination matches the Warren Commission's narrative. "'Docu-Game' Recreates JFK Assassination," Associated Press, November 22, 2004, reposted on Fox News.com, http://www.foxnews.com/story /0,2933,139213,00.html [accessed June 14, 2012].

58. Judy Keen, "JFK Relics Scattered Across U.S. Still Hold Mystique," *USA Today*, November 19, 2009, http://www.usatoday.com/news/nation/2009-11-19-JKF-relics_N.htm [accessed June 14, 2012].

59. Also included in this odd grab bag was Oswald's mother's death certificate. United Press International, "Brother Sues Over Oswald's Coffin," UPI.com, January 18, 2011, http://www.upi.com/Top_News/US/2011/01/18/Brother-sues-over-Oswalds-coffin/UPI-60551295389189/ [accessed June 14, 2012].

60. David Schwartz, "Purported JFK Ambulance Sold for $120,000 at Auction," Reuters, January 24, 2011, http://www.reuters.com/article/2011/01/24/us-ambulance-jfk-odd-idUS-TRE70N4FS20110124 [accessed August 7, 2012].

61. Roy Appleton, "Owner to Sell Rooming House Where Oswald Lived Before JFK Assassination," *Dallas Morning News*, May 8, 2013, http://www.dallasnews.com/news/jfk50/explore/20130508-owner-to-sell-rooming-house-where-oswald-lived-before-jfk-assassination.ece [accessed May 9, 2013].

62. Katya Kazakina, "Abraham Lincoln Glasses Could Fetch $700,000 at Auction," Bloomberg, April 23, 2012, http://www.bloomberg.com/news/2012-04-23/abraham-lincoln-glasses-could-fetch-700-000-at-auction.html [accessed August 8, 2012]. The glasses did not meet the minimum reserve price at this auction, and thus were not sold then. But another attempt in the future is probable.

21. THE PEOPLE'S PRESIDENT

1. For more information on Kennedy's enduring popularity, see Costas Panagopoulos, "Ex-Presidential Approval: Retrospective Evaluations of Presidential Performance," *Presidential Studies Quarterly* 42, no. 4 (December 2012): 719–29. Panagopoulos shows that Kennedy, of all presidents since and including FDR, had the highest average approval ratings during his presidency (80%) and one of the highest postpresidential approval ratings (88%). Roosevelt, whose average approval during his dozen years as president was 66%, had slightly higher postpresidential ratings than JFK (91%).

2. A score of 7–10.

3. It should be noted that this was an open-ended question asked at the start of the survey, without any comprehensive list of presidents presented to prompt respondents. People had to rely on their memories, and most simply named a recent president they liked.

4. John F. Kennedy, "Remarks during the Loyola College Alumni Banquet, Baltimore, Maryland, February 18, 1958," John F. Kennedy Quotations, John F. Kennedy Presidential Library and Museum, http://www.jfklibrary.org/Research/Ready-Reference/JFK-Quotations.aspx [accessed August 14, 2012].

5. John F. Kennedy, "Inaugural Address," January 20, 1961, Online by Gerhard Peters and John T. Woolley, *The American Presidency Project*, http://www.presidency.ucsb.edu/ws/?pid=8032 [accessed August 14, 2012].

6. Ibid.

7. Ibid.

8. John F. Kennedy, "Address at Rice University in Houston on the Nation's Space Effort," September 12, 1962, Online by Gerhard Peters and John T. Woolley, *The American Presidency Project*, http://www.presidency.ucsb.edu/ws/?pid=8862 [accessed August 14, 2012].

9. John F. Kennedy, "Speech of Senator John F. Kennedy, Civic Auditorium, Seattle, WA," September 6, 1960, Online by Gerhard Peters and John T. Woolley, *The American Presidency Project*, http://www.presidency.ucsb.edu/ws/?pid=25654 [accessed August 14, 2012].

10. Kennedy, "Inaugural Address," http://www.presidency.ucsb.edu/ws/?pid=8032 [accessed August 14, 2012].

11. 56% of Republicans singled out "Ask not . . . ," compared with 47% of Democrats and 42% of Independents.

12. Respondents viewed footage of the following: (1) "But why, some say, the moon? Why choose this as our goal? And they may well ask why climb the highest mountain? Why, 35 years ago, fly the Atlantic? Why does Rice play Texas? We choose to go to the moon. We choose to go to the moon in this decade and do the other things, not because they are easy, but because they are hard, because that goal will serve to organize and measure the best of our energies and skills, because that challenge is one that we are willing to accept, one we are unwilling to postpone, and one which we intend to win, and the others, too . . . We shall send to the moon, 240,000 miles away from the control station in Houston, a giant rocket more than 300 feet tall, the length of this football field, made of new metal alloys, some of which have not yet been invented, capable of standing heat and stresses several times more than have ever been experienced, fitted together with a precision better than the finest watch, carrying all the equipment needed for propulsion, guidance, control, communications, food and survival, on an untried mission, to an unknown celestial body, and then return it safely to earth, reentering the atmosphere at speeds of over 25,000 miles per hour, causing heat about half that of the temperature of the sun—almost as hot as it is here today—and do all this, and do it right, and do it first before this decade is out, then we must be bold." (2) "So, let us not be blind to our differences—but let us also direct attention to our common interests and to the means by which those differences can be resolved. And if we cannot end now our differences, at least we can help make the world safe for diversity. For, in the final analysis, our most basic common link is that we all inhabit this small planet. We all breathe the same air. We all cherish our children's future. And we are all mortal." (3) "And so, my fellow Americans: ask not what your country can do for you—ask what you can do for your country. My fellow citizens of the world: ask not what America will do for you, but what together we can do for the freedom of man." (4) "It shall be the policy of this nation to regard any nuclear missile launched from Cuba against any nation in the Western Hemisphere as an attack by the Soviet Union on the United States, requiring a full retaliatory response upon the Soviet Union . . . I call upon Chairman Khrushchev to halt and eliminate this clandestine, reckless, and provocative threat to world peace and to stable relations between our two nations." (5) "We are confronted primarily with a moral issue. It is as old as the scriptures and is as clear as the American Constitution. The heart of the question is whether all Americans are to be afforded equal rights and equal opportunities, whether we are going to treat our fellow Americans as we want to be treated. If an American, because his skin is dark, cannot eat lunch in a restaurant open to the public, if he cannot send his children to the best public school available, if he cannot vote for the public officials who represent him, if, in short, he cannot enjoy the full and free life which all of us want, then who among us would be content to have the color of his skin changed and stand in his place? Who among us would then be content with the counsels of patience and delay? One hundred years of delay have passed since President Lincoln freed the slaves, yet their heirs, their

grandsons, are not fully free. They are not yet freed from the bonds of injustice. They are not yet freed from social and economic oppression. And this nation, for all its hopes and all its boasts, will not be fully free until all its citizens are free."

13. All respondents were asked if they were "fairly" or "very" familiar with the following: Set a goal of putting a man on the moon within 10 years—66%; Stood up to the Soviet Union on the expansion of missiles into Cuba—65%; Used the authority of the federal government to protect the civil rights of African Americans in desegregating schools in Alabama and Mississippi—58%; Proposed the legislation that became the Civil Rights Act—52%; As the first Catholic president, spoke about the importance of the separation of church and state—46%; Developed the Peace Corps to influence public service—47%; Supported Berliners in their stance against communism—40%; Negotiated and signed the first treaty ending above ground testing of nuclear weapons—32%; Issued an executive order creating a commission on women, and signed the first equal pay law—30%; Passed a major tax cut—21%. More information on this poll, including the breakdown by age, is available at *TheKennedy HalfCentury.com.*

14. Here are our respondents' top choices of JFK's greatest accomplishments (combined percentages, all adults): Stood up to the Soviet Union on the expansion of missiles into Cuba—51%; Proposed the legislation that became the Civil Rights Act—48%; Used the authority of the federal government to protect the civil rights of African Americans in desegregating schools in Alabama and Mississippi—43%; Set a goal of putting a man on the moon within 10 years—38%; Issued an executive order creating a commission on women, and signed the first equal pay law—33%; Negotiated and signed the first treaty ending above ground testing of nuclear weapons—25%; Developed the Peace Corps to influence public service—19%; As the first Catholic president, spoke about the importance of the separation of church and state—17%; Passed a major tax cut—15%; Supported Berliners in their stance against Communism—10%.

15. All respondents were asked if they had "fairly" or "very" major concerns about the following: Under JFK, U.S. involvement in Vietnam escalated, which led us into the Vietnam War—53%; JFK approved the wiretapping of civil rights leaders, including Martin Luther King, Jr., and his advisers—46%; JFK was involved in several extramarital affairs while he was in the White House, including recent accounts of his relationship with a 19-year-old White House intern—33%; Through the CIA, JFK secretly supported coups and the assassination of foreign leaders in Latin America, Iraq, and Vietnam—30%; JFK was unable to push through major civil rights legislation during his own presidency, and it was not until Lyndon Johnson became president that the Civil Rights Act was passed—23%. More information on this poll, including the breakdown by age, is available at *TheKennedyHalfCentury. com.*

16. The final 3% said, a bit oddly, that the affairs made them feel more unfavorable to JFK as a president but did not affect their view of JFK as a person.

17. The "strongly agree" total for age 55+ was 38%, to 32% for those 54 and under.

18. Among those under age 55, 93% chose 9/11, with the Oklahoma City bombing second at 35% and the explosion of the space shuttle *Challenger* at 20%.

19. The other "clear and vivid" ratings were: Challenger explosion (63%), Oklahoma City bombing (36%), and the King assassination (34%). In each case, we included only respondents who were old enough at the time of the event to potentially recall it.

20. Respondents 55 and older were asked which major televised events they remembered

watching on live television during the assassination weekend. JFK's funeral procession—81%; John F. Kennedy, Jr., saluting his father's coffin—73%; JFK's coffin lying in repose in the White House—68%; Watching Air Force One land for the removal of JFK's coffin—57%; The lighting of the eternal flame and JFK's burial in Arlington—57%; Jackie Kennedy watching LBJ being sworn in as president—55%; Watching Walter Cronkite report on the JFK assassination—50%; The shooting of Lee Harvey Oswald—43%; The assassination of JFK in a convertible in Texas—31%. More information on this poll, including a breakdown of those who remember watching the events on television after they occurred or not at all, is available at *TheKennedyHalfCentury.com*.

21. The numbers for all responses add to more than 100% since respondents were permitted to choose up to two options.

22. The poll question on this topic was kept simple and structured to prompt respondents to make a basic choice: "There has been significant speculation about the circumstances surrounding the assassination of John F. Kennedy. Which statement do you agree with more?" (1) "There is nothing left to know about the circumstances surrounding the Kennedy assassination. Lee Harvey Oswald acted on his own to assassinate the president, and there was no conspiracy." (2) "There are still too many questions surrounding Kennedy's assassination to say that Lee Harvey Oswald acted by himself, or that there is not a larger conspiracy regarding the details of his death."

23. Younger voters, perhaps knowing less about the assassination, were not quite as firm in their beliefs. Only 11% strongly agreed that Oswald acted alone, while 41% strongly agreed that there were too many questions to claim there was no conspiracy. Of course, this is still a nearly 4-to-1 ratio in favor of the second statement among those with a strong opinion.

24. Note that the second statement in our polling query does not force people to conclude that a conspiracy existed, merely that there are "too many questions" lingering about the assassination to rule out the possibility (see note 22). In our view, this was a more realistic way to pose the choice.

25. Letter to the Author from Peter Hart and Geoff Garin, September 21, 2011, "Key Observations from the Focus Groups," Hart Research Associates, p. 1.

26. Ibid., 3.

27. Ibid., 9.

CONCLUSION: A FLAME ETERNAL?

1. "The Sound of Silence," Paul Simon website, http://www.paulsimon.com/us/music/paul-simon-songbook/sound-silence [accessed August 21, 2012].

2. "John F. Kennedy and the Press," John F. Kennedy Presidential Library and Museum website, http://www.jfklibrary.org/JFK/JFK-in-History/John-F-Kennedy-and-the-Press.aspx [accessed January 28, 2013].

3. Only William Henry Harrison, Zachary Taylor, Millard Fillmore, James A. Garfield, Warren Harding, and Gerald Ford served fewer days in the White House than John Kennedy.

4. In response to a March 21, 1962, press conference question about the unhappiness expressed by some military personnel about their status, Kennedy cited the unfairness of life, the fact that some people are sick and others well, some servicemen were killed in war while others never leave the country, and so on. See John F. Kennedy, "The President's News Conference," March 21, 1962, Online by Gerhard Peters and John T. Woolley, *The American*

Presidency Project, http://www.presidency.ucsb.edu/ws/?pid=8564 [accessed August 8, 2012].

5. E-mail from Ted Sorensen, October 22, 2010.

6. It is important to note that Kennedy was by no means the exception in an era when outlandish, dangerous sexual conduct was overlooked because it was categorized as "private life." The code of the times permitted even the CIA director, Allen Dulles, to have what his sister later described as a hundred or more affairs all over the world, with queens and commoners as he chose. Today's standards forced out CIA director David Petraeus after just a single affair in 2012. See Eleanor Lansing Dulles, *Chances of a Lifetime: A Memoir* (Englewood Cliffs, NJ: Prentice Hall, 1980), and Stephen Kinzer, "When a C.I.A. Director Had Scores of Affairs," *New York Times*, November 10, 2012, http://www.nytimes.com/2012/11/10/opinion/when-a-cia-director-had-scores-of-affairs.html?_r=1& [accessed November 12, 2012].

7. See Bryan Bender, "A Dark Corner of Camelot," *Boston Globe*, January 23, 2011, http://www.boston.com/news/nation/articles/2011/01/23/kennedy_family_limiting_access_to_rfk_documents/ [accessed August 21, 2012].

8. Barack Obama of Illinois is the sole exception, and he was born in the Sunbelt's Hawaii. Gerald Ford of Michigan was never elected.

INDEX

A Note on the Author

Dr. Larry J. Sabato is the founder and director of the renowned Center for Politics at the University of Virginia. He is also the University Professor of Politics at the University of Virginia, and has had visiting appointments at Oxford University and Cambridge University in Great Britain. A Rhodes scholar, he received his doctorate from Oxford, and is the author or editor of two dozen books on American politics, including *The Rise of Political Consultants*, *Feeding Frenzy*, *A More Perfect Constitution*, and *Barack Obama and the New America*. Dr. Sabato is a well-known election analyst who has appeared on television news shows hundreds of times. In 2013 Dr. Sabato won an Emmy for the documentary *Out of Order*, which he produced to highlight the dysfunctional U.S. Senate. He directs the Crystal Ball website, which has an unparalleled record of accuracy in predicting U.S. elections. Dr. Sabato has taught tens of thousands of students, and has received every major teaching award at the University of Virginia, which has also given him the university's highest honor, the Thomas Jefferson Award. For more information, go to www.centerforpolitics.org.

ASK THE AUTHOR

The Kennedy Half Century is accompanied by an innovative website, The KennedyHalfCentury.com. Additional features and updates will be posted on the site frequently, and readers can e-mail questions and comments to the author.